Cases in
**Operations Management**

We work with leading authors to develop the strongest
educational materials in operations management,
bringing cutting-edge thinking and best learning practice
to a global market.

Under a range of well-known imprints, including
Financial Times Prentice Hall, we craft high quality print
and electronic publications which help readers to
understand and apply their content, whether studying
or at work.

To find out more about the complete range of our
publishing, please visit us on the World Wide Web at:
www.pearsoneduc.com

THIRD EDITION

# Cases in
# Operations Management

**Robert Johnston**
Warwick Business School, University of Warwick

**Stuart Chambers**
Warwick Business School, University of Warwick

**Christine Harland**
School of Management, University of Bath

**Alan Harrison**
Cranfield School of Management, Cranfield University

**Nigel Slack**
Warwick Business School, University of Warwick

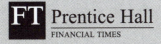
**FT** Prentice Hall
FINANCIAL TIMES

*An imprint of* **Pearson Education**
Harlow, England • London • New York • Boston • San Francisco • Toronto • Sydney • Singapore • Hong Kong
Tokyo • Seoul • Taipei • New Delhi • Cape Town • Madrid • Mexico City • Amsterdam • Munich • Paris • Milan

**Pearson Education Limited**

Edinburgh Gate
Harlow
Essex CM20 2JE
United Kingdom

*and Associated Companies throughout the world*

*Visit us on the World Wide Web at:*
www.pearsoneduc.com

———————————

First published 1993
Second published 1997
**Third Edition 2003**

ISBN 0 273 65531 0

**British Library Cataloguing-in-Publication Data**
A catalogue record for this book is available from the British Library

**Library of Congress Cataloging-in-Publication Data**
Cases in operations management / Robert Johnston ... [et al.].-- 3rd ed.
    p. cm.
   Includes index.
   ISBN 0-273-65531-0 (pbk. : alk. paper)
   1. Production management--Case studies. 2. Industrial management--Case studies. I.
Johnston, Robert.

   TS155 .C3158 2002
   658.5--dc21

                                                        2002027876

10 9 8 7 6 5 4 3 2 1
07 06 05 04 03

Typeset in 9.5/12.5pt Stone Serif by 30
Printed and bound by Bell & Bain Limited, Glasgow

*The publisher's policy is to use paper manufactured from sustainable forests.*

# Contents

# Contributors

## Authors

**Robert Johnston**     Professor of Operations Management, Warwick Business School, University of Warwick

**Stuart Chambers**     Principal Teaching Fellow in Operations Management, Warwick Business School, University of Warwick

**Christine Harland**     Professor of Supply Strategy and Director of the Centre for Research in Strategic Purchasing and Supply, School of Management, University of Bath

**Alan Harrison**     Professor of Operations and Logistics and Director of Research, Cranfield Centre for Logistics and Transportation, Cranfield School of Management, Cranfield University

**Nigel Slack**     Professor of Operations Strategy, Warwick Business School, University of Warwick

## Associate contributors

**Adam Bates**     Strategic Development Executive, British Tourist Authority

**Hilary Bates**     Research Fellow, Warwick Business School, UK

**Alan Betts**     Partner Bedford Falls Learning, UK

**Adrie Beulens**     Professor of Information Systems and Computer Science, Wageningen University, The Netherlands

**John Bicheno**     Reader in Operations Management, University of Buckingham

**Arnaldo Camuffo**     Professor, Department of Business Economics and Management, Ca' Foscari University of Venice, Italy

**Paul Chapman**     Senior Research Fellow, Cranfield Centre for Logistics and Transportation, Cranfield School of Management, Cranfield University

**Jaques Colin**     Professor and Director of the CretLog (Centre for Research on Transport and Logistics), Aix en Provence

**Jim Crew**     Managing Director, Eurocamp Travel Ltd

**Carole Driver**     Senior Lecturer in Operations Management, Plymouth University Business School

**Alan Fowler**     Reader, School of Management, University of Newcastle on Tyne, UK

**Andrew Greasley**     Lecturer in Operations Management, Aston Business School, UK

**Tammy Helander**     Independent Consultant

**Terry Hunt**     National Director/Chief Executive NHS Supplies 1991–2000

| | |
|---|---|
| **Eric Jackson** | Director of Operations, NHS Purchasing and Supply Agency |
| **Marie Koulikoff-Souviron** | Doctoral Fellow, Cranfield Centre for Logistics and Transportation, Cranfield School of Management, Cranfield University |
| **Keith Moreton** | Senior Lecturer in Operations Management, Staffordshire University, UK |
| **Sara Mountney** | Research Associate, Warwick Business School |
| **Jane Pavitt** | Research Fellow, Cranfield Centre for Logistics and Transportation, Cranfield School of Management, Cranfield University |
| **Mark Robinson** | Director, Wates Estates Agency Services, London |
| **Pietro Romano** | Lecturer in Supply Chain Management, Department of Management and Engineering, University of Padova, Italy |
| **Colin Samways** | Marketing Manager, Cadbury World |
| **Kevan Scholes** | Principal Partner of Scholes Associates and Visiting Professor of Strategic Management and formerly Director of Sheffield Business School, UK |
| **Roxanne Sutton** | Principal Advisor, Office of Public Services Reform, Cabinet Office |
| **Vinod Thayil** | Logistics Business Analyst, Finnforest Corp. |
| **Jack van der Vorst** | Assistant Professor of Logistics and Supply Chain Management, Department of Management Research, Wageningen University, The Netherlands |
| **Stephan van Dijk** | Researcher, Social Sciences Department, Wageningen University, The Netherlands |
| **Remko van Hoek** | Professor of Supply Chain Management, Cranfield Centre for Logistics and Transportation, Cranfield School of Management, Cranfield University |
| **Andrea Vinelli** | Professor, Department of Management and Engineering, University of Padova, Italy |
| **Adrian Watt** | Senior Lecturer in Operations Management, University of West England, UK |
| **Graham Whittington** | Marketing Specialist, Lancashire Enterprises plc |
| **Stuart Wicks** | Head of Marine Gas Turbine Support, Rolls-Royce plc, UK |
| **Kenneth Work** | I.S. Consultant, Logica UK |

# Preface

Case studies are essential to the teaching of practical and applied subjects such as operations management. To make life easier for teachers and students we have gathered together, in this one volume, a collection of case studies which we and our colleagues use in our teaching. The cases cover a wide variety of operations management issues in many different settings. Furthermore, these cases can be successfully incorporated into operations management teaching programmes at undergraduate and postgraduate levels and also in executive programmes.

This third edition of our case book contains an expanded and updated collection of over 50 cases. Before developing this edition we contacted many of our colleagues who we knew were using the book to ascertain their views. Although we were keen to introduce many new cases, we recognise that we have to maintain a balance by retaining some familiar cases that work well in our teaching. As a result we have kept eight cases as they were in the second edition, and made amendments to about 10 others. Some of our colleagues kindly provided some of their own cases to deal with areas which were not previously covered, such as operations strategy, interactive design, simultaneous engineering, supply chain reengineering, performance measurement, and TPM, for example. You will see that we have also included, as requested, many more short, one or two page, cases.

This case book continues to be structured to follow the themes of, and illustrate the main points contained in, many operations management texts, in particular, Slack, N., Chambers, S. and Johnston, R. (2001), *Operations Management*, Third Edition, Financial Times Prentice Hall, Harlow. We hope that this case book can be used as a companion to such texts, and also, because of the short introductions to each section, can be used as a stand-alone text for introductory operations management courses.

The introduction to this book deals with some issues concerning how to study operations management using cases and how to analyse case studies. Some students do not always see the value of case studies so this first section aims to address such concerns. This section sets out the importance of using case studies in studying operations management and identifies many of the benefits of so doing. It explains the nature of cases, what they are, what they are not, and provides some suggestions for their analysis. This section also explains the objectives for the whole book and describes the book's structure.

The main body of the book is structured into the seven 'traditional' operations headings which are likely to be covered in most operations management courses: Operations Management, Operations Strategy, Design, Planning and Control, Supply Networking, Quality Planning and Control, and Improvement. An introduction at the start of each part provides an overview of the area and some suggestions for further reading. Each case study is accompanied by a set of questions. The questions are indicative of some of the significant issues found in each case and should guide the students in their analysis. It is recognised that teachers may prefer to devise alternative sets of questions which better reflect their favoured teaching schemes and styles of approach to case analysis. Many of the issues and debating points that arise from the cases are considered in the *Lecturer's Guide* which accompanies the case book and can be downloaded from www.booksites.net/johnston.

Organisations on which cases are based have often been kind enough to allow their names to be used. Whilst all the cases reflect real issues facing the organisations at the time, the cases have been written for the purposes of class discussion and student instruction only and are not designed to illustrate the effective or ineffective management of an organisation.

We hope that you, both teachers and students, will derive as much value and pleasure as we have in our use of these cases. We would value any comments and suggestions you might have about the book and welcome your suggestions for future editions.

We would like to thank all those organisations, whether named or disguised, for their help with the preparation of the material used in this book. We are most grateful to the managers and staff of all those organisations for giving their time and their assistance, without which this book could not have been possible.

We are very grateful for the ideas and suggestions we received from Martin Lodge, University of Huddersfield, Andrew Greasley, Aston University, John Bicheno, University of Buckingham, Keith Moreton, Staffordshire University, Max Moullin, Sheffield Hallam University, Zoe Radnor, Bradford University, Eileen Saez, Northumbria University, and Richard Anderson, Coventry University.

We would like to thank our associate contributors for their work in the preparation and development of some of the cases and all of our past students who have participated in the discussion, and development, of these cases. Especial thanks to Hilary Bates at Warwick Business School for her invaluable help in developing the introductory sections.

We are grateful for the support of the highly professional team at Financial Times Prentice Hall, and in particular to Alison Kirk for her unfailing encouragement and support.

*Robert Johnston*
*Stuart Chambers*
*Christine Harland*
*Alan Harrison*
*Nigel Slack*

# Acknowledgements

We are grateful to the following for permission to reproduce copyright material:

Figures P1.1, P3.1, P3.2, P4.1, P5.1, P6.1 and P6.2 from *Operations Management*, 3rd edition, Pearson Education (Slack, N., Chambers, S. & Johnston, R., 2001); Figure P2.1 from *Operations Strategy*, Pearson Education (Slack, N. & Lewis, M., 2002); Figure 16.1 and Tables 16.1 and 16.2 from Back to the future: Benetton transforms its global networks in *Sloan Management Review*, Fall, Los Angeles Times Syndicate International (Camuffo, A., Romano, P. & Vinelli, A., 2001).

Every effort has been made by the publisher to obtain permission from the appropriate source to reproduce material which appears in this book. In some instances we have been unable to trace the owners of copyright material, and we would appreciate any information that would enable us to do so.

# Introduction to operations management case analysis

## Introduction

Operations management (OM) is a practical subject. Trying to learn about OM and the decisions that operations managers take each day in all organisations around us cannot easily be studied by reading texts or listening to lectures alone. Certainly these will give you important and helpful information, but the subject does not come alive until it is practised. You can learn how to fish from a book, but you will never understand the nuances of whirlpools and eddies until you have seen them for yourself. You cannot understand the excitement of playing sport from a book; you have to do it. You can learn recipes from a cookery book but you will not know how good the food tastes, or how difficult it is to cook, until you have tried them out for yourself.

Unfortunately, opening this book will not physically transport you into the office of an operations manager and allow you to take over their job. But it will get you close! It will provide you with information from over 50 different organisations, in many different sectors, from several different countries, and will give you some fascinating insights into what operations managers actually do and how they work, as well as the issues they face. Most importantly, this book will give you the opportunity, in a safe environment, to experiment with the situations they face – giving you the chance to assess, analyse and evaluate the situation they are in and make recommendations.

This casebook will provide you with many benefits:

- You will have at your fingertips real information about a real organisation without having to spend large amounts of time and effort interviewing managers, customers and staff or searching through company documents.
- You will have the chance to evaluate situations faced by real operations managers.
- You will be able to 'hold time still' – to assess a situation without it changing as it does in real time. You will have time to undertake analysis and evaluation without the pressures of managing the operation.
- You will have the opportunity, and the information, to debate and discuss the interpretation and use of the data and to undertake meaningful analysis.
- You will be able to develop and discuss possible solutions and their implications.
- You will not be sacked if you get a decision or the recommendations wrong, nor will you be taken to court if you cost the organisation millions of euros, dollars or pounds!

All of the cases in this book are real cases, based on real situations faced by real operations managers in real organisations. For many of them we have been allowed to share with you the name of that organisation.

Remember though, the case itself cannot tell us everything. The material has been selected to provide us with enough information to help us understand the particular topic. It has also been chosen with a topic in mind. Herein lies a problem for studying operations cases. The reality is that any operations problem involves elements of people issues, quality, scheduling, technology ... and every operations manager has to bring all their knowledge and experience to bear to deal with the issue at hand.

For the purpose of teaching and learning, we have had to divide the body of knowledge on operations management into convenient chunks. However, you will find that there are great overlaps when working on the cases. Bear in mind that the cases have been written to illustrate one particular topic but the nature of OM means that you will find, and indeed should look for, the links with all the other topics. That way you will start to understand the complexity, and the excitement, of managing operations.

## The aim of this casebook

The aim of this book is to demonstrate some of the problems faced by operations managers in various settings, both goods oriented and service oriented, through the provision of case studies. Its purpose is to promote discussion as to how operations managers might improve their operations and contribute to corporate objectives, and by so doing equip future and practising managers with the skills and techniques needed to be better able to understand and manage operations.

Using case studies will help you develop a range of other skills:

- *Analytical skills* – dealing with both qualitative and quantitative data to analyse situations
- *Application skills* – providing opportunities to practise using tools, techniques and theories learned in class or found in many operations management texts
- *Creative skills* – using imagination and ingenuity to assess and solve unique problems
- *Critical thinking skills* – applying clear and logical reasoning to the information available
- *Communication skills* – listening to colleagues and constructing and expressing your arguments, debating options and presenting findings
- *Decision making skills* – expecting you to reach conclusions and suggest decisions based on your analysis
- *Interpersonal skills* – working with peers, learning how to deal with them and with conflict situations
- *Time management skills* – scheduling time carefully to meet presentation or submission deadlines
- *Written communication skills* – developing effective writing skills through written case reports.

# What is expected of you

These skills don't just appear, they have to be worked at, and you should take personal responsibility for your own learning and development. The next two sections in this introduction will discuss the nature of operations management cases and provide some detailed information about the process of case study analysis. In this section we want to provide a few pointers to help you get the most out of the case approach.

The most important point to remember is to take an active role in your learning. What you get out of a case depends entirely on what you are prepared to put in. There are four different learning opportunities: personal preparation, syndicate work, class discussion and case assignment/examination.

## Personal preparation

Personal case preparation is the first and most important step in getting the most out of a case. There is often a temptation to skip or minimise effort on this stage. This is a serious mistake. There is nothing worse than being part of a small group or class discussion and not knowing what is going on! The section on The Process of Case Analysis (see later in this introduction) will show you how to do this. If you find yourself getting bogged down, leave that point and move on. Things often become clearer after a while.

## Syndicate work

Many lecturers encourage small groups to work together on particular questions, often culminating in a group presentation to the class. This is an important chance for you to test out your ideas and also take risks with your ideas. Every member of the group has a responsibility to ensure that everyone has a say. This, however, is not sufficient, everyone has to *listen* to all the views expressed and come to a *consensus* about the way forward. Group decisions are often better, more informed and better thought out than individual decisions, so see group work as a benefit, not as a threat to your own ideas; be ready to be persuaded! We find syndicate groups often spend too long on the first question. Consider starting the session by agreeing the amount of time you will spend on each part. As you know, deadlines focus the mind!

## Class discussion

We have run the same case with different classes and know that some classes have learnt a great deal while others have learnt little. The benefits to be gained in class depend upon the syndicate work, which depends upon your personal preparation. If different groups are making presentations, it is too easy to sit back, switch off and wait for your turn. You need to listen carefully and make sure you avoid repeating what other groups may have said. It is your responsibility to try to build on previous presentations and discussions. Also, there should be no need to remain silent. Use the class discussion time as a chance to ask good, pertinent questions. Make a point of asking critical (crucial) questions, not making critical (negative) points.

### Case assignment/examination

Sometimes case studies are used as assignments or as the basis for an exam or part of an exam. Sometimes you will be restricted to personal preparation only, but if possible and if it is permitted, try to make some time for group discussion about the case. As for all forms of examination, it is essential to answer the question. This may sound obvious, but we all know that the main reason why most students fail any piece of work is because they simply have not answered the question. Look at the marks allocated to each question (if they are given) and allocate your time in proportion to the marks. It is always a good idea to include your analysis, calculations, lists, tables and assumptions. Use diagrams and tables where you can; this can be an efficient way of conveying a lot of information without too many words.

## The nature of operations management cases

Operations management cases often reflect the nature of operations themselves. They can be complicated. Interacting within any operation there are different pieces of technology, different staff and different systems and procedures. This makes for a complex decision environment. Although some of the complexity has, of necessity, been taken out in the case writing process, you might still find that there are many different things to consider. So you must simplify. Extract what you believe to be important and classify issues, problems and pieces of information. This will give you a clearer picture of the case.

Operations management cases also often involve technology. This can cause people problems. They are reluctant to become too involved in strange technologies because they believe them to be difficult to understand. Yet it is usually not necessary to understand the nature or the workings of the technology itself to analyse the management situation. Just remember that, in essence, most technologies *are* quite straightforward. Just ask some simple questions. How big is the technology? How much of the work is done by machines as opposed to human beings? How integrated or connected is the technology? What are the effects on the people who staff the operation? How many different kinds of technology are there in the operation? Is it intended to be used for only one product or service (dedicated) or is it adaptable, capable of being 'set-up' for a range of different outputs?

This combination of complexity and technology can mean that you might have to speculate about the precise nature of the operation at some points in your analysis. Don't worry too much about doing this. Provided you are sensible and work from the facts that you do have, and you do not forget that you are only speculating and consider the difference it would make to your analysis if your speculation is misplaced, then your analysis will move forward.

## The process of case analysis

Case studies can ask you to do a number of things. Usually, though, they are either asking you to understand a situation and its implications or, alternatively, they are asking you to solve specific problems. Of course, in order to solve problems you first have to understand the situation and its implications, so the difference between these two types of case study is really one of emphasis. In fact one of the most useful ways of approaching case analysis is to treat them as problem-solving opportunities and follow a sequence of activities designed specifically for problem solving.

Figure A.1 shows this sequence of activities. First there is a process of observation or, for case analysis, of recognising the symptoms of possible problems described in the case. Next there is a process of understanding the overall objectives of the problem-solving process. This will involve understanding the objectives of the operation itself. After this the nature of the problem should be analysed and the interrelationships between different parts of the case established. It is now time to move on to considering the different options which might improve the operation. Eventually it will become necessary to evaluate and choose what you are going to recommend the operation to do. After this your recommended solution will need to be implemented within the operation. Finally, the effectiveness of the implemented solution should be observed and if any further action is needed, the whole cycle is started again. (You can, of course, only do this last step in a real situation.)

## Observe

Reading the facts as laid down in a case study is equivalent to observing an organisation in real life. During this stage be careful of jumping to premature conclusions. Something that seems significant when described in one part of the case study may take on a totally different aspect when placed in the context of information presented later. For this reason some authorities counsel against making notes on the first reading of a case study. Instead, read quickly through the case to get a picture of the overall 'story'. Then return to the beginning and work through more thoroughly, either highlighting points or making notes of facts and issues which seem particularly pertinent.

**Figure A.1 The stages of case study analysis**

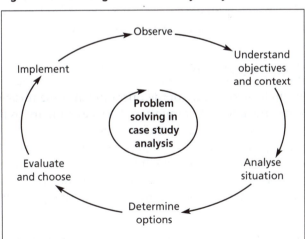

As you are noting what seem to be the key points, be careful to distinguish the strength of the evidence which is cited in the case. Relevant points can be drawn from the following:

- *Facts*. These are the hard pieces of information which are clearly in a precise form and seem unequivocal. For example, 'the turnover of the company is £5 million'. They are the bones of the case around which everything else is built.
- *Inference*. Reported facts are rearranged in such a way as to reach further conclusions. The inferred issue may never be explicitly stated in the case but can nevertheless be drawn from the logic of other statements. For example, if it is stated that the types of products produced by a company doubled over a period of time and if it is also stated that the management of that company invested heavily in more flexible machinery during the same period, it is safe to infer that the managers of the company understood the connection between product variety and operational flexibility.
- *Hearsay*. Many of the cases include statements from managers or other employees. These views are genuinely held and may be based on fact or, at the opposite extreme, they may be emotional responses to the situation. You will have to make judgements about the reliability of this data and weight it accordingly alongside other, more 'hard' evidence.
- *Speculation*. In some ways this is a weaker form of inference. Speculation must have a logical base in so much as it must be possible to make a case for the point you are noting. Furthermore, there should be some evidence to support it in the case study, though not to the point where one could in any way logically 'prove' the point.
- *Assumption*. When there is a clear gap or hole in the data in the case study, it may be necessary to make an assumption which, as far as you can tell, seems reasonable in the context being described. For example, we may assume that the behaviour of customers in different countries is sufficiently similar to recommend the same solution for all parts of a multinational's company. The important point is that assumptions must always be seen for what they are: 'best guesses' under the circumstances. The important caveat is that you should examine the possible effects if the assumptions you have made prove to be false.

## Understand objectives and context

Unless you know what the organisation described in the case study is trying to do, it is difficult to judge the nature of the problems it faces and, just as important, how the managers in the organisation might view things.

In operations management cases this stage is usually concerned with connecting the overall objectives of an organisation with the specific objectives of the issue or problem described in the case. So, for example, if a case describes the purchase of a particular piece of process technology for an operation, the questions to try to clarify could be as follows:

- What is the history of the organisation in terms of its use of process technology?
- What are the long-term objectives of the operation? Is it primarily a 'for-profit' organisation or do other non-financial objectives dominate? What are the implications (if any) for the way it uses process technology?

- How does the organisation serve its customers? Which aspects of what the organisation 'sells' to its customers are the most important to them? Is it:
  - the specification of the product or service?
  - the quality of the product or service?
  - the customer lead-time (how long you have to wait) for the product or service?
  - the dependability of delivery of the product or service?
  - the variety, customisation or flexibility of the product or service?
  - the cost of the product or service?
- What aspects of process technology in this particular case (size, cost, capacity, flexibility, etc.) influence the operations objectives?
- How does the way in which the organisation develops its process technology constrain and limit the strategic direction of the organisation?
- Conversely, how does the way in which the organisation develops its process technology enable the organisation to enhance its strategy?

## Analyse the situation

Be careful not to skip this stage. It is tempting to do so: the objectives of the organisation have been formulated and the issues already listed from the case study, so why not go straight into thinking of ways of solving whatever problems are described? Even when the decision seems clearly defined, it is worthwhile spending some time analysing the information in the case. Many organisations and individuals have suffered as a result of managers jumping to conclusions without adequate analysis of the situation.

The *Concise Oxford Dictionary* defines the verb 'to analyse' as to 'ascertain the elements of'. Analysis is the process of breaking down a complex situation into its component parts. This will help you to understand the underlying issues and the relationships between the problems in the case. The most likely outcome is that the nature of the problems in the case can be redefined so as to reveal their root causes.

Many of the cases comprise both narrative and data. It is important that your analysis should review both aspects. If you are dealing with narrative you may need to identify the different products or services provided by the organisation and ask which seem more popular and which are more difficult to provide and why? How are they made or provided, and can you identify the key steps or stages in the operations process? You might ask yourself what different people say about the situation and how good or bad things seem to be? If you are dealing with data, you might look for trends and for figures that seem out of line. You may need to calculate averages for comparison, or speeds of queues or of different production processes to identify bottlenecks or delays. Where possible you should identify and tabulate differences, for example between markets, volumes, skill requirements, etc. You may find simple tools like lists, graphs, charts and flow diagrams useful to summarise your findings.

Most questions will be concerned with understanding the nature of the problem and its causes. One useful way of getting to the root causes of the issues described in the case is by using cause–effect listings. This is simply a process of identifying the main symptoms, problems or 'effects' described in the case and then listing all the possible reasons, explanations or 'causes' of these which are described or referred to in the case study. So, for example, if you see an operation as having one major service quality problem which results in errors in the information presented to customers, the cause–effect listing could be as follows.

| *Effect* | *Possible causes* |
|---|---|
| Errors in information reaching customers | Lack of training? |
| | Errors in staffs' information sources? |
| | Out-of-date staff information sources? |
| | Customers given insufficient guidance on how to request information etc.? |

The next step would be to consider the connections and interrelationships between the possible causes based on your analysis of the information.

## Determine the options

Having spent some time breaking down the situation into its various elements (analysis), there comes a time to put it all back together (synthesis). This is the creative part of the whole process. It is where you should put forward the various courses of action that could be considered by the organisation in order to 'solve' the problems described in the case, or generally to improve the operation's performance. You will usually find that the questions associated with the case will help you do this. You may be asked to list the range of options, or identify the various ways that an organisation might go about doing something.

This is where the work you did in analysing the information in the case will again pay off. Although at an early stage you may have only thought of one or possibly two 'obvious' solutions, a good piece of analysis is likely to have helped you identify many more possibilities. Furthermore, it is more likely that these options will deal with the 'real' problems and the causes of these, rather than what you may have believed to be the situation on first reading the case.

As in most creative activities, two principles are worth bearing in mind in developing options. First, don't evaluate or criticise potential solutions too early. Go for quantity rather than quality of solutions to begin with. Try to 'brainstorm' all the possible ways of dealing with the situation. Do not reject any options at this stage, however crazy they may seem. Second, organise the solutions in some sets that naturally group together and check for overlaps, gaps and inconsistencies.

## Evaluate and choose

Evaluating means determining the value or worth of things. That is exactly what this stage consists of, determining the worth of the options generated in the previous stage and assessing how likely they are to contribute to improving the situation described in the case.

Your ability to evaluate a situation will be a function of the analysis you have already undertaken, though you may find that you have to undertake a little more analysis in order to evaluate all of your options. You should also test out your arguments against the material in the case to ensure that the evidence supports your conclusions.

The process of evaluation is best carried out by considering three questions about each option:

1 *How feasible is each option?* The feasibility of an option indicates the degree of difficulty in adopting it. It takes into account the time, effort and money needed to put it into practice. For example, you could consider whether the organisation has the technical or human skills required to carry out the option, whether it has the funding or cash requirements to invest in the option and generally whether it has the capacity or capability of implementing the option.

2 *How acceptable is each option?* By acceptability of an option we mean how far it takes the operation towards its objectives. In effect, it is the 'return' we get for choosing that option. Acceptability is best judged in two ways. First, by assessing the operational impact of the option: how it is likely to affect the operational performance of the organisation. For example, does the option increase the likelihood that the product or service of the operation will be closer to what customers want? Second, acceptability ought to be judged in terms of the financial impact of each option. If there is sufficient financial data in the case, it is useful to work out some of the more conventional financial evaluation measures such as return on investment or payback period.

3 *How risky is each option?* Perhaps the most robust way of evaluating the risk inherent in each option is to assess its 'downside risk'. That is, in effect, asking the question, 'What is the worst outcome that could happen if a particular option is chosen?' The next obvious questions are: 'What would be the effect on the operation if that worst outcome occurred?', 'Could the operation survive?' and 'Is it worth the operation taking such a risk?'

## Implement

If you are asked to, or choose to, make recommendations as part of your case study analysis, then they will be incomplete without some consideration of how they might be put into practice. The analysis of the case study may set the destination, but the implementation stage defines how you get there, which is a more difficult task.

The best way to consider implementation issues is to set an 'implementation agenda' – a set of basic questions whose answers set the basic plan for implementation:

- *When to implement?* Some times are better than others. What is happening in the organisation which could affect the chances of the recommended course of action being a success? Are some times of year quieter or more suitable for launching a change in the operation? It is clearly better to make changes when conditions are right. A word of warning though, there is never a perfect time, only some that are better than others.
- *How fast to proceed?* Should one implement the recommendations over a short or long period of time? Is there an advantage, for instance, in moving quickly to apply the recommendations throughout the organisation, or should a more gradual dissemination be planned?
- *Where to start?* In which part of the organisation should the recommendations be applied first? There are two schools of thought here:
  1 Start first where you will achieve the most improvement.
  2 Start first where you are sure you will succeed.

The advantage of the first is that the changes will quickly 'pay back' the cost, time and effort invested. The advantage of the second is that the risk of failure is minimised and the people involved in implementation learn the problems associated with the recommendations as they go along, without losing credibility.

## The structure of the book

This casebook has been structured to follow the main themes contained in most operations management texts, in particular Slack, N., Chambers, S. and Johnston, R. (2001), *Operations Management*, Third Edition, Financial Times Prentice Hall, Harlow.

Each part concentrates on a different aspect of operations management. Several cases are provided in each part which set out to describe some of the key issues involved and to show some of the difficulties and questions faced by operations managers. Introductions at the start of each part outline some of the key aspects of the topic. Some suggestions for further reading are also included.

### Part 1  Operations management

This part provides an overview of the nature and tasks of operations management. A framework is provided that encapsulates these and sets out the structure for the rest of the book and for the studying of the subject. It deals with the processing of materials, information and customers, and the creation of goods and services.

### Part 2  Operations strategy

This part investigates the role of operations in supporting, implementing and driving corporate strategy. Although many courses may leave operations strategy until the end, we find it useful to set out the context for operations management decisions and action near the beginning of our courses.

### Part 3  Design

This part and its associated cases demonstrate the processes involved in designing products and services and also the processes which create and deliver them. It identifies the importance of design and how products and services need to be designed not only to meet customer expectations but also to support the strategic intentions of the organisation. This part outlines the key stages involved in the design of a product or service, from concept to final specification. It also outlines the key activities involved in designing the process of delivery, the use of technology and job design.

### Part 4  Planning and control

Operations planning and control is a central, substantial and critical operations task. Thus planning and control issues have been split over the next three parts. Part 4 focuses on general planning and control, often a large and complex task. Simply put, this involves ensuring that the operation has sufficient resources to be able to meet demand. This part outlines some of the key planning and control activities, including the planning and control of capacity, inventory, just in time and *kaizen*.

## Part 5  Supply networking

No operation, or part of an operation, exists in isolation. Each operation is part of a larger and interconnected network of other operations. Supply networking is concerned with the flow of goods and services through the supply network, from suppliers through to customers. In large organisations, such networks might involve many hundreds of linked supply chains. Supply networking is concerned with both long-term consideration of an organisation's position in the supply network and the shorter-term issue of controlling the flows of materials through the supply chain. This part and its associated cases investigate managing relationships between suppliers and customers and designing the supply chain to meet market requirements.

## Part 6  Quality planning and control

Quality issues are covered in this part and also in the next part on improvement. In this part we focus on planning and control issues such as quality problems, and on quality control techniques and approaches such as statistical process control and control charting.

## Part 7  Improvement

This part and its associated cases outline what is emerging as an important operations task. It covers the importance of performance measurement and identifies several techniques that can be used to improve organisational performance, such as flow charts, scatter diagrams, cause–effect diagrams and Pareto diagrams. This part also covers total quality management (TQM), one of the best-known improvement philosophies.

### Recommended reading

Easton, G. (1992), *Learning from Case Studies*, (2nd edn), Prentice Hall.

Harrison, A. and van Hoek, R. (2002), *Logistics Management and Strategy*, Financial Times Prentice Hall, Harlow.

Johnston, R. (1994), "Operations: From Factory to Service Management", *International Journal of Service Industry Management*, Vol 5, No 1: 49–63.

Johnston, R. (1999), "Service Operations Management: Return to Roots", *International Journal of Operations and Production Management*, Vol 19, No 2: 104–124.

Johnston, R. and Clark, G. (2001), *Service Operations Management*, Financial Times Prentice Hall, Harlow.

Maufette-Leenders, L. A., Erskine, J. A. and Leenders, M. R. (1999), *Learning with Cases*, Ivey Publishing, London, Ontario.

Slack, N. and Lewis, M. (2002), *Operations Strategy*, Financial Times Prentice Hall, Harlow.

Slack, N. Chambers, S. and Johnston, R. (2001), *Operations Management*, (3rd edn), Financial Times Prentice Hall, Harlow.

Womack, J. P. and Jones, D. T. (1998), *Lean Thinking*, Touchstone Books, London.

# PART 1

## Operations management

# Introduction to Part 1

Operations management is concerned with the design, planning, control and improvement of an organisation's resources and processes to produce goods or services for customers. Whether it is the provision of airport services, greetings cards, plastic buckets or holidays, operations managers will have been involved in the design, creation and delivery of those products or services (see Figure P1.1).

## Designing products and services

Design is the activity of determining the purpose, physical form, shape and composition of products and services, and also, importantly, designing the processes that will be used to produce them. You will see from the Birmingham International Airport

**Figure P1.1  A general model of operations management**

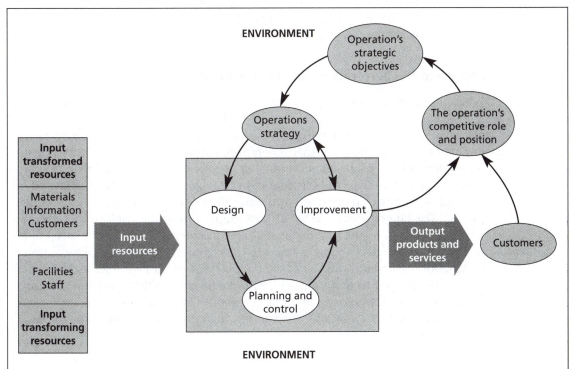

case (Case 1) that each part of the airport – terminals, baggage handling services, aeroplane servicing and catering, for example – has been carefully designed to fulfil not only its current role, but also with the possible demands of the next year and even the next 10 years in mind. In the case of Concept Design Services (Case 5) the fashionable designs of the 'Concept' range have accounted for the rapid growth and profitability of the business. Design is an important activity that will ensure the long-term success of the organisation and is covered in Part 3 of this book.

## Planning and controlling the operation

The planning and control of operations is a major task for all operations managers: coordinating all the different internal operations to ensure that materials and customers are in the right place at the right time for the right operation. Each part of Birmingham Airport's operation has to be planned so that it has enough staff, enough inventory, enough space, the appropriate passengers, the correct baggage, the right planes and the proper equipment in the right place at the right time. The staff involved, from the airport, airlines and associated organisations, have to undertake all the tasks they have been given so that the operation works smoothly, and management must then control these operations to ensure that all goes to plan and meets the needs of the customers – today, tomorrow, next week, next month and next year. Planning and control is the activity of deciding what the operations resources should be doing, then making sure that they really are doing it. For Frederic Godé of BonPain (Case 3) the success of the organisation depends upon the planning of all resources so that the appropriate mix of baguettes and patisseries are ready for delivery to the supermarkets as required. At Wace Burgess (Case 4) good planning ensures that greetings cards are ready in time for all the festivals and events. It's no good supplying the last batch of Christmas cards in January! This topic is developed in Part 4.

## Improving the performance of the operation

When products and services have been designed and the operation's work is being planned and controlled, this is not the end of operations management's direct responsibilities. The continuing responsibility of all operations managers is to improve the performance of their operation. Failure to improve at least as fast as competitors (in for-profit organisations) or at the rate of customers' rising expectations (in all organisations) is to condemn the operations function always to fall short of what customers expect and what the organisation as a whole requires from it. The Operations Director at Birmingham International Airport says that 'Our mission is to be the best regional airport in Europe. To do this we need to put on the right services at the right times to the right places.' It is through constantly looking for ways to improve what the airport does and how it does it that the airport will be helped to maintain and improve its competitive position. Executive Holloware (Case 42) needs to improve the quality of its products or it may well go out of business! Part 7 contains cases on how organisations go about the important improvement task.

## Operations strategy

Although the operations function is central to the organisation because it produces all the value-added goods and services, it does not exist in isolation. It has to work in conjunction with all the other functions of the organisation: marketing, accounting and finance, product/service development, human resources, purchasing and the engineering/technical functions, for example. Each of these influences, and is influenced by, the activities of the operation. Each of these functions has its own important role to play in the organisation's activities and they are (or should be) bound together, along with operations, by common organisational goals.

The strategic role of an organisation is to coordinate the activities of all these functions so that the organisation as a whole coherently and consistently meets not only the needs of the customers, but also fulfils the strategic intentions of the organisation. Operations strategy is concerned with helping the operation contribute to the organisation's competitiveness or strategic direction. This topic is dealt with in more detail later in this part and in Part 2.

There is a strategic issue in most of the cases in this book. For example, in Concept Design Services, the three markets described must be served in very different ways and so operations must be closely involved in supporting these different requirements if the business is to continue to grow profitably.

## The transformation model

All operations produce their goods or services by a process of transformation (see Figure P1.2).

**Figure P1.2  The transformation model**

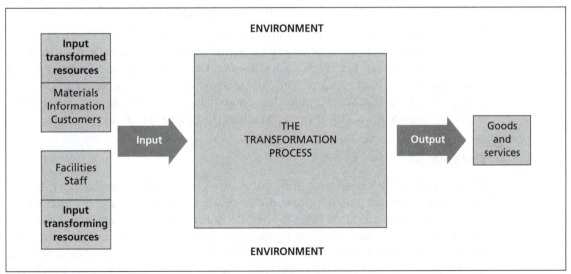

## The transformed resources

Operations transform a mixture of customers, materials and information.

### Customer processing

Birmingham International Airport, for example, processes *customers* through its termini. Individual passengers are processed into batches of customers ready to board the right planes at the right times. Plane loads of arriving passengers are processed through customs and immigration and reunited with their bags and transport.

### Materials processing

The airport also processes *materials* such as baggage, food and aeroplanes. In-bound aircraft, for example, are transformed into clean and refuelled out-bound aircraft. Incoming raw food is transformed into meals for staff and passengers.

### Information processing

The airport's operation also processes a large amount of *information* – plane schedules, air traffic control (ATC) information and individual requests from passengers. ATC information, for example, is transformed into departure and arrival times on the passenger information screens.

## The transforming resources

The materials, customers and information are transformed resources, they are changed in some way during the operation. What transforms them are the transforming resources: the operations facilities and staff. The cleaners, caterers and refuellers transform the aircraft; the check-in staff, departure lounges and restaurants transform the passengers.

## Customer/materials/information processing operations

Very few operations are exclusively engaged in processing only customers, or materials or information. Yet one usually predominates, for example Birmingham International Airport, like Hogsmeadow Garden Centre (Case 2) and Cadbury World (Case 11) predominantly transform customers whereas Wace Burgess and Concept Design Services predominantly transform materials. All of them, however, transform all three – information, customers and materials – to a greater or lesser extent.

## Outputs

The outputs of the transformation process are goods and/or services. Goods, like greetings cards and plastic household items, are tangible: you can touch them. Goods are usually produced prior to their consumption. Goods can often be stored, at least for a short time after their production, which may ease the planning and control task. There is often little contact between the staff producing the goods and the customer, so customers' perceptions of the quality of the goods is often based solely on the evidence of the goods themselves and not on the process by which they were made.

Services, such as festivals and music, tend to be intangible though they are seen and experienced by the customer. They can be difficult to store; space at a pop festival cannot be 'stored' and kept for use by paying customers a week later. Services are usually produced at the same time as they are consumed and so there is often contact made between the customers and the staff providing the service. As a result, the customers' views about the quality of the service will not just be about the 'service' itself, but also about the way in which it was produced – the process.

### Most operations produce goods *and* services

As most operations transform information, materials and customers, they produce combinations of goods and services. Hogsmeadow Garden Centre provides advice about gardening problems as well as the plants and other garden products that customers may take away with them. Wace Burgess does not only produce greetings cards but also provides technical and graphics advice to the designers, allowing them to explore the boundaries of creativity and innovation.

Some goods producers, such as computer manufacturers which have lost the ability to differentiate themselves from their competitors through the goods that they offer, are using the provision of services – after-sales support, distribution systems, care and warranty service, for example – to achieve a competitive advantage. Similarly, some service organisations, like airlines, whilst providing similar levels of service to customers, are forced to compete on their goods: their routes, type of food offered, type of video entertainment system and other on-board services, and types of aircraft.

## Operations within operations

Most operations are a complex set of interrelated smaller operations, each with a specific function. These smaller operations interact with each other to provide the main goods and services to customers, each having its own transformation process.

Birmingham Airport, for example, though one large operation, is made up of many interdependent and often autonomous 'internal' operations, or micro-operations – the catering operation, the cleaning operation, the baggage handling operation, runway maintenance, fire service and security service, for example. At Wace Burgess, a manufacturing business, there are a variety of micro, internal operations, including purchasing, customer support, graphics preparation, printing, cutting and folding departments. All these internal operations may be quite different from each other but they all have to be designed, planned, controlled, improved and coordinated with each other.

Just as operations have external customers, so all the different micro-operations have internal customers too. The airport's customers are the passengers who come to the airport to get on a plane and also the airlines for which the airport provides passenger facilities, fuel and landing services. These are the 'external' customers, customers from outside the organisation who desire and pay for the goods and services that it produces. The airport's internal customers include pilots who need ATC information and baggage handlers who need the bags after they have been processed by check-in staff.

Operations are usually a complex network of micro-operations that form internal customer–supplier relationships, which together provide the goods, services and information to the external customer. If any part of a micro-operation is not properly designed, planned or controlled, then the provision of goods or services to the external customer may be jeopardised. This is one of the foundations of total quality management (TQM) which is dealt with in Part 7.

As micro-operations act in a similar way to the macro-operation, then most of the ideas relevant to the macro-operation are also relevant to the micro-operations. In other words, many of the issues, methods and techniques which we treat in this book as applying to the operations function as a whole also have some meaning for each unit, section, group or individual within the organisation. All parts of an organisation, whether micro-operations such as catering or indeed other functions such as marketing or finance, can be viewed as operations in their own right. Each such operation will provide goods and/or services to internal or external customers, and each will have to design, plan, control and improve its outputs and the processes by which it creates those outputs. The implications of this are important. It means that every manager in all parts of an organisation is, to some extent, an operations manager. All managers need to organise their resource inputs effectively so as to produce goods and services.

## Types of operations

There are four particularly important dimensions which can be used to distinguish between different operations; the *volume* of their output, the *variety* of their output, the *variation* in the demand for their output and the degree of *customer contact* which is involved in producing the output.

### The volume dimension

With the exception of Hogsmeadow Garden Centre, all the cases in Part 1 of this book are high-volume operations supplying repetitive or standardised products and services. This allows for repeatability, specialisation and systemisation, usually resulting in relatively low unit costs. Operations such as Boys and Boden (Cases 17 and 18) and Thompson Telescopes Ltd (Case 29) are examples of lower-volume operations where a wide range of options is available, with less predictability and fewer opportunities for repetition and systemisation.

### The variety dimension

The greater the variety of products or services produced, the more flexible the operation has to be. Concept Design Services has recently introduced its 'Concept' range, thereby expanding the range of shapes and colours that it can offer, which has implications for the way in which the manufacturing process is organised to avoid large numbers of machine set-ups.

## The variation dimension

Variation is concerned with the change in patterns of demand for products or services. Little variation in demand allows some organisations to easily plan and control their activities, resulting in a high utilisation of resources. Variation is a real problem for Wace Burgess, which has to produce vast quantities of cards just for two big peaks, Christmas and Easter. Variation is an issue for many of the other cases in this book where demand is seasonal and/or uncertain; for example, Holly Farm (Case 24) and Fresh Salads Ltd (Case 26).

## The customer contact dimension

All operations have some degree of customer contact, but some have much more than others. Concept Design Services is a relatively low-contact operation but still gets orders and customer enquiries daily. Eurocamp Travel (Case 52) has much higher levels of contact between its customers and the operation.

# Operations strategy

Operations management is a very immediate occupation. It involves hundreds of minute-by-minute decisions throughout, the working week. Because of this it is vital that operations managers have a set of general principles which can guide decision making towards the organisation's longer-term goals. This is an operations strategy – the overall set of activities and decisions which create the role and objectives of the operations so that they contribute to and support the organisation's overall business strategy.

## Operations role

The operation may take three different roles within an organisation: as a *support* to business strategy, as the *implementer* of business strategy and as the *driver* of business strategy.

### Supporting business strategy
One role of the operations part of the business is to *support* strategy. That is, it must develop its resources to provide the capabilities that are needed to allow the organisation to achieve its strategic goals.

### Implementing business strategy
A strategy is only a statement of intent. It is the operations role, therefore, to make it happen: the role of operations is to 'operationalise' and *implement* the chosen strategy. Birmingham Airport has adopted strategies to help it become the 'best regional airport in Europe'. As a result, the operation had to oversee the development of new building projects to manage the growing number of passengers and meet their expectations. Apart from strategies aimed at increasing the customer base, it also has to ensure that the day-to-day running of the airport is seamless.

### Driving business strategy

The third role of the operations part of the business is to *drive* strategy by giving it a long-term competitive edge. It is important to realise that even the most original and brilliant strategy can be rendered totally ineffective by an inept operations function. Marks and Spencer (Case 6) shows how difficult a balancing act it can be to keep both market and operations strategies aligned.

## Operations performance objectives

So how does an operation go about ensuring that it contributes effectively to the organisation's strategy? It does so through five basic 'performance objectives': the *quality* of its goods and services; the *speed* with which they are delivered to customers; the *dependability* with which the operation keeps its delivery promises; the *flexibility* of the operation to change what it does; and the *cost* of producing its goods and services. Achieving high performance in any one of these can give competitive advantage to a business. For example:

● The quality advantage. By ensuring that the operation *does things right*, by not making mistakes or creating defective products or poor service, the operation can provide a quality advantage to the organisation.
● The speed advantage. By *doing things fast*, an organisation can minimise the time between a customer asking for goods or services and the customer receiving them in full. In so doing, it increases the availability of its goods and services to customers, thereby giving it a speed advantage.
● The dependability advantage. By *doing things on time* and keeping delivery promises that have been made to customers, the operation can provide the organisation with a dependability advantage.
● The flexibility advantage. By being able to *change what is done*, that is, being able to vary or adapt the operation's activities to provide individual treatment to customers or cope with unexpected circumstances, the operation can gain a flexibility advantage.
● The cost advantage. By *doing things cheaply*, that is, giving good value to customers whilst keeping to budget or providing the right level of return for an organisation, the operation can provide a cost advantage.

So, by translating organisational strategy into these operations performance objectives and identifying their relative importance, operations can focus on what is important and on doing it well.

## ● A framework for understanding operations management

We can now combine the three important themes to provide a unified framework for understanding operations management (see Figure P1.3).

The first theme is the key operations management tasks: the design, planning and control, and improvement activities. The framework shows these activities as being connected in, more or less, the chronological order in which they would happen if a totally new operation were being developed. It would first be designed,

**Figure P1.3  A framework for understanding operations management**

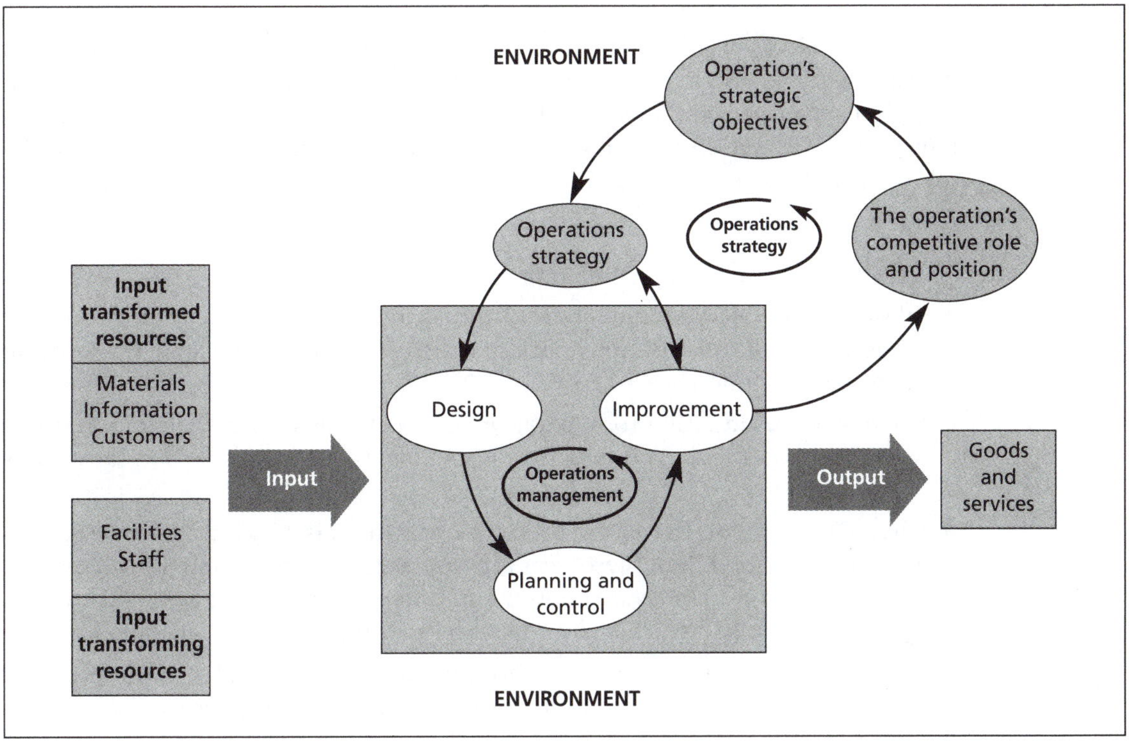

then be operated through planning and control activities and, over time, would be continually improved.

The second theme is the fundamental purpose of operations management: the transformation of input resources, both transformed and transforming, into goods and services, as illustrated by the input–transformation–output diagram.

The third area is operations strategy: understanding the organisation's strategic intentions and then translating them into operations performance objectives to guide operations decisions about the design, planning, control and improvement of operations resources and processes.

The model now shows two interconnected loops of activities. The bottom one more or less corresponds to what is usually seen as *operations management*, and the top one to what is seen as *operations strategy*. This book, like the associated text book, concentrates on the former but tries to cover enough of the latter to allow the reader to make strategic sense of the operations manager's job.

## ● The complexity and criticality of operations management

You should be starting to get an idea of just how complex and critical the operations management task is. It is complex because of all the different and yet interrelated activities, because of the large variety of tasks involved and because of the large number of associated tools and techniques. It is critical because if anything goes wrong, not only could it lose a customer or create bad will, it could also undermine the whole competitive strategy of the organisation.

## Summary

This part and its associated cases are provided to demonstrate the nature of operations management and also to provide a structure for studying the subject in more detail. Operations management deals with the processing of materials, information and customers, and with the creation of goods and services. This part has also considered the role of operations in supporting, implementing and driving corporate strategy.

### Key points

- All organisations have an operations function which produces their goods and services, and all organisations have managers who are responsible for running the operations function.
- The operations function (or 'operation' or 'operations system') is important to the organisation because it directly affects how well the organisation satisfies its customers.
- The most useful method of modelling operations is as an input–transformation–output system. Input resources can be classified as *transforming resources* (the staff and facilities) which act upon the *transformed resources* (materials, information and customers) which are in some way transformed by the operation.
- Outputs from the operation are usually a mixture of goods and services, although some operations are pure goods producers or pure service producers.
- Operations comprise many micro-operations; these micro-operations form a network of internal customer–supplier relationships within the operation.
- Operations can be classified along four dimensions which indicate their level of volume, variety, variation and customer contact.
- The key tasks of operations managers are the design, planning, control and improvement of operational resources and processes.
- By understanding the strategic intentions of an organisation and translating these into operations performance criteria, operations can support, implement and drive business strategy.
- The effective management of operations is critical to organisational success.

### Recommended reading

Chase, R. and Hayes, R. H. (1991), 'Beefing up Operations in Service Firms', *Sloan Management Review*, Fall: 15–26.

Chase, R., Aquilano, F. and Jacobs, R. (2000), *Operations Management for Competitive Advantage*, McGraw Hill.

Hayes, R. H. and Wheelwright, S. C. (1984), *Restoring Our Competitive Edge*, Wiley.

Hill, T. (2000), *Operations Management*, Palgrave Macmillan.

Slack, N., Chambers, S. and Johnston, R. (2001), *Operations Management*, (3rd edn), Financial Times Prentice Hall, Harlow, Chapters 1 and 2.

# CASE 1

# Birmingham International Airport

Case date
2002

## Robert Johnston

In the space of just 30 minutes every weekday, around 5.00 in the evening, around 20 flights arrive at and depart from the Eurohub Terminal. At the same time, aircraft are arriving and leaving the Main Terminal next to the Eurohub. Across the runway and acres of tarmac, at the site of the original airport, the overnight freight operation is just beginning to wake up with the arrival of staff and the preparations for the first aircraft from Europe or the United States.

Some of the 7000 staff from the 150 organisations based at Birmingham International Airport (BIA) see to the needs of their customers. The baggage handling operation is sorting, checking and dispatching bags to the many departing aircraft. The ground crews are loading and unloading aircraft, putting meals on board, filling the fuel tanks and cleaning the aircraft during their brief spell at the airbridge. The airlines' ticketing staff are dealing with lines of passengers, each of whom may have a different final destination. The information desk is fully staffed, dealing with the many queries, such as people wanting to know if their plane is on time, the location of a bank or hotel, or trying to work out how to get by road or rail to their final destination. Passengers flow through the lounges, passport control and security checks, and use toilets, duty free shops and restaurants, all of which have to be kept clean and stocked for their convenience. All of these activities, and more, are coordinated by BIA's Operations Director, Richard Heard. Richard explains his role:

'Out of all the people that work at the airport, BIA employs about 700 and I oversee about 600 of them. These operations people are basically concerned with the day-to-day running of the airport and the short and medium-term operational planning. This includes a whole raft of things on the airfield and in and around the terminals. The airfield side of things essentially involves maintaining the runways, agreeing slot allocations with the airlines, developing and implementing safety management systems and keeping the fire crew fully trained, for example. This is a heavily regulated area so we work very closely with the Civil Aviation Authority. The other side of the operation is about managing the terminal buildings and other facilities. This is almost like running a shopping centre with its focus on customer service but with special security arrangements. Airport security is a key task which we run in-house, employing about 300 people. I also have a facilities management team and an engineering services team that look after the maintenance of the whole site.

'In terms of long-term design and development, we set up teams to oversee the planning of new building projects, such as new catering outlets, car parks and people mover systems. This plan uses the forecasts of passenger numbers and guides our decisions about what to build and when, and how to pay for it. We have been growing at a rate of about 10 per cent a year over the last 10 years. In 2000 the airport handled 7.6 million passengers and our growth is set to continue, with an anticipated 10 million passengers expected to travel through Birmingham by 2005. This plan involves serious money; we are talking about a capital plan of about £50 million a year over the next 15 years. This is all very much driven by operational needs. Managing and developing the airport's operations are huge challenges.

'One of the major tasks for operations is not just to provide the infrastructure for all the other organisations on site – such as airlines, handling agents, retailers, cargo handlers – but also to provide the leadership and coordination for them. There are also groups off site, such as community groups, which we liaise with as we work to monitor and improve the environment. My personal job is about coordination and setting the safety and customer service standards for everyone to adhere to.

'All of us from the different organisations try to work together as a team and there is a great community spirit here that has built up over the years. Everyone wants their own bit to work well and the whole thing to work well together. We all have a great understanding of everyone's problems and there is an excellent spirit of cooperation.

'The real secret of managing operations, if you are ever going to sleep at night, is to make sure you have really good processes and procedures in place. We can't have people making it up on the spot. Everything has to be thought through and tried and tested. We spend a great deal of time reviewing and developing processes. We have to have procedures for fires, evacuations, bomb threats, ill passengers and even deaths in the terminal. Unfortunately, we do have medical emergencies, not surprising since we have about 30 000 people passing through the airport every day in the summer.

'Another key task is operational planning. We do this on an annual basis. Operational planning is about making the operation as efficient as possible by working out how we can best allocate our infrastructure to the airlines. For example, we need to decide who is going to get the airbridges, who is going to get certain stands, who is going to have their passengers bused to the terminal at peak times, and so on. However, you have to remember that the operational plans are just that, plans, and as ever, things go wrong – schedules fall apart because of plane delays or mechanical problems, for example. So we also have terminal duty managers whose job it is to sort out the day-to-day operational problems. Our team of terminal managers covers the airport 24 hours a day, every day of the week, with one senior manager overseeing each shift.

'Many of the things that happen are recurring problems, such as delays or diversions, and you know you will end up with a lot of passengers waiting around a lot longer than they want to. The job of the duty manager is to coordinate all our efforts, ensuring that the catering people know what's happening and making sure our information services people know so they can tell the passengers, for example. The terminal managers need to keep their ears and eyes open. Passengers may report that they have seen someone acting suspiciously and the managers need to know what to do. When passengers get off the plane and their bags are not there, although it's the responsibility of the airlines or their handling agents, our people may have to pick up the pieces. When people try taking prohibited items through security, such as a family heirloom with a large curved blade, we have to explain patiently to them that they have to leave it with us.

'The terminal managers also have to deal with major incidents – things like bomb threats or, like last year, when the Spanish coach drivers went on strike leaving many passengers stranded at the airport. The job of the terminal manager is to sort it all out and make sure everyone knows what is happening. It involves a great deal of common sense but it is not easy. If you have to do an evacuation, for example, everyone will be at different stages in the passenger processing and security clearance procedures, so when the incident is over, we have to try to put them all back where they came from without mixing them up or they all have to start the process again!

'We have the equivalent of the terminal duty managers looking after the airfield side: operations duty managers. Their job is about dealing with the day-to-day problems, such as changing stand allocations when delays occur or arranging snow clearance if we have a sudden fall. Again plans are in place and everything has to be thought through. We also have weekly communication meetings when we get the operations and duty managers to work with the operational planning department.

'Our mission is to be the best regional airport in Europe. To do this we need continually to try to improve everything we do. It sounds simple but it is not easy. For example, we have almost no capacity at the peak times, that is between 7.00 a.m. and 8.00 a.m. and between 5.00 p.m. and 6.00 p.m. when we are busy with short-haul European traffic, so we are trying to encourage other airlines to fill in the off-peak times. This is ideal for long-haul operators and we now have flights to South East Asia and America, and just last year we added an Emirates flight to Dubai. This allows us to use the middle of the day when we have runway and terminal capacity and it suits everybody as we can all make better use of our facilities.

'Running an airport is a fascinating and exciting challenge. No two days are the same. We know that we can make a real difference to our customers, both passengers and airlines, by what we do. We also make a major contribution to the impact on the local economy by encouraging inward investment and exports. As an operations manager, my job is to make it all happen. It's a fantastic opportunity and it really does make a difference – its great!'

## Questions

1  *Identify some of the micro-operations to be found at the airport. For each one:*
   (a)  *Identify the transforming and transformed resources.*
   (b)  *State which is the predominant transformed resource.*
   (c)  *Describe the output of each micro-operation and say who you think its customers are.*

2  *Summarise the job of the operations director. What are the main issues/problems he faces in managing the airport?*

3  *What do you think Richard Heard actually does each day (how does he spend his time)?*

4  *Discuss the relationship between the day-to-day tasks and the long-term issues and explain how Richard manages to oversee both at the same time?*

# Hogsmeadow Garden Centre

Case date
2002     Alan Betts

Don Dursley spread his arms widely as he surveyed his garden centre.

'Of course the whole market for leisure products and services, especially garden-related products, has been expanding over the last few years. Even so, we have been particularly successful. Partly this is because we are conveniently located, but it is also because we have developed a reputation for excellent service. Customers like coming to us for advice. We have also been successful in attracting some of the 'personality gardeners' from television to make special appearances. My main ambition now is to fully develop all of our twelve hectares to make the centre a place people will want to visit in its own right. I envisage the centre developing into almost a mini gardening theme park with special gardens, beautiful grounds and special events.'

Hogsmeadow is a large village situated in the Cotswolds, a popular tourist area of the UK. It has an interesting range of shops and restaurants, mainly catering for the tourist trade. About half a mile outside the village is the Hogsmeadow Garden Centre. The garden centre is served by a good network of main roads but is inaccessible by public transport.

Growth over the last five years has been dramatic and the garden centre now sells many other goods as well as gardening requisites. It also has a restaurant. It is open seven days a week, only closing on Christmas Day. Its opening hours are Monday–Saturday 9 a.m. to 6 p.m. and Sunday 10 a.m. to 5 p.m. all year round.

## ● Outside the centre

The centre has a large car park which can accommodate about 350 cars. Outside the entrance a map indicates the various areas in the garden centre. Most customers walk round the grounds before making their purchases. The length of time people spend in the centre varies but, according to a recent study, averages 53 minutes during the week and 73 minutes at weekends.

The same study shows the extent to which the number of customers arriving at the garden centre varies depending on the time of year, day of the week, and time of day. There are two peaks in customer numbers, one during the late spring/early summer period and another in the build up to Christmas, as Hogsmeadow puts on particularly good Christmas displays.

## Indoor sales area

The range of goods has increased dramatically over the past few years and now includes items such as:

- pets and aquatics
- seeds
- fertilisers
- indoor pots and plants
- gardening equipment
- garden lighting
- conservatory-style furniture
- outdoor clothing
- picture gallery
- books and toys
- delicatessen
- wine
- kitchen equipment
- soft furnishing
- outdoor eating equipment
- gifts, stationery, cards, aromatherapy products
- freshly cut flowers
- dried flowers.

## Outside sales area

In the open air and in large glasshouses there is a complete range of plants, shrubs and trees. Hogsmeadow quality is high, with plants looking well tended if a little more expensive than other smaller garden centres. Half a dozen bedding plants cost in the region of £2.99 compared to similar plants which could be obtained for around £2 from market stalls or other garden centres. Professionally qualified staff both tend the plants and staff the information centres located around the grounds.

In addition to plants, there is also a comprehensive array of outdoor stone ornaments. There is stock valued in excess of £50 000 on show. Prices range from £25 to £3700. There are also a large number of water features, compost and peat, garden sheds, conservatories, playhouses, decking, wooden furniture, garden machinery, playground equipment, fencing, slabs, rocks and stones.

## Inventory control

It has always been difficult for the centre to decide how much of each product to order at the beginning of the season. Some non-perishable products, such as barbecues, sold in quantity at the beginning of the spring season, often have to be discounted very heavily, sometimes at a loss, during the winter. Other items, such as bedding plants, have a limited shelf life as well as being difficult to sell later in the season. The proliferation of lines in recent years has made this problem even more acute. Don Dursley explains:

'We just never get this right. Every year we agonise over how much to buy – either we run out or we have stock left over. The weather plays such a huge part in determining demand and is impossible to predict so far in advance. In our worst seasons the money we lose by having to discount stock, or throw away in the case of some plants, can be as high as 20 per cent of our total revenue for the year.'

## Honeydukes Restaurant

Honeydukes serves morning coffee, lunches and afternoon tea. It is part self-service and part assisted service. Customers enter, pick up a tray, help themselves to cakes and pastries, and order meals from the counter staff. They then pass down the line and are served drinks, pay, pick up the cutlery and make their way to a table. A metal rail separates the queue from the seating areas.

At lunchtimes queues can reach 10 people during the week and sometimes in excess of 20 people at the weekend. At peak times it can take up to 15 minutes to move from the back of the queue to complete the purchase. Regulars often 'save' tables by putting their coats and bags on them whilst they wait in the queue.

On a normal weekday lunchtime there are 12 staff, seven of whom are in the kitchen preparing food, one is responsible for taking money, one serves drinks, one deals with hot food, one deals with clearing tables and the washing-up. In addition there is a manager, Christine Wilson.

During the week the majority of customers in Honeydukes are mothers with small children and older people. At the weekend there is more of a spread of all age ranges; with the exception of teenage children.

Christine Wilson feels that Honeydukes has almost become a victim of its own success.

'A lot of the people who visit Honeydukes have toddlers in tow; we've set up a family area with toys for the children to play with. We also recognised that children can be a bit fussy so they can ask for a children's lunch box which we make up for them according to their preference. The children's lunch boxes are very popular but they are time-consuming for the staff to make up and queues do tend to form. I know that at times people turn away when they see the queue which is very frustrating, particularly as often we are only half full. One step we have taken to reduce the queue is to advise customers that at weekend lunchtimes they cannot just have a drink. But that does tend to cause aggravation, particularly if the customer hasn't seen the signs and has had to queue for some time.'

Once seated, customers tend to spend around 20 minutes over morning coffee or afternoon tea and take around 30 minutes for lunch. Older couples and those with small children usually take longer.

## Staffing

Excluding Honeydukes Restaurant, which is run separately, there are 50 full-time staff working 40 hours per week, 15 part-time staff working 15 hours a week and 20 weekend staff working eight hours – who tend to be students. The centre also has up to 25 casual staff which it can call upon in busy times such as the run up to Christmas.

The centre is open for 61 hours per week but with setting up and closing down procedures of half an hour at both ends of the day, staff need to be present for 68 hours a week. Staffing numbers vary according to the time of the day, the day of the week and the time of the year. At peak times there could be up to 80 staff present; at the quietest times the centre can function on as few as 20. Excluding the casual staff who tend to do the more menial roles, the staff are broken down into the following categories:

| | |
|---|---|
| Cashiers | 18 |
| Customer service* | 6 |
| Gardening information* | 4 |
| Shelf stocking | 11 |
| Care of plants* | 8 |
| Pet care | 6 |
| Design studio* | 3 |
| Outdoor buildings | 6 |
| Receiving deliveries; etc. | 6 |
| Making deliveries | 3 |
| Sundry duties (carrying customers' goods, retrieving shopping trolleys, etc.) | 6 |
| Office staff and management | 8 |
| Total | 85 |

*Professionally qualified

Don Dursley admits that he is more comfortable organising plants than people.

'Trying to get the right numbers of staff with the right mix of skills can be a real nightmare. We have some flexibility in staffing through the use of part-time staff and casual workers but we need to be able to respond better than we can at present to the fluctuations that happen in this business. We are also conscious that the rapid growth of the centre has meant that many of the staff can only do one job and this restricts us even further.'

## ● The future

Although pleased by the growth in customer numbers, Don was troubled that sales revenue and profitability had not grown as fast.

'We know that the centre is attractive and we believe that the market for these types of products is likely to continue to grow. But we have to continue to develop new products, and especially services, which will continue to attract customers as competition hots up. More especially, we have to keep them in the centre for longer so that they will spend more money while they are here. In the last three years, the number of customers has grown by in excess of 30 per cent, while sales revenue, in real terms, has grown by a little over 10 per cent. At the same time our costs have escalated by more than 15 per cent. We have a great opportunity here, but to make it really work we need to become more professional in operating the business.'

## Questions

1 *List the main micro-operations at Hogsmeadow Garden Centre and describe the main input resources, transformation process and outputs for each of them.*

2 *Summarise the problems faced by Don Dursley in managing and developing his centre.*

3 *What are the main changes you would recommend Don to consider making to improve the profitability of his business?*

# A day in the life of Frederic Godé, Operations Manager, BonPain

Case date
2001

Stuart Chambers

Frederic Godé is the Operations Manager of one of France's largest bakeries, BonPain, Orleans, which supplies supermarkets throughout Europe with frozen, 'par-baked' (part-baked), French-style bread and patisseries (decorative pastries often incorporating fruit, nuts or jam). After delivery, these are thawed and re-baked in-store, providing delicious aromas and fresh-tasting, traditional-style products to Europe's quality-conscious consumers.

BonPain's largest volume of products comprises a range of baguettes (French sticks), which are made, baked and frozen on three high-volume, specially-built production lines. However, even for baguettes there is a very wide range of recipes and packaging requirements, so these lines have to be set-up for these differences several times per shift. The lower-volume, more complex patisseries and speciality breads are made in batches, and are hand-assembled and finished prior to baking in batch ovens and freezers. The total range of products comprises around 600 stock-keeping units (SKUs), most of which are bulk-packed and stored in BonPain's freezers for up to a maximum of four weeks. There is also a relatively small, flexible kitchen where new products are being carefully developed by experienced chefs, who have a clear understanding of the materials and processes to be used in full-scale production. This facility is an extremely important 'order-winner' when dealing with supermarkets which require a regular supply of attractive and tasty new products.

Frederic Godé recently attended a time management course arranged by the Human Resources department of the large international food manufacturing group which had acquired BonPain one year earlier. Reflecting on this course in the context of the complexity and variety of his daily job, Frederic decided to carry a dictaphone around for a day and record what he actually did. He chose a Wednesday in mid-October, which he considered would be a typical day in his working life. Later, his secretary carefully transcribed the tape as follows ...

**7:55**
Arrived at work, parked, walked to office.

**8:00 to 8:15**
Checked e-mail which included:

- Productivity report for yesterday's output (obviously well below target!).
- Quality report for last week, unfortunately showing above-average levels of scrap.

- A note from the night-shift plant engineering supervisor, reporting a serious four-hour breakdown during the night on the fastest baguette line. He contends that this was not the result of any lack of maintenance; it had apparently been caused by a failure of the production operatives to stop the machine quickly and correctly when the conveyors were jammed by a major material spillage.
- A note from Warehousing and Dispatch reporting that today's routine deliveries to our largest customer, Hypera (a supermarket group), could not be delivered at the scheduled times because of the production breakdown.
- One from an external equipment supplier, F-Robot, confirming their technical consultant's visit today at 11:30 to discuss one of the latest automation projects at the plant
- A request from Charles Lamouche, the Marketing Director, for an urgent discussion about production trials for one of the new product introduction projects. Replied, asking if he would be able to come to my office at 15:00.

### 8:15 to 9:00

Daily first tour of factory with the morning supervisor and the Senior Maintenance Engineer.

- During the tour it was pointed out that one of the three baguette production lines had only just restarted working. It had broken down in the middle of the night due to a bearing failure.
- Spent about 15 minutes in discussion with a group of production operatives who were concerned about our regular requests for extra staff to run the third line at the weekend. Although reluctant to come in, they were persuaded that we did need the extra output to satisfy demand, which had recently grown by around five per cent due to an export order for the UK.
- Noted that the finished baguettes from Line 1 (the oldest line) were showing wide variation in baked colour (but within the control limits) and asked to see the Quality Control charts, but routine notes on these did not highlight any reason for variations. Arranged for Pierre Moulin (the Quality Manager) to investigate root cause and to report back later.
- Was informed that we had run out of prepared apricots yet again, stopping scheduled production of the most popular Danish-style patisserie. Reminded me that I need to discuss this with Purchasing Manager, since this is the third stock-out this week!
- Spotted a guard missing from one of the conveyor drives. Plant Engineer arranging replacement this morning – temporary guard put in place immediately.
- Excessive flour and fat spillage in mixing room. Appears to be caused by carelessness, perhaps lack of training of night-shift operatives. Waste of this type severely erodes our tight profit margins. Will follow this up at meeting.

### 9:00 to 10:00

Regular scheduled morning meeting with: the three production line supervisors; supervisors from the mixing department, patisserie assembly and baking areas, and freezer warehouse; Pierre Moulin, the Quality Manager; and Monique Dumas, the Production Planning and Control Manager. The normal agenda included an overview of the previous day's production statistics, and of the rolling one-week averages including:

- the total output of each main production line
- performance against schedule per specific product
- utilisation and efficiency measures, and graphs showing these over 12 months

- records of delivery performance: on-time delivery of ordered quantities
- quality statistics: scrap levels for products and packaging.

Supervisors provided explanations of problems, and occasionally some suggestions on their resolution and prevention. However, many small improvements were increasingly being undertaken by *kaizen* (continuous improvement) teams. Generally, these were done on a day-to-day basis, without great supervisor intervention.

The meeting then continued by looking at forecast requirements for the next week and for the next three months. Monique pointed out that the market forecast suggested growth in bread sales of about two per cent per month, but only very slight growth for patisseries. She was concerned that it would be necessary to arrange increased levels of overtime to cover this extra demand and that there might be resistance from the operators, since they had already been working excessive levels of overtime over the last few months. It was certainly the time to consider purchasing a fourth baguette line!

Pierre was concerned that this pressure on output could lead to further deterioration in quality performance, which could not only create customer complaints, but might also lead to rising levels of scrap and waste. I also know that Monique is really getting stressed by the increasing prospect of being unable to meet a big customer's delivery schedule. Many supermarkets are trying to reduce their frozen inventory to only one or two days' demand, so if we fail to deliver, stores could be out of bread and then there will be big trouble! It's not made any easier by the pattern of consumer demand – up to twice as much bread and patisseries are sold in supermarkets on Fridays and Saturdays than on any other shopping day. We must address these issues when preparing our next operations strategy report.

I brought the team's attention to the apparently increasing levels of spilt materials (on the floor) observed on the morning tour. They agreed that a team would be formed to look at underlying causes of such waste.

### 10:00 to 11:30

Mostly alone in my office. I wanted to begin looking at the detail of proposals to automate the packing lines. If we make the right choice, it should be possible to eliminate two people per line by the robotisation of final packing. However, the equipment to do this is very expensive, with the best solutions seeming to be tailor-made for specific types of bread. This would therefore limit the future flexibility of this equipment. However, the project looked promising in terms of my calculations of the payback period, and I was therefore looking forward to the visit of our preferred supplier.

Some of this time spent reviewing Monique's calculations of the future capacity requirements of the plant. Use of overtime to provide extra capacity can only continue for a matter of months before that alone will not provide the solution. It is going to be necessary to invest in another line sooner rather than later if we are to avoid delivery problems in the coming spring. I should discuss the market forecast by volume and types with the Marketing Director, so I rang his secretary and made an appointment to talk with him this afternoon.

There were four phone calls during this period:

- Packaging supplier to discuss quality problem with one size of folding cardboard cases supplied in September. Agreed compensation/replacements and process changes to ensure non-recurrence.

- Group's IT consultant wanted to arrange a meeting with the Production team concerning implementation of new Materials Requirement Planning (MRP) system within the Enterprise Resource Planning (ERP) project. This would take over inventory control and placing of call-off orders currently done by two clerks in the Planning and Control Department.
- Discussion with Charles Lamouche about an opportunity to supply premium quality baguettes to a major sandwich/coffee bar chain. To win this order would require new process controls for bread quality, since the texture and general quality specification is known to be exceptionally demanding for this customer. It expects suppliers to use statistical process control (SPC) for several variables (weight, dimensions, moisture content) and attributes (colour, appearance, crustiness). This is much more demanding than the specification of any other customer.
- Message from Sales to expect a call from Sophie Chevalier, the Purchasing Director of Hypera, who wanted assurances directly from *me* that today's delivery problems would never reoccur. I have met her on several occasions when she first agreed to do business with us; she and her team had thoroughly inspected our facilities and quality control systems. I am not looking forward to her call!

### 11:30 to 12:30

Meeting with technical representatives of F-Robot, along with our Factory Engineer and Method Study Engineer. My main concern was to understand the flexibility of the proposed robot packers. There appears to be a choice between two types: high speed, specially-configured machines which can easily keep up with any future output speed of the improved standard baguette lines; and slower machines which are easy to adapt for different shapes and sizes of bread and even patisseries. The representatives also showed us information on state-of-the-art flexible equipment being developed for assembly of complex food products like patisseries.

We will clearly have to evaluate all these options on the basis of what return on capital investment could be achieved. However; there are also operations' issues to be considered in terms of capacity, flexibility, reliability and ease of maintenance, spare parts inventory, quality (will they be gentle enough to not cause damage? – trials will have to be conducted) and training of operators and maintenance staff.

### 12:30 to 13:00

Lunch in company restaurant. Sat with a group of supervisors from the Patisserie Production Department. Although generally very friendly and relaxed, I noted that they seemed to want to move the conversation towards the *kaizen* activities taking place in their department. I suggested that two of them come to my office immediately after lunch!

### 13:00 to 13:40

Continued discussion on *kaizen*. The supervisors were obviously still under the impression that this initiative was undermining their management role in the department since operatives were analysing problems, assessing solutions and implementing them with very little input from the supervisors. They were concerned that the operatives would not need supervision if this continued! I assured them that this was not the case, but that their role would gradually change and that their continued involvement and attention to detail was critical to the success of the department. (I must ensure that I sit down with Personnel to work out the future role and training needs of supervisors.) One of them was clearly under the impression that *kaizen* was simply a new version of total quality management – and that had not been a total success when we attempted it five years ago!

### 13:40 to 15:00

Another tour of the factory. Spent most of this time looking at SPC charts in each department because there was some evidence that these were not being used correctly. We may have to undertake some more training in this area if we are to get the full benefits of SPC.

Then spent some time with the Plant Engineer looking at possible locations for the installation of packing robots. The current packing area is badly laid out and needs reconfiguration, so I hope we can combine the installation of new equipment with a redesign of this area of the factory.

Finally, a short time looking at the freezer room, where we must consider capacity expansion. The increasing range and volume of product has recently led to a shortage of storage space. Also, if some of our large customers are moving towards just-in-time (JIT) deliveries, it may be necessary for us to support this with slightly increased inventory levels. The time has come for us to do a more detailed analysis of inventory, and if we leave this too late, we may end up having to rent more expensive storage space at external deep-freeze warehouses.

On the way back to the office, passed the training room where a *kaizen* team was conducting a brainstorming session. Did not interrupt this.

### 15:00 to 15:45

Scheduled meeting with Charles Lamouche, Marketing Director, and Sara Lepont, Product Development Manager, concerning development of a new range of mini-patisseries. The concept is to supply products of about a third of the normal size, which can be used at parties and receptions. Market research indicates a big potential growth in this type of 'snacking'. However, these products will be significantly more difficult to make on our existing equipment and will require the development of new recipes and packaging which would together reduce the drying-out of the products during the freezing stages. Although the recipes have proved successful in the trial kitchens, the time had come for full-scale production trials within the factory; most of the meeting was spent agreeing an outline schedule for this work. I reported on the capital equipment requirements for this project.

### 15:45 to 17:00

Began writing my monthly report for the monthly Board meeting. This summarises the production statistics for the previous month, and requires an explanation for any significant shortfall. The main problems reported included: lower than budgeted levels of productivity; and material usage variances which indicate an above-average level of waste and scrap. I reported on the actions being taken to improve process control. I also reported that the decline in productivity was largely caused by last-minute schedule changes which were outside the control of production management.

The next section included details of capital requirements for new equipment needed over the next two years. Many of these items had already been included in the main capital budget, but the need for some new items had arisen as a result of changes in capacity requirements and unforeseen new product developments.

I finally reported on each of the new product development projects for which I was responsible, including a set of Gantt charts showing progress. For each project there was a short explanation of the successes to date, and the main problems yet to be overcome.

Several phone calls during this period:

- Report from the Quality Manager that the variation in colour of baguettes on Line 1 had now been traced to a faulty burner control in the main oven. The plant maintenance team was preparing to replace the failed component during the scheduled weekend shutdown of this line.
- Report from the production supervisors in each department on output against daily target. Each section was on-schedule at this stage in the day. Good!
- Purchasing advised me that there was a potential delivery problem with important packaging from one of our main suppliers. They had had a serious fire in one of their plants, and were endeavouring to switch production to another. They assured us that everything was being done to ensure continuing supply. I phoned Monique to alert her to this situation, and asked her to continue to liaise with Purchasing.
- The expected call from Sophie Chevalier, complaining about today's late delivery to Hypera. Not a pleasant call, so I will not record the details here! The conclusion was that she will be sending an audit team to look at our planning and control procedures, and the plant maintenance systems. She is seeking assurance that these always give priority to production for Hypera. She also wants to know what we are doing about preventative maintenance (and in particular condition monitoring) so we will have to give that some attention before her visit!

**17:00 to 18:00**

Final plant tour. This afternoon I spent most of my time in the patisserie production area. Everything seemed to be going well, but there was the usual daily build-up of stock awaiting transfer to the freezer room. There always seems to be a capacity imbalance in this department. For now, the bottleneck is clearly caused by the availability of forklift trucks and drivers.

There are some material flow problems in this area which will need addressing before output volumes increase. I must arrange a meeting with the Industrial Engineer and production supervisors to discuss the issues and potential solutions. Because of the wide range of products, it is unlikely that we will be able to automate many of the processes, but some simple solutions could help to increase productivity.

I am also concerned about the relatively small batch sizes made in this area. The last time we calculated economic batch quantities for patisseries was about two years ago. Since then demand has increased significantly, so it may be possible to *increase* batch quantities, which would give us greater capacity because of the reduction in the number of set-ups. We have also recently done some work on reducing set-up time, which will also have an effect on economic batch quantities.

In general, there is a high degree of specialisation in this area. Many of the operators do the same job all day, every day. I know that the Human Resource Manager is concerned that this may lead to repetitive strain injury (RSI), so it is appropriate that we should look to more job rotation and enlargement. This should give more variety in individual operators' tasks, reducing the risks of RSI. This will be included as an important topic at our next departmental meeting.

**18:00 to 18:10**

Final check of production performance for today. Everything seems to be going well! Checked e-mail – only one significant new message, from the Operations Director. He is arranging a meeting with all his managers to begin work on the annual strategic review. This looks like being a big task ahead for me and the production team.

**18:10**

End of day, thank goodness. It's really amazing to see where my time goes! What a range of different things I seem to have been involved in today. But really, it is like that *every* day.

End of taped record!

## Questions

1 *Analyse the many things that Frederic does during his typical day. You should group these in terms of the five categories below, and provide a full list of sub-categories for each:*
   - *Strategic*
   - *Design*
   - *Planning and control*
   - *Improvement*
   - *Other (specify)*

2 *Assess the approximate proportions of Frederic's time that is spent on long-term and on short-term issues. Do think this is typical of operations managers in other industries (for example, banking, leisure, automotive component manufacture)?*

3 *What is Frederic's involvement in technology acquisition decisions? What are his main concerns when evaluating the capability of new equipment?*

4 *What main human resource issues are an important part of Frederic's activities?*

5 *In what ways can Frederic's operations contribute to the competitive advantage of the company?*

CASE
4

# Wace Burgess

Case date
1995

Stuart Chambers and Tammy Helander

## Background

Wace Burgess is a member of the Wace Group, a company in the pre-press and print technology market, with a mission:

'to become a world-class company providing complete production service for corporations, enhancing the perceived values of their products and services by improving the quality and efficiency of the communication process.'

The Wace Group operates in a wide range of communication-related sectors including imaging networks, advertising, promotional print, corporate literature, academic journals, rigid and flexible packaging, and labels. Wace Burgess, a business employing around 250 people, specialises in the colour printing of greeting cards, gift wrap, posters, calendars, book jackets and folders. Their customers are mainly creative publishers, supplying retailers.

## Greeting cards

The largest part of the business is the production of cards, which are of three types: Christmas cards, everyday cards (including birthday cards), and special days' cards (Valentine's Day, Mother's Day, Father's Day, Easter, etc.). Although Wace Burgess is the preferred supplier of many publishers, each order is typically quite small, but with many different designs. Until recently the card market mainly comprised specialist publishers who sold to all sizes of retail outlets such as newsagents, gift shops, card shops, etc. However, the situation had begun to change at the beginning of the 1990s. More and more cards were being sold through larger retailers including supermarkets, which had begun to take a greater interest in the highly profitable card market.

Wace Burgess had always been a company that wanted to be at the leading edge of the market and technology developments. If there was a market out there for supplying the larger retailers, they certainly planned to be part of it. Both as a result of their excellent reputation for quality and responsiveness, and as a result of considerable sales effort, it seemed that in the autumn of 1994 they had their first real chance to supply a big retailer – Marks & Spencer (M&S). Vicky Dockety, one of the account managers, had for some time been talking, via a publisher, to M&S and she now seemed to be close to actually getting the first order. She had already outlined the preliminary requirements to some of the technical specialists and several managers within the company.

## ● Orders

The vast majority of the orders were for print runs of between 5000 and 10 000 sheets, the average being about 8000. The most popular size of the cards was around 175 × 125mm (for some typical orders see Table 4.1). A sheet was a piece of thick paper printed in the lithographic printing machines, normally with standard sizes of up to 720 × 1020mm, and with typically 12 to 16 cards printed on it. However M&S had specified a smaller size of sheet, with smaller cards, very carefully arranged so that almost no paper would be wasted. They were asking for just five design variants. The delivery requirements were also unusual in that they would be precisely scheduled over several weeks, in contrast to the single delivery for most normal orders.

If they were to get the order from M&S, it would mean processing a single order of 600 000 sheets, so Vicky was somewhat concerned about their ability to deliver on time and to preserve their excellent reputation in the market. However, she had

**Table 4.1  Some typical card orders received by Wace Burgess in August 1994**

| Order number | Customer | Description | Quantity (sheets) |
|---|---|---|---|
| CI 164 | Creativity Inc. | Birthday humour (8 designs) | 5 000 |
| CI 165 | Creativity Inc. | Reasons to be happy | 12 000 |
| CI 166 | Creativity Inc. | Don't forget (B) | 15 000 |
| CI 167 | Creativity Inc. | Better late than never | 10 000 |
| GF 2378 | Gordon Fraser | Everyday gift cards: | |
| | | Portrait P56 | 5 000 |
| | | Landscape L78 | 10 000 |
| | | Landscape L83 | 8 000 |
| | | Landscape L98 | 10 000 |
| | | Animal A254 | 7 000 |
| | | Animal A342 | 6 000 |
| IN 4512 | INK Group | Christmas cards: | |
| | | Farside F34 | 5 000 |
| | | Farside F56 | 5 000 |
| | | Mix M87 | 7 000 |
| | | Mix M96 | 3 000 |
| | | Mix M105 | 8 000 |
| CV 34 | Cardivity | Economy Christmas cards: | |
| | | Angels A5 | 7 000 |
| | | Holly | 7 000 |
| | | Pudding | 8 000 |
| DC 75 | Descom Cards | Luxury Christmas cards: | |
| | | Bauble, twin pack | 4 000 |
| | | Mixed pack LP5 | 5 000 |
| | | Father Christmas FC30 | 5 000 |
| | | Sleigh | 6 000 |

recently been in a meeting with the management team, where Barry Jackson, the Managing Director, had made the case for pursuing the order:

'Our market is changing. We know now that the big retailers and supermarkets will play a larger part in the future of selling cards, as well as the specialist publishers, which have made up our traditional customer base. We must do *all* we can in order to be in that market when these changes take place. We don't want to lose our first-place position. I urge you all to ensure that you really have done everything you can to get these new accounts. As you all know we are totally committed and determined for Wace Burgess to grow with the developing market.'

Barry was, however, aware that Vicky was close to getting the contract with M&S and specifically urged her:

'Come back to me on that order, we could do with this business! If we can prove ourselves this time we might be able to win more of their work in the future. Check with the manufacturing and technical side once again to see that there aren't any issues we've overlooked, and come back to me as soon as possible. Because the prices will be tight, we cannot afford to have any problems with this one!'

## The factory

Although Vicky had been through the factory many times since she joined the company six months earlier, she paid particular attention to what John Wakeling, the Technical Director, had to say about the manufacturing details when they made a factory tour with some customers. They always started in the gallery, where the whole of the huge factory could be viewed from above through glass windows. It was always impressive to see the busy plant with its many separate operations.

They started at the beginning of the process by the printing machines, and walked past the stacks of printed card sheets being stored before going into the bindery, where they would be cut on the 'guillotines'. While the customers were being shown some details by one of the supervisors, John and Vicky started to discuss the M&S order. John reassured Vicky of their capabilities to handle the order, but admitted that capacity could be a problem:

'Of course there will be a strain on our capacity, because we already have a fairly full order book for the next two months. We work two eight-hour shifts now in the printing, bindery and packing sections. But we can always put on overtime or, if necessary, put on an extra shift on Saturdays and Sundays. We normally print several million cards a day, and most of these are small orders that take around a couple of hours to do. On average we print between 5000 and 6000 sheets per hour.'

'How about the set-up times?', Vicky asked.

'Oh, that is not really a problem, a litho print set-up takes about two hours for normal cards but changing to smaller sheets can take a little longer; perhaps about three hours – but that isn't too much of a problem. So, as for the printing, there is absolutely no need to worry! Set-ups are very fast both for guillotining and folding: around 10 minutes each for a typical job. It is possible to outsource die-cutting as well as the embossing, but it is more difficult with the folding and packaging. We could use home-workers, but it would take some time, and this takes a lot of organising and transport. If outsourced, this must also meet our very specific standards in order to meet the customers' quality demands.'

Die-cutting means that the edges of the cards are not cut straight, but into shapes, and embossing means that the paper surface is pressed between profiled plates to create an interesting surface.

'How about the quality?', asked Vicky. 'Can we hold the standards for such a large order – as that is one of the main reasons we would win the order? I am concerned that if something were to go wrong it might be the last order we will see!'

John Wakeling was just as concerned, as this order certainly was a big challenge:

'Of course there shouldn't be any problems. Our quality checks are rigorous and are built into the process. After each 500 sheets (about every six minutes) we take a sample and check it against the agreed specification, and we have other checks both at the beginning and the end of the process. On the rare occasions that we have had technical problems, such as in meeting an unusually difficult specification, we have been prepared to completely reprint an order to get the appearance the customers want. Only high quality, on-spec products will be sent out, and it is because of this that the customers trust us with their most demanding work. I am sure that we will be able to satisfy the M&S order without any problem, but we will certainly be extra careful as well!'

While they were continuing through the factory with the customer, they came across Simon Payne, the Planning Manager:

'Vicky, I just wanted to tell you that the special paper you were asking about for the M&S order has proved easy to get delivered quickly should it be needed. I checked it with the suppliers, and they reassured us that they would be able to make it.'

Later on, Vicky read a memo from one of the production schedulers about capacity. Although John had tried to reassure her, she had been anxious to have some more details. The note read:

---

Dear Vicky,

Concerning the questions on capacity you asked for, we do have somewhat different capacities on the different machines. The normal output rate for the printers using standard materials is 6000 sheets/hour, for the guillotines 4000 sheets/hour on average, and for the folders 24 000 cards/hour. As you know, we have 5 printing machines, 3 guillotines, and 5 folders – which gives us a lot of capacity, so we shouldn't have any problem with fitting in your job for M&S. Should you need any more details on capacity effects you should ask Simon Payne. He used to do detailed capacity scheduling, before he was put in charge of the reorganisation of the academic publications area.

Best regards, Tim

---

Vicky would remember to ask Simon during the day, but the scenario did not look too bad, and she trusted the judgement of John, who had been in the company for a long time, and knew everything worth knowing about the printing business and technology. The factory certainly worked very smoothly and was good at keeping delivery promises, producing high quality cards at short notice.

On her way back from the factory she passed the Customer Services and Pre-press room. Here the graphics were finalised before being checked by the customers and company specialists, before being made into printing plates. The staff here were among the best in the industry at ensuring that the artistic details in the card designs were reproduced accurately and to the required colour standards – routinely improving the customers' artwork using the latest computer imaging technologies, as well as using the staff's own design skills. Vicky had confidence in these technical skills, but also knew that the customers valued the department's organised approach to getting this work completed quickly. There could be no better supplier for M&S, she was sure of that! She had done absolutely everything to accommodate them, but she clearly understood that, with these huge volumes, the customer could be very particular with regard to quality and delivery performance.

She had earlier asked one of the supervisors about the issue of extra personnel, should they be forced to put on an extra shift. She dialled his internal number again; the reply was, again, positive:

'Yes, I have checked it with personnel as well, and there should be no problems. You know, it is quite easy for us to hire extra people when required, both students and others on a short-term basis, but only for the labour-intensive jobs such as packing. We usually put them in teams of two: one experienced and one new. It usually works out very well.'

## The M&S Christmas cards

The set of cards that M&S had ordered did not really appear so different from many past orders. All the cards were embossed, and the colours were mainly warm reds and greens, with some use of metallic inks and gold foil blocking, which had not often been required on this type of paper. The designs comprised simple, eye-catching images including Christmas trees, tartan teddy bears, nostalgic images of children, and a winter rabbit – they were really very charming. The publisher's graphics skills had been used very effectively, and the final designs were to be die-cut to give a more interesting shape. The quality of the special paper gave an unusually matt finish to the sample printing, and so the cards would have a very sophisticated, up-market appearance. Combined with Wace Burgess's manufacturing skills, this design concept would be a winner, and so Vicky felt sure that this would be the beginning of a successful long-term relationship with M&S.

The special paper could be obtained from one of the usual paper suppliers, but for the metallic inks and gold-blocking, they would have to use a relatively new supplier of whom they had little experience. The die-cutting and gold-blocking would be outsourced, as the factory did not have suitable equipment for the job. It seemed that there were no technical problems with the card or any unusual features that would have to be solved. In fact, it was not one of the most difficult cards they had tackled in terms of design or production. But with Christmas approaching, time was getting tight. The order should be received before the beginning of October, for delivery by mid-November – an unusually short lead-time considering the size and special requirements of the order.

## Questions

1 *What are the external performance objectives for the M&S business, and how do these differ from those for existing customers?*

2 *What are the potential risks and rewards of accepting the order from M&S?*

3 *Should the company accept the order if they get it?*

4 *Should management introduce any special or different practices in the factory to handle the M&S order, if it is received?*

**CASE**
**5**

# Concept Design Services

Case date
2002

Stuart Chambers and Nigel Slack

## Introduction

'Over a 10-year period we have totally transformed our outlook, our resources and our prospects. From being an inward-looking manufacturing company, we have become a customer-focused, integrated service provider. From a largely commodity supplier, we have become known for our value-added and innovative designs. Most importantly, our performance as a company has been little short of spectacular, and I see no reason why we cannot continue on this upward path [Table 5.1]. I know that the Group board is very impressed with our achievements, and uses this subsidiary as its best example of success-ful innovation.'

James Thompson, the CEO of Concept Design Services (CDS), knew his confidence was shared by his colleagues. After all, CDS was believed to be one of Europe's most profitable plastic household products ('homeware') businesses. Originally founded in the 1960s as Focus Plastics, the company's growth had come initially from the manufacture of complex injection-moulded plastic components for large industrial customers. Following the acquisition of the company by a large consumer products group, it had rapidly extended its range to include popular household items such as washing-up bowls, pedal bins, baby baths, buckets and dustpans. These were sold under the Focus brand name, initially through wholesale distributors and then increasingly to large national do-it-yourself (DIY) stores, often referred to as 'sheds'. By the early 1990s, the homeware business had grown to account for over 80 per cent of turnover, which had itself more than doubled in 10 years. Additional large injection-moulding machines had been purchased to cope with the rapidly growing volumes of products. These machines provided many economies of scale that enabled the company to compete aggressively in a market where barriers to entry were low. However, competition was increasing, mainly from small, specialised manufacturers with low overheads. The range of products supplied by these com-panies was often quite limited (just buckets or bowls, for example), largely because of the high costs of moulds, which could be up to £50 000 each.

## The products

By 1989 the company produced around 200 homeware stock-keeping units (SKUs), and had developed a reputation as a reliable source of supply of consistently high-

**Table 5.1 CDS Selected financial information (years ending 31 December)**

All figures in £000

| | 1989 | 1991 | 1993 | 1995 | 1997 | 1999 | 2001 |
|---|---|---|---|---|---|---|---|
| **Fixed assets:** | | | | | | | |
| Plant and equipment | 3366 | 3312 | 2394 | 2520 | 3672 | 5028 | 5880 |
| Moulds | 612 | 780 | 1020 | 1080 | 1920 | 3504 | 3720 |
| Total | 3978 | 4092 | 3414 | 3600 | 5592 | 8532 | 9600 |
| **Current assets:** | | | | | | | |
| Debtors | 2898 | 4464 | 5052 | 4902 | 7926 | 5778 | 8238 |
| Inventory | 1572 | 3516 | 6174 | 7554 | 9354 | 13458 | 15402 |
| Total | 4470 | 7980 | 11226 | 12456 | 17280 | 19236 | 23640 |
| **Total assets** | **8448** | **12072** | **14640** | **16056** | **22872** | **27768** | **33240** |
| **Financed by:** | | | | | | | |
| Share capital | 300 | 300 | 300 | 300 | 300 | 300 | 300 |
| Retained profits | 1680 | 2520 | 3180 | 3420 | 4980 | 10560 | 15960 |
| Loans from Group | 2700 | 3180 | 4920 | 5280 | 6720 | 4740 | 2940 |
| Total | 4680 | 6000 | 8400 | 9000 | 12000 | 15600 | 19200 |
| **Current liabilities:** | | | | | | | |
| Creditors | 3756 | 3192 | 3768 | 6804 | 10644 | 10464 | 10590 |
| Bank | 12 | 2880 | 2472 | 252 | 228 | 1704 | 3450 |
| Total | 3768 | 6072 | 6240 | 7056 | 10872 | 12168 | 14040 |
| **Total liabilities** | **8448** | **12072** | **14640** | **16056** | **22872** | **27768** | **33240** |
| **Sales and profits:** | | | | | | | |
| Net sales | 15132 | 17232 | 25272 | 26796 | 30648 | 32364 | 48126 |
| Net profit before tax | 876 | 1110 | 1644 | 2172 | 3372 | 4248 | 6300 |
| **Sales by market:** | | | | | | | |
| Industrial | 3020 | 0 | 0 | 0 | 0 | 0 | 0 |
| Focus Homeware | 12112 | 17232 | 18450 | 17480 | 15560 | 13244 | 13066 |
| Concept & Design House | | | 6822 | 9316 | 15088 | 19120 | 32420 |
| Concept Office | | | | | | | 2640 |
| Total | 15132 | 17232 | 25272 | 26796 | 30648 | 32364 | 48126 |

quality products. It was then decided to withdraw from the complex and cyclical industrial mouldings market in order to concentrate on developing the more profitable household products business. James Thompson explained:

'We recognised that the industrial markets were becoming more difficult and much less profitable. In the large white goods and automotive markets, order sizes (and therefore batch sizes) were getting smaller, and we were also losing some larger contracts as production moved abroad. Basically, many of our industrial customers were just too hard to do business with. They were always changing their schedules, but at the same time they would not guarantee long-term continuity of business. In the end, we decided that the industrial business did not fit well and was particularly difficult to plan and control alongside household products. Even in the Sales Office, it was felt that the commercial relationships with household product wholesalers and DIY sheds were clearer and under control, whereas business with the industrial customers was unpredictable and unstable. Schedule changes in quantity and delivery date were an everyday occurrence that disrupted the office and caused most internal communication problems. So, by 1990 all our industrial business had been terminated. But our decision to concentrate on one, relatively new market was recognised as carrying risks, and we were determined to differentiate ourselves from competitors. There were some very competent, smaller manufacturers that could compete in some of the volume business by undercutting our prices, not least because our overheads were higher than theirs! We were using the latest, precision equipment, bought the best-quality moulds, and generally positioned ourselves as 'technical professionals with a customer-focused service'. We knew that we had to exploit these differences, and that we would have to look for new markets that would really value our capabilities.'

## ● Market positioning

Linda Fleet, CDS's Marketing Director, joined the company in the early 1990s, having previously worked in a senior marketing role for a large retail chain of paint and wallpaper retailers.

'Experience in the decorative products industry had taught me the importance of fashion, even in mundane products such as paint. Premium-priced colours and textures would become popular for one or two years, supported by appropriate promotion and features in lifestyle magazines. Two years later they would look old-fashioned and people who care about their surroundings would redecorate individual rooms or even the whole house. The manufacturers and retailers which created and supported these fashion trends were dramatically more profitable than those who simply provided standard ranges. Instinctively, I felt that this must also apply to plastic homewares. At CDS, we decided to develop a whole coordinated range of such items, and to open up a new distribution network for them to directly serve individual up-market stores, kitchen equipment shops and speciality retailers throughout Europe.

'Our first new range of kitchen items was launched in 1992, under the "Concept" brand name. Within one year, we had over 3000 retail outlets signed up, and provided each with point-of-sale display facilities and high-quality brochures. Illustrated feature articles in well-targeted magazines and newspapers generated an enormous interest from the public, which was reinforced by the use of our products on several TV cookery programmes. Within one year we had developed an entirely new market! It was at this time that we changed the name of the company to reinforce our change of direction. "Concept" now provides over 70 per cent of our revenue and the bulk of our profits. The prices and margins that we can achieve with Concept are many times higher than for the Focus range, so we have proved that the market appreciates the value inherent in our designs. We quickly learned that the retailers liked the idea of a coordinated range of items. Customers could buy a few items to start a collection, and progressively add to this. Our research indicated that some customers kept our products on display in their kitchens as objects of beauty, or even as tokens or symbols of their lifestyle, rather than hiding them away in cupboards. We exploited this idea in our advertising, and guarantee to supply retailers any item in any colour for at least four years. To keep ahead, we continue to launch new ranges and colours at regular intervals. We now have the most comprehensive range of 'designer' items in the market: there are now six separate style ranges, and many of these are offered in up to 12 contemporary colours. The Concept ranges are highly profitable, both for us and for the many thousands of retailers throughout Europe that stock our products.

'In contrast to the success of Concept, we now clearly understand that many of the Focus products have effectively become commodities, as numerous competitors have gradually eroded market prices. Supply Services continues to provide a basic support to Focus customers in terms of routine order processing and production planning, whilst our Sales activity is largely confined to annual bidding for large contracts. I certainly intend that we should continue to replace this declining, low-margin Focus business with the exciting new Concept ranges and other growth opportunities that we have identified.

'In addition to continuing development of Concept, over the last two years we have been designing, manufacturing and distributing products for some of the more prestigious design houses. This sort of business is likely to grow, especially in continental Europe where the design houses now appreciate our ability to offer a full service. We can develop products in conjunction with their own design staff and offer them a level of manufacturing expertise they can't get elsewhere. Most significantly, we can offer a Europe-wide distribution service that is tailored to their needs. From the customer's point of view, the distribution arrangements appear to belong to the design house itself. In reality, they are based exclusively on our own call-centre, warehouse and distribution resources.'

## Manufacturing operations

All manufacturing was carried out in a large, leased, modern facility, which was located approximately 20km from the Head Office. The factory had areas for receiving and holding raw materials, and the moulding area included 24 large injection-moulding machines. The most recent had robotic devices to remove finished products from the machines and to place them on conveyors leading to the packing area. Adjacent to the moulding area was a large tool store with a capacity to store about 200 moulds on racks, and a small mould repair section with skilled craftsmen. Products, and individual components of products, were moved to the packing area, where they were assembled and/or labelled (where required), inspected, packed in bags or cartons and palletised. Finished goods were then taken to an adjacent large, narrow-aisle warehouse with high-level racking and special forklift machines. In one corner was an order-assembly and dispatch bay, with a platform access to load delivery vehicles. Grant Williams, the Operations Manager, described the development of these facilities over the preceding decade:

'The move away from industrial products allowed us to dispose of most of the older, more inefficient, and smaller injection-moulding machines. Having only larger machines now allows us to use large multi-cavity moulds. This increases productivity by allowing us to produce several products, or components, each machine cycle. It also allows us to use high-quality and complex moulds which, although cumbersome and more difficult to change over, give a very high-quality product. For example, it would have taken the same labour and machine time to make three items per minute on the old machines as 18 items per minute on the modern large machines with a six-cavity mould. That's a 600 per cent increase in productivity! We are also proud that we achieve such high dimensional accuracy, excellent surface finish, and extreme consistency of colour required for the Concept products. We can achieve all this because of our expertise derived from years in the technically-demanding industrial markets. The end product quality is second to none, and extensive benchmarking studies carried out by some of our European customers have confirmed our superiority in quality conformance. By standardising on single large machines, any mould can fit any machine. This is an ideal situation from a planning perspective, as we are often asked to make a run of Concept products at short notice on the next machine to become available. This standardisation has also enabled us to carry a complete range of spare parts for the machines, and the maintenance staff have become very skilled in caring for this specific size and type of machine.'

## ● Supply Services

The Supply Services Department of the company was regarded as being at the heart of the company's customer service drive. Its purpose was to integrate the efforts of design, manufacturing and sales. Essentially it had two functions: firstly to plan and schedule production in order to maintain appropriate inventory availability, and secondly to plan the distribution of products from the warehouse to customers. Sandra White, the Supply Services Planning Manager, was responsible for the scheduling of all manufacturing and distribution and for maintaining inventory levels for all the warehoused items. Supported by three other staff, she also prepared performance reports, monitoring the utilisation of equipment, output rates for each product and scrap rates. Although the organisation chart showed Sandra White reporting directly to Marketing, Linda Fleet did not often feel the need to intervene in the day-to-day workings of the department, preferring to concentrate on the more innovation-oriented activities of the Marketing Department. This relative autonomy allowed Sandra to optimise the planning throughout the internal supply chain.

'We try to establish a preferred sequence of production for each machine and mould. To minimise set-up times, we plan for each mould to start on a light colour, and progress through a sequence to the darkest. In this way we can change colours in around 15 minutes, with relatively small amounts of waste. Because our multi-cavity moulds are large and technically complex, mould changes take around three to four hours, so careful scheduling is important to maintain utilisation. The factory is usually not scheduled for weekend production, and maintenance is usually performed on Saturday mornings. Over recent years the general reduction in batch size has unfortunately brought down average utilisation, but with the wider product range, now at about 2500 SKUs, this was somewhat inevitable. However, our 'pick rate', which measures the availability of finished goods inventory, has been maintained at around 92 per cent. This means that, on average, there is a one in twelve chance of us not being able to supply any one SKU from stock. I know that Linda would like us to reach 100 per cent, but there is always some constraint that prevents us achieving higher availability. At the moment that constraint is warehouse space.

'Everything would be fine if we were able to stick to schedules, but short-term unplanned changes seem to be occurring more frequently than ever before. For example, last Monday we had an urgent request from Sales to produce a run of 500 rainforest-green pasta strainers because of unexpected demand levels. This involved complete rescheduling. Ideally we would like some stability, but the market is dynamic and continual schedule changes affect utilisation, efficiency *and* scrap rates. Certainly better marketing forecasts would help ... but even our own promotions are sometimes organised at such short notice that we often get caught with stockouts. Although Focus products have relatively stable volumes, the Concept products are much more seasonal, which makes capacity planning and scheduling very difficult at peak times around November (for the Christmas gifts markets) and Easter, just after the spring trade fair in London.

'At the same time, I have to schedule production time for new product mould trials; we normally allow three shifts (24 hours) for the testing of each new mould received, and this has to be done on production machines. From my perspective, it is often a difficult choice whether to schedule products that are needed urgently, or mould trials for new product launches which are equally urgent.'

Supply Services had become a large and strategically important part of the company. It maintained its own fleet of medium and small distribution vehicles for the UK market, but mainly used international parcel carriers for the continental European market. In the UK market a standard delivery timetable was used, delivering once or twice a week depending on the area. In addition, an 'express delivery' service was offered for those customers prepared to pay a small delivery premium. However, a recent study had shown that almost 40 per cent of express deliveries were initiated by the company rather than by customers. Often this would be to fulfil follow-up deliveries of orders containing products out of stock at the time of ordering. The express delivery service was not normally required for Focus products. Sandra White explained some of the issues faced by her department:

'Most of our time is spent planning the production and delivery schedules for Concept products, which involves a vast range of moulded parts, bought-in components, packaging, and finished goods. In contrast, the Focus planning is relatively straightforward, since the product range is simpler and the vast majority of deliveries are to a small number of important customers. The size of each Focus order is usually very large, usually with regular call-offs and deliveries to customers' own distribution depots. However, although organising Focus delivery is relatively straightforward, the consequences of failure are large. If we cannot fulfil an order, and therefore miss a delivery slot, we are inevitably upsetting a very large, powerful customer. My job is to ensure that we satisfy all our customers!'

## New product development

Grant Williams explained the new product development process:

'We receive detailed drawings of the new products from the Design Office, which is managed by Marketing. The Concept and 'design house' products are often high-precision, complicated objects, each of which presents its own technical challenges. However, we pride ourselves on our ability to overcome the technical and quality problems and, when we have decided on the basic mould requirements, orders are placed with our preferred mould makers, located in South Korea. Not only do these suppliers offer the highest standards of mould quality, but they are also significantly cheaper than comparable European mould makers. It usually takes around four to five months to get a new mould, which then has to be tested on our production machines. At the scheduled time, we fix the mould into a machine and undertake trials until we get perfect quality output. These then become the operating parameters and are recorded for future use. This whole process can take up to 24 hours, so we sometimes miss a night's sleep if there is an important trial in progress!

'The operators are as keen as we are to get the cycle times as fast as possible, since their bonus payments are based on good output. We make it easy for them by getting the settings right from the outset, but I'm afraid they don't all appreciate that. Sometimes, several operators spend most of a shift involved with normal production set-ups, and argue that they could have made more bonus wages on production. There is always a bit of tension here, but I still believe that we must continue to link wages and output if we are to retain our excellent record of productivity.'

## ● Latest developments

The 'Concept Office' brand had been introduced in late 1999, and was perceived as a very successful entry into a new market, employing many of the marketing ideas developed with the Concept household range. Concept Office items comprised filing trays, storage boxes and a range of desk items – all innovatively styled and in seasonal colours. Users were encouraged to change the colour in use every season to provide variety in drab, open-plan offices. Concept Office branded products were sold through specialist office equipment contractors and retailers.

James Thompson, the CEO, summed up his view of the current situation:

'Our alliances with several Italian and German design houses have been a particularly significant recent development for CDS. In effect, we are positioning ourselves as a complete service partner to the designers. We have a well-developed design capability ourselves, together with manufacturing, order processing, order taking and distribution services. These abilities allow us to develop genuinely equal partnerships which integrate us into the whole industry's activities.'

Linda Fleet also saw an increasing role for collaborative arrangements.

'It may be that we are seeing a fundamental change in how we do business within our industry. We have always seen ourselves as primarily a company which satisfies end consumer desires by providing good service to retailers. The new partnership arrangements put us more into the 'business-to-business' sector. I don't have any problem with this in principle, but I'm a little anxious as to how much it gets us into areas of business beyond our core expertise.'

The actual and prospective partnership deals fell into two broad categories, which are explained below.

## Design house collaboration

Some years ago, CDS had forged several partnerships with European design houses, the most successful of which was with a famous company of Italian designers. Generally it was the company's existing design expertise which was attractive to design-house partners. Not only did CDS employ professionally respected designers, but they had also acquired a reputation for being able to translate the most difficult technical designs into manufactureable and saleable products. Design house partnerships usually involved relatively long lead times but produced unique products with very high margins, nearly always carrying the design house's brand. Linda Fleet was enthusiastic about these developments.

'This type of joint-venture relationship plays to our strengths. Our design expertise gains us entry to the partnership; we are soon valued equally for our marketing, distribution and manufacturing competences. We gain access to the latest European design philosophies, ideas and market research, along with the rights to use their leading designer brand names. In return, they get a good royalty payment and access to our unique capabilities. It is certainly a win-win arrangement which is unique in the industry.'

## Major retailer services

This type of collaboration (one already established and one prospective) involved CDS taking responsibility for the whole category of plastic homewares for a large supermarket group. It involved having access to the retailer's sophisticated sales data systems and, based on this data, deciding what each store should have on its shelves. The product ranges supplied were not particularly adventurous in their design or colours, but most were clearly in the 'Concept' style and often carried the Concept brand. Where appropriate, competitors' products and the Focus range could be included where they filled gaps in CDS's ranges. Linda Fleet explained more about these category management services:

'Broadly speaking, the supermarkets do not seem to be as sophisticated in their non-food buying as they are in their food products. In effect, they have handed over part of the responsibility to us and trust us to supply ranges or products which are appropriate for their customers overall but, to some degree, selected to be appropriate for their individual stores. Their objective is invariably to use us to extract the best profitability from the category, particularly in terms of profit per square metre of shelf space. So far, this is working reasonably well, although the real costs of understanding their sales data are probably higher than we fully realise.'

### Questions

1 *How successful have Concept Design Services' strategies been since the decision to exit the industrial products market?*

2 *In what ways have the marketing strategies affected the activities of the Manufacturing Operations and Supply Services departments?*

3 *What have been the main features of the strategies adopted by Manufacturing and Supply Services during the 1990s? What operations-based competitive advantages were developed under the influence of these strategies? Were the strategies clearly developed or did they simply evolve, or both?*

4 *How might the development of the design house and major retailer services markets affect the operation of the Manufacturing and Supply Services departments? More specifically, what new capabilities may be required to serve these new markets effectively and profitably?*

5 *What changes, if any, would you recommend for the business to continue its growth in sales and profit?*

# PART 2

# Operations strategy

# Introduction to Part 2

Operations strategy reconciles two sets of pressures. One derives from the requirements of the markets in which the organisation operates. The other comes from the intrinsic characteristics of its resources – what they can and can't do. Figure P2.1 illustrates this idea.

This part:

- examines the difficulties in formulating operations strategies
- identifies four generic operations strategies
- identifies the key steps in formulating an operations strategy.

It also assesses four key challenges within creating an operations strategy:

- *ethical* – the moral imperative to develop ethical operations strategies
- *international* – the necessity to consider the international dimension of operations strategies
- *creative* – the need for creativity in devising operations strategies
- *implementation* – the ultimate challenge of implementing the chosen strategies.

**Figure P2.1  Operations strategy reconciles the requirements of the market with the capabilities of operations resources**

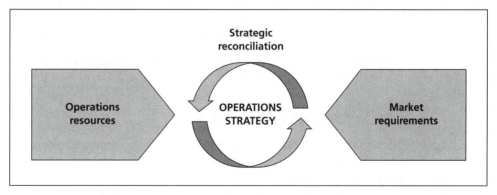

# The strategy challenge

By now it should be clear that managing most operations is a complex task involving the design, planning and control, and improvement of not only the products and services themselves but also the processes by which they are created. The complexity arises not just from the range of tasks, but also because these tasks are interrelated. The case of the Norrköping Plant A (Case 7) illustrates this quite clearly. The real challenge for operations managers, though, is not just their understanding and command of the detailed complexity of all the operations decisions, rather it is whether they can make enough sense of the operation to fit it into a strategic context, reshape and improve it, and then make sure that its contribution to competitiveness is both clear and ongoing.

Creating an operations strategy involves putting together a set of policies, plans and improvement projects which, when they are taken together, define the direction of the operation so that it becomes the source of competitive advantage.

## Difficulties in formulating operations strategy

Trying to make strategic sense of a business and the operations role within it is not easy for a number of reasons:

- Operations management is highly complex, involving many decisions about the effective use of most of an organisation's resources
- Operations managers may be geographically dispersed, located in all the operations parts of the organisation rather than grouped together at its headquarters
- Operations managers operate in 'real time', with pressure to deliver goods and services, and may not be able to allow their attention to move beyond the running of the operation for more than relatively short periods
- The cost of the resources under the operations manager's control is usually high and there is often a degree of difficulty in getting the organisation to accept innovative and imaginative changes
- Operations managers are often just not used to thinking, acting or influencing the organisation in any strategic manner; they tend to be more used to concerning themselves with the day-to-day detailed running of the operation.

The Marks and Spencer case (Case 6) demonstrates the difficulties inherent in developing operational strategies that can be as flexible and dynamic as the market they serve.

## Generic operations strategies

There are four generic operations strategies:

### The caretaker strategy
This strategy is often employed when an organisation believes that there is little competitive advantage to be gained by differentiating itself from its competitors. Operations managers are expected to make sure things do not go wrong, rather than provide much in the way of innovation or creativity.

### The marketeer strategy

Marketeer strategies are often used by organisations that experience increased competition and respond by enhancing or extending the level of customer service that they offer. This might include such things as broadening the range of their products or services, increasing quality levels or giving delivery guarantees. The operations function tries to do this by developing its infrastructural resources such as planning and control systems, working practices or quality management methods. After some poor financial results, Marks and Spencer developed new and innovative strategies for the market supported by considerable reorganisation of the supply chain, a strategic shift which helped to almost double its pre-tax profits from 2000 to 2001.

### The reorganiser strategy

This strategy implies a change in the way an organisation designs and manages its processes. This could mean investment in new technology and; more significantly, a different way of organising its methods of producing goods and services. Read Norrköping Plant A for an illustration.

### The innovator strategy

The innovator strategy is a combination of the marketeer and the reorganiser strategies. Not only does the organisation adopt an enhanced approach to designing its operations, it also expects enhanced customer service from its operations function. In other words, it enhances not only its structure but also its infrastructure.

## Formulating an operations strategy

There are several procedures available that can help organisations formulate their operations strategy. Typically many of the formulation processes include the following elements:

- A process which formally links the total organisational strategic objectives (usually a business strategy) to resource level objectives.
- The use of competitive factors (called various things, such as 'order winners', 'critical success factors', etc.) as the translation device between business strategy and operations strategy.
- A step which involves judging the relative importance of the various competitive factors in terms of customers' preference.
- A step which includes assessing current achieved performance, usually as compared against competitor performance levels (often referred to as 'benchmarking').
- An emphasis on operations strategy formulation as an iterative process.
- The concept of an 'ideal' or 'green field' operation against which to compare current operations. Very often the question asked is: 'If you were starting from scratch on a greenfield site, how, ideally, would you design your operation to meet the needs of the market?' This can then be used to identify the differences between current operations and this ideal state.
- A 'gap-based' approach. This is a well-tried approach in all strategy formulation which involves comparing what is required of the operation by the marketplace against the levels of performance that the operation is currently achieving.

## Judging the effectiveness of operations strategy

An effective operations strategy should clarify the links between overall competitive strategy and the development of the organisation's operations resources. More specifically, an operations strategy should be:

- *appropriate* – it should support the organisation's competitive strategy
- *comprehensive* – it should indicate how all parts of the operations function are expected to perform
- *coherent* – the policies recommended for each micro-operation must all lead roughly in the same direction, and interrelate positively with other functional strategies
- *consistent over time* – the lead time of operations improvement means that consistency must be maintained over a reasonable time period
- *credible* – the strategies and associated improvement targets should be seen as feasible and realistic.

At a broader level, operations strategies must also be ethical, international, creative and implemented.


## Strategies must be ethical

The concept of ethical decision making permeates operations management. There are ethical implications in almost every operations management decision area. Product or service design, for example, may affect customer safety or energy consumption; the layout of facilities may affect worker safety; process technology may affect waste product disposal.

In operations management, as in other areas of management, ethical judgements are often not straightforward. What might be unremarkable in one country or organisation's ethical framework could be regarded as highly dubious in others. Nevertheless, there is an emerging agenda of ethical issues which, at the very least, all operations managers should be sensitive to. The first step in this sensitisation process is to identify the groups to whom an ethical duty is due. These groups can be categorised as the organisation's customers, its staff, the suppliers who provide it with materials and services, the community in which the environment operates and the shareholders and owners who invest their capital in the organisation. Some of these issues are addressed in the Indian Metals Corporation case (Case 10).


## Strategies must be international

Few organisations can afford to limit their operations strategies to within their national boundaries. Only the smallest of organisations neither buy any of their supplies from abroad nor sell any of their products and services abroad, or are not considering doing so. For most operations managers, the 'environment' within which they make their decisions is, increasingly, a global one (see Case 6, New supply chain strategies at old M&S).

Large multinational organisations may also have the additional problem of different operating practices in different parts of the world because of differing cultures, economic conditions, history, market needs and demography, for example. The question, therefore, that a multinational has to face is whether it should allow its facilities in different parts of the world to develop their own operations strategies to suit their own conditions or whether it should encourage a uniformity of practice which reflects its corporate values.

## Strategies must be creative

Faced with a given set of circumstances, different sets of operations managers will probably come out with very different strategic solutions. Some might follow fairly conventional and orthodox routes while others might be more imaginative and creative in coming up with their own original strategic solutions. Many successful operations are successful because managers thought of an original way of creating their products and services and are therefore able to offer new forms of differentiation and associated competitive advantage. The relationship between customer and supplier in Norrköping Plant B (Case 8) illustrates how competitive advantage is not limited to the tangible aspects of business.

There are several blocks to creativity:

- *Trade-offs* – believing that prioritising operations performance objectives and improvements in one area will lead to a natural and consequential deterioration in another; for example, an increase in quality will have a consequent increase in costs.
- *Focus on efficiency* – developing operations planning and control systems which emphasise efficiency over creativity.
- *Specialising creativity* – dividing people's jobs into two categories and expecting one group to be creative and the other not, or expecting certain functions in the organisation (such as research and development or marketing) to be creative while other functions (such as operations and finance) are not expected to be creative.
- *Not rewarding creativity* – not recognising or rewarding those staff who generate creative solutions to operations strategy.

## Strategies must be implemented

Too often operations strategies fail at the implementation stage. A strategy may set the direction of the operation but implementation defines how it gets there, which is a more difficult task. Implementation of strategy within an organisation may run into problems and operations managers have to be prepared to counter and manage hostility from within – read Jossey Menswear (Case 9) for an illustration of this. Operations managers need to start the task by addressing their implementation agenda – the list of general questions whose answers set the basic plan for implementation.

The questions are:

- *When should it start?* Implementation should not begin until there is a clear idea as to how the strategy is to be implemented. Also, some start times may be better than others, such as during a relatively settled period rather than during the launch of a new product.
- *Where should it start?* Either start implementation where the operation is likely to get most benefit or where there is the best chance of success.
- *How fast should we go?* Managing the speed of improvement means understanding (and often combining) the two modes of improvement: breakthrough improvement and continuous improvement.

- *How should we coordinate the programme?* An operations strategy implementation needs to be managed like any other project. It requires planning, resource allocation and controlling to achieve the plan.

There are several important success factors that affect implemention of an operations strategy:

- *Top management support* – top management needs not only to offer support to the activity but also to allocate and coordinate resources.
- *Business driven* – the organisation's overall competitive imperatives must be linked to the operations strategy programme.
- *Strategy drives technology* – competitiveness should drive operations strategy which, in turn, determines the way technology is developed – not the other way round.
- *Change strategies are integrated* – successful operations strategy programmes involve change over several fronts: technological, organisational and cultural.
- *Invest in people as well as technology* – changes in methods, organisation or technology must be supported by changes in the knowledge and attitude of all employees.
- *Manage technology as well as people* – technology needs to be integrated into the operation and 'managed' after its implementation to achieve the most out of it.
- *Everybody on board* – any effective operations strategy must be understood and supported throughout the organisation, at all levels.
- *Clear explicit objectives* – if staff know what is expected of them and believe in the objectives, it is easier to succeed.
- *Time-framed project management* – objective setting, schedules, resource plans and milestones are as important here as for any other project.

## Summary

It has been suggested that a key challenge for operations managers is to be able to make sense of the operation and all its complexity and to fit it within a strategic context in order to ensure that it contributes to the competitiveness of the organisation as a whole. This task is complicated by a frequently held belief that improvement in one area will lead to deterioration in another. Operations managers need to work out how to do all things well and important things excellently. Furthermore, they have a responsibility to ensure that their decisions and actions are ethical, to take into account the global economy of which they are a part, and also to be creative in their development and implementation of operations strategies.

### Key points

- A key challenge for operations managers is fitting the operation into a strategic context and creating a set of policies, plans and improvement projects to provide the organisation with a competitive advantage.
- Operations strategies can be classified into four generic strategies: caretaker strategies, marketeer strategies, reorganiser strategies and innovator strategies.
- Formulating an operations strategy involves linking the total organisational strategic objectives (usually a business strategy) to resource level objectives.

- Nearly all decisions made by operations managers have some kind of ethical dimension.
- Managers need to understand the international implications of managing their operations.
- Creativity is needed to overcome trade-offs between performance criteria. This also involves overcoming some of the blocks to creativity present in most organisations.
- Successful implementation involves deciding when to start, where to start, how fast to proceed and how to coordinate the implementation programme.

## Recommended reading

Hayes, R. H., Wheelwright, S. C. and Clark, K. B. (1988), *Dynamic Manufacturing*, Free Press.

Hill, T. (2000), *Manufacturing Strategy*, Palgrave Macmillan.

Slack, N., Chambers, S. and Johnston, R. (2001), *Operations Management*, (3rd edn), Financial Times Prentice Hall, Harlow, Chapters 3 and 21.

Slack, N. and Lewis, M. (2002), *Operations Strategy*, Financial Times Prentice Hall, Harlow.

# New supply chain strategies at old M&S

Case date
2001

© Alan Harrison and Jane Pavitt

## Introduction

Marks & Spencer (M&S) is a leading retailer of clothing, food, homeware and financial services. Around 10 million customers per week are served in around 300 UK stores. The company was started in 1884, when Michael Marks (a Russian-born Polish refugee) opened a stall at Leeds Kirkgate Market. By 1997, M&S had grown into an international group with an annual sales turnover in excess of £8 billion – combined with one of the highest net margins in retailing.

M&S experienced a wrenching time since those glory days, having become highly vulnerable in its core customer base – women aged between 35 and 55. The very advantages that M&S had painstakingly built up became liabilities in the market downturn of autumn, 1998. For example, lengthy supply chain procedures meant that the company was buying 9 to 12 months ahead of the market. Traditionally M&S bought twice a year for spring and autumn with phased buying in between – that is, there were just two main sales 'seasons' per year. Nimbler competitors exploited many seasons per year for fashion items at one end of the market, and everyday low pricing that M&S could not match at the other. The M&S counter-offensive took a long time to formulate. Luc Vandevelde, the third CEO in as many years, said in his annual review to shareholders in 2001:

'...we have been able to conduct a thorough strategic review. Although some of the decisions we've taken are painful, they are necessary if M&S is to return to growth, and they will improve our ability to compete and respond more quickly to operational demands.'

As part of this strategic review, the UK retail management team, led by Roger Holmes, developed an operational plan that envisaged building on the strengths of M&S and exploiting new growth opportunities. A key part of the recovery plan included major improvements in product appeal, availability and value in order to rebuild relationships with the core womenswear customer base.

## A former supplier's view

Many of the 'painful decisions' related to Marks & Spencer's traditional UK supply base, which had been decimated in the scramble to reduce costs. In some ways, this had made the slowness to respond to market changes even worse. A former employee of a former M&S supplier, which has now closed most of its UK factories, commented on the recent changes:

'Three years ago M&S operated a very standard, very formalised route from order to contract, production and distribution. Each item had to have an M&S garment number as identification all the way through production, which precluded suppliers from manufacturing items for other retailers. More recent supplier rationalisation has changed this approach, but it is still very formalised and in reality a more informal approach is taken on a daily basis to actually get things done.'

Much of the manufacture of M&S products had been transferred abroad. There is very little capital expenditure in clothing. Typically, raw materials account for 50 per cent of the product cost, and labour for 30 per cent. Labour costs were much cheaper in countries like China, Cambodia and Bangladesh, but this has had a significant impact on lead-times: it takes four to six weeks to ship from the Far East. Airfreight is used sparingly, as it has not been possible to get the type of costs required for routine airfreight.

When buying standard ranges there is a balance between buying few colour ranges at higher volumes, or more colours at lower volumes. Combinations add to complexity: if there are eight colours and eight sizes, there are 64 stock keeping units (SKUs) in the range. M&S bought in a ratio across sizes based on sales history, but actual sales in a season – especially colours – were difficult to forecast. Responding to changes in volume and mix in the marketplace was difficult enough for the ponderous M&S systems, but the company's insistence on a single brand brought further problems:

'M&S procedures do not allow flexibility for short lead times. Had they agreed to sub-brand in the past, it would have been possible to produce to different quality standards for different product ranges.'

New product development was also slow and costly. All suppliers were asked to develop all ranges – M&S would then decide who would manufacture what and where. This increased development costs all round. The company has become more skilled at assessing supplier capabilities in advance. Suppliers who are low-cost producers receive orders for commodity products, while those with strengths in product or material development receive orders for more innovative lines.

## Improving the supply chain

M&S identified opportunities to reduce supply chain costs substantially, and achieved targeted savings of £120 million in 2000. The priorities were to eliminate duplication and to increase transparency. Some of the savings were achieved by using fewer suppliers and by working more effectively with them. This enabled M&S to get goods to the shops faster and to respond more quickly to emerging customer demands. By re-establishing closer working relationships with its supply partners – historically a unique strength – M&S wanted to achieve further improvements in quality, value, product appeal and availability.

Using information about customer preferences, buyers were better able to give suppliers the information needed to be more flexible and efficient in production. The company admitted that the speed of the changes made, and the replacement of a major supplier, did create availability problems in the autumn and spring of 2000/2001 – particularly in knitwear and lingerie. A focus on the 500 best-selling products, particularly basic items like socks and knickers, sought to ensure that customers noticed an improvement in availability.

## Improving the segmentation of clothing

M&S has concentrated on regaining the loyalty of its core customers, who prefer classically stylish clothes. In the past, the company had resisted splitting its traditional *St Michael* brand name, preferring to leverage the power of a single name that became synonymous with the company. As part of its new plan to segment products across different lifestyles, the company recognised that this was no longer tenable. For example, George Davies was appointed to design and supply a collection for the fashion-conscious woman. Davies had risen to fame as a result of making the retailer Next well known on the UK high street with his innovative designs and methods, and by his subsequent success in developing the *George* range of clothing at Asda supermarkets. His sub-brand at M&S was labelled *per una*, and 50 selected M&S stores were laid out by lifestyle to give impact and clarity to the display. Supply chain issues were also attended to.

'per una is "ring fenced" within the M&S system so that the range can be produced to a different standard. This enables George Davies to achieve a four-week turnaround.'

Another range called *The Autograph* was created by top designers to offer fashion items at High Street prices. A compromise was reached in sourcing this range, which was originally produced in UK factories but moved to Portugal. This had the benefit of cheaper labour costs than the UK and shorter lead-times than the Far East.

M&S also planned to regain the confidence of its customers in the quality and fit of its clothing. It chose to sharpen pricing by rebalancing the price structure and by extending the range of entry prices. The aim was to deliver 'aspirational quality at great value'.

### Womenswear ranges for autumn 2001

M&S further segmented its womenswear products to appeal to different lifestyles by introducing a number of ranges and sub-brands in addition to *per una* and *The Autograph*, including *The Perfect Collection* and *The Classic Collection*.

#### The Perfect Collection
*The Perfect Collection* focused on classically stylish merchandise for core customers. There are 60 lines for women and men which 'return to basics', and they include plain, white shirts, black roll-neck sweaters and jeans. With many items machine washable, non-iron and tumble-dry friendly, they're aimed at the customer with a busy lifestyle who is looking for quality and value at a reasonable price. The brochure described them as 'timeless essentials that you can wear with just about anything'.

#### The Classic Collection
*The Classic Collection* was aimed at the more mature customer, and the advertising concentrated on design, comfort, long-lasting style and versatility – 'Every piece in

The Classic Collection is designed to skim and flatter the natural body shape, whatever your size'. *The Classic Collection* is a range of smart, elegant clothes, made from high-quality fabrics at value-for-money prices. 'It's a timeless collection that reflects your style and finesse, and not just the latest fashion.'

### The Autograph range

The category manager, Liz Alcock, states: 'The *Autograph* philosophy is to bring cutting-edge design to a wider audience within a unique environment'. Like *per una*, *The Autograph* label, which was launched in the spring/summer 2000 range, was made available in selected stores only. M&S recruited some of the best designers in the business – such as Julien Macdonald, Philip Treacy and Sonja Nuttall – to create womenswear, menswear and accessories collections. For example, Philip Treacy's hat collection was launched in 15 M&S *Autograph* boutiques nationwide in March 2001 and comprised 18 hats and 10 bags with no more than 60 of each colourway and style. *Autograph* brings top designer collections to M&S customers at high street prices, within a designer boutique environment.

### per una

This high-quality range was designed to appeal to a broad catchment at competitive prices, and was launched in September 2001 into selected stores. The target customers were fashion-conscious women aged between 25 and 35, sizes 8–18. The aim was to provide 'superb designs at very affordable prices'. George Davies controls the supply chain, including sourcing and merchandising as well as control of the look of the selling space in store. In the brochure, he says *per una* embodies principles of 'the highest quality materials ... designs inspired by the very latest trends ... limited editions ... individual cuts for every size ... fanatical attention to detail ... ease of shopping'. The 300-piece collection was sourced from 90 suppliers from Hong Kong to central Europe. Production runs were short with no repeats, and speed of reaction was important to ensure that goods made it from design concept to shop rails in weeks not months.

In *Marks & Spencer Magazine*, September 2001, George Davies was quoted as saying:

'I know women don't want to see loads of the same thing around. It's OK for plainer pieces, but if it's distinctive, they want it to be rare. Which is why we'll have a series of limited-edition items introduced throughout the life of a three-month collection – so buy them because they won't be in store for long.'

Unlike other ranges in store where up to 20 of a style can be seen together, *per una* items were presented in small numbers, making each style 'special' and more exclusive. *per una* was 10 per cent more expensive than the M&S main range. However, the rollout programme had to be scaled down because the company could not keep up with higher than expected customer demand.

## Customer comments

Two M&S customers were asked: 'What are you looking for?' and 'What is important to you when considering buying a standard item or a high fashion item?' The first was a smartly dressed lady, aged 54, who said:

'For a standard item it's important that my size is available but quality and price are also important. In terms of quality, a jumper, for example, must be value for money, wash well and not require specialist washing (hand wash or dry clean!). For a premium item I don't want to be wearing something that is instantly recognisable as M&S – if I'm paying a premium price, therefore, "exclusive" design is a must. Quality is also important if I'm paying a higher price, as it must be well made and expected to last.'

The second customer, a fashionably dressed lady, aged 33, was asked the same questions, and said:

'I get very frustrated if an item is not available in my size. I am annoyed when I find that it is only currently in stock in sizes 8–10 as the larger sizes have sold out. They never seem to have enough of the bigger sizes. For a standard item I expect value for money and a "reasonable" quality – colour not to fade and it won't shrink when washed. Availability of a variety of colour shades for a shirt or jumper is helpful but not a key driver (size availability is key). For premium/high-fashion items, quality is not as important to me as design. If it's a high-fashion item I expect to wear it only a few times before replacing it. I would not make a specific trip to a store to buy such an item from M&S (unlike a standard item). It would tend to be more of an impulse purchase.'

## Questions

1 *What market segments do the three different product ranges serve? Assume that the* Perfect *and* Classic *ranges serve essentially the same segment.*

2 *What are the order winners and qualifiers for these different ranges?*

3 *What are the different logistics performance objectives for the different product groups? Fill in the following table:*

| | *Perfect* and *Classic* ranges | *Autograph* range | *per una* range |
|---|---|---|---|
| Product range | | | |
| Design changes | | | |
| Price | | | |
| Quality | | | |
| Sales volumes SKU | | | |
| Order winners | | | |
| Order qualifiers | | | |
| Operations priorities | | | |

The M&S website is at: *www.marksandspencer.com*

CASE
7

Case date
2001

# The Norrköping Plant (A)*

Nigel Slack

## Introduction

At the Vanden Corporate Park, just outside Norrköping in Sweden, is one of the largest pieces of converting machinery within the Carlsen group. Inside a room which is 20 metres wide and 120 metres long is housed a coater over 80 metres long with around 100 metres of film forming a web path from the unwind, through the coating processes and oven, to the rewinder. In June of 2001 when the coater went online for the first time it was, according to Lars Olafsen, Vice President of Carlsen's Industrial Division at the time:

'...the most advanced machine of its type in the world, which will enable us not only to increase manufacturing capacity but also achieve new standards of manufacturing excellence for products requiring absolute cleanliness and precision in production.'

The Norrköping plant was joining what are now Carlsen's two existing European plants, one in Stockholm and the other outside Copenhagen in Denmark. Both plants offered precision custom coating and laminating services to a wide range of customers. One of the most important of these customers, Agsten, used the firm to process its dry photoresist imaging films, a critical step in making printed circuit boards.

The Norrköping plant was developed especially to serve this photoresist market, though it was always seen by the company as more than simply 'providing capacity' for a growing market. Rather it was seen as a 'quantum leap in harnessing economies of scale, new technology and new forms of organisation to provide *the* plant of the twenty-first century'.

Yet the plant's origins lay some seven years earlier, in 1994.

## The 'Monster'

For Carlsen's photoresist imaging business, 1994 was a traumatic year. Prior to that time it had been the clear market leader based on high quality, a cost base comparable with its chief competitors and what it regarded as excellent working relationships with its customers. So when the downturn came, the shock was severe. Saviste Graphics, the company's major competitor, had introduced a new coating technology early in 1994 which enabled it to produce coated product at levels of cleanliness significantly in excess of those being achieved by Carlsen, who lost business as a result.

Birgit Deprez, Operations Vice President, Carlsen, outlined the situation:

'We paid out a fortune in customer rejections and the coating machine was down for eight months. Imagine it, we just didn't make any of this product line for eight months! It was a very painful experience for all of us who were with the company during that period. I guess it was this period which marked a clear turning point in the way Carlsen did business. Up to that time we had acted as though we pretty well knew what we were doing. We found out then that there was another guy on the street who could do things a little better than we could. It was a rude awakening for us. We learnt that if we were going to be successful in this business we always needed to be striving to be a little better. We had never been number two in any marketplace before and we weren't interested in being number two for very long.'

By working on its quality and clean-room standards, modifying its own coating technology, and by reorganising into business teams, the company overcame the worst of its problems and by August of 1995 was achieving sound business results. Yet the experience had convinced management that they should be considering more radical ways of deploying their process technology. Also, at that time it was judged likely that extra capacity would shortly be needed, so this seemed the ideal opportunity to explore some new ideas.

A team, led by Birgit Deprez, was formed to create a concept for a coating machine, the like of which had not been seen in the industry up to that point. The idea was to push the boundaries of process technology further than anyone had previously considered doing. This technology was to be at the forefront of sophistication, with a large capacity, faster speed, and with state-of-the-art instrumentation and automation, together with ultra-clean conditions, which would make it highly efficient with labour and capable of very high quality levels. Gregor Boisot, Engineering Manager, Carlsen, said:

'The concept of what became the Norrköping plant goes back to this time. Not only was this machine to have larger capacity, higher speed, and more computerisation than ever before, but also it would have significantly lower costs. We called this machine "The "Monster". It was a kind of design exercise I guess, but with a very serious intent. It was a "mind-expanding" experience yet with a clear business goal.'

However, shortly after the creation of the 'Monster' concept the need for this extra capacity evaporated as total market forecasts were revised downwards, but all who had participated in the 'Monster' team were convinced of the value of the process. Gregor Boisot explained:

'It was the ideas which were conceived at this time that allowed us to move ahead so effectively later. During the time of incubation which followed the exercise, many of the ideas that we had put into the "Monster" were changed and modified as new technology became available and as our ideas developed. But the "Monster" had planted the seed so the effort that we put in, although aborted at the time, did lead us to be able to be more effective when we got to the point of doing it in reality.'

## ● The 'Monster' resurrected

By 1997 forecasts of demand once again indicated a need for extra coating capacity and work started on examining how this extra capacity might be provided. At this time the working assumption was that any new capacity would be similar to the technology which was currently used at the company's Stockholm operation.

In December of that year David Leopard, Carlsen's CEO, visited Agsten, the company's most important customer for photoresist product, and became convinced that there was considerable business potential for Carlsen, especially if it could provide the most advanced coating service in the industry. From that point the scope of the capacity project expanded. Carlsen's operations team was charged with creating an operation which could ensure a competitive advantage and adequate capacity for decades to come. If successful, such an operation held out the prospect of securing a very large part of Agsten's future business – perhaps even an exclusive agreement to supply 100 per cent of its needs.

After consideration, three options were presented to the firm's new owners.

A. Expand the Stockholm site by building a new machine within existing site boundaries. This would provide around 12 to 13 million square metres (MSM) per year of additional capacity and require somewhat less than Kr100 million in capital expenditure.
B. Build a new facility alongside the Stockholm plant. This new facility could accommodate additional capacity of around 15 MSM per year but, unlike option A, would also allow for future expansion. Initially this would require around Kr120 million capital.
C. Set up a totally new site with a much larger increment of capacity (probably around 25 MSM per year). This option could also incorporate much of the 'Monster', ultra-clean technology which had been explored two years previously. Clearly this option would be much more expensive, almost certainly in excess of Kr120 million.

The three options represented an increased degree of risk but also an increased potential for profitable business. Birgit Deprez and his team initially favoured option B but in discussion with senior management opinion shifted towards the more radical option C. As he commented:

'It may have been the highest risk option but it held considerable potential and it fitted with the company's emerging philosophy of getting into high-tech specialised areas of business.'

The option of a very large, ultra-clean, state-of-the-art facility also had a further advantage – it could change the economics of the photoresist imaging industry. An examination of the worldwide demand and capacity at the time did not immediately justify investing in as large an increase in capacity as option C would provide. In fact there was probably some overcapacity in the industry. The real attraction of the 'Monster' type operation was that it would provide a level of quality at such low costs that customers would not be able to ignore it. If there was to be even further overcapacity in the industry, it would not be Carlsen's capacity which would be lying idle.

The option also needed costing – a process which, surprisingly, did not prove a major problem. Birgit Deprez explained:

'The process of costing the proposal for a large, state-of-the-art machine did not take too great an effort because we had gone through much of the analysis two years previously when we created the "Monster" concept.'

# Designing the new plant

The early part of 1998 was a hectic time for the team, especially Birgit Deprez, Gregor Boisot and, from June, Peter Walberg who joined the team as Plant Manager for the, as yet unbuilt, plant. Detailed decisions were needed in three interrelated areas:

- *Location* – where should the new plant be built?
- *Technology* – how many and what type of coating machines should be installed?
- *Organisation* – what shape of organisational structure and philosophy of working would be appropriate for the new plant?

## Location

A number of factors were important when the team were searching for a suitable location for the new plant. Probably the most significant was that any new site should be close to the company's headquarters near Stockholm. It also needed to have good communications – certainly it should be near good transport links. Furthermore, it also needed to be reasonably close to an airport. Just as important, it needed to be in an area from which professionals could be recruited, or which would attract professionals because of the 'quality of life' available. Gregor Boisot noted:

'When we were first considering the possibility of a green-field site, we contacted local government representatives in several places. Interestingly, those in Norrköping were much more receptive than the others, who did not seem to be as excited at the prospect of the new plant.'

## Technology choice

The design of the process technology itself again required a series of interrelated decisions. These were:

- What should be the final capacity of the process technology?
- How many separate machines should be installed to achieve this level of capacity?
- What type of drying technology to incorporate within the line?
- What kind of feed system should be installed to deliver the coating material to the coating heads?

The team soon found out that the first two decisions were impossible to separate. They considered two options. The first was to install two coating lines, each with around 15 MSM per year. This was a reasonably ambitious option given that the largest machine existing at that time had a capacity of around nine MSM per year. However, this paled beside the second option which was to install a single prototype machine with a capacity of over 25 MSM per year. This was clearly the riskier option and would require more technological development. However, it would be more effective in its use of capital and, potentially, would allow very efficient use of labour. Yet in spite of the potential advantages there was some feeling amongst the company's technical staff that there might be a penalty in terms of the yield achievable from the big machine and, more seriously, considerable changeover losses.

The decision over the drying technology was again a choice between traditional and radical options. A traditional approach to drying was to use relatively low energy levels applied to the material over a long web path, drying the material slowly and making for easier control of the drying process. The more radical solution was to subject the material to higher energy levels over a shorter web path. A major advantage of high energy drying was that it required a shorter machine and therefore a smaller plant to house it. However, again, there were risks in choosing the more radical solution. Certainly trials which Gregor Boisot and his team were conducting with suppliers seemed to indicate that there might be considerable problems in achieving an acceptable degree of quality with the high-energy solution.

### Focus or flexibility?

In the middle of all this decision making it became clear that there was one issue which was underlying all discussions – how flexible should the total system be? Should the team assume that they were designing a plant which would be dedicated exclusively to the manufacture of photoresist imaging film for the foreseeable future, and ruthlessly cut out any technological options which would enable them to manufacture beyond that technical brief? Alternatively, should they design a more general purpose plant which, although capable of, and suitable for, photoresist imaging film, could with relatively little effort be adapted to coat other products in the future? It proved a difficult decision.

The advantages of the more flexible option were obvious, as Peter Walberg commented:

'At least it would mean that there was no chance of me being stuck with a plant and no market for it to serve in a couple of years' time.'

In the end the design of the technology proved to be a mixture of the adventurous and the conservative. As opposed to the two or three smaller machines envisaged in the original plan, the team decided to go for a single large machine. However, the traditional drying technology was chosen for its robust, tried and tested nature. But perhaps most controversial of all, the team decided to focus on a relatively non-flexible dedicated design which would realise the economy of scale potential of the large machine. Peter Walberg commented on the team's feelings about this decision:

'You can't imagine the agonies we went through when we decided not to make this a flexible machine. Many of us were not comfortable with saying, "This is going to be a photoresist machine exclusively, and if the market goes away we're in real trouble". We had a lot of debate about that. Eventually we more or less reached a consensus for focus but it was certainly one of the toughest decisions we ever made.'

The capital cost savings of adopting a focused facility were attractive, but more influential were the team's estimates of operating costs savings of up to 25 per cent. Also the philosophy of total process dedication was seen as offering some advantages which could not be directly quantified but were nevertheless important, as Gregor Boisot explained:

'The key word for us was *focus*. We wanted to be quite clear about what was needed to satisfy our customer in making this single type of product. As well as providing significant cost savings to us it made it a lot easier to identify the root causes of any problems. In solving any problem we would not have to worry too much about how it might affect other products and other customers. It's all very clear. When the line was down we would not be generating revenue! The lack of flexibility forced us to understand our own performance. At other plants, if a line goes down, the people on the line can be shifted to other responsibilities. We don't have other responsibilities here – we're either making it or we're not.'

## Work organisation

In the same way that many of the technical ideas which found their way into the Norrköping plant had their origins some years earlier, so the pattern of work organisation and the concept of self-managed teamwork had been discussed for some time. As Birgit Deprez puts it,

'Norrköping gave us the opportunity to indulge in self-managed work teams and we jumped on the opportunity'.

However, before committing themselves fully, the team examined both the opportunities and problems associated with adopting self-managed teams. The key meeting took place in November 1998 and included Birgit Deprez, Peter Walberg and Vernon Vaughan, who had joined the team as Human Resources Manager for the plant. As part of that meeting the team drew up a list of reasons why they *should* adopt the self-managed work team approach and reasons why they *should not* do so.

**Reasons why we should do it**
1  It will allow us to change rapidly.
2  Enriches jobs for all employees.
3  Increased employee ownership.
4  More fulfilling for all employees involved. Leads to pride, high quality, etc.
5  If it leads to high quality, it will lead to lower cost.
6  Involves all employees in a joint venture to achieve customer satisfaction.
7  It will attract a higher calibre employee (flexible, thinking).
8  The Pygmalion effect – people are, or respond to, the way you think they are.
9  Our value statement – 'Let's walk like we talk regarding the worth and dignity of people, quality, customers, etc.'
10  The people we recruit will want change.

**Reasons why we should not do it**
1  We are currently successful.
2  We are inexperienced in using/implementing such a concept.
3  Starting a new operation – we have plenty going on as it is.
4  We do not have the support of middle management.
5  Risk of failure – 'It is a big piece of our business'.
6  Increased training costs/employee costs. We might have to pay more to get more.
7  Immediate impact on other Carlsen plants.
8  Uncertain consequences of failure. Would we be better off for having tried and failed or better off not to try?
9  Takes away some (or all) management control.
10  Human beings resist change.

By the end of the meeting the team had reached a number of conclusions. First, on balance they were in favour of going ahead with the team approach. Although there were obvious risks involved, it was felt that employees' expectations and the general values of the times were changing to the extent that a more traditional approach could be equally risky. Second, the risk of foregoing the advantages of teamworking, and thereby losing competitive edge, were too great.

## The plant goes up

The operation went online in June 2001, but the task of recruiting the workforce had started months earlier. Peter Walberg commented:

'It took two months to decide on the traits we considered necessary to be successful in the operation. It went beyond the technical ability of the person; it also included the ability to work as a team member with social skills.'

Over 500 applicants for the positions of production technician were interviewed. Four hundred passed this initial screening, from whom 50 were selected for team interviews that involved four people from the Marketing, Technical and Manufacturing functions. The team interviews whittled the 50 down to 28.

With this number the company started its first pre-employment class that lasted for nine weeks. The training programme consisted of a four-day-per-week programme, with each session lasting four hours. The pre-employment class was also intended to test the candidates' willingness to stretch themselves and their desire to join the company. Peter Walberg explained:

'We figured that if a person could manage to work through nine weeks of computer and maths training while working another job, even though we provided no guarantee of employment before the training classes began, then this person probably had the staying power that we needed for the company.'

Out of the 24 who completed the training programme, 19 who excelled in team exercises and interactive skills were selected to join the firm. All 19 accepted.

## Looking back

The plant started producing in June 2001. The capacity of the plant at start-up was forecast to reach 33 MSM per year, working on a seven-day basis. It was, from the start, a technical and commercial success. In fact a critical strategic objective had been met in October 2000 when a contract was signed with Agsten whereby 100 per cent of its needs for coated film were to be supplied by Carlsen over the next 10 years, with the contract taking full effect in July 2002. By the start of 2001 the plant was already meeting 50 per cent of Agsten's needs.

The process of building up the human assets proved almost totally successful. Peter Walberg notes:

'The teams worked well from the start, partly because we had always stressed the idea that respect is the basis of teamwork. However, you have to recognise that there will be times when the interests of an individual and those of the company will not be identical. This is why it is so important to define very clearly the "box" within which the teams are empowered to make decisions.'

Birgit Deprez is convinced that the advantages of Norrköping's team-based approach are the foundation of the plant's success.

'Our associates are now well used to the idea that nothing ever stays the same, that we have to adapt, change and improve no matter how successful we are. They understand business objectives and customer needs as well as any manager. They understood all this from day one. It was certainly the only time in my career when I saw a work team take over a machine which still had some problems to iron out and yet immediately took responsibility for it themselves.'

## Questions

1 *What were the significant events leading to the successful start-up of the Norrköping plant?*

2 *Why was the 'Monster' particularly important?*

3 *What risks did the company run by 'going for focus'? Was it wise or just lucky?*

4 *Did the self-managed team approach fit with the other decisions taken by the Norrköping team?*

# The Norrköping Plant (B)

Case date
2001

Nigel Slack

## ● Introduction

In July of 2001 Carlsen Industrial division's newest, largest and most focused plant had started production. The plant represented a calculated gamble that economies of scale and dedicated technology could produce quality and cost performance in coating photoresist imaging film well beyond the capabilities of any competitor. The plant was a totally new building, constructed using ultra-clean principles.

Central to the Norrköping investment had been the prize of securing the majority of business from one of the most important companies in the dry film photoresist market – Agsten. At the time of the Norrköping start-up, photoresist film produced by Carlsen was shipped to its converting facility in Alborg, Denmark. This distance caused a number of problems. Inevitably there was some waste caused by damage in transit. More seriously, the delays in communication were the cause of some frustration, especially when introducing technical changes to the product or solving minor quality issues. However, notwithstanding the problems of location, the relationship between Carlsen and Agsten was sound, helped by Agsten's cooperation during the Norrköping project. Peter Walberg, the Norrköping Plant Manager, summed up this relationship:

'They had a lot of confidence in us. We had worked closely with them during the design and construction of the new Norrköping facility. More to the point, they saw that they would certainly achieve cost savings from the plant, with the promise of more savings to come as the plant moved down the learning curve.'

In addition, the strategic position of Agsten made close links with Carlsen attractive. Agsten was the only company in the photoresist market without either its own in-house coating capability, or integrated coating/converting operations at the same facility. Also the market for dry film photoresist was becoming more competitive due to a growing number of global producers. The resulting margin erosion drove Agsten to investigate a sole source supply agreement with Carlsen. Agreement was reached in late 2000 (during construction of the Norrköping facility) to come into force in July of 2002.

With the agreement, Carlsen and Agsten increasingly adopted a partnership philosophy towards the business. To that end, the companies agreed to explore projects that would enhance the partnering, provided such projects were favourable for both companies.

## Co-location

The idea of a physically closer relationship between Carlsen and Agsten was not new. Conceptually, this approach had been considered by Agsten and discussed with Carlsen since the mid-1990s. However, Agsten's dedication to dual sourcing at that time made such an option unattractive. Once a sole source agreement was in place, co-location was seen as producing benefits for both companies. Birgit Deprez, Operations Vice President, Carlsen, commented:

'During the negotiations with Agsten for our 100 per cent contract there had been some talk about co-location but I don't think anyone took it particularly seriously. Nevertheless there was general agreement that it would be a good thing to do. After all, our success as Agsten's sole supplier of coated photoresist was tied in to their success as a player in the global market. In other words; to a significant degree, what was good for Agsten was good for Carlsen.'

From late 2000 through to the August of 2001, several options were discussed within and between the two companies. Agsten had, in effect, to choose between five options:

- Stay where it was in Alborg.
- Locate in southern Sweden but not too close to Carlsen.
- Locate on the adjacent site across the road from the Norrköping plant.
- Co-locate within an extension built to the Carlsen plant at Norrköping.
- Get Carlsen to operate the converting processes for Agsten at the Norrköping facility.

## The state of the Carlsen–Agsten relationship

A key factor when both companies were evaluating the options for co-location was the closeness of the relationship which had developed between them. This was partly a result of staff from both companies working together in solving the routine issues involved in constructing a large plant such as the Norrköping facility. It was also partly born from adversity. One issue especially had caused delays in commissioning the new facility. In the final stages of installing the new coating line, in early 2001, Carlsen's engineers had hit problems with the machine because of winding difficulties.

To solve the problems, they designed and installed a new winding mechanism. They also discovered that some problems were caused by 'bowed' paper cores. Moving to more rigid steel cores eliminated these problems. At the same time they tried to find paper or plastic cores that exhibited the straightness of the steel cores. However, using steel cores was a real issue for Agsten, whose staff had to cope with the heavier and cumbersome loads. Carlsen staff were impressed by their customer's willingness to help out by doing this while they worked on finding suitable lighter cores.

The winding problem, however, proved difficult to solve. So as not to cause Agsten problems, Carlsen decided to invest in an 'accumulator' mechanism which could be used in the event of the winding problem proving insoluble. The extra cost of purchasing the accumulator was almost Kr2 million. This time it was Agsten's turn to be impressed. Carlsen had clearly demonstrated its determination to meet its supply obligations. Peter Walberg commented on the strengthening relationship between the two companies:

'The winding problem was potentially very serious. But we made a conscious effort to keep the customer fully informed. In fact they were very helpful in doing anything they could to help us sort the problem. Partly because we worked together on that problem, the relationship has grown stronger and stronger. They have become a real part of the partnership rather than someone waiting on the sidelines expecting product to come to them. They agonised when we failed and they shared the sense of achievement when we succeeded. It may be no coincidence that a few months after we worked our way through the winding problem we signed the long-term contract.'

## Evaluating the co-location options

Relatively early in the discussions between the two companies, the two 'extreme' options of either doing nothing by staying in Alborg or, alternatively, Carlsen operating the conversion process themselves at Norrköping were discounted. The advantages of some kind of move, both in cost savings and in ease of communications, had convinced Agsten that staying in Alborg was too costly.

One option for Agsten was to move to a site some 50 km from Norrköping. This would be a relatively cheap option. The building was old and already owned by Agsten's parent company. Freight costs would be lower than for its current location, but communication would be only partially improved.

Agsten also strongly considered building and operating a converting facility across the road from the Norrköping plant. This option had several cost-related disadvantages to being located in a building attached to the coating plant. Yet for a while it was the preferred option. Birgit Deprez explained:

'There was a lot of resistance to having a customer on the same site as ourselves. At one stage we said we would never do it. No one in Carlsen had ever done it before and we couldn't imagine working so closely with a customer. The step from imagining our customer across the road to imagining them on the same site took some thinking about. It was a matter of getting used to the idea, taking one step at a time.'

Yet the more the options were discussed, the more it became obvious to both companies that the best plan was to have Carlsen build an addition to Norrköping and lease it to Agsten. One way of achieving this was to make the maximum use of existing space in the Norrköping plant and add only the extra space required.

A major justification for the co-location project would be its impact on Agsten's competitiveness by reducing its operating costs. This would enable it to gain market share by offering quality film at attractive prices, thus increasing volume for Carlsen. Other advantages for Agsten would come largely in two areas. First, there would be significant freight savings associated with the transportation of master rolls when coating and slitting were done at the same location. Second, the projected reduction of staffing for Agsten at Norrköping would generate a cost saving.

Carlsen would also derive tangible benefits from this closer operational relationship with the customer. Its ability to work hand in hand with the customer in solving master roll quality issues would reduce rejects through quicker and more accurate feedback. This would also be invaluable in reducing lead time on the introduction of new products or new procedures, while at the same time working together to contain costs and provide increased yields. For example, the possibility of longer rolls and recyclable racking for master rolls were two projects that would clearly benefit from such co-location. Currently both projects were difficult because of having to transport product to the Woburn converting location. Co-location would also give Carlsen added flexibility for coordinating coating and converting schedules to a greater degree, thus creating optimal coating efficiency, improved raw material utilisation and enhanced quality. Finally, co-location would enable Carlsen to bring its staff into daily, routine customer contact, allowing them to provide improved service and support.

## The proposal

By August of 2001, Carlsen's Norrköping management were in a position to present their proposal for extending the Norrköping plant to accommodate Agsten. The cost of the facility would be recouped through annual lease payments by Agsten for the 10-year period from 2003. Agsten would relocate all of its current converting, warehousing and other equipment from its Alborg plant.

The proposal was not well received by the main board of Carlsen. Birgit Deprez recalls:

'We were beaten up severely at that meeting. Providing factory space seemed a long way from our core business. Although we understood that this company is not in the real estate business, and expects higher returns than those companies which are, we felt we had a good package and could put together a leasing deal which was profitable in its own right and enhance our ability to make profit in our main business of coating.'

However, money was eventually approved during August of 2001. Nevertheless, there was still an element of concern over the arrangement.

'When the proposal was approved there was still some residual anxiety about the concept of actually sharing a facility. The board insisted, for example, that the door between the two companies' areas should be capable of being locked from both sides.'

Agsten took occupancy in early 2002 and were slitting sellable product within one week of moving in.

A significant benefit was also gained which had not been forecast. The Norrköping site, with Carlsen and the customer working side by side, has been used as a model in selling partnerships to new customers. In February 2002 alone, meetings were held with two large potential customers in Norrköping so that they could see first hand how strategic partnering and co-locating can work.

And that door separating Carlsen from Agsten which the board insisted be capable of being locked from both sides? 'It has never even been closed, never mind locked,' said Peter Walberg.

## Questions

1 *What were the reasons for Agsten considering a relocation?*

2 *What were the location options considered and what advantages and disadvantages did each option have?*

3 *What were the barriers to choosing the eventual 'solution' and how were they overcome?*

# Jossey Menswear – the supply chain project

Case date
2002

Nigel Slack

Founded more than a century ago, and now part of Amedox Fashion Retail division, Jossey had developed a reputation for skilful retailing. Its success had been due to several years of changes, not only to the 160 Jossey Ladieswear shops and 60 Jossey Menswear shops, but also in the separate Design, Manufacturing and Merchandising functions which backed up these two parts of the company.

Both Jossey Ladieswear and Menswear operated in the mid-range fashion sector. Not high fashion, but reasonably stylish, serving a middle to upmarket clientele. Menswear did not have as diverse a range of products or as wide a geographical spread. The nature of 'fashion' itself was also different. What constitutes 'fashion' in Ladieswear was regarded as being inevitably more subjective. Sometimes it was difficult to identify exactly why a particular product or look had sold. Whereas fashion in menswear was more evolutionary than revolutionary. There were relatively few of the major fashion swings which characterised even the middle-of-the-road sector of the Ladieswear market. However, Menswear fashion was moving towards Ladieswear. Brenda Wright, Merchandising Director, Jossey Menswear, explained:

'It is the overall "look" which is now becoming important. If single-breasted grey Prince of Wales check suits were in high demand, it would not necessarily be the right thing to do to go and buy more of that kind of cloth. Rather, it is important to ask ourselves, 'What is it about this product that is making it sell?' Then we can make an equivalent, or perhaps even better, product with the same look. You might even get the same customers who bought the first product returning to buy the second.'

## Market, demand and products

Traditionally, the fashion retail industry has, in the Northern Hemisphere, been based on two seasons. January to July as the spring/summer season and August through to December as the autumn/winter season. Both break points between seasons have traditionally been marked by 'sales' where surplus product is reduced for clearance. To some extent this neat division of the year has broken down in recent years, with 'transition' seasons between the two major seasons extending to provide more of a rolling change of product offering.

Tailored products – jackets, trousers and suits – were the backbone of the Menswear product range. The company had five suit 'blocks' which determined the underlying shape or style of a jacket (two classic blocks and three contemporary). Each of these was offered in a range of cloths to produce about 40 'suit cloths', each of which was offered in 21 sizes. These, along with knitwear, shirts and accessories were sold through around 60 shops. Shops varied by size. Larger shops offered a wider range of products. However, only one store, the flagship shop in London, offered all the 40 'suit cloths' which typically make up a season, while the average of all shops was around 12.

As far as retail business was concerned, the key indicator of sales success was the proportion of 'full price sales' (FPS) achieved by the company. These were the garments which were sold on to customers at full price (therefore full margin), as opposed to being sold at a discount (often significant) during the sales period or through factory shop outlets. The FPS in Jossey Menswear had been around 50 per cent for several years.

A number of factors seemed to determine the FPS percentage. A major influence was the appropriateness of the 'collection' (that is, the range of styles put together each season by the company's designers). Designers worked from an understanding of their customer base, the way styling trends had moved in recent years, the trends foreshadowed in the relevant 'directional' fashion shows, and any new cloths available on the market. However 'gut feeling' inevitably played some part. Inevitably, design decisions were better some years than others. According to David Jossey, Managing Director, Jossey Menswear:

'In a typical five year span we are going to have two quite good years because we get things right, probably two very good years, and one year where we just get it wrong. This can swing our sales volumes up and down by around 20–25 per cent.'

Getting the styles into the right locations was also a factor in determining FPS. Each style had a slightly different trading pattern across the country, so the better the match between the availability of stock and the characteristics of each location's trading pattern, the better the FPS. In addition, even with the right products in the right location, the sizes in which that style was supplied to the shops could be wrong. Brenda Wright explained:

'It is difficult to predict exactly what size of customer will want what kind of product. We tend to work on averages. So for example, we have an average for a double-breasted contemporary suit. However, in reality the size and shape of customers who actually buy a particular style will deviate from this average. I suppose it would be possible to look at the characteristics of a suit within a particular block and make a judgement of what sizes are likely to buy it. However, we just don't know our customer base well enough to do that.'

Choosing the right cloth for each style was also important. Designers would visit cloth shows, always on the lookout for new cloths which would enhance their styling decisions. Even so, often the choice of cloth was made on a relatively small sample, sometimes only a few square centimetres in area. As well as the obvious difficulties that gave the design team, it also made it difficult for the factory to predict how the cloth would behave during the manufacturing process. Brenda Wright commented:

'Six to eight years ago we used to say, "That is the right cloth for that style". We couldn't have used the cloth on anything else. If you got it wrong, well it was just too bad. Whereas

I think we've now got better at buying cloths that can work in different styles. The ultimate would be that we buy cloths that can be made into anything. Those cloths are few and far between.'

## Supply chain management and quick response

In recent years the company's management had been debating their overall supply chain issues, especially quick response (QR) supply chain management. Their hope was that fast throughput in the supply chain could not only save working capital but could also give the merchandising function sufficient flexibility to respond to the reality of a season's sales pattern rather than work entirely from forecasts made well in advance of the sales period. What was needed was the ability to cope with inherently uncertain markets. Within Menswear, a paper which had been put together raised a number of issues. Chief amongst them was the question of how Jossey Menswear could shorten time in its manufacturing process to enable it to make merchandising decisions closer to the point at which it sold the garment. David Jossey outlined the case for QR:

'Traditionally in this business we have made immense efforts to get costs down to save £1 or £2 on the cost of a suit. Yet if we don't sell a suit, the average markdown on that suit can be £100. It's far more important to make exactly what you can sell than it is to save a few per cent on the manufacturing costs of what you are making, especially if it is not what the customer wants to buy. By far the most significant way of improving our bottom line is by driving up revenue through increasing our volume of full price sales. To do this we have to have the right product in the right place at the right time. Typically our customers are not frequent visitors to our stores. They may come in, say, around twice a year. If they don't find what they want they are unlikely to return just in case we have it next time. What is really frustrating is our belief that sometimes customers come into our stores and might have purchased one of our products *if it had been there*. The reverse is also a problem for us. We don't want our stores full of product which, in hindsight, is not going to be a major seller. The faster we can replenish our stocks which are held in the shops, the less initial stock quantities are needed, and therefore the less risk we take of overstocking on low-selling items.'

Even so, not everyone in the industry, or even in the company, was convinced that QR would improve FPS. They argued that in the niche of the market a 50 per cent FPS was a given, though David Jossey disagreed.

'I just didn't believe that was right. OK, so you might have to change several things in order to improve it. Of course, if we carried on making decisions a year before the customer had the opportunity to buy the product, if we carried on buying our fabric nine months before, if we carried on making the stock three months before the sales period, and delivering it to the stores with no opportunity to back our winners once sales trends became evident, yes it *is* a given. But if we changed the rules of the game we were convinced that we could do better.'

Two issues were being seen as interrelated by the Menswear team. The first was the effectiveness of the design effort. The second was the effectiveness of their ability to get the right products in the right place at the right time. Yet a perfect range of products would be no good if the supply chain could not get them to the right locations in time. Furthermore, fashion products which were designed 18 months before the season were less likely to catch the right trends than ones which were designed nine months before the season. Brenda Wright commented:

'Clearly, however, there was a danger of improving supply chain systems merely to compensate for inappropriate design decisions. That would be a total waste of potential. Anyway, it would also mean that the factory would be busy making poor-selling products which adds to the complexity of the factory and makes it more difficult to maintain its quick response.'

## The Cornwall plant

The Cornwall factory manufactured all tailored menswear products for the company. In 1998 the plant was manufacturing around 1200 suit equivalents (SE) per week; by 2002 output had increased to 1900 SE per week; with fewer people.

The plant operated as a profit centre with its own set of accounts, with the price paid to manufacturing set on a 'cost plus' basis. The factory's costings were used as a basis for this, though there might be some negotiation between product managers and the factory. However, when reporting to the Division or to the Group, Menswear was judged as a single vertical business, a point stressed by David Jossey.

'It is useful to have Cornwall as a profit centre, even though by adjusting the transfer price we could swing profitability significantly up or down. But wholesale and factory shop production make genuine contributions to Menswear profits. It is also good to have the plant know that they are a contributor to overall profitability. However, it is also important that Cornwall management are not over-worried about their own profitability to the detriment of the whole business.'

In order to help the plant contribute to the supply chain initiative, an experienced operations manager, Frank Hawkins, was moved to an advisory role in the plant. When Frank arrived at the factory his task was to identify all the barriers which might inhibit the move to QR manufacturing. These barriers seemed to include limited factory space, a rigid payments system and limited skills flexibility and specialist machinery. Frank was also sounding out opinion in the factory. Rumours had already been circulating about QR and there seemed to be mixed feelings about any change to the work organisation. Some people were either enthusiastic, or at least willing to acquiesce in any changes; others were hostile, seeing the ideas as either unworkable or a threat to their earnings. Frank Hawkins found that many, however, took a wait-and-see attitude.

'As far as the factory floor were concerned, QR meant a move from traditional "individual operator" based training to "team" working. Team working was not welcomed by everyone, although it was being used by a number of other companies.'

Frank and his supply chain team soon reached the conclusion that not all the factory's resources need necessarily be organised on a QR basis to achieve substantial benefits. Their plan was to convert only 30 per cent of assembly to quick response, leaving the rest as conventional manufacturing.

'Looking back, partial conversion was not too risky. It allowed us to retain 70 per cent of our core machining processes as before, so we were not risking the whole factory to the new way of working.'

Even so, Frank's proposal meant an upheaval for the plant, whose operatives were in need of some reassurance. David Jossey outlined the assurances that were given:

'One of our commitments to Cornwall was that this supply chain project would not put them out of work. We promised them that we would give them something to make every working hour. Exactly what we would be asking them to make might not be known until a week before, but there would always be something. We also warned them that we might have to change our minds; we may have said that we wanted 500 navy-blue suits but now we only want 300. We can either make them and put them in the warehouse or we can change our minds and make something that we know we are confident that the customer wants.'

## ● Forming the teams

Frank's proposal called for two QR teams, one for jacket assembly, the other for trouser assembly. One debate was the basis for selecting these QR team members. Should they be volunteers, or should the management team select them on the basis of overall factory skill deployment? The obvious advantage of volunteers was that they would be the people presumably most committed to making the new system work. On the other hand, if the volunteers were the most skilled then how could the remainder of the sewing department manage without them? The pivotal meeting came in March 1998. The Plant Foreman at Cornwall reported:

'The workforce had been regularly briefed on the progress of the whole supply chain project. Now, with Frank's proposal agreed, was the time to ask the workforce for volunteers for the QR teams. I explained the reasons for such a radical change in some depth and demonstrated my own support for the project and belief that it would be essential for our continuing success. We were delighted by the response. We needed 25 volunteers but got 168!'

The issue of whether the teams should have supervisors was also debated. The majority of team members preferred to do without them, a decision welcomed by Frank who nonetheless knew that the teams would need careful handling. Because of the novelty of the system, many people would come and see the teams. Presenting them as the 'elite' of the factory would merely demotivate the rest of the workforce. In fact, whenever visitors came or information needed to be passed out, it was the conventional manufacturing parts of the department who were visited first before the QR teams. The teams were also encouraged to give themselves names, the 'Supreme 14' and 'The Commitments' for example. This seemed appropriately informal and, if the team members chose their own name, they would feel more comfortable with the idea of working in the new system.

## The payment system barrier

The payments system proved to be one of the biggest implementation issues. How could a payments system be devised for the new teams which would at the same time keep the operators motivated to maintain output levels while still allowing them to maintain their earnings levels? Frank Hawkins outlined the payment system issues:

'Getting the team payment system right was probably the single most important thing that we had to decide. The system was far from ideal. The more skills an operator had, the higher was their base rate. However, the skill differential was relatively small. In fact the common opinion on the shop floor appeared to be that the slightly higher rates for multi-skilled operators was compensation for not being able to make the incentive performance levels because they were continually changing jobs. It certainly wasn't regarded as a motivator to acquire more skills. The QR team payment system had to be better. If the operators liked the payment system and it seemed to them equitable and progressive then they would buy the whole team idea, but if they distrusted the payment system then it would be difficult to sell them the idea no matter how good it was. On the other hand, if the payment system was too generous and after a few months we had to go and take some money out of the system, again they were going to be less than happy. We never had to do that because we spent a long time simulating the payments system before the new teams went in.'

## Not everyone liked the changes

At a regional level, the changes were supported by the trade union, though a minority of its members at plant level remained hostile. Frank Hawkins recalled, 'At one public meeting one of the workforce looked me straight in the face and said "You, you're going to close this factory with your ideas".' The vast majority of the workforce, though, seemed willing to give the new system the benefit of the doubt. Even so, some parts of the plant were more welcoming of the new system than others. In the jackets assembly section there was general enthusiasm for the idea and no shortage of volunteers to staff the new teams; in the trouser section there was less enthusiasm. Eventually a team was selected but they were not regarded as being amongst the top performers in their department. In fact their performance had, historically, been lower than the departmental average. Yet, a year later there had been a transformation, as Frank Hawkins commented,

'These people who were previously low-skilled, low-performance operators were developing into a multi-skilled team achieving a higher performance than they would have been able to in the conventional system.'

## Measuring supply chain performance

Brenda Wright outlined the supply chain performance issue:

'We felt, early on in the project, that it was very important to set up measurements of supply chain performance that were not conflicting. For example, if we were too obsessed with output from the factory or standard hours of production, that could be in conflict with the retailing imperative of getting the right product to the right place at the right time.'

The set of performance measures used by the supply chain team to assess the effectiveness of the new QR system operated at a number of levels, listed below from macro to micro:

- Net achieved margin – the margin delivered, including all sales, as a percentage of revenue (without value added tax)
- Full price sales volume:
  - for the whole of Menswear
  - on 'key lines' (constituting 7 per cent of lines offered, but 25 per cent of sales)
  - the 15 top key lines (mainly sourced from Cornwall)
- Throughput time for orders placed to Cornwall
- On-time delivery of all orders from Cornwall (monthly)
- A 'root cause' report on all problems affecting supply chain performance – late cloth deliveries, late design decisions, process blocks, etc.

## The future

Several opportunities were on the supply chain team's agenda for the future.

### Extend the proportion of work made on a QR basis
The team had already decided to increase the proportion of trousers being made under quick response conditions from 35–40 per cent of production, and increase the proportion of jackets from 30–35 per cent in July 2000. This would mean enlarging the quick response teams in both sections. Even further expansion of both teams was likely.

### Speed up the product development process further
Brenda Wright explained the need for speeding up the product development process:

'One of our major opportunities is still in product development. What we have been concentrating on is how we can replenish within the season. What we need to be able to do more is trial new products so we are not taking the same risks in launching new designs. This means we have to get a brand new idea from nothing to being in front of the customer in the shortest possible time. We've still got some work to do around that.'

### Rethink how market information is captured
The merchandising team were acutely aware that, although they had made big strides in sharpening up their market information, an increasingly flexible supply chain, giving faster response, would even further increase the potential for appropriate and timely market information to increase sales effectiveness. Brenda Wright commented:

'One way of getting good information is through appropriate categorisation of our product groupings, which is a key issue for us. You have to find ways of grouping the products such that emerging trends can be spotted early.'

### Explore ways of choosing even more flexible cloth

The supply chain team were aware that even with perfect information on market trends, they would always be limited by the availability of cloth. One of the benefits of the supply chain project was seen by the team as increasing the awareness by designers of how their decisions influenced the performance of the factory. In spite of some initial resistance by designers in moving towards more flexible cloth purchasing, the supply chain team believed that designers had achieved a far more sensitive understanding of the flexibility implications of their choice of cloth. The task was to do this without inhibiting their design skills. David Jossey summed this up:

'You must not undermine the confidence of your product design people. Remember they are putting a lot on the line. It's them who are taking the risk with their reputations by accepting some curbs on their creative process. Getting the whole team aligned to the single supply chain goal of improving full price sales helped us get the message over.'

### Improve cloth suppliers' responsiveness

The big limiting factor on getting appropriate availability of styles into the shops was seen as the lead times from cloth suppliers. To some extent designers could mitigate this by flexible styling – buying cloth which is not limited to a single style – thereby increasing the chances of being able to use surplus cloth in the styles and designs that were selling well. But far more potential for shortening the overall product development *and* 'in-season' lead times was seen as coming from more responsive cloth supply.

### Work on cloth development with suppliers

Typical of this issue was the way the average weight of cloths had been getting lighter over the last few years. This itself had made the cloths more difficult to machine, although by working with machinery suppliers the company had largely overcome problems associated with lightweight cloth. However, cloths, even of the same weight, could vary considerably in their machinability. Frank Hawkins outlined a further aspect of this issue:

'We are a lot closer in understanding which characteristics of a cloth make it more or less machinable, but we still can't fully predict it. What disappoints me is that when we do have to abandon a cloth because it just isn't machinable, we don't get close to the suppliers and brainstorm the issue until we know exactly why it didn't work out.'

## ● Finally

The QR supply chain project was regarded by the whole team as having profoundly affected their views. Brenda Wright summed this up:

'Having capacity under our own management has the potential to give us a tremendous edge in the marketplace. It also allows us to develop ourselves as managers. If you are a buyer who has no responsibility for manufacturing problems it is easy to say to your supplier, "I want it, just sort it out". Having to understand the implications of our decisions for our own manufacturing plant has made us better managers. It has helped us to develop our thought processes and think around problems to find solutions.'

## Questions

1 *Why was the QR approach significant in improving the company's supply chain performance?*

2 *Do you think the Cornwall plant's approaches to introducing QR ideas were appropriate?*

3 *Which of the possible future actions identified by the supply chain team do you think worth pursuing and why?*

CASE
10

# Indian Metals Corporation

Case date
1996

Sara Mountney, Kenneth Work and Stuart Chambers

## Introduction

'The problem isn't the plant itself, it's the way it's being run.'

After four weeks in this remote part of north India, John Daley had seen at first hand the immense problems at the Lead and Zinc Processing Plant and was pleased to be heading home. He stared at the views from the taxi for the final time. The only signs of industrialisation in this isolated, mainly agricultural area were the makeshift sheds at the side of the road which had been put up by local villagers to service the trucks going to and from the plant.

John was part of a UN development team which had visited the site at the request of a team of European technical experts who were already on-site. The large processing plant and adjacent mine were owned by the Indian Metals Corporation (IMC). The complex had become operational in 1990.

## The Refinery

The plant used a method known as the Dual Refinery Process (DRP) to extract lead and zinc from the mined ore. This method had been a new venture for IMC and John's UN agency had been involved in the development of the plant.

The mine was a great success. The refinery, however, was experiencing immense problems and it was hoped that the European team and the UN team could help to resolve them. Despite processing half the company's zinc output, the plant had only ever operated at a maximum of half its capacity level. The layout of the plant is shown in Figure 10.1.

A mixture of the ore (from the mine) and other inputs are brought into the plant and processed into pre-product. Pre-product is a blend of inputs of a certain size and composition designed to enable the next stage, the furnace, to operate at maximum performance. The pre-product is broken down inside the furnace and both molten lead and molten zinc are tapped off and sent to the separate refineries for further processing. Lead processing is run in batches, but only when enough stock has built up to enable the refinery to run economically. Any contaminated or scrap lead can be recycled back into the furnace. The zinc refinery has to run continuously to prevent damage to the equipment. Large levels of buffer stock are needed to keep the refinery running because the furnace and pre-product units are unreliable and liable to shut down.

**Figure 10.1 The plant layout**

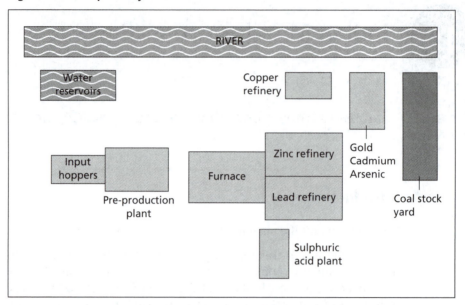

Other than zinc and lead, useful by-products produced are sulphuric acid, gold, cadmium and arsenic, all of which are processed and sold. A non-toxic black sand is also produced which is sold as landfill.

## John's visit to the plant

John's taxi arrived back at *The Colony*, seven kilometres away, where the plant workers lived. A sketch of *The Colony* is shown in Figure 10.2.

With the surrounding area being so isolated, the company had built it for staff at all levels. The houses, for staff and their families, ranged from fairly luxurious for senior management to communal barracks for contract workers, most of whom sent money home to their families. Basic living expenses and transport costs to and from work were paid for by the company. In all, the residents seemed satisfied with the amenities. John, however, did not like the surrounding barbed wire fence nor the look of the local militia who patrolled it. Back in the hotel, he began to think about the main aspects of his visit to be included in a presentation to his superiors on his return.

### Working conditions

He remembered how shocked the team had been at conditions inside the plant on their first visit. This visit had been the cause of some controversy – the team of European experts had been unhappy at the decision to allow the UN team inside as they thought it too dangerous. John and his team wore hard hats and masks, but had never received any safety briefing.

The first area they visited was the zinc refinery. The most obvious sight was the piles of lead and zinc dust everywhere. Zinc buffer stocks were also stored near equipment, and often across walkways and emergency exits. The team watched as a

**Figure 10.2 The Colony**

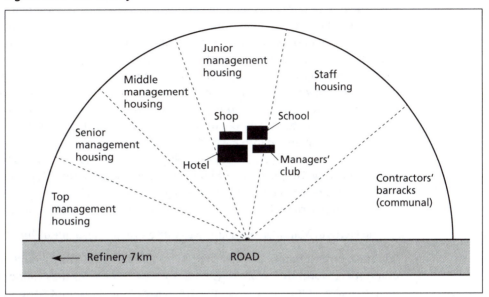

man stood on a 50mm girder over a conveyor belt from which hot zinc blocks (at around 250°C) were emerging. As each block appeared, he aligned it with the belt. This was repeated every 10 seconds. The man was not wearing any protective clothing. Their guide told them that, as a contractor, he was not entitled to any. The team watched, impressed by the contractor's balance. If he had fallen down onto a block he would have burned to death before anyone could help him. The entire area was hazardous. As John had leaned back and put his hand out to support himself on what he thought was a horizontal sheet of aluminium, the guide swiftly stopped him. The aluminium sheet was in fact molten zinc.

## The staff

The next area he visited was the pre-product plant, where the ore and inputs were crushed and processed for the furnace. Here, John talked to Mr Singh, the shift manager:

'I've worked here since the plant opened five years ago. As a shift manager, I work seven days a week, from 5.30 a.m. to 8 p.m. and I'm on call all night. The hours are excessive compared to other places, I must say. The pay here is low, but we do have some perks if we don't make waves and are liked by our managers. Perks include your own tea boy.

'Although I'm the shift manager, I'm not really too sure where my responsibilities lie, or sometimes even what I can and can't do. If there's a problem, I pass it on to my manager. That's how it is supposed to go – up the chain of command. Eventually, it comes down again. The management is very strict here and I prefer not to make a decision unless I really have to, because I could be punished.

'I had a situation only a few weeks ago. I was called in at night because that waste recycling machine over there wasn't working properly – it was making odd clanking noises. I didn't really know what to do about it – I wasn't going to close the plant down, that would be unthinkable, so I phoned my manager at home in The Colony. That took a bit of time because there's only one phone line. Anyway, he really didn't know what to do either so I left it with him. Nothing was done until about three hours later, when the General Manager phoned me. In the meantime, the clanking noises had got louder and more frequent, but there was nothing I could do. As I spoke to the General Manager, the machine literally fell to pieces in front of my eyes! Imagine having to tell *that* to him! In the end we managed to repair the machine by stripping out parts from an older one. We managed to get it going again in three days. In order not to stop the plant operating, the waste that would normally be crushed by the machine and fed back into the process was pumped into a wood at the back of the plant.

'I live with my family on The Colony, where all the company workers live, about seven kilometres away. They pay for our house, our bills and transport. Our house is quite small, a bit crowded really, but we won't get a bigger one unless I'm promoted. I can only go up one more step because I have a higher education certificate and not a degree.'

The General Manager, Mr Paul, was quite unequivocal about his staff:

'My staff, unfortunately, are lazy, half-witted and useless! They should be whipped into doing some work! Unfortunately, I am stuck with them, as they cannot be dismissed. I have to make all the decisions in this company because I cannot trust anybody! You ask any worker here to think of the answer to a problem, even a trivial, simple one, and they cannot do it! They are all idiots!'

The organisational structure was extremely hierarchical. The team identified up to 16 levels of management in some areas. A total of 2800 people worked in the plant. A comparable plant in Europe or the US would typically employ 800. Of the 2800, 800 were staff, identifiable by the company uniform, and the remainder were contractors, gangs of people who were hired casually.

The staff carried out the technical and administrative roles within the organisation, such as running and monitoring equipment, maintenance and repairs. Many members of staff were also employed as tea-makers, chair-setters and general helpers for management. These earned privileges could also be removed as punishment. Half of the staff had university degrees and the remainder had higher education certificates.

## Contractors

The contractors were paid for non-technical manual labour, such as digging trenches, loading and unloading raw materials and cleaning. This was gruelling and dangerous work – two contractors had been killed since the plant opened. Half the contractors were female because they cost less, even though employment of women in lead mines and processing plants is illegal. Hans Schmidt, a member of the European team, commented:

'We'd heard that women were working in the plant but when we arrived we couldn't see any of them. It turned out that they'd been hidden from us as we toured the plant! A manager showed me an official letter he'd received from the General Manager. It told him to say that no women were employed in the plant. The manager told us that the General Manager hadn't said anything about showing us the letter!'

The staff were reluctant to criticise the plant at first, but they became more honest as the teams stayed. The head of the pre-product plant, Mr Chandra, told the team how the contractors had died:

'One woman was digging a trench and it collapsed in on her. The other, a man, was cleaning out a machine. It crushes the waste from the furnace into a fine powder, but debris does build up around the inside and this has to be knocked out with a stick. Normally this is done from outside the machine but the man's stick wasn't long enough so he climbed inside. When he hit the roof with the stick, all the debris fell down and crushed him. Of course, the company paid a reasonable pension to both of their families, but it wasn't really that much money.'

## Chemical poisoning

There was an exhibition on health and safety in one of the office blocks, with an example of a protective suit to be worn in dangerous and high temperature areas. Unfortunately, the staff did not know about the exhibition and the contractors were not allowed access to the building. The protective suit was also the only one in the whole of the plant.

The major health and safety issue within the plant was lead poisoning. Regulations were in place to protect employees, such as wearing respirators, but they were largely ignored. Most of the staff did not wear their respirators and the contractors were not issued with them. There were no safety posters within the plant itself, although some were pinned up in the office blocks. The posters were very dirty and neglected.

The UN team were concerned about the exposure of the employees to lead and were convinced that many were showing symptoms of lead poisoning, including dizziness and lethargy. Yet blood tests showed the levels to be acceptable. Paul Buchanan, a member of the UN team, decided to investigate:

'The average reading from the plant's laboratories always showed less than 30 parts per million (PPM), but many of the staff tested had symptoms that you would relate to more than 55 PPM. We queried the levels with the laboratory officials, but their explanation was that lead was removed from the body far more quickly than in Europe because of the high levels of pulses in the Indian diet! This explanation was highly suspicious so we decided to carry out our own tests in the UK to check the plant's results. We took two blood samples each from six staff members and analysed them at the plant and at our testing centre in London. The plant tests revealed 30–35 PPM, an acceptable level, but the London results showed 55–65 PPM – twice the Indian level. When we showed this to the IMC officials, we were bluntly told that there must be problems with the testing facilities at London.'

Another major health and safety concern was the transportation of sulphuric acid to the customer. The customer's tankers used were old and rusty and liable to spill. In fact, many spillages had occurred inside and outside the plant. The driver of the tanker was often responsible for loading the acid and had not been issued with any protective clothing (except gloves) nor had he received training. The plant management were reluctant to do anything about this, seeing it as the customer's problem.

Despite these obvious health and safety breaches, the UN team discovered that the plant regularly passed all its inspections. These were carried out by a regional inspector.

## Planning

Annual production targets for the plant were usually set in October for the following year and were reviewed every quarter. They were decided at a meeting at HQ which was attended by the general managers of the larger business units and the government, the plant's main customer. Junior management were not consulted, and the targets were generally fictitious – there was usually no possibility of them being achieved. Demand was theoretically steady, but in practice the plant produced as much zinc as it could. As the financial year progressed and successive monthly targets were missed, the production office reworked the production estimates. Mr Chandra commented:

'The production targets are seen as a joke which is not at all funny. We are all aware that they cannot be met but we have a conspiracy of silence. If you fail your target, which we always do, it is readjusted for the next month. There are no reprisals as long as the plant keeps running.'

There was no long-term planning within the company. The staff did not carry out short-term planning because their roles mainly involved minute-to-minute troubleshooting.

## Maintenance

The policy at the plant was always to continue operations until a breakdown. At this point, a combined repair and preventative maintenance team would carry out emergency repairs and maintenance work, where time allowed, simultaneously. The consequences were that the maintenance was only partially effective, there were frequent machine breakdowns and plant utilisation was as low as 50 per cent. Equipment which was expected to last 10 years normally lasted just three.

A conventional approach for a plant of this type would be to have separate repair and maintenance teams. The repair team would carry out running repairs and fix plant breakdown, and the preventative maintenance team would work during scheduled plant downtimes, preparing equipment and spare parts while the plant was in operation. A plant using this strategy could expect to operate at 75 per cent to 80 per cent utilisation. The mission of the preventative maintenance team would be to ensure that the repair team never had any work to do.

The plant was not shut down, even when serious problems developed, on the orders of the General Manager. The heads of the pre-product, furnace and refinery units saw a plant breakdown elsewhere as an opportunity to carry out repairs on their own equipment. When a breakdown did occur, a witchhunt was carried out to find out who was to blame. Mr Chandra explained the consequences to the team:

'The General Manager will record who is to blame every time the plant stops. Then, if it's your fault, you will be verbally berated and some of your privileges will be removed, or you will be demoted, or your promotion will be blocked. I have to say that we are frightened to stop the plant, even in the most extreme circumstances. The Furnace Manager stopped his area once because somebody's life was in danger. He was severely disciplined.'

Another problem had occurred in the furnace. It was noticed that the roof above the furnace was unsound but the General Manager had refused to stop the plant. Three weeks later, the roof collapsed into the furnace, releasing carbon monoxide gas. Fortunately the area was clear at the time and nobody was killed or injured.

Modifications were carried out to the equipment and process in the pre-product unit to increase output. This was only partially successful because the pre-product produced was of such poor quality that the furnace took longer to process it into lead and zinc, leading to poor energy efficiency. The modifications to the pre-product plant also resulted in the release of sulphur dioxide into the atmosphere. This could be noticed by a foul sulphurous taste in the mouth up to half a mile away. With the wind in the right direction, the gas blew over local villages. Due to the inefficiency of the plant, traces of lead had been found in water samples from an outlet pipe which was fed into a nearbly river. This river was the source of the local water supply.

The plant drew its power supply from the public electricity supplier. Originally, the plant was supposed to have its own independent power station but this was never built. The electricity grid was unreliable and often the plant electricity supply failed or was reduced to a level where efficient operation was impossible. There were two back-up generators in the plant but neither of them worked.

The original machinery installed in the plant was of a high specification and from suppliers known to be world leaders. The equipment was controlled by basic electrical switching and was robust enough to deal with the fluctuating power supply. However, the quality of the equipment used in the plant had been affected by a process known as 'Indianisation'. The Indian government levies a 105 per cent tax on all imported industrial equipment. In order to reduce spares bills and to obtain them quickly, some equipment and spares were replaced by cheaper Indian goods. Unfortunately, these companies had not reached the same quality standards of the original suppliers and there were comfort stocks (long lead-time parts kept as duplicates in case of breakdown) in the warehouse which may not have worked when fitted to the equipment.

## Quality

Product quality was fairly well monitored. The zinc and lead produced were regularly checked for conformance to specification, and feedback occurred to ensure that the equipment was adjusted if the products started to fail. However, if a product was produced out of specification it was still sent out and not reprocessed. There were no reprisals for producing poor quality product as long as the plant was not stopped.

In the pre-product unit, John noticed several gangs of contractors clearing up a huge pile of ore and coal around a conveyor belt. A week earlier, a ten-tonne hopper containing this pile had fallen off the steel girder which supported it and crashed down through a conveyor belt. Luckily, nobody was nearby at the time. It seemed that these 'near misses' happened regularly yet nothing was done to prevent them.

## The kidnap

Outside the plant, a local village had decided that enough was enough. They told John how they had kidnapped a manager and held him hostage overnight. A man from the village commented:

'Since that plant opened a few years ago it's done nothing but spill out dangerous chemicals! We've had clouds of chemicals over the village. You couldn't see anything but you could taste it. I've also heard people say that there is lead in the water. I really worry about my health and my family's. We're all being slowly poisoned. We complain but they never listen, so we decided to do something to make them notice. As it was, it was useless. The manager said he'd be punished if he said anything.'

As he packed, John pondered over the problems at the plant. The staff themselves were highly skilled and very good at their jobs individually. They certainly did not need the European team to tell them how to run the plant. Yet they all said that they were unable to do their jobs properly. The problems at the plant were far more complex than was first thought. There was much more to be done than just replacing some machinery or installing a computer. John wondered, realistically, if the plant could ever be changed.

## Questions

**1** *Evaluate the ethical issues concerned with the operations management decisions of the IMC plant.*[1]

**2** *Comment on the maintenance strategy at the plant. Are there any alternative methods that would be suitable?*

**3** *'John wondered, realistically, if the plant could ever be changed.' If you were to carry out improvements at the plant, what would your ethical priorities be?*

### Reference

1 You may find it useful to refer to Slack *et al.*, (2001), *Operations Management*, (3rd edn), Financial Times Prentice Hall, Chapter 21; Tables 21.2 and 21.3.

PART **3**

# Design

# Introduction to Part 3

The usual image of a designer is of someone who is concerned with the appearance of a product – a fashion designer or a car designer, for example. The design activity, however, goes far beyond this narrow aspect of design. In fact, all operations managers are designers. Many of their day-to-day decisions shape the design of the *processes* they manage, which in turn influences the products and services that they produce. The purchase of every machine or piece of equipment is a design decision because it affects the physical shape and nature of the operation. Similarly, every time a machine or piece of equipment is moved, a method improved or a member of staff's responsibility changed, the design of the operation is changed.

**Figure P3.1  Operations management design activities**

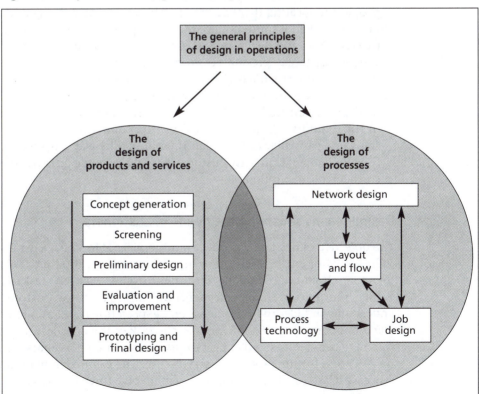

Operations managers also have an important influence on the 'technical' design of the *products and services* they produce by providing much of the information necessary for their design as well as providing the systems that produced them. This is why operations managers need to understand the basic principles of design, no matter whether it is a product, service or process that is being designed.

Design involves two distinct but closely related tasks: the design of the products and services themselves and the design of the processes for creating those products or services (see Figure P3.1). Each of these will be covered in later sections but first let us consider some of the general principles of design in operations.

## General principles of design in operations

### Design is important

Design is placed early in this book because it is one of the first things that operations managers have to be involved in when setting up an operation. The decisions they make during the design process are important for a number of reasons:

- They involve a lot of money. Most of the decisions described in the Cadbury cases (Cases 11 and 19) involve considerable amounts of expenditure. The capital cost involved in purchasing bits of equipment, facilities and technology is rarely going to be very low and often can be exceptionally high. Most operations, especially those with very expensive facilities, can't afford to get these decisions wrong.
- The decision process happens relatively infrequently. Choosing equipment and people and locating them in the operation is not something that any operations manager would want to do too often. The process is time-consuming and disruptive. The Boys and Boden cases (Cases 17 and 18) give a good example of how the general day-to-day pressures of work make organisations reluctant to go through the disruption which redesigning the system entails.
- Design sets the limits of the operation's capability. Once layout decisions are made, they constrain the way in which the operation can be run. For example, in the Cadbury World case (Case 11) the company chose to locate the attractions in a particular order which then limits the way customers can flow round the whole operation. Any customers trying to go against the flow would cause considerable disruption.

### Design means satisfying the needs of customers

The objective of designing products and services is to satisfy customers by meeting their actual or anticipated needs and expectations. Product and service design, therefore, should start and end with the customer. First, the task of marketing is to gather information from customers (and sometimes non-customers) in order to understand and identify their needs and expectations, and also to look for possible market opportunities. Following this, the task of the product and service designers is to take those needs and expectations, as interpreted by marketing, and create a specification for the product or service – see the Campaign planning for Red Nose Day case (Case 13). The specification will involve three key parts:

- a *concept*, which is the set of expected benefits that the customer is buying
- a *package* of 'component' products and services that provide those benefits defined in the concept
- the *process* by which the operation produces the package of 'component' products and services.

## Good design provides a competitive edge

Through careful design an organisation can achieve competitive advantage. It can support a quality objective by eliminating weaknesses in products or services or in the processes used to create them. It can develop ways in which products or services can be made quickly, and can make each part of the process, or the service or product produced by the process, more dependable which, for example, is critical for the RAC Motoring Services in the rescue of stranded motorists (see Case 20). Flexibility can be designed into the products/services and processes to make future changes easier or cheaper than they might otherwise be. Design can also have an important effect on the cost of the product or service. Good design can ensure a high utilisation of resources or could reduce the number of components in a product or stages in a service.

## Product/service design and process design are interrelated

The design of the products/services and the processes of creating them are sometimes undertaken as separate activities, but this seems unwise as the two clearly need to be closely related. Indeed, these two activities should be seen as overlapping, as shown in Figure P3.1. A close relationship between the two can significantly reduce the cost of the overall product or service, and may also reduce 'time-to-market', allowing products and services to be introduced to customers ahead of those of competitors. Merging the activities of designing products/services and the processes that create them is sometimes called *interactive design*.

In service operations it is more difficult to see these two activities since being distinct as in many service operations it is difficult to separate the process from the service itself. For example, at Cadbury World the service 'products' are completely entwined with the process, facilities and interactions experienced by the customers.

## The design activity is a transformation process

The design activity is an operation in itself and therefore the input–transformation-output process can be applied just like any other operation. The inputs will be market forecasts, market preferences and technical data, together with materials or parts which need to be tested for the suitability of their performance, design staff and equipment, such as computer-aided design (CAD) systems and development and testing equipment. The output is a definition of the concept, the package and the process.

## ● Design of products and services

Take the example of Cadbury World. The design of its service involved the development of the 'chocolate experience' concept. The idea was checked, or screened, to ensure that it could meet the rates of return required by the company and also deal appropriately with the needs of visitors in their expected numbers. Preliminary designs were developed, not only for the tour but also for the car parks, retail areas and restaurant and, in conjunction with leisure consultants, these designs were evaluated and improved until a final design was decided upon. This process of taking an idea for a new product or service and turning it into a final specification is referred to as the *design process* and involves five stages – see Figure P3.2. Cadbury World is also constantly being redesigned to reflect changes in customer requirements and volumes.

### Concept generation

Ideas for new product or service concepts may emanate from customers through formal mechanisms like focus groups or questionnaires, or through less formal means such as staff passing on suggestions from customers to the designers. Ideas may also come from other, often competing, organisations or from the organisation's own research and development department.

These roughly formed ideas for new products or services need to be honed into a product or service concept: a clear and simple statement of the overall form, function, purpose and benefits of the idea.

**Figure P3.2 The stages in product/service design**

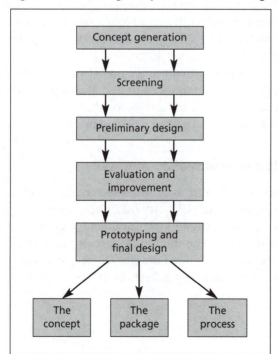

The concept of the 'Fun Factory' (Cadbury World case) was in response to discussions and other feedback from children who had enjoyed the more tangible aspects of the service and wanted more 'hands-on fun' of this type.

## Concept screening

Not all concepts generated will necessarily be capable of further development into products and services. Designers need to be selective as to which concepts they progress to the point of designing the preliminary aspects of the package and processes. The purpose of the concept screening stage is to take the flow of concepts emerging from the organisation and evaluate them for their feasibility, acceptability and 'vulnerability' (or risk). See The Reltex Project case (Case 15) for an illustration of some of these issues.

## Preliminary design

The next stage in the design activity is to try to develop a preliminary design for the product or service. Designers need to consider an initial specification for the package and the process. The process involves the way in which the package of goods and services will be delivered – what will be the flow of materials, the allocation of tasks, how will customers be dealt with, how will their orders be taken and completed? Several techniques are available to help with this activity, such as process flow charting or creating route sheets. Several of the cases in this part provide opportunities to document and evaluate flows, such as Cadbury World, Cadbury Ltd, Denby Constabulary (Case 21) and Cartes sans Frontières (Case 14).

## Design evaluation and improvement

The next stage is to take the preliminary design ideas and to test and refine them. Three particularly useful techniques are quality function deployment (QFD), value engineering (VE) and Taguchi methods (for more information see Slack *et al.* 2001).

## Prototyping and final design

The next stage is to turn the improved design into a prototype so that it can be tested. Organisations may consider making a mock-up of the proposed layout to check the feasibility of the flows or may just go ahead with the actual implementation of the new product or service on a trial basis to test customers' reactions to it. In the case of Cadbury World, changes were made to the design of flows of customers, but these were not tested or simulated before 'going live'. Some organisations may use much more sophisticated techniques such as the development of computer prototypes using computer-aided design and simulations. The outcome of this stage is the final specification for the concept, the package and the process of delivery.

## Simultaneous development

Although these design stages have been described as sequential, some organisations try to overlap these tasks to reduce time-to-market of their new product or services and to try to overcome what might be problems for later stages, without the need to halt the process and move back to a previous stage. This is usually referred to as *simultaneous* or *concurrent development* (or engineering).

## Design of the process

Getting the products and services designed is only part of the design activity. The process of creating the products or services has to be designed. The design of the process involves decisions about the operations network, layout and flow, process technology and the design of jobs – see the Denby Constabulary case.

### Network design

This will involve decisions about the sources of materials and service from suppliers. Cadbury will clearly provide the chocolate, but what about the ingredients for the Inca chocolate drink, the food for the restaurant, and even the materials, models and backdrops for the exhibitions? It will involve decisions about the location of the exhibition. The factory had spare land and buildings, but Bournville is not the easiest location to get to by road or rail. These issues were weighed up in the location decision. The size of the facility needs to be carefully considered. What are the excepted numbers, what happens if the numbers grow rapidly, is there room for expansion? What capacity is the facility to be designed for and how well will it cope with fluctuations in numbers?

Through successive redesigns and modifications, Cadbury World has successfully doubled its capacity (from 250 000 to 500 000 visitors per year) and improved the quality of the experience simultaneously. Similar improvements in capacity, quality and flexibility were achieved at RAC Motoring Services through the use of new technology. See also the Benetton Group case (Case 16) for issues related to network design and development.

### Layout and flow

Layout concerns decisions about where to put all the facilities, machines, equipment and staff in the operation. This decision will also affect how the materials, information and customers will flow through the operations. This is an important and very visible issue in the design of products and services. There are four 'basic' types of layout: fixed position layout, process layout, cell layout and product layout. See Boys and Boden (A and B) for discussion of issues related to process layout.

#### Layout by fixed position
Although this is called a layout type, it is not really a layout as such since the things to be processed stay where they are and the facilities and/or labour visit them in order to carry out their processing tasks. Usually this type of layout is used where the things being processed are too heavy or too inconvenient to move between facilities. A motorway, for example, is too large to be manufactured and then transported to where it is needed. Rather the facilities and labour necessary to manufacture it are moved to where the motorway is to be situated.

### Layout by process

In this kind of layout all similar facilities or people are concentrated together. The materials or customers being processed move between these concentrations of processors as they need them.

### Cell layout

A cell layout is one where the transformed resources entering the operation are pre-selected (or preselect themselves) to move to one part of the operation (or cell) in which all the transforming resources to meet their immediate processing needs are co-located. The cell itself may be arranged in either a process or product layout (see next section). Consider the staircase cell in Boys and Boden B.

### Layout by product

Layout by product means putting facilities and people in the order that they are required to process a particular type of product or service. All materials and customers will then flow in a determined and predictable manner from one set of facilities to the next. The Cadbury World case is a classic example of this type of layout. Customers flow in a set route from the ticketing area to the exhibition area, through to a holding area for the Marie Cadbury room and then continue all the way through to the shop and restaurant at the end. It is interesting to note that next door, in the Cadbury chocolate factory itself, chocolate bars are made in exactly the same way. The material moves predictably from the chocolate preparation area through to the moulding area, through to the packing area and so through the rest of the process.

## Process technology

Whenever operations purchase process technology they have choices to make. Factories need to decide what kind of machines they are going to use, banks need to decide what kind of computers and cashpoints they are going to invest in and airlines have choices to make between the different kinds of aircraft they purchase. In examining the choices which operations make, it is useful to think of the technology they use on three different dimensions:

- *Its degree of automation* – how much it still relies on human beings to operate it and how much the technology does itself without human assistance
- *The scale of the technology* – not its physical size but rather its capacity: how much it can process
- *The degree of integration* – how separate pieces of technology are linked with other technologies in the system.

### The degree of automation

Process technology varies in terms of the amount of human intervention that it requires. Some technology requires little human intervention in its use; some requires the human to be the brains and eyes of the technology, such as the technology described in the RAC Motoring Services case. The automation of doors described in Cadbury World required no human intervention, but did not operate quite in the way conceived by the designers.

### The scale of technology

Some operations, such as petrochemical plants, food processing factories and steel-making plants, really do benefit from using large-scale technologies. They use these technologies because with the high volumes they process they can achieve low costs – see Norrköping Plant A (Case 7). However, there are also disadvantages of using large capacity pieces of technology. If demand is not very high then they can be left only part utilised which can increase the operation's costs. For example, if an airline chooses to buy only a few very large jumbo jets, it will be fine provided it is transporting large numbers of passengers on relatively few routes. On the other hand, if it wants to provide its passengers with a large number of alternative destinations at lower volume, then it would be better advised to buy a larger number of smaller aircraft. In other words, it is the volume and variety of its services which will, to a large extent, dictate the mixture of large and small aircraft which it buys. This type of decision was also important in the Concept Design Services case (Case 5) where different sizes of injection moulding machines could be purchased for different volumes and varieties of plastic products.

### The degree of integration

The integration of technology, or its joining up with other pieces of technology, is also partly dependent on volume. Joining computers up into networks, for example, can make for lower costs and increase convenience, provided the needs and functions required by all the users are broadly similar. However, connecting up all these functions does make the whole process more vulnerable. If the whole computer network goes down, everyone is affected; if they weren't connected and one individual computer went down, only its user would be inconvenienced.

## Job design

For most operations the decision about job design is important. This is partly because of the large numbers of people usually employed in the operations function, and also because the actions of these people, individually and collectively, can have a significant effect on the quality of the goods and services and on the productivity and profitability of the operation as a whole.

Many decisions need to be taken about people's jobs. How many people will be required, what will they have to do, what skills will they need, how should they interface with the technology and the customers? These are issues considered in the Cadbury World case and in the RAC Motoring Services case.

Many tools and techniques exist to help the operations manager design, plan and control the tasks performed by the workforce: work measurement; method study; ergonomics; behaviour approaches to job design; job rotation, enlargement and enrichment; and empowerment. (See, for example, Slack *et al.* 2001.)

Several cases here provide opportunities to determine and evaluate how management might use people to improve operational performance in different work situations. They provide information to allow analysis of the work flows and the work content of many operations tasks. The cases also examine the critical nature of operations personnel, both customer contact staff and back office support staff, in providing a high-quality, efficient and profitable operation.

The RAC Motoring Services case describes the variety of processes and tasks that have to be coordinated in the provision of service to the stranded motorist. This organisation recognises that it needs to improve its performance to keep ahead of the competition. Its use and motivation of staff will be a key element in this strategy.

## Summary

This part and its associated cases try to demonstrate the processes involved in designing products and services, and the processes which create and deliver them. Although many operations managers are not directly involved in the process *per se*, they have a major stake in its outcome, the specification of the products, services and processes. As such they need to be aware of the design process and be concerned to take an active part in the process.

### Key points

- The overall purpose of the design activity is to meet the needs of customers.
- The design activity is itself a transformation process.
- The design of products and services is a multi-stage process which moves from concept through to a detailed specification.
- During the last few years many organisations have been moving away from the sequential approach to product and service design and have been applying interactive design methods. This approach shortens the time-to-market, reduces the number of operations problems, particularly quality problems, reduces development costs and provides an earlier return on investment.
- The process of creating the products or services has to be designed and it involves decisions about the operations network, layout and flow, process technology and the design of jobs.
- The two activities of product/service design and process design are interrelated and should not be done independently of each other. Bringing them together has many benefits including better designs and faster time-to-market. In the design of services it is often difficult to separate out the service from the process which produces it.

### Recommended reading

Chase, R. B. (1978), 'Where does the customer fit in a service operation', *Harvard Business Review*, Vol 56, No 6, November–December, 137–142.

Grinyer, C. (2001), *Smart Design*, RotoVision.

Pugh, S. (1994), *Total Design – Integrated Methods for Successful Product Engineering*, Addison-Wesley.

Shostack, G. L. (1984), 'Designing services that deliver', *Harvard Business Review*, Vol 62, No 1, January–February, 133–139.

Slack, N., Chambers, S. and Johnston, R. (2001), *Operations Management*, (3rd edn), Financial Times Prentice Hall, Harlow, Chapters 4, 5, 6, 7, 8 and 9.

Ulrich, K. T. and Eppinger, S. D. (1999), *Product Design and Development*, (2nd edn), McGraw-Hill Education.

**CASE**
**11**

# Cadbury World: Ten years of improvements

Case date
2001

Stuart Chambers, Colin Samways, Mark Robinson and Adam Bates

This case tracks the successful development of Cadbury World over its first decade of operation. For clarity, it is divided into four sections: following a brief introduction, it is described as it was during its first full year of operation in 1991; then the changes introduced by 1995 are explained; and finally the major redesigns that were undertaken in the late 1990s are outlined. Each of these date-specific sections can be analysed independently. However, the nature and sequence of developments over the whole period can also be explored to evaluate the impact on customer flow and on quality.

## Introduction

Cadbury has been a renowned English manufacturer of chocolate products for more than 100 years. Today, as Cadbury-Schweppes, the firm is a major food products conglomerate, but one with very deep roots. Indeed, the current mission statement of the company echoes the philosophy of John Cadbury, the committed Quaker who founded the company in 1794. Cadbury's mission stresses 'social responsibility' and the desire to be a good neighbour. It also explicitly sets out a commitment to encourage the personal fulfilment of employees. Although such corporate sentiments are not unique to Cadbury, they are rarely so deeply held.

John Cadbury saw his 'drinking cocoa' as a moral alternative to the cheap liquor sold to the working classes in nineteenth-century industrial England. The high quality of Cadbury's products, manufactured in the centre of Birmingham, was rewarded by its commercial success. In 1879, the chocolate factory, by then in his sons' control, was relocated four miles to the south in a rural setting on the River Bourn. The Cadburys initially purchased about seven hectares for the factory, but then bought more and more land. On this holding they developed the first 'model' village to follow a programme of mixed development. This was an environment for all social classes, developed as a balanced mixture of house types. By contrast, earlier 'model' villages were massed collections of a repeated dwelling type: the artisan's cottage. The new site was called 'Bournville' to give Cadbury products a French-sounding origin – at that time French chocolate was considered to be the world leader. Since then, the range of products, the factory and Bournville itself have all grown. Today, Bournville (now a pleasant suburb of Birmingham) extends to 400 hectares and comprises 6500 dwellings, housing 20 000 people.

### The development of Cadbury World

A factory visit to Cadbury's at Bournville has been a highlight for children since the 1920s. Even today, many adults fondly remember their childhood tours and gift of a presentation tin of chocolates. These trips included the production areas and Bournville village. At the end of 1965 (when 160 000 visitors came), Cadbury decided to stop the tours due both to tighter legislation on the hygiene of food production and to the possibility of intentional or inadvertent contamination of chocolate by visitors. For years after, however, Cadbury continued to be innundated by requests from educational groups and individuals that were interested in visiting the factory. In the face of this interest, management decided in the mid-1980s to reintroduce the popular outing to Cadbury. A number of major changes over the intervening 20 years meant that this new 'service product' would be very different from the old tours. Firstly, rationalisation at the factory had released a large area of land for non-manufacturing uses. Secondly, the production process itself had become much more automated and enclosed since the 1960s, and was no longer likely to be of such interest to visitors. Finally, the economic climate was more favourable to leisure businesses than had been the case for many years. The new venture was intended not only to be a contemporary 'leisure experience', but also to have educational value and to be guided by the spirit of the old tours. It was this combination of factors that influenced the decision to create Cadbury World.

In the words of the Cadbury World promotional material,

'Cadbury World is a permanent exhibition devoted entirely to chocolate ... where it came from, who first drank this mysterious potion, when it became eating chocolate, and the part that Cadbury played in this fascinating story.'

The scheme involved building a new Visitor Centre adjacent to the main production plant, constructing car parks and a play area, and hiring and training 87 staff – at a total cost of around £5 million. Advance estimates by leisure consultants indicated that it would attract around 250 000 visitors a year; based on an average ticket price of around £3.50, the return on investment (low for Cadbury) would be just under 10 per cent. After much planning, Cadbury World opened to the public in mid-August 1990.

The 1990 Cadbury-Schweppes Annual Report commented on this new venture:

'Its success as a unique and absorbing leisure experience can be measured by the 185 000 visitors who enjoyed the Cadbury World experience between August and the year end.'

## ● Cadbury World: 1991

Nearly all visitors arrived by car or coach. Parking for cars was arranged in three areas, with a total capacity of 484. Separate spaces could accommodate 24 coaches and there was a 'picking up/setting down' area close to the main exhibition. Records suggested that on a representative weekday (during school term time), 15 pre-booked coaches and about 204 cars came to Cadbury World. Typically, there were about 35 visitors per coach and three per car.

The site was served by two other means of transport, inheritances from its industrial past: to the rear of the factory were a railway station and a canal pier. Some visitors came by train and there were a few commercial barge operators who ran tourist trips from the centre of Birmingham out to Bournville. However, the plant layout meant these visitors had about a 10-minute walk around the perimeter of the factory before reaching Cadbury World. This path has been signed as 'The Factory Trail'. In practice, less than five per cent of customers arrived by train or barge.

The exhibition's reception area had three tills. Two were for individuals and the other was for the leaders of coach visitor groups. The ticketing system had been the subject of experimentation, the latest being a 'timed ticket'. This printed out a specific 10-minute time slot on a batch of tickets. However, computer problems meant that this had not been successfully implemented during 1991.

Ticket prices and times of opening and entry are set out in Table 11.1.

The booking system for groups required organisers to specify their group's time of arrival and to pay a £25 deposit. The maximum size for any single group was set at 60 people. Cadbury World scheduled coaches at regular times throughout the day to space the arrival of groups. Because of the difficulty of estimating the duration of road journeys, coaches often arrived late and missed their agreed times. This added to the queues of visitors at the exhibition's entrance at busy periods.

The relative numbers of visitors in a typical week during school terms was:

| Monday–Friday | 60% |
| Saturday | 18% |
| Sunday | 22% |

The main categories of Cadbury World visitors were families, pensioners and school parties.

## Entering the exhibition areas

The entrance to Cadbury World had low barriers funnelling individual visitors toward the tills. Beyond these, the reception area gave access to the exhibition, the shop and the restaurant. Sometimes this area was used for attractions such as a 'honky-tonk' piano player. At other times, a TV continuously played a four-minute video previewing

**Table 11.1 Ticket prices and opening times in 1991**

| | |
|---|---|
| Opening times | Open every day except Christmas Day<br>Monday–Saturday: 10.00 a.m. to 5.30 p.m.<br>Sunday:   12.00 noon to 6.00 p.m. |
| Last admissions | Monday–Saturday: 4.00 p.m.<br>Sunday:   4.30 p.m. |
| 1991 prices (includes VAT) | Adult £4.00<br>Child £3.00 (5 to 15 years inclusive)<br>Under fives FREE<br>Family rate £12.85 (2 adults and 2 children)<br>Senior Citizens £3.60 (Monday–Friday only)<br>Groups (20 or more) must book in advance |

many of the features visitors would see at Cadbury World. This included many parts of the interior of the exhibition, the packaging plant, and short extracts of other videos which were running inside Cadbury World. A sketch of the Cadbury World site as at 1991 is reproduced in Figure 11.1.

The entrance to the exhibition itself was via a pair of unmarked double doors. A ticket collector stationed here controlled the number of visitors entering. The ticket collector judged the number of visitors to be admitted at any time, simply by periodically entering the exhibition and checking the number of visitors before 'Bull Street', which marked the end of the first part of the exhibition. On average, in a busy period, 15–20 visitors were let in every two and a half minutes. For most of the exhibition, visitors had no guides.

The first section of the tour described the ancient origins of chocolate and tried to capture the atmosphere of a South American jungle. Visitors entered a darkened room which was 'dressed' with artificial trees and lianas. Among these, static wax models of South American Indians were shown making and drinking chocolate. The narrative of the story was carried on a variety of short sign-boards and continued, a little further on, by a continuously playing video 'documentary' lasting three minutes. 'Jungle sounds' were played over loudspeakers. Most visitors passed quickly through this section, treating it almost as a decorative entrance to the exhibition.

The visitors then passed a scene featuring a representation of Hernando Cortes, the Spanish conqueror of Mexico, beyond which the jungle abruptly ended. This area had a serving hatch and a sign invited visitors to take a small plastic cup of liquid chocolate ('like the Incas used to drink'). A swing-top bin was positioned next to the hatch for the disposal of used cups. This section was supervised by a member of staff, who explained: 'We have problems with some of the children. They take five or six of the cups, cover themselves in chocolate and make themselves ill.'

Visitors then passed a pictorial wall-mounted display, and moved (still at their own pace) into the European Room, which described the introduction of chocolate to Europe. To the rear, the faint sounds of the jungle could usually still be heard. Beyond this section, visitors entered 'Bull Street', a replica of a cobbled Georgian street, with authenic-looking shop windows. An attendant in Bull Street halted the flow of people to form groups outside a door to the next part of the tour, the Marie Cadbury Room. This had seating for 16 and surrounding standing room. At peak times as many as 70 people could be accommodated in the room, although it was originally designed for only about one-third of this number. After the doors closed, there was a five-minute automated 'show' explaining the early days of Cadbury, using taped voices and three static, illuminated scenes. This was controlled by an attendant, who was responsible for closing the doors and starting the automated sequence. Completion of the show was indicated to the attendant by an unobtrusive light, which was the prompt to open the doors to allow the next group in. However, the attendant generally waited for about one minute before opening the entry doors. In this time, some of the preceding group, realising that the show was over, started to look at the wall-mounted exhibits in the room, whilst others began leaving the room via the marked exit, moving to the next section of the exhibition. Only when the attendant finally opened the *entry* doors, the remainder finally began to make their own way out. Filling and emptying the Marie Cadbury Room took an average of about four minutes, although this did increase for very large groups.

Figure 11.1 A sketch of Cadbury World site (1991)

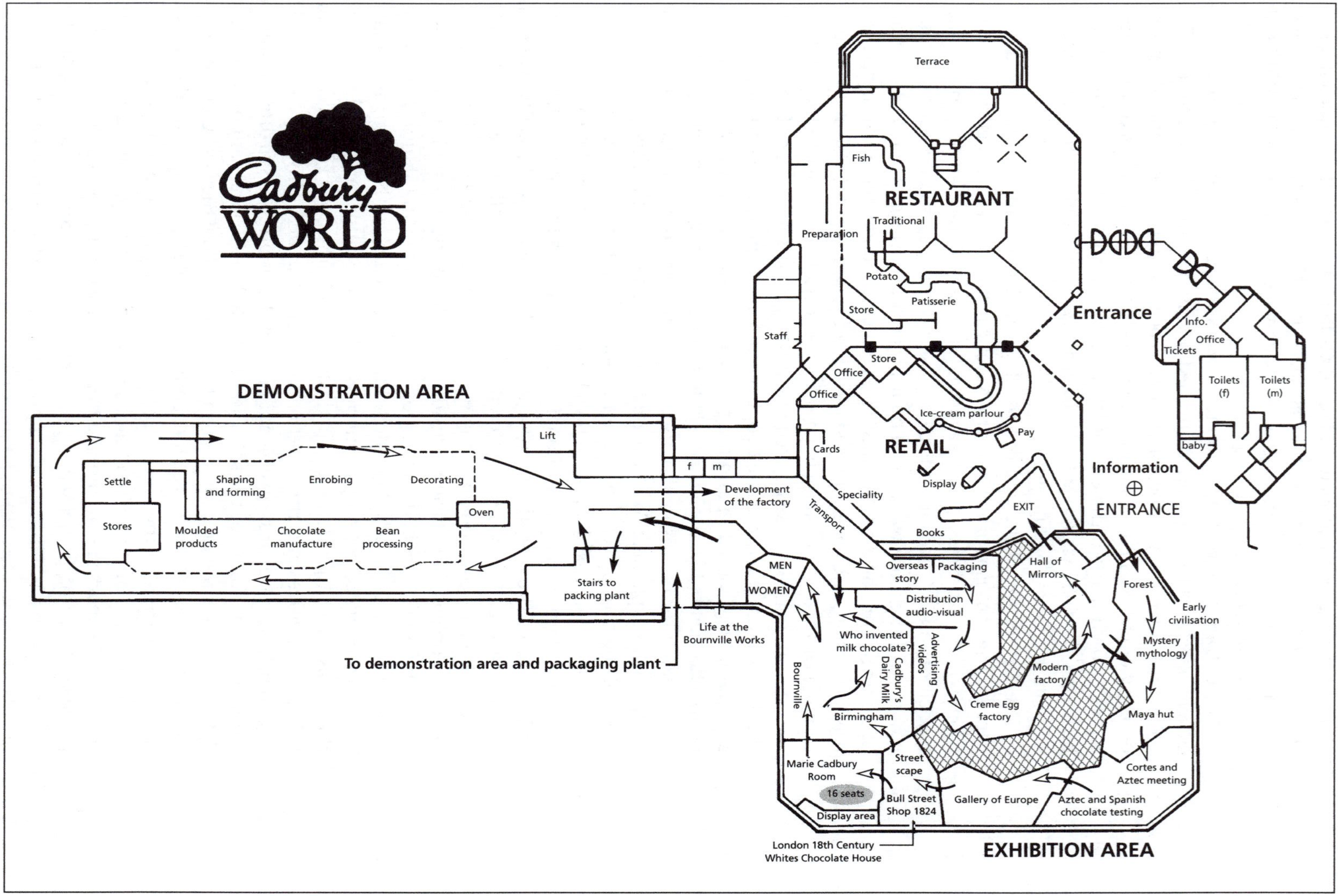

The next area comprised pictorial exhibits explaining the history of Cadbury, Bournville village and the social background to the firm. At one end of the room, a video entitled 'Making Chocolate' ran for three minutes. Beyond this was a mock-up of an old factory entrance, with a working 'clock' and 'clocking-in' cards. The entrance has two gates marked 'MEN' and 'WOMEN', as did the original factory. Families were momentarily separated at this point. This interactive section of the exhibition was often a cause of amusement, with older visitors explaining to children how the 'clock' worked.

Throughout the exhibition, different types of visitors spent their time in different ways. Most pensioners liked the videos, but skipped most of the written materials. School groups, however, tended to focus on the notices and narrative material. An educational 'task sheet', available for children from the reception, was a way of holding these visitors' attention. From here, visitors left the new building and directly entered part of the factory, originally known as the East Cocoa Block. The contrast was marked: the ambience here was typical of a factory built in the 1930s. The floors and stairs were concrete, and the walls bare, cream-painted brick. Surprisingly, there was little smell of chocolate.

What the visitors saw next depended on whether the factory itself was running. The factory had scheduled maintenance shut-down periods of about 37 days per year. When the factory was working, visitors could see the Packaging Plant. At other times they missed this out and went directly to the Demonstration Area. It was clearly indicated in advance that the Packaging Plant was not guaranteed to be open every day. Nevertheless, a few visitors became quite annoyed if they could not visit it because of these shut-downs.

## The Packaging Plant

This was located at second-floor level and reached by the original factory stairs. There was a ground-floor waiting area for visitors in wheelchairs who could not reach the packaging plant since there was no lift. At the top landing a queue formed in front of a TV playing Cadbury's adverts. The tour comprised a route with three stopping points or 'stations'. A guide collected a group of around 30 people from the landing and led it to the first station. Here there was a short video showing the factory, with a commentary added by the guide. Following this halt of about three minutes, the guide led the group to the next station. On the way, they would usually pass the preceding group returning from the second station. This caused some confusion and delay, as the groups passed on a narrow walkway. The guide then marshalled the group at the second station (about 30 metres from the previous one) from where the packaging machinery could be seen and heard. The Packaging Plant itself was a very clean area in which white-coated attendants and engineers could be seen monitoring the wrapped bars of chocolate rolling off the line. The format here was the same: a brief video explained the packaging process, and a live commentary was added by the guide. Visitors were sometimes surprised to see that some guides read their commentary from handwritten prompt cards. Next, they followed the preceding group and retraced their steps, meeting another group on the walkway. Before leaving this area the guide halted, giving another brief explanation, and then offered visitors chocolates from a tray. On warm days, visitors were offered paper towels on which to clean their fingers. The Packaging Plant section of the tour was generally completed in about eight minutes.

## The Demonstration Area

This part of the tour was run in guided groups of about 15 people. At peak times, up to eight guides were on duty. Guides had the option of addressing their groups with their own voices or, for larger groups, by means of a portable microphone. Visitors were encouraged to ask questions. There were normally several groups on the circuit round the demonstration area (which is shown at Figure 11.2).

The Demonstration Area was on the ground floor and showed a number of production processes carried out by about seven staff on small, 'old technology' machines. These machines had been chosen to enable operations, such as the coating of nuts with chocolate, to be seen and understood. The visitors were separated from these operations by chest-high perspex screens. The demonstration staff, who had been recruited from the factory, wore white production clothing, and had been trained to interact with visitors. After watching a process (for example, vibrating chocolate into moulds or turning out blocks), visitors were offered samples of chocolate. Overhead, a number of suspended photographs showed the full-scale production equivalent of each of these machines. This section of the tour continued with a number of demonstrations of the production of luxury, handmade chocolates. As before, staff were behind clear screens; they carried out a number of dipping, enrobing (coating) and finishing operations. After being given more free samples and asking questions, the group moved out of the demonstration area and back into the new building. Although there was not a set number of points of interest, visitors could see up to eight different processes in this area.

It was often noticed that some visitors roamed, moving from one guide's group to the one ahead, and completed this section in as little as six minutes. By contrast, other visitors took the opportunity to ask many questions, looking at all the points of interest and sampling all the free chocolate. In this case, they and their guide could take up to 17 minutes to get round. No overtaking of guides by the following guides was allowed. Therefore, they needed to adjust the length of their explanations in order to match the speed of their group to that of any preceding group, which could include an unusually slow visitor. Guides noticed that they found it easier to control the coherence and behaviour of their groups when they used the microphones.

**Figure 11.2  The Demonstration Area (1991)**

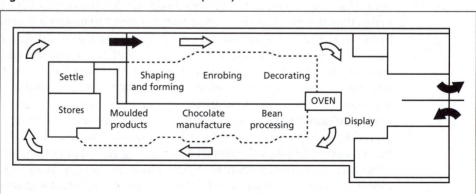

## Exit

The remainder of the tour was unaccompanied, and focused on marketing material. This included a video on the making of a Milk Tray TV advert (the 'Man in Black'), and video compilations of advertisements which could be selected by visitors pressing buttons. The end of the route led directly into the rear of the shop.

## The shop

This sold a wide range of Cadbury products as well as 'branded' mementoes such as tea towels, mugs and T-shirts. Most of the goods were on self-service display and pilferage by children was believed to be a minor problem. There were three checkouts and most goods were bar-coded. Observations showed that, on average, during busy periods one customer could be served at each till every 15 seconds. While most tour visitors entered the shop through the back entrance (having completed the tour), a number of customers also browsed and bought before the beginning of the tour.

## The restaurant

The Centre Services Manager described the restaurant: 'The restaurant is modelled on that of a "Food Court", such as those typically included in modern indoor shopping centres. There is a good choice of foods and there is something for everybody.'

Approached from the reception area via a single entrance, it was a self-service restaurant with five serving points arranged in a row. Four of these were labelled: 'Patisserie', 'Baked Potato', 'Traditional' and 'Seafood'. The fifth was a heavily-used point serving tea and coffee. The range of food choice could not be seen from the entrance to the restaurant. Visitors entered, observed the various serving points, and then made their decision on food type and thus decided which queue to join. This could take a little while, especially in the case of some old people and families. The popularity of the adjacent 'Baked Potato', 'Tea and Coffee' and 'Traditional' serving points resulted in severe congestion at busy times. Payment was taken separately at each sales point.

Customers took their selections to the seating area. This was a large, airy room providing comfortable surroundings. Fifty-three tables of various sizes provided 169 covers.

On average, people spent 25 minutes in the restaurant. Tables were promptly cleared and cleaned by pleasant staff based in a 'refuge' in the centre of the seating area. Most visitors to Cadbury World came into the restaurant.

## Coffee and ice-cream parlour

This small area was approached via the shop and had 46 'covers', comprising stools at the island bar and separate tables around it. The design of the parlour was similar to an American-style diner. The parlour sold coffee, tea and ice-cream. On average, a visitor stayed in the parlour for 18 minutes. At any one time, about 25–30 people could be found there.

## The Alternative Exhibition

This was located close to the coach park, 300 metres from the main exhibition. It was a converted factory building, about 250 square metres in area. In 'feel', it was more like a traditional museum than the rest of Cadbury World. It housed static displays of old machinery, a fire engine and other historic items. More than 95 per cent of visitors to the main exhibition came here. A small shuttle bus was provided to take visitors between the two sites. The Alternative Exhibition was staffed, and visitors (some of whom were retired Cadbury employees) often asked detailed technical questions.

### Questions relating to 1991

1 *Draw a process flow chart showing how customers were processed through the operation. What does this suggest about the process design of Cadbury World?*

2 *Calculate the hourly capacities for each micro-operation. How does Cadbury World management vary capacity to respond to changes in demand? How could the service be amended to increase bottleneck capacity?*

## ● Cadbury World: 1995

'Since opening in 1990, Cadbury World has exceeded all of our expectations' explained Jeremy King, Sales and Marketing Manager, to the new Centre Services Manager, Peter Bales. 'Having originally designed the operation for 250 000 visitors annually, current forecasts for the remainder of 1995 are that numbers will top half a million.'

During Peter's induction into the organisation, Jeremy had suggested that he focus on assessing three major operational issues that had recently been raised. Firstly, automatic doors had been installed at the entrance to the Cadbury Room, and Jeremy was concerned that queues were developing in the areas leading up to this part of the exhibition. Secondly, queues for the Packaging Plant were extremely long during periods of high demand, and he wanted to evaluate whether this had been affected by the new doors at the Cadbury Room. Finally, the tour guides had adopted a 'free-flow' system for the Demonstration Area. This comprised guides stationed at fixed points giving their commentaries, and allowed visitors to be processed at a faster rate than the conventional guide-led tours. It was not known what effect this new system had had on the visitor flow and on service quality.

Cadbury World had been fine-tuning its visitors' experience over the first five years of operations, altering both the design and layout of the facility, and the flows and processes within it. Demand for the attraction had continued to be largely from the leisure market, but the recent inclusion of the study of the Aztecs (who have associations with chocolate) in the National Curriculum for Schools had also generated a reasonably-sized educational market. Originally the centre was open 364 days per year but, in order to reduce its operating costs, and in response to known patterns of demand, opening had been reduced to 294 days, with closures occurring most Mondays, Tuesdays and Fridays from November through to March. Ticket prices had increased annually, slightly ahead of inflation, and the 1995 rates are shown in Table 11.2.

### Table 11.2 Ticket prices at Cadbury World in 1995

| Opening times | Every opening day: 10.00 a.m. to 5.30 p.m. | |
|---|---|---|
| Last admissions | Every opening day: 4.00 p.m. | |
| 1995 prices (includes VAT) | Adult | £4.90 |
| | Child (5 to 15 years inclusive) | £3.35 |
| | Under fives | FREE |
| | Family rates (2 adults and 2 children) | £14.00 |
| | (2 adults and 3 children) | £16.85 |
| | Senior Citizens | £4.20 |
| | Adult group (each) | £4.25 |
| | Child group (each) | £2.90 |
| | School/Senior Citizen group (each) | £2.90 |

## Reservations and ticketing

Reservations were now required to guarantee entry, and this was clearly marked on all Cadbury World literature. Most visitors' first direct contact with Cadbury World, therefore, now occurred on the telephone, and every effort had been made to ensure that this was as satisfactory, informative and friendly as possible. If the Packaging Plant was planned to be closed, as happened at certain times throughout the year, visitors were informed at this time. The reservation system was free to the visitors, and was used to book up to 80 per cent of any day's capacity. After that, visitors were told that no more reservations could be taken, thus allowing Cadbury World some slack, and not disappointing too many visitors that might turn up on the day without a reservation. Groups of 20 or more people made their reservations using the same system, but were required to pay a nominal deposit to guarantee the booking.

No significant alterations had been made to the parking areas. Set-down and pick-up areas for cars and coaches were clearly identified directly in front of the main doors. A 'flexi-barrier' queue system was set up in front of the ticketing area. A notice at the entrance to the queue advised visitors that only one member from each group need join in order to obtain tickets. Tickets were issued with specified entry times, with each day being broken into 10-minute 'slots'. Originally 72 tickets had been made available for each slot, increasing to 78 when the Packaging Plant was closed; however, this had now been reduced to a single rate of 68 persons per 10-minute slot. Jeremy explained:

'We had received feedback from our market research that customers' perceived quality of the attraction was diminishing at the highest levels of demand, and in order to improve the experience we felt justified in reducing the numbers of visitors. Four people less may not sound like much, but it can mean approximately £4000 less revenue per week in the high season.'

Average arrival times of casual visitors were also problematic, as Jeremy remarked to Peter:

'Most people who turn up without reservations tend to do so between 11.00 a.m. and 1.00 p.m. This is also a popular period for the arrival of our pre-booked visitors, and so the people who just turn up can have long waits: sometimes up to a few hours. We have considered limiting the number of coach parties over this period and only allowing them to visit during the shoulder periods, 10.00 a.m. to 11.00 a.m. and 1.00 p.m. to 4.00 p.m., which would improve the experience of those visitors who had not booked. What effect this might have on our coach groups is hard to gauge.'

Apart from changes in the reservation and ticketing arrangements, much work had been done to improve the layout and flow within the exhibition. The main changes to the layout are highlighted in Figure 11.3, and are described below.

### Entrance to the exhibition

'Flexi-barrier' queues were again used in the area leading up to the exhibition entrance, and a permanent TV monitor displayed a four-minute video previewing the main features of the exhibition. The ticket collector at the entrance to the exhibition no longer had to control the number of visitors entering at any particular time, as this was determined by the timed ticketing. The ticket collector was required to give the first chocolate sample to the visitors (usually a popular product such as Crunchie, Curly Wurly or Wispa) and also to hand out activity sheets to the younger children. It was only possible to answer the questions by referring to specific information boxes at various points in the exhibition.

### Chocolate and the South Americans

The first section of the tour remained largely unchanged, giving a brief history of the earliest discovery of chocolate by the South American Indians. The booth, housing a guide responsible for issuing small samples of the 'chocolate' drink, had been moved to the other side of the corridor, allowing him/her a view back into the Aztec area and the jungle. This had been necessary when the attendant (who is dressed in the distinctive Cadbury shirt and tie) used to control the flow of visitors into the later stages of the exhibition. This task had now been made obsolete by the changes to the admissions to the Cadbury Room, described later. This very first section of the exhibition had capacity to hold approximately 50 people, and average throughput time at peak demand periods was seven minutes, two minutes of which could be spent queuing for the chocolate drink. Next, the visitors passed into the Gallery of Europe with its static displays of King Charles II and various portraits of eminent European royals and nobles. This room could hold about 20 people, with seating for 12. A commentary described how chocolate became adopted within the European courts, recounting how British pirates, raiding the early Spanish ships returning from South America, thought that the cocoa beans were sheep's droppings, and so threw them overboard! The commentary lasted 2 minutes and 15 seconds, but only about one quarter of all visitors stayed throughout this time; most others moved through within one minute.

### Bull Street and the Cadbury Room

In the original design, an attendant would halt the flow of visitors at the end of Bull Street, forming groups for entry to the Cadbury Room, but later this person had

Figure 11.3 A sketch of Cadbury World (1995)

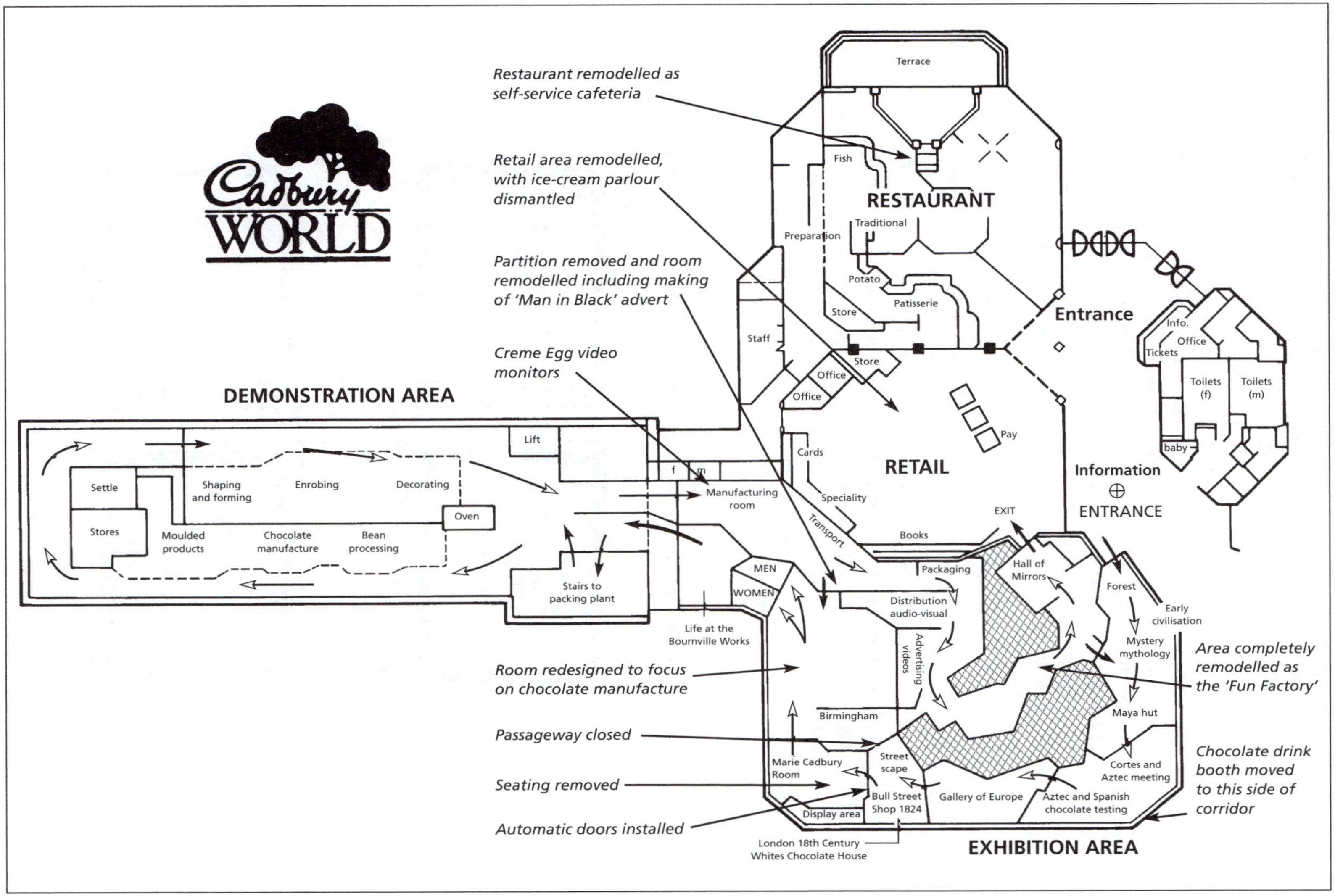

been removed and visitors were then allowed to flow in freely. Two weeks before Peter's arrival, an automated door system had been introduced, with the intention of regrouping the visitors in Bull Street so that they would only move into the next area in time to see the *beginning* of the automated presentation being given in the Cadbury Room. The aim had been to ensure that everyone had the chance to see one complete cycle of the 'show'. Bull Street had no animation or displays of any note, and was perceived by many of the visitors as a relatively uninteresting waiting area for the Cadbury Room. As many as 70 people could wait in the Bull Street area, although queues could sometimes develop as far back as the chocolate booth. This was most common in busy periods when flows become irregular, or if large coherent groups (such as school parties) were moving at abnormal speed through the exhibition and were either catching up with, or being caught up by, other visitors. A small TV monitor, located below shoulder height beside the entrance door, informed visitors exactly how long they would have to wait, and when to enter. The messages it showed are reproduced in Figure 11.4.

Whilst seating had originally been provided in the Cadbury Room, this had now been removed and there was only standing room in which visitors could view the displays located on two adjacent sides of the room. The automatically-opened doors stayed open for one minute, allowing an average of 45 people to enter before they closed. Although the room had a maximum holding capacity of about 80 people, visitors' viewing pleasure was known to deteriorate above 45 persons. Therefore,

**Figure 11.4  TV monitor messages at entrance to the Cadbury Room (1995)**

1  Show starts in Cadbury Room and doors close

2  Message asks guests to wait for the next show, now doors have opened

3  Message change each minute, informing guests how long they have to wait

4  Doors open and guests are requested to enter the Cadbury Room

this lower number was set as the optimum capacity, and the timing of the automatic doors had been adjusted accordingly. The show lasted seven and a half minutes, and the entry doors reopened 30 seconds after the end of the show, during which time most people in the Cadbury Room would have identified the exit and made their way out.

## Chocolate manufacturing area ('Making Chocolate')

The next section had been entirely remodelled, with the relocation to the Cadbury Collection of most of the pictorial exhibits explaining the history of Bournville village and the social background of the firm. This area now focused on the manufacture of chocolate, the processes used, and the location of Cadbury's manufacturing plants worldwide. It had also gained a large video monitor describing the chocolate production process, from the cultivation of beans to completion of the packed products. On one of his visits, Peter had overheard a conversation between two visitors: 'It's a bit difficult to hear all of the video, isn't it? You can still hear the commentary from the last room, and there is something else that sounds like a helicopter and thunder!' They were right, and Peter had noticed that none of the walls between any of these sections in the exhibition extended to the ceiling, allowing noises from one area to spill over into others. This room held up to about 40 people, and visitors stayed there for an average of four minutes. Beyond this, the mock factory entrance had been retained, separating visitors through two gates marked 'MEN' and 'WOMEN' with an antique clocking-in clock and cards for the visitors to punch-in. This section could hold a further 30 people but most visitors found it only briefly amusing, passing through in an average of two minutes.

## Packaging Plant

The visit to the Packaging Plant had been improved by the construction of a second staircase, which allowed one-directional flow. A diagram showing the layout and flow for this part of the tour is reproduced in Figure 11.5.

As before, visitors left the main exhibition building and entered part of the main chocolate factory. If the factory was operating, visitors were escorted upstairs to the Packaging Plant, where they joined a queue for the start of their tour.

During the wait, visitors were given a second chocolate bar, and were entertained by a TV monitor slung from the ceiling that showed videos of Cadbury adverts over the ages. Visitors were grouped into batches of about 30 people, and each group was taken by a guide to three separate points in the plant on the second and third floors. At each point the group was halted, and the guide plugged a microphone into the newly installed sound system, giving an explanation of the activities occurring in front of the visitors. If excessive queues built up in the entrance to the packaging area, the size of groups was increased, and it was not uncommon for the number of people in a group to approach 50. At the second stop a pre-recorded video was shown of the unseen activity on the floor below, with a live commentary being given by the guide. However, there continued to be problems with the guides' commentaries. In the words of Jeremy:

**Figure 11.5 Packaging Plant layout and flow (1995)**

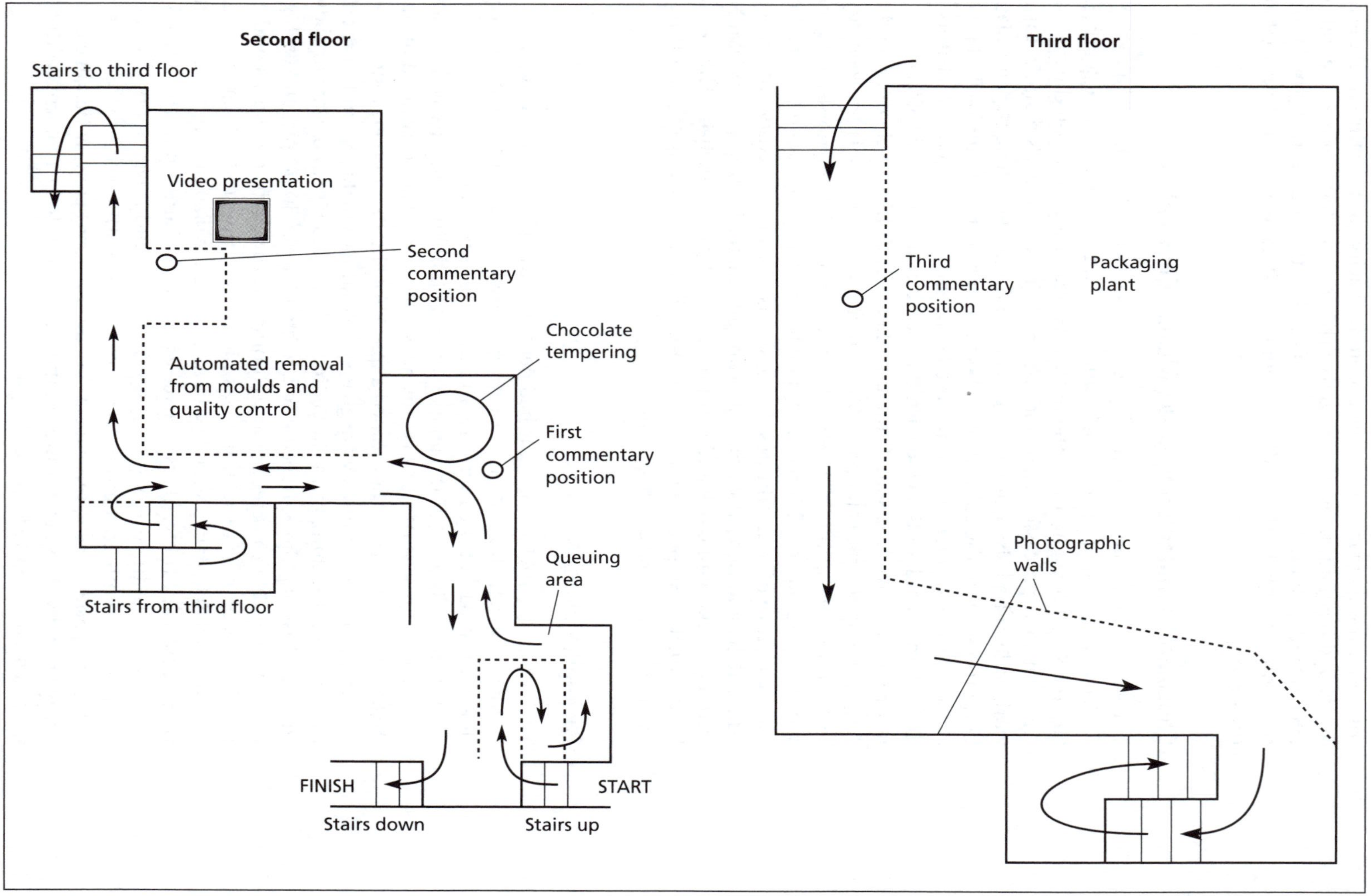

'Unfortunately, the sound system is not having entirely the beneficial effects that we considered it would. There are issues of the number of people in the group, the visibility of the guide, the use of the microphones by the guides, the use of seasonal staffing, and competition with the loud radio music for the operatives in the factory. These factors impact on the visitors' experience and reduce the overall effectiveness of the commentary. But we are making every effort to ensure that the perceived quality of Cadbury World's visitor experience is at the same level as that conveyed by its food products.'

The groups of visitors used to have to return along the same corridor, causing difficulties when one group met another, but this had been resolved by introducing a second staircase allowing the tour to take a circular path. The queuing area could hold up to 50 people, and up to three groups could be touring the Packaging Plant at any one time. The tour lasted approximately 15 minutes, after which the group was led directly downstairs to the Demonstration Area. If the Packaging Plant was closed, either as a result of a factory holiday or because of planned scheduled maintenance, visitors moved directly to the Demonstration Area. Some visitors were openly annoyed when the Packaging Plant was closed, despite all published material clearly indicating that there was no guarantee that it would be open.

## Demonstration Area

The Demonstration Area could take two groups at a time, with each group consisting of no more than 30 people. A guided batch of visitors took about 10 minutes to move through the area. They were shown many of the old methods for producing and finishing the chocolates that would have been used in the factory at the turn of the century, and were able to sample fresh chocolates produced within the last few minutes. At the end of this section the visitors were told that the type of handmade chocolates that were produced in front of them could not be bought anywhere other than in the Cadbury World shop, and would therefore make an exclusive memento of their visit. As they left the Demonstration Area they were given a sample bar of Cadbury's Dairy Milk. If the Packaging Plant was closed, the size of this free bar was increased, and another chocolate bar might also be given by way of an apology.

If the queue became excessively long, three guides were permanently positioned at different points to give a running commentary. This allowed throughput times to be reduced to eight minutes because visitors tended not to dwell so long and could be encouraged by the guides to move on. However, feedback showed that many of the visitors disliked this system; 'It was much less personal than when we last visited,' mentioned one dissatisfied visitor. This free-flow system did not alter the total number of visitors in the area, which remained at about 60.

## 'Man in Black' and the Fun Factory

The remainder of the tour had been extensively remodelled to make it 'more fun'. The Manufacturing Room had video monitors, set in life-size mockups of Cadbury's Creme Eggs, showing how various products were manufactured; the videos deliberately had no commentary. Other amusing novelties, like a 'Measure your height in fudge bars' and other 'Fun Facts', improved the overall enjoyment, particularly for the younger visitors. Most people passed through this section within 90 seconds and the room had capacity for around 25 visitors. Next, a large video screen showed a short feature on the making of the latest 'Man in Black' Milk Tray advert, shot on location in Jamaica. The film showed how both real and model helicopters were used to produce an advert lasting just 30 seconds and containing some 27 scenes. Sixteen seats were provided here, but up to an additional 14 people could stand and watch the video which lasted 3 minutes and 5 seconds. There was a 15-second gap between showings. Many people found this an interesting show, and approximately one quarter of all people watched it twice. A little further on, other displays and video screens showed Cadbury adverts from across the years, adding an average of 3 minutes and 40 seconds to people's visits, and the capacity of this area was about 30 persons.

The newly-constructed Fun Factory followed, giving (in the words of the Cadbury literature), 'A light-hearted look at chocolate-making with help from Mr Cadbury's Parrot, the Bean Team and a touch of Cadbury magic…' There were many bright colours, flashing lights, lots of noise and plenty of buttons for the children to press. This area was found to be very popular with young and old alike, and had a capacity of approximately 35 persons, with most people spending an average of five minutes in this section before entering the final part of the exhibition, the Hall of Mirrors. By the use of opposing mirrors, this room gave the impression that you could see up, down and sideways into infinity. It could only hold about 10 people, and most visitors did not linger, passing directly through – spending on average a mere 30 seconds before emerging in the shop.

## The shop

Cadbury World Shop had gone through a significant number of costly changes in response to extensive customer feedback. Most significant was the expenditure of over £100 000 on air conditioning, which required the whole complex to be closed for the month of January 1994. This had improved both the quality of the chocolate on display, and also the visitors' comfort, causing them to linger longer than they might otherwise have done.

The floor area had been increased by 40 square metres, following the dismantling of the Ice-cream Parlour. Five tills now operated, rather than the original three, and these were all located in a single row at the exit, similar to a checkout at a supermarket. Electronic point of sales (EPOS) systems had been installed to improve the sales information, and to tie in with monitoring and control of stock. Some customers expressed disappointment that chocolate prices were not lower, but they were actually competitive against prices in normal retail outlets. Clearly, Cadbury World could not deliberately undercut its local retailers, but as well as selling chocolate, it offered a wide range of souvenirs and giftware. A 'Bargain Corner' had been introduced, which sold misshapen goods (seconds), and customers could also buy the 'exclusive' handmade chocolates they saw being made in the Demonstration Area.

## The restaurant

The original Food Court concept had been scrapped, and the restaurant redesigned as a self-service free-flow, offering a narrower range of items, including pizza, fried chicken, salads, fish fingers, a selection of sandwiches and ice-creams. This had led to a reduction in staffing costs of up to 54 per cent. There were two tills, and the number of covers had been increased from 169 to 250. An additional Outside Catering Unit, located in the Children's Play Area, also acted as an overflow and during the summer months could generate significant revenues.

## The Cadbury Collection

Originally called the 'Alternative Exhibition', this had been moved from its original location at the far end of the parking area, and was now situated on the lower ground floor of the factory, next to the Children's Play Area. The Collection still resembled a more typical museum, with static displays explaining the history of Bournville, the production methods employed, as well as the social history of the firm and samples of many of its products over the years. A mockup of an old sweet shop and a 1930s film on the factory were also offered. Entrance to the Cadbury Collection was free to exhibition ticket holders.

## Peter's observations

A week after his arrival Peter met with Jeremy King to review his findings:

'In Bull Street, I got the impression that people regarded this as a waiting area for the next stage. They would probably not have stopped here for more than a few minutes had they not been obliged to wait for up to eight minutes by the automatic door. Visually, the street is well designed, authentically reproducing the Birmingham street as it was in 1794, with a London scene and Whites of St James on the other side of the room, but it lacked animation! There were sounds of horses on the cobbled streets, but I can't help thinking that this audio equipment could have been better employed.

'The doors are not proving as effective as I believe had been anticipated. I studied the flows of visitors through this area on four separate days, admittedly at periods of high demand, and found the problems were as follows: The safety sensors on the doors react so that whilst people continue to stream past the open doors, they were unable to close. The TV monitor located by the door never signalled people to stop, and so they continued to fill the room beyond its capacity. Children playing with the door handle caused it to open, as did someone wanting to return from where they had come. Once reopened, it took over a minute for the door to close with people continuing to stream in. Groups entering just as the doors were about to close also caused the doors to stay open for far longer than should have otherwise been the case.'

The findings also showed the numbers of people entering, and the delays in closing the door, which Peter had noted on the back of an envelope, and are reproduced in Figure 11.6.

'The effect of this was that people's enjoyment of the Cadbury Room deteriorated, and I also found that as the number of people in the room increased, the number of people leaving the show before it was completed also increased. [These findings are reproduced in Figure 11.7.]

'The queue lengths at the Packaging Plant entrance have apparently not reduced dramatically, but from talking to the guides, they believe that there are fewer fluctuations in the queue length. Before the Cadbury Room doors were introduced, the queue to the

**Figure 11.6 Numbers entering the Cadbury Room and delays in doors closing**

| Visitors entering | Delay to doors closing (seconds) |
|---|---|
| *- Fri 11th August (visitor total = 1998)* | |
| 36 | 0 |
| 57 | 20 |
| 60 | 12 |
| 74 | 56 |
| 31 | 0 |
| 64 | 43 |
| 46 | 32 |
| 37 | 0 |
| *- Thur 17th August (visitor total = 2369)* | |
| 64 | 10 |
| 49 | 15 |
| 32 | 2 |
| 56 | 18 |
| 70 | 41 |
| 61 | 26 |
| 32 | 0 |
| 51 | 12 |
| *- Tue 22nd August (visitor total = 2420)* | |
| 69 | 25 |
| 47 | 33 |
| 76 | 47 |
| 69 | 63 |
| 64 | 51 |
| 94 | 192 |
| *- Wed 30th August (visitor total = 2510)* | |
| 49 | 15 |
| 38 | 22 |
| 32 | 0 |
| 63 | 26 |
| 45 | 31 |
| 56 | 28 |

**Figure 11.7 Numbers entering the Cadbury Room and numbers leaving before the end**

| Visitors entering | Leaving before end |
|---|---|
| *- Fri 11th August* | |
| 36 | 0 |
| 57 | 6 |
| 60 | 5 |
| 74 | 6 |
| 31 | 0 |
| 64 | 0 |
| 46 | 2 |
| 37 | 0 |
| *- Thur 17th August* | |
| 64 | 2 |
| 49 | 2 |
| 32 | 0 |
| 56 | 5 |
| 70 | 3 |
| 61 | 0 |
| 32 | 3 |
| 51 | 0 |
| *- Tue 22nd August* | |
| 69 | 9 |
| 47 | 0 |
| 76 | 6 |
| 69 | 16 |
| 64 | 2 |
| 94 | 42 |
| *- Wed 30th August* | |
| 49 | 1 |
| 38 | 4 |
| 32 | 0 |
| 63 | 6 |
| 45 | 4 |
| 56 | 2 |

Packaging Plant occasionally became extremely long; up to a 20–30 minute period, whenever one group accelerated through the first part of the exhibition and joined a slower group. Now the arrival of visitors seems to be more constant, which even though it may lead to queues, does not produce queues of excessive length.

'The free-flow in the Demonstration Area seemed to be effective at rapidly processing the visitors, reducing times from an average of 10 minutes to an average of 8 minutes. This clearly helps reduce queue lengths, but at what cost? The guides do not enjoy it as much, which comes over in their performance, and they suggest that the customers also prefer being given a tour by a single guide, with whom they feel more relaxed and able to question. But if the maximum number of visitors that can be taken around by each guide is 30 and the processing time is kept at 10 minutes, how else can we put more capacity into the Demonstration Area?

'Finally there do appear to be one or two "dead areas" where queuing takes place, and I am concerned that the queue lengths appear excessive to the visitors simply because these areas are not entertaining enough. I am keen to discover whether there are any low-cost ways of improving entertainment in the queues, perhaps through the use of material that is not very effective in its current position.'

### Questions relating to 1995

1 *Calculate the hourly capacities for each of the areas in the exhibition.*

2 *Where could queues build up and why? What has been done so far to overcome bottlenecks? What else can be done to overcome excessive queue lengths?*

3 *What are the benefits and drawbacks of introducing the electronic doors?*

4 *What else could be done to improve the visitors' satisfaction at Cadbury World?*

## Cadbury World: developments from 1996 to 2001

### 1997: Cadabra

Market research and customer feedback collected during the first few years of operation had indicated that the original design under-provided for the needs of young children. Whilst the addition of the Fun Factory (now known as the Fantasy Factory) in 1994 had successfully provided some additional interactive activities for children, this was of limited value to the under-fives. A leisure consultant was contracted to design a new attraction that would appeal to the younger audience, whilst adding to the overall experience of visitors of all ages.

The chosen design, known as 'Cadabra', comprises a short 'enchanting ride' in one of the four-seat 'Beanmobiles', which follow a guided track on a 'magical journey through an animated chocolate wonderland'. The capital scheme of £1.2m was approved and an area of offices above the Demonstration Area was relocated to make space for this large new attraction. Cadabra was then installed, and has proved to be a very attractive addition to the package of activities. It is included in the standard route around the facility, so normally every customer travels on this ride. Whilst it is technically possible to bypass it by removing (or ducking under) a tape barrier, there is no member of staff positioned at the appropriate location to facilitate this. In practice, even pensioners enjoy Cadabra, and very few customers wish to omit the ride!

In normal operation there are twelve cars in the loop of track, each of which can seat four people. Very small children are allowed to sit on parents' laps, but most prefer to occupy a front seat! At busy times, filling every car is important, so this is a key task of the Cadabra guide who assists in the loading of the cars. This can present problems when family groups have to be split up or have to share a car, but in general customers cooperate with the loading arrangements suggested by the guide, although some seats may not always be filled, even on very busy days. There is only 20 seconds allowed in the automated cycle for loading or unloading a stationary car, so any delay in these activities can require a guide to temporarily disable the automatic cycle (for safety reasons), which stops all the cars on the loop of track for a few seconds. There is one car designed to carry a single disabled-person's wheelchair plus two other passengers. This can be inserted into the loop of track in place of a standard car by a simple transfer mechanism at right angles to the track just prior to the loading station. This changeover takes less than 20 seconds, which is within the cycle time of loading or unloading adjacent cars, so it has no effect on the process times.

The ride operates on a standard cycle, with a car departing from the loading area exactly every 30 seconds, unless the manual override is activated. At the loading area, it takes 10 seconds for a departing car to move away from the area, whilst the next empty car moves forward from an awaiting position and comes to a complete halt. Therefore, the remaining 20 seconds are available for loading, assisted by a guide as described above.

On completion of the ride, customers are assisted to disembark by a second guide, a process that normally takes under 15 seconds. Departing passengers are segregated from the queuing customers by a simple tape barrier. After being stationary for a total of 20 seconds, the car moves forward to an awaiting position. Meanwhile, the remaining nine cars move slowly around the track, on view on CCTV monitors, and under the control of a third guide, responsible for overall safety. This guide is able to stop the system in the event of problems (such as a passenger leaving the car during the ride), and is able to mobilise maintenance assistance if technical problems arise.

On busy days, substantial queues can build up for Cadabra, snaking back along the corridor from the Packaging Plant. Colin Samways, the Marketing Manager of Cadbury World, commented:

'We do everything we can to keep the flow going through Cadabra. In the first few years of operating this attraction, we had a tear-off portion of the admission ticket that had to be removed by a guide at Cadabra to ensure that customers only went on once! In practice, this could actually slow down the loading stage, particularly as some customers had mislaid their tickets. We now do not inspect tickets at this point, on the basis that on busy days, customers would not wish to rejoin the back of a long queue, and certainly would not be able to queue-jump. Some small children liked Cadabra so much that they wanted to go around again, and behaved obstructively when being requested to get out! With the ensuing pleas from parents, and the guide's polite refusal, this could delay the process for a few valuable seconds at times. Short delays can occur loading wheelchairs, but on average we only have about five of these per day. When a reservation is accepted for a large group of disabled people, we have to ensure that they understand the need to spread out their Cadabra rides. If this has not been pre-arranged correctly, the corridor can become obstructed by a queue of wheelchairs!

'A number of very short delays occur where the 20-second loading time is exceeded, where the ride is stopped momentarily for safety reasons; and occasionally, where a mechanical or electrical fault activates cut-outs. However, this technical downtime only accounts for about two per cent of available time – we have excellent maintenance staff! If the queue gets really long, say over 20 minutes, one of the managers will pass down the line offering the opportunity to bypass Cadabra, but we usually get very few volunteers. We had a serious fault with one car at a busy period, which affected capacity for about a week. If the whole of Cadabra is out of action, we compensate customers with vouchers that can be spent in the shop. But that has only occurred for about three hours over the whole of the first year of operation.'

## 1997: Revised Packaging Plant visit

The main alterations to the Packaging Plant visit are in the video presentation area and the elimination of guiding around the plant. At the main presentation area, there are now three video screens, and 10 groups of three seats. In addition, there is standing room for up to 20 people, although in practice it feels very overcrowded if more than 10 occupy this area. It takes about 30 seconds for customers to move to the seats and sit down, after which a guide takes up a microphone. This is needed because this area is very noisy, being located beside the working factory. The guide's welcome and introduction takes up to two minutes, followed by a video that lasts three and a half minutes. It takes a further 30 seconds for the customers to leave their seats, passing awkwardly through the next group of arriving customers, particularly if access to the remainder of the Packaging Plant upstairs is closed off. On busy days, the guide's introduction can be reduced by about half a minute, but care has to be taken to retain the feeling of personal service given by the interaction between the guide and the customers. This overall contact, of course, was reduced by the cessation of the guided tours around the Packaging Plant, although the majority of the visitors actually preferred free-flow to guiding.

## 1998: Coronation Street

The original 'Man in Black' area had shown a video on the making of a Milk Tray commercial. By the middle of the 1990s this exhibit was looking dated and uninteresting to most visitors, and this advertising campaign had been discontinued, so this was ready for replacement in the exhibition. Cadbury had begun sponsoring Coronation Street, a popular 'soap' drama on television, where each episode began and ended with an amusing animated 'bumper' featuring an imaginary scene from the drama, where everything appeared to be made of chocolate. This ended with a sponsor message linked to one of the famous brands.

A new exhibit was built featuring a large chocolate-coloured miniature film set used for filming these adverts. A large-screen video shows a four-minute explanation on the filming of the painstakingly slow animation processes, where mouldable models are changed slightly between frames. There are four other smaller videos screens for which customers can use fixed keypads to select from a choice of eight video clips. This area has no seats, and comfortably accommodates about 25 people standing. About half the customers pass straight through without stopping to look at the film set or the videos. Children like pressing the buttons, but often do not wait to see the result of their choice! Those people that do stay spend an average of five minutes in this area.

## 1998: Planet Astros

The Hall of Mirrors had caused some problems with customers being frightened of the visual impression of being suspended in the middle of infinitely high and wide space created by opposing mirrors, and was not felt to add much to most people's visit. This was replaced by a small exhibit called Planet Astros, which was an attempt to build a contemporary element in the exhibition, and to target teenagers via a new product, Astros, aimed at them. The set was a replica of that used for the only TV commercial that ran in the UK for the brand, and had limited appeal. Most visitors had no interest in the set or the brand, and continued directly on to the retail shop. The relatively few that were interested were able to indulge without hindering the main flow through.

## 1999: Cocoa Road, and 2000: Manufacturing Set

Since opening, there had been a dead area of the exhibition immediately after visitors passed through the Demonstration Area, and attempts to fill it with information about warehousing and distribution or manufacturing processes were unsuccessful. With the development of the CadburyLand brand, an opportunity was seized to provide an interactive area called Cocoa Road, through which visitors pass on their way to the Coronation Street set. The area is potentially a bottleneck, though its limited appeal, principally to under-eights, helps reduce that risk. At the same time, the videos of production of three brands were repositioned, with some additional benefit in terms of the visitors learning more about how chocolate brands are made.

However, the real advance was achieved in 2000 when a new set was installed to replace the 'Life in the Bournville Works' factory set, with its segregated entrances, clocking-in machines, and black and white chronicling of the life of the Bournville factory in the early years (about 1910). The new set comprises four self-contained PCs and monitors, and a back projected screen, with subtitles, showing a continuous reel of production of seven famous products. Visitors are able to select any or all seven, which provide a video guide and authentic factory sound on screen to illustrate more detail on production. Watching all seven films can take up to 14 minutes, though most visitors spend no more than five minutes watching just a couple of the brands. The layout of the room can lead to queues at the entrance while monitors further on lie idle, but some visitors choose to skip the whole area, and others curtail their stay.

## 1999: Liquid Chocolate

A primary objective for most visitors is to get close to fresh, liquid chocolate, and in 1999 the technology became available to deliver measured samples of freshly tempered, and therefore warm, chocolate. The initial sampling was to some extent hindered by some customers' fear that it was a further sample of the Aztec drink. A significant proportion of the visitors had not liked the taste of this spiced liquid chocolate drink previously offered to them in a small plastic cup in the Aztec section. This had always been a problem area, since it was a bottleneck at busy times, and required one employee to serve and keep the area tidy at all times. Also, however it was presented, the use of plastic cups and waste bins was an incongruous feature within a historically-themed area of the exhibition. It was decided to remove the spiced Aztec chocolate drink altogether, saving a unit of labour, and to provide visitors with a taste of freshly prepared liquid chocolate within the Demonstration Area, where this was a more relevant activity.

## 2000: Yowie

The Planet Astros exhibit was replaced by a new exhibit featuring Yowie, based on six Australian animal characters representing ecological themes to young children and targeted at three to eight-year-olds. The Astros brand had been discontinued, and the new youth brand from Cadbury was to be Yowie. The set was created once again in the three weeks of closure at the beginning of January, and although it was very different in style to the rest of Cadbury World, it attracted very little attention. In part this may be due to the low effectiveness of the marketing of this brand in the UK, but visitor flow problems have never been encountered in this area, despite the fact that it would be possible to spend 12 minutes or more in the area.

## 2000: CadburyLand

Situated slightly away from the main building, adjacent to a renewed play area, CadburyLand is the largest new investment (£2m) since Cadbury World opened in August 1990. An advertising brochure describes it thus:

'Meet your favourite Cadbury Land characters... The CadburyLand show will take you on a fantastical journey into a magic chocolate land where no one is too old to join in the fun! Meet Dudley Sidebottom and his friends – Bouncy Button, Friendly Fudge and the rest of the gang in their crazy adventures in CadburyLand!'

The central part featuring the 'electronic pantomime' is complemented by the renovated play area, also branded CadburyLand, and by retail and catering units. The show runs for about six minutes and can hold about 80 visitors, while the 'pre-show' runs for three minutes before visitors enter the main auditorium. From an operations perspective, this micro-operation is decoupled from the main part of Cadbury World. It does, however, have a big impact on customers' perceptions of value, for two main reasons: it is new, up-to-date and enjoyed by most visitors, and it extends their dwell time on-site by up to an hour, to around three and a half hours. In the summer, outdoor entertainment (such as jugglers) is also provided, ice-cream and refreshment booths are opened, the playground is busy, and many families stay for four hours or more. Visitors are not tied to a specific time to enjoy the show, and generally the show opens and closes later than the main Cadbury World building, to fit with the standard practice of visiting the main exhibition first, before going on to CadburyLand.

## 2001: Cadbury Story and Making Liquid Chocolate

The Marie Cadbury Room had always presented operational difficulties, described earlier in this case. Not only were there problems with the flow of visitors, but the presentation was seen as dated and of diminishing value to them. The next area in the exhibition, known as the Making Chocolate area, which used video to explain the manufacturing processes for milk chocolate, was also in need of major refurbishment and updating. It was decided to rebuild both areas in order to provide a much higher standard of presentation and an enhanced visitor experience, and to lead in to the new Manufacturing set opened a year earlier. During a three-week shutdown ending on 20th January 2001, these two areas were replaced.

The new Cadbury Story is a small theatre-style room, decorated as if part of a historic industrial building. To the rear of the narrow stage is a large video projection screen, and there are smaller screens to each side. Above the proscenium arch is a video-animated head. All four videos work together to relate the interesting story of Cadbury at Bournville, presented by historic Cadbury family characters, played by actors. The room has 12 bench seats, 10 of which are long enough for seven average-size people each, but the front two benches only hold five each.

Visitors arrive from the earlier parts of the attraction, and wait in Bull Street. There is a new, large, high-level video monitor, based on the design of a large town clock, giving an indication of waiting time. For the final couple of minutes' wait, a video of John Cadbury talking is used to prepare visitors for the show. Eventually, the (original) double doors open, and the guide encourages everyone to enter, ensuring that the room is not overloaded. The doors remain open for only 80 seconds, and close automatically, after which the lights dim and the show begins immediately, lasting for seven and a half minutes. The theatre lights come on again, and all the visitors leave via the exit doors, taking about 50 seconds, although the doors are actually open for 70 seconds. They then close and the entry doors open, starting a further cycle. Movement of the visitors is supervised by the guide at all times, to ensure that the doors are not obstructed. The guide also clears away any litter in the few moments between shows.

The exit doors from the Cadbury Story lead directly into a second theatre, referred to as 'Making Liquid Chocolate'. Here there is a single large projected video screen on one long wall. Facing it are seven rows of low padded benches, each approximately five metres long, each of which comfortably seats about 12 average-sized people, although 15 children would sit comfortably on one. The six front benches are mechanised to shake or vibrate at a certain point in the show, to illustrate in an amusing way what is happening to the chocolate ingredients at certain points in the production process described in the video. The last row is reserved for people with medical conditions that require avoidance of rapid movement, and there is an audible warning of this. In addition, the show includes other surprise elements that impact the senses. From the opening of the entry doors, a loading time of about 80 seconds allows everyone to take their seats. The video presentation then lasts 7 minutes 20 seconds, after which exit doors open, allowing 80 seconds for visitors to leave, before closing automatically. Again, this exiting actually only takes about 50 seconds for a full theatre. The entry doors then open, starting the next cycle.

## 2001: Television adverts

The area just beyond Coronation Street, dedicated to showing adverts from four decades of television, was remodelled in 2001. Six linked large-screen videos dominate this area, and there are 10 large, round padded seats arranged either side of a winding pathway along which visitors move towards the Fantasy Factory. Although the display of videos lasts six and a half minutes, only about one in four visitors actually stops to watch any of this display. The area could comfortably hold about 20 people seated (two per seat), plus about 20 standing.

## Demonstration Area

Guiding around the Demonstration Area was discontinued soon after the opening of Cadabra in 1997. Customers are no longer grouped or guided here, but are free-flowing, past employees stationed in designated positions (see Figure 11.8). The sequence is now:

- At the entrance there is a 'Heroes' set photo-opportunity featuring an Elvis cut-out for photographs of customers' heads within an Elvis costume
- Liquid chocolate tasting – cups of chocolate served by one employee
- Employees making handmade chocolates on traditional marble slabs
- 'Nuts About Caramel' display for children – photo opportunities for parents
- Dipping chocolate – customers are invited have a go and dip a fudge centre into liquid chocolate
- Demonstration of a photo image being transferred to chocolate by computer technology
- Production of personalised plaques (for example, *Happy Birthday, Susie*) handwritten by skilled worker.

The whole area is sufficiently long for about 60 customers to stand and watch comfortably. The average customer has been observed to spend about five minutes here, although some move considerably slower as they become engrossed in the various activities.

## Parking

The number of spaces for coaches has not changed since the original opening, and has generally been adequate. An additional 50 car park spaces have now been made available by relocation of some employees' cars to an alternative site.

## Changes in demand patterns

Annual visitor numbers have remained at about half a million, and although there was a slight drop in 2000 to 480 000, this was balanced by the success of 2001 with 529 000. On the whole, such levels did not normally cause any severe operational problems, as Colin Samways explained:

'After all these developments over the last five years, we are now able to increase the customer flow throughout Cadbury World. At busy times we will now allow 80 customers through every 10 minutes, a big increase from the original capacity of 72, which had later been reduced to 68. We do get some build-up of queues at various bottlenecks, but our staff are now better at managing these to prevent them getting out of control. Customer satisfaction surveys indicate that the overall quality of the visit is high, and we continue to have very low levels of formal complaints about service.

**Figure 11.8 A sketch of Cadbury World (2001)**

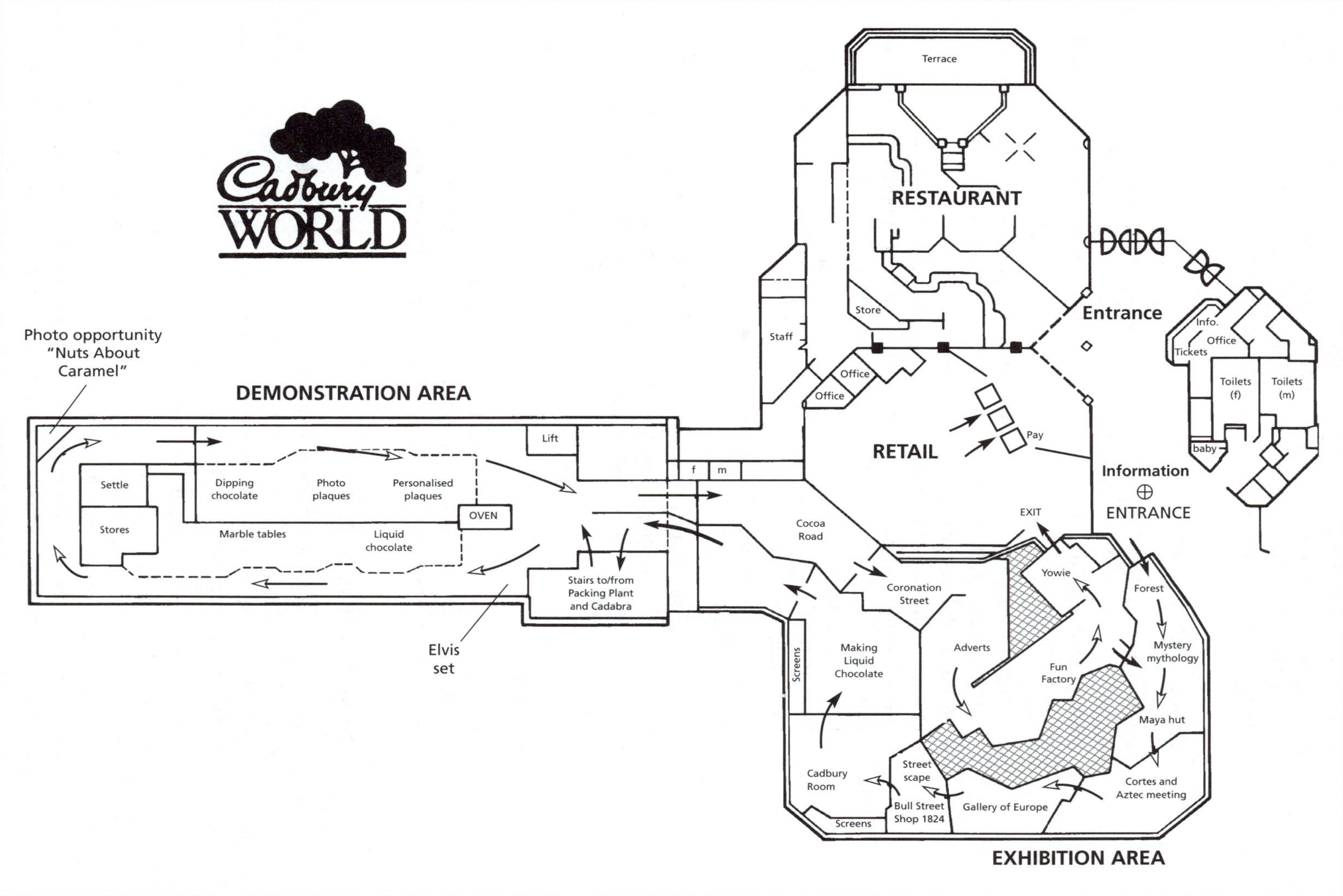

'There is much greater awareness of our reservation service, so we get far fewer people just turning up without a reservation. This has meant that we have been able to remove the need to staff a checkpoint on the entrance roadway, where we used to turn away some potential customers on busy days. That was never an easy job! We are also more flexible on the actual operating time. If we find that we have not cleared demand by the official closing time for admissions, we may allow an extra group to enter. We generally find that these late groups do go around a bit faster than average anyway, so we do not have to keep the staff on any later. Thus we get satisfied customers and the extra revenue, but without significant additional costs. There are many alternative things for the non-reserved customers to do whilst waiting for entry to the main attraction. Even if a family had to wait for several hours, as part of their ticket package they could visit CadburyLand and see the show there, go to the Museum, and let the children enjoy the excellent play equipment. Various catering options are also available. Outside the coldest months, we set up a marquee for the professional children's entertainers. Oh, and there's the shop too – everyone likes to go there for a while! In fact, all customers spend much more time on-site here than they did in the earlier years. On average, about two hours are spent within the main attraction, and a further two in the other facilities. Some families make almost a whole day of it now!

'The opening plan is crucial. We have found that demand is low on weekdays during school terms, and very high at most holiday periods except Christmas and the New Year. However, we are less busy at the Spring Bank Holiday, when there are lots of competing events. There is very low demand after three in the afternoon during school terms. We have gained an understanding of the typical patterns of variation in demand, so this has enabled us to cut costs in the hours when demand is expected to be lower. Thus we now have six different operating hours (shown for 2001 as Appendix 11.1). At the busiest times we allow admissions over an eight-hour span, but in quiet times this has been as little as four hours. One objective of this schedule is to avoid the fixed cost of staffing the attraction for periods with hardly any customers present, since it takes about 35 people to operate the main exhibition alone, plus contractors for catering and cleaning. There are also the considerable costs of heating and lighting the centre. By designing this better schedule, we have certainly been able to increase utilisation, whilst reducing the times when there are so few customers that they lose the sense of enjoyment of being with a crowd!'

## Questions relating to 2001

1 *Evaluate the design of Cadbury World in terms of the five operations objectives and the Four Vs (volume, variety, variation and visibility). What would this imply about the most appropriate choice(s) of process design to be used for the customer-processing operation?*

2 *What are the main elements of the service concept, and are these of equal importance to all customers? What trade-offs have had to be made in the design to deliver a quality service package to all of Cadbury World's customers.*

3 *What process type(s) was actually used in the original 1991 design, and how has that been changed during the 10 years of improvements?*

**4** *Draw process charts for the main exhibition, highlighting where the main changes in process design have been implemented over the 10 years of operation.*

**5** *Calculate the hourly capacities for each of the micro-operations described in the case. You should do this for 1991, 1995 and 2001. How has the change in process affected the position of bottlenecks, and how have these been managed?*

**6** *Calculate the utilisation of the attraction for both 1999 and 2001, based on the attendance figures given in the case. Why is the utilisation below 100 per cent even at busy times, and has it changed over the two-year period? How has productivity been affected by the changed schedule?*

**7** *What does queuing theory suggest about the average queue length before the bottleneck operation(s) identified above? You could test a queuing model for various admission rates from 68 to 80 per hour. What does this indicate about the management tasks of running Cadbury World on busy days?*

*Please note*: While we gratefully acknowledge Cadbury World's help in the development of this case study, we must ask students preparing answers *not* to contact Cadbury World and its managers for any further information. However, much more detail on the operation can be obtained by undertaking the tour as a normal paying visitor. You should not interfere with the other customers by attempting any unauthorised questioning or filming.

## Cadbury World: 2001 Schedule of admission times:

| Month/Day | January | February | March | April | May | June | July | August | September | October | November | December |
|---|---|---|---|---|---|---|---|---|---|---|---|---|
| Sunday | | | | | | | | | | | | ▦ |
| Monday | | | | | | | | | | | | C |
| Tuesday | | | C | | | | | | | C | | C |
| Wednesday | | | B | | | | | D | C | | ▦ | C |
| Thursday | | | B | | F | | | D | B | | B | C |
| Friday | A | B | B | | F | | | D | B | C | B | ▦ |
| Saturday | ▦ | B | B | | F | | F | D | B | C | B | ▦ |
| Sunday | ▦ | B | B | B | F | | D | F | B | C | | ▦ |
| Monday | B | E | C | C | D | | C | D | B | E | D | B |
| Tuesday | B | E | C | C | D | D | C | D | B | E | D | C |
| Wednesday | | E | B | C | B | B | D | D | B | F | | ▦ |
| Thursday | A | F | B | C | B | B | D | F | B | F | B | B |
| Friday | A | F | B | C | B | B | D | F | B | F | B | B |
| Saturday | | F | B | C | B | B | D | F | B | F | B | ▦ |
| Sunday | | D | B | C | B | B | D | D | B | F | | ▦ |
| Monday | B | D | C | D | C | C | C | D | B | E | C | C |
| Tuesday | B | D | C | D | C | C | C | D | B | E | C | C |
| Wednesday | | B | B | D | B | B | B | D | B | B | | ▦ |
| Thursday | | B | B | D | B | B | B | F | B | B | B | B |
| Friday | | B | B | D | B | B | B | F | B | B | B | B |
| Saturday | | ▦ | B | F | B | B | B | F | B | B | B | ▦ |
| Sunday | | ▦ | B | F | B | B | B | D | B | B | | ▦ |
| Monday | | B | C | E | C | C | C | D | B | C | C | D |
| Tuesday | | B | C | E | C | C | C | D | C | C | C | D |
| Wednesday | | | B | E | B | F | B | D | C | B | C | ▦ |
| Thursday | | A | B | E | B | | B | F | | B | C | |
| Friday | | A | B | E | B | | B | F | | B | B | |
| Saturday | | | B | E | B | | B | F | | B | B | |
| Sunday | | | B | E | B | | B | D | | B | | ▦ |
| Monday | | B | C | E | C | C | C | D | B | C | C | D |
| Tuesday | | B | C | E | C | C | C | D | C | C | C | D |
| Wednesday | | | B | D | B | F | B | D | C | B | | |
| Thursday | | A | B | B | B | | B | F | | B | C | |
| Friday | | | B | B | B | | B | F | | B | B | |
| Saturday | | | B | B | | | B | | | B | B | |
| Sunday | | | B | B | | | C | | | B | | |
| Monday | | | E | | | | C | | | | | |

Daily hours:

| | | Grey shaded area |
|---|---|---|
| Closed | | |
| 10:00 to 14:00 | A | |
| 10:00 to 15:00 | B | |
| 10:00 to 16:00 | C | |
| 09:30 to 16:30 | D | |
| 09:30 to 17:00 | E | |
| 09:00 to 17:00 | F | |

# The development of the Hovis Crusty White Loaf

Adrian Watt and Stuart Chambers

## Introduction

The Hovis brand and the British Bakeries (BB) company had evolved dramatically since 1997 to become the dominant force in the UK mass-market bread industry. Cathy, who had a history as a successful brand manager at a number of other major fast-moving consumer goods (FMCG) companies, had been asked to join the new BB Strategy and Marketing Team when it was formed at the end of 1997. She was to be brand manager of Hovis White Bread. The team was given the key objective of making Hovis the number one brand in white bread, a position it had always held in the brown sector. To achieve this it would mean growing its overall brand share from 12 per cent to at least 18 per cent of the UK market.

## Hovis – a history of baking bread

Hovis had a long and illustrious history in bread production as the leading bread brand in the UK. It began as Richard 'Stoney' Smith's patented wheatgerm flour in 1884 (renamed *Ho[minis]vis* [The strength of man], following a public competition in 1886). The flour was sold to craft bakers across the country, who were allowed to use the unique Hovis recipe to bake their wholemeal loaves. Only if the Hovis company's quality inspectors had approved the loaves baked to its recipe, using this special flour, could a baker display the Hovis sign over his shop. The brand image capitalised upon the nation's increasing interest in healthy nutritious food, the growing understanding of the value of wheatgerm (with its high iron content), and the use of the whole of the grain in flour and bread production. As a result, Hovis had continued to occupy an almost unique position in the minds of consumers, being synonymous with quality and healthy eating.

Following the Second World War, the Hovis company started manufacturing bread in its own bakeries, as it was realised that baking the bread as well as milling the flour would increase profits without compromising brand quality. This vertical integration and expansion was achieved throughout the 1950s and 1960s largely by the acquisition of independent bakeries, purchased at a number of key locations across the UK considered convenient for distribution nationwide. In 1967 the production of all Hovis, other-branded and own-label breads that the company manufactured was rationalised and amalgamated under the umbrella of British

Bakeries. However, the company continued to license the production of its Hovis branded loaves at craft bakeries.

Throughout the 1970s the success of Hovis brown bread continued. Meanwhile, the other brands within the BB portfolio also achieved great success. By the mid-1980s, bread consumption had reached a steady state for both market penetration and consumption volume, with market penetration reaching 99 per cent of people in the UK eating bread, and an average consumption of 1.5 loaves per household per week. Of the total market, just 30 per cent was brown bread, which was most popular with older consumers. White bread held the dominant 70 per cent market share, and was popular across the whole consumer spectrum, but most notably amongst younger consumers and children.

Circumstances in the late 1980s led the main board of BB, and its parent company RHM (Ranks Hovis McDougall) to examine their existing bread brand portfolio. It was evident that the only growing sector was in the *premium* white loaf market. The increasing depth of the economic recession and the high cost of the advertising needed to support a major brand meant that it was unrealistic to attempt to support more than one major bread brand. Hovis, with its extremely strong brand recognition, had a dominant share in its market. Yet this success was only in the *brown* bread segment, as Hovis had never produced a white loaf. The other major BB brand was Mother's Pride, a brand that had ridden high on the fashion and lifestyle image of the 1970s and 1980s, which was strongly associated with convenience, the standard by which all great developments are now judged and epitomised by white sliced bread! The decision on which of the two brands to support and build was not easy. However, following a detailed review of the dynamics of the marketplace, Hovis was chosen as the most suitable brand to focus support on, given the direction in which consumers were moving. Customers were becoming more conscious of the taste, health, nutritional benefit and value that premium quality loaves were offering. Thus in 1990, over 20 years after adopting the advertising slogan, '*Don't say brown, say Hovis*', BB launched its first ever Hovis white loaf: the Hovis Premium White Loaf (HPWL). Active marketing and advertising support was withdrawn from Mother's Pride in England and Wales, although it continued at a reduced level in Scotland and Northern Ireland.

## The Hovis white loaf

The launch of the HPWL was an immediate success, and it rapidly established itself with a significant market share. Hovis had successfully made the transition from a brown bread brand to a brand name associated with quality loaves of either colour. However, the brown bread image still held the strongest association in the mind of the consumer. The entry of competitors' brands such as Allied Bakeries' Kingsmill into the higher-margin premium end of the market, competing with and winning market share from the HPWL, led to the launch in 1997 of the Hovis Farmhouse in white and wholemeal varieties. This had a creamier texture and more yeasty flavour, and was favoured by adults rather than child consumers.

Somehow, during the development phase of the Hovis Farmhouse, Kingsmill learnt of the planned launch and pre-empted it by launching Kingsmill Gold one week before the Hovis Farmhouse launch. The Kingsmill loaf was soft, without the yeasty flavour, and so appealed more to children, giving it a much broader market. In addition, although still weighing 800g, it was baked in a larger tin to make it appear bigger and was very well presented in shiny gold packaging. Kingsmill Gold strongly outperformed the Hovis Farmhouse, taking a larger market share. As a result, the Hovis Farmhouse was relaunched a year later in a modified style with new packaging and baked in a larger tin. Immediately the relaunched loaf met with great success and soon outsold Kingsmill Gold. As an additional holding measure before a wider examination of its white bread portfolio, Hovis decided to launch the Square Cut Premium White Loaf (SCPWL). This is a medium-sliced, high-sided loaf, with a moister crumb than HPWL, baked in a lidded tin to give a flat top and hence rectangular cross-section. Its market share has grown steadily since its launch to become the best-selling loaf in the UK.

## Planning the future

After the launch of Hovis Farmhouse, it was evident that if Hovis was going to become dominant in the bread market it would need to achieve further substantial growth in the white bread sector. The question was whether this could be achieved by growing the existing brands in their present markets, or through new product development (NPD). If it was to be the latter, what form should the product take and what target market segment should it be aimed at? Deciding on, and then recommending, the project plan was Cathy's first task. She would then be responsible for its implementation, and was required to grow the Hovis market share as quickly and profitably as possible. In order to achieve this, her team was given a budget of £3 million to cover: all market research; product, process and packaging research and development; the acquisition of equipment; adaptation of the production lines; and sundry additional capital expenditure.

Cathy outlined the overall strategy behind achieving the objectives set for the new product: 'We really wanted to develop a product that would give us a sustainable long-term competitive advantage in the bread market.' She explained that this meant the new features should satisfy customer needs and requirements in ways not previously achieved. This required truly innovative solutions that would provide a unique selling point (USP). At the time, competition was driven by sales volume rather than by margin. There was very little differentiation between bread brands, as supermarkets fighting for customers drove down prices, often selling basic staple products such as bread and milk below cost price (an average 58p for an 800g loaf). They demanded promotions such as cut-price offers, or even a BOGOF (Buy One Get One Free!). This meant that margins were always extremely tight, with the brand leader at any one time being the one on special offer, with the top position switching as one brand came off promotion and another went on. This meant that far from long-term competitive advantages being obtained, the company could suffer from margins being cut to below profitable levels, while production schedules would be disrupted as volumes fluctuated dramatically within short periods of time.

'At Hovis, we wanted to gain a competitive advantage in the product design, with a specification and production techniques that couldn't be copied easily by the competitors. This would enable us to avoid having to compete on price, helping us maintain our retail price and margins, and differentiating our offering by competing on true product advantages.'

## Market analysis

Cathy's first action was to commission additional market research to supplement the data that the Hovis team regularly collected on the bread market. The aim was to understand all aspects of the market, including consumers' current buying patterns to see how the market was moving and how well all its segments were served. A series of taste tests were used to explore customers' perceptions and preferences for different types and characteristics of bread, thereby identifying potential profitable gaps in the market that Hovis could fill. Cathy explained:

'Before the design process could begin in earnest, it was vital for us to really understand the customer and what they wanted, so that we could design a product that satisfied their needs.'

The market analysis results were very revealing. They confirmed the 70:30 percentage split between white and brown bread, and also that premium white bread was by far the biggest bread sector at 27 per cent. It showed that customers primarily selected their ideal bread on taste, and most had clear preferences for the type of bread they wanted. They also demanded good value for money. There were four distinct taste clusters in white bread; Rustic, Crusty, Functional and Fodder. The second largest segment, Crusty, represented 30 per cent of the population's preference (compared with 32 per cent for the Rustic), and this sector was dominated by In-store Bakeries (ISB) and Craft Bakers (CB). This was also the only segment in which Hovis was not represented across its brand portfolio. The qualitative research indicated that the customers' perception of the ultimate bread was *real bread fresh from the bakers* in the form of a loaf with a soft, moist crumb, a yeasty flavour and a crisp crust. The main problem with real crusty loaves made at ISBs or CBs is that they had a very limited shelf life of one to two days, and lacked the convenience of being ready sliced. At the same time, although Crusty and Rustic loaves were by far the most significant segments in terms of the customers' taste preference, when it came to actually purchasing bread there was a complete reversal, with 70 per cent of people making their actual purchasing decisions based on value and functionality.

The previous substantial episode of rapid growth within the bread market had been due to the development of ISBs. However, by 1998 this growth had slowed, and the segment was now relatively static. Sales of ISB loaves were greatest at the weekend and significantly lower at the start of the week, despite relatively level bread usage throughout the week. This indicated that families were more inclined to purchase long-life value and functional loaves for weekday use, but favoured a short-life ISB loaf for taste and a treat at the weekend. This meant that there was an opportunity to grow the market by getting consumers to purchase premium loaves based on flavour, crustiness *and* an extended shelf life.

From these results, Cathy decided that there was a major opportunity to exploit the crusty premium white loaf sector within the Hovis portfolio. Cathy concluded:

'This gave Hovis a major marketing opportunity and provided the basis for the product concept: a premium pre-sliced crusty white loaf that lasted for up to four days, and therefore would last for most of the working week.'

## The problem

Why was this potentially lucrative market not already being served by Hovis or by its competitors? Strategically, was this a market sector that Hovis wanted to be in? If so, was it technically one that BB had the core competences to enter and dominate? The answers were simple. Strategically, it was important for Hovis to enter this segment if it was to achieve its objectives of dominating both the white and brown bread market, but the technical solutions were not nearly so easy to solve. Cathy was certain that BB had the skills and manufacturing capability to produce a loaf that met all the technical requirements. However, there are two main problems faced by all bread producers in maintaining the freshness of their bread. Firstly, loaves dry out as moisture is lost to the atmosphere, and this is a non-reversible process. Secondly, bread goes stale because of a chemical reaction, with starch converting from one form to another, accompanied by a change in flavour and texture. Existing baking and packaging processes and technologies had largely solved these problems, maintaining moistness and preventing staleness for up to five days. However, a third problem would be maintaining the crusty nature of the loaf (the primary reason for the consumers' purchase) for the required four days. This had never been solved before, and hence all crusty loaves had short shelf lives, and therefore remained the preserve of the ISB and CB.

## Forming the team

Once the marketing opportunity had been defined, the project team was formalised. Cathy explained

'I thought it was important to have a fully cross-functional team to cover all the aspects of the project from design to launch. I wanted them involved right from the start so that we could all consider every aspect of the development, and any implications of the problems and design suggestions.'

A core NPD (new product development) team comprised: BB skilled craft bakers, food scientists, technical and engineering staff from BB and RHM Technical (RHMT), production and marketing representatives, all of whom were involved throughout the project. Beyond the core team, further parties became involved as their specific skills were needed. These included: outside marketing research agencies; the Hovis advertising agency; brainstorming facilitators; food flavour research analysts; the production, research and development departments from some of the BB manufacturing plants where the loaves would be manufactured; packaging experts; food scientists, and finance and sales representatives. Thus the team was not purely marketing-led, but had a strong operations and technical involvement.

RHMT comprised a wide range of experts concerned with all aspects of food science, production and packing facilities. Cathy commented:

'RHMT is a very valuable resource. They are available to work with all companies within the RHM group, and provide a pool of expertise and equipment that we couldn't possibly have permanently based in Hovis.'

They also have access to small-scale production facilities, which complement the BB NPD craft baking team, along with a detailed knowledge of baking, production and equipment on an actual full manufacturing scale.

## Devising the concept and identifying the problems

In January 1998, the full team held their first major meeting. The overall brief had simply been to increase the Hovis market share from 12 per cent to 18 per cent, and from the general marketing data it was obvious that this meant increasing their white bread share. Detailed market research identified the most appropriate market segment to enter and the general concept of the type of product that should be developed to meet that segment's needs. The product concept was for a premium pre-sliced white loaf that lasted up to four days. Cathy explained: 'We now needed to refine the concept and determine how to translate the initial idea into an actual product.' The first meeting was primarily a brainstorming session led by skilled facilitators.

'It was very fruitful as everyone contributed to all areas of the discussion, and as no limits were imposed or any ideas rejected out of hand. All contributions were considered and discussed further.'

It also enabled the technical and production teams to discuss and conceive innovative solutions for the use, modification and introduction of new equipment beyond the simple adaptation of existing equipment. As Cathy remarked:

'Some of the more outrageous ideas formed the basis for the final solutions! A good example was that, when considering how to maintain the moisture in the loaf, someone mentioned how currants in a currant bun act as a source of moisture, rather like water capsules in the dough. They developed this idea further, which helped the technical team to gain a better understanding of the baking process and techniques of moisture retention, and to derive a solution to the problem.'

Describing this first session, which involved the entire NPD team and lasted the whole day, Cathy continued:

'The session really helped us to focus on our objectives and finalise a firm concept of what we wanted to achieve, and gave us new angles from which to look at the problem. We wanted to produce a pre-sliced, long-life wrapped sliced loaf with a crusty texture and flavour, rather than a primarily craft-baked loaf that was cut and would only last two days. This gave us a clear perspective on the types of problems we would encounter, their priority, and how to go about tackling and solving them. At the same time, we allowed the teams to be very flexible in how they achieved this. A large number and a wide range of scenarios emerged from the brainstorming session, all of which needed to be investigated and turned into detailed specifications to actually make the product. Initially this was the task for RHMT, working with our craft bakers to test and develop in their trial bakery. We needed to test the ideas against a number of criteria; primarily, was it feasible? Did the idea solve the problem, enabling us to make a product that met the specification, and did we as a company have the skills, capacity and resources to achieve it? This process took us nearly three months!'

## Solving the problem

From the initial brainstorming and the RHMT follow-up work, it became apparent that in order to produce a white crusty loaf and keep it crusty, there would be three aspects of the production and packaging process that required attention and innovative development. These were: the recipe and ingredients; the production process itself (particularly the proving and baking process); and the packaging and storage conditions needed to keep the bread fresh and crusty for four days. To get the recipe correct and produce a crusty loaf, each one of the ingredients had be selected for its baking properties, particularly the types and grades of flour, their characteristics and gluten content. New process techniques, technology and equipment would be required to enable the proving and baking process to produce crusty loaves, and then new high-speed packing techniques would be needed that could use the new types of packaging. It was also necessary to develop visually striking packaging for the point-of-sale presentation to attract customer attention, and produce innovative technical developments for the packaging to maintain the correct combination of moistness and crustiness of the loaf.

At every stage of the product and the production development it was important to balance the acceptability of the solution with the risks, financially and operationally, of the consequences of any failures. At the extremes, this could entail either not adopting a particular innovation opportunity, and hence failing to fully match the agreed product concept, or the final product being too difficult and/or uneconomic to produce. Either scenario could lead to the development being a commercial failure.

In order to identify and source suitable ingredients, to develop recipes and technical solutions and to find new equipment and packaging, it was necessary to involve companies that would be acceptable to RHM under its usual terms of supplier selection. These companies would also have to be willing to, and capable of, building a long-term relationship with BB, and of working in partnership and as part of the team in order to solve the various problems. This was not easy to achieve, and eventually RHM had to go to Germany to find a company that was both willing and capable of working with it to develop the packaging solution.

## The NPD process and teamwork

The core NPD team worked closely with the production and management teams at selected Hovis baking sites within BB. Cathy described the process:

'We wanted to ensure the maximum amount of contact and communication between all the members of the project team. Formal meetings involving all the team members were held once a month, with weekly follow-up meetings to discuss problems and check on progress. All information was shared either in letters, e-mails, phone calls, dialogue, etc. Face-to-face encounters with continuous informal discussions and 'corridor meetings' were encouraged, so that everyone knew what was going on and could share ideas and work out solutions more quickly. We found that as the NPD core team was developing ideas and using the site production teams as a sounding board, they would all discuss the pros and cons, and a constructive debate would ensue. Thus they never spent long developing complex theoretical solutions only to realise that they were impractical on a mass-production scale. As each stage of the recipe and manufacturing process was developed, plant trials were conducted to confirm they worked and to fine-tune the production process. This also ensured that the bakeries' expertise and capabilities were always used to the full extent and that they also had time to develop their own production systems.

'It was during these development stages that we really managed to get complete staff buy-in. At every step, we involved the actual operators at the bakery plants; after all, they knew their part of the job better than anyone else, and so could really help by giving ideas and suggestions for improvements and implementation. Initially, some people at a variety of levels were quite shocked about us talking directly to the shop-floor employees, but as these staff were bought into the project, they too were really keen to make it work.'

A good example of this involvement was in the development of the automated bagging process. As the loaves reached the end of the production line after the slicing process, they were to be packed in unique hybrid paper/plastic bags, the development of which is described later. Each bag was inflated and pulled over the loaf, tied tight to keep the sliced loaf together, with enough of the bag spare to ensure that it was tied securely, but not with too much surplus which would present difficulties when packing loaves into the plastic transportation crates. Obviously, running an entirely new combination paper/plastic bag on equipment designed to run only plastic bags presented technical difficulties. However, the suggestions and efforts of bakery line staff, working closely with the site engineers the main project engineers and the suppliers ensured success. It was an iterative process of virtually weekly experiments at the plant, with RHMT running trials on the packaging and machine modification, listening to the suggestions from the packaging staff, going away to make changes and coming back the following week to try the new design. This really helped speed up the process of solving problems and implementing solutions.

The debrief review meeting of each production trial was chaired by the Bakery Manager. This ensured that the lead bakery owned the project as much as the core NPD team. The overall effect of this close involvement of all key personnel was to minimise any adverse effects of hierarchy and internal politics. It ensured that everyone understood that the project was of benefit to all at BB, and not just to a single individual.

## Recipe and technological innovation

A great deal of effort was expended on perfecting the recipe for the new loaf. New and specific ingredients and recipe combinations were selected and trialled so that the flavour, moisture and crustiness of the loaf were exactly those required. It was important to obtain proprietary ingredients if possible, with a unique recipe that competitors couldn't simply discover and copy, to help ensure the long-term competitive advantage of the product.

Technologically there were two major sets of innovation. The first was in the proving and baking process. This is still so confidential that it is discussed only on a need-to-know basis. It was important to ensure that the production process helped lock moisture and lightness into the loaf, and then produced a baked product that was crusty and still internally moist. A variety of mixing techniques was investigated to produce a dough that had the right consistency and moisture. The proving process is where the dough is allowed to rise, and this ensures the right level of lightness and the moistness of the loaves' internal structure. The baking process is on a continuous production line passing through oven zones set to different temperatures. The temperatures and the speed at which the loaves pass through the ovens determines how well baked the loaf is, particularly with regard to its internal moisture and external crustiness. A considerable amount of time and effort was spent perfecting these parts of the process to give the desired finished product, and also to ensure that the result could be achieved on the existing production lines, after making any necessary modifications and adjustments.

The other major innovation was the packaging. Having created a loaf that was crusty on the outside and moist on the inside, it was important that it was kept that way. If the packaging was made of the usual polythene, the loaf would be kept moist, but the crusty texture would be lost after a day. If the packaging was just paper, the loaf would dry out too quickly. Marketing analysis also showed that using paper in the packaging was essential for the presentation, giving the customer the perception of a premium loaf, and a transparent plastic top was important so that customers could see the primary sales feature of the crusty top. Thus the packaging had to be a combination of paper for the lower half and plastic for the top. Perforating the plastic allowed the correct ventilation in the desired areas, allowing some controlled loss of excess moisture to prevent the loaf from going soggy and therefore maintaining the crustiness, but not so much that the entire loaf would dry out. The bag also had to be strong and tight enough to hold the loaf together, otherwise it would open up and be poorly presented, and the slices would dry out.

Having designed the dual component packaging concept, the first technical challenge was to get the dual bag to run at full speed on a plant designed to run polythene bag only. This was eventually solved by selecting a stiffer form of plastic with physical properties more similar to the paper. The second challenge was to stick the two materials together. This was especially difficult as the bag had perfor-ations, which meant that the glue could unintentionally stick the bag's sides together so that it could not be opened to wrap the loaf. Also, all the bags in a stack could stick together! Cathy recalled that even after the product launch, it was found that the glue bond could fail when consumers stored loaves in their freezers, so the bags fell apart as they took the loaves out. 'As soon as we started to get complaints from consumers about this, we took action and searched for a more suitable glue.'

This range of very complex problems was solved by the close collaboration of the core and extended teams, the production staff and the packaging and equipment suppliers, all of whom had to develop new equipment and techniques. As the various team members worked together, which allowed them to overcome the R&D problems simultaneously rather than in a sequential manner, the project continued at good speed.

Cathy summarised the development process:

'Through the NPD process we had started from a clear strategic objective which gave us a general but vague concept. We then clarified and refined this concept, filtering a vast array of suggestions and selecting the best possible ones. These gave us technological and operational procedures and innovations that helped us to achieve our aims and which met all our criteria. The result was a loaf that was, and still is, vastly superior to anything our competitors can offer. This has given us a significant competitive advantage in the marketplace.'

## Production

A critical stage in the NPD process was ensuring that the loaves could be manufactured within the current production facilities, with the addition of any modifications that were required for this product. The basic production layout consisted of a typical food production line. First there was the recipe mixing room, from which batches of ingredients were added to the mixer. The mixer blended the ingredients according to the three key criteria of moisture, temperature and the energy used to mix the dough (which gave a measure of the elasticity in the mix). The dough was then added to a hopper from which it was automatically measured out into the baking tins. The tins were carried on a conveyor belt into the 'prover' where the dough was allowed to rise, before going into a sequence of oven zones at a range of temperatures. After baking was complete, the loaves were cooled, sliced, packed and put into crates to be loaded onto lorries for distribution.

The new loaves had to be manufactured on this production line with the minimum of alterations. It was important that the line was flexible enough to accommodate the range of products, with the minimum of set-up time to ensure that product changeovers could be fast. BB already had the essential capabilities to produce high-quality loaves with a considerable degree of flexibility to enable them to change the type of loaves being manufactured. Working as part of the NPD team, the plant operations staff ensured that the new loaf could be produced on the existing line. In some cases this was simply a matter of feeding the new recipe information into the existing database and menu from which it could be selected, such as for the weighing equipment. In other cases, it meant ascertaining the optimum production parameters, and adjusting the production programming or sequences to fit this – such as for the actual mixing process and in particular the baking process as the loaves moved through the oven. In some cases additional process steps had to be added which only applied to the new loaf. Finally, at specific parts of the process, significant equipment modifications or the purchase of new equipment was essential to cope with the new production or packaging. This included the wrapping of the loaves as they came off the production line.

Thus from a production perspective, working closely with the members of the NPD team was an essential part of integrating the manufacture of the new loaf into the existing production system, and ensuring that the process was flexible enough to cope with the strategic requirements. Due to the high standards of Hovis' existing operational processes and expertise and the rigorous work of the team, this was managed successfully.

## The product launch briefings

As the technical problems were nearing solutions, the launch procedures were put into place with internal and external briefings. The Avonmouth bakery (near Bristol) had been the main development site, so many people at the site already knew about the new loaf. However, three other plants would also be involved in the production, so presentations and training were held at each site for all the relevant staff. These were given by all members of the team, involving representatives from Marketing and RHMT, as well as from the Avonmouth bakery staff. They explained the strategy and commercial importance of the crusty loaf to Hovis, BB and RHM, as well as the technical breakthroughs the project had developed, the forthcoming launch plans and the changes to the production processes.

At about the same time as the production briefings, the sales team started to approach the supermarket retailers. The supermarket buyers usually demanded three months' notice before a product launch to give them sufficient time to incorporate it into their retail and logistic systems and to allocate the appropriate shelf space. The sales presentations detailed the market research and analysis that underpinned the decision to produce a crusty loaf, as well as details of the planned substantial pre- and post-launch advertising and promotional support. However, Hovis was cautious about providing too much information too early, after the experience with Kingsmill Gold. The retailers were extremely impressed with the brand proposition, market analysis and predicted sales profiles, and listings rapidly followed.

The objective for the Hovis Crusty promotional strategy was to try to break away from competing on price and BOGOF promotions, and to compete on the product benefit: 'A real style loaf that kept crusty for up to four days'. The product launch was to reflect this approach. The recommended retail price was 69p, 10p above the standard price for a premium white sliced 800g loaf. However, at launch a 10p discount was given to equate the price to standard loaves, and to encourage customers to trial the Hovis Crusty without feeling they were risking money by purchasing it.

Research into consumer behaviour had shown that the average time spent browsing the supermarket bread shelves was around three seconds, so Cathy believed it was important to ensure a strong visual display to attract customer attention. This was achieved using gondola ends as well as special in-store point-of-sale units, shelf and window displays, and in-store advertisements and promotional visuals. It was all backed up by a very strong nationwide television and printed media advertising campaign. The total launch advertising spend was £2.4 million, with plans to increase this to £5 million for the full 12 months.

## The launch

In the two months prior to the launch a number of final details were completed. The production process and baking parameters were confirmed and final trial production runs were conducted. New equipment was installed, and modifications to existing machinery completed. The packaging designs were approved, and print runs scheduled. Forecasts and provisional production schedules were drawn up and integrated with existing product plans. These would be confirmed just prior to the launch, and thereafter adjusted according to the actual demand. Orders for the quantity and delivery dates for raw ingredients were issued, ensuring sufficient flexibility to adjust these if necessary. Logistic and delivery plans were finalised. Avonmouth and Nottingham were to be the two bakeries that would manufacture the loaves initially. Byfleet and Wigan would come on-stream later when greater capacity was required (this was anticipated to be three to six months post-launch). This required additional planning and capital expenditure, and was only due to occur when the launch review could quantify the success and provide more accurate forecasts of demand.

Two weeks before the launch, the production lines tested the final set-up procedures. Raw ingredients and packaging arrived just before the launch date. On 27th June 1999, 24 hours before the launch, the lines went into full-scale production. Crates of bread were loaded onto lorries which, once full, rolled onto the roads heading for stores nationwide. By 9 a.m. on 28th June 1999 the supermarkets opened their doors and the Hovis Crusty loaf went on sale to the public.

## Fifteen months later

The success of the Hovis Crusty white loaf was immediate, with demand reaching the anticipated six-month level after just one month – before capacity could be increased fully to meet it. As demand outstripped supply, the increased supermarket orders could not all be met in full, although all the anticipated and planned orders were completed. However, this had a fortunate side effect: some of the large supermarket retailers had initially tried to impose the standard lower retail price; now, because consumer demand was so high, Hovis was able to resist any pressures to cut the supply price. By the time the retailers had fully accepted these higher prices, Hovis had increased capacity to meet the elevated demand. Its ability to resist the pressure to cut prices was purely the result of the product being of such high quality that it was unique and clearly differentiated. Thus it enabled Hovis to break out of the vicious circle of having to compete on low price and promotional offers. Having achieved all its sales targets in the first year, Hovis Crusty has continued to hold its market share despite the entry of competitor offerings into the market.

The new loaf met all the technical and marketing specifications. Subsequently, there were follow-up launches of brown versions and crusty rolls, which served to maintain the consumers' interest and the high profile of the brand, whilst capitalising on the momentum of the initial launch. The marketing team examined their complete bread portfolio, and an improved, revamped range was launched in June 2001. A year after the launch, Hovis Crusty was selling 650 000 loaves per week and had a three per cent market share. Market research indicated high customer satisfaction and an extremely high customer repeat purchase rate.

As a recognition of the truly innovative nature of the packaging design, Hovis (on behalf of British Bakeries and its suppliers, who had worked so closely with the company), won 'Packaging of The Year' prize from the Packaging Industry for its innovation. It was also awarded two Silver Stars for 'Design Excellence and Technical Innovation' at the Star Pack Awards Ceremony, both in 2000. In addition, this success has helped to foster further innovation, with retailers now looking to British Bakeries to lead bread market development.

Hovis was now the overall dominant brand in both the brown and white bread market segments. After the growth achieved from the introduction of the Hovis Crusty, the Square Cut White (soft regular white) grew to being the top-selling loaf in the country. Hovis also introduced the first non-price promotional activity on regular white bread in 2000 with an on-pack competition across the white bread range. These activities had grown the value of the white bread sector, as sales moved from low-priced lines to premium brands. Hovis consistently outperformed Kingsmill, and its market share rose from 12 per cent to 18 per cent. Cathy's job was now complete, and she had really enjoyed working with such an enthusiastic and committed team, which extended to include the whole company. She and the rest of the team had achieved all the objectives they had been set.

A chronology of the key events in the launch and market development of Hovis Crusty is given in Appendix 12.1.

## Questions

1 *What were the main performance objectives for the Hovis Crusty loaf concept, and how did these differ from those for existing RHM white breads?*

2 *To what extent did the development follow any of the conventional screening 'funnel' approaches to arrive at the final concept and package design?*

3 *Summarise the main elements of the design approach taken by Cathy and her team for the development of Hovis Crusty. What were the advantages and risks of this approach?*

4 *How would you describe the organisation structure used for this development project?*

5 *What impact, if any, would the introduction of Hovis Crusty have had on the volume and variety characteristics of a BB bakery operation?*

## Appendix 12.1

### Key events in the launch and further development of Hovis Crusty

| | |
|---|---|
| January 1998 | Started market research and concept development work |
| June 1999 | Launched Hovis Crusty White: sliced and unsliced |
| | Supporting activities: |
| | Advertising on TV from late July to October 1999 |
| | First six weeks (June/July/August): 10p off introductory price in main retailers (puts at equal price to in-store bakery crusty breads) |
| | Second site merchandising |
| | Sainsbury's supermarkets link Hovis Crusty to delicatessen purchases. |
| January 2000 | Launched Hovis Crusty Golden Brown |
| January 2000 | Upgraded to better bags that rip less when taken out of freezer |
| April–May 2000 | Competitor entries: Rathbones, Harvestime, Kingsmill |
| May–June 2000 | Hovis ran on-pack coupon for 10p off next purchase |
| January 2001 | Hovis Crusty bread made 'even crustier' |
| June 2001 | Launched Hovis Crusty rolls |

# Campaign planning for 'Red Nose Day'

© Alan Harrison and Jane Pavitt

## ● Introduction

Comic Relief is a charity 'seriously committed to helping end poverty and social injustice in the UK and the poorest countries in the world'. The charity was launched from the Safawa refugee camp in Sudan, on Christmas Day 1985, in response to growing needs in the UK and Africa. Jane Tewson, Richard Curtis and leading figures in the comedy world set it up. The aim was to take a fresh and fun approach to fundraising and, through events like Red Nose Day, inspire those who hadn't previously been interested in 'charity' to get involved.

It began with a few live events, drawing support from across the comedy community until the first Red Nose Day, in 1988, which instituted the unique union of comedy and charity on national television. The first big night of television was presented by Lenny Henry, Griff Rhys Jones and Jonathan Ross, and raised more than £15 million.

Since then the organisation has gone on to raise over £228 million. There have been eight Red Nose Days so far and the most recent, in March 2001, raised more than £54 million and money is still coming in (see Figure 13.1).

Comic Relief aims to enable the poorest and most vulnerable people to develop the strength and skills they need to solve their problems themselves, and to develop long-term solutions. In Africa, it has made more than 1200 grants to projects making long-term changes to the profound poverty and injustices people experience there. From educational schemes for disabled children in Tanzania, to support for widows of the Rwandan genocide, Comic Relief cash is hard at work in

**Figure 13.1  Money raised by Red Nose Day (1988–2001)**

*There have been 8 Red Nose Days*

1988 - *£15.8 million*
1989 - *£26.9 million*
1991 - *£20.3 million*
1993 - *£18 million*
1995 - *£22 million +*
1997 - *£27.1 million +*
1999 - *£35 million +*
2001 - *£49 million +*

over 40 African countries. In the UK, Comic Relief has made over 4000 grants to projects in England, Northern Ireland, Scotland and Wales over the last 15 years. The money is currently helping projects such as a refuge in Gwynedd for women and children fleeing violence at home, a project in Antrim which reaches out to young drug and alcohol users, a programme in Fife providing care and support for people infected with, or affected by, HIV, and a project in Exeter helping vulnerable older people take control of their lives.

## The charity

Comic Relief is the operating name of Charity Projects, which is a company limited by guarantee and a registered charity. The company has the approval of the Charity Commission to use the name 'Comic Relief' as an operating name of the charity. Charities have only limited powers to carry on trading activities and many charities therefore have subsidiary companies to undertake activities that they cannot. Comic Relief Limited is a trading company owned by the charity.

The trading company pays its entire profits up to the charity in a tax-efficient way. The board of trustees meets eight times a year and is the main policy-making body of Comic Relief, having the power to take strategic and management decisions relating to the company in the same way as the board of directors of a commercial company, but with the additional responsibilities of charity trustees.

The trustees are responsible for distributing the grant funds of Comic Relief. This is done with the assistance of expert committees (UK and Africa Grants Committees). Through these committees and the executive, the trustees are in a position to take informed decisions on making grants.

## Managing the event

Planning and controlling the Red Nose Day event, which is now held in March every two years, is a major operations challenge. Behind the scenes a massive amount of organisation and planning goes into putting together the many events that make up this unique occasion.

For the core campaign planning process there is an Operational Management Group, which includes all managers within the organisation and BBC producers, who are included in all stages of the process to help their planning. A 'huge debrief process' starts after each Red Nose Day (RND), before the process of planning for the next event begins. The time plan for each campaign is based on experience from previous years. The team already knows that the public launch date when the BBC media and trails are launched will be the first week in February – five weeks before RND. Activity will then visibly increase up to the live seven-hour TV show on BBC One. The planning process must work backwards from that key date. The next RND will be on 14th March 2003. The next section gives an overview of the main activities that are involved, illustrated with comments from Carolynne Evans, National Fundraising Manager, Terry Mills, Promotions and Merchandise Manager and Jack Lundie, Internet Manager.

## Key Red Nose Day activities

There are many activities involved in planning for a Red Nose Day. The main ones include the following:

1 The theme
2 TV production
3 Public fundraising
4 Internet and telephone fundraising
5 Merchandising and corporate partnerships
6 Building the website
7 Press and PR planning
8 Artist/celebrity liaison
9 Staff and recruitment

### The theme

Ideally Comic Relief comes up with a theme early on, such as the *Say Pants to Poverty* theme of 2001, and then the planning of other activities should flow – but this does not always happen!

'There is a cut-off date for the theme, otherwise, for example, we can't get merchandise produced and into the shops for sale in time. There is also a contingency plan because you've got to think what if we don't have a theme?

'The theme is important to the design of merchandise, but we know from experience the theme can take longer than desired because you've got to have something that is really cutting edge. But if you're deciding 18 months in advance, what was really cool and trendy then may not be by RND! We run a parallel strategy where we design a T-shirt, which is general but will fit, so if we don't get a specific theme, we have a design that can go into production.'

The theme is central to the campaign and to the marketing mix as a whole, as it will have an impact on the design of many items, such as the fundraising packs and pre-recorded TV trailers or programmes, not just merchandising.

### TV production

TV is planned very closely with the BBC who produce the live television show. The BBC team must consider production and content for many different TV productions such as a variety of campaign trails, the launch programme, pre-recorded light entertainment programmes and documentaries, as well as the seven-hour live TV show itself.

To produce documentaries for broadcast, the Comic Relief Grants Team works closely with a separate BBC documentary team in liaison with the production team working on the live show. The planning starts about 18 months prior to RND with a shortlist of issues to cover and they start to look for suitable stories which represent projects both in the UK and in Africa. The production team then plan and look at the area before they cast the crew or approach a celebrity to do the shoot. They will film pieces to make 10-minute documentaries, two and five-minute trailers and undertake separate commissions for 50-minute documentaries. This filming can take place up to six months prior to RND.

'We often get calls saying there's a TV programme being recorded tomorrow, which will be shown during the campaign, and can we get T-shirts there so the children or celebrities are seen in our T-shirts? We have to respond and get some printed up so you need to be flexible. If you get the opportunity to shoot a picture with a celebrity you send 50 red noses or some T-shirts by DHL and you get a fantastic PR shot.'

## Public fundraising

The Fundraising Team starts developing education themes and ideas for fundraising packs about 18 months prior to the event. Packs must go to print over Christmas before RND. Comic Relief produces a variety of packs to suit different audiences, such as nurseries, schools, universities, sports and leisure groups, youth groups and people at work, as well as a generic pack. The specific RND packs and the ongoing education pack are proactive in style to develop active thinking in givers and to encourage involvement. Fundraising packs hit doorsteps at the launch of the campaign in early February. The public can apply for packs via the Internet or premium rate telephone lines, which pay for the cost of packing and mailing, and they are encouraged to do this through trailers on the BBC.

## Internet and telephone fundraising

Corporate partnerships are developed with a wide variety of organisations to provide the services and resources required to maintain and operate areas of the event such as 'donation logistics'. Agreements are made with credit card companies, banks and building societies for online transactions and telephone donations. Companies such as BT and Cisco Systems provide equipment to enable telephone and online donations. Other organisations provide facilities and volunteer staff to operate call centres, for example Yellow Pages provided one of upwards of 60 such centres, which between them handled in the region of 760 000 telephone calls on the night.

'The thing to say around functionality that depends on corporate relationships is that "sign-off" is something you have to plan around. The bigger the partner, the longer the sign-off because it has to go across more desks. If things happen late in the day then we have to ask people to suspend the normal sign-off process in order to secure the necessary approval.

'The sensitive network of relationships is something you want to plan. So when the corporate sponsorship team go in they know that Internet is something they should talk about in their formative discussions. You need to build flexibility into your plan so there are things you can put in place early, such as relationships, sorting out hardware, equipment and legal requirements.'

## Merchandising and corporate partnerships

There are a number of key merchandising products including the Red Nose (see Figure 13.2), the Clothes Nose (a buttonhole badge), the Car Nose and the T-shirt, as well as books and a pop single that are produced for each event.

**Figure 13.2**

'The nose is the one thing people want to buy as it demonstrates a visual sign of support so we try to make that as exciting as we can within the constraints of the corporate budget we've got, whilst still retailing for £1 and getting the maximum donation possible on each item.'

The Comic Relief logo is also licensed for use by certain partner organisations on products, particularly fast-moving consumer goods (FMCG) such as Mr Kipling cakes, Persil washing powder, Virgin Cola and Flora margarine. Organisations approach Comic Relief and the merchandising team also actively seeks new partners. That type of work starts at least 18 months prior to an event to allow time for production planning. The merchandising team also brief creative agencies in January (14 months prior to event) for a new red nose design.

'Comic Relief produced five Red Nose items and worked with 12 different corporate partners on branded products selling 40 million items during the campaign in 2001. The planning process starts at the end of each campaign with the evaluation of what was done before. Comic Relief evaluates each project and every partner they work with.'

Comic Relief has to be careful about which organisations it agrees to partner with:

'The preparation time for each campaign is getting longer and longer just because there is so much to bring together. We are generally proactive in going out to companies and asking them to work with us. We had approaches in to us within 2 weeks of RND from brands saying they want to work with us for the next campaign. You have to assess whether they're suitable partners to work with, although it's a difficult one because we are here to raise as much money as possible for the charity but it isn't just about money. It's about brand fit and consumer perception of that brand as well. Some brands we can't work with.

'We start thinking about items like the various noses and T-shirts from end of December (about 15 months prior to the event). The logo is also licensed to partners such as Mr Kipling, Persil and Virgin Cola and that process needs to start 18 months ahead of RND to get into their production planning. If Comic Relief has worked with them before then the evaluation process will highlight learning points and ensure that the processes are understood and where possible improved for the next event. Comic Relief makes approaches to new potential partners about 18 months ahead of RND. We start negotiations with existing partners about working together for the next event in January and February (13 to 14 months prior to the event).

'In the background contracts are going back and forth. We contractually agree before we even start how much money they're going to give us so that there is some sort of guarantee and that contract can take three or four months at least.'

The planning process for production of merchandise must take a number of factors into account.

'So talking about running parallel strategies for the merchandise you're running lots of things all the time. It's about project managing. You've got to think how is that relation-ship going, when do I need to do this by and being quite formalised about things but also being open to opportunities. You've got to be very focused and very methodical but also flexible. Next week we could get on radio or tomorrow an auction on the Internet and you have to think: can we do that, what does it deliver for us, does that get us more awareness, will it raise more money? If it meets those criteria then you have to respond very quickly.

'I guess the key is that you know where you want to be and you work backwards. For example, we speak to the T-shirt manufacturers, find out their time frames and work back from that point because we then know when to make certain decisions and we can start to put key dates in. You know when the campaign date is going to be in March and that the launch date is in the first week of February. You know then you have to get T-shirts into store in mid-January so you work it backwards from there. That is crucial, so if the manufacturer says production will take three months and has to start in March (12 months prior to RND) and you plan to ship by sea from the Far East to keep costs down, then you start to see key dates.

'So with red noses, for example, we allow time for companies to come up with ideas and samples because we know from experience we need to be ready to go into produc-tion in July or August because we know it takes many months for production and shipping and we work it back from there. If we decide to go with a theme you have to balance the timing. Suppliers come up with ideas, which may influence the theme, but you know they may make samples and we say yes that's great, but we've now got a dif-ferent theme. So it's quite difficult to decide when is the right time.

'It takes time to develop different designs and from experience if we start asking them to make samples in the Far East this may take two to three weeks. We may say we like this but can it be bigger/smaller/rounder/whatever, we get them to produce visuals rather than samples but you get to the point where you actually need the physical sample so you can see if it does what you want, like this year's Whoopee Nose design with the rubber tongue and raspberry sound from Aardman. It is critical that we carry out an ethi-cal check of production facilities and we must also allow time for that visit to take place.

'You also have to build in time for legal and safety checks. We are very thorough with European and American safety standards. Even so there were safety issues with one item despite the fact it passed all the safety and legal requirements. From this we learnt that however much you plan and are careful with your processes you still have to have contingencies and be aware that things can go wrong. However careful you are, be more careful; however much you think you've checked it check it again and also have a contingency plan.

'At the planning stage you build in leeway to allow for delays in production or shipment. To be fair the suppliers are generally quite experienced and they build in leeway as well so you're building in all this contingency time! We had an issue this year where the boxes used to display the noses would not stand up so if they were sent to store like that they wouldn't display properly. We had to rework those and it got down to the last few days before we managed to sort it out. It's about being open and flexible, and if there is an issue you have to think how you get round it. If there had been a major disaster like a ship had sunk then you can't plan for that as you can't suddenly have two factories producing double the amount just in case.'

## Building the website

'We were lucky to get Cisco Systems to be our headline sponsor for our Internet activity. They brought together an unprecedented coalition of technology providers who could deliver the backing for our donation machine and for the rest of our web requirements, involving world leaders such as Compaq, Oracle, Zeus, Sun, and Energy Squared. They put in place a world-beating machine, which stood up on the night of 2001 March 16th.

'During the campaign we processed about 85 000 donation transactions online – 90% of which happened the weekend of RND. With an average donation amount of £35 it added up to around £3.6million, which at the time was a world record for a single event.

'We had a machine that was capable of processing 200 donations a second and we were keen to give ourselves the necessary bandwidth. In the end we had loads to spare. The processing power was tested so we could have done with more capability. But we don't think we turned anyone away. We don't know if we promoted it enough because on the night we had the telephone number displayed for two-thirds of the time and the web address for one-third. In hindsight we could have driven more people to the website and taken more there. You can never know whether we missed any, or whether the fact we had a website actually added new money.

'We turned around the website in about three weeks when anyone sensible would allow at least a couple of weeks for testing a site with infrastructure of that magnitude. We didn't have the time. We had an Internet Service Provider (ISP) lined up who dropped out on Christmas Eve. We had to put another in place for January and build the site and content. There was testing but not enough. It didn't fall over so that is academic now. I suppose the flip side of working with people of that size and standing within the global technology marketplace is they cannot afford for their brand to fall over. So there was a timetable and we had plans that simply got moved and moved. There was a real concertina effect going on.

'At the end of January it was decided we would have a *Celebrity Big Brother* website. Now that is a huge commercial property and there was a huge amount of traffic going through the servers for this microsite. It was an unprecedented alliance of Channel 4, the BBC and Endemol [TV production company] working together around a single project. At the 11th hour they decided yes, we're doing a website and you will have the news 24 hours before either of the TV programmes on Channel 4 and BBC. Suddenly it's happening and we have to make it work. The corporate partners who have the donation machine in place say, well you can't have it on these servers. But we didn't have any other servers so it had to go on them and we made it work. It had a dynamic side that was database-driven, running on the same servers as the donation machine. Planning for that was difficult. The biggest planning lesson is that we have to plan for last minute things to drop into play.

'Planning was already under way when I joined in June 2000. An agency had been appointed but we didn't have a headline sponsor. We were trying to get a sponsor in place by the end of the summer and that simply didn't materialise. So all the time we were running two parallel plans. We either do a budget thing and just concentrate on donations or we do full interactivity, dynamic with online event registration, fun stuff with games and movies and all the other things we did eventually end up giving our supporter base.

'Our headline sponsor, Cisco Systems, didn't come on board until 24th October 2000, which is much later than we wanted so we were already up against it. Suddenly we had the necessary resource to make it fly. We like to be cutting edge and use technology to raise money in new ways, involve our supporters in new, exciting and creative ways.

'Currently out of an event we use a service provider to process donations but during an event with the corporate technology providers we had in place for RND 2001 money went straight into the bank at NatWest. On the night it was something like 67 000 donations online. In the four minutes either side of the news at 10 o'clock we counted around 35 000 donations. The spike was huge.

'A spike like that is not something that Amazon or other e-commerce sites have to deal with. There is not much threat to the business model of someone like Tesco if the customer can't buy online there and then, as they'll try again. But for us it's a one-off opportunity. If someone doesn't give their money then there is no guarantee they will give it later, so we have maximum risk. We cannot afford for it to fall over so the resilience of our architecture is key.

'Time issues highlight the importance of being flexible to adopt ideas, to react to things that happen outside of your control like losing the ISP, taking on opportunities that arise and a headline sponsor coming on board late. We had crashes through the campaign. We wanted to launch on 6th February when we had the PR launch but we couldn't because everyone came on board late so we had an online launch of 20th February, which was not a success. It was difficult because we had a crash midway though the campaign, which was a very basic technology failure. If it had happened on 16th March (RND, 2001) we would have been absolutely up the creek.'

New technology developments also need to be considered seriously when planning for future events:

'The Internet is calming down and predictions are that by 2003–4 interactive TV will have taken over and there'll be a new medium in which we will again aspire to be the leading edge. To be the first charity to do things on an interactive TV platform. We'll be doing text updates in 2003.'

## Press and PR Planning

The Comic Relief media team's overall objective for the Red Nose Day campaign is to maximise publicity across all four mediums (press, TV, radio and the Internet) in order to mobilise the public and ensure fundraising targets are met:

'We serve the whole organisation's publicity needs, so we face the challenge of juggling each department's demands, constantly reassessing priorities, giving back value to our corporate partners in PR terms and ensuring our celebrity supporters' time is maximised to the full.'

The media team work with the press and PR agencies of their corporate partners to ensure they maximise any opportunities that may be available to them. They also benefit from gifts in kind from media and PR agencies that support Comic Relief on elements of the campaign such as brainstorming for the theme.

## Artist/celebrity selection

In order to grow the brand and keep people interested, it is important to get new artists and celebrities involved. As an example of the diversity involved, the TV listing for RND in 2001 read:

On TV, over 300 artists are taking part in Red Nose Day 2001. The show will be presented by Davina McCall, Lenny Henry, Ant and Dec, Jonathan Ross, Graham Norton, Zoe Ball, Cat Deeley and Dermot O'Leary. Other artists involved include Billy Connolly, Dawn French, Jennifer Saunders, Ali G, Richard Blackwood, Jamie Oliver, Harry Hill, David Baddiel, Michael Greco, Jack Dee, and Vic and Bob. A live seven-hour TV show on BBC One includes specials from *One Foot in the Grave*, *The Royle Family*, *Robbie Williams and The Fast Show*, *EastEnders*, *Alan Partridge*, *The Weakest Link*, *Smack the Pony*, and appeal films from projects in Africa and the UK. A special Comic Relief *Celebrity Big Brother* will also be broadcast.

Relationships with this star-studded cast must be managed:

'We have a department that makes sure our representation of Jack Dee or Lenny Henry or Ali G, or whoever, is appropriate and delivers as much as it possibly can without asking too much of the particular celebrity.'

Celebrities are taken on project visits to get them involved and to show them what their participation means to Comic Relief.

## Staff and recruitment

Comic Relief has approximately 50 full-time staff that are aided by a large number of temporary staff and volunteers recruited for the six months prior to RND (October through to March).

'In planning terms, when you bring new people on board to something as intricate as Comic Relief you have to build in time to allow those people to get up to speed on the sensitivities around the brand. They must be aware of the very different relationships we have with all our supporters, on many levels – from the person organising an underwater dinner party to the corporate partner.'

All new staff participate in a one-week intensive induction programme, which is designed to bring them up to speed as quickly as possible. The programme involves spending time with every department within the organisation and new staff will also go on project visits so they can see first hand what Comic Relief is all about.

## Planning issues for RND

Comic Relief believes itself to be an opportunistic organisation, which has to be flexible. The success or size of a campaign can very much depend on opportunities that present themselves quite late in the day, such as the offer of two books by J.K. Rowling and *Celebrity Big Brother*. In terms of planning, the RND brief is *do everything earlier*. Within the RND campaign, activities have to be performed flexibly against a fixed deadline, where much of the fundraising takes place in a very short 'window of opportunity':

'Planning is very much about not limiting expectations but having realistic expectations. What are the most important core objectives for us to achieve, and what are the things that it's okay to drop? We are not going to drop online donations, so on the night of RND it is imperative that machinery doesn't fail, that the technology delivers, that we have servers that can withstand a huge spike of activity. Although we have global ambition we are keenly aware that our key audience is very much UK based. It's about making informed decisions about what you can realistically achieve, given that we have no resource and that we have an immovable deadline.'

Comic Relief has to be careful about the fundraising opportunities it chooses:

'So that our targets or aspirations aren't unreasonable and 'pie in the sky', we have to weigh up the opportunities. We may have 100 brilliant, creative ideas and if 30 to 35 of them come off, that will be good. Experience has taught us it will bring in record amounts of money. If we can deliver more of those, so much the merrier, but we have a strategy of delivering fewer fantastic things than lots of things averagely. We can only do so much, therefore we try to be focused in what we do.'

The workload has peaks and troughs in terms of resource:

With merchandise we tend to peak activity-wise from the six months before RND because you've virtually signed off all your partners for products and production is underway, so a lot of our stuff is front-loaded. You do go through a big peak before the campaign starts, and on an ongoing basis you may go through peaks if you're doing marketing activity or a TV ad. We go through this massive peak around the event and then a massive trough a few weeks after, but it is such a big campaign that you're pretty much straight back into the planning stage. So we finish in March, we're doing evaluations through into May and early June, a bit of a lull, then from September you're back into making approaches again.

'Yet it's often difficult to plan because you don't know what's going to happen. Something may be a challenge but it is important to be flexible, to learn and to respond to opportunities. All the lessons we learned when planning for the Internet are based on "give yourself more time". But you also have to allow for the fact that creative properties like J.K. Rowling and Robbie Williams, who did an online auction, *Celebrity Big*

*Brother* – any of those things – can arrive at any time and you simply can't turn away gift horses. You have to believe that the brand of Comic Relief has so much goodwill imbued in it that people will stretch time!

'When you think you are stretched to your absolute utmost, suddenly something will arrive and you would love to say that we couldn't do that because we're at capacity, but if it's going to generate money you can't say that. I can't tell you that one of our planning criteria is "be realistic at all times" because I don't think that is a realistic option, not within the time frame or the given resource. There is so much goodwill and passion within the organisation, which I think is a key ingredient for making plans work. People are extremely committed to the cause, which is important for making all these things happen.

'The process is now starting to build up to the next event. There is a website year round and we're keen to show people where the money is going from RND 2001. The first batch of grants is being processed and we're beginning to spend the money. We're beginning to put plans in place for 2003. We're putting strategies, relationships and the necessary resource in place to deliver against those ambitions, but there's a part of me that knows it will still be manic.'

### Questions

1 *Draw an outline bar chart for RND 2003 based on the nine main activities listed.*

2 *What principles should Comic Relief use to plan its human resources? What personal attributes would you seek when hiring full-time staff, and when recruiting temporary staff and volunteers in the run-up to RND?*

3 *Based on the above information, if you were a consultant to Comic Relief, what advice would you give about the way that RND is managed?*

Visit the Comic Relief web site at: *www.comicrelief.com*

# CASE 14

## Cartes sans Frontières

**Case date 2001**    Alan Harrison

## Introduction

Cartes sans Frontières (CSF) is a € multi-million organisation that produces maps for the European traveller. Based at Lyons in France, CSF produces several different types of product ranging from large scale (1:10,000) to small scale (1:100,000) maps, road atlases and travel guides. A Surveying and Designs Division does the designs and also earns substantial royalties by licensing those designs to various external organisations. Small scale maps are produced in five major ranges for different European countries as follows:

- France: covered by 510 individual maps (called 'sheets'), with annual sales of some 1.5 m sheets.
- UK: covered by 220 sheets, with annual sales of about 1.0 m
- Italy: covered by 260 sheets, with annual sales of about 0.7 m
- Germany: covered by 320 sheets, with annual sales of about 1.2 m
- Spain: covered by 460 sheets, with annual sales of about 0.8 m.

Sales for smaller west European and east European countries total some 1.0 m sheets. All maps are available either as folded (and mounted on card), or as unfolded sheets.

Average annual sales per sheet show a typical Pareto pattern, with a few 'blockbusters' at one end and a lengthy 'tail' of maps that show only small annual sales per sheet. Figure 14.1 gives a Pareto analysis of last year's annual sales by sheet.

**Figure 14.1 Average sales per customer for the year 2000**

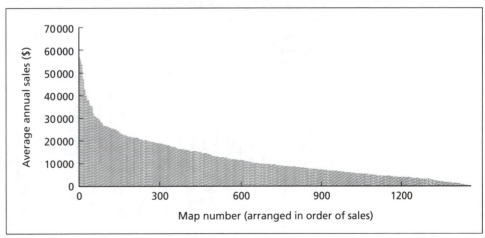

When asked why there was such a lengthy tail of maps with low annual sales, the Sales Manager replied:

'Regional maps are a more complex business than, say, the mass market for books. The reason is that a customer in the north of France will not sell the same maps as someone in the south of the country. These are just two of the many possible extremes. Our top-selling maps very much focus on the key holiday areas. But that doesn't mean to say that someone in the Côte d'Azur would sell the same maps as someone on the west coast. It is important that a customer can go into a shop anywhere in our chosen territories and find the local maps on display.'

Another characteristic of map sales is that there is a strong seasonal peak around Easter. Figure 14.2 shows the seasonal nature of demand for CSF maps. This can be described, in broad terms, as consisting of two fairly distinct levels of demand. The first, lower level occurs from September through to January. During this period, monthly sales volumes amount to between 5 per cent and 7 per cent of the annual total. The second, higher level of demand occurs from April through to August. During this period, monthly sales volumes amount to between 9 per cent and 11 per cent of the annual total. The transition between these two levels of demand is marked by a significant growth in sales during February that continues and peaks in March, where sales are 13 per cent of the annual total. The March peak is more than double the sales typically made during the winter months and around a third more than sales during the summer months.

The case presents an overview of the CSF demand fulfilment system in Section 1, and then provides details of the trade orders system (Section 2), stock picking (Section 3) print planning (Section 4) and printing (Section 5). The study questions ask you to prepare a flow diagram for Sections 2, 3, 4 and 5 and then to compare the order processing system as a whole with the stock replenishment system.

# 1 Demand fulfilment system

CSF's demand fulfilment system is shown in Figure 14.3. The system can best be described by following the progress of a customer order through the system. An

**Figure 14.2 Seasonal nature of demand**

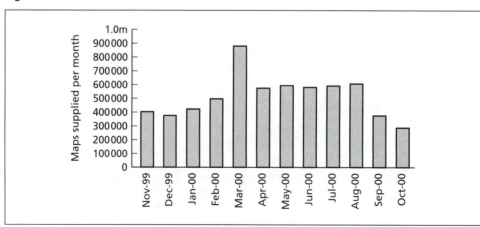

**Figure 14.3  An overview of CSF's demand fulfilment system**

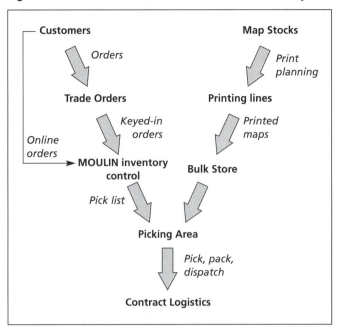

order from a customer is entered into the inventory control system directly through 'online' ordering via Electronic Data Interchange (EDI). Alternatively, a member of staff in the Trade Orders Department keys in an order that arrives via telephone, fax, post or e-mail. The order is processed through the inventory control system (a SAP R/3-based system called 'Moulin'), where it is assigned an order number. The Moulin system also generates pick lists for the flat stock and folded stock stores. ('Flat stock' comprises sheets that come directly from the printing lines; 'folded stock' are sheets that have been folded and mounted onto printed cards.) In the folded stock Picking Area the pick list is downloaded into hand-held bar code scanning guns that inform operators which maps to pick. Upon completion of the picking operation, the order is packed. Packed orders are dispatched near the end of the working day when a contract logistics service provider picks up the orders for next-day delivery to the customer (or in two days for more distant areas like Scotland and the south of Italy).

When order picking has been completed, the hand-held bar code scanning gun uploads a confirmation of the order to the inventory control system. If, as a result, inventory levels in the Picking Area are found to be below a prescribed level, an instruction is sent to the Bulk Store for additional inventory to be delivered to the Picking Area.

Inventory in the Bulk Store is replenished as a result of periodic checks of inventory levels in the store. These checks are undertaken by the map stock team who use the information to forecast the time remaining until current stocks run out. Six months before a predicted zero stock time a works order is issued to the printing lines to print a map. Once they have been printed, the resulting maps are delivered to the Bulk Store. Key performance measures of the overall system are the lead-time from order receipt to dispatch and the level of inventory held.

A performance target has been set for order fulfilment. This is that the order should be dispatched within three days of order receipt. Also, the order is to be met in full and dispatched for delivery on time – within four days of order receipt for most areas of Europe, and an additional day later for the more remote areas.

The corporate target level, that is the percentage of orders dispatched to meet this level of dispatch performance, is 88 per cent. While this is exceeded most of the time, the service level provided to a key customer was reported by its Sales Manager to have been much lower at certain times – particularly around Easter – during the last 12 months. These periods of low service were stated to have been caused by problems with the contract logistics service provider.

Benchmarking of stock turnover management of other publishing organisations showed that CSF's performance is one of the lowest of the companies included in the sample used. In spite of the excess inventories, CSF is unable to satisfy every order in full.

## 2 Trade orders

Orders are received in the CSF Trade Orders Department in a number of ways depending upon customer preference. Between 50 per cent and 60 per cent of orders are received by EDI, with the remainder arriving by other channels either fax, telephone, post or e-mail. EDI orders can be automatically input into the Moulin system. Other ordering channels require the order to be manually keyed into the system by staff. The procedure for keying orders includes date stamping orders upon receipt and allocating record numbers. The date stamp is used to begin the process of measuring the turnaround time from receipt to dispatch of orders.

Whilst EDI receives the highest volume of orders, use of this channel is limited to a small number of CSF's largest customers. Amongst the other ordering channels, fax is the most popular and e-mail is the least.

The Moulin system checks the integrity of orders entered into it, for example by checking that valid product codes have been used. The system is able to correct simple mistakes such as by replacing superceded codes with current numbers. Other errors result in a discrepancy report being created which staff in the Trade Orders Department use to take corrective action. Around 97 per cent of orders pass smoothly through the process.

A number is allocated to each order by Moulin, and separate pick lists for folded and flat stock are generated. The Trade Orders Department performs a number of functions in addition to carrying out the basic steps of this process. For example, when a large order is received, the person who keys the order notifies the Bulk Store straightaway, so it can arrange the delivery of the necessary stock to the picking area. The department also deals with customer feedback, especially customer service problems. A recent development that will facilitate order fulfilment performance is the policy of requesting the largest accounts to make more regular orders for their stock replenishment.

## 3 Stock Picking Area

Maps are stored and picked in two separate areas, depending upon whether they are folded or flat. The majority of maps are supplied folded, so the folded stock area is described here. The picking process for folded stock begins when the pick list for an order, created by the Moulin system, is downloaded into a hand-held scan gun. Bar-code labels are printed at this stage that will be used later in the process to label the box or boxes in which the order is subsequently to be contained. A customer card is also written out at this stage, which will be placed in this box when the order is packed.

Maps are picked from a dedicated area in the stores. This area is laid out in aisles, with the maps arranged by country and then by numerical order. The scan guns have a display that tells the picking operator which map number to pick, and the quantity required. The picking sequence starts with the lowest map numbers first. The order in which the maps are picked is maintained throughout picking and packing as this allows for easier checking both by CSF and the customer.

When all the maps in an order are picked, the information from the scan gun is uploaded into Moulin and a delivery note produced. The maps and their accompanying documentation are packed in a packing area and palletised with other orders where they await dispatch. This action concludes the process.

## 4 Planning procedures for printing

We next turn to the right 'arm' of Figure 14.3, starting with the planning procedures in the Map Stocks section, and moving on to the printing lines in Section 5. The planning procedure in Map Stocks is applied on a monthly basis, and determines the need for placing a map on the printing schedule. This will happen when the inventory holding of a map is projected to provide six months of cover until it runs out. This procedure is shown in Figure 14.4, which shows the timing sequence for planning and printing a map. The aim of the map stock team is to schedule the delivery of a batch of printed maps to the Bulk Store three months before stock is projected to run out ('nil stock' point). The typical time from raising a works order to delivery to the Bulk Store is three months. Therefore, the works order is raised six months before the projected nil stock point.

**Figure 14.4 Planning and printing timings**

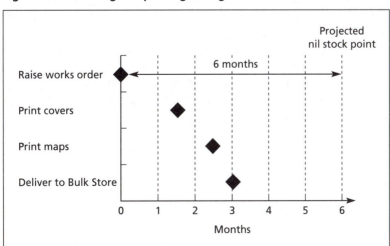

The print planning procedure is carried out as follows. The Map Stocks section reviews all Moulin projections for those map numbers where stock will run out within the next six months. A check is made of physical stocks of flat maps, and of outstanding orders and production runs over that period. If the flat stock is insufficient to meet the projected demand, then the latest design is called up from the Surveying and Design Division. This must be loaded onto the cartography section so that the printing plate can be made. Next, the print run size must be set, and the new print run loaded onto the printing section. The map covers must also be loaded for printing – they are produced on different printing presses. Two weeks prior to printing, the Moulin projections are rechecked, and the size of the print run confirmed. Finally, a day-to-day check is made of the print priority list, and adjustments made with the Print Room Manager in the light of current priorities.

If there is sufficient flat stock to meet the projected demand, then only the covers will need to be loaded for printing.

The number of maps printed (the print batch size) is the decision of the map stock team. Formerly, the batch size was equal to 18 months of demand. In 2000, this policy was changed and the print batch size was reduced to 12 months of demand. By printing 12 months of stock and planning the batches to be in store three months before the nil stock point, the amount of stock in the Bulk Store should, on average, fluctuate between a minimum of three months and a maximum of 15 months of stock.

## 5 Printing lines

The process for printing maps at CSF is as follows. The current ISBN design for a scheduled print run is downloaded from Surveying and Designs Division, and used to produce the plates. When the line is ready for the next batch, the plates are loaded onto the printing machines, and adjusted so that the colours are perfectly aligned. This set-up process takes about four hours for the Alpha machines, and about two hours for the Beta machines. Once the batch has been printed, it is laid down as flat stock to dry. Meanwhile, the covers are printed eight at a time on smaller machines, and then guillotined ready for assembly. The flat maps must also be guillotined, then folded into the familiar fan shape ready for assembly. Finally, the map and cover are assembled and glued together. The batch of folded maps is then transported on pallets into the Bulk Store.

CSF has four printing machines which work two seven-hour shifts. Two of these are Beta machines, which can print at the rate of 8000 maps per hour. The other two are older Alpha machines, which produce at half that rate. Some 40 per cent of printing capacity is currently taken up with production of brochures and reports, mostly for organisations outside the CSF group.

## Questions

1 *Prepare flow charts for trade orders (Section 2), picking (Section 3), map stock planning (Section 4) and printing (Section 5).*

2 *Compare the left 'arm' of Figure 14.3 with the right 'arm'. What is the P:D ratio? (Refer to Slack, Johnston and Chambers,* Operations Management, *3rd edn, p. 312.) Why are there such huge differences in responsiveness between the two arms?*

3 *What actions could CSF take to reduce stock levels **and** improve service levels to customers?*

# The Reltex Project

Case date
2001

Nigel Slack

Globestelle is the world's largest precision diecasting company. It is a global enterprise, with 20 plants in 15 countries, providing a diecasting service, from designing and prototyping to full-scale production runs, in specialist equipment.

Diecasting is a process where molten metal is injected into a die which forms it into its required shape after which it is rapidly cooled. The process allows very complex and high-precision components of a range of sizes (but particularly small) to be reproduced consistently in large volumes. Often, diecasting can replace conventional metal forming processes such as machining, turning, moulding, pressing and fabricating. Examples are car lock mechanisms and connectors for the automotive industry, battery shields in mobile phones and payphone push-buttons. Globestelle also has a large plastics injection moulding operation which produces similar results using plastic material.

## ● The project starts

In November 1998, Globestelle's sales office in Cologne received an order from Reltex, a nearby automotive components manufacturer. Reltex required 'Xway magnesium connectors' as part of its contract with another automotive supplier, AGT, a division of a major vehicle manufacturer. The Xway connector project was the largest single project Reltex had ever undertaken. Furthermore, it was both outside its core business and far more complex than anything it had produced before. It was also unfamiliar with the diecasting process, hence the involvement of a specialist supplier. The Programme Manager for Reltex explained:

'This was a huge project for us. Previously the biggest project we had handled was worth around €18 million. This one was €100 million of which the Xway connector was around €60 million. It was also the first time our customer, AGT, had gone outside its own vertical structure for a product like this. I guess we didn't really understand the implications of all this, especially as it impacted on supplier development.'

The development and manufacture of the Xway connectors (which even for Globestelle, was technically complex) was due to take place at Globestelle's Stuttgart plant. A consultant, Franc Warde, was brought in to head the project in November 1998. By December, a prototype die had been developed to be used in a trial run.

## 1999 – during which not much happens (until the end)

Throughout the whole of 1999, development progressed on the new product. Franc Warde continued to assist the project on a consultancy basis although it was not until August that he was brought in full time (still on a consultancy basis). However, in December Joseph Zemel from Globestelle Tustin was also seconded to the project full time to help Franc.

Prototype castings were being made at the Stuttgart plant, which was, at this stage, the only unit to have a suitable magnesium machine. In August Reltex specified an annual volume of five million pieces. Shortly after this Reltex also changed the product specification to add a 'Leak test' requirement. This modification to the specification came as a result of a repositioning of the connector within the engine cavity to a point where the product was, at least potentially, more likely to have to withstand damp conditions. Unfortunately Reltex did not immediately inform Globestelle of the additional Leak test requirement. This was the first of several changes that Reltex made to the product specification. In December 1999, trials on the pre-production samples of the connector failed a required salt spray testing. Under the new requirements, there was a real possibility that the product would never be satisfactory if made in magnesium. A Globestelle engineer commented:

'We were pushing magnesium casting technology to its limits on this project with such a smooth surface finish and thin cast walls. We just could not protect the magnesium under such severe spray conditions.'

## 2000 – during which many things happen

It quickly became clear that magnesium was an unsuitable material for the component. The best solution would be to use aluminium as an alternative. Not only would this require a change to the component, but it would also require the modification of the die itself for use in the conventional diecasting process for aluminium. It was during this period of crisis that Franc Warde eventually became a full-time employee of Globestelle. In January he and others involved in the project met with both Reltex and Reltex's customer, AGT, to review the position and examine the changes which would be required if the material was changed from magnesium to aluminium. Within days of this meeting, Globestelle had drawn up capacity plans for aluminium casting and worked with the die suppliers to adapt the prototype die for aluminium. Twelve days after the meeting with Reltex and AGT, the first castings in aluminium were being produced. One of Globestelle's engineers said:

'I think that our responsiveness impressed Reltex. They had been, of course, very concerned at the prospect of changing to aluminium, but at least we showed them that we could move fast when required. However, it seemed that Reltex had the impression that we had a larger base of resources than we actually had.'

Both companies now needed to understand the full implications of this change. Reltex had informally indicated that they would accept the change in material to aluminium. Within Globestelle, capital expenditure plans were being drawn up and quotes being prepared. However, the project was put on hold until firm costings had been established. By late February, Globestelle was ready to submit its revised piece part price to Reltex, which was not well received. Nevertheless, by March Reltex had reluctantly accepted the new price and issued the relevant documentation. Now that the decision had been made, development of the component in aluminium started in earnest. Even so, some 12 to 15 months of project time had been lost due to the failure of the magnesium product.

By the end of March the project had received the go-ahead for expenditure on the first production cell. Shortly after getting approval for the production cell development Joseph Zemel retired due to ill health. This left the project, already under-resourced, even shorter staffed. As one of Globestelle's engineers commented:

'We didn't have the resources available, especially in the early days of the project. Nor did we make resources available fast enough. There was always the question of what to do with people once the project was finished. Nor did we always document everything in as detailed a manner as we should have done. Our limited resources and lack of documentation sometimes let us down. For example, no one really knew about trim-presses after Joseph Zemel left.'

The next two months of development progressed reasonably smoothly. This in spite of the unit which would eventually produce the product moving to an entirely new site. Even at this time it was obvious that the site move would cause problems. In effect, it would mean that aluminium diecasting and production facilities would not be available within the company until January 2001. This would mean using a subcontractor initially and then moving production facilities into the new plant during 2001. A Globestelle engineer commented on the relocation:

'There is no doubt that the Reltex project impacted on our relocation to the new plant. We had been operating at capacity with no room for future growth, so the building of the plant was seen as providing growth capacity for the future. The Reltex project came along as an additional piece of business. Then the delay in the Reltex project and the change to aluminium delayed decisions and our move. Suddenly the future seemed less certain. Things also worked the other way round. The move did not help the project. During the time when critical decisions were being made on the Reltex contract, many of us were focused on the new building. This may have taken some of the resources away from the Reltex project itself.'

There were also other irritations during this period. The Leak test specifications demanded by Reltex were too tight for Reltex's own equipment to measure. Therefore, Globestelle became involved with Leak test manufacturers in ongoing discussions over the viability of various Leak testing equipment. Perhaps more significantly in the long term, in May Reltex informed Globestelle that it had not secured the contract for the 2Xway connector (an advanced version of the Xway connector) which it had bid for earlier. The Globestelle engineer explained:

'I guess our development resources could have been transferred to the 2Xway product if we had got that contract. Ironically, one of the reasons that we lost that order was that Reltex didn't want to put a problem onto a plant that didn't have the resources for the current project it was handling.'

Meanwhile discussions on issuing a contract for the Leak tester were dragging on. In June, Reltex asked for a further quote from one potential Leak test manufacturer.

This would add a further 10-week lead-time to the eventual purchase of the Leak testing machine, an issue which caused some concern at Globestelle.

The end of June brought two problems in two days. At a senior management meeting between Globestelle and Reltex, Reltex accused Globestelle of being insufficiently committed to the project. It was clear that there was some considerable dissatisfaction from a customer who represented a potentially very large piece of business. The next day, over at the subcontractor where the first aluminium components were being produced with the modified die, an untrained operator neglected to connect part of the water-cooling system to the diecasting machine, which seized up, causing damage to the die. Both events came as a shock to the Globestelle engineers, who had to spend precious resources dealing with the issues.

'Part of our problem was that we did not seem to recognise that things will sometimes fail along the way. You have to plan for the fact that something may not work and put in appropriate contingencies. We did very little pre-planning in the early stages of the project. Part of our style was that we were much better at solving problems once we encountered them than we were at anticipating problems. In fact we were far better at putting together requests for capital expenditure to satisfy our own internal requirements than we were at planning the actual progress of the project in consultation with our customer.'

Meeting to discuss Reltex's accusations some days later, Globestelle decided to transfer prototype development, and eventually production, to a larger subcontractor who would be able to cope with higher volumes until the new plant became available. Meanwhile, over at the original subcontractor, the repaired die had arrived and had started producing product which, in spite of some further die modification, looked promising.

During the summer, development on the production processes proceeded fairly smoothly, although by July it was clear that the whole project was at least 20 per cent over budget. The Leak testing issue, however, was not much closer to being settled, with several meetings between Globestelle, Reltex and potential equipment suppliers. Also, Globestelle was becoming concerned with the way in which Reltex was specifying the product. Not only had there been numerous changes to product specifications but Globestelle believed the product was overspecified. Reltex also insisted on 100 critical dimensions, or key product characteristics (KPCs) and very tight specifications – in some cases tightening AGT's original specified tolerances. Given their experience in the diecasting process, Globestelle believed many of these specifications to be unnecessary.

September and October of 2000 brought good news and bad news. Production trials were going reasonably well and the parts required by Reltex for the end of September were shipped on time. Yet a meeting with Reltex in early September had been a strained and, at times, bad-tempered affair. Reltex was itself under pressure from its own customers. At Globestelle the project was now 30 per cent over budget. The Leak testing saga also dragged on. More design consultations within Globestelle were held and further discussions with manufacturers took place. In an attempt to resolve the issue, on 30th September a meeting was held at Reltex with representatives from companies who had submitted quotes to build the Leak test machine. However, the only decision taken was to meet again.

In October Reltex asked Globestelle to quote for yet another product, the 2Xway header housing. Two days later a quote was sent to Reltex. Two weeks after that Globestelle was again told it had not won the order. Partly, at least, the failure to obtain the contract was due to Reltex's view of Globestelle's planning processes. Reltex was a company that adhered very strongly to systems and procedures, and undertook project planning very efficiently and in great detail. Its methods of working, particularly with quality systems and project management, were tried and tested. Globestelle did not work in this way. A manager at Reltex explained:

'Globestelle's core technology is first rate. Their tool building is a key advantage for them, and they are the industry leader as regards to cost. We know because we have looked elsewhere. But in the end we placed the 2Xway contract with a higher costs supplier. There is more involved in a project like this than just making a damned good die. We are buying more than technical expertise here.'

## 2001– during which many things continue to happen

The build up of capacity continued through the year. Production was transferred to the new plant in January. The first truck-load of production castings was shipped to the Reltex plant in March, and by early April Globestelle was seeing the first profits from the Reltex contract. However, two technical issues were to dog production during 2001. Periodically, the machining centres in the new plant were shut down due to machine damage caused by the machining fluid. It was found that the fluid was causing the seals in the machines to perish. A request was made to Reltex to change the fluid, but Reltex did not seem keen to discuss the issue. In August, the fluid suppliers confirmed that the problem fluid was incompatible with the machining centres. In spite of this, Reltex were still concerned about changing the fluid, but eventually agreed. Globestelle, meanwhile, had requested that Reltex pay for the damage to the machining centre caused by the fluid. The issue was not resolved until December when Reltex agreed to the use of the alternative machining fluid. The second technical problem surfaced in June when problems were discovered with another lubricating fluid used in the diecasting process (which had been specified by Reltex). By July, Globestelle was sufficiently concerned to officially request that Reltex allow it to change the die face lubricant. A meeting was organised with the lubricant supplier but Reltex declined to attend. Further investigations revealed that the problem was due to bacteria and a cleaning solution was used to rectify the situation. By the end of August a satisfactory replacement for the lubricant had been agreed with the suppliers and samples of it submitted to Reltex for analysis. Although both problems had been solved, they had proved a significant distraction. A Globestelle engineer commented on the problems:

'The time and resource spent on both the machining fluid and the die lube issues was considerable. In projects like this, one of the things that would help us most is some way of keeping the customer out of our processes.'

There were also tensions between the companies because of their different attitudes to documenting the project.

'We couldn't believe how much documentation Reltex required. Everything had to be detailed at, what seemed to us, a ridiculous level. To some extent this caused us to avoid getting involved in documentation which was not strictly necessary.' (*Globestelle engineer*)

'We didn't believe how little documentation Globestelle had traditionally used. We are used to dealing with very comprehensive quality and specification manuals which fully document all parts of the project.' (*Reltex engineer*)

At one point during this time, Reltex refused the payment of an invoice to Globestelle because the documentation was not complete. Again, there were significant differences in attitude between the two companies.

'We did relatively little to communicate with Reltex when it wasn't strictly necessary. We came to believe that the best things we did were the ones that kept Reltex off our backs. We would say, "Today is a good day, we haven't heard from Reltex yet".' (*Globestelle engineer*)

'Our suppliers varied considerably in their ability to manage their part of the overall project. Our best suppliers, were the ones that were calling me up all the time. All our good suppliers' salesmen are the ones who are often regarded as pests.' (*Reltex programme manager*)

During the project, relations between the two companies had been strained at times, yet by mid-2001 both sides found that communication improved as they became familiar with each other's different methods of working. Globestelle had not dealt with such a demanding customer before and certainly had very little experience of quality manuals. Its expertise was in using its specialist technical skills to deliver the required product. Therefore, it was unhappy with many of Reltex's specifications, which had been designed by engineers with no previous experience of the diecasting process. It took until September 2001 before Reltex was confident enough to reduce the number of critical dimensions (from 100 to 22), something Globestelle had been urging for 18 months. If Globestelle was unhappy with the technical demands of the Reltex project, Reltex was unhappy with Globestelle's methods of project management. Globestelle believed that Reltex planned for every conceivable, and often unnecessary, detail, and Reltex believed that Globestelle were not sufficiently committed to the project, partly because it did not have the supporting documentation and partly because it seemed to be reluctant to devote resource to the project. Into 2001, however, Globestelle was becoming more skilled at handling the documentation and had introduced two more engineers to work on the project, though it never had the same type of dedicated programme manager as Reltex did. A Globestelle engineer explained:

'From the beginning of the project Reltex had a single programme manager who AGT saw as the single point of contact. All issues were coordinated through the programme manager, including relationships with Reltex's suppliers. We never really had an equivalent person, as such. Reltex would need to contact one person for technical issues, another person for quality issues, and yet another one for general business issues.'

As the year drew to a close so, it seemed, did the Leak testing saga. In August, the first set of Leak test heads had been approved and sent to the machine builders for incorporation into the Leak testing machines, which were due in September. Although initially repeatability and reliability tests proved disappointing, by October the Leak testing equipment was finally available for use.

Two months later, Reltex informed Globestelle that Leak testing was 'no longer deemed critical' and should be 'put on the back burner' for the time being.

## Questions

**1** *What were the significant events in the history of this project?*

**2** *How do you see these significant events influencing each other and affecting the whole product development process?*

**3** *What were the worst mistakes made by Globestelle during the production development process?*

# Benetton Group: The evolution of a network to face global competition

Arnaldo Camuffo, Pietro Romano and Andrea Vinelli

## Benetton – the united colors of success

The Benetton you thought you knew no longer exists. The new competition brought about by globalisation and information and communication technologies (I&CT) have shaken its consolidated business model from the roots, pushing the Italian company toward a radical strategic change.

In the 1980s, Benetton's tremendous growth, outstanding financial performance and innovative strategies were widely celebrated by the press, researched by scholars, admired by practitioners and studied in business schools almost everywhere in the world. Thanks to this success, Benetton became a world-famous company and, for many years, represented, worldwide, the prototype of the network enterprise.

However, this stereotype about the 'Benetton network system' – the hollowed-out corporation that (a) produces garments through a web of small companies located in the north-east of Italy and (b) sells them through a worldwide chain of small independent stores – is no longer true.

Indeed, the most evident example of this comprehensive change concerns the transformation of the upstream and downstream web of business relationships which links raw materials suppliers, outside contractors, agents and retail outlets. For years, this network structure, coordinated by Benetton, had ensured high performance, reaching simultaneously production flexibility and efficiency, market growth and customer satisfaction.

Today, however, Benetton's top managers are aware that this model will not *per se* guarantee success in the future. If the Treviso-based company is to be able to remain competitive in the new global arena, it ought to get first-hand contact with the end customers, take more direct control over the supply chain and respond in real time to market solicitations.

Hence, Benetton's management has recently undertaken a number of initiatives aimed to effect this major strategic change. For example, it vertically integrated upstream by taking direct control of its main suppliers of wool and cotton and, through the family holding, even by going so far as to purchase large sheep ranches in South America.

In addition, over the past two years, Benetton has begun integrating downstream, too. Opening its own megastores – the so-called 'Retail Project' – has represented a major discontinuity in Benetton's approach to distribution, being part of the firm's intent to directly monitor consumers in crucial markets, thus challenging its major competitors – large pure international retailers – on the same terrain.

**Figure 16.1 Benetton Group's financial and economic indicators**

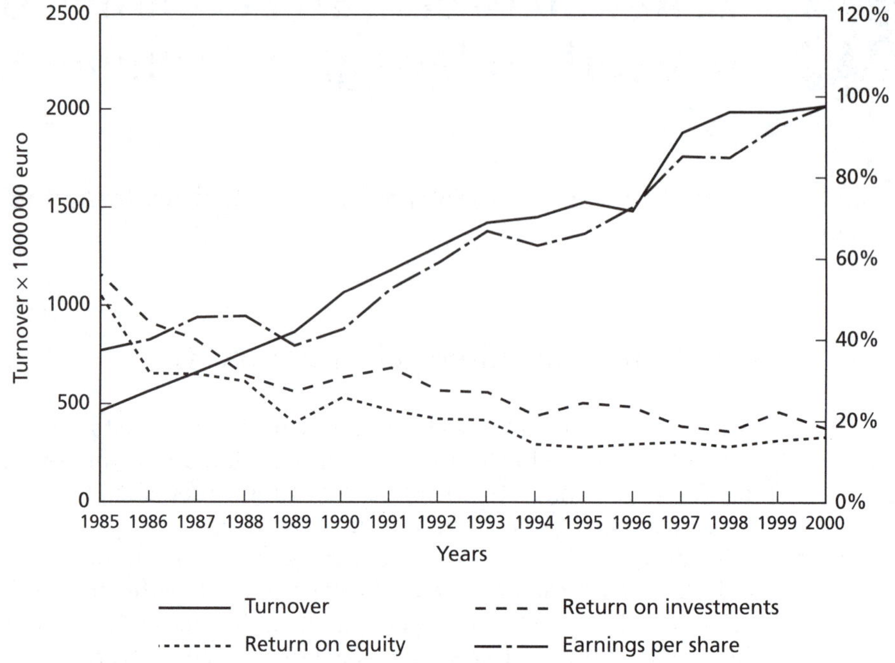

*Note*: In 1998 a 1/10 stock splitting was carried out.

Finally, in 1998, Benetton completed its diversification strategy by merging with Benetton Sportsystem, a completely separate company also owned by the Benetton family holding, which included the sports-related business activities (sportswear, sports equipment, shoes and accessories) acquired and/or developed over the last two decades. Diversification has meant facing competition in a diverse, though adjacent, industry, characterised by production and commercial logics which are considerably different from those of the core business, and which require innovative strategies, markedly diverse from those of the conventional Benetton model.

Today, Benetton is therefore facing perhaps the most critical transformation since its foundation, and its business model, which has made it famous worldwide, is, in its turn, undergoing modifications and adaptations in order to keep up with the changing realities of competition.

Interestingly enough, this transformation does not derive from a financial crisis or a significant performance demise. Data in Figure 16.1 shows that, although slightly worsening in the mid-1990s, the overall financial performance of the Treviso-based company has remained excellent. Thus, Benetton's efforts should be interpreted as an anticipation strategy, aimed at interpreting and reacting to the changing environment and to the new competition.

## The Benetton Group

Benetton's early history is closely bound with the life story of its founders: Luciano, Giuliana, Gilberto and Carlo Benetton. In the 1950s, Luciano – the eldest brother – took a job in a men's clothing store. In 1955, Luciano – then in his early twenties – convinced Giuliana that he could market the original bright-coloured sweaters she had been knitting as a hobby for her family and friends. The outcome was that he succeeded in selling to local stores the first collection Giuliana put together. Sales increased steadily over the next few years and, in 1965, Benetton was formally established as '*Maglificio di Ponzano Veneto dei Fratelli Benetton*'. Luciano and Giuliana decided to involve their younger brothers, Gilberto and Carlo, in the company operations. In the same year, the first Benetton factory went up in the village of Ponzano, a few kilometres outside Treviso. In 1968, Benetton opened the first shop and, over the next decade, a further 1000 shops followed, both in Italy and abroad. By the late 1990s, there were more than 6000 shops in 120 countries. By 1987 exports, which had amounted to two per cent of turnover at the end of the 1970s, had grown to 65 per cent. In 1986, only 20 years after the firm had been founded, turnover reached €500 million; it then grew continuously, at an average annual rate of 18 per cent until 1990, when it passed the €1 billion mark. In 2000, the €2 billions turnover threshold was hit. In the late eighties, Benetton was listed in some of the most important stock exchanges, such as Milan, Frankfurt, New York and Toronto.

Today, the Benetton Group is currently one of the world largest garment producers and retailers – with stores and manufacturing facilities located all over the world, a turnover of €2 billion and 7000 employees. The Benetton Group is controlled by Edizione Holding, a financial company all in the hands of the Benetton family, which owns a portfolio of businesses in a variety of industries ranging from garments to catering (Autogrill), from sport to telecommunications (Telecom Italia, Tim and Blue), from agriculture to services (Host Marriott Services) and highways (Autostrade). Benetton Group's activities can be clustered into three distinct businesses:

1 Casual wear business: garments, accessories and footwear, distributed under the United Colors of Benetton and Sisley brands; this represents the core business of the Group (74 per cent of total turnover in 2000).
2 Sports business: clothing, accessories and footwear, mainly marketed under the Playlife and Killer Loop brands, and sports equipment (ski boots, skis, roller blades, skateboards, snowboards, scooters, tennis rackets, etc.), distributed under the Nordica, Prince, Killer Loop and Rollerblade brands (20 per cent of total turnover in 2000).
3 Complementary activities: royalties, sales of raw materials, industrial and advertising services (6 per cent of total turnover in 2000).

## Benetton: the archetype of the network organisation

According to the conventional, now outdated, picture[1] of Benetton, the firm's success was based on the following factors:

- Unique and original marketing and communication strategy: the United Colors of Benetton brand has become a world recognised example of counter-intuitiveness, irony, and disruption both in marketing and in advertising.

- Network organisation for distribution: Benetton sells and distributes its products through a number of agents, each responsible for developing a given market area. Benetton does not own the stores, rather, agents set up a contract relationship with the independent store owners (a licensing agreement similar to franchising) who sell Benetton products. Benetton supports the sell-out process by providing the retailers with a number of services (merchandising, etc.).
- Network organisation for manufacturing: the extended use of a network of 'contractors' and 'subcontractors' (mainly small and medium enterprises, many of which owned, completely or partly, by former or current Benetton employees) which supply Benetton factories. This 'hollow' structure has given Benetton a significant cost advantage (lower manufacturing and labour costs), risk reduction (investment selection and risk shifting onto suppliers) and unbeatable flexibility (rapid adjustment to changes in demand).
- Innovative operations management techniques, such as resequencing for postponement: the Benetton manufacturing process postpones garment dyeing for as long as possible, thus, decisions about colours can be delayed in order to better satisfy market trends (so called *tinto-in-capo* strategy).

However, emerging challenges have now caused Benetton to move away from this previously successful strategy.

## The emerging challenges

Globalisation and I&CT are changing the name of the game in the textile-apparel industry. Globalisation of markets implies an increasing cross-country homogenisation of consumers' lifestyles and market preferences and encourages firms to offer 'global' products, with no major national customisation. Factors like marketing economies of scale and brand equity gain more and more importance, triggering firms' size increases and concentration of market shares in the hands of companies – usually big buyers – able to control markets through capillary retail structures.

Globalisation also affects manufacturing. For example, during the last decade, some US retailers have played a major role in shaping overseas production networks in the garment industry. In other cases, like Benetton, globalisation has encouraged both a move towards the internalisation of certain operations – in order to maintain control over the supply chain and to take advantage of economies of scale – and the relocation of production abroad, in order to take advantage of cost (namely labour cost) differentials.

New I&CT have a double-fold profound impact. First, they dramatically reduce information costs, facilitate communications, eliminate barriers related to geographical distances, and allow real time response to market change. Second, they enhance product development and manufacturing, widening the possibility to achieve, simultaneously, better quality, higher efficiency, and faster time to market.

### Challenges in the casual wear business

In recent years there has been a profound transformation in the rules of competition within the textile-apparel industry.

Table 16.1 provides a snapshot on the different strategies of some key actors in the casual wear business (Benetton, The Gap, Hennes & Mauritz, Zara). Almost all Benetton's competitors are international retailers that shape their international production network on the basis of economic considerations (labour cost global scanning, minimisation of foreign trade constraints effects, etc.), realising basically no in-house operations.

This strategy seems to represent a benchmark in the industry, since it allows quick response to market changes, product mix and volume flexibility, and cost efficiency. One of the main features of such a strategy is constituted by the role of retail outlets that no longer merely sell a product, but, rather, draw the customer into the firm's world, communicating its image and philosophy. Since this is harder to do in small retail outlets, ample spaces are needed to display the entire range of garments and accessories. Consequently, the so-called 'megastores' (ranging in size from 1000 to 3000 square metres) have become 'the rule'. They have increasingly substituted small retail outlets not only because they serve to implement this new approach to the relations with customers, but also because they often allow twofold, if not threefold, turnover increases per square metre, when compared with traditional small shops.

**Table 16.1 Global competitors in the casual wear business**

| | Features of the business network | |
|---|---|---|
| **Competitors** | **Supply and production network** | **Distribution and retail network** |
| Benetton (Italy) | • Strong upstream vertical integration<br>• In-house production in 32 production centres: 22 in Italy and 10 abroad<br>• Outsourcing of production to a network of SMEs directly controlled by the Italian and foreign production poles | • Turnover ≈ €2 billions<br>• Retail outlets managed by third parties: about 5500 stores in 120 countries<br>• Retail outlets managed directly: about 60 worldwide<br>• Average size: 120 m² (traditional shops); 1000 m² (megastores) |
| The Gap (USA) | • Complete outsourcing of production | • Turnover ≈ €14 billions<br>• Retail outlets managed directly about 3700 stores mainly in North America<br>• Average size: 700 m² |
| Hennes & Mauritz (Sweden) | • Complete outsourcing of production | • Turnover ≈ €4 billions<br>• Retail outlets managed directly: around 700 stores in 14 countries<br>• Average size: 1300 m² |
| Zara (Spain) | • Partial upstream vertical integration<br>• In-house production in 23 production centres<br>• Outsourcing of production to a network of small shops in Spain and Portugal | • Turnover ≈ €2 billions<br>• Retail outlets managed directly: about 450 stores in 29 countries<br>• Average size: 750 m² |

## Challenges in the sports business

Unlike in the casual wear business, where there is a very special relationship between Benetton and retailers, in the sports business Benetton interfaces with a variety of different actors: big distribution chains, small specialised shops and, also, retail agents. None, apart from the agents, have an exclusive relationship with Benetton, which, therefore, competes with the other producers in each distribution channel. Indeed, the worldwide distribution chains effectively dictate the rules of the game. In large display areas, all the competing sports brands are compared directly by customers. This is particularly important for technical equipment (such as skis) as customers need to have the opportunity to evaluate the features of the various products made by the different makes (for example Nordica, the brand for Benetton skis, compared with Atomic, Rossignol, Fischer, Head, K2, etc.) in order to be able to choose the article that best fulfils their expectations. Design, style, technical performance, technology content, wearability and price are only some of the factors that are critical for success in sport equipment and sportswear. Indeed, the sports industry, though differentiated, is highly competitive and the world market is already virtually saturated, with the exception, perhaps, of some niches.

## Benetton's new global network

Today, Benetton is therefore involved in global competition on two, very different fronts, both of which pose a considerable challenge. On the one hand, there is the traditional casual wear business which has to face up to innovative and aggressive competitors; on the other hand, there is the sports clothing and equipment business which is having to develop and establish itself in a market that is not going to expand much further and in which many of the firms have already consolidated their positions.

### Product design in the casual wear business

Since its beginnings, Benetton has always operated as an international enterprise and has tended to offer the same or a similar range of products in all the national markets it has entered. However, until recently, more than 20 per cent of the models in its ranges were customised in order to satisfy the specific demands of each country (for example smaller sizes for the Far East, specific colours for Middle East countries, etc.). The task of selecting the models best suited to each different clientele was left to the individual retail agents. Effectively this was a 'partial globalisation' resulting in a different image of Benetton in different geographical areas. Today, however, in order to communicate just one image all over the world, Benetton has decided to develop just one, more limited range of products that will be offered in every country. Indeed, nowadays, only 5–10 per cent of the models it offers in each collection have been differentiated in order to meet the specific needs of individual countries. The spring/summer and autumn/winter collections for the year 2001 have been reduced, in terms of the number of articles offered, by as much as 35–40 per cent.

At the same time, Benetton is developing the 'flash' collections – introduced during each retailing season in order to renew the articles offered to customers and to keep up better with the fast-changing market trends – that will, eventually, make up 35–40 per cent of its total products. Thus, a more thorough understanding of customer's expectations and lifestyle, and an increase in the numbers of flash collections launched during each season should strengthen the United Colors of Benetton brand.

The year 2000 was also the year in which Benetton streamlined its brands. The brands related specifically to babies, children and expectant mothers' garments have all been eliminated and unified under the United Colors of Benetton brand. The whole range is now divided on the basis of age with, obviously, different collections for each group (four for children, one for men, women and expectant mothers).

In the field of design, major efforts have been put into the search for new materials, especially easy-care textiles, in order to produce garments that are easy to look after as they can be machine washed and do not need to be ironed. This also is part of Benetton's attempt to reinforce the image of its products, which are fast becoming truly global (the same article is on sale all over the world), young (no specific age group is targeted, rather a lifestyle is), 'easy' (to use and, again, to get hold of) and, above all, of high quality.

## Operations management in the casual wear business

The Benetton conventional network system was characterised, among other factors, by heavily outsourcing the labour-intensive phases of production – such as tailoring, finishing and ironing. Small and medium size firms, mainly located in the north-east of Italy – in the Treviso county in particular – usually specialised in one of these operations and worked as main contractors. However, strategic activities and operations which require heavy fixed investment (amounting to around 30 per cent of the value of production), such as weaving, cutting, dyeing, quality controls at entry and on finished goods, quality control of intermediate phases and packing, have always been carried out within Benetton itself.

In the mid-1990s, as volumes increased, this strategy led Benetton to the setting up of a high-tech production pole at Castrette, not far from the Ponzano headquarters. Undoubtedly, the Castrette pole can be considered one of the most advanced in the world within the textile-apparel industry. It covers an area of more than 100 000 square metres and is divided between the five technical divisions – Wool, Cotton, Tailoring, Shirts and Jackets, Accessories and Shoes – which are responsible for all garments and accessories production, both casual wear and sports clothing. Castrette has an overall production capacity of about 120 million items per year.

Moreover, Benetton has recently changed its relationships with suppliers. In order to take advantages of labour cost differentials, Benetton has relocated some of its outside contractors abroad (Table 16.2).

However, interestingly enough, Benetton has adopted the original Castrette model in the countries it has relocated to – Spain, Portugal, Tunisia, Croatia and Hungary, etc.– recreating, on a smaller scale, directly controlled production poles. Thus, foreign poles are composed of a subsidiary (totally or partially owned and directly managed by Benetton) which coordinates the production activities of a group of the SMEs (small to medium-sized enterprises), often set up and managed

**Table 16.2 Localisation of the foreign production poles**

| Name | Headquarters | Workshops location | Benetton's equity share |
| --- | --- | --- | --- |
| Benetton España S.L. | Castellbisbal | Spain | 100% |
| Benetton Lda. | Maia | Portugal | 100% |
| Benetton Tunisia S.àr.l. | Sahline | Tunisia, Morocco | 100% |
| Benetton Ungheria Kft. | Nagykallo | Hungary, the Ukraine, the Czech Republic, Poland, Moldavia, Bulgaria and Romania | 100% |
| Benetton Croazia | Osijek | Croatia, Slovenia, Serbia | 100% |
| Benetton Korea Inc. | Seoul | Korea | 50% (joint venture) |
| Egyptian European Clothing Manufacturers | Alexandria | Egypt | 50% (joint venture) |
| DCM Benetton India Ltd. | New Delhi | India | 50% (joint venture) |

by ex-Benetton employees or Italian contractors. For example, Benetton Hungary (a foreign subsidiary of the group) coordinates the production activities of outside contractors in Hungary, but also in the Ukraine, the Czech Republic, Poland, Moldavia, Bulgaria and Romania. These production poles make to order: the Castrette pole chooses what is to be produced by each of the foreign production poles, which then, independently, decide how they allocate production tasks among the SMEs they are linked to. Articles produced abroad return to Italy, where they are prepared to be shipped to the final customers.

The foreign production poles focus on one particular type of product and use skills already existing in the area: T-shirts are made in Spain, and jackets in Eastern Europe. Consequently, high-quality production is ensured. At the moment the foreign contribution to Benetton's production is still limited, given that the 70 per cent of Benetton's output is still produced in Italy, but it will increase in the future.

Lastly, it should be noted that even the system of production in the original Italian establishment of Castrette has changed. Indeed, activities that used to be considered critical, such as quality controls at entry and on finished goods, cutting out and dyeing, have been transferred to subsidiaries. Currently, the Castrette pole focuses on such operations as: elaboration of the marker sheets for the computerised fabric cutting system (using CAD and CAM systems), which are then sent, using electronic support, to foreign production poles (for example in Tunisia and Hungary); cutting out prototypes; and, quality control of diverse intermediate phases. Clearly the process of moving production to international subsidiaries and contractors has increased both the necessity for, and the needs, of integration and communication between Castrette and the foreign production poles. Through improved communications, the separate actors of the supply network can coordinate the timing of the various phases in the best way, so as to reduce production lead-times to the minimum. Today, production lead-times are between 35 and 40 days whatever the product may be. However, in the garments sector, the critical factor in time compression does not depend so much on the tailoring phase, but rather on the supplies of raw materials.

In order to overcome this potential problem, Benetton has, over the years, gradually increased the degree of upstream vertical integration to incorporate its textiles and threads suppliers. Indeed, Benetton's main supplier of raw materials – which provides and guarantees 60 per cent of the woven fabric, 90 per cent of cotton knit fabric and 90 per cent of carded and combed wool – is 85 per cent controlled by Benetton itself.

Both upstream vertical integration and partnership relationships with external suppliers have made it possible for Benetton to transfer upstream quality controls on textiles/threads. This, in its turn, allows the materials purchased to be sent direct to workshops and external producers without further controls, thus reducing transport costs and cutting production lead-times overall.

Nevertheless, Benetton has decided to maintain direct control of the logistics phase and has invested heavily in automating logistics processes in order to achieve total integration within the production cycle – from customer orders to packing and consignment. Indeed, today, the average time for consignment is seven days and 10 million garments could be sent out all over the world each month.

## Reshaping the retail network

Benetton's traditional approach of direct retailing entrusted to third parties represented one of the Group's most successful strategies for many years. However, this strategy no longer seems to be able to sustain Benetton's presence on the market. The retail market has recently been characterised by a general tendency to increase the average size of retailing outlets, up to 1500–3000 square metres – the so-called megastores. On the contrary, the average size of Benetton's retail outlets has remained much smaller. Benetton risks seeing its locations suffocated by the aggressive market penetration strategies of its international competitors, whose retail outlet's average size is larger.

In order to face this challenge Benetton has decided to reorganise its commercial policies and change the size of its retail outlets by:

- enlarging its retail outlets, wherever possible, so as to be able to display the whole range of Benetton (or Sisley) products, garments, shoes and accessories
- focusing, where such expansion is not possible, each retail outlet in one market segment and/or product (for example only men's, or only women's products, or only knitwear, or lingerie and/or garments for the seaside etc.)
- opening new large retail outlets (500–2000 square metres) in the main shopping streets and areas of big cities.

Alongside the strategy of rationalising retail outlets, which are still organised using the traditional licensing formula, Benetton has taken on a far greater challenge: the Retail Project. Since November 1999, Benetton has been working on a project which seeks to flank its traditional retail network of licensed retailers with a direct sales network, which will be made up of medium to large-size shops directly owned and managed by the Treviso-based company itself.

The Retail Project, which entails complete downstream integration, represents a marked change in the traditional Benetton model of business organisation. With the Retail Project, Benetton is seeking to challenge competitors, focusing on selling garments with a high styling content, on continuous rotation of the products displayed in outlets and on very large display areas. By opening and directly managing its own retail outlets, Benetton is also able to get closer to the final consumer, thus obtaining more information and reinforcing its image, in a business where fashion is more and more unpredictable, subject to lightning changes and where, as a result, quick response to the market is a key success factor. Moreover, through an information system that directly links Benetton's own retail outlets with headquarters, the firm knows exactly how many, which size and what colour of article has been sold, how much it was paid for these and what remains on the shelves in the shops. Thus, Benetton is able to design and produce collections on the basis of continuously updated information.

By the end of 2000 Benetton had already set up more than 60 megastores throughout the world, and a further dozen have been opened so far during the year 2001. Benetton aims to have 100 megastores worldwide by the end of 2002. So as to give maximum visibility to the Benetton brand, the first megastores have all been opened in major cities, such as Paris, London, Rome, Milan, New York, Tokyo, Sao Paulo, Moscow, Hong Kong, Wien, Brussels, etc.

## Reorganisation of the sports business

After the merger with Benetton Sportsystem, the Benetton Group has had to develop a way of coping with two, distinct businesses: casual wear and sportswear/sports equipment. In doing so, Benetton has tried to exploit to the utmost the possible synergies between such businesses. In the short term, the greatest and most easily realised synergies concern all activities linked to sportswear, while the biggest differences are found in the area of sports equipment.

The world market for sports equipment and clothing is, typically, made up of 20 per cent sports equipment and 80 per cent soft clothing (sportswear and footwear). Currently, the 88 per cent of Benetton Group turnover in the sports business derives from sports equipment and only 12 per cent from sports clothing. Benetton intends to expand its sportswear (clothing) business with respect to its sports equipment activities, given that, usually, in the clothing sector – both casual and sports – a leading firm can aim to achieve a 20 per cent margin, whereas in the sports equipment sector even a leader can only hope to achieve an 8 per cent margin. The short to medium-term aim is to attain a turnover in the sports sector where 60 per cent derives from equipment and 40 per cent from sports clothing, while in the medium-long term Benetton aims to mirror the distribution typically found in the world market (20 per cent sports equipment and 80 per cent soft clothing).

In order to support its strategy, Benetton has been investing heavily in sportswear development, trying to offer very wide Playlife and Killer Loop collections, ranging from the top level to the most economic items, and offering not strictly technological clothing items, but rather items designed to attract a broader spectrum of consumers. On the contrary, in the sports equipment business, Benetton is seeking to consolidate the images of its brands by continually offering products which are highly innovative, both in terms of performance and in terms of the features they incorporate.

The initiatives so far set up are:

## Design of sports equipment

Over the past two years Benetton has invested more than $5 million in high-technology systems specifically for designing sports equipment. The aim is to offer products with a high technological content, which the final consumer will really be able to perceive as being better than those of competitors. This strategy wishes – to a certain extent – to persuade the large distribution chains to necessarily include Benetton's products in the range they offer because final consumers do expect this. From the organisational point of view, all the sports equipment-related R&D activities have now been concentrated in Italy, in Venegazzù, Treviso county, whereas formerly they were spread out all over the world (rollerblades in Minnesota, skis in Austria, etc.). In this way, the decision-making process should become more effective and the management of common services more efficient. The concentration of all R&D activities in one place – an open space of about 2000 square metres where more than 100 people work together every day – also aims to exploit possible synergies within the product innovation process to the maximum. Indeed, such choice multiplies cross-fertilisation opportunities, as project leaders and researchers can easily share information and knowledge about both materials and production processes. Moreover, people involved in R&D activities can also share their distinctive cultures and skills which once were not only part of different 'worlds' (different companies, products, brands, etc.), but also of different mentalities, such as the US one – typical of Prince and Rollerblade – and the Italian one that refers to Nordica.

## Operations management

The reorganisation of the production process has been based on two main guidelines: on the one hand, the need not only to minimise manufacturing costs but also to cut the costs of transporting materials and part-finished items from one site to another; on the other hand, the need to both maintain and constantly expand the know-how associated with the quite handcrafted style of production activities. This reorganisation of operations has been carried out by:

- concentrating production of ski boots, skates, skis, attachments and accessories in the production plant at Trevignano, in Treviso county. The Trevignano plant has been designed similarly to the Castrette pole centralising just the high value-added manufacturing and logistics activities
- delocating the whole or part of production of some products in countries where labour costs are lower (for example, part of the rollerblade production in Hungary and China)
- concentrating management and control of sportswear production at Castrette so as to exploit as many synergies with the production of casual wear as possible.

## Retail network

The process of merging with the casual wear business has also affected commercial and marketing activities which previously were entrusted to the Benetton Sportsystem European subsidiaries. This made possible both more direct monitoring of the market and closer relations with major customers (for example with large specialised chains). Moreover, concentration has also helped to eliminate all the fixed costs that arose from maintaining intermediary structures, such as trading companies, which were replaced by agents. In this way, both warehousing and distribution have been completely rationalised. More specifically, Benetton has tried to optimise its distribution network structure in two ways: (1) by developing, within the large sports shops of the distribution chains, special areas dedicated to displaying and selling Benetton's sports equipment brands, and (2) by constructing a new specific network of Playlife retail outlets, repeating the model successfully developed in the casual wear business. In 2000, Playlife brand reinforced its image in the sportswear market after it was chosen as the official supplier for the Italian team sent to the Olympic Games in Australia. The other brand with which Benetton commercialises its sportswear products is Killer Loop, which is destined for a young, extrovert public. Moreover, interestingly enough, Benetton is attempting to develop partnership commercial relations with its direct customers, the big specialised distribution chains. This allows Benetton to change from a make-to-stock production approach (usually imposed by the large distribution chains) to a make-to-order one, according to a new kind of commercial agreement that is called Blade Express Formula. Benetton offers special commercial credit to customers that accept the Blade Express Formula and does not produce on the basis of forecasts any more, thus avoiding warehousing (very risky, given the rapid rate of obsolescence in the sports products sector). Currently the Blade Express Formula covers 70 per cent of total orders.

## Fabrica and United Web

One of the distinctive traits of Benetton is the way in which it is continually seeking new means of communication. Such a search, in recent years, has led the company to undertake advertising campaigns that have been based on social and universal themes, such as racism, AIDS, nature conservation, and life and death.

Benetton's interest in communication led it, in 1994, to set up a centre for the research and development of communication, Fabrica – a Latin word which means workshop – an incubator and a catalyst for the cultural inheritance of the Group. Headed by an international scientific committee which ensures the strategic, cultural and communication validity of the project, Fabrica has invested in creativity and brought young people and experimental artists from all over the world, as guests, to the huge complex near Treviso, which was designed by the architect Tadao Ando and inaugurated in September 2000. Fabrica occupies a total area of 11 000 square metres. It has a cinema, an auditorium, libraries, laboratories and photographic studios. The projects so far carried out by Fabrica have involved many different non-profit organisations, such as the Food and Agriculture Organisation (FAO) and SOS Racism, as well as both cultural institutions and museums in various countries. It has been recognised as an emergent, lively cultural centre, esteemed and appreciated at the international level. Some successful examples are the special award won by the movie *Blackboards* at Cannes Film Festival, 2000 and the Golden Lion won by the movie *Dayereh* at Venice Film Festival, 2000.

Even in the world of the net-economy, Benetton has found an original approach. In order to manage its e-commerce venture, Benetton has founded a company – United Web. The declared short-term aim of United Web is not increasing sales by introducing a new form of distribution, but is rather exploring and being present in an area which is considered to be potentially very interesting as a means of (1) reinforcing contacts with customers, and (2) making Benetton's products and style known to an increasing number of potential customers. The Benetton.com site has been conceived not simply as a virtual shopping centre where customers can buy Benetton products online, but rather as a horizontal portal, through which Internet navigators can find a far wider and more varied offer of services. These services range from critics' reviews of the latest LP by the singer Björk to holiday offers in Thailand, from the chance of listening to the latest CDs by Ricky Martin and Britney Spears to a summary of the spiciest gossip about VIPs in the public eye. All the time, while the visitor is listening to pop music, or reading reviews and gossip, images of products on offer that can be bought online run along a banner at the bottom of the screen.

United Web seeks to take advantage of the development of electronic transactions and confirms Benetton's attitude to innovation in a medium – the Internet – compatible with its business philosophy and global image. Entering the e-business world is consistent with Benetton's communication strategy and with the attempt to provide consumers with a comprehensive experience, a lifestyle. Therefore, United Web represents not only an additional distribution channel (business-to-customer B2C), but also an opportunity to transform all the relationships among the actors of the network.

As to the future, e-procurement and online services for the distribution network are only a few of the projects on which Benetton managers are currently working.

### Questions

1 *Identify and summarise the main differences between the conventional and the new Benetton networks, addressing product design, supply and production, and retail networks, both in the casual wear and sports businesses.*

2 *Identify and discuss the major characteristics of Benetton's innovative strategy to design and manage its global supply network.*

### Reference

1 Some versions of the Benetton story can be fund in Signorelli, S. and Heskett, J. (1984) 'Benetton', *Harvard Business School case no. 6-985-014*, Harvard Business School Publishing Corp.: Boston; Dubini, P. (1991) 'United Colors of Benetton' in *Corporate Transformation*, ed. A. Sinatra, Kluwer Academic Publishers: Norwell, Massachusetts, 415–446; Harrison, B. (1994) *Lean and Mean: The New Landscape of Corporate Power in the Age of Flexibility*, Basic Books: New York.

# Boys and Boden (A)

Case date
1988
Stuart Chambers

'There *must* be a better way of running this place!' said Dean Hammond, recently recruited General Manager of Boys and Boden, as he finished a somewhat stressful conversation with a complaining customer, a large and loyal local building contractor.

'We had six weeks to make their special staircase, and we are still late! I'll have to persuade one of the joiners to work overtime this weekend to get everything ready for Monday. We never seem to get complaints about quality, as our men always do an excellent job ... but there is usually a big backlog of work, and something always gets finished late, so how should we set priorities? We could do the most profitable work first, or the work for our biggest customers, or the jobs which are most behind on. In practice, we try to satisfy everyone as best we can, but inevitably someone's order will be late. In theory, each job should be quite profitable, since we build into the price a big allowance for waste, and for timber defects. And we know the work content of almost any task we would have to do; this is the basis of our estimating system. But, overall, the department is disappointingly unprofitable, and most problems seem to end up with a higher-than-anticipated cost, and with late deliveries!'

Boys and Boden was a small, successful, privately-owned timber and building materials merchant based in a small town. Over the years it had established a large Joinery Department, which made doors, windows, staircases and other timber products, all to the exact special requirements of the customers, mostly comprising numerous local and regional builders. In addition, the joiners would cut and prepare special orders of timber, such as non-standard sections and special profiles, including old designs of skirting board, sometimes at very short notice, and often even while the customers waited. Typically, for larger joinery items, the customer provided simple dimensioned sketches of the required products. These were then passed to the central Estimating and Quotations Department which, in conjunction with the Joinery Manager, calculated costs and prepared a written quotation, which was faxed or posted to the customer. This first stage was normally completed within two or three days, but on occasions could take a week or more. On receipt of an order, the original sketches and estimating details were passed back to the Joinery Manager, who roughly scheduled them into his manufacturing plan, allocating them to individual craftsmen as each became available. Most of the joiners were capable of making any product, and enjoyed the wide variety of challenging work.

The Joinery Department appeared congested and somewhat untidy, but everyone believed that this was acceptable and normal for job shops, since there was no single flow route for materials. Whatever the design of the item being made, or the quantity, it was normal for the joiner to select the required bulk timber from the storage building across the yard. This roughly-sawn timber was then prepared using a planer-thicknesser machine which gave it smooth, parallel surfaces. After that, the joiners would use a variety of processes, depending on product. The timber could be machined into different cross-sectional shapes, cut into component lengths using a radial arm saw, joints were formed by hand tools, or using a morticing machine, and so on. Finally the products would be glued and assembled with screws and nails, sanded smooth by hand or by machine, and treated with preservatives, stains or varnishes if required. All the large and more expensive floor-standing machines were grouped together by type (for example, saws) or were single pieces of equipment shared by all 10 joiners. Every joiner also owned a complete set of hand tools which they guarded and cared for with pride. Dean described what one might observe on a random visit to the Joinery Department:

'One or two long staircases partly assembled, and crossing several work areas; large door frames on trestles being assembled; stacks of window components for a large contract being prepared and jointed, and so on. Offcuts and wood shavings are scattered around the work area, but are periodically cleared when they get in the way or form a hazard. The joiners try to fit in with each other over the use of machinery, so are often working on several, part-finished items at once. Varnishing or staining has to be done when it's quiet, for example towards the end of the working day or at weekends, or even outside, to avoid sawdust contamination. Long offcuts are stacked around the workshop, to be used up on any future occasion when these lengths or sections are required. However, it is often easier to take a new length of timber for each job, so the offcuts do tend to build up over time. Unfortunately everything I have described is getting worse as we get busier … our sales are increasing so the system is getting more congested. The joiners are almost climbing over each other to complete their work. Unfortunately, despite having more orders, the department has remained stubbornly unprofitable!

'Whilst analysing in detail the lack of profit, we were horrified to find that, for the majority of orders, the actual times booked by the joiners exceeded the estimated times by up to 50 per cent. Sometimes this was clearly attributable to the inexperience of newly employed joiners. Although fully trained and qualified, they might lack the experience needed to complete a complex job in the time an Estimator would expect; but there had been no feedback of this to the individual. We then put one of these men on doors only; having overcome his initial reluctance, he has become an enthusiastic "door expert" and gets closely involved in quotations too, so now he always does his work within the time estimates! However, the main time losses were found to be the result of general delays caused by congestion, interference, double-handling, and rework to rectify in-process damage. Moreover, we found that a joiner walked an average of nearly 5 km a day, usually carrying around heavy bits of wood.

'When I did my operations management course on my MBA, the professor described the application of cellular manufacturing and JIT. From what I can remember, the idea seems to be to get better flow, reducing the times and distances in the process, and thus achieving quicker throughput times. That is just what we needed, but these concepts were explained in the context of high-volume, repetitive production of bicycles, whereas all the products we make are one-offs. However, although we do make a lot of different staircases, they all use roughly the same process steps:

1 Cutting timber to width and length
2 Sanding
3 Machining
4 Tenoning
5 Manual assembly (glue and wedges)

'We have a lot of unused factory floor space, so it would be relatively easy to set up a self-contained staircase cell. There is a huge demand for specially-made stairs in this region, but also a lot of competing small joinery businesses with low overheads, which can beat us on price and lead-time. So we go to a lot of trouble quoting for stairs, but only win about 20 per cent of the business. If we could get the cell idea to work, we should be more competitive on price and delivery, hence winning more orders. At least that is the theory. I know we will need a lot more volume to justify establishing the cell, so it's really a case of whether to construct a cell in anticipation of higher demand, or to try to win more business first. To do the latter, we would have to reduce our selling prices and lead-times, and then allocate more joiners to complete the higher volumes of orders until we had enough work to set up the cell. I personally favour setting up the cell first so that we can have a "capacity leads demand" strategy.'

### Questions

1 *To what extent could (or should) Dean expect to apply the philosophies and techniques of JIT to the running of the staircase cell?*

2 *What are likely to be the main categories of costs and benefits in establishing the cell? Are there any non-financial benefits which should be taken into account?*

3 *At what stage, and how, should Dean sell his idea to the Joinery Manager and to the workers?*

4 *How different would the cell work (job design) be to that in the main Joinery Department?*

5 *Should Dean differentiate the working environment by providing distinctive workwear, such as T-shirts, and distinctively-painted machines in order to reinforce a cultural change?*

6 *What risks are associated with Dean's proposal?*

# Boys and Boden (B)

Stuart Chambers

This case study should only be used after Boys and Boden (A) which gives background information on the business and on the issues involved in setting up the cellular manufacturing system for special staircases.

## ● Cellular production

The staircase cell had been a great success! In well under a year, the company had established an enviable reputation for high quality, quick delivery and very competitive prices.

The best production configuration had proved to be a rectangular area of the factory, equipped with a full set of the requisite machinery (bench-saw, planer-thicknesser, spindle moulder, tenoning machines, surface sander, assembly benches, etc.) and two skilled joiners (carpenters). They worked well together and their productivity was dramatically higher than had ever been seen in the job shop environment. As a result of the increased competitiveness, volume was increasing, but attempts to use three men had proved unsatisfactory. Given the limited space available, they seemed to be getting in each other's way, and productivity fell, reducing the benefits of cellular manufacturing which had been found in the earlier months of the experiment. There was always a feeling that 'two's company and three's a crowd', as the two-person cell seemed to work as a better team than three.

Dean Hammond, General Manager of Boys and Boden (B&B), reflected on their experience of changing the staircase production system:

'This has been one big learning experience for us all! We knew what machinery we would need, but it was not at all clear in advance how much space would be used productively and how the men would take to more repetitive work. Hardly any of their staircases are identical, but they do only make staircases, whereas before they would have moved on to windows, doors, and all sorts of other special items required by a multitude of customers. In practice we should not have worried, since the two men immediately took responsibility for their work area, sorted things out, and developed a pride in their specialised work.

'With only one cell, our output was clearly limited, so we began to think about adding a second identical cell. This would certainly introduce an element of competition, which could have a positive impact on productivity and quality. However, we felt that this was not really the only way of expanding capacity. Perhaps there were ways of introducing technology to simplify all the manufacture of these specialised staircases. In fact, this seemed to be one of the few industries left where most of the technologies had changed very little during the micro-electronics revolution. Making specialised joinery remains the domain of a diminishing number of highly skilled craftsmen, and the number of good quality apprenticeships had declined dramatically over the last 20 years. I knew we had to rethink what we were doing, and I knew this was an opportunity to focus on high-value-added products with relatively certain levels of future volume.

'For each job, the joiners start by "setting out" the strings (the long sides of a staircase), drawing at full scale the overall shape and positions of cuts and grooves to be made in the wood. They get the required information from detailed drawings included with the production specification. This specification is sometimes provided by the customer, but more often is prepared in the drawing office here. The setting out is a very time-consuming step, taking up to two days for all the components of a really complex staircase, for example, a flight of stairs which turns through 90 or more degrees, known as a "winder". The selling price of large, complex staircases can be very high, but the work content is correspondingly large, so our margins are not always that great!'

## ● The seed of an idea…

'Whilst watching the staircases being made, I came to realise that the men were, in effect, duplicating the work done in a drawing office – the data is the same, but scaled up from the drawings. If we were to grow this business, we would need to find ways of increasing the overall productivity of the system. We knew that there should be a way of getting the data directly transferred to the wood, and I know this has been achieved in many industries using CAD/CAM, so a few months ago I started investigating the possibility of purchasing suitable systems. There are several reputable manufacturers that make large computer-aided manufacturing (CAM) machining centres for use in the metals industry, but there appears to be only a few specifically developed for the woodworking industry. I then identified one German supplier that can modify and enlarge one of its largest machines for our application, but there will be an element of experimentation and innovation involved here. They do have some experience with wood machining, but only for small components. Our staircase strings are up to five metres long! By the time the clamping tables have been extended, this will be an extremely expensive piece of equipment!

'It is clear that there are a few very large manufacturers of staircases in the UK, but they specialise in standard sizes which are sold in huge quantities to large builders and merchants. They are, in effect, making commodities and their manufacturing systems are designed to make large batches of standard components, which are then assembled on production lines. It is clear that we will never be able to compete profitably in this part of the market. However, an increasing number of house builders are using staircases as an attractive feature of hallways, and some of these require more complex shapes (including winders) and better finishes [an example is shown in Appendix 18.1]. In addition, refurbishment of existing houses often requires the installation of special staircases designed to fit into awkward spaces, and with non-standard heights. There is also increasing demand for expensive feature hardwoods such as oak and beech, which are not usually mass-produced. These changes are providing an opportunity for us to become a specialist, not just serving our local area, but providing non-standard stair-cases throughout the country. For this to be competitive, our quality will have to be excellent, our delivery time will have to be quicker than the average local joinery shop, and our production costs will have to be much lower to more than offset our higher delivery costs.'

## The new brand: going for growth

'Even with our somewhat limited cellular production system, I knew that we should start marketing our capability, and so we have branded this business "Pear Stairs", with an eye-catching new logo provided by a local image consultant, who also prepared an excellent new brochure. Our regional marketing campaign has already brought in a high level of enquiries, most of which are for special staircases, with delivery often required very quickly, often in less than two weeks. It is increasingly apparent that there is a huge opportunity to roll out our capability over an expanding geographical area, only limited by our ability to continue to supply quickly. I am now even more certain that we will need to mechanise some or all of the time-consuming processes, from design to final assembly.

'During our first year of running the cell, our monthly turnover of staircases has doubled from around £4000 to £8000, and is now only constrained by capacity. The monthly management accounts indicate that our staircases are now very profitable. Even within the local trading area (mostly agricultural and small market towns, with low population density, covering a radius of about 80 kilometres) demand seems to greatly exceed supply, and we are in effect limiting sales by quoting fairly long lead-times and high prices. If we could double turnover so easily, there is surely good potential to broaden our area to take in some larger centres of population, but only if we could increase our capacity substantially. The time is now right for deciding whether to invest in a state-of-the-art technology.'

## CAD/CAM

'The system we have devised includes computer-aided design (CAD) and computer-aided manufacturing (CAM). No single firm supplies both for this type of joinery product, so we will have to take responsibility for linking the two systems. We have identified the best supplier of CAD systems for special stairs, and have already ordered a two-workstation system, so that we can begin trials of this as soon as possible. Even if we decide not to go ahead with the manufacturing system, we can continue to supply joinery design services using this new design technology. The digital output of the CAD is adaptable to the input requirements of the proposed CAM. This initial CAD system will cost us around £15 000 for hardware and software. But the really big decision concerns the CAM system, which will cost in the order of £240 000, the single largest investment ever made in this small business! Everybody thinks I'm mad even contemplating it, but we have already prepared a business case for raising the money, and our bank manager has agreed to support this radical innovation. In practice, the bank's risk is relatively low, since the loan would be secured on our real estate, and for that reason we have been able to agree a very low interest rate. The shareholders (this is a family business) are supportive in principle, but a little nervous, I think! This could be a make-or-break decision not only for the future of joinery manufacture within the company, but also of the company itself!

'In my view, the future of any generalist joinery job shop is under threat anyway. Already, window specialists have acquired the processes and technology to make bespoke windows efficiently, and the same is happening with doors. That will take volume away from the thousands of small joinery businesses that make a wide variety of "specials", threatening their very survival. This trend will be compounded and accelerated by the scarcity of trained joiners in this country! Eventually, specialisation and technology will displace the slow and inefficient traditional generalist craftsmen. There is a real window of opportunity here – to be the first to adopt these technologies for staircases – and there will be first-mover advantages, so we need to get this underway as soon as possible. The technology is extremely precise – positional accuracy is better than one-tenth of a millimetre for every cut, which is an order of magnitude better than can consistently be achieved by skilled joiners. This means we can get very accurate and tight joints, and, hopefully, the elimination of mistakes where drawings are misread! This CAD/CAM technology could actually be used to machine virtually any joinery components, but I feel that we simply must not be distracted by this capability. We want to specialise just in stairs, and therefore should not get into making windows, doors or any other special products, even in quiet periods. This is a strategic issue – if you believe in the benefits of focus, you mustn't get distracted from focus!'

## The proposed design process

'On receipt of customers' orders, their sketches and any other forms of information supplied by the customer detailing their requirements will be delivered to the small design office. Here, the two CAD designers will extract the dimensions and apply them to the CAD staircase templates held on the system. Trials indicate that this will be a relatively quick process, taking between half an hour and two hours depending on the complexity of the design. Thus a detailed drawing of the whole staircase can be produced very quickly, and a copy can then be sent back to the customer for their confirmation. The system holds all the details on each staircase, so that when confirmation and approval is received, the details can be immediately passed electronically to the CAM system. In theory, it should be possible to e-mail the drawings to a customer, but at present most builders prefer paper and many sites do not even have faxes! It will be a few years before we can link electronically to both the buyers and the site managers of even the larger builders. Smaller builders may never adopt this technology.'

## The proposed manufacturing process

'Briefly, the process will work something like this: one of the factory team workers will select and prepare the pre-planed timber for all the components to be produced for a staircase, working from a detailed cutting list and drawings supplied by the CAD system. This will involve him selecting planed timber from stock, cutting it to length, and sometimes gluing pieces together. He will then pass these components through a sanding machine. He will continue until a full set of pieces is ready on a trolley. This "kit" of materials will then wait in a small buffer area prior to being machined on the CAM.

'The CAM operator will then carefully position each piece of timber in turn on an adjustable vacuum clamping device forming part of the bed of the CAM machine. Precise alignment will be facilitated by a laser light outline projected from the ceiling, corresponding to the staircase and component reference stored in the CAM server. The operator then will initiate the automatic machining of the components. The CAM machine will select appropriate tooling from its own tooling "library" and will complete the entire machining of the component with no further operator involvement. In the meantime, the operator will be able to position the next component on the opposite end of the CAM bed, and also clean away the wood chippings and sawdust at that end. In this way it should be possible to virtually eliminate set-up time. The machined component will then be unclamped from the bed and placed on another trolley; when filled, this will be taken to the assembly area. Every component of a staircase can be prepared in this way, including handrails, treads, risers, newels, etc. No setting-out will be required, saving enormous amounts of time. For example, a very complex string will take only about five minutes to machine; whereas a skilled joiner might take several hours just to mark out such a component, followed by up to a day using hand tools to cut the various features.

'The other three workers on each shift will be responsible for assembly and packing. Additional special clamping tables will be purchased which facilitate accurate assembly of all the components. Most of the assembly work involves gluing and wedging, but some components will be nailed or stapled using compressed-air-driven hand tools. Finally, the completed staircase will be lightly sanded, inspected and packed as a builder's kit ready for despatch. Where separate components will be assembled on-site, an additional step will include trial assembly within our factory. None of the workers will be traditionally skilled joiners, but will be newly trained to do these specific jobs. Both of the existing skilled joiners in the staircase cell are being trained as CAD operators, which is where we expect them to work when the new machine is installed.

'By keeping the components on a limited number of trolleys between each stage of production, we can limit work-in-progress. This should keep the cell tidy and orderly, eliminating damage and shortages. It will also ensure quicker throughput times, supporting the short delivery lead-times required by many of our new customers.'

## Developing a business plan

'I have set up a working party to fine-tune the business plan for this project, prior to agreeing the loan conditions and ordering the machinery. We have contracted out a limited piece of market research to confirm the prospects for serving national builders and merchants. This indicates that there is a vast market for specials in the UK – far in excess of our capacity. Our UK market share would in fact be quite low, and our proposed differentiation based on delivery speed is confirmed as an important criterion in this market. We have therefore projected volumes growing to £50000 per month by the end of Year 1. This represents sales of approximately 100 stairs, or around four or five per working day. I am quite confident that we can easily achieve this level before the end of 2000, given our experiences to date, so subsequent years should easily reach the forecast sales shown on the spreadsheet.

'Regarding costs, we have had to make a number of broad assumptions. Since this technology has never before been used to make staircases, the actual output speeds can only be based on estimates derived from the CAM supplier's experience with much smaller timber components. Therefore, we have had to make all such estimates relatively pessimistic – "playing safe". In that way, if the system performs better than expectations, the breakeven point will be lower and the profit even higher. The detailed times per component and per staircase indicate that the breakeven output could easily be achieved by two teams of five operatives, working two shifts. This will be the first time we have used two-shift working, so we will undoubtedly experience some unforeseen problems. I have asked our accountant to prepare budgets for the first four years of the system [see Appendix 18.2], which clearly indicate that excellent profits should be achieved when we can reach the forecast 2003 sales of £80 000 per month. The entire team has endorsed my view that we should actually achieve this level before the end of 2002!

'So…this is not only a strategic investment which will ensure our future in bespoke joinery, but it will also give outstanding returns and positive cash flow after the learning period of Year 1! What do you think –  have we missed anything? Do you agree that we should go ahead?'

### Questions

1 *Evaluate the proposed CAD/CAM system in terms of its contribution to each of the five operations performance objectives. In doing this, you could make comparisons between the existing and proposed system.*

2 *Analyse the degree of automation inherent in the proposed system. What other process elements could be automated, and what are unlikely ever to be automated? Explain your rationale.*

3 *Is there any evidence that the CAM technology could be purchased at a smaller scale? and if so, why has Dean not considered that option? Is the proposed scale too big/ambitious a change from the existing jobbing processes?*

4 *Where is there any integration between technologies? What risks will there be at this interface(s), and how could these be minimised?*

5 *To what extent does the proposed CAD/CAM system provide future opportunities to integrate customer, information, and material processing technologies? Could this provide any USPs (unique selling points) for the company?*

6 *Carry out a net present value calculation for this project, based on a discount rate of 8 per cent. What does this indicate about the viability of the project?*

7 *Summarise the pros and cons of this investment. On balance, do you feel it should go ahead, either as proposed or in a modified way?*

## A typical non-standard staircase

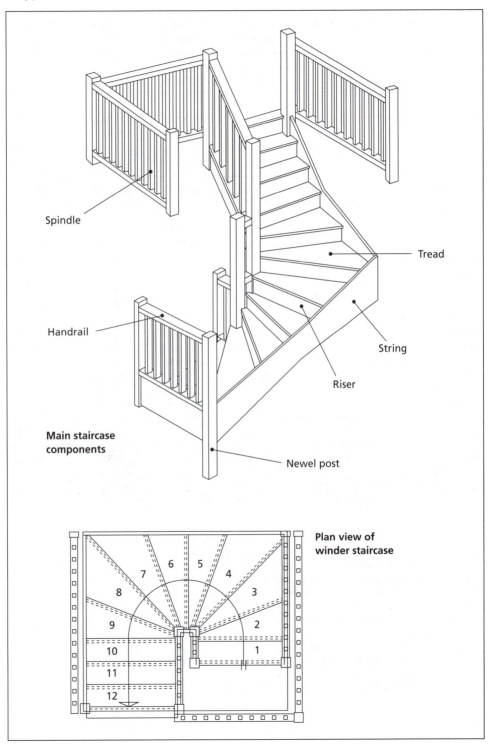

Spindle

Tread

Handrail

String

Riser

**Main staircase
components**

Newel post

**Plan view of
winder staircase**

## Appendix 18.2

## Financial projections and cash flow

| Boys and Boden: Staircase CAD/CAM cell proposal | Note | Average month: Break-even | Forecast Year 1 (2000) | Forecast Year 2 (2001) | Forecast Year 3 (2002) | Forecast Yrs 4/5 (2003) & (2004) |
|---|---|---|---|---|---|---|
| Turnover: Sales | | 50000 | 520000 | 720000 | 840000 | 960000 |
| **Direct costs** | | | | | | |
| Materials (46%) | 1 | 23000 | 239200 | 331200 | 386400 | 441600 |
| Production wages | 2 | 12000 | 146000 | 172800 | 201600 | 230400 |
| Contract delivery | | 1000 | 10250 | 11750 | 14250 | 15750 |
| Total | | 36000 | 395450 | 515750 | 602250 | 687750 |
| **Contribution** | | 14000 | 124550 | 204250 | 237750 | 272250 |
| **Overheads** | | | | | | |
| Salaries | 3 | 2000 | 24000 | 26000 | 28000 | 30000 |
| Wages | 4 | 4500 | 54000 | 65000 | 75000 | 80000 |
| Postage and stationery | | 200 | 2400 | 3000 | 3500 | 4000 |
| Telephone | | 100 | 1500 | 1700 | 1900 | 2100 |
| Car expenses | 5 | 200 | 3000 | 4250 | 4250 | 4250 |
| Gas/electricity | | 200 | 1800 | 2000 | 2200 | 2400 |
| Rates (local tax) | | 100 | 750 | 850 | 950 | 1050 |
| Advertising | | 100 | 1200 | 2000 | 3000 | 3000 |
| Interest charges | 6 | 900 | 10800 | 10800 | 10800 | 10800 |
| Repairs and maintenance | 7 | 700 | 8400 | 10000 | 12000 | 14000 |
| General overheads | 8 | 2000 | 24000 | 26000 | 28000 | 30000 |
| Sundries | | 0 | 2350 | 2500 | 2750 | 3000 |
| Total | | 11000 | 134200 | 154100 | 172350 | 184600 |
| **Depreciation** | 9 | 3000 | 40000 | 40000 | 40000 | 40000 |
| **Profit** | | 0 | −49650 | 10150 | 25400 | 47650 |
| **Annual cash flow** | | | −9650 | +50150 | +65400 | +87650 |
| **Cumulative cash flow** | 10 | | −9650 | +40500 | +105900 | +193550 |

*Notes*

1 Average percentage of materials from recent history of cellular production
2 Based on two shift x 40 hours production, five people per shift.
   Semi-skilled rate including shift allowance and employment costs: £7.50 per hour
3 Staircase Business Manager, including employment costs
4 Weekly paid: two designers and estimator, including employment costs
5 Pool car for manager and estimator
6 Bank loan: fixed interest for purchase of machine and for extra working capital, less 25% down-payment (deposit) from B&B's reserves
7 Mostly cutting tool repair and replacement
8 Fixed costs of whole business, apportioned to departments by % turnover
9 £240000 depreciated linearly over six years
10 Excluding initial investment of £240000, financed by loan

# CASE 19

# Cadbury Ltd:
# A routine investment decision?

Case date 1992
(additional text
added 1995)*

Stuart Chambers

## Introduction

Cadbury Ltd was founded by a Quaker, John Cadbury, in Birmingham, England in 1794 and sold tea, coffee, cocoa and drinking chocolate. In 1866, his sons started producing chocolate bars, which proved so successful that, in 1879, the business moved to a larger site on the edge of the city. The company built a new factory, along with housing and recreation facilities at Bournville which became internationally famous as a model community. Cadbury is now market leader in UK chocolate confectionery (see Table 19.1), with worldwide exports, and volume is continuing to increase by about five per cent per year.

Chocolate-making starts with a series of primary processes, which convert full cream milk, sugar and cocoa into a wide range of recipes of thick (viscous) liquid chocolate. This chocolate is used at secondary processes to mould bars such as Cadbury Dairy Milk (CDM), to coat biscuits and assortments, and to make speciality products such as Easter eggs. Often, UK and export markets require different recipes to cater for legislative and climatic differences.

The conching process is a later stage of the primary processes. These enormous machines take fatty powders from earlier primary stages and, through a shearing action between large contra-rotating rollers, release fats and disperse the solids to produce liquid chocolate with various controllable physical properties, such as temperature and viscosity. The main steps in the primary processes are outlined in Figure 19.1. Late in 1991, at a regular meeting of the Management Committee, a routine discussion centred on the purchase of additional equipment for the Chocolate Department. David Manuel, Manufacturing Director of the Bournville

**Table 19.1  UK market share of chocolate confectionery (1988)**

| Company | % Market share | |
| --- | --- | --- |
| | By volume (kg) | By value (£) |
| Mars | 30 | 24 |
| Cadbury | 26 | 29 |
| Rowntree-Nestlé | 26 | 27 |
| Others | 18 | 20 |

* Based on research originally conducted by Helen Valentine. Names and data have been disguised.

**Figure 19.1 Primary chocolate processes**

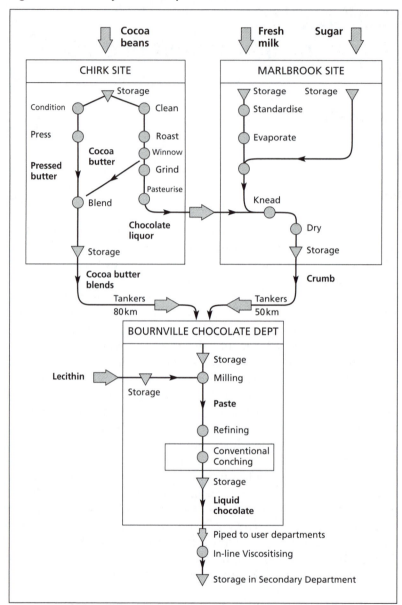

site, was supporting his recent £1.5m. capital application for a fifth conventional 'conch' machine, to provide an additional 25 per cent capacity for the department.

'We really should not delay this decision again! If we can't approve the purchase of another conch machine, we will not be able to meet the forecast growth in demand for 1992/3, and we will be forced to cut back on all our expansion plans. We are already experiencing frequent capacity problems in the chocolate plant ... it is certainly our worst bottleneck! It is now sometimes nearly impossible to plan an efficient sequence of production of different grades of chocolate to satisfy the various needs of all the secondary user departments. My proposal is that we should purchase another conventional conch machine which could be installed and working in under six months. Because it would be identical to the existing four machines, we would have considerable flexibility ... for example, to move staff around the different conches, to plan for any type of chocolate on any conch, and to hold standard spare parts. There would also be greater opportunity to dedicate one conch to one grade of chocolate, so cutting out many costly change-overs. I really cannot support Chris' proposal to buy the "new technology conch". Because it could take 12–15 months to make and install, it's certainly not going to solve next year's capacity problems. It would require completely different skills, both in production and maintenance, and would even require different planning rules. All this would be far too disruptive at a time when we need to concentrate on output and new product development. I'm sorry, Chris, I do think that you've done a good job on the development of the new small-scale conch, but I would rather invest the extra capital at Bournville in more in-line viscositising and much more chocolate storage, to decouple primary and secondary processes.

'However, I am certain that the new technology conch would be well-suited to a greenfield development such as at one of our new joint-venture operations in Eastern Europe where we could standardise on this new equipment. This would also eliminate the risks of potential subtle changes in taste being noticed by our customers. With the greatest respect to Chris and his team, I cannot understand how we've ended up with a new technology without first establishing a clear market need for it!'

Mark Mitchell, Marketing Director, commented:

'I really must agree with David. I too support the idea of purchasing another conventional conch, as otherwise we can get into production by mid-1992; the new technology conch would not be into production until at least six months later. But, even more importantly, while we know that the small trial machine has made chocolate which the tasting panel cannot distinguish from our standard product, there is no guarantee that would be the case for a machine 10 times larger. We know that conching is critical in creating our unique "Cadbury Dairy Milk" (CDM) flavour and texture, so we should take no risks and stick with the type of process we have been using for at least 80 years. At least 70 per cent of our customers, particularly in the UK, can distinguish the taste of CDM from competitors' products such as "Galaxy" (Mars) and "Yorkie" (Rowntree-Nestlé). The early commissioning of the extra capacity will allow us to go ahead with our schedule of planned trials and new product launches, which are already being disrupted by capacity and planning constraints. How could we possibly justify the delays and risks associated with the new technology, Chris?'

Chris English, the Director of Engineering Development, had been expecting resistance to his proposal from Marketing, but had already made some attempts to convince David of the advantages of the new conch technology in manufacturing. It seemed that all his colleagues were against his proposal, even the Finance Director objected on the grounds that the new process would cost about £2m. as opposed to £1.5m. for conventional conching of similar capacity. It appeared that two years of research and trials had been for nothing but he sprang to the defence of his proposal:

'I am convinced that the new technology offers too many advantages to be dismissed so lightly. I accept that it could delay the availability of capacity by around six months and would cost more – but there are at least six advantages which I have listed separately [see Appendix 19.1], some of which could be quantified in money terms, to justify the extra capital cost. You will understand that I am not in any position to calculate all these cost savings throughout the company, but I think that they could be obtained if we required them, but that would create months more delay. Our conventional capital expenditure (Capex) applications have always had to demonstrate clear departmental cost savings such as reductions in direct labour and associated overheads which result from automation technologies. The opportunities for further automation of high volume production processes are diminishing as the variety of our products is expanding. Payback periods for this type of investment are extending ... perhaps we are experiencing the law of diminishing returns. The days are long gone when we can design dedicated production lines for single products.

'The relative annual cost saving of the new technology conch (compared to a conventional conch) in the primary processes would be around £140 000. The labour saving is only small, perhaps half a person or around £10 000. Space savings are estimated by Finance to be worth around £20 000 in opportunity cost. Improved control of cocoa fat content will save the department around £30 000 based on our trials on the prototype machine. The biggest saving is reduced material wastage at change-overs: we could expect a £80 000 reduction here, since there will be dramatic reductions in the quantity of mixed grade outputs which are used up on the lower specification products. But the big benefits will be seen in the secondary departments, where there will be much more control of coating thickness and less quality and productivity problems. Unfortunately, these savings are much more difficult to predict. I believe that we cannot survive and grow without this type of development. In my view, the old technology is often barely able to achieve the demands placed on it by the complex new products being dreamed up by our Development Department. These modern and efficient process technologies will be critical in our future developments. Mars and Rowntree-Nestlé are certainly investing heavily in their factories.'

The Chairman was alarmed to find that there was no agreed strategy for the purchase of conching capacity but recognised that the decision had to be made quickly and appropriately:

'Before we decide what to do next, let's just have another look at our marketing strategy; that might give us some insights on the best solution. Mark, what do you think are the key aspects of our strategy in this context?'

Mark was well prepared to brief the Board, having just completed his first draft of the marketing strategy.

'As you all know, chocolate eating is an obsession in the UK [see Table 19.2], which gives us a solid base of loyal consumers. However, the environment is changing quickly! While Cadbury holds the top position in the UK consumer's mind (70 per cent refer to Cadbury when questioned about chocolate), we know this is based on volume brands like CDM and Roses. There is ample evidence that they are demanding more varieties and experimenting with new tastes. The European manufacturers are already making major attacks

**Table 19.2 Consumption of chocolate confectionery per capita in selected countries**

| Country | Per capita consumption kg/year |
| --- | --- |
| Switzerland | 8.8 |
| United Kingdom | 8.0 |
| Germany | 6.7 |
| France | 4.2 |
| Italy | 1.1 |
| Spain | 1.1 |

on our market and some of our comfortable dominance of retail chains could be lost in the 1990s. Competition for retail shelf space will be intense. Our strategy is clear. First, we will have to defend existing volume brands by maintaining price competitiveness and quality. The factories must be able to continue to support this by corresponding cost reductions. Second, we must be able to launch new, high quality, high margin products (based on the trusted Cadbury name) at a faster rate than ever before, to satisfy the niche opportunities provided by changing consumer and retailer demand. If we can't do this successfully, I know there are plenty of eager competitors out there ready to erode our shelf space in the corner shops and supermarkets. Realistically, not all of these new products will be a success and few will ever even reach 10 per cent of the weight of sales of CDM. But, together, they will be very profitable and will provide most of our projected growth.

'We will also continue to export existing and selected new brands, particularly into Europe. The marketing strategy recognises that this decade will bring unprecedented competition but, also, unbelievable opportunities for our chocolate business. With the right support from the factories, I am confident we will become the leading European manufacturer. I think you can see why I favour the conventional conch technology. It minimises the fixed-cost burden of extra capacity and ensures low-cost production without any risks associated with new processes.

'I have heard it said that one of the strengths of Japanese companies is that they would almost never make new products on new, uncertain processes. They first try out any new technology on well-established products in order to minimise any impact on the market of unforseen problems. Thus they always have the back-up of the old processes in case of problems. In my view, the new conch would be an expensive distraction at a time when we should be concentrating on the new product launches. The last thing we want is any unnecessary delays or risks!'

The Chairman leaned back thoughtfully in his chair and sighed:

'Well, we have a problem but I'm not prepared to put this issue to the vote today. I propose that we wait just two weeks, while you give one last thought to Chris' proposal, and re-examine the Capex. We must see an analysis of the likely savings from receiving more consistent chocolate at the secondary processes; perhaps that would put a better perspective on the incremental cost. I always feel that new technology is only of use if it helps us competitively. What we must decide is how the new conch process would help, if at all. Clearly, this is not one of our routine investment decisions!'

A report was received from the secondary processes manager ten days later. A summary of her findings is shown in Appendix 19.2.

## Questions

1 *What are the main concerns of the managers involved, when choosing between the 'conventional' conch and the new technology conch process?*

2 *How did Cadbury compete for sales of its various chocolate products, and how is that expected to change in the 1990s?*

3 *The Manufacturing Director refers to flexibility when considering the purchase of the new asset. What is meant by 'flexibility', and what will be the main differences in flexibility between the two types of conch machine?*

4 *What do you think the management should decide to do?*

## Appendix 19.1

## Memorandum on the advantages of the new process

To:     Members of the Board                                         30th September, 1991
From:   Chris English,
        Director of Engineering Development

**NEW CONCHING PROCESS**

Trials have now been completed on the one-tenth scale new technology conch. All output has been used successfully on our full product range. The tasting panel reports no detectable changes in taste, texture or aroma.

There are at least six advantages of this technology, which I list below; not all can be evaluated in money terms:

1  **Fat content**
   Trials have indicated that, for about half of our recipes, fat content can be reduced by up to 1% without significant changes to flavour or texture. As cocoa butter is expensive, this could give significant savings for some products.

2  **Viscosity***
   The new process gives much greater control over viscosity, allowing more precise coating of biscuits and fondants. This should reduce the level of rejects on all coated products, but the greatest saving would be that the chocolate can be used immediately without further adjustment, eliminating the need for 'in-line viscositising'.

3  **Change-over time and cost**
   Conventional conches take eight hours to completely clear of material during a recipe change, during which time the output is a mixture of two recipes, which can, therefore, only be used on the 'lower quality specification' product (usually a product that sells at a lower price). The new conch, in comparison, fully clears all material in less than half an hour, reducing the cost of materials.

4  **Variety capability**
   The new conching process will allow a much wider range of chocolates to be produced, as it can produce to a higher viscosity and to tighter tolerances.

5  **Scalability**
   We believe that the technology will work at any size from one-tenth to double the size of conventional conches. They can be custom-built for our specific needs.

6  **Reduced size**
   The new conch occupies 150 m$^2$ on one level, whereas a similar sized, conventional machine occupies 200 m$^2$ on three levels (total 600 m$^2$). The saved space would provide opportunities for further expansion.

* Viscosity is the thickness of a liquid; it is a measure of how quickly it flows.

## Appendix 19.2

## Edited memorandum on the advantages of the new process in the secondary processes

To:    Members of the Board
From:  Christine Thompson,
       Secondary Processes Manager

**NEW CONCHING PROCESS**

Now that we have had experience of using the chocolate from the small scale conch, we have been able to estimate the potential costs benefits to the secondary processes. These are entirely due to the improved viscosity consistency which gives us more control over the thickness of the chocolate in the case of coated products and shells (e.g. Easter eggs).

**1 Material savings**
We estimate that the tighter performance to our viscosity requirements will yield savings on these products of approximately £100 000 per year based on current output levels. This saving has been calculated from our statistical records of standard deviation of coating/shell thicknesses.

**2 Reduced scrap/rework**
Where viscosities have been too low, some coatings or shells have suffered from defects such as holes, and are therefore rejected, as are underweight eggs. The improved viscosity control should eliminate at least 75 per cent of this problem, saving £140 000 per year.

We should like to point out that this improved control means that we should not need any more in-line viscositising between primary and secondary processes. The improved consistency of the chocolate will eliminate many of the uncertainties in our department, which should, in turn, allow us to give a more reliable service to our customers.

# RAC Motoring Services

Case date
2000

Stuart Chambers

'I think that we all now fully understand the need for some fairly radical reorganisation of the way we plan and operate a rescue service, but I'm not convinced that we yet fully appreciate just how difficult this is going to be! The changes to our business environment in the last few years have been quite dramatic, and if we are to remain profitable we must now complete our negotiations with the unions in order to implement the new systems we have devised. Lex bought the RAC on the basis of its strong brand, large customer base and good profitability. However, if we don't get this work completed quickly, our service levels will continue to be worse than some leading competitors, and could even fall. We will certainly lose market share, and our costs will rise inexorably. At the moment, the only big winners seem to be the contractors who provide capacity during the night and when we are overloaded. And whilst our own patrol staff are earning more and more, their productivity is continuing to decline. We have no choice: we must solve this one, or we will be in serious trouble.'

Martin Connor, the Director of Operations, was addressing the monthly meeting of the operations team, just prior to the commencement of a series of negotiations with representatives of the Transport and General Workers Union (TGWU), which was the recognised union for the majority of the manual employees.

## The RAC

RAC Motoring Services had been established in the vehicle breakdown and recovery industry for over 100 years. It had its own branded patrol force which was deployed to rescue and fix customers vehicles at the roadside. The RAC was perceived to offer a high-quality service at a relatively high price. However, its image had sometimes been seen as somewhat old-fashioned. Its brand was very well established and trusted, but it was the number two in terms of customer awareness behind the AA (Automobile Association). For all of their long histories, until very recently both these organisations were owned by a specific group of their members, and were therefore not required to produce profits for external shareholders. Some commentators believed that this type of mutuality inevitably led to a sense of complacency, where market share was the most important measure of success. Underlying this image, however, the RAC had continued to invest in state-of-the-art technologies to efficiently receive members' calls and to dispatch rescue patrols. It had also constructed eye-catching control centres at highly visible points on the motorway systems, signalling its presence as a modern service provider.

In order to overcome its slightly dated image, in 1997 the RAC had rebranded and changed its corporate colours, the aim being to project a more modern and dynamic image to appeal to younger market segments. This was primarily done to address the continuing erosion of market share, but the main reason for its declining customer base had been the increasing level of competition in the market. For many years the RAC and AA had dominated the market, but recent new players such as Green Flag had entered by offering a cheaper product using third-party contractors. This introduced price competition and redefined customer service expectation. Green Flag advertised aggressively that it would reach all customers within 35 minutes, and if it did not, then it would refund £10. This led to Green Flag rapidly gaining market share at the expense of the AA and RAC.

In 1999 both the RAC and the AA gave up their mutuality when they were taken over by a large companies. The AA was acquired by Centrica, a utility services company, and the RAC by Lex plc, which included vehicle servicing businesses, vehicle leasing and the British School of Motoring. This brought a more commercial focus to both organisations. The RAC was determined not only to arrest the decline in customer numbers, but also to rapidly increase it. It could not do this by acquisition, and therefore the only option was to invest so that it could lead the market in terms of service quality.

A recent independent survey, carried out by J D Power, ranked the RAC second behind the AA in terms of customer satisfaction. The AA was ahead in two key areas: the quality of its call-taking (when customers phone the organisation to request roadside assistance) and the efficiency of its dispatch system (getting patrols to the customer quickly). The roadside services provided by patrols from both organisations were similar. The AA's more advanced call-taking and dispatch system resulted in quicker response times and better customer management during the period that customers were waiting for service. Therefore, for the RAC to grow its market share, it definitely needed to improve its call-taking and dispatch processes. It should be noted, however, that a leading 'new' competitor had scored consistently low in the J D Power survey for all aspects of its service, but continued to compete on the basis of lower annual membership charges.

Customers were getting more demanding too. Expectations of service quality are continuously rising, and motorists who have broken down invariably feel stressed and anxious. The quality of every interaction between the RAC and its members will be of concern. Thus customers will perceive waiting time as critical, and the reliability of arrival time of the patrol will be under scrutiny. Martin Connor was only too aware of the importance of reliability, as failure to meet lead-time promises had a major effect on customer satisfaction levels, and these were measured regularly by independent market researchers.

## ● The patrols

By 1999, the RAC was employing about 1350 patrols, and most of these had followed an earlier career as mechanics, undertaking garage servicing of vehicles. In many ways these were considered to be the elite of the mechanics trade, since they were capable, through experience and further training, of servicing a very wide range of vehicles and associated faults, usually in the presence of the distressed customer and in harsh roadside conditions. These skills were well rewarded by good earnings, including overtime payments, well above those of the garage trade. However, the average age of the patrols was becoming fairly high, and many were beginning to contemplate retirement. Surprisingly, patrol turnover was remarkably low, at around three per cent,

Patrols worked on rotating patterns of shifts referred to as 'Earlies' (7:00 to 15:00), 'Mids' (11:00 to 19:00) and 'Lates' (15:00 to 23:00). However, very few patrols (around five per cent) were scheduled for the Mids, because demand for roadside assistance tended to be lower through the middle of the day, certainly on weekdays. Together, the normal patrols in any cell evenly covered all seven days of a week, with every patrol working a third of the days on Earlies, a third on Lates, and a third taking a break period. Each of the patrols was issued with its own fully equipped rescue vehicle, which was only needed during working hours. When not required, this vehicle would usually be parked outside home, ready for the next use. Although this resulted in low utilisation of this very expensive asset, this had been found to be the best way of ensuring that the equipment was kept in a good condition ready for use. It also ensured that the patrol could continue to work on a broken-down vehicle even beyond the end of its shift, without worrying about the delay in handing over to another patrol. It also allowed the patrol to be on 'standby', awaiting a request to attend a motorist outside the normal shift time. This provided the patrol an opportunity for overtime earnings, whilst giving the RAC extra capacity to call on at off-peak times.

## Managing the patrols

The patrols were organised into geographic 'cells'. These varied in size from about 8 to 15 patrols, covering an area that allowed a patrol to travel to reach a motorist within about 20 minutes. Under average conditions, this would allow a patrol to attend about one job per hour: say 20 minutes travel, 20 minutes to undertake the repair and 20 minutes average delay awaiting the next call-out. During busy periods the average waiting time would become much lower. The office-based dispatching operations were conducted on the basis of these cells; motorists breaking down within a particular cell were normally serviced by a patrol from that cell.

About 50 service managers were each responsible for teams of up to 28 patrols covering two or three cells. Their job was to ensure that service standards were achieved in their areas, within target productivity levels. However, an activity survey in 1998 indicated that they generally attempted to achieve this by undertaking a large number of odd jobs to ensure that their patrols were kept on the road. For example, they would obtain and deliver replacement uniforms and consumables to individual patrols. It was becoming very apparent that, in effect, they were spending their time circumventing or supplementing poor processes, rather than getting involved with the detailed operations management of their teams.

## Use of contractors

There was extensive use of private contractors during weekends and at night-time. Sometimes they would even be used to supplement capacity during the day if unexpectedly high demand occurred. Whilst these were responsible for the same activities as patrols, they did not carry the full RAC branding, and were often found to lack the full capabilities of the patrols. Market research indicated that members were generally less satisfied with the service provided by such contractors, but it had been necessary to use them to provide capacity at times when it was uneconomical to maintain a full coverage of RAC patrols. The cost of contractors was high (averaging £36 per job) and rising, and there was considerable concern that the amount of work put out to contract was increasing, at the same time that the productivity of the patrols was actually falling.

The proportion of jobs covered by patrols was measured every month; the Patrol Attendance Rate (PAR) was averaging 80 per cent in 1999. It had been calculated that a one per cent fall in PAR would cost about £1 million per year in contractor fees. Therefore, in order to generally minimise the use of contractors, patrols had always been offered incentives to do some of the jobs at off-peak times. The PAR was often low at times when the patrols took holidays, for example many were on leave at the end of the holiday year (March), and many patrols wanted to take their holiday in August to be with their families. The PAR reached a record low of 77 per cent in August 1998.

## Overtime and standby

The patrols were contracted to work shift rosters, as described earlier, over a standard 40-hour week. In general, when demand was expected to be sufficiently high, they were offered overtime work or per job payments known as 'standby'. Overtime was paid at time-and-a-half rates (approximately £10 per hour) with double time on Sundays (approximately £14 per hour). On this basis, there was really no incentive to work fast and productively, since the patrols would be paid even whilst they waited for further instructions.

Patrols could also choose to be on standby. For this to apply, they had to 'log on' to the communications system in their vehicle, awaiting jobs to be issued to them. For every job completed they would be paid a flat fee of £6. For simple jobs (starting problems, flat battery, etc.) a patrol in a busy area could complete up to four jobs in an hour. Thus their earning potential could be very high, but they retained the right to 'log off' at will. Experience indicated that this would often happen if a difficult job was offered, which the patrol knew would take a long time. If none of the patrols in a cell would accept that job, it would then be passed to a contractor.

In 1999, only about 50–55 per cent of jobs were done within the duty roster. The remainder was covered by overtime, standby and contractors. A particular problem that arose from this system was that of inconsistent service level. The operation ran with the risk that off-peak but unexpectedly busy periods could not be adequately covered by patrols; the alternative use of contractors would often impact customer perceived service quality. Analysis of the customer feedback forms, filled in by motorists after receiving assistance, indicated a strong negative correlation between their overall satisfaction level (known as the Customer Satisfaction Index, or CSI) and the time they had waited for the patrol to arrive (known as the Average Time of Arrival, or ATA). Moreover, there was a significant seasonality in the CSI scores, with below-average levels in the winter months for two years running.

The net result was that the productivity levels achieved by the RAC patrols had been falling for five years. During this period new competitors, such as Green Flag, did not carry the cost of directly employed patrols and their associated vehicles and equipment. They simply contracted all work to third parties.

Clearly this situation could not be allowed to continue! Martin and his team had to rethink how the existing numbers of patrols, and their area service managers, could be reorganised to increase productivity and PAR. For the RAC to satisfy the changing demands of its customers and its employees, things would have to change! No longer could the organisation continue to place more and more work in the hands of contractors: it was much too costly and was certainly affecting customer satisfaction. Martin knew that there would be resistance to almost any proposed change. After all, many of the patrols were of an age where their families had left home so their living expenses were falling, and therefore they were seeking more social hours and a generally easier working schedule.

## Demand patterns

The annual number of breakdowns attended by the patrols peaked in the mid-1990s at around 2.9 million, but had then fallen steadily to about 2.4 million in 1999, despite an increase in membership. This fall was attributed to several underlying factors. Firstly, the most obvious reason was that new cars had become significantly more reliable! Secondly, because of strict testing requirements, many older and more unreliable vehicles were being scrapped earlier, or were being used less, as families became multiple car owners. Thirdly, the RAC had been proactive in encouraging its members to prevent common failures. For example, a very common task for patrols involved starting cars with flat batteries. Where one was found to be old and in poor condition, the member was now required to replace it immediately, with a clear understanding that failure to do so would disqualify them from receiving this service again. This change was known to account for a reduction of approximately 150 000 incidents of this type. A second change was the introduction of the 'Fair Call Policy' which entitled a member to a maximum of six free call-outs per year; the seventh and subsequent ones would become chargeable. About three per cent of customers had created about 20 per cent of call-outs, so this policy helped to contain demand, freeing capacity and responsiveness for the less-frequent users. Despite the significant reduction in the number of breakdowns, the number of patrols was maintained at around 1350. It was calculated that even with the reducing volume of demand, the RAC would need around 2000 patrols to cope with demand without the use of contractors and overtime working. Clearly, a 50 per cent increase in numbers employed would be impracticable and too costly in terms of both capital and revenue.

**Figure 20.1 RAC national total annual service breakdowns (by month)**

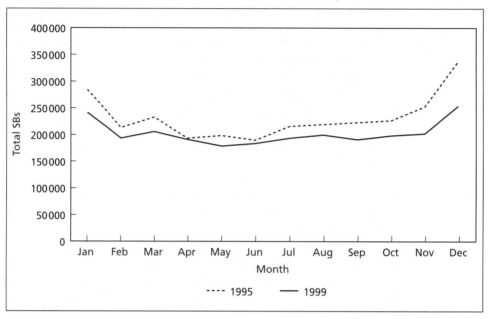

There was a significant seasonality in breakdowns, as shown in Figure 20.1. There are more call-outs in the winter, much of which can be explained by the weather. For example, electrical faults occur more frequently because extra loads are placed on the system by the greater use of lights, which are also used more of the time, providing more opportunities for failure to be noticed. Starter motors and alternators are subject to more load, and electrical systems can be affected by dampness and water ingress. In the summer, a greater proportion of the motoring population will be abroad on holiday, reducing demand on the motoring rescue services. However, to an extent offsetting this effect, a proportion of motorists take their cars on unusually long journeys on their summer holidays, sometimes heavily loaded and without adequate servicing, resulting in breakdowns such as overheating.

There were 'normal' weekly and daily patterns of service breakdown (referred to as SB) volumes that varied relatively predictably throughout the year, but this could be greatly distorted by unusually severe weather conditions. These demand patterns had gradually changed during the latter half of the 1990s as a result of gradual social, behavioral and economic changes. For example, the working population of the UK increased, leading to more home-to-work travel by car at peak times. Many organisations, ranging from manufacturers to financial services' call-centres had introduced new working patterns such as 'continental shifts', which required employees to cover operations for up to 168 hours a week. Weekend and evening shopping became much more popular, with some supermarkets staying open overnight. Fast food outlets, leisure facilities, and even universities began operating longer hours. These types of changes gradually led to a more spread-out pattern of car travel both for worker and consumers, and had noticeably reduced the weekday morning peaks SB levels. Figure 20.2 shows typical weekly patterns of demand in 1995 and 1999, Figure 20.3 shows the daily SB patterns for Saturdays, and Figure 20.4 shows the corresponding SB pattern for Mondays.

**Figure 20.2  RAC total annual service breakdowns (by day of week)**

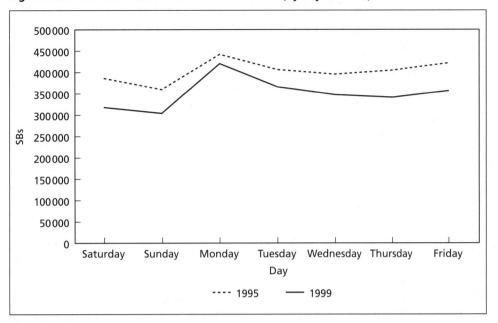

**Figure 20.3  RAC national service breakdowns (by half hour for average Saturdays)**

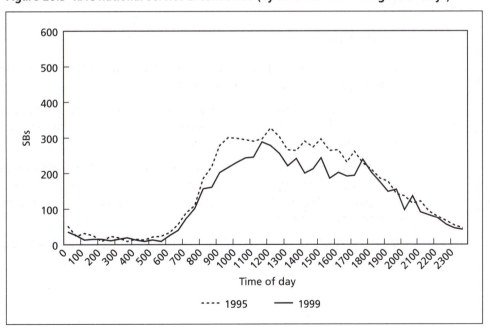

**Figure 20.4 RAC national service breakdowns (by half hour for average Mondays)**

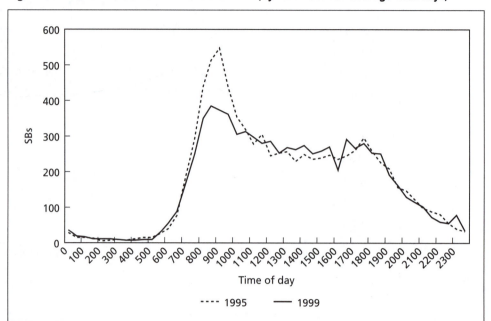

## Questions

**1** Evaluate the competitive position of RAC Motoring Services in terms of its operations-based strengths or weaknesses.

**2** What are the advantages and disadvantages of the current cell-focused service management structure? What alternatives might give better results in terms of increasing quality and productivity?

**3** How could the employment contracts, payment systems and working practices be redesigned to help to increase the patrol productivity, to increase PAR and to reduce waiting times? What resistance is likely to be faced, and how should this best be countered?

**4** What are your overall recommendations for an implementation plan?

# Denby Constabulary

Andrew Greasley

## Introduction

There are 43 police forces in England and Wales, each with a chief constable responsible for the deployment, direction and control of staff. The police service is based on a hierarchical rank command structure. The chief constable and assistant chief constable are known as Association of Chief Police Officer (ACPO) ranks and constitute top management. The middle ranks of superintendent, chief inspector and inspector have responsibility for either territorial or functional divisions. Sergeants, the lowest level of management, supervise the police constable (PC) rank that accounts for approximately three-quarters of police staff. Most police officers work within territorial divisions, responsible for geographical units, with the average police service having between three to six divisions.

In private sector organisations, improving quality and efficiency of service usually leads to an increase in revenue which more than pays for the cost of introducing changes. If changes are not made, market share is lost to competitors who do invest in innovation and process improvement. Public sector organisations face a problem, though, in that more effective service provision may not actually generate income to pay for changes. This leads to a situation of internal efficiency gains or a 'lowest cost' approach to service provision taking precedence over meeting customer needs. This can mean management is focused on measuring resource expenditure, within departmental budgets. An alternative approach is to analyse the performance of processes across functional boundaries against measures such as customer service quality, speed of delivery and dependability of service. As a way of improving performance in the public sector, the Best Value initiative was introduced by the Labour Government in 1997. The government definition of Best Value is as follows:

*'Best Value will be a duty to deliver to clear standards – covering both cost and quality – by the most effective, economic and efficient means available.'*

The approach requires the public sector organisation to take account of stakeholders such as customers, users and the wider community and provide an efficient and effective service, and not simply the 'least cost' or most economic option. The head of the Best Value Unit at Denby Constabulary provides an account of the review into improving service delivery:

'We know that one of the main measures of the public of our effectiveness is the visibility and amount of time our police constables spend on front-line duties tackling crime. A business-led process review team was set up with team members chosen with a mix of operational, administration and information systems experience. The team was not part of the IT function but reported directly to senior management. The previous information systems review had identified a number of priority areas for investigation including custody, case preparation, accounting and personnel. It was decided to focus on the custody operation first because it is legally bound by nationally structured procedures. This would allow the team to gain experience in redesign before moving on to more loosely defined processes.'

## The custody suite case study

The custody suite is the point of call for any arrests carried out by police officers in the field. The custody operation involves taking details of the arrested person by a designated custody officer and then the possible detention and interview of that person at a later date. The objective of the study was to identify a custody of prisoner process which is legitimate and best practice, and provide recommendations for computerisation. A particular focus of the study would be on reengineering the use of human resources within the area. The main activities involved in the custody process are as follows:

- *Booking-In* – recording of arrested person details, reason for arrest and other information
- *Interview* – secure rooms and taping facilities for interview purposes
- *Detention* – secure facilities for detention of suspects awaiting interview or court.

Personnel involved in the custody of prisoner process include the inspector, custody officer (sergeant rank), police constable and jailer. These are ranked from top to bottom. The high rank can always legitimately perform the task of any person beneath them in the order of ranking, however a low rank cannot legitimately perform any function of a person above them in the order of ranking. Authorisation from inspector level is required for an extension of the normal detention period. The custody officer role is to organise, supervise and ensure the efficient operation of the custody suite. The custody officer is responsible for the documentation and explanation of rights to arrested persons and so requires a thorough knowledge of relevant legislation and guidelines. The police constable will often be the officer responsible for the arrest of the person and will usually escort them to the custody suite and provide information for the booking-in process. The jailer role (undertaken by a PC or civilian jailer) includes the transportation of the arrested person between the booking-in area, the interview rooms and cells and general welfare, such as the organisation of meals and visits.

## Process improvement techniques used in the study

The following techniques were used to provide an analysis of the custody of prisoner process:

## Process mapping

Process mapping involves a study of how activities link together to form a process. The technique involves interviewing personnel and observation of the relevant process, which provides information that is used to draw a process map. The analysis shows the interrelationships between activities and identifies the elements and roles involved in process execution. The study considers the arrest process, from the initial arrest of a suspect by a PC, through the booking-in process at a custody suite to possible detention and interview. The main activities in the arrest process are shown in a process map (Figure 21.1). Each decision point (shown by a diamond in the process map) will have a probability for a yes/no option. For example, the first decision point in the arrest process is whether to conduct a search of the location of the arrest. The staffing rank required for each process is indicated above the process box. Personnel involved in the arrest process include the PC, custody officer, jailer and inspector. The process map indicates the role of each rank for each activity.

## Simulation modelling

Statistical techniques are utilised to facilitate business decision making by understanding the underlying causes of variability in business situations. Business processes consist of a number of activities that are linked and so their performance is dependent on the variability in individual activity times and the linkages (interdependencies) between the activities in the process. Simulation modelling is increasingly used to analyse these systems to provide information for decision making. The simulation method refers to both the process of building a computer model and the conducting of experiments on that model. The model building stage will include collecting data on process durations and decision point probabilities and programming the model using simulation software. An experiment consists of running the simulation for a time period for a number of runs in order to provide data for statistical analysis. An experiment is conducted in order to understand the behaviour of the model and to evaluate the effect of different input levels on specified performance measures.

## Activity-based costing

The wide range of activities that a people-based organisation undertakes often leads to a situation of management of resources by inputs (budgets) because of the difficulty of classifying the wide range of outputs that personnel can perform. The amount of resources (people) deployed is based on historical departmental budgets with a large proportion classified as overhead and fixed, with an annual addition for inflation. Departments are then managed by tracking variances in expenditure from budgeted amounts. However, resource allocation decisions can be informed by moving from costs defined in a general organisational budget to an output-oriented budget. The activity-based costing (ABC) approach allows the user to distinguish between resource usage and resource expenditure, the difference being unused capacity. Once identified, this capacity can either be eliminated, reducing costs, or redeployed, improving effectiveness.

**Figure 21.1 Arrest process map**

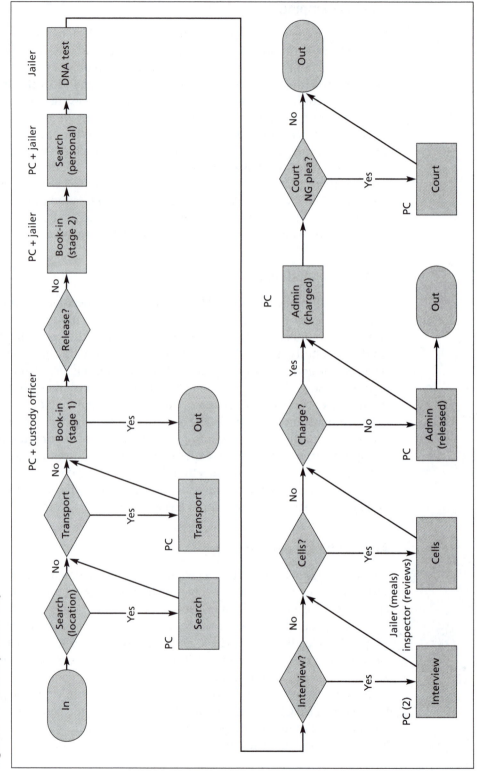

# Improvement areas identified in the case study

The following main improvement areas were identified as a result of the case study analysis:

## Job design

### Task reallocation

The focus of the simulation study was an investigation into the effect of reallocating tasks from the custody officer to the jailer. This would release a senior officer, the custody sergeant, for other duties. To implement this change, a radical rethink of the custody officer role was required. The role contains important tasks in that the custody officer must ensure that the required information and correct actions are taken in respect of a person brought in by a police constable for arrest. The role has evolved over a number of years and it was assumed that most tasks carried out by the custody officer could only be carried out by them or by a person higher in the hierarchy (for example a superintendent). However, after a study of legal requirements it was found that this was not the case. In fact many of the tasks were of an administrative nature and did not require the authorisation of the custody officer. The custody operation was redesigned from scratch from a process perspective. A procedure was designed which involved the custody officer carrying out a series of tasks required by law and then handing over the 'case' to the jailer to process. From the simulation study it was found that there is scope to increase jailer utilisation and to make better use of the custody officer. The results of the study showed that custody officer utilisation had dropped from 29 per cent to 9 per cent while jailer utilisation has risen from 25 per cent to 67 per cent. The study also indicated the utilisation of custody desk personnel, the number of cells occupied and the number of interview rooms in use at any one time.

### Civilianisation

An increasing number of posts are being civilianised in areas such as IT, finance, personnel, scene of crime work and administrative support. The increasing role of civilianisation is due to lower wage costs, demands for professional management and a wish by the public for a police presence in the community. The possibility of civilianisation of the jailer role was also investigated. This would include tasks such as the taking of fingerprints, photographs and DNA samples. Further tasks include undertaking the breath test procedure and attendance at court if required. The personnel would be supplied by a contracted provider who would be responsible for training, replacement for sickness and absence leave, and pension provision for the staff.

### Centralisation

A study was initiated to assess the feasibility of replacing local custody suites throughout the county with a centralised facility. This would reduce costs and smooth demand. However, the logistics of transporting personnel and arrested persons to a centralised facility had to be considered carefully. The following options were considered for centralisation of custody operations:

1 Prisoner arrested by PC and taken to be booked in locally. Later conveyed to custody suite by PCs.
2 Prisoner arrested by PC and taken to be booked in locally. Later conveyed to custody suite by civilian jailer.
3 Prisoner arrested by PC and taken to be booked in locally. Later conveyed to custody suite by private security firm.
4 Prisoner arrested by PC and awaits pick-up by civilian jailer. Then conveyed to custody suite. Jailer then returns PC to section.

All options would need to be considered in terms of cost feasibility. In particular, option 4 is unlikely to be a feasible option as it means the PC and prisoner would be in limbo as they awaited transportation, which may have been deployed elsewhere.

## Capacity planning

This part of the analysis studied the mix of arrest types that was dealt with by a typical custody suite. The simulation was able to estimate the amount of resource required for each arrest type. This was derived from not only the number of arrests but also from the likelihood of an arrest leading to interview, detention and court procedures. A Pareto analysis was undertaken and showed that relatively trivial theft offences (usually involving children shoplifting) are causing a heavy workload. This finding could lead to policies to decrease this workload through crime prevention activities, for example. Also, once the costs for a certain mix and volume of arrest types has been made, the model can be used to predict the costs for different activity mix and volume scenarios. For example, it was used to analyse the effect of a change in the demand pattern of arrests as a result of legislation regarding extended drinking hours in public houses.

### Questions

1 *Evaluate the job design changes made at the police custody suite.*

2 *What strategies could the police follow in order to reduce their apparent cost to the public?*

3 *Evaluate the difference between managing costs by budget and an activity-based approach.*

# PART 4

# Planning and control

# Introduction to Part 4

One of the most important tasks of an operations manager is to ensure that the organisation has sufficient input resources to be able to meet demand. This is the task of operations planning and control, the objective of which is to ensure that the operation runs effectively and produces products and services as it should do. It is concerned with the timing, quantity, quality and choice of transformed and transforming resources to ensure that the supply of products and services meets customer demand (see Figure P4.1). Planning and control involves both managing demand for its products or services from actual or potential customers and matching them against its capability to supply them, today and in the future.

## Planning versus control

A plan is a statement of intention based on expectations about the future. Planning the future allows an organisation to commit itself to longer-term expenditure which will be required to ensure that it can cope with the future. The plan may need to be reworked, or re-planned, to deal with known or anticipated changes as the date of implementation nears.

When the plan is implemented many things may go wrong and thus control is required to try to cope with whatever changes have occurred. Control is about making the necessary measurements and changes to allow the operation to meet its

**Figure P4.1 Reconciling demand with supply**

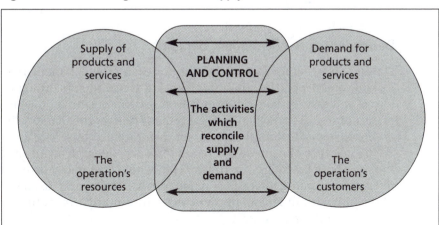

objectives – the objectives set by the plan. The closer to implementation, the more the task concerns control; the further away, the more it concerns planning.

## Long, medium and short-term planning and control

In the long term, the planning and control task is primarily concerned with long-range planning. It is concerned with taking long-range forecasts and making appropriate long-term investments, or divestments, to try to meet the level of expected demand. This is done at a broad, or aggregate, level and may affect the number and size of operations locations, the approximate number of employees needed and the broad skills required, for example.

By the medium term, some of the resources will be fixed and the forecast a little more certain. Planning is still usually at an aggregate level. Most operations use some form of master plan, schedule or timetable. This should be a realistic, achievable statement of what the organisation is planning to do, so it is checked against the operation's expected ability to supply to see if meeting forecast demand is feasible. If it is not, the plan must be altered. Any imbalances are usually dealt with using one, or a combination, of the following approaches: level capacity, chase demand, demand management (see below).

In the short term, the master plan provides the base for detailed planning of the day-to-day provision of goods or services.

- *Loading*. This task involves assigning customers/products to work centres, i.e. staff and/or machines. Essentially it is about deciding who, or what, will do what.
- *Sequencing*. This concerns determining the order of jobs at each stage of the process. It is usually approached by allocating priorities to the jobs using predetermined rules, such as 'first come first served', or is based on a sequence of sizes, such as wide to narrow or large to small. See 'I'll Phone You Back!' (Case 23) for an example of sequencing.
- *Scheduling*. Scheduling is the allocation of start and finish times to each task and involves statements of the detailed timing of activities – see 'I'll Phone You Back!'

Furthermore, as the actual demand and mix will vary from day to day and hour by hour, control is needed in the short term to deal with the impact of queues, staff shortages, material shortages, equipment failures, etc. by reloading, resequencing and rescheduling the work.

## Dependent and independent demand

Planning is easier for some organisations than others. If demand is relatively predictable and dependent upon some known factor then planning will be relatively logical and easy, certainly in comparison with an organisation which can only base plans or forecasts on what its management *believes* the market will require, based on, for example, historical demand for their products or services.

The first type of demand is referred to as dependent demand and is illustrated in the Aylesbury Pressings case (Case 31) in which customers, being mainly automotive, provide rolling forecasts of requirements. Other cases document the problems of dealing with independent demand, without any firm future orders – see, for example, Holly Farm (Case 24).

There are many important activities involved in planning and controlling an operation. Most of these are addressed below, while others will be dealt with in Parts 5 and 6.

- *Capacity planning and control* – planning and control at an aggregate level
- *Inventory planning and control* – managing physical inventory to meet intermediate or end demand
- *Supply chain planning and control* – ensuring the best flow of goods and services through the supply network (see Part 5)
- *Materials Requirements Planning (MRP)* – planning and control of independent demand with the aid of a computer-based information system
- *Just-in-time planning and control* – producing goods and services exactly when *needed*
- *Project planning and control* – the planning and control of large and complex sets of interrelated activities
- *Quality planning and control* – ensuring the quality of the goods and services produced (see Part 6).

## Capacity planning and control

Capacity planning and control is also sometimes referred to as *aggregate planning and control*. This is because demand and capacity (or resource) calculations are usually performed on an aggregated basis which does not discriminate between the different products and services which an operation might produce. Holly Farm uses customers and litres of ice-cream, Ice House Toys (Case 25) uses the number of orders and Peas (Cases 28) uses tonnes of peas harvested. The essence of the task is, at a general and aggregated level, to reconcile the supply of capacity with the level of demand that must be satisfied.

Capacity planning and control, as dealt with here, is concerned with setting capacity levels over the medium and short terms *in aggregated terms*. That is, it is making overall, broad capacity decisions whilst not concerned with all of the details of the individual products and services offered. Thus aggregate plans assume that the mix of different products and services will remain relatively constant during the planning period.

### What is capacity?

The capacity of an operation is the maximum throughput of an operation over a period of time. Capacity may be measured in terms of inputs, process or output capacity, and there will usually be some constraints upon the organisation's capacity. For Holly Farm, for example, there is a limit to the number of cars and coaches that it can accommodate (input capacity) although maximum depends on the mix of cars and coaches and how long they stay. The organisation's ice-cream processing has a maximum daily capacity, limited by its ability to fast freeze its output. Its ice-cream storage is also limited by its freezer capacity.

## Capacity plans

There are three main ways of managing capacity, that is, trying to reconcile supply and demand at an aggregate level:

- *Level capacity plan* – ignore demand fluctuations and keep activity levels constant
- *Chase demand plan* – adjust capacity to reflect the fluctuations in demand
- *Demand management* – attempt to change demand to fit capacity availability.

In practice, most organisations will use a mixture of all of these 'pure' plans, although often one plan might dominate.

### Level capacity plan

In a level capacity plan, the processing capacity is set at a uniform level throughout the planning period, regardless of the fluctuations in forecast demand. This means that the same number of staff operate the same processes and should, therefore, be capable of producing the same aggregate output in each period. Level capacity plans of this type can achieve the advantages of stable employment patterns, high process utilisation, and usually also high productivity with low unit costs – see Mandexor Memory (Case 27). Unfortunately, they can also create considerable inventory which has to be financed and stored. Perhaps the biggest problem, however, is that decisions have to be taken as to what to produce for inventory rather than for immediate sale. Some organisations have little alternative but to adopt a level capacity plan because they are physically constrained.

### Chase demand plan

An alternative capacity plan is one that attempts to match capacity closely to the varying levels of forecast demand. This is much more difficult to achieve than a level capacity plan, as different numbers of staff, different working hours, and even different amounts of equipment may be necessary in each period. Also, for particularly capital-intensive operations, the chase demand policy would require a higher level of physical capacity, some of which would only be used occasionally. Ice House Toys, for example, is a mail-order operation serving the Christmas gifts market, so most of its order processing is conducted on a chase demand basis in October to December.

### Manage demand

A third approach is to try to 'manage' demand to match the organisation's productive capacity more closely. There are several ways of doing this, for example: changing the level of demand through the price mechanism or using promotions; creating alternative products or services to use spare capacity; or attracting customers away from heavily used capacity – a good example of this can be found in Chicken Run (Case 34). Careful target marketing is crucial to get the best demand profile/capacity match.

The Holly Farm case provides opportunities to investigate these capacity plans. Sometimes the capacity plan is influenced by the supply of transformed resources (inputs) and this is illustrated in both the Peas case and Fresh Salads Ltd (Case 26).

# Inventory planning and control

Inventory is the stored accumulation of physical material resources in the operation. These could be stocks of ice-cream, for example. In some organisations the value of the inventory might be quite small, in others it is large. Maintaining optimum inventories is difficult, as evidenced by the Water for Africa case (Case 30).

## Types of inventory

Inventory is often classified into raw material, work-in-progress and finished goods. However, it is often more useful to categorise it in terms of its role in the operation's system:

- *Buffer inventory*. Buffer inventory is also called safety inventory; its purpose is to compensate for the uncertainties inherent in supply and demand. By holding buffer inventories, organisations can help ensure that they can meet demand even if it is greater than anticipated or in case the supply of goods, either from the operation or a supplier, does not arrive on time (see the Aylesbury Pressings case, Case 31, and The Royal Navy, Case 32).
- *Cycle inventory*. Cycle inventory occurs because an organisation chooses to produce or purchase in batches or lots in quantities greater than are immediately required by subsequent operations or customers.
- *Anticipation inventory*. Anticipation inventory is made in anticipation of changes in demand or supply. It is most commonly used when seasonal demand fluctuations are significant but relatively predictable. It might also be used when supply variations are significant, such as in the freezing of seasonal foods (see the Peas case, for example).
- *Pipeline inventory*. Pipeline inventory exists because material cannot be transported instantaneously between the points of supply and the points of demand. Material 'in transit' is referred to as pipeline inventory. The Cadbury Ltd case (Case 19) includes an example of *internal* pipeline inventory.

## Inventory decisions

There are three key decisions associated with inventories:

- How much to order – every time a replenishment order is placed, externally or internally, how big should it be?
- When to order – at what point in time, or at what level of stock, should the replenishment order be placed?
- Which items are the most important – should different priorities be allocated to different stock items?

### How much to order?

This decision usually requires balancing two sets of costs: the costs associated with purchasing the items and the costs associated with holding inventory. One option would be to hold very small stock and to purchase when needed. Although this approach has the benefit of only spending money when materials are needed, there may be a high cost in terms of time and inconvenience in having to make frequent purchases. Alternatively, purchasing very large amounts infrequently would have the effect of minimising the cost and inconvenience of making the purchases but would result in very large stock holding. This is an important issue raised in the Ice House Toys case. Organisations therefore have to make a balance of judgement between all the costs involved in stock holding and replenishment, including:

- the costs of placing orders (or setting up processes)
- price discounts for bulk purchases
- working capital costs
- storage costs
- obsolescence costs.

### When to order

If stock arrived immediately after it was ordered this would be a simple decision. However, in reality there may be a variable lag in the system between order and arrival and also variability in the use of the item, so both supply and demand is uncertain. Operations managers can try to use their understanding of order lead-times, and their variability, and the demand variability in order to make decisions about the most appropriate levels of safety stock and when it is best to order.

### Which items are the most important

In any inventory which contains more than one stocked item, some will be more important to the organisation than others. Some items, for example, may have a very high usage rate, so if they ran out many customers would be disappointed. Other items may be of particularly high value, so excessively high inventory levels would be particularly expensive. One common way of discriminating between different stock items is to rank them by their usage value (their usage rate multiplied by their individual value) and categorise them into class A, B and C items:

- Class A items – those 20 per cent or so of high-value items which account for around 80 per cent of the total usage value
- Class B items – those of medium value, usually the next 30 per cent, which account for around 10 per cent of the total usage value
- Class C items – those low value items which, although comprising around 50 per cent of the total types of items stocked, probably only account for around 10 per cent of the total usage value of stocked items.

## MRP

The purpose of MRP is to help organisations plan and control their resource requirements with the aid of computer-based information systems. Over the last 20 years, the concept of MRP has developed from an operations tool which helped in planning and controlling materials requirements (MRPI) to become, in recent years, a broader business system which helps plan all business resource requirements (MRPII).

## MRPI – materials requirement planning

Materials requirement planning, usually referred to as MRPI, is a computerised control and information system that provides a formal plan for every part, raw material, component and sub-assembly. It coordinates all manufacturing decisions, based on forecast demand and actual orders, from ordering, through the control of stock levels and work-in-progress, to the supply of the finished products. Its aim is to help organisations calculate how many materials of particular types are needed and when they are needed in order to manufacture their products to meet the actual and anticipated needs of their customers.

Because of the often complex nature of this activity, due to the numbers of different components involved in products and the varieties of products produced, this activity is usually undertaken by computer.

MRP generates purchase orders and work orders for items, based on forecasts and actual orders, and so is a dependent demand system. It involves a number of stages:

1 *Demand Management* – this involves generating customer order and sales forecasts for the products and also the physical distribution of the finished items. This information is fed into the master production schedule.
2 *Master production schedule* – this provides the main input into the MRP system and is a statement of time-phase records of each end product, current and expected demand, and available stocks.
3 *MRP* – the MRP system takes the master production schedule together with the bills of materials (BOM) for the products and the inventory records of all existing component parts and effectively explodes the top level demand through bills of materials, taking into account inventory and lead-times at each level in order to generate:
    - purchase orders
    - works orders and
    - material plans.

The Aylesbury Pressings case provides an opportunity to understand in detail how MRPI works and to discuss some of the problems of using MRP systems.

## MRPII – manufacturing resource planning

During the last 20 years the concept of MRPI has expanded and been integrated with other parts of the business, each of which may have held their own computerised databases. A product structure or bill of materials, for example, may be held in the engineering department and also in materials management. If engineering changes are made to the design of products, both databases have to be updated. It is difficult to keep both databases entirely identical and discrepancies between them cause problems, which often are not apparent until a member of staff is supplied with the wrong parts to manufacture the product or stocks of the required items are unavailable. Similarly, cost information from finance and accounting, which is used to perform management accounting tasks such as variance analysis against standard costs, needs to be reconciled with changes made elsewhere in the operation, such as changes in inventory holding or process methods. (See the Aylesbury Pressings case for an illustration of MRPII in practice.)

Manufacturing resource planning, or MRPII, is based on one integrated system containing a database which is accessed and used by the whole company according to their functional requirements. This ensures the updating of bills of materials as design modifications are made, allowing for updates of stock costs and product costings to take place, for example. However, despite its dependence on the information technologies which allow such integration, MRPII still depends on people providing the right information at the right time and doing the right things with that information!

## Just-in-time planning and control

The aim of a just-in-time (JIT) approach is to produce goods and services exactly when they are needed, with perfect quality and no waste, and is a philosophy of manufacturing embodying a collection of tools and techniques. It is a technique associated with large industries such as the automotive industry, but it has also been usefully applied to smaller-scale, low-volume organisations as well. For an interesting example, see The Royal Navy case.

### The JIT philosophy

JIT is a philosophy founded on doing the simple things well, or gradually doing them better, and on squeezing out waste every step of the way. It involves three core principles:

- *The elimination of waste* – the removal of any activity which does not add value
- *The involvement of everyone* – JIT is a 'total system' approach which aims to pull together everyone in a system
- *Continuous improvement* – the JIT objective, which, being an ideal, aims to promote continuous improvement through an organisation.

### JIT tools

JIT comprises a collection of tools for reducing waste and these include:

- *Basic working practices*, such as the use of standards, fair personnel policies and working practices, flexibility of responsibilities, autonomy, 'line stop' authority (allowing people to stop the process if problems occur) and an improvement in problem solving, data gathering and personal development.
- *Design for manufacture* – fostering a close relationship between design and operations to ensure that what is designed can be made well.
- *Operations focus* – focusing on simplicity, repetition and experience.
- *Small simple machines* – using several small machines instead of one large general purpose machine as small machines may perform more reliably, are easy to maintain, and produce better quality over time. Small machines are also easier to move and modify.
- *Layout and flow* – layout techniques can be used to promote the smooth flow of materials, of data, and of people in the operation. Long complex process routes may cause large quantities of inventory and slow the process, both of which are contrary to JIT principles.

- *Total productive maintenance (TPM)* – TPM aims to eliminate the variability in operations processes which result from unplanned breakdowns.
- *Set-up reduction (SUR)* – set-up times can be reduced by a variety of methods, such as cutting out time taken to search for tools and equipment, the pre-preparation of tasks which delay change-overs, and the constant practice of set-up routines, all of which contribute to the elimination of waste.
- *Total people involvement* – total people involvement is concerned with providing people with the training and support to take full responsibility for all aspects of their work, including dealing directly with suppliers, measurement and reporting, process improvements, budgets and plans, and dealing directly with customers and their problems.
- *Visibility* – problems, quality projects and operations checklists are made visible by displaying them locally so that they can easily be seen and understood by all staff.

### JIT planning and control techniques

There are three techniques which deal specifically with the planning and control of operations using JIT:

- *Kanban control* – kanban is the Japanese for card or signal. It is sometimes called the 'invisible conveyor' which controls the transfer of materials between the stages of an operation. In its simplest form, it is a card used by a customer stage to instruct its supplier stage to send more materials. This is a key signal to produce and ensures that production only takes place when items are required, in the quantity in which they are required (see the Aylesbury Pressings case).
- *Levelled scheduling* – this activity attempts to equalise the mix of products or services made each day to create a simple and repetitive cycle. This makes control easier and more visible.
- *Synchronisation* – many companies make a wide variety of parts and products, not all of them with sufficient regularity to warrant levelled scheduling. Synchronisation dictates that parts need to be classified according to the frequency with which they are demanded and tries to make production as regular and predictable as possible.

## Project planning and control

A project is a set of activities, often large scale and complex, which has a defined start point and a defined end state, pursue a defined goal and use a defined set of resources. Projects have several elements in common:

- They have a defined objective or end result
- They are complex consisting of many related events
- They are unique, that is they produce 'specials' – non-repeated outputs
- They are, therefore, also uncertain and contain an element of risk
- They require a temporary allocation of resources until completion
- They follow a predictable life cycle which affects the nature of planning and control activities.

# The project planning and control process

Project management planning and control can be categorised into four stages relevant to project planning and control.

**Stage 1** *Understanding the project environment – the internal and external factors which may influence the project*
The project environment comprises all the factors which may affect the project during its life, such as political, geographic, economic, other projects being carried out, or even the history of previous projects carried out for the customer. Each of these may influence how the project is carried out and will affect the degree of risk inherent in the project.

**Stage 2** *Defining the project – setting the objectives, scope and strategy for the project*
Before starting the complex task of planning and executing a project, it is necessary to be as clear as possible about what is going to be done; the objectives, the scope of the project and the strategy for meeting the objectives. Some projects are simpler to define than others. Projects where all the major tasks have been done before, where methods and equipment have already been proven, can be defined reasonably well in advance. Completely new projects may be much more difficult to define – see the case, Campaign Planning for 'Red Nose Day' (Case 13).

**Stage 3** *Project planning – deciding how the project will be executed*
Project planning involves the detailed step-by-step planning of all the activities involved in the project. It involves breaking the overall complex task down into separate activities, estimating the time and resources required for each activity and the relationships and dependencies between them. This information is used to create a schedule of activities and to identify the time critical or resource critical activities in the project.

The planning process fulfils four distinct purposes:

- It determines the cost and duration of the project. This enables major decisions to be made – such as the decision whether to go ahead with the project at the start.
- It determines the level of resources which will be needed.
- It helps to allocate work and to monitor progress. Planning must include the identification of who is responsible for what.
- It helps to assess the impact of any changes to the project.

**Stage 4** *Project control – ensuring that the project is carried out according to plan*
This stage deals with the management activities which take place during the execution of the project. The process of project control involves three sets of activities:

- Monitoring the project in order to check on its progress using a variety of measures such as cost, overtime and delays.
- Assessing the time performance of the project by comparing monitored observations of the project with the project plan.
- Intervening in the project in order to make the changes which will bring it back to plan. This can be a complex decision because the activities in a project are interrelated; making changes in one area will have knock-on effects elsewhere.

## Summary

Planning and control is a central and critical responsibility of operations. It involves ensuring that the operation has sufficient resources to be able to meet demand. It involves decisions in the short term to ensure current demand for products and services can be met and also long and medium-term decisions to prepare for future anticipated demand. Key planning and control activities include:

- planning and controlling the use of resources (capacity planning)
- managing physical stocks to meet end demand (inventory planning and control)
- planning and control of independent demand with the aid of a computer-based information system (MRP)
- producing goods and services exactly when needed (just-in-time planning and control)
- the planning and control of large and complex activities (project planning and control).

### Key points

- The purpose of planning and control is to ensure that the operation runs effectively and produces products and services as it should do.
- Planning is the act of setting down expectations of what should happen. Control is the process of monitoring events against the plan and making any necessary adjustments.
- The balance between planning and control changes over time. In long-term planning and control the emphasis is on the aggregated planning and budgeting of activities. At the other extreme, short-term planning and control usually operates within the resource constraints of the operation but makes interventions into the operation in order to cope with short-term changes in circumstances.
- In planning and controlling, three distinct activities are necessary: loading, sequencing and scheduling.
- The capacity of an operation is the maximum level of value-added activity which it can achieve under normal operating conditions over a period of time.
- There are three basic plans for capacity planning and control: the level capacity plan, the chase demand plan and demand management.
- There are three major types of decision which operations managers need to make regarding the planning and control of their inventory. These are:
  - How much to order
  - When to order
  - Which items are the most important.
- Materials requirements planning (MRPI) is a system for calculating materials requirements and creating production plans to satisfy known and forecasted sales orders.
- Manufacturing resource planning (MRPII) incorporates engineering, financial and marketing information in an integrated business system for manufacturing businesses.

- The aim of just-in-time (JIT) operations is to meet demand instantaneously with perfect quality and no waste.
- JIT can be seen both as an overall philosophy of operations and also as a collection of tools and methods which support its aims.
- A project is a set of activities which have a defined start point and a defined end state, that pursue a defined goal and that use a defined set of resources.
- Project management has four stages relevant to project planning and control: understanding the project environment, defining the project, project planning, and project control.

### Recommended reading

Chopra, S. and Meindl, P. (2000), *Supply Chain Management*, Prentice Hall.

Christopher, M. (1998), *Logistics and Supply Chain Management*, Financial Times Prentice Hall.

Juran, J. M. and Godfrey, Blanton A. (2002), *Process Management*, McGraw-Hill, e-book.

Maylor, H. (2001), *Project Management*, (3rd edn), Financial Times/Pitman Publishing.

Meredith, J. R. and Mantel, S. (2001), *Project Management: A Managerial Approach*, (4th edn), New York, Wiley.

Sandras, W. (2002), *Just-In-Time: Making it Happen*, (2nd edn), John Wiley and Sons.

Slack N., Chambers S. and Johnston R. (2001), *Operations Management*, (3rd edn), Pitman, London, Chapters 10, 11, 12, 13, 14, 15, 16 and 17.

# AEB Mortgage Services

Nigel Slack

'It is quite difficult to know exactly how long operators should be spending on each call. Sometimes a client really does need detailed advice or reassurance, at other times the call could be dealt with very quickly indeed. There's a minimum amount of time just to go through the courtesies. But there's also an upper limit. No matter how complex the call, our systems should be able to cope with it within a set time limit. My main concern is that we really do not know how much we should expect calls to vary.'

Duncan Hindes, Mortgage Services Manager (AEB) was speaking in early 1997 just after AEB had made a considerable investment in its new call centre information technology project. The new system had been up and running for several weeks now and was generating considerable amounts of data. All of this data was monitored and stored, but Duncan felt that he should be making more use of the information. The average length of phone calls was a particular concern to him. He had a suspicion that the calls were varying too much and that operators should be able to control even the longer calls. He also felt that it should be possible, at the same level of service quality, to get the average call time down to under two and half minutes (it was a little above this at the moment).

'If operators spend too little time with clients, we can lose both valuable opportunities to collect important information from them, make them feel "dismissed", and sometimes waste an opportunity to sell them further services. On the other hand, if operators spend too much time we are obviously reducing the effective capacity of our unit and wasting valuable operator time.'

Duncan decided that he could exploit the data monitoring system in the call centre in order to chart the average call length, and its variability, over time. As a first attempt to do this, he used the system to sample six conversations at random every hour. He then requested the system to calculate the average length of call for the sample and the range of call lengths (the difference between the longest and the shortest call in the sample) for each sample. This data is shown in Table 22.1. Duncan commented:

'I'm not sure what this tells us. Certainly there is more variation in the length of call than I would have expected, but I am not sure what we can do to reduce this.'

Duncan was convinced that he could take actions which would both speed up the process and reduce the variability of the length of calls. Several options were open to him. He could easily get the new IT system to reinforce the idea of the

**Table 22.1 Call length sampling results – six calls per sample**

| Sample | 1 | 2 | 3 | 4 | 5 | 6 | 7 | 8 | 9 | 10 | 11 | 12 | 13 | 14 | 15 |
|---|---|---|---|---|---|---|---|---|---|---|---|---|---|---|---|
| Average call length | 2.55 | 1.47 | 2.49 | 3.15 | 2.57 | 2.58 | 2.18 | 2.1 | 2.34 | 2.36 | 2.41 | 2.16 | 3.24 | 2.39 | 2.06 |
| Range of call lengths* | 3.49 | 3.13 | 5.33 | 5.47 | 5.37 | 6.18 | 3.37 | 5.23 | 3.21 | 3.14 | 3.19 | 5.17 | 5.48 | 5.21 | 2.52 |

*Range = longest call time in sample – shortest call time in sample.

'target call length' in the operators' minds by putting reminders on screen when the calls exceeded a certain length of time. He could even reinforce the bonus system to put greater emphasis on the number of calls handled by each cell per week – currently the payment system gave a small bonus related to both productivity and quality. More controversially, he could put pressure on the operators to make better use of the new IT system. Although the new system was much more sophisticated than the old, operators often reverted to using the old system, which was still online, because they were familiar with it and made fewer mistakes. Finally, he could increase the emphasis on the degree of monitoring carried out by the supervisors. The new system could allow supervisors to sample average call lengths for each operator and flash up warning messages when average call times got above a certain level. Duncan outlined his favoured approach:

'I guess what we should do now is change some of these parameters to try and reduce the variability of calls. Personally, I am in favour of using all four options. In particular, we could easily get the system to flash up messages to the operators if their calls exceed a certain time. At the same time, it is important that we quickly move them on to the new IT system. We can do this easily, simply by accelerating our existing programme of decommissioning the old system. As it is gradually taken off-line, the operators will be obliged to move on to the new system.'

### Questions

1 *Why should most of the calls at the mortgage centre be within specified limits? What are the advantages and disadvantages of controlling the time staff spend on each call?*

2 *What are the advantages and disadvantages of using the mechanisms suggested to reduce call variation?*

3 *Do you think Duncan Hindes is right in his approach to controlling this process?*

# I'll Phone You Back!

Stuart Chambers

Dave McDonald, owner of Oilpartz Ltd, took off his jacket and sat down at his desk. It was the early morning of his first day back at work after the two-week annual holiday shutdown, and the beginning of Week 1 of the company's financial year. Dave had been pleased that his production team had managed to complete and despatch all existing orders before their holiday. However, this meant that the only new work for them would be any that had come in while they had been away. Dave had about 30 regular customers who valued the exceptional quality and reliability of Oilpartz' workmanship, and its almost unique capabilities for producing small quantities of very complex, special components.

Oilpartz specialised in producing some of the larger pipeline components used on rigs, production platforms and on-shore facilities of the oil industry. There were also a few customers in the chemicals and heavy engineering industries. Because of the size and complexity of the parts, machining times were long, and could be up to five hours per component, per operation. As these were mostly used for major capital projects and for planned maintenance, customers usually were happy to accept Oilpartz's normal quoted lead-time of six weeks. Sometimes, however, a regular customer might ask for a quicker delivery, perhaps because of a late design approval or because of an ordering error. Dave always liked to help, but tried to ensure that other customers never suffered as a result of doing such a favour. Also, for the same reason, he never accepted orders for repetitive, high-volume work. Customers usually arranged for all their special raw materials requirements (such as tubes, forgings and rings) to be delivered to the company shortly after placing their orders, a system known as 'free issue'.

By 7.30 a.m., Dave had checked through the new orders received, and was just starting to prepare the schedules, ready for the start of production in half an hour, when the telephone rang. It was Mike Rowlands of Nitro Chemicals, one of Oilpartz' larger and very profitable accounts.

'Dave, it's Mike … Sorry to bother you so early, but I've a big problem down here that I hope you can help me with! As you know, our main plant has just been shut down for its annual overhaul, and already we've run short of those stainless steel sealing rings – the smaller diameter ones. One of the contract welders used the wrong process settings when fitting them, and we've had to scrap most of his work and start again. You must remember the part – you did some of them for us just a month ago, they're your reference NC11! We really need 20 of them … well, like yesterday! What could you do to help us out? We only have less than two weeks before the whole plant must be back on stream. If you could start straightaway, we could send the material down to you immediately. I would really be extremely grateful if you could help – and if you need to work overtime, I would be only too willing to pay the extra costs. I just need to know when you could get them ready for us to collect. As you can imagine, this is really critical to us!'

Dave stretched back in his chair and paused a moment before responding:

'I've just got back from holiday, Mike, so I haven't finished the schedule yet. I will see if I can fit in your order, but it sounds a really difficult request. From what I remember, your job took us at least *six* weeks last time, and that was at a relatively quiet time for us. Today we've got quite a full order book after our shutdown. However, we still have the drawings and machining times from before, so I will work out what we can do for you. I understand the urgency, so please give me half an hour or so, and I'll call you back, Mike!'

Dave looked at the list of four jobs that he had just entered in the order book, all of which were for familiar work of a type that was ordered fairly regularly. He then pulled out the corresponding job record cards from the filing cabinet, which gave machining times per operation, per component. Because of the small batch quantities, all operations were undertaken by highly skilled machinists, and any set-up time for each operation was insignificant compared to the long machining times involved. During the machining, each employee normally operated only one machine at a time, so that full attention was given to the quality of each component. This was critical because of the high cost of materials involved, and the high value-added at each stage.

Dave's four highly skilled machinists worked eight hours a day, Monday to Friday. They were usually willing to work some evenings and occasionally at weekends, but Dave had agreed that no one would normally be asked to do more than

**Table 23.1 Analysis of orders – in sequence of order placement date**

| Customer | Part ref. | No. reqd. | Operation route (sequence) and hours per component | | | | Delivery end of week No. |
|---|---|---|---|---|---|---|---|
| | | | Op 1 | Op 2 | Op 3 | Op 4 | |
| Alpha Oil | AO6 | 10 | Turn 5 | Mill 3 | Drill 4 | Grind 2.5 | 4 |
| British Pipelines | BP23 | 5 | Turn 10 | Mill 5 | Drill 2 | Turn 4 | 3* |
| Gamma Gases | GG7 | 10 | Mill 2 | Drill 3 | | | 5 |
| Delta Engineering | DE31 | 5 | Turn 3 | Mill 4 | Grind 4 | | 6 |
| Nitro Chemicals | NC11 | 20 | Turn 1 | Mill 0.5 | Drill 1.5 | Grind 1.5 | urgent |

*British Pipelines' order had been sent at the end of the first week of the holiday, and it had requested delivery within five weeks. This customer is Oilpartz's largest and oldest account.

10 hours of overtime. Experience had shown that beyond those hours too many expensive mistakes were being made. Each machinist was multi-skilled and could operate any of the machines. Oilpartz owned two lathes (used for turning, or cutting cylindrical surfaces), one milling machine (used to cut flat areas and slots), one drill (for cutting holes) and a grinding machine (for extremely precise cutting and smooth finishing of surfaces).

Dave summarised the details of all the orders, including the urgent one from Nitro Chemicals, on his office whiteboard. His next tasks would be to turn that into a schedule, and then to phone Mike. He then added the processing times for the current orders and for the Nitro Chemicals enquiry. A copy of this completed information is shown as Table 23.1.

## Questions

*To answer these questions you should first prepare a blank Gantt chart for scheduling the five machines.*

**1** *What is the best delivery date (week number and day) that Dave could quote to Mike? Will this affect delivery to the other customers and, therefore, should it be taken on?*

**2** *If Dave decided not to give priority to Mike's order, he would then be able to schedule the other four orders in several different ways. Compare and contrast the schedules for:*

- *First come, first served (FCFS)*
- *Due date (DD)*
- *Longest operation time first (LOT)*

*In preparing the LOT schedule, you will have to decide whether to consider the operation time for each order at each machine, or overall for all operations. State which assumptions you have made, explaining what you have done, and why.*

This case was developed from an unpublished Hancock's Half Hour case with the kind permission of Roy Staughton.

# CASE 24

# Holly Farm

Case date
1999

Stuart Chambers

## Introduction

In 1993, Fred and Gillian Giles decided to open up their mixed (dairy and arable) farm to the paying public, in response to diminishing profits from their milk and cereals activities. They invested all their savings into building a 40-space car park, a six-space park for 40-seater coaches, a safe viewing area for the milking parlour, special trailers for passengers to be transported around the farm on guided tours, a permanent exhibition of equipment, a 'rare-breeds' paddock, a children's adventure playground, a picnic area and a farm shop. Behind the farm shop they built a small 'factory' making real dairy ice-cream, which also provided for public viewing. Ingredients for the ice-cream, pasteurised cream and eggs, sugar, flavourings, etc., were brought out, although this was not obvious to the viewing public.

Gillian took responsibility for all these new activities whilst Fred continued to run the commercial farming business. Through advertising, giving lectures to local schools and organisations such as Women's Institutes, and through personal contact with coach firms, the number of visitors to the farm increased steadily. By 1998 Gillian had become so involved in running her business that she was unable to give so much time to these promotional activities, and the number of paying visitors levelled out to around 15 000 per year. Although the farm opened to the public at 11.00 a.m. and closed at 7.00 p.m. after milking was finished, up to 90 per cent of visitors in cars or coaches would arrive later than 12.30 p.m., picnic until around 2.00 p.m., and tour the farm until about 4.00 p.m. By that time, around 20 per cent would have visited the farm shop and left, but the remainder would wait to view the milking, then visit the shop to purchase ice-cream and other produce, and then depart. The entry fee was £4.

## Visitors to the farm

Gillian opened the farm to the public each year from April to October inclusive. Demand would be too low outside this period: the conditions were often unsuitable for regular tractor rides and most of the animals had to be kept inside. Early experience had confirmed that mid-week demand was too low to justify opening, but Friday through to Monday was commercially viable, with almost exactly twice as many visitors on Saturdays and Sundays than on Fridays or Mondays. Gillian summed up the situation:

'I have decided to attempt to increase the number of farm visitors in 1999 by 50 per cent. This would not only improve our return on "farm tours" assets, but would also help the farm shop to achieve its targets and the extra sales of ice-cream would help to keep the "factory" at full output. The real problem is whether to promote sales to coach firms or to intensify local advertising to attract more families in cars. We could also consider tie-ups with schools for educational visits, but I would not want to use my farm guide staff on any extra weekdays as Fred needs them three days per week for "real" farming work. However, most of the farm workers are glad of this extra of work as it fits in well with their family life and helps them to save up for the luxuries most farm workers cannot afford.'

## The milking parlour

With 150 cows to milk, Fred invested in a 'carousel' parlour where cows are milked on a slow-moving turntable. Milking usually lasts from 4.30 p.m. to 7.00 p.m., during which time visitors can view from a purpose-built gallery which has space and explanatory tape recordings, via headphones, for 12 people. Gillian has found that, on average, spectators like to watch for 10 minutes, including five minutes for the explanatory tape.

'We're sometimes a bit busy on Saturdays and Sundays and a queue often develops before 4.00 p.m. as some people want to see the milking and then go home. Unfortunately, neither Fred nor the cows are prepared to start earlier. However, most people are patient and everybody gets their turn to see this bit of high technology. In a busy period, up to 80 people per hour pass through the gallery.'

## The ice-cream factory

The factory is operated 48 weeks per year, four days per week, eight hours per day. The three employees, farm workers' wives, are expected to work in line with farm opening from April to October, but hours and days are by negotiation in other months. All output is in one-litre plastic boxes, of which 350 are made every day, which is the maximum mixing and fast-freezing capacity. Although extra mixing hours would create more unfrozen ice-cream, the present equipment cannot safely and fully fast-freeze more than 350 litres over a 24-hour period. Ice-cream that is not fully frozen cannot be transferred to the finished goods freezer, as slower freezing spoils the texture of the product. As it takes about one hour to clean out between flavours, only one of the four flavours is made on any day. The finished goods freezer holds a maximum of 10 000 litres, but to allow stock rotation, in practice it cannot be loaded to above 7000 litres. Ideally, no ice-cream should be held more than six weeks at the factory, as the total recommended storage time is only twelve weeks prior to retail sale (there is no preservative used). Finished goods inventory at the end of December 1998 was 3600 litres.

Gillian's most recent figures indicated that all flavours cost about £1.00 per litre to produce (variable cost of materials, packaging and labour). The factory layout is by process with material preparation and weighing sections, mixing area, packing equipment and separate freezing equipment. It is operated as a batch process.

# Ice-cream sales

The finished product is sold to three categories of buyers. See Appendix 24.1 for sales history and forecast.

## Retail shops

The majority of output is sold through regional speciality shops such as delicatessens and food sections of department stores. These outlets are given a standard discount of 25 per cent to allow a 33 per cent mark-up to the normal retail price of £2.00 per litre. Minimum order quantity is 100 litres, and deliveries are made by Gillian in the van on Tuesdays.

## Paying visitors to the farm

Having been shown around the farm and 'factory', a large proportion of visitors buy ice-cream at the farm shop and take it away in well-insulated containers that keep it from melting for up to two hours in the summer. Gillian commented:

'These are virtually captive customers. We have analysed this demand and found that on average one out of two coach customers buys a one-litre box. On average, a car comes with four occupants, and two one-litre boxes are purchased. The farm shop retail price is £2.00 per box, which gives us a much better margin than for our sales to shops.'

## 'Farm shop only' visitors

A separate, fenced road entrance allows local customers to purchase goods at a separate counter of the farm shop without payment for, or access to, the other farm facilities.

'This is a surprisingly regular source of sales. We believe this is because householders make very infrequent visits to stock up their freezers, almost regardless of the time of year or the weather. We also know that local hotels buy a lot this way, and their use of ice-cream is year-round, with a peak only at Christmas when there is a larger number of banquets.'

All sales in this category are at the full retail price of £2.00.

Appendix 24.2 gives details of visitors to the farm and ice-cream sales in 1998. Gillian's concluding comments were:

'We have a long way to go to make this enterprise meet our expectations. We will probably make only a small return on capital employed in 1998, so must do all we can to increase our profitability. Neither of us want to put more capital into the business, as we would have to borrow at interest rates of up to 10 per cent. We must make our investment work better. As a first step, I have decided to increase the number of natural flavours of our ice-cream to 10 in 1999 (currently only four) to try and defend the delicatessen trade against a competitor's aggressive marketing campaign. I don't expect that fully to halt the decline in our sales to these outlets, and this is reflected in our sales forecast.'

## Questions

1 *What are the issues that Gillian faces?*

2 *Evaluate Gillian's proposal to increase the number of farm visitors in 1999 by 50 per cent. You may wish to:*

- *evaluate the sales forecasts*
- *analyse the capacities and identify the capacity constraints within these businesses.*

3 *What factors should Gillian consider when deciding to increase the number of flavours from four to ten?*

Note: *For any calculations, assume that each month consists of four weeks. The effects of Bank Holidays (statutory holidays) should be ignored for the purpose of this initial analysis.*

## Appendix 24.1

### Analysis of annual sales of ice-cream (£000s) from 1994 to 1998, and forecast sales for 1999

|  | 1994 | 1995 | 1996 | 1997 | 1998 | 1999[b] forecast |
|---|---|---|---|---|---|---|
| Retail shops | 8 | 26 | 39 | 62 | 75 | 65 |
| Farm shop total[a] | 10 | 16 | 20 | 25 | 27 | 40 |
| Total | 18 | 42 | 59 | 87 | 102 | 105 |

*Notes:*

[a] No separate records are kept of sales to the paying farm visitors and to those who only visit the farm shop.

[b] The selling prices and discounts for 1999 will be as 1998. Gillian considered that 1998 was reasonably typical in terms of weather, although rainfall was a little higher than average during July and August.

## Appendix 24.2

### Records of farm visitors and ice-cream sales in 1998

|  | Jan | Feb | Mar | Apr | May | June | July | Aug | Sept | Oct | Nov | Dec | Total |
|---|---|---|---|---|---|---|---|---|---|---|---|---|---|
| Total number of paying farm visitors[a] | 0 | 0 | 0 | 1200 | 1800 | 2800 | 3200 | 3400 | 1800 | 600 | 0 | 0 | 14800 |
| Monthly ice-cream sales (£s): |  |  |  |  |  |  |  |  |  |  |  |  |  |
| to retail shops | 3900 | 4050 | 7950 | 5100 | 6600 | 8550 | 8250 | 7500 | 7350 | 4800 | 3450 | 7500 | 75000 |
| Farm shop total | 600 | 1000 | 800 | 1600 | 2400 | 4000 | 4400 | 4800 | 2400 | 1600 | 1000 | 2600 | 27200 |

*Note:*

[a] Farm visitors are those that pay the £4.00 entrance fee. This figure does not include local customers who only visit the farm shop and are able to use a separate entrance and sales counter.

# Ice House Toys

Stuart Chambers and Graham Whittington

## Introduction

Robin Baker, the Managing Director of a small group of toy shops, suspected that he had a problem. His company, formed in 1962, consisted of five profitable shops and a catalogue sales (mail-order) business which, although profitable, had never been able to capitalise fully on the quality of its products and the loyalty of its customers.

Ice House Toys, its mail-order operation, was run from a renovated eighteenth-century ice house (originally constructed on a dockside for storing imported blocks of ice) in Bristol, which the company acquired in 1981 when such old industrial property was cheap and easy to find. The current state of the property market made relocation unrealistic, and alternative modern warehouse space in the Bristol area was both inconveniently situated and too expensive.

The building consisted of three floors, each of which was divided by the stairwell and lift-shaft into two working areas of 600 square metres each. One of the ground floor areas was used to store stock for the company's shops, but it had been decided to reallocate this space to the mail-order operation from the beginning of September 2000. The other ground floor area was used as the packing room for the mail-order operation. Of the remaining four work areas in the building, three (two on the first floor and one on the second) were mail-order stockrooms, while the fourth contained the office. As is often the case in a historic industrial building, ceiling height was restricted and stock was stacked to use all the available height.

## Sales and purchasing patterns

Ice House Toys distributed three mail-order catalogues every year, each of which contained approximately 300 different toys and games, all of which were standard products manufactured in the UK, Europe and the Far East. The major catalogue was the Christmas one, sent to 160 000 customers in the first week of October. In 1999, this had resulted in a total of 22 600 orders with an average order value of £42. The Winter Sale Catalogue and the Spring Catalogue were each sent to 45 000 regular customers, and in 1999 achieved a combined total of 6900 orders with an average order value of £23.

The stock for the Christmas Catalogue was ordered before the end of July, and was received in two phases. The first, representing approximately 75 per cent of

**Table 25.1 Orders received in 1999**

| Month | Week | Orders |
|---|---|---|
| October | 1 | 0 |
| | 2 | 300 |
| | 3 | 800 |
| | 4 | 1800 |
| November | 1 | 2900 |
| | 2 | 3300 |
| | 3 | 3700 |
| | 4 | 3500 |
| December | 1 | 2800 |
| | 2 | 2200 |
| | 3 | 1300 |

total requirements, arrived in the first week of October, filling the stock areas to capacity. The remainder was ordered after the first 2500 customer orders had been processed and the sales patterns had been analysed, and was delivered during the fourth week of November. The feasibility of receiving deliveries of smaller quantities of stock had been considered on several occasions in the past but, taking loss of discount and advantageous terms of payment into account, the resulting eight per cent reduction in gross profit margins had been considered unacceptable. Appendix 25.1 gives a detailed breakdown of costs.

In 1999, stock with a total resale value of £1.1 million was ordered. This was based on a projection of 21 000 orders with an average value of £45, plus a margin for error which Robin always added to guard against unexpected higher demand for a particular item or the failure of some suppliers to deliver an order in full. Any surplus stock at the end of the Christmas Catalogue period could be disposed of through the Winter Sale Catalogue, or through the retail shops. Robin liked to maintain a minimum stock level at any time to cover 10 working days, allowing a buffer for late delivery from a supplier or for a sudden unexpected demand for a particular item.

The recorded volume of orders received from the Christmas Catalogue in 1999 is shown in Table 25.1. This pattern had been found to vary little from year to year.

Given the 24th December delivery deadline for Christmas, all orders had to be dispatched by the end of the third week in December. Any customers whose orders were received in the fourth week of December (there were only 75 orders in 1999) were contacted by telephone, and most usually agreed to their order being dispatched when the warehouse reopened in the first week of January.

## ● Operations

Any order arriving at the warehouse passed through three stages, in the following sequence: recording, assembly and packing, dispatch. A detailed analysis of each of these stages follows:

## Recording

All orders were entered into the computer on the day on which they arrived so that the earliest possible notice could be given of any stock shortages. There were facilities in the office for up to seven VDU operators, who were hired from a local agency and were paid by the hour. They each worked a seven-hour day. Each operator was able to process an average of 22 orders per hour, which involved entering either an existing customer's account number or a new customer's name and address into the computer, followed by the customer's order and payment details. Picking lists, packing notes and address labels were then automatically printed out two floors below in the Parcels Room, where both the assembly/packing and dispatch operations were situated.

## Assembly and packing

The assembly operation was divided into two stages, both of which, according to internal and external work studies, were performed efficiently. For every batch of 20 orders, the computer produced an aggregate picking list, which enabled each of the three stock collectors to go round the stockrooms and, in an average of 45 minutes, select the stock required for their 20 orders. This stock was then given to teams of two packers who worked together to allocate it to individual orders, to check that each order was correct, and then carefully to pack each order into a suitable-size box. The completed orders were then passed on, with packing note attached, to the dispatch stage of the operation. Each packer completed an average of 4.3 parcels per hour, which enabled a single stock collector to provide sufficient stock for six packers.

The total space allocated to the packing operation was 330 square metres, which was sufficient for a maximum of 16 packers at any one time. This department, like the dispatch department, was staffed entirely by part-timers who worked either four-hour (morning) or five-hour (afternoon) shifts. The warehouse was operated Monday to Friday from 9 a.m. to 6 p.m.

## Dispatch

The workers in the dispatch department were, like their colleagues in assembly and packing, employed as and when they were required. Their job was to take each parcel, attach an address label, which had been printed by the computer, and enter the order number into the computer to confirm that the order had been fully processed. The parcels were then stored in a secure area on the loading bay, and were collected by a parcel carrier at regular intervals six times each day. Each person in the dispatch team could complete 9.5 orders per hour, and required at least 30 square metres to be able to operate effectively.

## ● Future plans

Robin was determined to expand catalogue sales considerably in 2000:

'The 1999 ratio of 22 600 orders from 160 000 catalogues sent out was close to the average for the last 10 seasons. For 2000, however, there are three major changes. Firstly, we have made an agreement to share part of our customer database with a company that sells upmarket children's clothes by mail order. Of course, these are clearly identified customers who have signed an agreement to allow their details to be used in that way. In return, this company will provide us access to its database of similarly disposed customers, and this will add some 30 000 names and addresses to our current list. Our second initiative is to spend a further £18 000 on advertising. In the past, each £1000 spent on advertising has finally led to 190 additional orders.

'Thirdly, we finally launched our new website, aimed at existing customers only, at the end of November 1999, and expect this to have a significant impact in our market this year. Unfortunately, it was late for the season just finished because the design had to be reworked to remove a number of very irritating bugs that were identified by around a thousand trial customers. Now, however, anyone who accesses this site will be able to obtain more comprehensive descriptions and photographs of all the products we supply, and it will make ordering much simpler for the customer. They will simply fill their virtual shopping baskets by clicking on the products they require. There will be no need to copy out product descriptions and codes: the system will do all that for them. We learnt a lot during the trial, and found that the average order value for the Internet customers was around £60. From discussions with some other mail-order retailers who have similarly gone online, I would expect about five per cent of our existing customers to use this service in the 2000 season, and overall usage of this channel is expected to double every year as new customers find our site.

'Orders received this way will remove the need to key in data in the Recording Office. The data-entry staff will simply check the details deposited by the online customers and, if these are correctly and fully completed, will allow the order to pass into the further processes as normal. Our trials indicate that this will allow each operator to completely process and authorise these orders at a rate of about one per minute. That will eventually have a significant impact on our costs, and will increase our capacity to enter orders into the system at the busiest times of the season.

'The only thing that worries me is that this ongoing expansion will either lead to us completely running out of warehouse space due to the sheer volume of stock, or to us being forced to pay overtime to run the operation during evenings or weekends. This would undermine our tight control of costs and erode our hard-won profits. Also, at present, it is our policy to dispatch all orders within three days of receipt; I am very concerned that this may become increasingly difficult to achieve as our sales volumes should grow by a forecast annual rate of 15 per cent per year from the 2001 season.'

## Questions

1 *Evaluate the impact on operations of Robin's sales targets for the 2000 Christmas Catalogue. You may wish to consider the following:*

- *What are the main capacity constraints within the mail-order operation?*
- *To what extent can they be resolved by the planned 2000 increase in the amount of warehouse space allocated to the mail-order operation?*
- *In what other ways could Robin attempt to influence demand so as to overcome capacity constraints?*

- What will be the impact on operations of the website, based on Robin's forecast of customer uptake? What would the effect be if this channel failed to grow as rapidly as expected?

Assume that selecting smaller toys for the catalogue is not a solution!

2 What are the longer-term capacity planning issues? Evaluate the impact of the projected 15 per cent growth over five years.

3 Is it possible to construct an argument which could justify the company accepting a 7.5 per cent reduction in gross profit margin through the adoption of an alternative purchasing policy, which would significantly reduce stock levels? Ignore any effect of price inflation, and take account of your answer to Question 2, above.

4 Is it reasonable for Robin to be horrified at the idea of overtime payments?

## 1999 Christmas Catalogue: cost analysis

**Breakdown of costs for one average parcel (1999 figures)**

|  | £ |
|---|---|
| Sales | 42.00 |
| Cost of stock, packaging materials, carriage | (23.00) |
| **Gross profit** | **19.00** |
| Share of fixed costs[a] | (10.08) |
| Catalogue production[b] | (3.25) |
| VDU operator wages | (0.35) |
| Stock collector wages | (0.12) |
| Packer wages | (0.77) |
| Dispatcher wages | (0.35) |
| **Net profit** | **4.08** |

*Notes:*
[a] Total fixed costs £288 000 per year, absorbed over 22 600 orders.
[b] 160 000 catalogues were printed and mailed at a cost of £0.46 each, resulting in 22 600 orders

# Fresh Salads Ltd:
# The Iceberg lettuce harvest

Case date
2000

Stuart Chambers

## Introduction

Fresh Salads Ltd is an important division of a privately-owned farming company specialising in vegetable growing and distribution. Its most important customer group is the major UK supermarkets which require fresh produce to be delivered to them 364 days a year. The company has all the staff, expertise and specialised facilities needed to supply these supermarkets throughout the year. One of the most important products of this company is Iceberg lettuce, which is grown in England during the summer and in south-east Spain during the winter. Iceburg lettuces are dense and round, but are easily bruised so have to be harvested with great care, after which they are stored and transported in chilled conditions to avoid deterioration. From the time of cutting, they must be packed quickly to minimise water loss and taken rapidly to a cool store. Market demand varies greatly, dependent on the season and on weather conditions, with demand rising rapidly in periods of hot, dry weather and in the preceding day. Supermarkets rely on weather forecasts to predict demand for salads and fresh sandwiches.

## The harvesting rigs

The company has developed specialised machinery to assist in the harvest of millions of Iceberg lettuces every year. Each of the company's six Iceberg lettuce picking machines (known as 'rigs') is a large mobile factory which is mechanically powered to move very slowly across the enormous lettuce fields, at a speed and direction controlled by the supervisor using a simple joystick control. The rig runs on caterpillar tracks which allows it to cross the soft, deep peaty soils on which lettuces thrive. However, in very wet conditions, this very heavy piece of equipment can get stuck and may need assistance from an additional crawler tractor. At the very back of the rig is attached an open-fronted road trailer, into which the trays of packed lettuces are carried and stacked. This trailer can be released when full, and attached to a four-wheel drive tractor for subsequent transportation to the company's local cold store. Another trailer is then connected in its place to allow picking to continue uninterrupted.

Each crew (picking team) comprises 17 people and a supervisor; there are nine cutters, five packers and three people preparing cardboard trays, labelling the individual supermarket lettuces and carrying completed trays and crates to the trailers. The supervisor, who is fully responsible for product quality and output of the rig, also provides assistance at any point on the rig to relieve any short-term bottleneck and to cover any short period when an operative needs to leave the rig. The crew members are paid piecework, and usually work eight-hour days (plus breaks), although overtime may be necessary on very busy days in mid season. Crew members of the most successful teams can earn more than double the UK hourly minimum wage, but this requires sustained effort and concentration, and cooperative crew behaviour.

## The picking process

The nine cutters work on the ground in a wide line just in front of the rig, which slowly moves towards them. They stand astride the rows of lettuce, working slowly backwards. The average cutting speed per person, in good conditions, is eight seconds per iceberg lettuce. Within this cycle time the picker selects and cuts each lettuce using a sharp, slightly hooked knife, trims away the outer leaves (which are often muddy and/or damaged), and then drops the prepared lettuce into a polythene bag pulled from a bundle attached to the cutter's waist belt. The cutter can choose to leave uncut any lettuces exhibiting defects, for example, under-size, poor shape or damaged, and these are later ploughed back into the soil. They are also very skilled at judging lettuce weights, and will avoid under- or over-sized specimens. The best-quality wrapped lettuces are then thrown carefully forward to a packer. Others are thrown further forward straight into plastic crates of 20 for subsequent industrial processing, depending on quality. These are known as 'process grade' and are used to make prepared salads and bulk chopped lettuce for the sandwich industry. In persistently wet weather, the average picking rate can slow by up to 25 per cent, as a result of a combination of mud slowing the picking and packing process, rigs getting stuck and a general deterioration in morale of the crew.

The five packers sit on seats attached to the front of the rig, in front of the pickers and just off the ground. They seal the bags with tape, and place the lettuce in a single layer in cardboard trays, selecting (grading) them – the best quality for the supermarkets in trays of 10, the remainder for wholesale markets in trays of 12. On average, this task takes five seconds per lettuce. The full trays are then quickly pushed forward to the final group of employees who work further back on the rig, higher up and level with the trailer floor.

These three workers have several tasks. Firstly, they have to erect the cardboard trays from flat 'cut and creased' blanks which the company buys in from an outside supplier of cardboard packaging. This tray preparation entails a folding and tucking action, and one skilled worker can make and stack the trays in an average of about seven seconds each. Typically, half of this person's time is spent on this activity, and the remaining time on labelling.

The next task is to label all the supermarket lettuces. Self-adhesive labels are provided on a long roll, and are simply peeled off and stuck on each lettuce bag. These labels customise the lettuce for individual supermarkets and also provide the bar code and sell-by/use-by dates. Although they have to be positioned carefully with minimal creasing, a skilled worker can apply a label about every two seconds. On completion, each tray is then pushed forward, ready for conveyance to the trailer by another worker.

Each filled tray or crate has to be carried from the deck of the rig into the transport trailer, where it is stacked. Although the walking time for this action depends on the extent to which the trailer has been filled, an average time is approximately 15 seconds, which includes the time needed to return for the next tray or crate. This is the heaviest task, so the three workers rotate the jobs on the upper level of the rig. The supervisor is based here too – weighing equipment and quality records are kept at the back of the rig – so is able to assist with these jobs when needed.

Trailers are changed approximately every two hours, but this does not stop the operation of the picking, packing or labelling part of the rig. Two workers are needed to uncouple the trailer and reconnect the empty replacement. This takes approximately 10 minutes.

On average, during a normal working period, each worker uses about five per cent of the time for personal needs and for occasional activities; such as collecting packaging material. Breakdown time averages approximately two per cent of the available time, and this is usually used for cleaning and preparation.

Although the supervisor is able to assist others when the need arises, he or she spends about two hours a day on quality assurance. Statistical process control (SPC) is used to ensure that lettuce weight is within the requirements of each customer, and samples are inspected to ensure that their appearance remains within tolerance. Records of quality and output are maintained per rig.

## Output statistics

During a busy period of sustained good weather in August, the average daily (eight hours) output from each rig was as follows:

| | |
|---|---|
| Supermarket | 1800 trays |
| Wholesale | 230 trays |
| Process | 200 crates |

### Questions

1 *What are the inputs and outputs of the transformation process described in this case?*

2 *What are the main operations objectives for the macro-operation?*

3 *How would you describe the type of process and the layout used in this unusual operation?*

4 *Calculate the capacities for each part (micro-operation) of the Iceberg rig, and from this estimate the total capacity. To what extent does the overall capacity depend on the product mix? What problems are encountered when attempting these capacity calculations?*

5 *How well balanced are the capacities, and what could adversely affect this balance?*

6 *Compare the actual output to the capacity. What does this suggest about the operations management tasks involved in running all six rigs?*

7 *In a typical UK summer, the weather can cycle frequently between cool, dull periods with spells of heavy rainfall, and periods of hot, dry and sunny weather. What capacity management problems could arise during such variations in the weather, and how can management best respond to such fluctuations?*

# Mandexor Memory

Nigel Slack

In November 1999, Mat Frankel was promoted to the post of Operations Manager of the company's European Disk Drive Division, located just outside Dublin. An American, he had been given the job for two reasons. First, the parent company in the USA was concerned at the poor record of the Dublin plant in terms of meeting production targets which, it was felt, he could improve. Second, the whole of the European operation was about to reorganise. The reorganisation would take away each division's sales and marketing function and centralise them into a Marketing Division. It was hoped that this new division would rationalise distribution, reduce overall stock investment and improve the quality of sales forecasts. Each manufacturing division would then sell to the sales division at cost, plus a small percentage. The Marketing Division would take responsibility for all finished goods stocks. This form of organisation had been used by the US company for some years and it particularly wanted an American Operations Manager during the changeover period.

Previously, Mat had been the Production Controller of an equivalent plant in the USA. His experiences there had developed his ideas on how operations should be run. At his first management meeting in December 1999 he addressed his new team.

'The main problem with running a plant like this, especially in the computer business, is that there is such a lot that we don't know. Of course, we never know what sales are going to be. Sure, we have forecasts, but I suspect that our forecasters do little more than guess. And who can blame them? With so much technical innovation, who knows what lies around the corner? But it is not only external unknowns that are the problem. We are not even sure of the true cost of our actions. For example, what is the real cost of holding inventory? A million dollars worth of inventory can halve in value overnight if the technology changes. At other times, its value can actually increase if there is a shortage in the market. Nor do we have any real idea of the true cost of lost sales if we run out of inventory, or the cost to our reputation if we fail to meet delivery dates.

'I know what you might say. "How can we find out true costs when we are continually changing schedules because the forecasts are changing?" Well, while I have some sympathy with that, we cannot always blame other people. I know better forecasts would help us significantly, but we must also put more effort into both planning to cope with inaccurate forecasts and being able to respond flexibly when we need to. Also, what is the use of complaining when it is the very nature of management to cope with some fundamental tensions? Different parts of the business have always wanted different things. The finance people are concerned with minimising inventory levels so that they can cut our levels of working capital. Marketing are only concerned with having plenty of product to sell at any time. In operations, we like to minimise our own costs by minimising any disruption to our production plans.

'But from now on we are going to take a lead. We are going to plan the production levels for our factory in such a way as to give everybody what they want. From now on we schedule in such a way as to minimise our own costs, give marketing the goods they want when they want them, and keep inventory levels at a minimum. I know that's one hell of a task, but if we don't do it, no one else can.'

## ● Marketing considerations

Mandexor Memory produced and sold three basic ranges of disk drive, modified only slightly for different markets. The first range of products was known as the 'Consumer' range. These products were relatively small disk drives which were sold into the consumer market as added memory products. Some were intended for external use while others were mounted internally. Also, both external and internal drives were made with different storage capacities. However, there was a very high degree of parts commonality between the different types and every model within the range could be manufactured on the same production line, without modification. The products in the second range, known as the 'PC Drive' range, were large disk drives sold to personal computer manufacturers for assembly into their products. Again, these came in different sizes and with slightly different specifications, but had a very high degree of similarity and parts commonality. The third range was known as the 'Professional' range. These were stand-alone drives of very high capacity mounted within their own enclosures and sold to a wide range of professional information technology (IT) users.

The Consumer product range was sold primarily through large computer retailers, both physical retailers and Internet retailers. More recently, Mandexor had started selling direct to the public through its own Internet site. As yet, this only accounted for three to four per cent of total Consumer range sales. The PC Drives were sold to computer manufacturers under short and medium-term contracts. Typically, a computer manufacturer would place an order for several thousands drives of various types to be delivered on specified dates. Usually this contract allowed the PC manufacturer to vary quantities and delivery times at relatively short notice without compensation. Although there was considerable price competition in this market, Mandexor realised good margins on its PC range. This was because it had an excellent reputation for the quality and reliability of its products. The top-end PC manufacturers were willing to pay slightly more for Mandexor drives because of their proven reliability. The Professional range of disk drives was sold through a variety of channels. Some were sold directly through the company's Internet site, some to the larger computer manufacturers for installation as part of their own systems, but most were sold through specialist IT systems suppliers.

Mandexor sold disk drive products from stock all over the world; because of this market fluctuations were, to some extent, smoothed out. However, forecasting was notoriously difficult for three reasons. First, computer sales as a whole were dependent on overall economic growth. While this had been strong in most markets throughout the late 1990s, regional economic downturns could still impact on Mandexor's sales. Second, technology was continually shifting both in terms of disk drives themselves and in other aspects of computing. Although technology changes had not had any major impact on the company for several years, press speculation surrounding technology change could cause fluctuations in the supply chain. Third, there was market seasonality in disk drive sales. This was a result of the Christmas gift market and, more significantly, financial year end points. Typically, the August low point was around 60 per cent of the December peak. The actual retail sales for 1999 are given in Appendix 27.1. Forecasts of the orders for each range were made every month for the next four-month period. Also, every quarter a four-quarter forecast was made and occasionally a 12 month forecast was made. At the monthly sales/production meeting, these forecasts were used to agree a month-by-month production plan with the Operations Manager.

## Manufacturing considerations

Manufacturing at the plant consisted of parts fabrication and assembly. Parts fabrication operations included metal shaping and forming which were done in batches on various machines. Unusually, Mandexor also produced some of their 'disk media'. This was the coated surface on which information was stored. The reason for this was partly historical, but was also justified in terms of keeping close to the technical developments in the media-coating process. Assembly operations were line-based, with the lines carefully balanced using standard times. More and more assembly and inspection jobs were being automated as cost reduction opportunities became evident. Mat Frankel had said his plant now had a five-day capacity of about 16 500 drives per week.

After the monthly sales/production meeting, the Plant Manager would translate the production plan into its 'standard hours' equivalent. This was the unit of production which enabled production to be aggregated and the loading on the plant calculated. The standard hours for each product was derived from the number of direct labour hours needed to manufacture it, and incorporated various allowances. Thus the monthly forecast for each product type was multiplied by its standard hour equivalent and summed to obtain the factory loading.

Appendix 27.2 shows the four-month forecasts and the actual factory loadings at each monthly meeting during 1999. Normally the model mix produced consisted of about two Consumer range products to three PC range products to one Professional range product. The standard hours content of the Consumer range products was 80 per cent of the content of the PC range products; the Professional range products was 120 per cent of the standard hours content of the PC range products. If mix changes occurred, assembly lines could be rearranged. Operators were transferred among the three production lines with only marginal loss of efficiency – about half the assembly personnel had been employed for at least four years, and they had developed a versatility in working on the different models. Many parts were interchangeable among the models and parts were made in job lots so that product mix changes did not significantly affect labour loads in the parts machining and processing departments. Because of this and the recent stability of the product mix, manufacturing personnel usually described output in terms of 'unit drives' rather than 'standard hours'.

The plant was heavily unionised but labour relations had been generally good for the last few years. The company's employment record had been good, with no redundancies and a minimum of four weeks' notice given for any working practice change or overtime. Wage rates were about average for the area, but fringe benefits were better than average. The whole plant shut down for the last two weeks in July and the first week in August.

## Fixing the production programme

January 2000 saw the Sales Division formed and Mat's first production budget meeting. This was the meeting at which the guidelines would be agreed between Production and Sales for production volumes over the coming year, and a preliminary overall production plan pencilled in.

Mat rather shocked the meeting by making what some regarded as a 'delaying' proposal.

'I am firmly convinced that we could save considerable amount of money by examining our production schedules. I propose that we set up a small working party to examine the costs involved in adopting a number of strategies, namely:

- keeping production levels constant and absorbing demand fluctuations by varying finished goods stocks
- using overtime on an extensive basis in peak periods and allowing underutilisation of labour during slack periods
- hiring an extra shift for peak production and laying them off later in the year, if necessary
- subcontracting out some of our parts fabrication over to assembly.'

Rather reluctantly, the meeting agreed to postpone any decisions for two weeks while the working party examined Mat's alternative 'strategies'.

## The working party

The working party met five days later and consisted of one representative from each of Production Control, Accounts, Sales and Marketing, and Distribution (now in the Marketing Division). They had two documents for consideration – a sales forecast for 2000 and some brief information prepared by the Accounts Department concerning each strategy. These two documents are shown in Appendices 27.3 and 27.4. In addition, the production control representative tabled a preliminary analysis of production requirements based on the 2000 forecast. This is shown in Appendix 27.5.

The production control representative put his view of the problem:

'We have to tackle this problem in the right order. First we need to look at the actual level of output that will be needed over the year, then we can decide how, ideally, we might like to meet this output requirement. Lastly we need to have some idea of how to increase or decrease output if our forecasts change, and under what circumstances we would break away from the production plan.'

## Questions

**1** *What level of output will be required each month for the plant to meet its demand?*

**2** *What combination of 'strategies' would you recommend in order to meet the production plan?*

**3** *How might production levels be changed in the light of changes in the forecast demand?*

## Actual average weekly orders (rounded) in unit drives 1999

| Month | Consumer | PC | Professional | Total |
|-------|----------|-------|--------------|--------|
| Jan   | 5500     | 7950  | 2750         | 16 200 |
| Feb   | 5190     | 7560  | 2650         | 15 400 |
| Mar   | 5950     | 8800  | 3050         | 17 800 |
| Apr   | 7100     | 10 400| 3500         | 21 000 |
| May   | 5500     | 8300  | 2700         | 16 500 |
| Jun   | 5050     | 7250  | 2500         | 14 800 |
| Jul   | 4900     | 7190  | 2410         | 14 500 |
| Aug   | 4750     | 7050  | 2350         | 14 150 |
| Sept  | 5050     | 7550  | 2550         | 15 150 |
| Oct   | 5600     | 7750  | 2700         | 16 050 |
| Nov   | 5150     | 8800  | 2600         | 16 550 |
| Dec   | 7550     | 12 150| 3800         | 23 500 |

# Appendix 27.2

## Forecast and actual factory loading in standard hours/week

| Sales/Prodn meetings at… | 1999 | | | | | | | | | | | |
| --- | --- | --- | --- | --- | --- | --- | --- | --- | --- | --- | --- | --- |
| | Jan | Feb | Mar | Apr | May | Jun | Jul | Aug | Sep | Oct | Nov | Dec |
| 19.1.99 | 14 500 (14 850) | 15 050 | 15 900 | 20 500 | | | | | | | | |
| 30.1.99 | | 14 000 (14 500) | 16 500 | 20 000 | 17 050 | | | | | | | |
| 27.2.99 | | | 16 000 (16 150) | 19 200 | 16 600 | 14 300 | | | | | | |
| 2.4.99 | | | | 18 900 (19 200) | 15 900 | 14 100 | 15 000 | | | | | |
| 30.4.99 | | | | | 15 100 (15 400) | 13 500 | 13 500 | 13 100 | | | | |
| 9.6.99 | | | | | | 13 600 (13 600) | 13 200 | 13 000 | 14 200 | | | |
| 24.6.99 | | | | | | | 13 100 (13 300) | 12 700 | 14 000 | 14 800 | | |
| 29.7.99 | | | | | | | | 13 100 (13 000) | 14 000 | 15 100 | 16 300 | |
| 3.9.99 | | | | | | | | | 13 900 (13 900) | 15 500 | 15 200 | 18 700 |
| 7.10.99 | | | | | | | | | | 14 900 (14 700) | 15 100 | 19 000 |
| 4.11.99 | | | | | | | | | | | 15 100 (15 150) | 19 900 |
| 2.12.99 | | | | | | | | | | | | 20 100 (21 500) |

*Note:* Figures in brackets are actual demand in hours.

## Average weekly sales forecast for 2000 in unit drives (as of January 2000)

| Month | Consumer | PC | Professional | Total |
|-------|----------|------|--------------|-------|
| Jan | 5960 | 8940 | 2980 | 17800 |
| Feb | 6090 | 9550 | 3220 | 18860 |
| Mar | 6030 | 9510 | 3160 | 18700 |
| Apr | 6540 | 9770 | 3290 | 19600 |
| May | 5800 | 8450 | 2900 | 17150 |
| Jun | 5000 | 7500 | 2500 | 15000 |
| Jul | 5000 | 7500 | 2500 | 15000 |
| Aug | 5000 | 7500 | 2500 | 15000 |
| Sep | 5000 | 8000 | 2500 | 15500 |
| Oct | 5500 | 8200 | 2800 | 16500 |
| Nov | 5600 | 8500 | 2900 | 17000 |
| Dec | 8000 | 12000 | 4000 | 24000 |

## Preliminary costings

### Cost of stock
Finished goods stocks are no longer a factory item. Previously we have charged at an annual rate of 20 per cent of factory cost to include all warehousing and handling costs.

Current warehouse capacity is 20 000 drives. Occasionally extra storage space is rented.

### Overtime
Current union agreements require four weeks' notice for any overtime. However, in practice some weekday overtime can be arranged at shorter notice. Up to two hours a day can be worked over the eight-hour weekday shift. Weekday and Saturday overtime rates are 150 per cent of standard rates. Sunday rates are 200 per cent of standard rates.

### Hire temporary workers
Recruitment would incur costs but much of the 'personnel' effort required could come from existing resources. Productivity of new workers would also be low, but again this is difficult to quantify.

### Subcontracting
We have put out some work to local subcontractors before – usually simple parts fabrication work. We generally expect to pay subcontract prices of between 120 per cent and 125 per cent of our own factory costs.

## Appendix 27.5

### 2000 Volume planning (all figures are in unit drives)

| Month | Production weeks | Sales weeks | Forecast | | |
| | | | Average weekly demand | Total months' demand | Cumulative demand |
|---|---|---|---|---|---|
| Jan | 4 | 4 | 17 880 | 71 520 | 71 520 |
| Feb | 3 | 4 | 18 860 | 75 440 | 146 960 |
| Mar | 4 | 5 | 18 700 | 93 500 | 240 460 |
| Apr | 4 | 4 | 19 600 | 78 400 | 318 860 |
| May | 5 | 5 | 17 150 | 85 750 | 404 610 |
| Jun | 4 | 4 | 15 000 | 60 000 | 464 610 |
| Jul | 3 | 4 | 15 000 | 60 000 | 524 610 |
| Aug | 3 | 5 | 15 000 | 75 000 | 599 610 |
| Sep | 4 | 4 | 15 500 | 62 000 | 661 610 |
| Oct | 5 | 5 | 16 500 | 82 500 | 744 110 |
| Nov | 4 | 4 | 17 000 | 68 000 | 812 110 |
| Dec | 4 | 4 | 24 000 | 96 000 | 908 110 |

# Peas

Stuart Chambers and Tammy Helander

## Introduction

John Lincoln nodded goodbye to the guard and drove out of the gates of his large factory, situated in a fertile coastal region of eastern England. He drove home through a soft rolling landscape, surrounded by shimmering green fields towards a darkening early September sky, but the sight of this beautiful summer scene gave him little peace of mind. It just made him worry more about peas and pea fields. Peas that had to be harvested, transported to the factory, cleaned, processed, frozen, and packaged. And soon plans had to be completed for *next year's* pea crop, because as Factory Manager, he had to look ahead to ensure that all the production processes would be prepared to cope with the requirements of the increasingly demanding customers.

This year had been difficult. The weather had been exceptionally good, which meant that the harvesting period had been much shorter than usual, putting pressure on the factory, which only had a limited daily processing capacity. The factory was designed to produce a range of frozen vegetables including carrots, cauliflowers, beans, peas, petit pois, broccoli, and sprouts. It belonged to a large specialist food group, and had an enviable reputation for its high quality standards.

Despite John's many years of production management experience, the pea processing operation had always been his greatest headache during the summer season. The previous year had turned out to be an exceptionally long harvesting period of 65 days, which was relatively easy to cope with. However, this year's season, because of the fine weather, had shrunk to a more normal 44 days, which had meant an immense pressure in getting about the same tonnage of peas through the factory in the much shorter period. Peas always caused the worst problems, as they were by far the largest crop handled by the factory, and had to be processed in a very short time after being picked.

John had discussed many times with the Crop Planning Manager, Dave Ronson, the possibility of extending the pea growing season to lessen the pressure on the factory but it was difficult to make any further changes. As Dave explained:

'Well, unfortunately you can't plan the weather! Certainly, we do influence when the peas should be ready for vining (picking) by using the best possible planning to ensure that the harvest is spread out over as long a time as possible. You know as well as I do, that the distribution of harvest times can be manipulated; for example, by using selected south and north facing fields, different varieties of seed, and planting at different altitudes above sea level. We have continuously worked to make this planning better, and to have better cooperation with the growers. We have managed to get them to agree on a target growing plan period of 44 days instead of 36, which is the normal contract period for growers supplying other factories. But there is a limit in how much we can extend the season – the peas will simply not grow over a longer period, and I believe we have reached the limit. The yields are also different, depending on the harvesting period. For the first and last quarter of the period the yield is only around 3.5 tonnes per hectare, whereas in the middle the yield is as much as six tonnes per hectare. The growers are naturally more interested in having their main harvest in the middle, for obvious economic reasons.'

It was only two weeks after the last of this year's harvest had gone through the factory, and the group's operations director had scheduled the following Wednesday to meet with John and the management team. They would go through this year's output figures compared to targets. Each year's targets were set on how many tonnes of frozen peas they would have to produce to satisfy anticipated customer demand.

## The company

Although the frozen vegetable business had achieved only slow organic growth, it had continued to invest in improved processing facilities, and to develop better product quality through agricultural technology and practices, as well as by using leading freezing technology. In this way, the company ensured that the products were fresh and of high quality, and this was controlled by taking appropriate measurements on samples at every stage of processing from the field to the final packing in the factory. Most of the immediate customers were large and powerful retailers with very specific requirements for taste, colour, size, tenderness, etc.

The number of factory employees varied between 400 and 200, depending whether it was the peak harvest season or not. Most of the important functions were all on-site, including production and marketing, but some additional cold storage and transportation resources were provided by contractors.

## The market for peas

The total market for vining peas (the pea type that is best suited to quick freezing) in the UK is about 200 000 tonnes per annum and the growing area is around 40 000 hectares. The human consumption markets (there are some sorts of peas used for animal feed) are quite static, but remain important for vining pea growers, who have invested in expensive, specialised equipment for harvesting the crop.

The typical annual pattern of demand in the UK for frozen peas is just the opposite of that of supply. Peas from growers all come in during three summer months with the harvesting lasting between 40 and 60 days, and with the main peak in July. In contrast, sales are at a minimum in the summer, because of the good availability of fresh vegetables, but peak during the winter from October to May, as shown in Figure 28.1. The company's sales target throughput of frozen peas for this year had been 15 115 tonnes, measured in the frozen state. Actual output had been slightly higher at 15 396 tonnes as shown in Table 28.1, much to the satisfaction of the management team.

**Figure 28.1 Market for peas in the UK (previous year)**

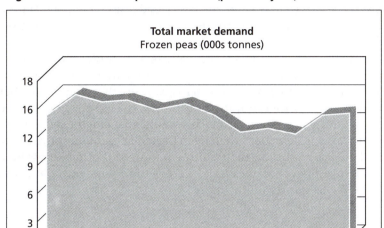

**Table 28.1 Current year pea output in frozen tonnes**

| Date | Tonnes | Date | Tonnes | Date | Tonnes |
|------|--------|------|--------|------|--------|
| 28/6 | 29 | 13/7 | 467 | 28/7 | 489 |
| 29/6 | – | 14/7 | 449 | 29/7 | 370 |
| 30/6 | 134 | 15/7 | 411 | 30/7 | 404 |
| 1/7 | 241 | 16/7 | 463 | 31/7 | 350 |
| 2/7 | 320 | 17/7 | 524 | 1/8 | 450 |
| 3/7 | 349 | 18/7 | 492 | 2/8 | 488 |
| 4/7 | 454 | 19/7 | 452 | 3/8 | 514 |
| 5/7 | 543 | 20/7 | 358 | 4/8 | 435 |
| 6/7 | 500 | 21/7 | 337 | 5/8 | 351 |
| 7/7 | 476 | 22/7 | 336 | 6/8 | 226 |
| 8/7 | 462 | 23/7 | 335 | 7/8 | 120 |
| 9/7 | 461 | 24/7 | 179 | 8/8 | 102 |
| 10/7 | 376 | 25/7 | 305 | 9/8 | 36 |
| 11/7 | 379 | 26/7 | 363 | 10/8 | 13 |
| 12/7 | 401 | 27/7 | 452 | TOTAL | 15396 |

## ● Retail customers

Most of the total market is held by the bigger retailers, including Asda, Safeway, KwikSave, Iceland, Somerfield, Tesco, and Sainsbury. For a producer to be approved by a large retailer, it is critical to offer the right price and the right quality. John's factory focused mainly on the needs of these very demanding UK retailers.

Sales can be either in bulk form (which are subsequently prepared for retail sale by contract packers), or in branded or own-label retail packs within cardboard cases, according to requirements. Exports are only in this packed form and only account for a small proportion of sales. Prices depend on which quality the customers ask for, as the peas are graded in qualities ranging from AA to D, where AA is the top grade. The goal is to make as many AA graded peas as possible. The factory had built up an enviable reputation with the retailers for the quality of the product and services provided.

Despite this, everyone was continually seeking ways of further increasing quality. For instance, it was known that the recently installed steam blancher should improve final pea quality. A blancher is basically the equipment where the peas get a rapid pre-cook, either in water or in steam, to stop enzymes action which breaks down natural sugars in the peas. This would give tangible benefits in terms of texture and taste, which could then be marketed at premium prices. By improving the overall quality of output, the resulting improved profitability would make it possible to reinvest in order to further improve the equipment, thereby achieving even higher levels of quality in the future.

## Marketing and competitors

There were about six direct competitors that operated on a sufficiently large scale to supply the major retailers. One in particular was privately owned, and sometimes used aggressive pricing, apparently to gain market share. In contrast, John tried to maintain high utilisation of capacity in order not to increase unit fixed costs, but some competitors were known to hold considerable spare plant capacity which was only in full use during the peak harvest season.

According to the Marketing Manager, Chris Johnson, the most important factor in the success of the business was its ability to enhance the customers' frozen vegetable business, and to initiate quality projects, in line with detailed knowledge of the retailers' requirements. They had the market understanding, and good development resources and skills to achieve this success. Unlike many competitors which offered a wider range of frozen foods including pizzas, pies, and gateaux, the account managers here were able to focus only on selling vegetables, which kept their knowledge and interest high.

Chris was very conscious of the necessity of close cooperation between the factory and Marketing, in order to sustain and improve success in terms of customers. He liked the fact that the marketing function was now located at the factory, creating an understanding and ambition for the site from the customers account managers. Chris was quite proud both of their external and internal relations:

'I think our customers like dealing with us, because we are usually able to provide them with exactly what they want. We specialise in vegetables and we always try to help them with all their special requirements, for example special pack sizes and graphics to assist in their promotions. We have good cooperation with the factory as well. We simply would not ask the factory to do something that it could not do. We talk every day to the planning people at the factory.'

## Factory processes and customer service

Another important factor was the short line of communication along the supply chain, and the ability to adapt. The company had extremely good trade relations and supply partnerships, and the factory tried to always be very responsive. The target service level of 98.5 per cent delivery dependability was usually met or exceeded. Marketing was constantly updating its demand forecasts, and checked these against the factory capabilities. They also gained from having big company back-up, as they at any time could call upon the technical or commercial help of the group.

An important characteristic of the operation was that it had good control of the whole process, from the farms to the cold storage rooms. Some of the competitors had great difficulties in controlling their supply chains, and tended to depend more on the open market for the vegetables as it unfolded each season. In contrast, the close and detailed cooperation here between the marketing and factory operations, and between the suppliers and factory, impressed most customers.

However, there were some unique difficulties in the planning of the pea business. The sowing/growing plan had to be set nearly one year ahead of the demand for peas in the following year. Therefore, the forecast from the marketing/sales department had to be made long before getting firm orders from any of the customers. The customers committed themselves firstly around May, by which time all the peas were planted and some of them were in flower.

## Conditions for pea growing

Commercial pea crops are mainly grown in the east of England because of the particular weather pattern needed for a good quality crop. High summer rainfall would make it messy and expensive to harvest and to clean, so reasonably dry weather is an advantage. In the eastern areas these conditions are met, as there is usually less than 75mm of rain in the whole of July and August.

The economics of pea growing is affected by things like crop rotation, soil condition, feed, weed control, machinery, as well as post-harvest handling. The crop has to be rotated, using a field only every fifth year or sometimes even only each seventh year before it is possible to grow peas or related crops again. The peas provide a valuable soil-improving crop, since they 'fix' nitrogen from the air into the soil. There are many types of peas, but vining peas are harvested mechanically for processing and quick freezing.

## Suppliers: the pea growers

The farmers that supply the factory are members of trading groups, which mutually own equipment and hire personnel for the vining pea season. The factory closely cooperates with five of these farmer groups. In cooperation with the growers, a sowing plan and a harvesting plan are prepared each year, which details the number of hectares and tonnes to be harvested every day during the season. The sowing of peas usually starts in the last week of February.

Some of the farmer groups have exclusive contracts with the business, but there are also some who have contracts with other processors. The crops are normally situated within a 60 kilometre radius of the factory, because the growers have to be able to deliver within a short elapsed time from beginning each harvest run. This is to ensure that the time from picking to blanching does not exceed 140 minutes, a demanding internal specification designed to produce the highest quality peas.

# The vining in the fields

Before vining can begin, the 'sample man' visits the fields and measures the tenderness of the peas, and when this reaches exactly the right level, it is time to begin harvesting the following day.

At each farm, a foreman is responsible for the detailed control of the vining process, and maintains constant radio contact with the control room at the factory. He is in charge of the planning and ordering of lorries, and for the timing of the emptying of the peas from the vining machines, which is done during harvesting, without having to stop. The tractor and trailer simply drives alongside the vining machine, and the crop is discharged in one or two tonne batches into the trailer. These are then driven to lorries, and the peas are discharged into them up to the maximum required weight.

The work shifts are different for each of the farmer groups, but in most cases the vining machines are used for around 19 hours a day, with five hours for cleaning and preventative maintenance. There is an average of three harvesting machines per farming group. Usually, two machines work all the time and the third is held in reserve, to be used if one suffered a breakdown or if the pea factory asks for more peas. The workers are employed on two shifts; a night shift from 6 p.m. to 6 a.m., and a day shift from 6 a.m. to 6 p.m., continuing seven days a week, every week until the pea season is over. This is demanding work, and sometimes stressful when vining on sloping fields. The huge machines, known affectionately as 'big drums' by the drivers, eat their way up and down the fields, irrespective of the weather. The only break in the humming driver's cab is the contact with the staff in the other viners and the tractor using the walkie-talkie radio. There is one full-time maintenance man, as it is important to keep these £250 000 machines going, not least because of the potential costs of delays in terms of lost revenue and scrap peas, but also because of the importance of keeping a reliable supply for the factory.

When the peas are being vined, the whole plants are cut and rolled over drums to separate the peas from the pods and stems. They then pass into a drum, where the peas roll down to the transporter belt, which takes them up to the hopper, where they can be seen from the driver's seat. The normal harvesting speed is around six tonnes/hour, but in ideal conditions can achieve around eight tonnes/hour.

# Transportation to and arrival at the factory control room

The time from the beginning of harvesting to arriving at the factory should be below 90 minutes. This is vital in order to ensure a consistent high quality of the frozen peas, and so the farmers are careful to keep within the time, particularly as they are being paid on the quality of the peas they are delivering. The lorries are owned both by large haulage firms and by individual lorry owners who come back and operate during the pea season year after year. The capacity of the lorries ranges from four tonnes to eighteen tonnes, but they do not normally load more than about five tonnes per journey, as the lorries need to get quickly to the factory. They average around 45 km per hour on the journey along country roads and lanes.

When the lorries arrive at the factory, they first stop at the control room for the quality check, to see if the load will be accepted. A collection tube is put into the

**Table 28.2  Actual and planned intake of peas in dirty tonnes**

| Date | Actual | Daily plan | Date | Actual | Daily plan | Date | Actual | Daily plan |
|------|--------|-----------|------|--------|-----------|------|--------|-----------|
| 28/6 | 36 | 40 | 13/7 | 568 | 564 | 28/7 | 609 | 562 |
| 29/6 | – | – | 14/7 | 543 | 496 | 29/7 | 460 | 505 |
| 30/6 | 169 | 196 | 15/7 | 496 | 521 | 30/7 | 496 | 547 |
| 1/7 | 295 | 374 | 16/7 | 524 | 488 | 31/7 | 438 | 491 |
| 2/7 | 394 | 437 | 17/7 | 633 | 622 | 1/8 | 558 | 573 |
| 3/7 | 427 | 392 | 18/7 | 596 | 608 | 2/8 | 600 | 615 |
| 4/7 | 562 | 557 | 19/7 | 548 | 621 | 3/8 | 626 | 711 |
| 5/7 | 661 | 616 | 20/7 | 433 | 496 | 4/8 | 527 | 625 |
| 6/7 | 613 | 624 | 21/7 | 408 | 474 | 5/8 | 428 | 435 |
| 7/7 | 590 | 624 | 22/7 | 401 | 416 | 6/8 | 273 | 376 |
| 8/7 | 565 | 566 | 23/7 | 418 | 420 | 7/8 | 148 | 220 |
| 9/7 | 559 | 580 | 24/7 | 220 | 366 | 8/8 | 122 | 110 |
| 10/7 | 466 | 513 | 25/7 | 379 | 382 | 9/8 | 46 | 88 |
| 11/7 | 464 | 480 | 26/7 | 451 | 455 | 10/8 | 17 | 48 |
| 12/7 | 486 | 488 | 27/7 | 560 | 469 | Total | 18813 | 19791 |

load, and sample peas are extracted and taken directly into the quality room. Three samples are taken, from which the tenderness of the pea, percentage of unwanted material, and dirtiness is measured. Should any of the values not be within control standards, the load will not be accepted. The whole checking procedure takes between five and ten minutes. Once accepted, the lorries are weighed with the full load of peas and after having tipped the load into the receiving hoppers, the lorries are weighed again empty. The drivers are given receipts detailing the tonnes delivered and quality. The whole weighing-tip-weighing procedure takes ten minutes on average, provided that there is a receiving hopper immediately available.

Records are kept of the total daily deliveries from farmers, and of the expected tonnage (the 'daily plan'), based on the previous day's field inspections by the Sample Man, as shown in Table 28.2. The expression 'dirty tonnes' simply means that the peas are delivered as they are without being cleaned. They are cleaned when they come to the factory, and go into processing. The target for the supply from growers this year in dirty tonnes had been 18 660 tonnes, but the actual deliveries were slightly higher at 18 813 tonnes.

## In the control room

John Lincoln often talked to the staff in the control room, the hub of the linkage between the harvest, transport and production processes. He was thinking back to some of the comments he had heard during the day. When John had come in to the control room, Tim Wallace, the shift manager, had been explaining their role to a visitor:

'You can see, from this position, how the whole factory is planned and run. Whatever is done here affects the whole process. From the tipping of the lorries of peas, to the feeding of the lines, blanchers and freezers.'

Behind him was the babble of voices of the other people working in the room. One had just received a call from a farmer, apologising that they could not deliver as many peas as planned at their sceduled five minute 'slot' one hour later. One of the new summer planners had immediately changed the figure on the board, the main planning instrument, according to the new information. Tim had crossed out and changed the figure just written down, and had quietly explained to the visitor:

'You have to keep an eye on them all the time! We have so many new employees during the summer. Our workforce increases from 200 in the winter to almost 400. You have to teach them everything, from the start.'

On his way back to his office, John had walked past the cleaning lines, one of which was standing idle, so he asked an operator what the problem was.

'Oh, it has just clogged again, but it will soon be back running! It was much worse yesterday ... a load of peas was accidently tipped outside the hoppers, which prevented us from tipping there for a time while we cleared up. They had to stop one of the viners for an hour or so, I heard.'

There are three shifts in the control room: one night shift from 23.00–7.00; two day shifts, from 7.00–15.00, and from 15.00–23.00. There is a CB (citizens band) radio to communicate with the viners and lorries, and everything that has affected the schedule of deliveries is recorded in detail.

## The factory

Once the lorries have been emptied into the hoppers, the peas are conveyed in segregated batches into one of three production lines in the factory. According to the control room manager, the maximum planned input is 12 tonnes/hour of dirty feed for Lines 1 and 3, and 10 tonnes/hour for Line 2. The peas go into bulk feeders and up on to the weighing belt, and then to the 'pod and stick machine' to take out stones, pods, small lumps of earth, and other unwanted materials. When processing peas, approximately 10 per cent of tonnage is removed in transforming dirty peas to clean, and around a further 10 per cent is lost when transforming clean to frozen. The segregation of batches is critical, to maintain traceability and to ensure that different grades are not inadvertently mixed.

The peas then go into small hoppers known as 'scacos' which hold a small buffer of inventory to smooth out the flow, and then to collecting points, from there they are transported in water, pumped along pipes. These lead directly to the water or steam blanchers, where the peas are heated in approximately 90 seconds to 98 degrees Celsius. After the blanching, there is a cooling down process and quality check, where the content of starch can be sampled.

The peas are then pumped in water to the freezer house, where there are three freezers, with capacities which are detailed in Table 28.3. The peas flow continuously into the freezers and are collected at the end into bulk pallet containers, each of about one tonne capacity. The output of frozen peas is weighed and labelled, allowing traceability of each harvested batch, before being transported into the cold

**Table 28.3  Nominal capacity of the three freezers**

| Freezer number | Tonnes/hour |
|---|---|
| 1 | 10 |
| 2 | 7.5* |
| 3 | 10 |
| Total | 27.5 |

* No 2 revised from 10 to 7.5 because of age (19 years)

store by fork-lift truck. Peas must exit the freezers at, or below, minus 18 degrees Celsius. Figure 28.2 illustrates the main process stages.

Each freezer is made up of five separate sections, each with refrigeration coils (cold surfaces behind which refrigerant is passed). The outside of these tend to 'ice-up' fairly quickly, reducing their cooling efficiency, so each section is automatically defrosted while the peas continue to be frozen in the remaining sections. Depending on certain factors, such as temperature, the moisture of the inputs and the weather, the rate of icing-up increases, and overall effectiveness of the process declines, being detected by an upward trend in the output temperature of the peas. At this point, the input feed rate must be reduced, affecting the actual output capacity of the freezer, and slowing down the feed rate for the cleaning and blanching process because there is almost no in-process storage between blanching and freezing. For the same reason, any problems with the cleaning and blanching processes quickly deprive a freezer of its input, wasting valuable freezer capacity.

**Figure 28.2  Factory processes and layout**

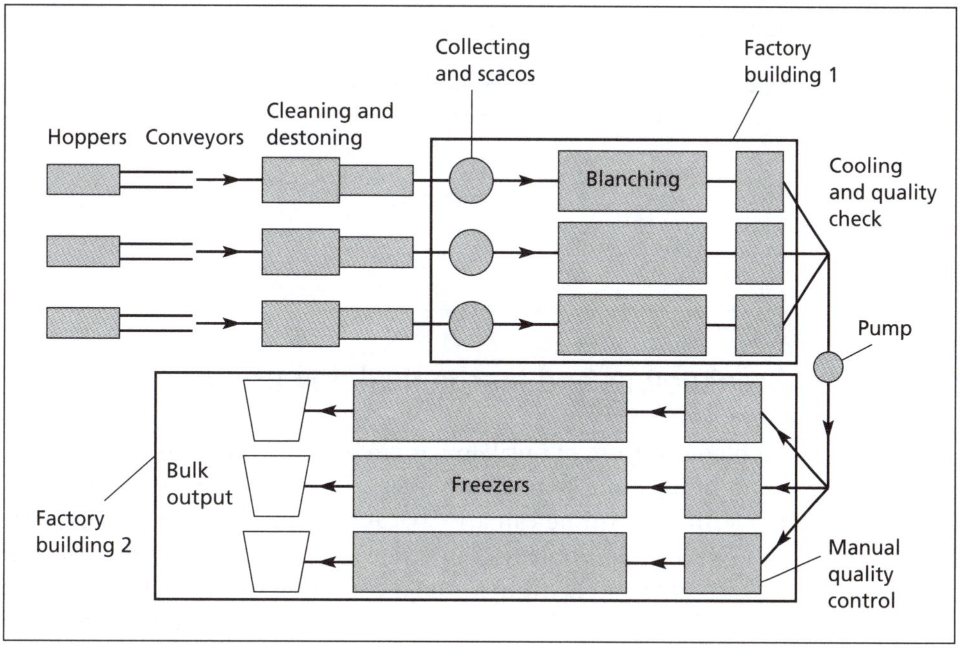

# Quality and hygiene requirements

Through the whole process there are stringent quality checks, and if batches of peas are not immediately accepted, they are quarantined and labelled accordingly. There are three standard places for quality checks: one in-process quality check; one check at the freezer output, and one when the peas are repackaged later for retail sale. Whenever capacity is a constraint, the bulk pallet containers of quarantined peas are taken into cold storage and dealt with later. Up to 30 per cent of the peas may be quarantined, but this does not seem to be a problem, as they can be dealt with later. The frozen peas can be fed through the automated 'Sortex' colour sorter, where any that are discoloured (and may therefore have a sour taste) or are otherwise bad are extracted.

In order to operate under hygienic conditions and to operate the freezers at as near to maximum capacity as possible, they are scheduled (see Table 28.4) to be regularly defrosted, completely cleaned out and sterilised. It takes eight hours for each freezer to be defrosted. Visiting the inside of a working freezer, one can see why defrosting is so essential: they are very big, with a length of about 15 metres and a width of about six metres. Before entry, it is necessary to wear insulating clothes, since the air temperature is around minus 35 degrees, and a wind is blowing, making it quite a frightening and breathtaking experience!

A series of conveyor belts go through the whole freezer, and cold air is blown up from underneath making the peas jump and circulate some centimetres above the conveyor while they freeze. Snow can build up on the floor to more than ten centimetres deep, and icicles hang from everywhere in the roof. The walls are covered with snow and ice.

Table 28.4 Typical 'hygiene' cycle schedule

| Day | Freezers defrosted |
| --- | --- |
| 1 | 3 and 2 |
| 2 | Nil |
| 3 | 1 and 2 |
| 4 | 3 |
| 5 | 2 |
| 6 | 1 |

# Breakdowns and mechanical downtime

Problems in form of breakdowns are dealt with by the Process Manager, who has a team of full-time skilled employees, plus contractors if required. Unplanned engineering downtime can arise because of mechanical, electrical, refrigeration, or other technical problems. Time is planned for preventative maintenance, in order to keep the equipment in optimal condition to cope with the pressures of the harvest. This planned downtime reduces operating utilisation on each of the cleaning/blanching lines to 95 per cent of operating time. Planned maintenance of the freezers is carried out during the hygiene downtime described above.

**Table 28.5  Actual recorded downtime, this season.
Total for cleaning and blanching lines**

| Downtime | Hours lost |
|---|---|
| Engineering | 83.59 |
| W.F.P. (Waiting for Product) | 125.97 |
| Production problems | 39.97 |
| *Total* (unplanned downtime) | 249.53 |
| Planned hygiene | 82.30 |
| *Total* (Recorded Downtime) | 331.83 |

Because of the complexity of the equipment, and variability of the condition of the peas, small unplanned breakdowns are frequent, and records are kept of the time, time lost, the line involved, and the type of breakdown. One of the most common reasons is 'WFP' (waiting for product; that is input of peas); another is clogging (the produce getting stuck and making the lines stop), which is recorded as production downtime. In the control room any changes to the plan are recorded on the wall charts, using a blue pen for changes originating from factory problems, and using a red pen for changes created by the growers. The actual downtime for the year turned out as shown in Table 28.5.

## Packaging

There is a review of the sales plan every fourth week. It is prepared by the sales department covering 13 weeks ahead, and is given by specified product in cases per week. This plan is downloaded on the systems for all departments to use. A weekly plan is delivered, first and foremost, to the packaging department for repackaging from bulk into retail packs and outer cases.

Sometimes the department has to deal with lingering quality problems, which can slow down the process. These can normally be completely sorted out by running the bulk peas through the Sortex colour sorter, if necessary several times. The packaging shift manager, Andy Burton, was not always happy with having to do this rework:

'There have always been some arguments between production and packaging about quality. There are quality checks, both in the beginning of the line, at the flow-end, and in the packaging area, but in spite of these checks it is this department that has to deal with any remaining problems, which can take quite some time to sort out! When we get in bulk packs of peas, which are clogged, iced, or contain sours, it means that we have to run them through the Sortex several times. This sometimes results in time delays in delivering to customers, since most of the packing is planned on a just-in-time basis.'

From time to time, especially in the spring season, the factory can run out of peas, which then have to be bought in. Usually there are the right amount of peas in store, but not the right mix of quality and grade of peas required. Other quality problems can involve the supply of cases, labels, or polythene bags.

# Cold store

In addition to the factory cold store, the company uses six contractors' stores, all at temperatures around –30 degrees Celcius. Only 2700 tonnes can be stored on site, comprising 1500 tonnes in bulk containers on pallets, with the remainder kept for cases of packaged peas awaiting dispatch to customers. Over the whole year there is a need for a maximum of 22 000 tonnes of cold storage, not only for peas but for all other vegetables produced at the site. The cold store manager, Martin Stover, commented:

'We have a much better system in the cold store after the recent reorganisation. Now we can access the piles of containers from all sides. However, the piles of peas bought in from other companies cause a bit of a problem as they often don't fit in well with our own bulk containers. It is quite expensive to buy in from others, of course. But even though we have lots of peas, we do not always have the right quality grade according to the retailers' wishes, and we have to do everything we can for these customers. They pay our salaries, you know.'

## Questions

1  *What are the capacities at each main stage of the pea processing?*

2  *Which is the bottleneck process, and how is this managed to maximise throughput?*

3  (a) *What is the design capacity of the overall operation?*
   (b) *What is the effective capacity?*
   (c) *Calculate the efficiency and utilisation for the operation over the current year's pea season. Would this give a good indication of the factory performance, for example in benchmarking against other factories in the group, such as frozen pizza manufacturing?*

4  *Prepare graphs showing:*

   (a) *the daily output compared to design and effective capacity*
   (b) *cumulative output compared to cumulative design and effective capacity*

   *What do these tell us about the operation?*

5  *Summarise the reasons why capacity is lost on some days in mid-season. What could be done to reduce this problem?*

6  *Do you think that John Lincoln's desire to extend the pea harvest period is the best strategy for the overall operation?*

# CASE
# 29
# Thompson Telescopes Ltd

Case date
2002

© Alan Harrison

## Introduction

Thompson Telescopes Ltd is a division of Murray Engineering. It was formed following the acquisition of a US company by Murray's parent group, the large conglomerate, PH Holdings plc. Initially, Thompson acted as the UK sales arm, and marketed a range of standard telescopes for amateur astronomers and clubs. Telescopes were manufactured in the USA and sold via the UK company to markets in Europe, the Middle East and Africa (EMEA). However, customers increasingly demanded specific designs to meet their own tastes. Some, for example, would want their own specification of motion drives to be fitted, others wanted CCD camera attachments and accompanying software. It was found that, while the US company could supply special orders, Thompson's sales were suffering because of the costs and the relatively lengthy delivery times involved.

It was therefore decided some six years ago to establish manufacturing facilities in the UK. A factory was built on an industrial estate at Ebbw Vale in Gwent, South Wales, and the machines and equipment purchased to enable Thompson Ltd to carry out manufacturing and development of many of the components and systems themselves. This helped considerably to reduce costs and improve capability of meeting specific customer orders, and sales surged ahead. By 2000, Thompson Ltd was buying only 50 per cent by value of the parts and systems that it used from the USA.

## The company

Although Thompson had grown rapidly after it had established UK manufacturing facilities, sales turnover had flattened in recent years. Table 29.1 shows the profit/loss statement, and Table 29.2 the balance sheet for this period. Thompson is currently regarded as a poor performer within Murray, and finds it difficult to attract investment for the further growth in sales the company believes is possible.

The organisation chart for Thompson is shown in Figure 29.1, and the main functions can briefly be explained as follows:

**Table 29.1  Consolidated profit and loss account (£000)**

|  | 1996 | 1997 | 1998 | 1999 | 2000 | 2001 |
|---|---|---|---|---|---|---|
| Turnover | 2784 | 4192 | 6462 | 8961 | 8349 | 9073 |
| Cost of sales | 1953 | 2934 | 4394 | 5735 | 5594 | 6069 |
| Gross profit | 831 | 1258 | 2068 | 3226 | 2755 | 3004 |
| Admin expenses | 1011 | 1360 | 1807 | 2320 | 2210 | 2720 |
| Trading profit | (180) | (102) | 261 | 906 | 545 | 284 |

**Table 29.2  Consolidated balance sheet (£000)**

|  | 1996 | 1997 | 1998 | 1999 | 2000 | 2001 |
|---|---|---|---|---|---|---|
| **Fixed assets** | | | | | | |
| Tangible assets | 270 | 1021 | 1507 | 2294 | 2095 | 1943 |
| **Current assets** | | | | | | |
| Stocks | 1189 | 1487 | 1589 | 1907 | 2288 | 2794 |
| Debtors | 565 | 979 | 1152 | 1356 | 1648 | 2010 |
| Cash in hand | (200) | (103) | (53) | 752 | 505 | 230 |
| **Creditors** | 432– | 621– | 1207– | 1564– | 1156– | 1023– |
| **Net current assets** | 1122 | 1742 | 1481 | 2451 | 3285 | 4011 |

**Figure 29.1  Thompson Telescopes: organisation chart**

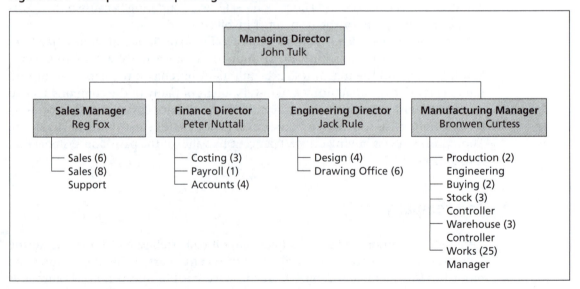

## Managing director

John Tulk has been with Thompson from the start. He has been successful in establishing the company as a force in the marketplace, and has led the sales initiatives
'from the front'. In common with Murray Group policy, he is required to prepare

and have approved an annual budget and to submit monthly reports of current and forecast financial performance. He is under increasing pressure to improve return on capital employed (ROCE) to the Group target of 15 per cent.

'After our initial sales successes in the European and Middle Eastern markets, competition has become much more intense in recent years. Further progress depends on improvements in the level of service we provide to our customers while at the same time making substantial inroads into our cost base. It is apparent that our manufacturing operations have a major role to play in achieving these twin objectives.'

## Sales

Reg Fox joined Thompson four years ago, and his responsibilities now range from the sales force to sales support. Sales support handles telephone and e-mail orders and enquiries, and processes contracts and orders from the sales force. Sales have led the development of Thompson, and take full ownership of processing customer orders from pricing, quoting delivery dates through manufacturing to delivery. In the last year, Reg has become increasingly concerned about Thompson performance.

'We are getting a lot of complaints about late deliveries. My salespeople are wasting a lot of their time chasing orders through manufacturing, and are increasingly delivering urgent orders themselves. I know that opportunities are being missed; we are simply finding it difficult to keep our promises.'

Thompson holds about 18 per cent of the EMEA market for its range of products; the major player holds about 35 per cent and a number of smaller players each hold less than 10 per cent.

## Finance

Peter Nuttall is responsible overall for Thompson's budgets and period financial reports. Sales produce a forecast in November for the 12 months commencing January. The forecast covers each main product range in financial terms. Peter operates a standard costing system with direct labour performance reporting. Prices are negotiated by the sales team, but Peter or John Tulk sign off contracts above £10k in value. The overall product cost breakdown is as follows:

- direct material – 67 per cent
- direct labour – 8 per cent
- works overhead – 12 per cent
- commercial and administrative overhead – 13 per cent.

Peter echoes John Tulk's concern about ROCE:

'It is not surprising that we are under pressure from Group about our financial performance. In spite of our commitment to improve returns last year, our performance this year has actually deteriorated. I estimate that the cost of holding and servicing these inventories alone is 20 per cent per year. Murray's patience is not inexhaustible!'

### Engineering

Jack Rule started with Thompson at the same time as John Tulk in order to develop a sound technical base for the UK operation. Initially presiding over a sales and service operation, his responsibilities now cover design and systems development. The main activities of these areas of the business are maintenance of designs for standard products and the ongoing design of make-to-order contracts.

'We have made considerable progress in transferring American designs to European practice in recent years. My aim is to be importing less than 20 per cent of our parts from our US affiliate within the next two years.'

### Manufacturing

Bronwen Curtess was hired six years ago to develop Thompson's product support expertise. She soon found herself making the major decisions on factory layout and equipment. She comments:

'The job has grown like crazy. I am now responsible for product support, production engineering, buying and the factory. In the factory, we have six machine operators, six technicians and eight assemblers, together with some support staff. We intended to install sufficient equipment to meet peak sales demand easily. However, sales forecasts in this business are notoriously unreliable, and the sales force do tend to drop lots of orders with short delivery dates onto us with no warning! I must admit that our production planning leaves much to be desired, and I'm starting to look much more closely at this.'

## The product

Thompson's sales catalogue describes some 200 types of standard telescope. These are produced in eight different sizes and two different finishes. The basic types are further subdivided into products with different mountings, automatic controls, etc. All of the standard telescopes are quoted for delivery within two weeks of placing an order. Customers may also specify their own individual requirements, which are made to order with delivery dates quoted individually. Sales by type of telescope range from about £1k for the most popular to about £10k for lower-volume types. Sales of new telescopes for 2001 were 70 per cent standard designs and 30 per cent made to order; the made-to-order sales have been increasing by 10 per cent to 15 per cent each year.

There are some 2500 active components listed in the stores system, of which about 500 are raw materials (bar, tube, sheet and castings); 1250 are made in-house and 750 are bought from outside – mostly from the US affiliate. The part numbering system became somewhat disjointed after Thompson set up its UK factory. Parts from the US affiliate are numbered on a different system which starts with a prefix 'A', and the designers tend to use suppliers' catalogues when selecting a part. This has resulted, among other things, in a very limited number of common components used in the different types of telescope.

The manufacturing lead-times for a batch of standard products vary from three weeks for smaller types to 12 weeks for the larger ones – urgent jobs can be rushed through in three days for smaller jobs to 12 days for larger ones. Lead-times cover purchase of bought-out materials – which takes up about half of the lead-time – through to delivery of the telescopes into the finished goods warehouse. Component machining takes from one to three weeks, and the rest is allowed for assembly and test. Because of the manufacturing and shipping times involved, the US affiliate requires four months advance notification of UK requirements. Minor substitutions only are allowed up to one month prior to production at Thompson, and no changes at all are allowed after this time.

Parts are controlled by means of a stock control system, which is similar for both components and finished products. The key points of this system and the accompanying manufacturing operations are described briefly below.

## Component stock control

Stock records are maintained on file for every component used in a standard type of telescope. An example is shown in Appendix 29.1 for raw material from the tube store. The record contains the following information:

- size and spec: the tube size and specification
- parts made: the part number of the Thompson component(s) which are made from this
- bar code: the Thompson part number for the tube
- conversion factor: allows the stores to convert from delivered measure (weight) into used measure (length)
- safety stock: the stock balance which triggers a requisition to be raised for more parts to be ordered
- reorder quantity: the weight of steel ordered each time a requisition is raised
- receipts: records date received into store, the supplier, order number, weight and length
- movements: records issues (ISS) and receipts (REC) into and out of stores, together with the quantity moved and the balance.

If the stock has been physically checked, the letters 'S/C' are entered in the movements record, together with the physical quantity. Stock records are maintained by a stock controller; some 300 entries are made onto the stock control system every day. Requisitions for fresh deliveries of parts are automatically raised by this system when the stock level falls below the reorder level. Reorder quantities are based on the last three months' usage, but this usage figure is rarely adjusted and so is typically out of date. The requisition is passed to a stock controller who checks the order details against the stock record. It is then routed to buying (for raw materials and bought-out parts, such as the steel tube in Appendix 29.1) or to production control (for made-in parts). The cost of raising a purchase order is reckoned to be £30.

Reorder levels on the stock records are based on estimated lead-times. If the stock has already fallen to zero, or a large demand arises which cannot be covered by existing stock, the stock clerk will enter 'ASAP' in the delivery date box on the requisition. Otherwise, buying or production control assume that the usual lead-times will apply.

Most of the deliveries to stores of made-in parts were executed in not one but several part-batches. This was usually traceable to production exigencies, whereby only part of a batch would be made so that a machine could be set up for the next part which was also urgently wanted. The rest of the batch would be completed when it too became urgent.

It was hoped that a 100 per cent service level to production would be provided on this system, but in practice stocks of many parts are excessive while stocks of others are nil. Appendix 29.2 shows a representative sample of 35 bought-out parts from the range held at Thompson, which serves to illustrate this and other points. Further, stock record accuracy, determined by comparing stock check quantities with the stock cards, averages only about 40 per cent. This is a matter of grave concern for Peter Nuttall.

## Finished goods control

Stock records are also kept for each standard type of telescope held in the finished goods warehouse. The record carries similar information to the component stock control cards described above:

- description: the description of the type of telescope stocked
- part number: the Thompson part number for this type of telescope
- safety stock: the stock level at which the clerk raises a new factory order for a fresh batch of telescopes to be made
- reorder quantity: the batch size for the factory order
- receipts: the number of telescopes received from the factory
- order quantities: the outstanding number of telescopes on factory orders
- issues: the number of telescopes issued to meet a given customer order.

When the balance on a finished goods stock record falls below the reorder level, the clerk raises a factory order which is signed by the Warehouse Controller and passed to the Production Controller. The reorder quantity is intended to represent six weeks' usage of the more popular types to 10 weeks' usage of the less popular. These quantities were last set two years ago after discussion with Sales.

The warehouse processes customer orders in the sequence in which they are received, unless Sales instruct otherwise – which they frequently do. If there is insufficient stock to meet a customer order, a note is made of the customer order and this is entered onto the stock record so that the order can be cleared as soon as a fresh batch of telescopes arrives from the factory. No regular report is made of the outstanding orders and their age, but the usual procedure is for Sales to circulate lists of unfulfilled orders, currently expected by customers, to members of the senior management team, production control and the Warehouse Controller.

## Stores procedure

A stock check of stores and work-in-progress is held twice each year. Volunteers from the shop floor and from offices come in over a weekend, and enter the stock check figure onto the stock cards. If there is a major discrepancy between the physical figure and that on the stock record, a stock controller is expected to identify the reason. 'Major' is not specifically defined, and the controllers do not have time to investigate more than a few items.

Keeping track of component stock is particularly difficult. When batches are split for the reasons outlined above, the operator is expected to identify the part-batch with a slip of paper. Urgently-needed batches of made-in components often bypass the stores, and the supervisor is supposed to notify the stock controller of his actions. Issues from raw material and component stores are made on requisitions that can be authorised by many different members of staff: the Production Controller, stock controllers, supervisors and service engineers. A frequent problem in the finished goods warehouse is that salespeople enter the stores in search of telescopes that are missing or reported as out of stock.

Assembly orders are raised by production control one week in advance of the assembly of a batch of telescopes. The stores assembles kits of parts and report any shortages to production control. It is up to the assembly supervisor to accept a kit which has shortages; if he rejects it, then it will have to wait until the shortages have been made good. Meanwhile, he will bring forward a batch from another week to maintain satisfactory labour productivity figures.

## Questions

1 *What problems are being created for Manufacturing by:*

- *Sales*
- *Engineering*
- *Current procedures for stock control and production control.*

2 *Thompson's customers are complaining that deliveries are unreliable and that promises are often broken, but stocks are high and stock turns are sluggish. How should Thompson plan to overcome these problems?*

## Appendix 29.1

## Example of steel stock print run

STEEL STOCK PRINT RUN: 01-03-00 TO 31-10-01

| SIZE: 0.6756 × 0.6134 | SAFETY STOCK: 100 | BAR CODE: | T6756 |
|---|---|---|---|
| SPEC: 16 MNC R5 | ROQ: 317 | CONVERSION FACTOR: 22.096 | |

| | RECEIPTS | | | | | ISSUES | | |
|---|---|---|---|---|---|---|---|---|
| DATE | SUPPLIER | CODE | WEIGHT | LENGTH | DATE | ISS/REC | LENGTH | BALANCE |
| 25-3-00 | Desford | C8125 | 7452 | 337 | 22-5-00 | ISS | 108 | NIL |
| 17-6-00 | Desford | C9225 | 6780 | 307 | 17-6-00 | REC | 307 | 307 |
| 26-8-00 | Desford | C8409 | 4154 | 788 | 23-6-00 | ISS | 110 | 197 |
| 6-10-00 | Desford | C8409 | 3600 | 163 | 11-7-00 | ISS | 101 | 96 |
| 12-1-01 | Desford | C0877 | 7980 | 361 | 26-8-00 | REC | 188 | 284 |
| 22-5-01 | Desford | C0501 | 8802 | 399 | 5-9-00 | ISS | 96 | 188 |
| 24-8-01 | Desford | C1657 | 2868 | 130 | 12-9-00 | ISS | 77 | 111 |
| | | | | | 2-10-00 | ISS | 111 | NIL |
| | | | | | 6-10-00 | REC | 163 | 163 |
| | | | | | 6-11-00 | ISS | 61 | 102 |
| | | | | | 9-11-00 | ISS | 51 | 51 |
| | | | | | 14-11-00 | ISS | 51 | NIL |
| | | | | | 12-1-01 | REC | 361 | 361 |
| | | | | | 15-1-01 | ISS | 58 | 303 |
| | | | | | 16-1-01 | ISS | 109 | 194 |
| | | | | | 24-1-01 | ISS | 111 | 83 |
| | | | | | 5-3-01 | ISS | 83 | NIL |
| | | | | | 22-5-01 | REC | 399 | 399 |
| | | | | | 22-5-01 | ISS | 58 | 341 |
| | | | | | 24-5-01 | ISS | 45 | 296 |
| | | | | | 5-6-01 | ISS | 48 | 248 |
| | | | | | 8-6-01 | ISS | 58 | 190 |
| | | | | | 5-7-01 | ISS | 44 | 146 |
| | | | | | 7-7-01 | ISS | 45 | 101 |
| | | | | | 10-7-01 | ISS | 51 | 50 |
| | | | | | 6-8-01 | ISS | 50 | NIL |
| | | | | | 24-8-01 | REC | 130 | 130 |
| | | | | | 28-8-01 | ISS | 57 | 73 |
| | | | | | 3-9-01 | ISS | 45 | 28 |

*Notes*:
1 Steel is ordered and delivered by weight. The CONVERSION FACTOR (22.096 in this case) converts from weight (kg) into metres. All of the stock movements are recorded in metres.
2 The numbers in the 'CODE' column refer to the steel mill cast code for traceability purposes.
3 Under 'SIZE', the dimensions refer to the external and internal bores of the tube, and '16MNC R5' to the specification of the steel. 'BAR CODE' refers to the Thompson part number for the material. 'ROQ' refers to the reorder quantity. According to records in the buying department, the purchase price is £717/tonne.
4 If the stock has been physically checked, 'S/C' is entered in the movements record.

## Appendix 29.2

## A representative sample of component parts from the Thompson range

| Part number | Unit cost (£) | Annual usage | Annual expenditure | Physical stock | Physical value | Order quantity |
|---|---|---|---|---|---|---|
| B-010 | 2.34 | 106 | 248 | 126 | 295 | 40 |
| C-011 | 63.45 | 111 | 7043 | 28 | 1777 | 30 |
| D-012 | 31.68 | 5 | 158 | 15 | 475 | 5 |
| E-013 | 34.38 | 42 | 1444 | 24 | 172 | 50 |
| F-014 | 3.00 | 1133 | 3399 | 363 | 1089 | 300 |
| G-015 | 38.04 | 244 | 9282 | 121 | 4603 | 100 |
| H-016 | 9.91 | 13 | 129 | 6 | 59 | 10 |
| J-017 | 0.89 | 180 | 160 | Nil | Nil | 200 |
| A-018 | 29.90 | 10 | 299 | 59 | 1764 | 10 |
| A-019 | 4.06 | 51 | 207 | Nil | Nil | 50 |
| B-020 | 37.20 | 4 | 149 | 43 | 1600 | 20 |
| A-021 | 0.90 | 5353 | 4818 | 3167 | 2850 | 2000 |
| B-022 | 25.32 | 23 | 582 | 2 | 51 | 10 |
| C-023 | 14.65 | 13 | 190 | 108 | 1582 | 10 |
| A-024 | 440.86 | 30 | 13226 | 1 | 441 | 20 |
| B-025 | 0.45 | 618 | 278 | 1701 | 765 | 2000 |
| C-026 | 92.44 | 9 | 832 | 3 | 277 | 20 |
| A-027 | 0.42 | 360 | 152 | 90 | 38 | 300 |
| B-028 | 2.00 | 811 | 1622 | 1630 | 2656 | 20 |
| C-029 | 1.78 | 66 | 117 | 7 | 12 | 50 |
| D-030 | 0.36 | 246 | 89 | 3 | 1 | 300 |
| A-031 | 125.55 | 20 | 2511 | 13 | 1632 | 10 |
| B-032 | 8.10 | 40 | 324 | 27 | 8 | 30 |
| C-033 | 15.00 | 73 | 1095 | 3 | 360 | 50 |
| D-034 | 37.20 | 4 | 149 | 43 | 1600 | 20 |
| E-035 | 243.90 | 16 | 3902 | 24 | 5854 | 10 |
| F-036 | 0.27 | 396 | 107 | 136 | 37 | 300 |
| A-037 | 1.34 | 102 | 137 | Nil | Nil | 100 |
| A-038 | 10.95 | 68 | 745 | Nil | Nil | 100 |
| A-039 | 42.80 | 4 | 171 | 1 | 43 | 10 |
| A-040 | 94.00 | 1 | 94 | 5 | 470 | 1 |
| A-041 | 0.45 | 822 | 368 | 280 | 126 | 200 |
| B-042 | 13.98 | 145 | 2027 | 190 | 2656 | 20 |
| C-043 | 27.30 | 6 | 164 | 7 | 191 | 10 |
| D-044 | 3.13 | 214 | 671 | 600 | 1878 | 50 |
| Totals | | | 56 889 | | 35 362 | |

*Notes:*
Part numbers have been simplified and shortened for the purpose of this analysis. Those beginning with 'A' are purchased from the American affiliate. The sample of 35 parts has been chosen to be representative of the 2500 total in the range held by Thompson.

# WFA (Water for Africa)

Case date
2002

Robert Johnston

Mike Riley is the operations director for WFA (which used to be known as Water for Africa). WFA is a charitable trust that was set up in the 1970s to provide long-term help for victims of environmental and political crises. WFA specialises in helping the inhabitants of disaster stricken towns and villages install their own water supplies and improve sanitation facilities.

Because all of the funds have to be raised through the efforts of volunteers, the Directorate is concerned about minimising costs. Mike is constantly under pressure to reduce his stock of sanitation equipment and supplies. Indeed, over the last four years he has reduced stock holding across all of the stores from around £10m to £5m (cost of capital (10%) × cost of an item). But now it seems he has gone too far in reducing inventories. His field managers are complaining of shortages, particularly of copper pipe and sealant. From his main store in the UK, Mike supplies 14 regional stores which are close to where the 47 projects are underway. The field workers can e-mail orders for any items, in predetermined order quantities, at any time and delivery is usually within three weeks. The exception is portable electricity generators which are delivered directly from the supplier and take around six months. The cost of administration and delivery for any part is calculated at £45.

**Table 30.1 Sample from a stock record at a regional store**

| Item | Usage items/year | Cost per item (£) | Number in stock | Order quantity |
|------|------------------|-------------------|-----------------|----------------|
| Plastic joints | 12 000 | 0.30 | 450 | 2 000 |
| Blankets | 10 000 | 0.70 | 4 000 | 10 000 |
| Soil pipe (4m lengths) | 8 500 | 2.80 | 6 420 | 10 000 |
| Compression joints | 7 500 | 3.80 | 8 500 | 10 000 |
| Tinned food | 5 500 | 0.35 | 240 | 1 000 |
| Copper pipe (2m lengths) | 4 600 | 3.65 | 0 | 50 |
| Buckets | 3 500 | 0.50 | 320 | 1 000 |
| Sealant (tubes) | 3 200 | 0.20 | 20 | 1 000 |
| Dehydrated food packs | 2 050 | 0.40 | 3 800 | 5 000 |
| Petrol cans | 60 | 2.90 | 10 | 50 |
| Water pumps | 9 | 555.00 | 9 | 10 |
| Portable generators | 4 | 1050.00 | 1 | 1 |
| Water trailers | 3 | 450.00 | 2 | 5 |

On a visit to a new project, Mike called into the regional store and checked the stock records on the computer. Being short of time, he selected 13 items from the 105 on the database – the results are shown in Table 30.1. Walking around the store he was concerned to see large quantities of many items. He also noticed that some of the dehydrated food was more than 12 months old and past its sell-by date. He could not find any tubes of sealant but noticed about 100 lengths of copper pipe in a corner.

Mike was bewildered. The Directorate thought too much money was tied up in stock, he thought he had reduced it as far as he could – so much so that the field operators complained of shortages – yet there were heaps of equipment and rotting supplies in the store.

## Questions

1 *Evaluate the stock holding policies at WFA.*

2 *What changes should Mike make?*

**CASE**
**31**

**Aylesbury Pressings**

Case date
2001

John Bicheno

Aylesbury Pressings is an automotive metal components supplier that employs some 280 people. Formerly family-owned, it is now one of a number of companies owned by a large German automotive components group. The company manufactures a variety of components and sub-assemblies for car manufacturers in Britain and on the continent. Typical products include sub-frame assemblies and internal metal brackets. Around 80 main products are made, several of them in multiple versions. Customers include Nissan, Ford, Vauxhall, Honda and Rover.

## Manufacturing

The plant is organised in a manner that is fairly typical for modern component manufacturers (see Figure 31.1).

### Raw material
The primary raw material is steel that is sourced from steel service centres, usually as slit coils averaging two to six tonnes in weight. In addition a wide variety of components are bought in from other suppliers.

### Blanking
The first process is to uncoil the steel and cut it into blanks – flat sheets of steel ready for pressing. Typically these might be of a size ranging between 100mm and 500mm. There is a blanking cell with two blanking presses. Blanking involves changeover time of around 15 minutes but blanking operations typically take place at a rate of 10 pieces every two seconds. These supply blanks to all subsequent press lines and blanks are moved in stillages by forklift, usually via an intermediate store. In some cases, ready-cut blanks are purchased from the steel service centre primarily because of restricted capacity in the blanking cell. Steel supply has proven erratic over the past few years.

### Pressing
The second process is for the flat blanks to be pressed into shaped parts. The press shop comprises 10 presses ranging from 40 tons to 300 tons, including one progression press. Three of the presses are arranged in line for operations requiring several subsequent operations. This gives progression press possibilities but requires manual movement between presses. On a single press a typical cycle time is the

**Figure 31.1 Outline of key processes at Aylesbury pressings**

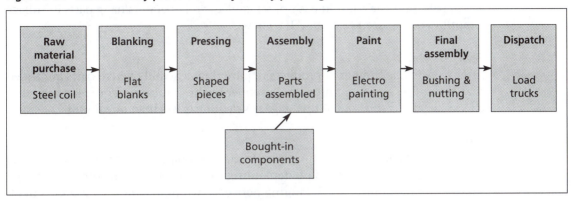

equivalent of two seconds per part because several parts are pressed in one opera-tion. Typically there are two changeovers per shift. The maintenance staff aim to limit downtime to five per cent. Some presses work at only 80 per cent of their rated speed. The press shop is a common use facility serving assembly, although some presses are dedicated more or less full-time to the production of specific parts. The press shop and the blanking cell are situated in a separate area away from assembly both for noise reasons and the fact that they are common facilities. The press shop is a common-use facility serving assembly, although some presses are dedicated more or less full time to the production of specific parts. The press shop and the blanking cell are situated in a separate area away from assembly, both for noise reasons and the fact that they are common facilities. There is a large warehouse (known in the company as 'the fridge' on account of it not being heated) after the press shop into which all parts are moved by forklift and stored for between one day and four months before being moved into the cell 'supermarket' prior to assembly. Pressings typically weigh between 0.5 kg and 10 kg. A steering bracket weighs 2 kg.

### Assembly
Aylesbury has 13 assembly cells, each entirely dedicated to the production of a family of parts for a specific customer. Here the pressed parts, typically between two and four, together with any 'bought-in' components, are assembled using spot welding stations. Most cells do drilling, some punch and some attach components. Cycle times vary between 12 seconds and 1.5 minutes per part for each process. Changeover time between batches of different products is five minutes. There are typically five processes in each cell, which are staffed by between one and four oper-ators. For instance the making of steering brackets requires four operators and makes four types of bracket, all in similar quantities. The bracket has individual operator cycle times of 45, 80, 55, and 38 seconds. In many cases the automotive customer not only audits the cell but also sends quality experts and improvement engineers to assist.

### Paint
There are two paint plants for electro-painting of finished assemblies. All products go through one of these two lines. Each paint line is a continuously moving over-head conveyor. Products are hung on hooks by operators and unhooked after the

cycle; this takes 90 minutes, during which time less than three minutes is used for actual painting. The paint line is not scheduled, and operators hang parts in stillage quantities on a first-in-first-out (FIFO) basis.

### Final assembly

After painting, a number of products require final assembly where parts are added that cannot be painted, for example rubber bushes, nuts and bolts. Final quality checks are also carried out at this stage. Cycle time is less than one minute.

### Dispatch

In the final dispatch bay, vehicles are loaded and parts dispatched to customers typically several times per day, depending on volume and distance to the customer's plant. A buffer stock ranging between two hours and two weeks is held. Usually the 'timed delivery schedule' is received overnight, which details the exact quantities and times required during the next day. These may or may not match what is expected.

Each section has its own supervisor. In assembly there are four supervisors who manage the 15 cells. All sections are organised into teams. Each team has its own team leader, some of them elected by team members themselves. Teams cover both shifts and team members work on both shifts during every quarter. An annualised hours scheme has recently been introduced.

## ● Scheduling

The company runs an MRPII system that is used for raw material orders and for daily scheduling of the blanking and press shops and weekly scheduling of all other areas and cells. The company is currently in the process of implementing an ERP system from SAP which, it is hoped, will unify all information flows but will extend the MRPII functionality to quality control, maintenance and personnel. SAP also has a finite scheduling module that is being considered for detailed scheduling.

All products can be considered as *runners* or *repeaters*. Typical volumes are between 150 and 500 parts per day, made over two shifts. For example, a steering bracket has been called off Monday to Thursday at a fairly consistent 170 pieces per day with 80 on a Friday (a five-day week is worked). The scheduling function tries to promote the 'EPE' (every product every) idea in assembly cells so that the full range of products made in each cell are produced preferably every day, or at least once per week. Although weekly schedules are issued to each cell, detailed scheduling at cell level is the responsibility of assembly supervisors. There is always a mix of growth, steady, and decline products, but the company works with customers to ensure that the relatively stable period is reached as soon as possible.

All the automotive customers provide rolling forecasts. Typically these are a six-month forecast, a monthly forecast, weekly requirements and daily call-offs. The stability of these forecasts varies by customer. Generally, the Japanese forecasts are very stable. The Japanese tend to keep schedules stable for longer periods, typically six months or even a year. Aylesbury also provides monthly forecasts and weekly orders to the steel services centres. Some parts are pulled in under *kanban* control.

In the press and blanking shops, batch sizing using the economic order quantity (EOQ) was abandoned some six years ago. This led to a sharp drop in work in progress. An MBA graduate in the company explained that a reorder point system was simpler and more effective provided that demand was fairly constant. Today schedulers look at the MRP records (for future requirements) but also monitor inventory levels in the warehouse before deciding on batch quantities. Batch sizes are also decided by the loading in the press shop – when presses are heavily loaded, batch sizes are increased.

The schedulers use the MRP system to coordinate the delivery of bought-in components. These parts are received at the receiving dock and are then taken to the warehouse and from there to the cell 'supermarket'.

Different customers have their own peculiarities on scheduling and the cell operations reflect this. The Japanese favour high visibility. Nissan favours *kanban*. Honda favours a synchronised approach. Ford is now encouraging Aylesbury to adopt the Ford Production System (FPS). Rover has good stable schedules but tends to allow the company more flexibility. All insist on excellent performance in each of the key areas of cost, quality, and delivery (Q, C, D). Aylesbury is considering adopting the Toyota *heijunka* system that is used in a sister company.

## Blanking and press operations

Because of changeover, blanking and press operations have to take place in batches. First, parts are inspected visually and sometimes using statistical process control (SPC) methods. There is typically a one per cent scrap rate as a result of changeover. Lubrication and other minor stoppages, for example taking SPC samples, account for some 10 minutes per batch. Some of the dies used in pressing are old or are difficult to adjust during changeover, resulting in defective parts. As a result, once a press has been set up there is a motivation to make more parts than are strictly required by the schedule. This is also encouraged by stillage quantities that do not match schedule quantities. As an example, the quantities of the steering bracket made over one month are shown in Table 31.1.

**Table 31.1 Steering bracket production in one month**

| Day | Steel delivery (part equivalent) | Blanking (parts) | Pressing (parts) |
|-----|-----|-----|-----|
| 2   | –    | –    | 466  |
| 5   | –    | 1100 | –    |
| 7   | –    | –    | 590  |
| 9   | –    | 1235 | –    |
| 10  | 1800 | –    | –    |
| 16  | –    | 770  | 1130 |
| 21  | 2200 | –    | –    |
| 24  | –    | –    | 1340 |

## Assembly cell operations

The cell supervisors are able to achieve the daily product targets with good consistency provided they have the parts available. Schedules are issued weekly through the MRP system and finalised in conjunction with the supervisors from subsequent operations and dispatch. A daily production meeting is held for this purpose. Parts are delivered to the general cell supermarket from the warehouse in stillages by forklift. This is supposed to take place under *kanban* control, with a card from a stillage being used to trigger a pull signal. The forklift drivers are under pressure: congestion in the warehouse means they have to shift stillages to gain access so that sometimes parts arrive late or occasionally the wrong parts are delivered, delaying the cell. A 'catch up' is sometimes required, but buffer stocks held in subsequent operations ensure that customer deliveries are near perfect.

At the 'supermarket', parts are taken out of the large stillages and decanted into small plastic containers that can be handled by operations. Each cell has its own pre-cell inventory staging area which is considered necessary to ensure that the three or four parts that typically make up a product are all present before work starts in the cell.

When the output rate changes by more than a given amount, cells have to be rebalanced. This involves allocating work elements between operators and determining the rate at which the cell should flow. Operators now do balancing themselves, working with the supervisor, on what Ford and the Japanese call a *yamazumi* board. This contains magnetic strips of length proportional to the work elements that have to be rearranged to fit in with the new output requirements. The cell that makes the steering bracket also makes one other product with very similar characteristics and approximately the same volume. At present there are three operators for each shift in this cell, manning the five machines. The operators bring parts to the cell from the cell buffer, carrying the parts in plastic tote boxes weighing up to 15kg.

## Quality

Aylesbury has to meet exacting quality standards from its customers. A total quality programme was started some eight years ago that had a slow but steady impact on defect rates. The workforce was educated in the '7 tools of quality' and a suggestion scheme was put in place. Today the level of suggestions is very low and fishbone diagrams are seldom seen. Over the past eight years, period final defect rates as measured by the customer have declined from around 40 000 parts per million (ppm) – 4 per cent – to 1600 ppm – 0.16 per cent. Today there are only four staff in the quality section serving the whole plant. One of these people spends most of her time in the metrology room where samples are taken for exacting measurement. Another spends the majority of his time with manufacturing engineers to improve machine capability. A third works full time with suppliers and customers. The three programmes that made a significant impact on quality were:

- The introduction of SPC after blanking and pressing. Originally quite frequent samples were taken, but with improving capability, far fewer samples are now taken.
- The introduction of *pokayoke* devices in the assembly cells. This programme was

initiated by an enthusiastic outside consultant who was able to identify numerous 'failsafing' opportunities and to motivate operators to think of their own ideas.

● The supplier development programme.

Nevertheless the current defect rate of around 1600ppm is considered good in the industry but poor by the customers. This level of defect has seemed to 'plateau'. Defect rates are measured at each stage, and (encouraged by Ford) the 'first time through' (FTT) rate is measured for individual products. FTT measures parts that go through without any rectification. The FTT rate varies from 95 per cent to 87 per cent. Staff from the quality department are now enthusiastic about six sigma and one of them has been identified to attend a black-belt training programme in the New Year. The six sigma level of 3.4ppm seems a long way off.

## ● Delivery

Automotive customers expect defect-free products to be delivered exactly on time (not too early or too late) in the exact required quantity. The performance measure therefore combines three elements multiplied together. Customers measure this by individual delivery and regard a shortage of one part in a container as a zero performance on that element. When Aylesbury started measuring performance for each product in this way some five years ago, its performance, often in the 20 per cent range, was a cause for alarm. Today its performance is consistently in the high 90 per cent range. The greatest problem is now in part quantities where, despite quite large downstream buffer inventories, part shortages still persist. Of course one problem is customers who do not stick to their own schedule forecasts but nevertheless expect perfect delivery performance.

## ● Inventory

Inventory is kept at every intermediate stage. For the steering bracket, a snapshot of equivalent parts revealed the results shown in Table 31.2.

### Table 31.2  Steering bracket inventory

| Stage | Part equivalent |
|-------|-----------------|
| Coil steel | 500 estimate |
| After blanking | 200 (1 stillage) |
| After pressing | Nil |
| In warehouse (fridge) | 1780 |
| In cell supermarket | 230 |
| In cell staging area | 35 |
| Before assembly | 16 |
| In the assembly cell | 13 |
| After assembly | 324 |
| At paint | Nil |
| At final assembly | Nil |
| In dispatch bay | 623 |

## ● *Kaizen*

The company established a Kaizen Promotion Office (KPO) some three years ago, with the aim of encouraging waste reduction and promoting lean initiatives. The Kaizen Promotion Manager also has responsibility for the MRPII system production control office. Early initiatives were a 5S campaign and an attempt to put in standard operating procedures (SOPs). All operators and supervisors were put through an education programme devised and delivered by the KPO which covered the seven wastes, 5S, and SOPs. These programmes were subsequently rolled out to the shop floor by the three KPO staff. However, subsequent audits by the KPO have shown that many SOPs are not being followed. The 5S campaign was an initial success with large amounts of accumulated rubbish being thrown away under the first S (Sort), and quite successful work being carried out under the second S (Straighten) whereby an attempt is made to locate everything in the correct place. The KPO thinks that the 5S programme has gone backwards since the initial work, and is now considering a new round. A recent audit of shop floor staff showed that most operators and supervisors could remember only three or four of the seven wastes, with the second shift showing the poorer retention.

Some changeover times have also been addressed. The KPO decided to work systematically through the presses with the aim of reducing changeover times to below 30 minutes. This has been achieved with four of the presses, but some changeovers still take double this time. Nevertheless, benchmarking reveals that 30 minutes is an excessive time. Operators are supposed to record each changeover time on a chart held at the press, but tend to fill in the data at the end of a shift. Dies are located in a store adjacent to the press shop.

The KPO has also run three *kaizen* blitz events during the last year. The initiative came from a KPO member who attended a blitz event at another company. A typical format is as follows: An assembly cell is chosen and the supervisor from the cell, two supervisors from other cells, four operators from the cell and three people from the KPO participate. Sometimes an outsider from within the Group attends. Events are held over four days and end with a presentation to appropriate managers. The emphasis is on doing, and the expression 'just do it' has been adopted as the blitz event motto. All of the three events held were considered a success, with one of them resulting in a 32 per cent inventory reduction and a halving of lead-time. The KPO has noticed, however, that the gains have begun to be lost, in one case rather rapidly. The company has now been persuaded by one of its customers to allow Industry Forum, a group sponsored by the DTI and the Society of Motor Manufacturers and Traders, to conduct the next event.

## ● **Current situation**

In common with all first-tier automotive suppliers, Aylesbury is under pressure to reduce costs and improve quality. Most automotive customers expect annual price reductions of between two per cent and six per cent, demand perfect delivery performance and expect defect rates to be reduced below 100ppm (0.01%). As a result, there are several initiatives in place. Volumes, which grew steadily during most of the 1990s, are now under pressure.

## The meeting on 15th October 2001

On 15th October, the Managing Director, Brian Franks, and the Kaizen Manager, Stuart Archer, held a short meeting. Both knew that despite the achievements of the past few years; the company was now in danger of a big decline in business. This was due not just to the economic climate but also to the relatively slow rate of improvement in company performance. It was felt that with several new cars in the pipeline, the company would be able to continue to grow if it could put in place more effective improvements. It was felt, however, that without improvement in delivery performance the company would not win new business.

### Question

*What improvements do you consider that the management team at Aylesbury should be giving priority to, and why?*

# CASE 32

# The Royal Navy: JIT based ship spares provisioning

Case date 2001

Alan Fowler

## Introduction

JIT methods are commonly associated with mass production industries, for example car manufacturing, in which investment in developing and implementing radical new processes can be justified against savings in large volume turnover. However, Womack and Jones[1] identified several successful applications of this practice in different industries around the world, and claimed that it could be applied in low-volume operations and office activities as well as in mass production on the scale typically found in the automotive industry. The question therefore arises as to whether these methods can yield cost-effective benefits in the small quantities that are turned over in industries such as defence. Spares provisioning for the Royal Navy typifies such a requirement where, in addition to potential concerns about higher set-up costs for small batch production, development costs are high relative to material costs. For a service that is becoming increasingly aware of the need to reduce costs, whilst simultaneously maintaining a high level of operational availability, JIT based methods of spares provisioning appear potentially promising.

## Contending models for warship spares provisioning

Traditionally, spares support for warships, as depicted schematically in Figure 32.1, can be divided into two categories: Forward Support, including carried-on-board (COB) spares, and Base Support (base spares).

Ships carry a limited range of spare parts, mechanical and electrical, so that repairs and some maintenance can be performed whilst at sea.

The range of COB spares is limited by the ability to conduct the related maintenance at sea while the quantity is determined by stock-out risk (SOR) criteria. This is typically set at 95 per cent which means that the warship crew can be 95 per cent confident that they will not run out of spares during a standard mission (for example 90 days). This calculation assumes constant random failure rates for all equipment (no account is taken of wear-out rates within this simplified assumption). In practice this is a reasonable assumption, since it is generally true for the electronic products which comprise the largest population of COB spares. Conversely, the rate of demand for mechanical items is so low as to make the required spares quantities insensitive to the inaccuracies of this assumption.

**Figure 32.1 Conventional warship spares provisioning system**

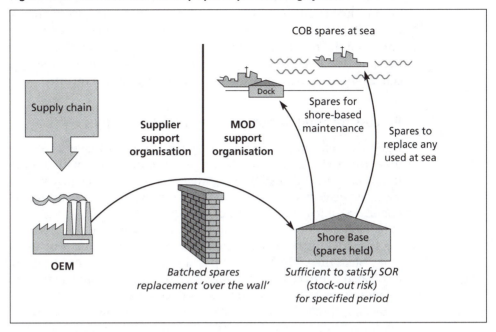

The majority of maintenance and repair work, other than emergencies at sea, is performed at the dockside by a 'prime contractor' working for the MOD/Navy (the MOD Support Organisation). When a warship returns to base, any COB spares used on deployment must be replaced. Further spares may also be required for base maintenance. These are drawn from stores, either held at the shore base or at a central depot. Currently, the level of spares inventory for each 'Line Replaceable Unit' (LRU), sometimes called a 'spareable' item, is again determined by a SOR criterion for some initial period of the warship's operational life. By definition, the stock-out risk criterion is demanding: almost twice as many spares are held as are expected to be needed, just in case. The rationale for this is that the Royal Navy is charged with the defence of the nation, implying that operational availability is crucial and should not be jeopardised by lack of spares. The situation is exacerbated by MOD's requirement for insurance spares. These are required since occasionally damage is incurred to warships through fire, accident or combat. Under these circumstances spares may be required on a range and scale that would not normally be anticipated. These often include large quantities or high-value items that represent a significant cost.

The prime contractor is supplied by original equipment manufacturers (OEM) who, in turn, are supplied by component manufacturers comprising the 'spares supply chain'. Collectively, this comprises the supplier support organisation, depicted in Figure 32.1.

Finally, Figure 32.1, also alludes to the current state of relationships within the supply chain which may be characterised by an 'over the wall' mentality involving limited integration and transparency.

Currently the MOD is beginning to contract with prime contractors to provide the Support Organisation for a Contractor Logistic Support (CLS) period (Tasker and

Willcox[2]) which corresponds to the period for initial support. During this initial period the actual spares demand is monitored and further spares are ordered as required. However, there are some fundamental problems with this existing system. For example, the initial support period is not long enough to determine future demand; too much stock is procured initially; shortages develop quickly; obsolescence problems arise and excessive inventory costs are incurred.

## Process reconfiguration drawing on JIT principles

Figure 32.2 illustrates how a JIT approach to replenishment could enable base-spares inventory to be reduced to give an equivalent SOR but with a shorter replacement lead-time. First, it should be noted that there is no real change at the COB end of the spectrum, except a stronger emphasis on providing timely information when a failure occurs which necessitates a call on spares.

Notably the MOD shore base stores are reduced and responsibility for provisioning is passed further back upstream, moving from a just-in-case to a JIT concept. The system therefore depends upon a fundamental change in the relationship and associated contract with the supplier. This entails arrangement for replacement of spares in a guaranteed lead-time with fixed prices.

By adopting this approach based on JIT principles, featuring a shorter replacement lead-time, it may be possible to reduce base-spares inventory and tackle the problems outlined above, whilst continuing to provide an equivalent SOR. This also allows insurance spares to be largely eliminated by making alternative arrange-

**Figure 32.2 JIT based warship spares provisioning**

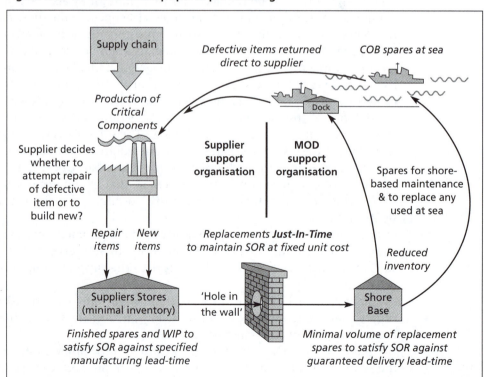

ments for timely replacements in the event that they are needed. This would be achieved by changing the structure of the contract with the supplier whereby instead of a one-off buy of equipment and spares, the supplier would be contracted to provide a service level commitment for a specified period of time.

Reduced bureaucracy should also characterise this system. Currently, when defective items are returned to industry for repair or refurbishment, there is a protracted contractual debate about whether it is economical to repair the item, how much this should cost and how long it should take. This debate can often take place between the MOD and several tiers within the supply chain. Consequently it is disproportionately expensive and time-consuming. With the JIT concept, all defective items are simply returned directly to the supplier who then takes the decision on repair independently. Since the supplier is already contracted to provide a replacement in a guaranteed lead-time at a fixed unit price, the customer can be indifferent to the decision outcome. However, the supplier must also provide information on the diagnosis of the failure and any repair activity carried out to maintain 'Corrective Actions' and 'Configuration Management' records.

Since it is envisioned that a fixed price would be paid for this service, then the supplier should be motivated to take the most cost-effective decision to maintain margins. Indeed, by assessing the expected number of items that will be capable of repair, and the likely repair costs, the fixed unit price for replacements can be negotiated to a weighted average of new build and repair costs with an agreed margin. This means that the aggregate unit price for spares could be less than that paid for the original equipment. Under such a system, the supplier would also be motivated to improve the reliability of its equipment, since this is the other way in which margins can be maintained or improved.

In contemplating the potential of such a system, there are a number of current developments which illustrate the trend towards alternative approaches. For example, there is notable evidence that many in the defence industry are attracted to the idea of moving spares stock from the customer's premises to those of the suppliers. This view, which appears to be gaining popularity, is referred to as 'vendor managed inventory' (Walmsley[3] and Coles[4]). The benefits are seen as reducing the cost of holding the inventory and enabling suppliers to manage inventory levels. However, suppliers naturally expect to be paid for providing this service and taking on additional risk. Furthermore, Coles alludes to doubts over the sincerity of industry in its espoused willingness to participate in such projects:

'Only those in industry can truly know whether they are prepared to work in this way, and there is still some way to go before we can confidently predict what the exact result will be.'

These initiatives have the potential to facilitate more rapid introduction of new technology into service since the switch to upgrades can render large spares inventories obsolete overnight. However, the most significant factor impacting on the more rapid introduction of new technology is the adoption of commercial off-the-shelf (COTS) components. This is because commercial development moves at a rapid pace and is supported by a much larger market. Use of COTS, therefore, enables the MOD to take advantage of new technologies as they emerge without the time and cost penalties of developing bespoke military equipment.

Conversely, there are penalties associated with having to accept commercial specifications, which may require concessions on military requirements such as shock resistance. Design must also be modular to allow frequent upgrades in components to be accepted without affecting form, fit or function.

However, on balance, the policies of increasing use of COTS and vendor managed inventory would appear to be entirely complementary with JIT spares provisioning. For example, JIT may be seen to facilitate the more rapid introduction of COTS upgrades by maintaining the supply chain and reducing inventory while COTS components will be more suitable for JIT provisioning because of the larger manufacturing base and expanded production volumes.

These smart procurement policies are mostly enablers for defence projects to achieve greater efficiencies through modern information systems, streamlined bureaucracy and clear data standards. All are potentially significant contributors towards the development of a JIT spares provisioning system, although amongst the various approaches proposed RAMP (rapid acquisition of manufactured parts) appears to be the most relevant. This envisages the holding of electronic parts data and/or partially manufactured components at the suppliers' premises so that they can be completed and shipped quickly when required. In this way, the long lead-times and risks associated with process planning, sourcing exotic materials and elaborate forgings, and organising complex manufacturing processes can be managed upstream, leaving the relatively straightforward stages of manufacture to be completed when the parts are required. The MOD pays for the extent of the work completed plus a fee for storage and only completes the balance when the part is actually delivered.

## Some issues of concern

Although the JIT system potentially has several advantages, it is also necessary to sound a cautionary note. The JIT model may work in situations where the accounting trade-off between the risk of losing a sale, due to the absence of immediate availability, can be balanced with the cost of inventory. The question is, does this logic transfer directly to the case of the defence industry? The MOD is charged with the defence of the realm. What higher priority can there be, and what price can be placed on success? Understandably, the MOD is preoccupied with operational availability as well as cost. A simple trade-off between the costs of the traditional system and those of a JIT system may not be sufficient to justify a change in policy.

Additionally, JIT production is usually considered to depend on predictable demand and level scheduling, but both factors are significantly absent in the context of spares provisioning. Also, there is the broader issue of whether JIT really eliminates cost from the supply chain or just moves the costs to some point upstream. For example, some evidence indicates that only those suppliers who themselves also implement JIT manufacturing and purchasing techniques are able to supply JIT without increases in raw material and/or finished goods inventory (Germain and Droge[5]). Furthermore, some would say that only where manufacturing lead-time is less than the required response time can increases in finished goods inventory be avoided.

This highlights the main threat to the application of JIT in the low-volume operations of the Royal Navy. Short response times are required at irregular and unpredictable intervals for the supply of high-value, complex equipment with long manufacturing lead-times. The implication is that this can only be achieved through holding finished goods inventory.

In summary, it is essential to remember that still the most significant issue for the MOD, which differentiates it from much of industry, is the importance of operational availability. Achieving a trade-off between inventory cost and availability is a difficult problem to solve.

## Cost modelling of the spares provisioning process

Financial viability is a primary consideration in contemplating a transition to JIT based spares provisioning. Towards this end, a limited modelling exercise may be readily conducted using available suppliers' data on component cost, reliability and production lead-time. Extending this context, it is also important to ask the question: What happens after the initial in-service support period? With the conventional approach, the stock level would be topped up to restore the desired SOR for some follow-on period, taking account of the actual demand rate experienced during the initial in-service support period. For analysis to proceed, it would have to be assumed that the predicted failure rate is accurate so that the predicted demand rate, after the initial period, can be expected to remain unchanged. JIT replacements would then continue to be provided, as before, with prices assumed to remain stable. Furthermore, the advantage of the JIT based approach could actually be enhanced further when factors such as obsolescence and technology upgrading are taken into account. This is because with JIT, accommodating changes to the in-service equipment configuration is easier, quicker and cheaper because there is less inventory to become obsolete.

Finally, it must always be emphasised that the operational availability of vessels is of paramount importance to the MOD. Consequently, it is imperative when comparing the resulting spares availability under the two competing policies, to bear in mind that the availability of spares must remain at least as good as it is at present and, ideally, should actually be improved following the implementation of a JIT policy.

### A comparative illustration of a typical spares provisioning situation

Presented below is a snapshot of some typical data pertaining to spares provisioning for warships. The Royal Navy is considering the alternative JIT based approach as a means of potentially reducing the cost of spares inventory and is using, as an example, the case of a particular high-tech part for a radar system. This is supplied by a single supplier who does not supply anything else to the Navy.

Under the existing arrangements, the Navy carries two years' stock whilst also subscribing to the 95 per cent stock-out risk criterion (this means that there is a 95 per cent confidence of not running out of spares). Alternatively, this may be thought of as a 95 per cent 'stock-held' confidence criterion. In addition, Naval operational requirements dictate that, irrespective of risk criteria based on probability, there should be a minimum inventory level of one item to provide for immediate availability.

Under the alternative JIT based spares policy that is being considered, the customer (the Navy/MOD in this case) will hold reduced stock at its shore base, while still achieving 95 per cent SOR against a guarantee of delivery on demand to the Navy, within five days, at a fixed unit price. The supplier will also maintain additional buffer stock, at an agreed level, to achieve 95 per cent SOR against its manufacturing lead-time, to maintain availability (replacing any parts drawn down by the Navy during the support period). This service will be provided, in return for a fixed fee to be agreed between customer and supplier. It is assumed that any failed parts will be discarded.

For the purpose of calculation, the following customer data is available:

- There is one of these parts fitted on each of 10 ships.
- The anticipated utilisation is 1000 operating hours per year for each part.
- The mean time between failure (MTBF) of these parts is 10 000 operating hours.

The following supplier data is also available:

- The supplier has a manufacturing lead-time of 90 days.
- The cost of each part to the supplier is £100 000. This is marked up by 10 per cent for sale to the Navy.
- The supplier proposes to charge a fee of £35 000 per annum to the Navy for providing the JIT type service, plus the initial cost of setting up the buffer stock.
- The contract will run for two years (to be directly comparable with the existing arrangements).

In comparing the JIT based proposal with the existing arrangements, the following questions thereby arise:

(a) What is the cost to the Navy in the existing, traditional arrangement, when there is a need to carry two years' stock in accordance with the 95 per cent stock-out risk criterion?

(b) Under the alternative JIT arrangement, what level of stock needs to be carried by the Navy and by the supplier respectively? What will this arrangement cost the Navy, in total?

(c) Is the proposed JIT arrangement financially advantageous to both the Navy and the supplier (that is, what are the respective profits/benefits)?

(d) Suppose that a sensitivity analysis is also to be performed in which the mean time between failure is assumed to be respectively:
    - 1000 operating hours.
    - 20 000 operating hours.
    How does this affect the predictions of benefits/deficits accruing to the respective parties?

(e) Are there any other sensitivities that should be considered and how influential are they with respect to the viability of the proposal?

In performing the above analysis it should be assumed that cumulative Poisson probability data will be used to assess the value of the stock-out risk criterion for different scenarios. In performing your calculations you may choose, for convenience, to use the cumulative Poisson function provided in the standard Excel spreadsheet facility.

## Questions

*In addition to consideration of the financial and operational advantages that might accrue when implementing the changes suggested above, it is inevitable that political, cultural, social and economic issues will also impact on, and influence, the potential success of the JIT based proposal. A full analysis should therefore focus on a number of questions which may be summarised as follows:*

1 *How does the proposed JIT system compare with/differ from the existing conventional spares provisioning process?*

2 *What are the qualitative benefits that might accrue, based on the data made available in the case study?*

3 *The stakeholders involved in implementing this proposal may be broadly grouped into three categories: the MOD/Navy, the prime contractors (organisations who provide first-line and dockyard services to the MOD) and subcontractors (the organisations in the industries that supply and support the prime contractors). What do you believe the issues/problems would be in applying JIT principles to spares provisioning from the perspective of each of these groups respectively?*

4 *Based on the illustrative numerical data presented above, how attractive is the JIT proposition from a financial perspective, assuming this simplified quantitative example is typical of others (work through the calculations to produce your answer).*

5 *Weighing all the evidence available, do you believe that it would be feasible and advantageous to move towards a JIT based system for spares provisioning to Royal Navy warships? Explain your reasoning.*

## References

1 Womack, J. P. and Jones, D. T. (1996), *Lean Thinking*, Simon & Schuster, New York.
2 Tasker, P. H. and Willcox, N. (1999), 'The Royal Navy ASTUTE Class SSN,' *Journal of Naval Engineering*, 38(3), 376–390.
3 Walmsley, R. (1999), 'Smart Procurement', *Journal of Naval Engineering*, 38(2), 155–157.
4 Coles, J. (1999), 'Smart Procurement, the UK model', *Journal of Naval Engineering*, 38(3), 372–376.
5 Germain, R. and Droge, C. (1998), 'The context, organizational design, and performance of JIT buying versus non-JIT buying firms', *International Journal of Purchasing and Materials Management*, 34(2), 12–19.

# PART 5

# Supply networking

# Introduction to Part 5

No operation, or part of an operation, exists in isolation. Each operation is part of a larger and interconnected network of other operations. This network will include suppliers and customers. It will also include suppliers' suppliers and customers' customers and so on. Including government agencies, labour markets and other similar bodies as customers, suppliers or both, an organisation's network becomes its total business environment.

Supply chain planning and control is concerned with the flow of goods and services through the supply network, from suppliers through to customers. In large organisations there may be many hundreds of strands of linked operations passing through the operation. These strands are more commonly referred to as supply chains. A supply chain as a whole can be viewed as the flow of water in a river; organisations located closer to the original source of supply are described as being 'upstream', those located closer to the end customer are 'downstream'. See Chicken Run – the poultry supply chain (Case 34) and Fastflowers.com (Case 45).

Many of the topics covered in this part of the book are relatively new, and the concepts overlap in the sense that they refer to common parts of the total supply network. Therefore it is useful to distinguish between the different terms used. These are illustrated in Figure P5.1.

At a strategic level, operations managers are involved in designing the shape and form of the network in which their operation is set. Fundamental to the strategic design of any operations' resources are network-related questions such as: Should we carry out this activity or should another company do it for us? Which of our current suppliers do we want to buy and incorporate into our current operation? How should we develop trading relationships with suppliers and customers? See Wheatco Ltd and Chemco Ltd, B (Case 37) for a discussion of trust in buyer–supplier relationships.

There are three main areas in understanding supply chain planning and control:

- *Purchasing and supplier management* – the role of the purchasing function in forming contacts with suppliers to supply the organisation (upstream activities).
- *Physical distribution management* – the movement of products or services to the customer (downstream activities). Logistics is an extension of physical distribution management and usually refers to the management of materials and information flows from a business, down through a distribution channel, to end customers.
- *Materials management* is a more limited term than supply chain management and refers to the management of the flow of materials and information through the immediate supply chain, including purchasing, inventory management, stores management, operations planning and control, and physical distribution management.

**Figure P5.1 Some of the terms used to describe the management of different parts of the supply chain**

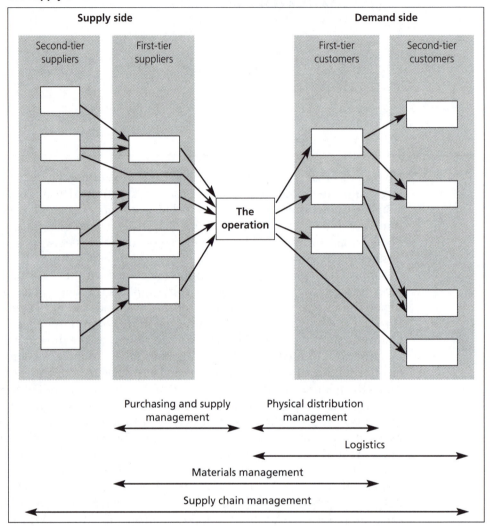

## Purchasing and supplier development

At the supply end of the business, the purchasing function forms contracts with suppliers to buy-in materials and services. Some of these materials and services are used in the production of the goods and services sold on to customers. Other materials and services are used to help run the business, for example, staff catering services or oil for machinery. These do not make up part of the finished goods or services but are still essential purchases for operations. Those responsible for purchasing need to understand the requirements of all the processes within the operation and also the capabilities of the suppliers.

There are six key objectives for the purchasing function – see the Marsden Community Stores case (Case 35):

### Purchasing at the right quality

The quality of incoming goods and services will have an important impact on the quality of the processed goods and services and also on their reliability and dependability. While in the past many organisations would carefully inspect all incoming items, purchasing functions are now working closely with suppliers to ensure that incoming goods and services will conform to the agreed quality specifications, through supplier quality programmes, for example. The Smart car final assembly time of 4.5hrs is only achieved because of this type of buyer–supplier collaboration – see The Smart Car and smart logistics (Cased 33).

### Purchasing for fast delivery

In some organisations where competition is based on fast response or where demand is uncertain, a major purchasing objective will be to find suppliers who can themselves respond quickly (see the Chicken Run – the poultry supply chain case).

### Purchasing for delivery at the right time and in the right quantity

Purchasing at the right time and in the right quantity can also have an important impact on the operation's overall performance. Success in this area requires the purchasing function to understand the operation's processes and forecast activity, and the intricacies of lead-times, volumes and seasonalities, for example. Successful management of timing and quantities has a big influence on inventory levels (working capital). See the Ice House Toys case (Case 25) for an illustration of the impact of inventory.

### Purchasing to retain flexibility

Supply flexibility, whether in terms of changing specification, changing delivery time or changing quantity, will be particularly valuable to those organisations that themselves are operating in fast-changing or uncertain markets.

### Purchasing at the right price

This is an important way of providing the organisation with a cost advantage as the cost of materials may have a significant effect on an organisation's overall costs. Historically, this objective of purchasing has been emphasised in purchasing theory and practice.

### Purchasing from the right source

One key function of the purchasing department is to make choices between the various suppliers. Decisions may not only rest on price and quality but also on future potential, and willingness to develop what they do and to work with the downstream organisations. A second issue here is the decision of whether to have just one organisation provide the goods or services (single source) or to reduce the risk in problems of supply through multi-sourcing.

## Purchasing, the Internet and e-commerce

For some years, electronic means have been used by organisations to confirm purchased orders and ensure payment to suppliers. The rapid development of the Internet opened up the potential for greater changes in purchasing behaviour. The Internet also provides the opportunity to search through a wider pool of potential suppliers for new sources of supply. Both e-commerce, the trade that takes place over the Internet, and e-procurement, when groups of organisations group together to link e-commerce systems into a common exchange, have seen considerable growth over the past few years, although they are still not as widely used as was expected. (See E-commerce in the NHS, Case 39.)

## Physical distribution management

On the demand side of the organisation, products (and sometimes services) need to be moved to the customer, involving the physical transportation of materials through the supply chain (see both Chicken Run – the poultry supply chain and the The Smart Car and smart logistics cases). These are the main issues which confront the manager concerned with distribution:

- The mode of transport to be used – for example, road, rail, water, air or pipeline.
- The use of warehousing, or hubs, to simplify routes and communication, whereby many products can be distributed to regional warehouses so that end customers only need deal with one warehouse instead of many. See the case of The Smart Car and smart logistics for a discussion of innovative distribution mechanisms.
- Deciding contract terms, in particular agreeing who takes the risks involved in transporting the products and deciding when the products will be paid for.

## Materials management

The concept of materials management originated from purchasing functions that understood the importance of integrating materials flows and its supporting functions, both throughout the business and out to immediate customers. It includes the functions of purchasing, expediting, inventory management, stores management, production planning and control, and physical distribution management. In retail operations, the purchasing task is frequently combined with the sales and physical distribution task into a role termed *merchandising*. A merchandiser typically has responsibility for organising sales to retail customers, for the layout of the shop floor, inventory management and purchasing.

## Objectives of supply chain management

In the past some organisations have seen purchasing, distribution and even inventory management as almost independent and distinct functions. This approach tends to underrate the importance of management of the whole flow of materials from upstream suppliers to downstream users through many distribution channels. Supply chain management is concerned with the management of the *whole* supply chain, from raw material supply right through to distribution to the end customer.

The three main objectives of supply chain management are discussed below.

### To focus on satisfying end customers

Because supply chain management includes all stages in the total flow of materials and information, it must be based on consideration of the needs of the final customer. It is only the final customer who has the only 'real' currency in the supply chain. When a customer decides to make a purchase he or she triggers action along the whole chain. All the businesses in the supply chain pass on portions of that end customer's money to each other, each retaining their margin for the value they have added. If each link in that chain does not understand their role in the supply chain, the final customer's needs may not be met.

### To formulate and implement strategies based on capturing and retaining end customer business

The key operation in a chain is the strongest business, which is in a position to influence and direct the others so that they work together in the common cause of capturing and retaining the end customer's business. This organisation may then take responsibility for setting the standards and determining the design of the infrastructure, such as the information systems used, to which the downstream dealer network needs to comply.

### To manage the chain effectively and efficiently

Taking a holistic approach to managing an entire supply chain opens up many opportunities for analysis and improvement, especially in shortening time-to-market, dealing with 'bottleneck' organisations, and performing cost and value analysis of the whole supply chain to try to generate cost savings across the whole supply chain.

## Summary

Supply chain management is a strategy concept, which includes the long-term consideration of the organisation's position in the supply network as well as the shorter-term control of flow through the supply chain. One of the key issues for operations, therefore, is how to manage the relationships with their immediate suppliers and customers, and how to maintain these over time (see the Wheatco Ltd and Chemco Ltd B case). The behaviour of the supply chain as a whole is made up of these relationships which are formed between individual pairs (or dyads) of operations in the chain. Another important consideration is that supply chains are dynamic and need to be adjusted to ensure that they are in line with market requirements (see Supply Chain Redesign at Finnforest Corp., Case 38).

### Recommended reading

Child, J. and Faulkner, D. (1998), *Strategies of Co-operation: Managing Alliances, Networks and Joint Ventures*, Oxford University Press.

Ford, D., Gadde, L., Hakansson, H., Lundgren, A., Snehota, I., Turnbull, P. and Wilson, D. (1998), *Managing Business Relationships*, John Wiley & Sons.

Harrison A. and van Hoek R. (2002), *Logistics Management and Strategy*, Financial Times /Prentice Hall, Harlow.

Slack, N., Chambers S. and Johnston, R. (2001), *Operations Management*, (3rd edn), Financial Times/Prentice Hall, Harlow, Chapter 13.

# CASE 33

# The Smart Car and smart logistics

Case date
2001

© Remko van Hoek and Alan Harrison

At the beginning of October 1998 most of the parking places in downtown Amsterdam were filled with one or ... two cars. The variety in colours and the remarkable design of the two-seater car attracted great attention. The message was clear: Smart had come to town and it's here to revolutionise the concept of car production, logistics and marketing.

Micro Compact Car AG (MCC), a wholly-owned subsidiary of Daimler-Benz (formerly a joint venture of Daimler-Benz and Swatch), is the company behind Smart. Together these manufacturers have developed what they call a new mobility concept that relieves the heavy environmental pressure caused by present traffic while still ensuring continuous individual mobility. Overlooking the period preceding the introduction of the car, MCC management could look back on many peaks: a completely new brand had been developed; pilot marketing of brand and product concept had raised high levels of customer awareness and interest in European markets; a production site of 68 hectares had been developed and constructed from scratch; a dealer and marketing organisation had been developed and was ready for product launch. Moreover, the supply chain concept developed went beyond existing practices in the automotive industry on a number of points:

- Customers can say how they want their product to be configured
- Lead-times for cars are counted in weeks
- Suppliers have co-invested in the production location and take a greater share in the final assembly process
- The value added during final assembly is just 10 per cent of the production cost price
- Supplier facilities are integrated in the assembly hall of MCC.

From the time of the first feasibility study by Mercedes in 1993 and the foundation of MCC in 1994, the management team realised it was facing a new set of challenges in terms of developing and integrating the supply chain. How should the supply chain be managed, coordinated, controlled and further developed? These questions were not only of relevance to MCC, but to the Daimler-Benz Corporation as a whole, which earmarked Smart as a strategic learning project. Moreover, the concept being brought to practice by MCC is widely considered by leading car manufacturers as of key importance to future industry developments. Manufacturers and suppliers therefore monitor the successes and failures of MCC, as the results will in future influence organisation of many other supply chains.

**Figure 33.1 The Smart City Coupé**

# The car

The Smart City Coupé is a two-seater car measuring 2.5 metres in length, 1.51 metres in width and 1.53 metres in height (Figure 33.1). It has been developed mainly for in-city use. It's a safe and environment-friendly car; despite its micro credentials, it combines driver comfort, safety and customer choice. According to MCC, the car is an answer to mobility problems in urban areas. A key target was to minimise the burden on the environment caused by individual mobility. By using changeable body parts, the life cycle of the car can be extended. Moreover, the car and its components are fully recyclable after use. Its size also makes it friendly to the environment, as it needs a relatively small and fuel-efficient engine – and two Smarts can be parked in a single parking slot.

The Smart is based on a rigid integral body frame/safety cell (called 'Tridion'), to which such flexible body panels as doors, the front and rear panels and the optional glass roof are attached. The customer can specify the product by combining two colours of the frame (black and silver) with the various colours of the body panels. This way the customer is given the impression of a high level of choice, although product variation in the production process is kept to a minimum.

Product variations differ in interior trim, body colours, comfort features and engine power. The modular product layout enables MCC to supply customer choice with minimum product complexity. As most of the features are easy to add, both at the assembly line and during the life span of the car, variation in customer demand hardly interferes with production processes. For example, the interior trim (fabric and colour) consists of exchangeable panels, easy to mount at the assembly line and even easy to be exchanged by the owner afterwards. Moreover, features that might disturb production, if made optional (such as ABS, electric windows, etc.), are integrated as standards in the car. The after-sales extras include a wide range of easy-to-attach peripherals such as stereo and children's seats.

On top of this customisation, the modular concept enables the customer completely to renew and upgrade the product during its lifetime. Product features can be added and coloured body parts can be changed in the dealership (called the 'Smart Centre').

Moreover, the modular concept makes it possible for designers and engineers of MCC and its suppliers quickly to develop and implement minor and major product redesigns. For example, the first extension of the product offering was introduced within six months of launch. Two additional colours (on top of the basic ones) were introduced. The gimmick here is that a form of cubic printing is used. This technique uses not only a basic colour but adds a colour film on top of it (orange and green in this case) in a random pattern (like the spots on a cow), making each panel unique. That introduction is an important indicator of future policies. The input of Swatch, the Swiss watchmaker, in concept development is clearly present here. Within the existing product architecture of easy-to-assemble products, new options and features are introduced at a rapid pace. This adds to the fashionable character of the product: constant change and improvement.

Further ahead, the modular concept permits engineers to renew the car completely or extend the product line within short time frames. This can be achieved by changing the form of body panels and interior components, while keeping the basis of the car (the Tridion safety cell) unchanged. Through 'smart' product development, the engineers at MCC have achieved high levels of customer-perceived choice, while limiting product variation and production complexity.

## Selling the concept

Smart was launched into its target European automotive market which is stagnating and where competition in existing channels is rapidly intensifying. To lend leverage to the remarkable design of the product, the marketing organisation is geared not only to promote Smart as a new car concept, but also to create new sales opportunities by using unconventional channels and sales processes.

The market winners of the car are:

- design and technology
- high levels of customer choice
- new distribution channels
- safety
- space (small size but large interior)
- environment (fuel efficiency, recyclability).

Technology relates to such features as the tip-touch gearbox, features that differentiate the product from the smaller cars of other brands that are positioned as basic and low cost. Design (form and colours) reveal the Swatch input in the concept development and give the car a trendy and different look. Customisation is actively included in the sales process by making sales channels establish a dialogue with customers and sell on a consultative rather than a 'move-the-metal' basis. In addition to the initial choices, a relationship with the customer is developed by additional customisation opportunities during the period of ownership. While customisation is not new in the automotive market, the combination of a two or three-week lead-time based on production flexibility, and direct distribution (as opposed to multilayer distribution), certainly is. VW currently has a lead-time of up to six months for some models. Space relates to the smallness of the car, allowing it to reduce congestion on roads and in parking areas. Environment, furthermore, refers to recycling and lower emission rates of the car.

After the launch of the product, the target segment of DINKies (double income, no kids) turned out to be too narrow, as the Smart proved attractive to senior citizens and also to students. The target markets were redefined to include customers that are young or young in mind and fashion conscious. Dealerships are located in highly frequented places in urbanised areas such as shopping centres on the outskirts of cities. In addition to the Smart Centres, satellites (smaller sales outlets related to a centre) are used. The function of the satellites is to increase product exposure and market penetration by adding a sub-channel. Satellites display one or two cars. Sales advisors in the satellites do not take orders; they do prepare product proposals but their main function is to attract prospective customers to the nearest Smart Centre. In Germany a satellite centre is located in a McDonald's restaurant, and in future satellites may also work through supermarkets, department stores and as shops-within-shops.

Cars are mainly built to customer orders, which the plant in Hambach receives from the Smart Centres. For the purpose of display, test rides, promotion and for 'take-away' sales, Smart Centres do have cars in stock and, if needed, the car can be customised at the centre according to the client's specification by the exchange of such components as body parts. Some further final assembling tasks, like adding special features or light final assembly, can be performed at the centres. Postponement thus plays a major role in customising the product to client's needs in the centres, but also takes place in the factory.

The single-stage sales concept allows Smart centres to procure their cars – via the sales logistics department – directly from the production plant in Hambach instead of through a dealer or import organisation. This distribution system is very different to the tiered sales structure in the traditional automotive industry, in which national sales organisations and importers add another layer between dealers and the manufacturer. Through this concept, Smart aims to minimise ordering and delivery times and to reduce cost. The dealer organisations use multimedia systems to enable clients to 'engineer' their car in the showroom and to forward orders directly to MCC headquarters. This allows production planning to be based on point-of-sale (POS) data. The centres are connected to Hambach by satellite.

## SMART-ville

At the launch of the product in selected European markets, a total of DM830 million had been invested in developing and building a factory. The full capacity of the plant is 200 000 vehicles a year, or 750 a day, a volume that is targeted for the year 2000. The factory, located in Hambach, France, covers 68 hectares with 20 production buildings. A test site was built in an 18-month period. The facility is referred to as 'Smart-ville'. Suppliers and partners of MCC occupy a number of on-site buildings, and investment in factory development was shared with suppliers. MCC invested approximately DM445 million, its suppliers and partners about DM385 million. Suppliers invested a further DM300 million in machinery and facilities in the Hambach factory. Employment started with 1500 (only 650 of which are on the MCC payroll) and is expected to rise to 2200 over the next few years. MCC also invested DM700 million in the development of the car and in machinery, and DM550 million in establishing a dealer and distribution organisation. Total investment before launch reached DM2.4 billion.

Right at the start of the production, the management of MCC addressed the question of how to expand capacity in the near future. The whole concept has been developed to enable MCC to expand capacity by replicating the site, its layout and its supply structure, anywhere in the world, wherever the market may be.

Flexibility, just-in-time operation and short supply lead-times were goals for production and plant layout. According to MCC, this has resulted in a reduction of transport and logistics cost to the absolute minimum. Moreover, final assembly of the car takes just 4.5 hours, which is far less than in any other factory in the world. It is impressive to see how easily the modules and parts can be bolted to a car. Design for assembly has been taken beyond current levels. The high performance levels of the final assembly facilities could only be attained through innovative outsourcing concepts – described in the next section.

## The supply chain structure

Before the supply chain is detailed, it is important to understand the product structure of MCC and how the product is divided into modules. It is impressive to see how MCC has succeeded in limiting the number of components supplied by direct (tier 1) suppliers. The modular concept, as well as technological innovations, have enabled MCC to produce a car from no more than 40 to 50 modules and parts. Table 33.1 specifies these modules and parts in terms of integrated (in-house) and non-integrated supplies.

**Table 33.1  Modules and parts sourced by MCC**

| Integrated direct suppliers | Non-integrated suppliers | | | | |
|---|---|---|---|---|---|
| | Ordered according to production plan | | Parts and components on-the-shelf (TuF) | | After sales parts, available at Smart Centre |
| Front module | Seats (including optional side airbags) | Rear axle | Seat belts | Brake system | Cassette-, CD-box |
| Body panels | Wheel system | Front axle | Locking system | Drive shaft | Cup holder |
| Paint and body protection | Exhaust system | Under shield | Carpet | ABS cable system | RPM revolution counter |
| Rear module drive-line (incl. engine) | Transmission | Cooling system | Rear light | Relays box | Audio system |
| Safety body cell | Headlights | Wheel arch and sill panels | Side direction indicator | Driver pedal module | Other parts – not specified |
| Dashboard/cockpit, including airbags | Engine | | Sunshade for glass roof | Fuel tank flap | |
| Doors | Front window | | Aerial (antenna) | Fog lights | |
| Cubic printing | Glass roof | | Upper interior trim | Rear window | |
| | Roof module | | SE-drive unit | 10–15 other components – not specified | |
| | Fuel tanks | | Crash management system | | |
| | Centre console; Luggage box | | | | |

**Figure 33.2  MCC basic plant layout**

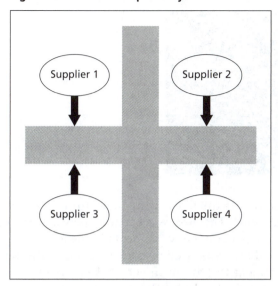

Smart is based on an integral body frame (the Tridion) to which modules are attached. Apart from the body, the car consists of several main modules:

- rear module, including the driveline
- doors
- cockpit.

Each module contains sub-modules and components. The modules are supplied in sequence for final assembly by a small number of first-tier suppliers. Seven of these are fully integrated into the final assembly site. Modules are bought by MCC only when needed for the final assembly process. For example, a complete rear module includes rear axles, transmission, suspension and engine. It is pre-assembled by a supplier, who starts assembling the module only on demand by MCC. The assembly sequence by the supplier begins 1.5 hours before the module is needed on the final assembly line. The same is true of the doors (three hours lead-time) and the dashboard system (one hour lead-time).

To ensure a smooth flow of goods within the plant, the car is moved along the workstations of the assembly line, which is laid out in the form of a cross (see Figure 33.2).

Reasons for this plant layout were to permit frequent deliveries at a large number of delivery points, while keeping transport to a minimum. Sub-sections can also work independently to avoid system disruptions in case of malfunction at one particular point along the assembly line (Figure 33.3). Furthermore, 'integrated suppliers' are able to supply their finished products directly to the final assembly line or by means of a conveyor system.

At Smart-ville, the manufacturing process starts with Magna assembling the body (Tridion) in white. This process is highly automated and standardised: Magna employs 130 robots. In fact, this is one of the very few automated process steps; operators mostly perform subsequent steps. The finished body is then passed on to the next partner in the adjoining facility. In this step Surtema (an Eisenmann

**Figure 33.3 The Smart Car assembly line**

subsidiary) primes and paints the body using paint tunnels for each of the two colours (black and silver/grey). The process is based on powder coating – it has been developed especially for Smart and is environmentally friendly.

After painting, the body is transferred by conveyor belt to the beginning of the assembly 'cross'. Starting at the top of the cross, VDO assembles cockpits and mounts them to the body. In the three other sections of the cross, MCC goes on assembling the car, starting with the mechanics and chassis, followed by external and internal trim assembly, inspection and testing. The rear module (including the drive train) is pre-assembled by Krupp Hoesch and undergoes several additional assembly tasks by MCC workers on a small island adjacent to the cross. Following assembly, the rear module is brought to the line on a telescopic carrier that raises it to shoulder height, enabling operators to guide it into the car.

During the assembly process, modules and components are delivered line-side (within 10 metres of the workstation) on a just-in-time basis. For example, complete front-end and rear-end modules are delivered by Bosch and Krupp respectively. Dynamit Nobel delivers the plastic outer body panels moulded on site. The door panels are delivered to Magna Door Systems, who pre-assemble the doors before delivering them line-side. The seven 'integrated' suppliers are responsible for the supply of 70–80 per cent of the volume and 30–40 per cent of the value of the finished product. In addition, 16 non-integrated suppliers deliver sub-modules and parts to both MCC and the integrated suppliers. These non-integrated suppliers add about another 20 per cent of the volume to the car. Their supplies include seats, wheels, windows, etc. and are delivered to the relevant docking station of the assembly line, at a maximum distance of 10 metres. The remaining 10 per cent of the volume consist of standard and small parts not linked to a particular module, which are stored in an on-site warehouse, operated by a third party.

MCC has selected suppliers to integrate at the site and suppliers that could supply from a distant location by a straightforward process. Logistics management at MCC made a calculation based on the frequency at which a module was used and its size. The outcome of this exercise showed the volume of the various flows of components. Apart from special cases in which the characteristics of the manufacturing process did not allow on-site assembly (as with engines), the components causing the largest transport flows were integrated in the premises of MCC. Table 33.2 lists the integrated and non-integrated suppliers of MCC.

**Table 33.2 Selection of MCC suppliers**

**Integrated module suppliers**

| | | |
|---|---|---|
| 1 | Bosch | Front module and headlights |
| 2 | Dynamit Nobel | Synthetic body panels/wheel arch and sill panels |
| 3 | Surtema | Paint and surface protection |
| 4 | Cubic | Cubic printing |
| 5 | Krupp Hoesch | Rear module (rear-wheel suspension, integration of engine, etc.) |
| 6 | Magna/Magna Doors System | Safety body cell/doors |
| 7 | VDO | Dashboard/cockpit, battery and wiring harnesses |

**Non-integrated main suppliers**

| | | |
|---|---|---|
| 1 | Behr | Cooling system |
| 2 | Bertrand Faure | Seats |
| 3 | Continental | Tyres |
| 4 | Eberspächer | Exhaust system |
| 5 | Getrag | Transmission |
| 6 | Magneti Marelli | Dynamo/starter/relays |
| 7 | DaimlerChrysler | Engine/front and rear axles/drive shaft |
| 8 | Splintex | Windows and glass roof |
| 9 | Meritor | Roof-module, sunshade for glass roof |
| 10 | Bosch | Control/stability system |
| 11 | Solvay | Fuel tanks |
| 12 | Stankiewicz | Carpet |
| 13 | Simoldes | Centre console and luggage boxes |
| 14 | Rieter | Undershield |
| 15 | Johnson Controls Interiors | Upper interior trim |
| 16 | Lemförder | SE-drive unit |
| (17*) | Dynamit Nobel | Crash management system |
| (18*) | Bosch | Headlights/brake systems |

**'TuF' suppliers = non-integrated suppliers of off-the-shelf products**

| | | |
|---|---|---|
| 10 | Various suppliers | Ranging from, among others, heater-aircon systems, |
| (16*) | | driver pedal systems and side airbags, to fog lights |

Suppliers marked with * supply in multiple supply chain setting; they perform both as integrated and as non-integrated suppliers.

The system also differs from traditional supply chains with respect to the activities that are outsourced. Even activities traditionally considered core activities of the OEM (original equipment manufacturer), such as the pressing of body parts and painting, and even the coordination of internal logistics, are no longer performed by MCC. Not only do suppliers closely participate in the final assembly of the car, they are also deeply involved in the development and planning of the product. What can be said about the outsourcing of components and modules manufacturing is equally true of supporting services. The whole information system supporting the processes of MCC in manufacturing, logistics and distribution is outsourced to a third-party service provider, who owns and exploits the hardware and the software, as a facility-management arrangement. Panopa controls lorry traffic on site, which is important because 100 lorry deliveries will be made during each shift once full capacity is reached. TNT logistics manages a spare-part facility and Rhenus operates a storage facility for small standard components and parts. These parts are replenished to the line by a *kanban* pull system, operated by Rhenus. MTL, finally, ships finished cars to the dealers. Production output is shipped instantly and directly to the dealers without intermediate hold-ups or inventory layers.

## Supplier relations

The plant in Hambach was in every sense a greenfield. The car was novel, supplier relations had to be built up, the plant was completely new, and even the organisation and its staff had been built from scratch. Therefore, the building of supplier relations was not saddled with history. Following the first crude drawings of the car and its modules, several suppliers were invited to send in competitive bids for product concepts. The concept competition (Konzept-Wettbewerb) resulted in proposals of suppliers with respect to, among other things: the modules in terms of functions, materials, layout, design, etc.; suggested production technologies, processes and location, as well as logistic systems; and target cost.

In developing the supply chain, a detailed supply chain map was developed including descriptions of processes and sub-processes involved, and establishing which company would be solely, partially or informally responsible for each of the 140 assembly activities in the process. To develop the modules, project teams consisting of MCC and selected suppliers worked together and reported to an MCC team coach. The supplier involvement in design was structured within the general product architecture specified by MCC.

Contracts with suppliers are intended to last the entire life cycle of the product, and are based upon single-sourced modules. In line with that principle, the contract with only one supplier has so far been terminated because it could not meet quality standards over a period of time.

The initial rationale for involving suppliers was in fact a financial one. At the time the project was proposed to the Daimler board, the automotive industry had reached the stage of saturation and a (temporarily) stagnating demand, and many automotive companies were busy restructuring their programmes. The go-ahead for the project was based on the relatively low investment costs for Daimler, given the large share contributed by suppliers.

To facilitate communication and the exchange of ideas among staff and partners, a central area of the factory is designed as a meeting room. Its function as 'marketplace' is reinforced by its use for open discussion of problems and for quality management and quality improvement meetings. Furthermore, standardised performance measures for each sub-section of the process are displayed electronically at the 'marketplace', for everyone to see. Measures include assembly line stoppage times, delivery performance, product reclamation and scrap, productivity targets and trends, as well as qualifications of teams/sections along the line. The open architecture of the factory makes quality problems and line-stops clearly visible to clerical employees as well as to assembly workers. Cars that need to be fixed because of quality problems or missing components are parked at the 'marketplace'.

## Questions

*Despite the innovative achievements, MCC management was facing a number of immediate and longer-term issues, centring on how to manage and control the supply chain.*

1 *Why should MCC assemble cars itself when suppliers are already integrated on the site? VW, for example, at its truck plant in Latin America, involves suppliers in assembly, thus further lowering the financial commitment of the OEM. In line with the question whether car makers should assemble cars at all, or should leave this to suppliers, an interesting topic is how to assure a lead over suppliers when these perform most of the value-adding activities and how to maintain an integrated environment. One might reason that suppliers are becoming too 'smart' and might (in a consortium or stand-alone) bypass MCC and gain the lead over the supply chain. The Lear Corporation, for example, is a consortium of suppliers that used to supply car-interior parts to manufacturers and is now beginning to supply entire car interiors and so is becoming increasingly dominant in relations with manufacturers.*

2 *Another problem was how to control and assure performance in the supply chain, not on the basis of ownership but through cooperation with suppliers. MCC is heavily focused on integrating the flow of information between players and levels in the chain, but how should the performance of partners be measured and assured?*

3 *The order to delivery lead-time is generally faster than other manufacturers. However, visiting the Smart user club at **www.thesmartclub.co.uk** revealed such problems as:*

> *'Just picked up my new Smart Pash tonight. Been dead excited all day. However, there were a few things not quite right when I got to Smart Milton Keynes (MK Smart):*

> – *Colour was wrong. I ordered a blue one. Def ordered blue. Car is silver, but I think I prefer the silver one now!!!!*
> – *No CD multi-changer fitted, as ordered. More gutted about this really, I have no tapes at all, so the weekend driving will be listening to crappy radio! MK Smart say they will get me in early next week to have this fitted.*
> – *No velour mats as ordered. They say they had none. Fair point, mats are not essential (unlike CD player!), but they will supply my mats when they are in.*

> *'All in all, I was a little disappointed, but the total handover was very well explained by Giles, and they were very apologetic about the missing bits and bobs.*
> *'I wanted to specify it with Boomerang Red seats, but was told that this would be a special order taking up to 12 weeks (!!) as there is a run on Smarts at the moment. So I accepted a car they already had in stock with Blue seats, but had all the clock/rev counter/speedo/controls with red trims ... and I collected it three weeks later ...'*

*Taking into account that (a) it is possible to have order-specific modules such as dashboards produced at two hours' notice, and (b) the final assembly process* takes less than five hours, why is a response time of two to three weeks such a challenge for MCC?

4 The modular product concept of MCC permits customisation of the product in the dealer channel through logistical postponement. However, at present the final assembly is done at the plant in Hambach. What could be the rationale behind that decision?

# CASE 34

# Chicken Run – the poultry supply chain

Case date
2000

Stephan van Dijk, Jack van der Vorst and Adrie Beulens

## Introduction

At Wings & Legs, a large poultry processor in the Netherlands, the working day starts very early in the morning. Before a single cock-a-doodle has sounded, live chickens are delivered at the processing plant where they are cleaned, processed, packed and stored. The next day, packages of fresh poultry meat are distributed to several large retail distribution centres and a large number of smaller retail stores. In the evening of that second day, many people will enjoy their chicken Tandoori or fried chicken leg. The product is simple and the whole operation seems efficiently executed. However, at the weekly plenary meeting of senior managers, a serious discussion arises. The Sales Manager complains that the delivery performance has decreased in the last couple of months. Moreover, he complains that retailers are less satisfied with the quality of products they receive. Product freshness and product weight have not been according to specifications several times this month. The Operations and Purchase Managers respond with the remark that the sales department makes sales-agreements with retail that cannot be met in such a short time. They want to know in advance information on promotional activity so they can respond more effectively. They want to have better forecasts of future sales so they can match the supply of chicken with the demand for poultry products.

This discussion sounded very familiar to the General Manager. He has already heard the complaints of the senior managers many times. Last year they implemented some major improvements to their production line. It now operates more efficiently, with shorter set-up times and less waste. In addition, the coordination between the sales department and operations has been improved. A new planning system has been set up and more frequent meetings between sales and operations have been initiated. The General Manager wonders if, in the big scheme of things, these improvements actually were effective at all and had any real impact on performance to consumers. He thinks it is time to take a broader perspective on their problem. Flexibility is needed not only in their own operations, but in the whole supply chain, as the processes in their supply chain are so strongly coupled.

## Market developments

The food and retail market that Wings & Legs serves is very dynamic. During recent years, the product assortment of most retailers has increased by a factor of four to five times. A single retail outlet used to store 4000 to 5000 different products; now it has

20 000 to 30 000 different products. Obviously, this has had an effect on the assortment of Wings & Legs itself. It introduced a large number of new fresh poultry products to remain competitive. Poultry meat was packed in more variations and combinations, and processed in many more different ways. It introduced new seasonings and microwaveable ready-meals based on poultry products. Its own assortment grew from 100 different products to 450 different products and product variations.

Although it introduced a large number of original and easy-to-prepare poultry products, most of its turnover was still generated by straightforward commodity poultry products. These commodity products typically have low profit margins. Low cost is, for most food products in the Netherlands, still an absolute market-winning factor. This holds true for the end consumer who buys Wings & Legs' products in retail outlets, and for the retailer, who is the direct customer of Wings & Legs.

One could argue that, because of the growing attention on food safety and the recent outbreaks of animal disease in Europe, guaranteed product quality is becoming more and more a market-winning factor. Wings & Legs is audited many times a year by its customers and by independent food safety and quality organisations. Everybody at Wings & Legs realises that if its food quality and quality management systems are not up to standards, it will be out of business very soon.

## Demand and product characteristics

The demand for poultry products by end consumers shows a very variable pattern and seems unpredictable. This may look strange at first sight, but is explained by the heavy use of promotional activities at the retail stage in the supply chain (which are not always communicated in detail to Wings & Legs). The size of the consumer reaction to a promotion is not easy to predict. If there were no promotional activities, the demand of end consumers actually shows a more or less seasonal pattern, which is relatively predictable. The promotional activities initiated by the larger retail companies place heavy strains on Wings & Legs and the upstream supply chain. An opportunity to level demand is to eliminate all promotional activities. However, this encounters much resistance from the retail companies involved; promotions of poultry products are a favourite instrument for competitors to bring in new customers. Meat products are the most expensive components of evening meals, and a reduction of sales price is therefore very appealing to consumers.

In addition, the poultry processor itself initiates promotional activities. This is, in most cases, motivated by the need to sell overproduction of products. Overproduction of specific poultry products will always occur, because the demand for the different component poultry products is not equal or 'balanced'. Wings, chicken breast and legs are all part of the same chicken but demand for each product is not the same most of the time.

An important characteristic of fresh poultry products is 'product perishability'. Processed poultry stays fresh for a limited number of days, after which the quality deteriorates and the products are not allowed to be sold for human consumption. Product freshness is an important performance indicator in the poultry supply chain. Retail companies demand the highest product freshness possible. One can see that there exists a strong relationship between product freshness, lead-times and inventory turnaround. If turnaround is low and lead-times are long, the chance of product obsolescence increases. All products of which the best-before date has been exceeded are written off and sold to downstream food-processing industries for a lower price.

Furthermore, the end of the supply chain is characterised by very short required lead-times (retail companies demand a delivery time of between 18 and 48 hours). Retail companies place their orders every day and products are delivered on a high frequency (many times per week). Because of the small lead-times, stock is held at the poultry processor. The required service levels for poultry products are high. The poultry processor has to comply with a minimum delivery reliability of 99 per cent, even in the case of promotions.

## Supply characteristics

The supply chain of Wings & Legs can be characterised as a chain of strongly interconnected processes with minimal possibilities for buffering of products and materials. This is caused by the nature of the 'product' exchanges in the supply chain. At the hatchery, eggs are hatched during three weeks and the newborn chickens are immediately transported to the broiler houses. At the broiler houses, chickens are fattened over nine weeks and, when reaching the agreed delivery date or specified weight, delivered to the poultry processor. Because the 'goods flow' in this supply chain concerns *living* chickens, processes cannot be buffered very easily and short-term coordination is of utmost importance. The average lead-times of each phase in the production of chickens and poultry products are shown in Figure 34.1.

The chickens supplied by the broiler houses have to comply with specific quality characteristics. Chickens have to be from certain races, of a specific weight, fattened with high-quality certified feed, and fattened according to several quality systems

**Figure 34.1 Overview of Wings & Legs' supply chain**

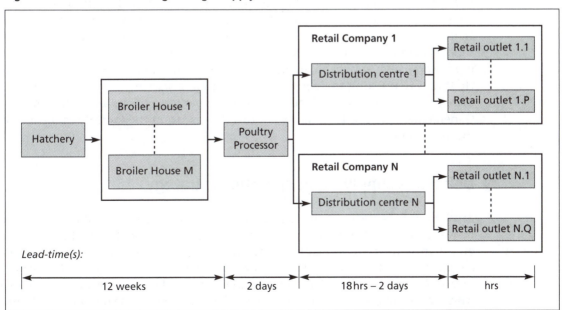

(such as HACCP (Hazard Analysis and Critical Control Points) and the Dutch Integral Chain Control policy for poultry). Only broiler houses and hatcheries that comply with these quality specifications are allowed to supply Wings & Legs. These high-quality specifications are necessary to guarantee the food safety of the consumer product. The number of certified broiler houses and hatcheries that are able to supply to Wings & Legs is therefore limited.

Because of the longer lead-times upstream of the poultry supply chain, the planned volume of supply is not easily changed. If estimated demand exceeds the planned supply it is possible to purchase chickens from other broiler houses, but only if they are able to comply with the mentioned quality specifications. Another option is for Wings & Legs to purchase finished poultry products from other poultry processors. Most of the time these products have to be repacked and have different quality characteristics with regard to weight and processing procedures. These different quality characteristics sometimes give rise to complaints from the retail companies. However, the purchase of finished poultry product from other processors does not have the disadvantage of overproduction of divergent poultry products at Wings & Legs itself.

## Matching supply and demand

In short, demand uncertainty is relatively high. As a result, the need for production capacity, and thus the need for raw materials (living chickens) fluctuates. The production capacity itself is planned for maximum utilisation (to keep production costs per kg of product as low as possible) resulting in low production flexibility. Finally, the supply of certified chickens from suppliers has to be planned 12 weeks ahead because of the duration of the hatching and fattening stages. The potential for buffering and inventory storage is limited in the supply chain since the quality of the supply of chickens and of the consumer products will deteriorate.

The General Manager and all other employees of Wings & Legs are faced with the above-mentioned characteristics of market supply and demand every day. For the General Manager it is clear that a better match of supply and demand within the supply chain is of central concern. The improvements he is looking for have to fit in the company's supply chain and in an overall supply chain operations strategy. He thinks that taking the whole supply chain as a starting point for the analysis prevent a narrow-minded focus on local company problems and solutions. The General Manager wants to find solutions that are from the 'outside in' instead of the 'inside out'.

## Defining a supply chain operations strategy

At Wings & Legs, the General Manager and the other managers find it hard to choose between a lean and an agile strategy. During the last couple of years they have predominantly focused on leanness and efficiency improvements. However, their commodity poultry products do not show a relatively stable demand, as already mentioned. On the contrary, demand is relatively unpredictable and shows similarity with the demand pattern of innovative products. Moreover, the importance of product availability is increasing as relative shelf-space in the retail outlets is becoming smaller and the total assortment in the outlet has grown enormously. They realise that responsiveness is needed in their supply chain, but that physical costs and quality are still of utmost importance due to low profit margins Maybe a combination of a lean and agile operations strategy, a so-called hybrid strategy, is the solution?

A hybrid supply chain operations strategy means that part of the supply chain adopts a lean approach and the other part is geared towards agility and responsiveness. The challenge for Wings & Legs is to find the right combination of leanness and agility. The General Manager understands that a central notion in a hybrid 'lean and agile' strategy is the supply chain decoupling point. Processes upstream from this decoupling point could focus on leanness; processes downstream from the decoupling point could focus on agility.

He starts to consider two types of decoupling points. First, the *information decoupling point* (IDP) – this represents the furthest point to which information on real final demand penetrates the supply chain. Upstream from the IDP, processes could be forecast driven and based on planning; downstream processes could be demand driven and based on real-time demand. The idea here is that the IDP should lie as far as possible upstream in the supply chain.

Second, there's the *material decoupling point* (MDP), at which strategic inventory is held in as generic a form as possible. This is closely related to the concept of 'postponement', or 'delayed configuration'. By delaying product differentiation, one delays as far as possible the moment when different product versions assume their unique identity, thereby gaining the greatest possible (mix) flexibility in responding to changing consumer demands. This resembles the production control situation 'assemble to order' – the fabrication process is standardised and the assembly and distribution processes are customised. Postponement is based on the principle of seeking to design products using common platforms, components or modules but where the final assembly or customisation does not take place until the final market destination and/or customer requirement is known. Downstream from the MDP, products or goods are differentiated to specific customers or markets. Upstream from this point (production) processes are 'generic', which means no customer or market-specific attributes or value is added to the products. Ideally the MDP should lie downstream in the supply chain and as close to the final marketplace as possible.

Finding a good location of the material decoupling point is, according to the General Manager, of central importance to the solution of the problems at Wings & Legs. Delaying the point of product differentiation could solve a part of its matching problem because in several cases the amount of raw material supplied seemed sufficient, but the wrong amount of product variants had been produced and demand could not be met. Because of the divergent product structure of poultry products, opportunities for *postponement* seem obvious: the divergent structure naturally offers 'modular and common components'. Moreover, taking a closer look at the current information decoupling point and information exchange in its supply chain could generate several improvement opportunities it would not have identified before.

## Postponement and the material decoupling point

At Wings & Legs, several customer and consumer-specific product variants are produced. The end consumer has the choice between several volume variants at the retail outlet. For instance, he or she can choose between 4, 6 or 10 chicken legs in a pack (three product variants). Moreover, each retail company has its own specifically labelled and packaged poultry products (private labels). So, the two customer/market-specific attributes that will be addressed are 'retail-specific label variant' and 'consumer-specific volume variant'. Two production processes are related to these attributes:

1 The packaging process, at which a specific number of components, for example chicken legs, are combined into one pack (or stock-keeping unit).
2 The labelling process, at which a retailer-specific label is printed and attached to each product.

The position of the MDP relative to these processes could be in one of three places, as shown in Figure 34.2.

The processed semi-finished poultry products are perishable. This means that products can only be held in stock for a limited time span before they become non-consumable, or obsolete. The vacuum packaging of semi-finished components in very small batches extends the lifetime of these components. When components are stored together in large batches (not vacuum packed), quality deteriorates much faster and the risks of cross-contamination increase, for example, the spread of salmonella bacteria. At this time, the costs associated with advanced forms of meat storage which do not have the above-mentioned drawbacks are too high compared to the costs associated with reduced mix flexibility of strategic inventory. These quality and cost constraints also apply to the postponement of the packaging or labelling process further downstream – to the distribution centre, for instance. Moreover, packaging of fresh poultry products at the distribution centre requires an advanced production line in a low-temperature environment. This is only feasible if more fresh meat products are packaged at the distribution centre (for reasons of economies of scale).

## Improving information exchange in the supply chain

As stated before, the information decoupling point concerns the most *recent* undistorted information about *past* sales. Downstream of the IDP each stage in the supply chain has the same view on marketplace demand, and is able to coordinate its distribution and production activities accordingly. The difference between IDP information and actual end consumer orders is important – there are two alternative positions of the IDP, as shown in Figure 34.3.

The enhanced information exchange about past sales (Situation 1 shown in Figure 34.3) could benefit Wings & Legs and its supply chain. However, the exchange of information about past sales only is probably not enough to accomplish major improvements. As a large part of total demand is generated by promotional activities, longer-term information about future promotions, but also about category management decisions at the retail outlets concerning the product assortment, needs to be communicated to Wings & Legs at an earlier stage and on a more structural basis. Cooperation between retail companies and Wings & Legs on promotional activities should be extended. The information about promotions and category management can be characterised as middle-term tactical information in the supply chain. This information tells a lot about the tactical movements of the retail companies and therefore has to be handled with great care.

**Figure 34.2 Postponement options at Wings & Legs**

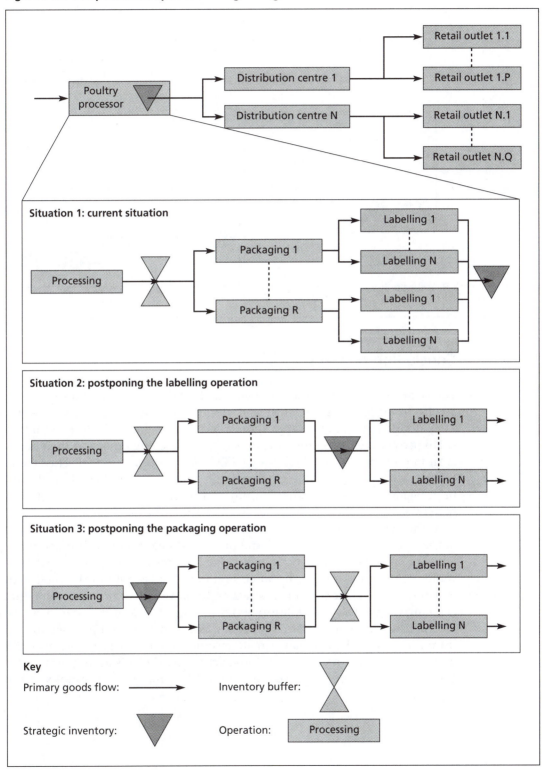

**Figure 34.3 Information exchange in the poultry supply chain**

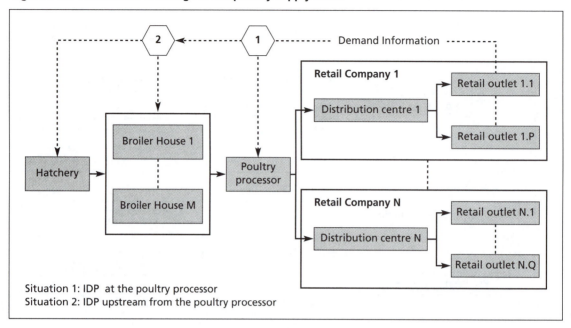

Situation 1: IDP at the poultry processor
Situation 2: IDP upstream from the poultry processor

### ● Concluding remarks

The General Manager and senior managers find the first explorations of designing an effective supply chain strategy and supply chain improvements very promising. They decide that Wings & Legs should continue to find solutions from a supply chain perspective. Postponing the packaging or labelling process in their operations is an important option which they will work out in more detail. The Operations and Logistics Manager will form a project team that will address these details. The improvement of the exchange of information in the supply chain will be given high by sales and operations managers throughout the organisation.

At the plenary meeting, the above mentioned findings are presented. At the end of the meeting everybody has his and her own thoughts and doubts about the proposed improvements. Everybody agrees that a supply chain operations strategy that combines the lean and agile paradigms is most feasible, but how to implement this is still not very clear to some managers. In particular, the improvement of the exchange of tactical information about promotions does not seem very easy to accomplish. The General Manager acknowledges this and wants to set up a project team with one of the company's main customers to explore in more detail how to improve the planning of promotional activities. He feels an important step has been made in developing a cost-efficient, high-quality and responsive poultry supply chain.

## Questions

1 *How might Wings & Legs combine a lean and an agile approach in its supply chain?*

2 *What are the relative merits of each possible position of the material decoupling point and of the information decoupling point. How do they relate to each other with respect to supply chain planning and control?*

3 *Most managers of Wings & Legs see the exchange of tactical information about (price) promotions between Wings & Legs and the retail companies as difficult to accomplish. What are the advantages for the retail companies of exchanging more timely and more accurate information about promotions with Wings & Legs?*

4 *The network-based approach of an agile operations strategy could solve part of the matching problem for Wings & Legs. In supply chain management much attention is paid to improvement of the* vertical *processes in a supply chain. However, Wings & Legs also outsource part of production (they buy poultry products from other poultry processors) which means that* horizontal *processes and* horizontal *cooperation are of importance.*

   (a) *What advantages are there for Wings & Legs in outsourcing part of their production to other poultry processors? What advantages are there for these other poultry processors?*

   (b) *How should Wings & Legs outsource part of production to other poultry processors, with respect to production planning, quality control and product specifications?*

5 *The information decoupling point only concerns information about changes in demand and market. This is information that flows upstream in the supply chain. In the poultry supply chain, living chickens and perishable products are exchanged. Wings & Legs therefore not only have to take into account variations in demand, but also variations in supply. What information should flow downstream in the supply chain (to the poultry processor) so that Wings & Legs is able to match supply with demand in a better way?*

# Marsden Community Stores

Keith Moreton

## ● Background

Marsden Stores is a £480m turnover regional 'community' grocery chain (see Appendix 35.1) with 215 outlets located in the villages and suburbs of major towns and cities along the M6 motorway corridor in England – from Walsall in the west Midlands to Lancaster in the north-west. Marsden's national market share of predominantly food retailing is quite small (approximately 0.8 per cent), however, its regional market share in the Midlands and north-west approaches 1.5 per cent (see Appendix 35.2).

Store sizes range from 600ft$^2$ to 16000ft$^2$ sales area, with the average store size being approximately 6500ft$^2$. There are a number of Marsden Store formats:

- *Community Supermarkets* – These compete for 'primary' shoppers and they range in size from 9000ft$^2$ to 16000ft$^2$. However, none of them fall within the 'superstore' definition – stores with retail areas of 25000ft$^2$ to 50000ft$^2$ – and consequently they are not intended to compete with the mainstream supermarkets such as Sainsbury or Tesco. These stores stock almost the full Marsden range of 16000 product lines plus a limited range of consumer durables.
- *Community Convenience Stores* – These are located in high streets and have petrol forecourts. Marsden has 30 of these stores in its portfolio. All are co-branded stores – the Marsden brand and the brands of major petroleum companies.
- *Community Village Stores* – These are located in small rural communities to serve everyday shopping needs and represent some of the smallest stores in the company.
- *Metropolitan Community Range* – These are almost all located in and around Liverpool and Manchester. These stores supply ethnic products, convenience foods and food for immediate consumption such as sandwiches. The format is similar to the Tesco 'Metro' Stores.

The stores are mostly located within 'cohesive' communities which the major chains such as Tesco, Safeway, Morrison and Sainsbury are not really interested in. This 'niche' strategy was formulated in 1984 by Duncan Marsden, the founder and currently the Chairman and Managing Director of the chain.

Prior to this, in the late 1970s and early 1980s, the Marsden chain had, inadvertently, positioned itself in almost direct competition with the really 'big boys' such as ASDA, Sainsbury, Tesco and the emerging, but relatively large, Morrison chain. This was a 'no-win' situation for Marsden and although volume was growing at the time, it did not match that of the predominant chains. In addition, the company did not have the same purchasing power or economies of scale as these larger organisations and as a consequence it was being forced into 'price competition' and its margins were being eroded.

Price was, and still is, regarded as important, but Marsden does not compete on price alone: convenience (stores are open from 7.30 a.m. to 10.00 p.m.), location and an adequate product range were seen as major criteria for maintaining customer loyalty.

Whether by luck or judgement, the change of direction proved to be fairly successful and Duncan always insisted that several events during the 1990s proved the efficacy of the strategy which was implemented and developed from 1984 onwards, for example:.

- The near bankruptcy of ASDA in 1992 was the result of ill-timed, highly geared growth in order to capture trade from the market leaders, Tesco and Sainsbury.
- The start of the decline, in 1994, of KWIK SAVE, the discount grocery chain with over 1000 stores. It was being 'out discounted' by the new 'super discounters' such as Aldi and Netto and the mainstream chains, whose prices were as good as KWIK SAVE but who also had larger product ranges and superior economies of scale.
- The bankruptcy, in 1993, of the Isosceles group following the highly geared (£2.1bn) takeover of the Somerfield and Gateway chains in 1989.

As the 1990s unfolded there were major structural changes in the supermarket industry, which intensified price competition. To begin with, there were the 'store wars' which were precipitated by Tesco in 1994/95. More recently, in 1999, the takeover of ASDA by the American giant, Wal-Mart, has intensified price wars, as ASDA now has access to the enormous global resources and supply chains of Wal-Mart. All this led to unprecedented food price deflation during the period 1995–2001, putting increasing pressure on supermarket margins.

Even though Marsden had no intention of competing on price alone, it was not immune to price pressures and as early as 1997 was taking initiatives to reduce its cost base, including supply chain costs. The latter involved a deliberate policy of 'leaning out' the product range through a combination of product and supplier rationalisation.

The purchasing function was also centralised and distribution was consolidated into a 60 000ft$^2$ ambient grocery distribution centre which supplies all outlets. Prior to 1997 there had been three smaller distribution centres. The distribution centre stocks approximately 16 000 product lines. This is a significant reduction from the 20 000 lines which were stocked in 1997. Because of the wide variety of stores in the chain, not every line at the distribution centre is displayed in all outlets, of course. The distribution centre is also strategically located in North Cheshire which is close to the junction of the M6 and M62 motorways and is almost at the geographic centre of the chain.

## Mary Johnson and the malt whisky issue

Mary Johnson, the Purchasing Director on the management board of Marsden Stores, had experienced, as usual, a very busy day. It was 6.30 p.m. now and she had just completed a very successful negotiation with a major spirits supplier. She had squeezed a £5 reduction in price per bottle to fund a promotional offer of own-brand malt whisky. This was something of a breakthrough: up until now the maximum a supplier would fund in this category was '£3 off'. There was, however, a quid pro quo – Mary had agreed to offer more volume to the supplier and this involved a further reduction in suppliers. Nevertheless, this perfectly fitted the overall rationalisation policy and the 'slimming' of the malt whisky range. She had also anticipated this deal and had made provisional arrangements with marketing to assess the sales effectiveness of the offer when it went on the shelves in June 2001.

Mary had worked for Marsdens for 15 years since leaving university with a first degree in mathematics and philosophy ('What a combination,' she often thought). However, qualifications do not provide a short cut up the greasy pole of promotion in grocery retailing. Mary was no exception: she had started off on the checkouts, worked in almost every type of store at Marsden and in almost every department. Ten years ago her hard work and eagerness to improve her qualifications started to pay off: she had been continually promoted, from Senior Supervisor to Store General Manager to Area Manager. Then in 2000 she was promoted to the management board, which was only a 'heartbeat' from the main board.

At 'thirty something' she had not discontinued her intellectual pursuits; she was an active member of the Chartered Institute of Purchasing and Supply (CIPS) and was a frequent guest speaker at CIPS branches. She not only used these occasions to outline the most contemporary issues relating to purchasing strategy and supply chain management in the industry, but also to obtain feedback from actual and potential Marsden customers. She inevitably conveyed her enjoyment of supermarket retailing – it was 'fast moving' and 'exciting' – but, as she always insisted to her audiences, the industry required meticulous attention to operational detail and routine.

One set of routines which she observed religiously at the end of the working day was to check her voicemail and the intranet. There was nothing on voicemail which was urgent and the intranet was similar: confirmation of vendor rating issues, imminent promotional activities and so forth, all of which she was either actively involved in or aware of.

However, there was one intranet message from 'the boss', Duncan Marsden, and it was marked urgent. 'Better open it up,' she thought. It was also addressed to Michael Wilkes, the Marketing Director on the main board.

---

Dear both of you,

What ARE you up to?

The malt whiskys proposed for the upcoming review would hardly stand up against a Londis store. Offering a paltry seven can't be in line with our strategy of matching the competition. Have you done a gap analysis?

I can't see how this range will attract customers or, more importantly, retain the existing ones. This is one opportunity to improve the whisky fixture, please let's not miss out on it.

I know we have a rationalisation policy, but isn't this taking it too far?

Wanna see you both in the morning.

Regards Duncan (a worried malt aficionado).

---

Mary gasped with surprise and exclaimed: 'But we *agreed* on this weeks ago *and* we did a gap analysis with the other major stores. And there is another error,' she thought. 'You're not a "malt aficionado"; your favourite tipple is a cup of tea.'

It had been agreed a month earlier that the malt whisky range should be reduced from seventeen to seven lines. The seven selected were based on the sales value of these lines at Marsden, which closely correlated with value and volume data obtained independently through wine and spirits merchants (see Appendix 35.3). They had also undertaken a competitor stores audit (gap analysis) and the following was reported:

| Multiple grocer | No. of malts in store |
| --- | --- |
| Sainsbury | 20 |
| Safeway | 27 |
| ASDA | 15 |
| Morrison | 26 |

It was no surprise to discover that Morrison had 26 malts on its fixtures. It had, after all, been awarded 'The best supermarket off-licence retailer' for many years. However, it was interesting to note that ASDA, one of the fastest growing multiples, was working with a fairly limited range, especially compared to Morrison. The Marsden buyers who had audited the stores also made the comment that 'Very few, or none, of the products had been 'shopped' in these stores over the duration of the audit'. This suggested that the majority of malts in these stores were, in fact, 'shelf warmers' and they were on the shelf to merchandise the faster-moving products in their range.

## The meeting

Both Mary Johnson and Michael Wilkes were anticipating a roasting from Duncan, but it became clear that malt whisky was not Duncan's only concern, and he was unusually apologetic:

'I'm sorry about the e-mail. I know you've done a gap analysis on the malts and all that, but I'm very worried about all of our offering. The malt reduction was only a catalyst for my concern.

'I know that we've agreed that it's important to reduce supply chain costs, but it's far too easy, as the marketplace becomes more aggressive, to become obsessed with cost cutting at the expense of losing sight of the customer at the end of the chain.

'It seems to me that we're pursuing a range and supply base rationalisation programme as though it was a "fashion accessory", the "flavour of the month", the "in thing". Tell me, is there any hard evidence readily available that this "lean" programme will lead to increased overall sales and profitability and justify our store development plans? Are we chopping down our range on a whim, a piece of received wisdom that's past its sell-by date?

'We've been pursuing the "lean" policy for almost three years now and it's only just occurred to me that no one in the business, including myself, has really analysed the impact that these changes could have on the future of the business."

Michael, who had been with the business almost from the start, knew Duncan very well. When the boss was worried, his arguments become rhetorical and circular. This was happening now and Michael decided to break it:

'When do you want this analysis, Duncan?'

'Yesterday would have been preferable, but tomorrow will do. Go on, tell me that's impossible!' Duncan replied.

Michael considered. 'It is, but would three to four weeks be acceptable?'

'OK, what's your plan?'

Michael was now addressing both Duncan and Mary:

'Mary has already made arrangements with me to audit the sales of the malt whisky fixtures and, if you have no objections Mary, I'd like you to broaden the scope of our audit into a pilot which covers other categories and suppliers – the project would combine supply chain management with marketing. That's "right up your street" isn't it, Mary?'

Mary nodded, not quite sure what she was letting herself in for. Michael continued:

'Very well, if we both come back tomorrow with a plan of action, a set of objectives which addresses your concerns, will that be OK?'

## The project

It was OK. The research proposal was approved the following day. Mary usually disliked being 'volunteered' for any task, but this was a challenging one. Michael Wilkes was a pragmatic 'super marketer'. Nevertheless, he provided clarity of thought in his interpretation of Duncan's worries. Consequently, Mary and Michael had produced the 'aims' of the project very quickly.

The aims of the pilot research were:

- To seek clarity on the ranging policies that the major multiples practise. This would be extremely difficult to achieve because these chains were notoriously 'tight lipped' about their operational activities. Everything was commercially confidential in the supermarket business and Marsden was no exception. Nevertheless, they believed the aim was marginally achievable and that it would either confirm or confound Duncan's worries and scotch any possible future disagreements in the business.
- To identify the advantages of range reduction and examine the theory which supports this principle.
- To establish consumer attitudes towards ranging in general and analyse the extent to which supermarket customers have actually noticed any significant changes at Marsden and other supermarkets over the past two years.
- To examine the relationship between ranging and merchandising of produce, for example, the way in which the display of the products affects purchasing decisions and how this affects category turnover.

## A supply chain approach

To address these aims, a 'supply chain methodology' was to be adopted. The areas and possible types of research are illustrated in Table 35.1.

**Table 35.1  Possible areas for Marsden's pilot research**

| Supply chain research area | Type of research |
| --- | --- |
| Product and customer | Primary customer research |
| Product in store | Perceptions of change and effects of merchandising (primary and secondary research). |
| Competitor policies | Questionnaires to leading retailers and closer study of ranges in the major outlets |
| Internal supply chain:<br>● Warehousing, distribution and delivery<br><br>● Stock control and administration<br>● Buyer and supplier negotiation | Interviews to assess understanding of the rationale for range reduction at Marsden |
| ● Suppliers and product | Discussions with key suppliers and secondary research of suppliers who advocated range reduction |

Mary knew that it was impossible to research each one of these areas of the supply chain in detail if the three to four week deadline was to be met. She therefore decided to concentrate on four major areas:

● Attempt to gain some information about the top supermarket ranging policies through a postal questionnaire and more detailed observation of in-store activities
● General customer attitudes to products and ranging
● Assess attitudes to range reduction inside the company through face-to-face interviews with some key Marsden personnel, for example, in warehousing, general managers of the larger outlets and purchasing staff
● Target suppliers who, in Mary's experience, advocate the practice of range rationalisation and conduct telephone and/or face-to-face interviews with them.

Even this, in the short term, represented a lot of unproductive activity and so she set up a small team from Marketing and Purchasing to undertake some of the 'donkey work'.

## The supermarkets

Mary quickly developed a brief but comprehensive questionnaire (see Appendix 35.4) to be posted to five of the large chains. She was reasonably well known in the industry and she did not expect to receive any responses to these questionnaires. She was tempted to resort to subterfuge by disguising her name, however she discarded this idea – it was a little unethical for a company director and CIPS member. Nevertheless, she posted the questionnaires using her own name, but from her home address with a polite, and truthful, request for information to assist in retailing research. Unsurprisingly, the request for information only elicited two replies from the major supermarkets: Morrison and ASDA.

Morrison apologised and said that due to the confidential nature of the answers required, it was unable to complete the questionnaire. This response was expected, but at least it was a response.

However, ASDA, to Mary's surprise, completed the questionnaire in full. There was a certain amount of ASDA public relations language used, particularly in the qualitative responses on 'Pricing' and 'Range depth'. However, the quantitative responses were more specific. ASDA had reduced the live product lines in an average store over the last five years from 30 000 to 25 000, but this depended on store size – some hypermarkets may carry as many as 40 000 lines. There had also been a corresponding reduction in the supplier base from approximately 2750 five years earlier to approximately 2000. ASDA also apparently attached equal importance to branded, own-label and tertiary brands, but indicated that their importance varied within each category of product.

This appeared to confirm some secondary research which Mary had undertaken. It was apparent that all supermarkets had reduced their ranges. For example, in the annual report of one large chain it claimed to have 27 000 product lines in every store in 1996. However, in 2001 the range was described as 'over 20 000 products'. This subtle change in language suggested that the range had actually been reduced. This appeared to contradict Marsden's own buying intelligence section who asserted that 'ASDA, Tesco and Morrison have in fact increased the number of products in their ranges'.

Had the impact and perception that range rationalisation imposes upon customers been overlooked or was rationalisation a fact? Understanding customer perceptions was Mary's next task.

## Customer perceptions of products and ranging

Mary undertook this research herself. She carried out a survey in Manchester of the first 100 shoppers she came across who were willing to cooperate. The questionnaire used was very brief, but it covered the following areas of buyer behaviour and perceptions:

- Why do you choose certain products?
- How does the variety of your favourite brand category compare to what it was a year ago?
- How 'brand loyal' are you and what would you do if your favourite brand was not in stock?

### Reasons for choosing

The results for this area of research are shown in Table 35.2.

It appeared from the survey that neither price nor special offers played a significant role in a purchase decision. The most important factor, it seemed, was 'favourite brand' (61 per cent) or, possibly, being persuaded by children (20 per cent). When asked, 63 per cent also considered themselves to be 'brand loyal' and 80 per cent of these said that if their normal supermarket did not stock their favourite brand they would shop elsewhere; 50 per cent of these people indicated that they would switch supermarkets permanently if their favourite brand was not available.

**Table 35.2  Reason for choosing certain products**

| Reasons | % |
|---|---|
| Attractive pack | 1 |
| Not tried before | 2 |
| Special offer | 3 |
| Price | 5 |
| Not tried for a while | 8 |
| Kids asked for it | 20 |
| Favourite brand | 61 |

**Table 35.3  Customer perceptions of variety**

| Response | % |
|---|---|
| A lot better variety | 24 |
| A little better variety | 31 |
| The same variety | 39 |
| Variety a little worse | 5 |
| Variety a lot worse | 1 |

### Customer perceptions of variety

The results for this section of the survey are shown in Table 35.3.

Customers were asked: 'How does the variety of your favourite brand category compare with what it was a year ago?'

Just over 50 per cent of the respondents suggested that their favourite brand category was beer. These results were a little surprising because it was well known in the trade that some multiples had significantly reduced the best category range – one by as much as 40 per cent. The majority of respondents in Mary's survey perceived that choice had increased (55 per cent); only six per cent thought choice had deteriorated. Was this because there were more facings of the leading brands on a display fixture – the ones that most customers were looking for? This was another question she would have to address later.

## Internal attitudes to range reduction

The interviews Mary held internally revealed two camps of opposing views on range reduction: those who were for and those against. However, the interviews were not very informative. They tended to confirm Duncan's worry that no one really understood the rationale for range reduction. Those who were for range reduction, even amongst general managers of outlets, could barely provide a 'textbook' argument for rationalisation. A typical response when asked why Marsden encouraged range reduction was '... well, I don't know, we just do it don't we. Everybody does it!' None of these people could provide evidence or cases to support their view.

Most interviewees who could be described as being in the 'anti-rationalisation camp' had 'reservations' about range rationalisation, but were not totally against the principle. A number of managers in this group were concerned that Marsden was cutting back its range too far at the expense of customer choice, but their concerns were based mainly on their own and their families' shopping experiences. However, one general manager in a large store, whilst not being totally critical of rationalisation, was more concerned than the others about Marsden's increasingly 'leaner' operations:

'To be sure, it reduces product duplication and marginally saves manpower requirements at store level. And no doubt that by utilising fewer suppliers we gain economies of scale, it's very probable that scheduling is simpler and we require less space and fewer personnel in the distribution centre. But what about the disadvantages? What if a major supplier fails to deliver? We're stuck with them and we might not have a substitute.

'Using fewer suppliers, I believe, could lead to a reduction in competitive pressures and expose us to supplier opportunism, such as unexpected price increases or deficient quality. In the long run a smaller supply base is an invitation for those in it to become more complacent and less innovative.

'But my real concerns are these. This trade is totally unpredictable, but "lean operations" tend towards rigidity and standardisation. In addition, it almost assumes that our own criteria of cost and quality are the factors which influence customer satisfaction. We don't satisfy customers by eliminating waste (it's invisible to them), but by configuring our range to maximise customer satisfaction.

'Rather than just rationalising the supply base, Marsden should have more flexible relationships with suppliers – a supply base with fluid groups of suppliers who are more "agile" and have a fast response. But I don't know how a second division chain like Marsden can achieve that. I suppose that's "marked my card".'

Mary assured him it hadn't and that interviewee responses would remain anonymous. In fact, she went as far as informing him that he and Duncan Marsden shared similar misgivings. To Mary, the debate between 'agile' versus 'lean' was similar to a non-physicist being able to differentiate between a 'quark' and a 'proton'.

It was also true that with 16 000 product lines in total, Marsden was 'second division' compared with the offerings of the larger superstores. However, the reduction in Marsden's product range over the previous three years seemed to have gone unnoticed by its customers – while Mary had been conducting her research, Marketing had undertaken a 'quick' survey of Marsden customers. The survey revealed that 85 per cent of customers thought that there had been no noticeable changes to the range of products on offer. This closely correlated with her own survey in Manchester.

## Suppliers

At the other end of the supply chain, the principal suppliers, particularly brewers, were keen to support range *and* supplier rationalisation. Competition in this industry was intense with diminishing profit margins, therefore any reduction in range and marginalisation of their own competition was welcome. It was a recipe for greater economies of scale and less competition. They were obviously acting to serve their own best interests, as was Marsden, but was it a 'synergy' of interests?

There were many people – even Mary's CIPS audiences – who believed that buyer/supplier relationships in the industry were one-sided: the supermarket chain had all the power. This simply wasn't true: suppliers were very 'canny' negotiators. They were well aware that the supermarkets *needed* well-advertised brands on their shelves. On the other hand, as much as 90% of a major supplier's production was sold through the fairly concentrated channels of supermarkets. This seemingly well-balanced 'opportunism' was, to Mary, an ideal environment for lean or agile initiatives.

## Product in store – merchandising

Product merchandising and ranging are inextricably linked and Mary believed that the pilot study would be incomplete without some further secondary and, possibly, primary research in this area. She had read a tremendous amount of literature on the subject in trade journals and had access to empirical studies undertaken by large confectionery and brewery companies. In addition, Marsden had also undertaken its own merchandising studies of fast-moving categories in its larger stores.

Most consumer/merchandising research indicated that 60 per cent of shoppers spend 10 seconds or less at a shopping display or fixture. Most, if not all, shopping fixtures have what is known as a 'hot spot' (see Figure 35.1). The hot spot is the area of the fixture that customers are most likely to shop from, quite simply because it is the part of the fixture that is at eye level and is at the centre of the fixture.

To encourage customers to spend more money at a fixture, it is also important to differentiate between brands. The well-known, highly advertised or popular brands should be positioned at, or near, the hot spot. These products yield higher turnover and are usually more profitable. The 'tertiary' products, such as the 'price-fighting,' own-label discount brands should be positioned at the bottom of the shelf or at the right or left-hand extremity of the shelf. The rationale for this is that, although 'tertiary' brands have high volume, they do not yield the same level of profit as premium or well-known brands.

**Figure 35.1 Fixture and theoretical shopping 'hot spot'**

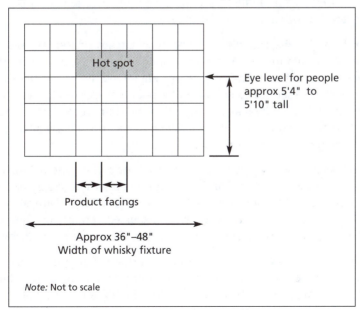

Other display/merchandising principles are also equally important, especially when working with a reduced range. Best-sellers should have multiple facings and be placed on the best sites of the fixture. This simply means giving more space to the best-selling products in order to grow sales. Obviously giving more space to the best-sellers means that an overall category range has to be reduced as retailers do not have elastic shelves. However, the question was: how can the retailer provide visual variety with a rationalised range and simultaneously grow sales?

Fortunately, a large confectionery supplier had published merchandising research it had undertaken in major stores with its own brands. The initial research indicated that an extra facing of a well-known brand would increase sales by between 23 per cent and 25 per cent and that third and fourth facings would grow sales by a further 17 per cent and 13 per cent respectively. To test the research further, the confectionery company chose three of its best-selling brands and persuaded retailers to move these into areas in or near the hot spot. Each of the brands was given one additional facing at the expense of slower sellers, which were removed from the fixture. The 'optimised' fixture provided an overall sales increase of 16 per cent.

Mary thought it would be worth trying out similar principles with the reduced malt whisky range in Marsden's larger stores. She quickly drafted a schematic of the malt whisky fixture as she thought it ought to be. The Marsden 10 year old (which was to be on special offer) was given four facings. Glenfiddich was given two facings (one each for 35cl and 70cl), both at, or near, the hot spot. Both of these products had quite high sales volumes and reasonable profit margins. Glenmorangie was given two facings just below the 'hot spot as it had similar sales and margin to Glenfiddich. The remaining three brands had one facing each. The layout was only a 'rule of thumb' and she also had to leave space on the fixture for three or four of the discontinued brands. The schematic is shown in Figure 35.2.

The following day she explained her logic for the layout to Michael Wilkes. He studied it carefully for about 10 seconds, murmuring a few 'umms' and 'ahhs', but his final reaction was a little unexpected.

'Beat you to it! Our merchandising people have already (yesterday, as a matter of fact) instructed the community supermarket managers to adjust their malt whisky fixtures. The new layout is almost identical to yours. We intend giving it a week to "bed down" and then we'll do a serious comparison of week on week sales this year compared with last year. The results will be available within the four-week time frame we promised Duncan. Perhaps the outcome will calm him down a little. I'll e-mail them to you at the close of trading on Sunday, 10th June.'

Two weeks later Mary was attempting to draw some conclusions from the pilot research, in her own time, on Sunday, 10th June. It was necessary to distil them into a series of bullet points for a very brief executive summary – Duncan wouldn't read a 'tome'. He insisted that major issues were discussed verbally but he expected everyone to be armed with 'the facts'. She commenced with the less controversial issues:

● Experience, and all the evidence, indicates that the major chains were all reducing their product ranges and, by implication, the number of suppliers.
● Supplier rationalisation has some obvious benefits in terms of reducing supply chain costs, which will not disadvantage us.

**Figure 35.2 Schematic of malt whisky fixture**

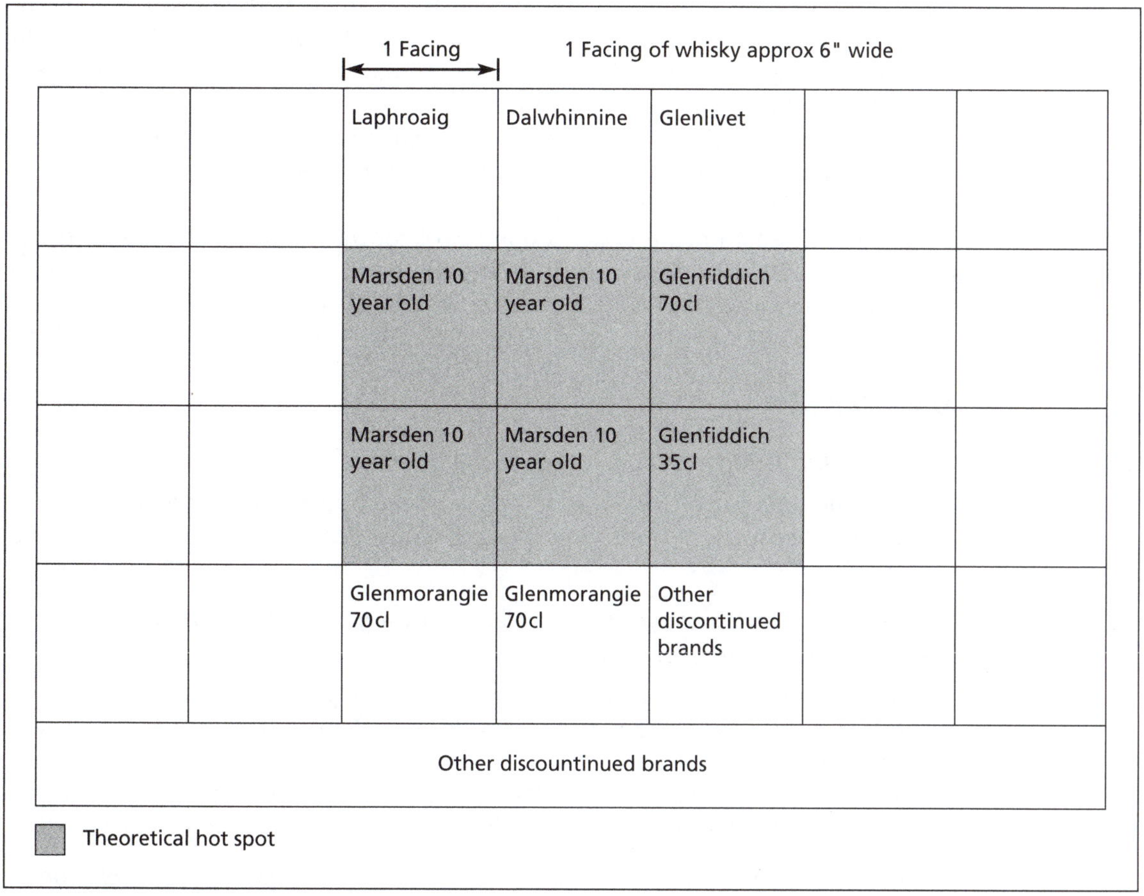

| | | | 1 Facing | 1 Facing of whisky approx 6" wide | | |
|---|---|---|---|---|---|---|
| | | Laphroaig | Dalwhinnine | Glenlivet | | |
| | | Marsden 10 year old | Marsden 10 year old | Glenfiddich 70 cl | | |
| | | Marsden 10 year old | Marsden 10 year old | Glenfiddich 35 cl | | |
| | | Glenmorangie 70 cl | Glenmorangie 70 cl | Other discontinued brands | | |
| Other discountinued brands | | | | | | |

▨ Theoretical hot spot

- There was very little understanding of the rationale for range reduction in the company (this raised other issues such as communication and education in the company).
- Customers appeared to believe that choice had increased. Was this the result of 'smart' merchandising by supermarkets?
- All the evidence of consumer and retailing economics indicated that consumers were price sensitive, but was price the only consideration in a purchasing decision or for shopping in a particular store? Most consumers cited 'favourite brand' as the major reason for choice. Therefore, is price a 'qualifying criterion' and brand availability the 'order winner'?

The last two issues might be clarified a little by the figures for malt whisky sales from the new layout fixtures. These were due in.

Mary opened her e-mail and sure enough Michael Wilkes had delivered his promise. The EPOS (electronic point of sale) data for sales of the malt whisky category were on the screen (see Appendix 35.5). The results were impressive. Malt whisky sales for the first week of June 2001 had increased by more than 90 per cent compared with the same period in the previous year – from 212 to 392 bottles. However, on closer examination the results were inconclusive. The Marsden own-brand malt whisky, which was on special offer, had increased volume by 800 per cent – at the expense of the branded malts whose volume had dropped to approximately 20 per cent of sales in the same period in 2000. Duncan and Michael would certainly be delighted with the overall sales results, but this would be short-lived. The offer was only running for three weeks.

It was obvious that the results had been 'polluted' by the own-brand offer and Mary cursed herself for not comparing like with like. She would now have to investigate the effect on sales of previous offers in the malt whisky category or other categories.

Her earlier research had revealed a number of contradictions, but the latest information only added to the confusion. She doubted the reliability of the whole project and she was certain it would not address the Chairman's concerns.

### Questions

1 *Evaluate the validity of the pilot research undertaken by Marsden. For example:*
   - *Was the supply chain orientation of the research sufficiently rigorous?*
   - *What other sources of information could have been explored in the timescale required?*

2 *What factors influence your own selection of a grocery retailer? Rank these as either 'order winning' or 'order qualifying' factors.*
   - *Do you believe that your own preferences can be generalised to a wider population or do you believe that Mary Johnson's research reveals your own preferences?*
   - *What are the implications of Mary Johnson's research in terms of Marsden's performance objectives for its own internal and external supply chain?*

3 *In the case study there is a brief debate between 'lean' versus 'agile' operations.*
   - *Is 'agile' merely a rebranding of 'lean' ideas, as some authors suggest, or are there any real differences in the two approaches?*
   - *What are the advantages and disadvantages of lean operation in the context of grocery retailing?*

4 *It is sometimes argued that the supermarkets have developed new paradigms for effective supply chain management which many organisations in non-food manufacturing are attempting or would dearly love to emulate.*
   - *What aspects of supermarket supply chains would these manufacturers 'dearly love to emulate' and why?*
   - *What are the performance standards, both qualitative and quantitative, which make supermarket benchmarking such an attractive proposition for manufacturers outside the food industry?*

## Appendix 35.1

### Marsden Community Stores
### Five-year summary of financial results (£000)

|                                    | 2001     | 2000     | 1999     | 1997     | 1996     |
|------------------------------------|----------|----------|----------|----------|----------|
| Turnover including VAT             | 480050   | 454200   | 442190   | 340100   | 324080   |
| VAT                                | 33100    | 31400    | 30000    | 20100    | 17800    |
| Turnover excluding VAT             | 446950   | 422800   | 412190   | 320000   | 306280   |
| Gross profit                       | 59080    | 53070    | 50010    | 37500    | 34200    |
| Operating profit                   | 19000    | 16305    | 16060    | 11800    | 9900     |
| Profit before tax                  | 17295    | 14605    | 12860    | 9320     | 7650     |
| Fixed assets                       | 155100   | 148100   | 145100   | 118000   | 109600   |
| Current assets:                    |          |          |          |          |          |
| Stock                              | 30400    | 32080    | 31100    | 21500    | 18300    |
| Cash                               | 13500    | 10500    | 9000     | 10500    | 10200    |
| Net current assets (liabilities).  | [16800]  | [19100]  | [23800]  | [9000]   | [8500]   |

## Appendix 35.2

### National and regional market share and turnover of UK grocery chains

|                              | 1996 | | 2000 | | Regional market share north-west and Midlands of England | |
|------------------------------|-----------------------|----------------|-----------------------|----------------|-----------|-----------|
| Company                      | UK market share %     | Turnover £bn   | UK market share %     | Turnover £bn   | 1995 %    | 1999 %    |
| Tesco UK                     | 14.2                  | 11.56          | 16                    | 17.00          | 12.6      | 16.2      |
| J Sainsbury UK               | 12.2                  | 10.91          | 12                    | 12.35          | 12.8      | 14.7      |
| Safeway                      | 7.7                   | 6.07           | 8                     | 8.30           | 5.8       | 7.2       |
| ASDA (Wal-Mart)              | 7.7                   | 6.04           | 8.8                   | ND             | 12.4      | 16.2      |
| Somerfield                   | 4.2                   | 3.16 ⎫         | 6.0                   | 5.90           | 5.0 ⎫     | 5.6       |
| Kwik Save                    | 4.3                   | 3.51 ⎭         |                       |                | 4.5 ⎭     |           |
| Marks & Spencer (Food UK)    | 3.3                   | 2.85           | 4.4                   | 3.20           | ND        | ND        |
| Wm Morrison                  | 2.6                   | 2.10           | 4.3                   | 3.10           | 5.7       | 7.1       |
| Waitrose                     | 1.8                   | 1.38           | 1.7                   | 2.00 approx    | NA        | NA        |
| Iceland                      | 1.6                   | 1.20           | 1.6                   | 1.90           | ND        | ND        |
| Marsden                      | 0.4                   | 0.32           | 0.7                   | 0.45           | 1.1       | 1.3       |

Notes:
NA = not applicable (do not operate in Midlands and north-west).
ND = no data (for example, ASDA accounts are consolidated in those of Wal-Mart).

Sources: Mintel, The Grocer, Taylor Nelson Sofres, Company Accounts and best estimates by the author based on declared sales areas.

## Appendix 35.3

## Marsden malt range pre and post-review

| Pre-review | MAT[a] – % | Post-review | MAT[a] – % |
|---|---|---|---|
| Lagavulin 70cl | 3.0 | Marsden 10 year old[b] | 11.0 |
| Laphroaig 70cl | 4.1 | Dalwhinnie 70cl | 2.0 |
| Macallan 70cl | 4.8 | Glenfiddich 70cl ⎫ | 23.0 |
| Oban 70cl | ND | Glenfiddich 35cl ⎭ | |
| Aberlour 70cl | ND | Glenlivet 70cl | 5.8 |
| Marsden 10 year old[b] | 11.0 | Glenmorangie 70cl | 17.0 |
| Highland Park 70cl | ND | Laphroaig 70cl | 4.1 |
| Cragganmore 70cl | ND | | |
| Dalwhinnie 70cl | 2.0 | | |
| Glenfiddich 35cl ⎫ | 23.0 | | |
| Glenfiddich 70cl ⎭ | | | |
| Glenlivet 70cl | 5.8 | | |
| Glenkinchie 70cl | ND | | |
| Glenmorangie 70cl | 17.0 | | |
| Glenmorangie 35cl | 17.0 | | |
| Glen Ord 70cl | ND | | |
| Knockando 70cl | ND | | |

Notes:
[a] MAT = moving average total of market share by value [data for December/January 2000]. MAT values are based on data supplied by wines and spirits merchants.
[b] The MAT value for Marsden 10-year-old malt is based on data for own-brand sales across the UK.
ND = No Market Share data available.

## Appendix 35.4

## Multiple questionnaire for a retailing project

**1** If possible, briefly outline your ranging strategy in the following areas:

Pricing     _____

_____

_____

Demographics    _____

_____

_____

Regional variances   _____

_____

_____

Range depth    _____

_____

_____

**2** Please indicate the importance of each part of your range by awarding the following categories with marks out of 10 – 10 being most important.

(a) Brand    _____
(b) Own label   _____
(c) Tertiary   _____

**3** Approximately how many live product lines do you have listed in total? _____
**4** How many were listed two years ago?   _____
**5** How many were listed five years ago?   _____
**6** How many were listed 10 year ago?   _____
**7** Approximately how many suppliers are on your supplier base?   _____
**8** How many did you use two years ago?   _____
**9** How many did you use five years ago?   _____
**10** How many did you use 10 year ago?   _____
**11** Which three aspects do you consider to be most important when selecting a supplier? Please indicate on a scale of 1 to 10 where 1 = unimportant and 10 = very important.

| Price | _____ | Product quality | _____ |
| Trading terms | _____ | Past performance | _____ |
| | | Promotional support | _____ |

Other – please state _____

## Appendix 35.5

### EPOS sales by quantity
### Category: malt whisky

| First week June 2000 | | First week June 2001 | |
| --- | --- | --- | --- |
| **Brand** | **Sales** | **Brand** | **Sales** |
| Glenfiddich 70cl | 7 | Glenfiddich 70cl | 7 |
| Glenfiddich 35cl | 31 | Glenfiddich 35cl | 13 |
| Glenlivet 70cl | 12 | Glenlivet 70cl | 12 |
| Glenmorangie 35cl | 29 | Macallan 70cl | 4 |
| Aberlour 70cl | 16 | Glenmorangie 70cl | 7 |
| Highland Park 70cl | 1 | Glenmorangie 35cl | 28 |
| Knockando 70cl | 1 | Marsden 10 year old | 313 |
| Laphroaig 70cl | 40 | Laphroaig 70cl | 1 |
| Macallan 70cl | 23 | Dalwhinnie 70cl | 3 |
| Glen Ord Malt 70cl | 2 | Other brands | 4 |
| Glenkinchie 70cl | 0 | **Total** | 392 |
| Cragganmore 70cl | 1 | | |
| Glenmorangie 70cl | 6 | | |
| Lagavulin 70cl | 1 | | |
| Dalwhinnie 70cl | 2 | | |
| Marsden 10 year old | 39 | | |
| Oban 70cl | 1 | | |
| **Total** | 212 | | |

# Supply chain relationships: Wheatco Ltd and Chemco Ltd (A)

Marie Koulikoff-Souviron, Alan Harrison and Jaques Colin

Wheatco and Chemco are two US-owned corporations that have much in common. Both are in the chemical industry, both are leaders in their chosen activities and both are of similar size (around $2bn in sales). Their culture is close, centred on quality of products and services, safety and profit. Ten years ago, the two companies decided to form a partnership with the strategic objective of gaining competitive advantage through mutual access to low-cost raw materials.

One of the outcomes of this partnership was the establishment in the UK of two units of a large Wheatco plant of 700 employees combined with a small Chemco facility of just 70 employees. The division between Chemco and the Wheatco plants was marked only by a fence, with selected employees being able to pass freely by means of swipe card access. The two firms form a 'closed' supply chain, whereby they are customer of, and supplier to, each other.

The Chemco plant was built in 1991. It is dedicated to the production of a chemical additive called 'A1' used in the production of rubbers, paints and other compositions. The feedstock used in the Chemco process is manufactured by Wheatco. The manufacturing process of the additive A1 generates a gas, 'B3', as by-product, which is recycled back into the Wheatco feedstock process. The supply chain 'loop' is illustrated in Figure 36.1.

**Figure 36.1 Outline of the production process**

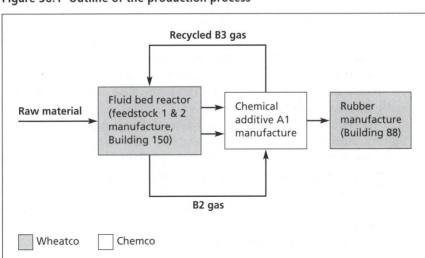

**Figure 36.2 Chemco organisation chart (additive A1 supply chain)**

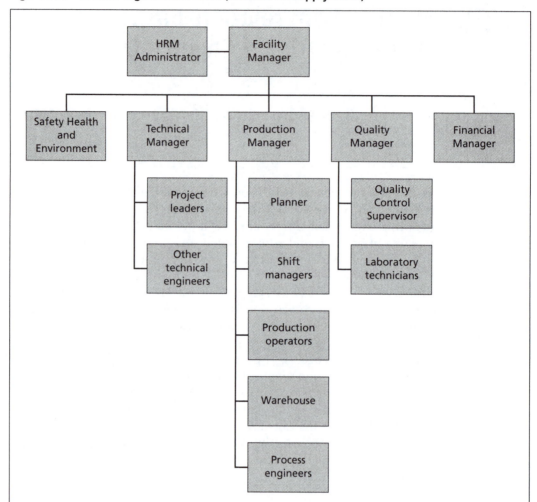

Half of the additive A1 made on the Chemco site is sold to Wheatco, and the rest to other customers in Europe and the USA. World capacity for A1 is limited, so Chemco can sell all that it can make. Capacity was extended in 1996 from 8000 to 13 000 tonnes. Another extension project is under discussion, which would bring Chemco capacity up to 20 000 tonnes within the next two years. Figure 36.2 shows the Chemco organisation chart.

The Wheatco plant is the largest plant in the world, and comprises 15 production areas. The production unit which supplies the feedstock to Chemco (Building 150) is located in the largest area, where about 100 people are employed. Figure 36.3 shows the Building 150 organisation chart. Only Unit 1 produces the additive A1. This area is geographically at the opposite end of the site from the rubber manufacturing area (Building 88), which is Chemco's customer. The two areas belong to different strategic business units (SBUs). Building 150 is in the Basic Chemicals SBU, and Building 88 is part of Specialities SBU. Figure 36.4 shows the Building 88 organisation chart.

**Figure 36.3  Basic Chemicals area organisation chart**

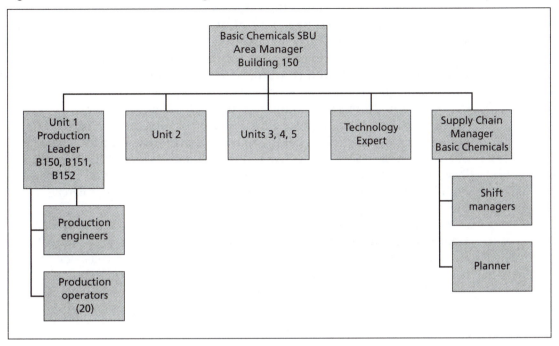

**Figure 36.4  Specialities area organisation chart**

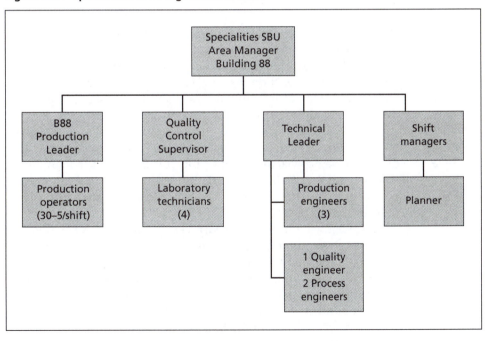

There is very little interaction between employees of these two units, although their Area Managers have regular meetings at site management level.

In order to avoid unnecessary investment, Wheatco supplies Chemco's utilities – such as water, electricity and compressed air. Wheatco also handles Chemco's waste products. Similarly, the overall costs for the Wheatco–Chemco partnership are reduced to a minimum with very little buffer stock both upstream (Building 150 to Chemco) and downstream (Chemco to Building 88). This creates a total interdependence between the members of the 'closed' supply chain.

The structure of the supply chain partnership is multifaceted, with interactions taking place at many levels. Locally it includes plant management, engineers and operators. In the USA, an executive contact (Business Manager) has been appointed by each firm in order to manage the relationship at a strategic level, especially in regard to the global contract agreement, which provides the commercial terms for the relationship.

Local management does not perceive the relationship between the two US Business Managers as being very good. Indeed contract negotiations can be a source of conflict as both firms pursue their own interests. At local level, however, collaboration appears necessary in order to meet the operational requirements of the joint process. Thus the local relationship is developed independently of corporate involvement. One of the managers said during a meeting: 'we don't understand the big picture: we don't understand the global relationship between Wheatco and Chemco.'

## ● The production process

Wheatco receives raw material from an external supplier. This raw material is a fine powder, which is heated up to 300°C together with the gas B3 supplied by Chemco. The powder is suspended in a fluidised bed reactor in order to allow perfect mixing and an optimum reaction process. The reactor is about 2m diameter and 9m high, with close temperature control. The result of the reaction process is a mixture of three components: feedstock 1, feedstock 2 and another gas, 'B2'.

Next, feedstocks 1 and 2 are purified, refrigerated and condensed into a liquid, which is supplied to Chemco via a pipeline. The B2 gas is also purified, and shipped direct to Chemco via another pipeline. It is important to maintain the ratio of feedstocks 1 and 2 at 40/60. Any variation within this ratio will negatively impact the quality of the additive A1 produced by Chemco. For the same reason, the B2 gas has to be extremely pure.

The rate at which the two feedstocks are produced is key to ensuring that a constant blend is maintained, and hence consistency of the batches of A1. The storage capacity of the feedstock tanks, when they are full, gives Chemco no more than 15 hours of production in the event that the Wheatco process is stopped. At Chemco, the feedstocks are mixed with gas B2 in a high-temperature process in order to produce the additive A1. The additive is a low-density powder, which is stored in silos and blown via pipeline to the Building 88 production unit. Temperature is a critical parameter in the chemical reaction: problems in the reactor can produce overheating, which creates variations in the feedstock, which in turn negatively impacts the quality of the A1 additive. The final properties of the additive A1 are therefore the result of the process control within Chemco as well as within Wheatco.

# Coordination of the supply chain

In keeping with the close product integration of the two companies, interaction within the supply chain takes place at many levels: production operators, engineers, logistics and management. Communication takes place both informally via telephone, e-mail or visits, or formally within inter-organisational team meetings.

## Formal interactions

The formal relationship structure of the local Wheatco/Chemco partnership consists of four teams, with different missions and time horizons, as shown in Table 36.1.

### Logistics Coordination Team

Annual forecasts of demand for the chemical additive A1 are defined contractually. Because of the constraints in world capacity of chemical loading, Chemco operates at full capacity; hence logistics coordination consists essentially of short-term adjustments. Every Monday morning planners from both firms meet on the Wheatco site

**Table 36.1  The Chemco–Wheatco formal relationship structure**

| Team | Objectives/*Measures | Participants | Meeting frequency |
| --- | --- | --- | --- |
| Logistics Coordination Team | Short-term forecasts and production issues <br> * On-time delivery of feedstock and A1 additive; inventory management | Chemco: Planner, shift managers <br> Wheatco: Planner, production engineers Building 150, shift managers Building 150 | Weekly |
| Technical team | Process improvements between Building 150 and Chemco (upstream of the supply chain) <br> * Consistency of feedstock rate <br> * Purity of B2 gas <br> * Less than 12 'trips' per year (reactor shutdowns) | Chemco: Technical Manager, Operations Manager, process engineers <br> Wheatco: Supply Chain Manager Building 88, Building 150 Production Leader, production engineers Building 150 | Every six weeks |
| Quality Improvement Team (QIT) | Quality improvement of chemical loading (downstream of supply chain) <br> * A1 additive quality and variability | Chemco: Production Manager, Quality Manager <br> Wheatco: Rubber production manager, quality engineer and rubber production leader, SC manager (Basics) | Quarterly |
| Steering Committee | Set the direction and tone of the Wheatco/Chemco relationship <br> Define and set performance improvements and metrics <br> Provide guidance to QIT and Technical Team | Chemco: Facility Manager, Production Manager <br> Wheatco: Basic Chemicals Area Manager, Rubber Area Manager, Supply Chain Manager (Basic Chemicals) | Every eight weeks (set up March 2000) |

in order to determine the weekly demand of additive A1 required by Building 88 and by other Chemco customers in order to calculate the weekly feedstock production volumes. Chemco shift managers also attend the meeting, as well as the production engineers from Building 150, in order to discuss coordination of production shut-downs for equipment maintenance.

### Technical team

The Technical Team meets every six weeks and focuses on upstream process improve-ment between Building 150 and Chemco. This involves joint discussion on causes of production shutdowns or variability of feedstock. Implementation of action plans can involve capital investments from one side or another of the process. In the Technical Team, Chemco is identified as Wheatco's customer.

### Quality Improvement Team (QIT)

This team meets on a quarterly basis and includes all members of the supply chain – representatives from the Building 150 production unit, from Chemco and from Building 88. Its aim is to work on long-term quality improvement for the additive A1 supplied to Building 88, together with cost improvements. The QIT emphasises Chemco's role as a supplier of Wheatco.

### Steering Committee

The Steering Committee was formed in March 2000. Its members are, for Chemco, the plant manager and the operations manager, and for Wheatco the supply chain manager from Building 150 in charge of the relationship, the Building 150 area manager and the Rubber Area Manager. The mission of this team is to determine the local operational strategy for the relationship and to provide guidelines for the QIT and the Technical Team.

## Informal interaction: the day-to-day coordination

The production processes are operated on a round-the-clock basis and there is very little buffer stock within the supply chain loop. This close interdependency of the process means that the three operating teams are in contact on a 24-hour basis: Building 150 with Chemco and Chemco with Building 88. There is a direct telephone link (called a 'bat phone' to mimic the fast response in *Batman* films!) between Building 150 and Chemco operators. This allows easy communication by either side in order to warn of any changes occurring in either of the processes (such as the production rate), or to inform of any shutdowns or production breakdowns. In the best case, shutdowns only last for an hour or so and do not induce downstream problems. In case of longer shut-downs (five hours or more), the process start-up needs to be synchronised, with no certainty that the process will start up again without further hitches.

Operators from Building 88 contact Chemco operators every morning in order to confirm their daily demand. Indeed, depending on the production problems within Building 88, volumes can vary between ±30% from the Monday morning forecasts. Chemco operators will adjust their production rates in line with this information. When the consumption is much larger than forecast, the silo of additive A1 will become empty quicker than expected, possibly causing an out-of-stock situation. A three-day buffer stock of bags of A1 is kept at the Building 88 warehouse.

Building 88 operators will immediately be aware of any deviation in the quality of A1 because it will cause the rubber to become either too hard or too brittle. In this case, it is very important that the information is immediately passed on to Chemco operators so that they can make adjustments to their process. However, it often happens that complaints are not forwarded on the spot but on the following day.

Every year the two production units agree on a date for the annual shutdown, which takes place over two or three weeks and allows each unit to do the equipment cleaning and necessary maintenance and repairs.

## Questions

1 *Map the supply chain management process, indicating the physical product flows.*

2 *What information flows should ideally underpin the physical flows?*

3 *What are the potential failure modes within the Wheatco–Chemco relationship?*

**CASE 37**

# Supply chain relationships: Wheatco Ltd and Chemco Ltd (B)

Case date 2001

## Marie Koulikoff-Souviron, Alan Harrison and Jaques Colin

*This case study should only be used after Supply chain relationships: Wheatco Ltd and Chemco Ltd (A) which gives background information on the businesses and the issues involved in the Wheatco–Chemco relationship.*

About eight years ago, shortly after the Chemco facility was built and the partnership was set up, joint 'team days' had been organised on two occasions to allow employees from each production unit to meet and get to know each other. This allowed people to 'put a face to a name' and thus make it easier to collaborate on the technical process. However, since these early days, such meetings have no longer been organised, and yet a number of reorganisations within Wheatco have introduced new faces, especially within the Building 150 operating room.

In 1997, a new very large production process was established on the Wheatco site. All of the operators who had originally installed the Building 150 production unit were promoted to shift manager status. A completely new team of operators was appointed. Moreover, Wheatco recently put in place a new procedure of 'operator cross-training' in order to increase the number of personnel who were qualified to operate each of the three production processes. Building 150 operators now rotate from one process to another instead of being dedicated to a single production process. There have been two impacts of these changes on employees at Chemco: on the one hand the new Building 150 operators are unfamiliar, and on the other hand they have to deal with more than one person during a shift, so they complain about a lack of follow-up in communication. Moreover, they have the feeling that the Building 150 process is a kind of training ground for new operators who, once they are suitably experienced, are moved to other, more strategic production units on the Wheatco site.

There is another cause of tension among production operators. Over the last two years a new incentive scheme has been put in place at Chemco, which is based on the performance of the additive A1 production process. Thus if the process is stopped, for whatever reason, the Chemco bonus is reduced. The Chemco operators blame the Building 150 operators for not being committed and capable of running their process, and in cases of shutdowns, they use the 'bat phone' to ask when the process will be running again. This annoys the Building 150 operators, who are busy looking for the cause of the problem. A Wheatco engineer comments:

'The Chemco operator will ring up our operator and say, "Are you ready yet?" And our operator will say, "No, we won't be ready for 12 hours". Another hour later, the phone rings again: "Aren't you ready yet? What? Are you the same person I talked to an hour ago?" Clunk (as the phone goes down).'

Several quality issues have recently arisen in regard to the supply of additive A1 from Chemco to Building 88. Thus during meetings in March, it appeared that some testing procedures had not been properly followed by the Chemco quality department. The Wheatco production engineer has become very upset: 'I can't trust them any more!'

## The new situation

The situation with regards to the Wheatco–Chemco partnership is currently very tense. It is being described as 'not a smooth supply chain at the moment'. Although Chemco has had its fair share of technical failures in the past, the current situation seems to be better with regards to the Chemco side of the supply chain 'loop'. Over the last four or five months it has been Building 150 which has been the source of most of the problems. This lack of reliability is due to the fluid bed reactor, whose temperature can rise beyond the 300°C limit and cause the reactor to 'trip' (cut out). It's usually possible to start up the reactor again without further problems. When this is not the case, it can take up to several days to succeed in starting up again (the number of these trips has been estimated at about 50 per year). These problems are a cause of tension and conflict. In the words of a Building 150 operator:

'Through a 12-hour shift, the feed trips then you put them back online, then it trips again and it does wear you down if you're constantly having to start the plant up again.'

When either of the two production units (Chemco or Building 150) shuts down, it has to carry the blame for the shutdown of the entire supply chain.

Several causes have been envisaged for the reactor hot spots. One solution has been identified, which engineers estimate would have an 80 per cent chance of success, but this requires purchasing a piece of equipment, which is on order but which will not be available until March 2002. Michael Bond was made Director of the Chemco facility in March 2000. He has a solid experience of plant management at other Chemco sites. However, it is the first time that he has had to face the task of managing such an intricate partnership. His challenge is to manage his own plant performance, whilst being aware that it is very dependent on an external company. Upon arriving at the Chemco facility, Michael Bond found the relationship with the Wheatco site very open and honest with excellent information sharing between both firms at management level. However, he is very much aware of tensions existing at other levels, especially among production operators.

Beside this he is under pressure because the decision to extend the site has been put on hold by the US corporate management because of the current unreliability of the Wheatco process. The final decision will be made in March 2002. Michael knows that he has no other alternative than to collaborate with his partners – but the situation is difficult and conflicting at various levels. Moreover, problems within his own quality organisation are such that Michael is mulling over changes within his own organisation to reinforce the quality drive within Chemco.

At Wheatco, a new Supply Chain Manager for the Basic Chemicals SBU – Jonathan Price – was also appointed in March 2000 to coordinate the partnership with Chemco. He has a very good experience of the Wheatco–Chemco relationship because nine years ago he was an Area Manager within Basic Chemicals – where Building 150 is located. He is very aware of the strategic problem caused by Wheatco to Chemco. Indeed Chemco's long-term development is threatened by lack of reliability of the Building 150 process. Jonathan has to convince Chemco that Wheatco has been channelling a lot of resources in order to resolve the technical issues encountered within Building 150. Could it be that a better collaboration between both firms with regard to human resource management could help resolve the numerous sources of conflict that exist at various levels? What could be done?

## Questions

1 *How can Michael Bond and Jonathan Price face the crisis situation within both firms, which is expressed through the lack of trust and conflicts that make the relationship difficult to manage?*

2 *How can Michael Bond manage the internal difficulties within Chemco, with most of his employees questioning the level of priority that Wheatco grants to Chemco? How convincing is the Wheatco position?*

3 *How different would the situation be if the two organisations were 200km apart instead of being on the same site? Focus in particular on the human issues involved in the case, and ignore the likely increases in stocks and transportation costs.*

# CASE 38

## Supply chain redesign at Finnforest Corp.

Case date
2001

Paul Chapman, Vinod Thayil and Alan Harrison

## Introduction

Finnforest Corporation is a €1.2 billion turnover timber products company, owned by about 125 000 private forest owners of Finland, with worldwide sales and operations. Here, we focus on the Corporation's European operations, where the company undertakes primary and secondary timber manufacturing, and the supply and distribution of finished goods to three main types of customer:

- home improvement/DIY retailers
- industrial and construction companies
- builders and timber merchants.

The case considers how the company supplies its major DIY retailers in the UK, and invites you to propose improvements to the design and operation of this supply chain that will help to achieve better customer service at lower operational costs.

Vinod Tayil, a Cranfield masters student, applied a three-stage approach to process redesign of the Finnforest DIY supply chain. The approach is summarised in Figure 38.1.

**Figure 38.1 Supply chain redesign methodology**

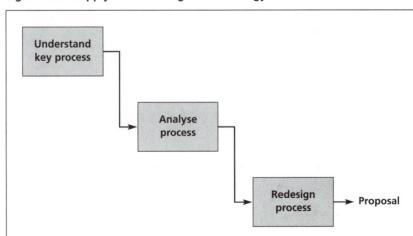

The first stage of this approach to supply chain redesign is to *understand the key* process. Vinod considered the existing supply chain of timber products from Finland to major DIY retailers in the UK, and described the supply chain with the aid of two tools: a flow chart and a pipeline map.

The second stage in the supply chain redesign is to *analyse the process*. To help undertake this analysis, Vinod used a tool called time based process mapping. This tool helps to identify where waste exists in the supply chain.

The final stage is to *redesign the process*. While results from Stages 1 and 2 are presented, you are asked to propose solutions that will improve the performance of the supply chain. These solutions should meet the objective stated above – by identifying ways that Finnforest can improve customer service whilst reducing cost.

## Stage 1: Understand the key supply chain process

Vinod began his analysis with a *diagnostic journey*. Diagnosing a supply chain starts by understanding the current operational system and processes. This understanding is also the first step in gaining widespread recognition of any symptoms of poor performance and helps to establish the need for change. Mapping and measuring a process establishes the performance base line that enables the effect of changes to process design on performance to be measured.

Vinod diagnosed the Finnforest supply chain in terms of five main stages, shown below in Figure 38.2. This 'block flow diagram' format uses a notation of boxes to represent each stage, and arrows to represent the flow of goods between these stages.

In order to gain a more thorough appreciation of the supply chain, Vinod conducted a more detailed investigation. This involved travelling to each of the supply

**Figure 38.2  An overview of Finnforest's timber product supply chain**

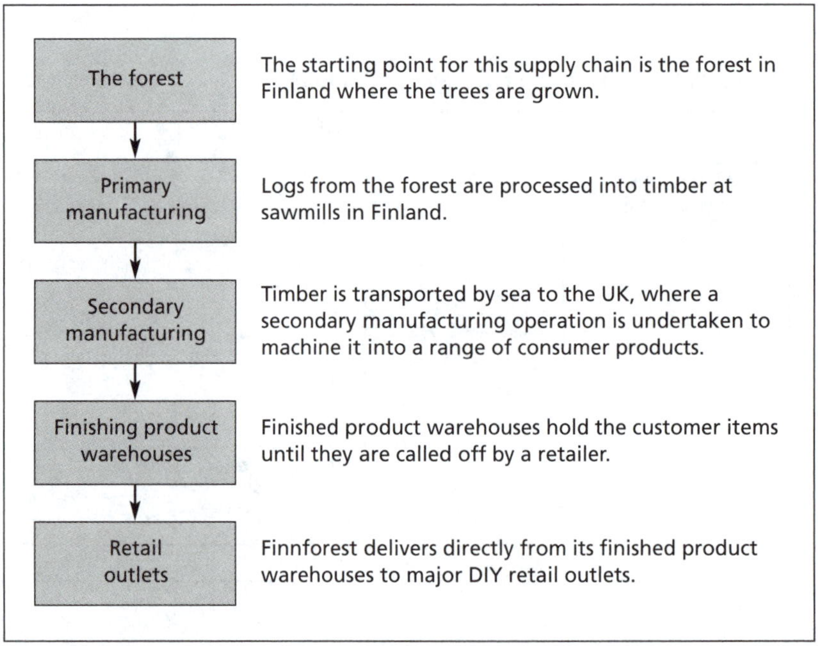

| | |
|---|---|
| **The forest** | The starting point for this supply chain is the forest in Finland where the trees are grown. |
| **Primary manufacturing** | Logs from the forest are processed into timber at sawmills in Finland. |
| **Secondary manufacturing** | Timber is transported by sea to the UK, where a secondary manufacturing operation is undertaken to machine it into a range of consumer products. |
| **Finishing product warehouses** | Finished product warehouses hold the customer items until they are called off by a retailer. |
| **Retail outlets** | Finnforest delivers directly from its finished product warehouses to major DIY retail outlets. |

chain stages shown in Figure 38.2 in order to gain first-hand data about the process. Physically following the supply chain enabled him to catalogue individual steps of the process at each of the five locations.

## Data gathering

Data was gathered at each of the major steps in the process. The principal unit of measure that Vinod used was time. Despite being a simple metric, time allows a rich understanding of the symptoms of poor performance and is effective in identifying and diagnosing waste. Its usefulness is based on the relative ease with which this understanding can be communicated to those involved in operating a process. It also helps in showing what and who would be affected if the process were changed. In addition to time, inventories were quantified at each step of the process.

Vinod collected data on three measures as follows:

1 *Activity time* – The time to physically undertake the activity involved in completing a process step for a single item.
2 *Lead time* – the time between when the item finishes the preceding step in the process until it finishes the current step in the process. This time will include the time spent undertaking any activity.
3 *Inventory* – the amount of inventories, either raw materials, work in progress or finished goods held, measured in terms of the number of days of demand.

This data was collated and is presented in Table 38.1.

**Table 38.1  Finnforest's supply chain steps with performance measures**

| Supply chain step | Activity time/days | Lead-time/days | Inventory/days |
|---|---|---|---|
| Harvest trees | 1.0 | 7.0 | 14.0 |
| Transport logs to mill | 1.0 | 2.0 | 1.0 |
| Grade logs | 0.1 | 1.0 | 10.0 |
| Primary manufacture | 0.1 | 1.0 | 1.0 |
| Kiln dry | 5.0 | 5.0 | 2.0 |
| Grade | 0.1 | 0.5 | 0.0 |
| Pack | 0.1 | 0.5 | 45.0 |
| Transport to port | 1.0 | 1.0 | 10.0 |
| Transport to UK | 11.0 | 14.0 | 31.0 |
| Secondary manufacture | 0.1 | 14.0 | 1.0 |
| Warehouse | – | – | 46.0 |
| Transport to retailers | 0.5 | 4.0 | – |
| Total | 20.0 | 50.0 | 161.0 |

The data in Table 38.1 showed that the overall lead-time for products to get from the forest to the retail outlet is 50 days. Contained within the 50 day overall lead-time is 20 days of activity time, when the timber is worked upon. Overall, the supply chain contains 161 days of inventory.

## Stage 2: Analyse the process

Having collected data on the structure and performance of the supply chain, the second stage of supply chain re-engineering is to analyse the process. To aid the analysis, the data in Table 38.1 were presented graphically in two ways:

- a pipeline map
- a time based process map.

These two process mapping techniques are introduced below.

### Pipeline map

A pipeline map allows process lead-times and inventory holdings to be shown together. The data on elapsed time and on inventory holdings is shown in Figure 38.3.

**Figure 38.3  A pipeline map of the Finnforest supply chain**

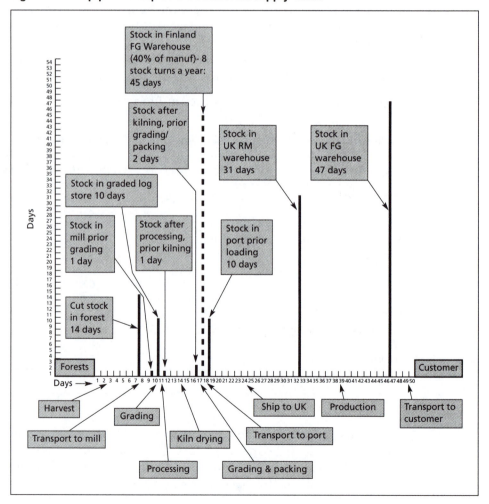

**Figure 38.4 Finnforest's time based process map (TBPM)**

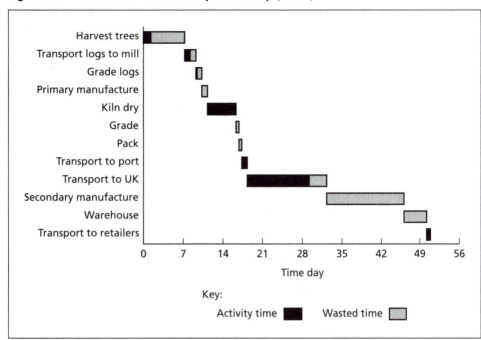

The format of a pipeline map is to show lead-time as a horizontal bar and inventory as a vertical bar. In both cases the length of the bar is proportional to the number of days it represents.

## Time based process map

The format of the time based process map, TBPM, is to show lead-time data for the supply chain process in a format similar to a Gantt chart. The TBPM presents data for both lead-time and activity time for every step along a process. It complements the pipeline map by providing additional data on the breakdown of the lead-time data for the supply chain process.

The lead-time for each process step contains a value for the amount of activity time involved in undertaking that step. By definition, the remainder of the lead-time must consist of time where no activity was undertaken. An assumption is then made that all lead-time which has not been classified as activity time must be 'wasted time'. Thus, the TBPM provides the means to present performance data and highlight the incidence of wasted time. Through highlighting where wasted time exists, the TBPM helps direct attention onto the most significant areas of waste. A TBPM based on data in Table 1 is shown in Figure 38.4.

## ● Stage 3: Redesigning the supply chain

Measuring inventory and lead-time using time allows supply chain performance to be classified in the same units. There is an important relationship between lead-time and inventory. Specifically, supply chain lead-time increases the need for cyclical stock and safety stock. Therefore, reducing lead-time allows inventory levels to be reduced, thus reducing working capital, and improves responsiveness to changes in customer demand.

### Questions

1 *What proportion of the supply chain process lead-time is made up of wasted time?*

2 *Which steps in the supply chain contain the largest amounts of wasted time?*

3 *Using the information supplied, list where opportunities exist to reduce the overall supply chain lead-time.*

4 *Propose actions that Finnforest could take to realise the opportunities you highlighted in Question 3.*

5 *Suggest the effect your proposed actions would have on the supply chain in terms of:*

*Working capital:*
- *raw and finished goods inventories*
- *warehouse space in the UK*

*Performance:*
- *supply chain lead times*
- *delivery performance, for example no supply or late deliveries*

*Ability to respond to supply chain risks, such as:*
- *Fashion driven demand swings in the UK DIY market (the 'Changing Rooms' effect – Changing Rooms is one of a number of TV programmes that encourage viewers to enhance their lifestyle through home improvements)*
- *Exaggerated but generic demand swings, for example warm Easter period or prolonged, wet summer*
- *Limited raw material availability, for example, in spring the thaw in Finland waterlogs the ground, preventing trucks from transporting harvested logs from the forest.*

CASE
39

# E-commerce in the NHS

Case date
2001

Roxanne Sutton, Eric Jackson and Christine Harland*

## Introduction

In March 1999, Tony Blair, the UK Prime Minister, said[1]:

'The Government has a mission to modernise – renewing our country for the new millennium. We are modernising our schools, our hospitals, our economy and our criminal justice system. We are modernising our democratic framework...

...But modernisation must go further. It must engage with how government itself works. Modernising government is a vital part of our programme of renewal for Britain.'

The Government set out five key aims for delivery; one of those aims was to exploit new technology to bring government into the Information Age. When *Modernising government* was launched, the Government embraced the concept of the 'third revolution'[2] – the information revolution – 'carrying society forward in another major leap equivalent to the earlier agrarian and industrial advances'[3]. Its idea of an 'Information Age Government' was about translating this into practice for the citizens and business of the UK: how the government does business with its citizens, how the government handles its internal workings and how government (and the broader public sector) interacts with industry and the commercial sector, shown in Figure 39.1.

Each part of government was required to deliver this agenda, by:

- appointing its own Information Age Government Champion at a senior level
- preparing its own e-business strategy
- meeting key targets for electronic service delivery and electronic access by citizens
- ensuring implementation in all its agencies, non-departmental public bodies and other public bodies it sponsored.

This was the scenario across the public sector at the beginning of the year 2000.

---

* All figures in this case are attributed to Roxanne Sutton and Eric Jackson

**Figure 39.1  Modernising UK Government**

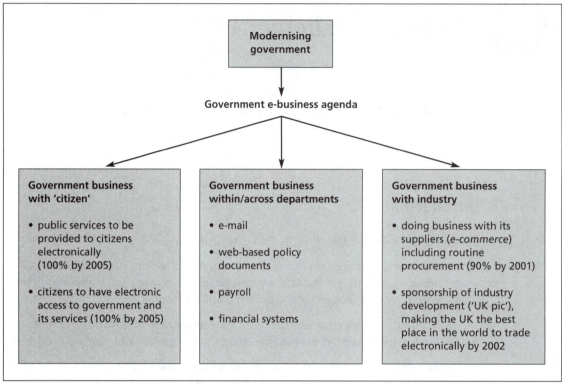

*Source*: NHS Purchasing and Supply Agency (RYS) – 2000

## ● Supply in the NHS

As part of the wider public sector, the National Health Service (NHS) was required to meet the Government's targets; however, there were other pressures in addition to these targets. Since the NHS spends as much as 25 per cent of its annual budget of around £55 billion with the commercial sector on goods and services which are necessary for it to provide health care, any opportunity to reduce this cost, or stretch its value further, was a source of management interest.

Suppliers, too, worried about inefficiencies in the NHS – fragmentation of demand, for example, and arcane and inconsistent processes, added to their own costs. Therefore, at this interface between the public and commercial sectors, was a shared objective to reduce the costs of the supply chain. E-commerce was being promoted to the NHS as a new way of doing this and across the NHS there were some very receptive audiences.

The Government's *Modernising government* agenda provided a more general lever – modernisation, for its own sake, became almost a 'moral' obligation and an overriding government policy. The NHS became one of the highest priorities for this modernisation programme, and in turn, this shone the spotlight back on to the agenda for supply in the NHS.

Supply systems in the NHS are huge and complex. The NHS is not a single corporate body. Whilst there are national policies and priorities, service frameworks, action programmes, regulation and performance management arrangements, from an operations perspective the NHS is a confederation of several hundred independent organisations including hospital trusts, primary care trusts and health authorities. The philosophy about the balance between local autonomy and central control of the NHS varies over time as national policy changes. Arrangements for supply management have tended to reflect the mainstream management culture of the time, oscillating between the influences of centralisation and devolution. Purchasing and supply has remained an operational/transactional process, with little professional or strategic influence exerted by its practitioners, either within their own NHS organisations, or 'across' them.

Until the beginning of the 1990s, the quality, status and sophistication of supply arrangements relating to purchasing, storage and distribution varied widely across the country, reflecting regional variations in NHS management 'style'. A more streamlined, standardised and integrated approach was developed with the creation in 1991 of a single national organisation – the NHS Supplies Authority. This organisation was charged with bringing together and managing the disparate and variable supply operations across the whole English NHS and to operate as a successful commercial venture.

The NHS Supplies Authority gained economies of scale for the NHS by aggregating purchasing spend on around £0.5 billion worth of goods commonly used across the NHS; these were purchased, stored and distributed to hospitals across the country. In addition it created framework agreements with suppliers that fixed national prices, allowing hospitals to contract with suppliers at pre-agreed prices for particular goods and services. However, the NHS Supplies Authority did not have the authority over other parts of the NHS to prescribe how they would spend their own local budgets, and how they would contract with suppliers. Local hospitals were free to choose which brands of which items they wanted to purchase, and which suppliers would provide these. Effectively, there was little or no management of variety across the NHS for most of the goods and services purchased. It was also not possible to find out how much the NHS was spending with each supplier and how many goods of a particular type were being purchased across the NHS as there was no common coding of suppliers or purchased items.

A Cabinet Office review of procurement in the NHS led to the separation of the strategy and purchasing roles from supply transactions. A new agency – the NHS Purchasing and Supply Agency (hereafter referred to as 'the Agency') – was established in the Department of Health. Unlike the NHS Supplies Authority, as a central government agency, the Agency was given powers to act on behalf of the NHS, and to develop policy on supply for the NHS. The Agency provided the NHS with the capability to act strategically in response to the fragmented pressures for 'e-commerce'. From a practical point of view, it was *only* the Agency that could develop a strategy for the NHS as a whole that would take e-commerce beyond fragmented and purely local, piecemeal implementation.

## E-commerce for the NHS

The UK Government had defined e-commerce as[4]:

'...the exchange of information across electronic networks, at any stage in the supply chain, whether within an organisation, between businesses, between businesses and consumer, or between the public and private sectors, whether paid or unpaid.'

In its early stages of thinking about a strategy for the NHS, the Agency provided some clarification of the components of e-commerce, as shown in Figure 39.2.

**Figure 39.2  Clarification of the components of e-commerce**

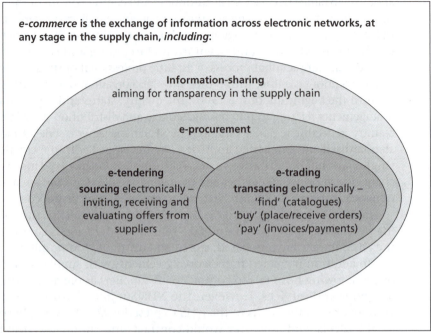

*e-commerce* is the exchange of information across electronic networks, at any stage in the supply chain, *including*:

**Information-sharing**
aiming for transparency in the supply chain

**e-procurement**

**e-tendering**
**sourcing** electronically – inviting, receiving and evaluating offers from suppliers

**e-trading**
**transacting** electronically – 'find' (catalogues) 'buy' (place/receive orders) 'pay' (invoices/payments)

*Source*: NHS Purchasing and Supply Agency (RYS) – 2000

E-commerce was viewed in the NHS as relating to transactional and operational systems, the availability, use and transparency of information throughout the supply chain, and the relationship of players to each other (specifically, customers and suppliers). The Agency drew a distinction between e-commerce and e-business in order to ensure that its own role in relation to the NHS's commercial interface was not confused with the wider NHS's responsibility in responding to the government's full range of expectations for Information Age Government. This is shown in Figure 39.3.

**Figure 39.3  The e-business environment**

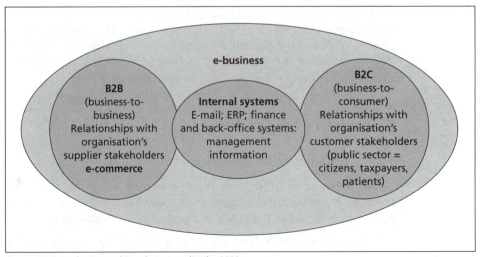

**e-business**

**B2B**
(business-to-business) Relationships with organisation's supplier stakeholders
**e-commerce**

**Internal systems**
E-mail; ERP; finance and back-office systems: management information

**B2C**
(business-to-consumer) Relationships with organisation's customer stakeholders (public sector = citizens, taxpayers, patients)

*Source*: NHS Purchasing and Supply Agency (RYS) – 2000

This distinction is particularly helpful in the public sector as government e-business refers to the work that government departments do internally between government departments, with taxpayers/citizens (and, in the NHS, for patients) who receive public services, and with the commercial sector with whom the public sector contracts.

As the Agency investigated the growing market more and more deeply, it came to the view that the scope of e-commerce in the NHS would have to include:

- undertaking electronically traditional and discrete procurement-based activities, such as: electronic tendering (sourcing); electronic catalogues (display of products, prices); electronic purchasing (ordering of goods and transacting with suppliers)
- overlapping financial and probity processes, such as: invoice receipt, invoice matching, payment of suppliers, audit trail and authorisation procedures
- generation of management and strategic supply information, such as: budget planning, reporting and control; demand forecasting; supply chain performance management and strategic sourcing and supply decisions.

The potential benefits of applying e-commerce across the NHS could arise at three levels, as shown in Figure 39.4. However, there was not an obvious solution as to how these three levels of benefits might be achieved through using existing B2B offerings. Most developments of B2B at that time involved individual organisations and their relationships with other individual organisations, whereas 'the NHS' encompassed many hundreds of organisations, doing business with many thousands of suppliers, who in turn had a myriad of relationships with their own suppliers. The NHS supply network, therefore, was substantially more complex than the supply networks of other private sector organisations implementing e-commerce solutions.

**Figure 39.4 Potential benefits from e-commerce**

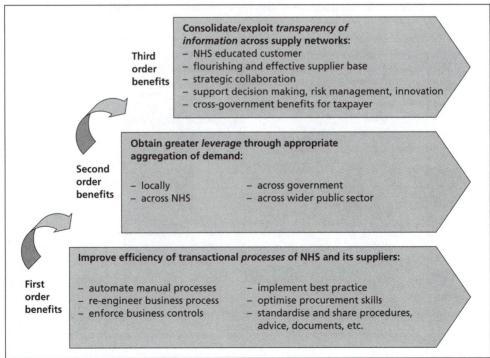

*Source*: NHS Purchasing and Supply Agency (RYS) – 2000

The Agency studied the marketplace and drew several key conclusions that would affect its strategy for e-commerce. First, despite what e-commerce providers claimed, it was apparent that there were no existing models, either in the public or the private sector, which replicated the circumstances of the NHS. Second, system-based 'solutions' of computer software programs which 'do' part of the procurement process, and the technology to run them, would be a relatively small component of e-commerce compared to the scale of business change that e-commerce was going to require. Third, system 'solutions' do not achieve 'e-commerce'; designing and making systems available does not necessarily mean that they are in widespread operation.

It was predicted that the overall objectives of e-commerce in the NHS would take three to five years, and part of the Agency's strategy would have to be about managing expectations accordingly. An enormous programme of change was needed to underpin the overall objective of changing business practices throughout the NHS, and for undertaking development work with the supplier base which – with notable exceptions – was far from ready for such upheaval. Even if all transactions were dealt with by a common information systems platform, without a common coding platform for goods and services and for suppliers it would still not be possible to find out exactly what the NHS was spending on each item and with each supplier, therefore potentially prohibiting a more rational, coordinated and strategic approach to purchasing.

In the light of this, the Agency developed a policy platform, which would drive its creation of an e-commerce strategy for the NHS. There were four clear intentions set out, as shown in Figure 39.5. From this, a 'vision statement' was created, describing seven substantial business changes that would characterise the successful implementation of e-commerce across the NHS, shown in Figure 39.6. This vision statement was presented to, and endorsed by, the Agency's Ministerial Advisory Board in January 2001.

**Figure 39.5  The policy platform for e-commerce in the NHS**

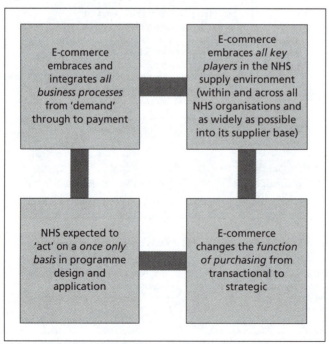

*Source*: NHS Purchasing and Supply Agency (RYS) – 2001

**Figure 39.6 The Agency's vision statement for e-commerce**

A vision for e-commerce in the NHS

When the NHS has achieved, and is fully exploiting an e-commerce environment...

Every transaction with a supplier, from demand through to payment, will be **electronic**

This process will be **standardised** throughout the NHS (subject to agreed variations necessary in certain selected markets)

This process (processes) will be **integrated** with other systems (including supply chain systems)

There will be the ability to **customise choice** (i.e. product range, supplier)

There will be the ability to aggregate across the **whole NHS trust** (demand, contracting, ordering, payment and supply chain)

There will be the ability for aggregation across the **whole NHS**

There will be the ability to collect, analyse, use and make decisions on this information, creating added value for the whole NHS (synergy)

*Source*: NHS Purchasing and Supply Agency (RYS) – 2001

In January 2001, with its vision statement accepted as the 'policy' for e-commerce in the NHS, the Agency faced the huge task of turning this into an overall strategy for action.

## Questions

**1** *What are the key elements of a strategy for e-commerce for the NHS?*

**2** *What are the main barriers to such a strategy being effective across the NHS?*

**3** *How might the Agency remove those barriers and enable an effective e-commerce strategy to be implemented?*

**4** *If you had responsibility for this project, what initiatives would you start?*

## References

[1] *Modernising government*. Presented to Parlament by the Prime Minister and the Minister for the Cabinet Office, March 1999. HMSO. Cm4310.

[2] Alvin Toffler, *The Third Wave*, Pan, 1981.

[3] *E-commerce@its.best.uk*, Performance and Innovation Unit Report, Cabinet Office, September 1999.

[4] (e-commerce@its.best.uk, Cabinet Office, September 1999).

# CASE 40

# NHS Supplies – supply for the National Health Service

Case date
April 2000

Christine Harland, Roxanne Sutton and Terry Hunt

## ● Introduction – the public sector context for supply

The National Health Service (NHS) is a public sector health care provider for England and Wales. In the UK, the service sector represents 79 per cent of gross domestic product (GDP) and, despite significant privatisation programmes over the last 15 to 20 years, about half of that sector is still publicly managed. As about 40 per cent of GDP is under government control, this means that public sector spending is of significant interest to the UK economy and taxpayers.

However, government spending is still a relatively fragmented and uncoordinated activity. Government can be divided into central government, the wider public sector and quasi-autonomous non-government organisations, as shown in Figure 40.1.

There have been recent attempts to coordinate spend across government. For example, formed in April 2000, the Office of Government Commerce (OGC) brought together three former Cabinet Office agencies with the former Treasury units concerned with procurement policy, practice and development, and the Private Finance Initiative (PFI), with a remit of improving the efficiency and effectiveness of the government's annual procurement budget. The OGC had four high-level objectives:

1 Provide guidance and expertise to support the successful delivery of procurement-based projects and other forms of commercial activity.
2 Develop the government market so it is more efficient and attractive for both suppliers and customers.
3 Develop a clear and supportive framework for best-in-class procurement activity to help achieve better value for money.
4 Deliver efficient and effective services to external and internal customers, gaining widespread recognition for excellence and as a leading contributor to government modernisation.

The OGC was targeted to deliver £1 billion of savings by 2002–2003. However, rather than centralise spending to pursue purchasing economies of scale, the OGC has provided standardised processes and models for improving the performance of devolved spending together with some cross-government framework contracts.

In defence, the Defence Procurement Agency (DPA) and the Defence Logistics Organisation (DLO) have respectively helped to coordinate large capital spend and revenue spend across the three forces, though many operational contracting decisions are still taken separately.

**Figure 40.1  Different types of UK public sector organisation**

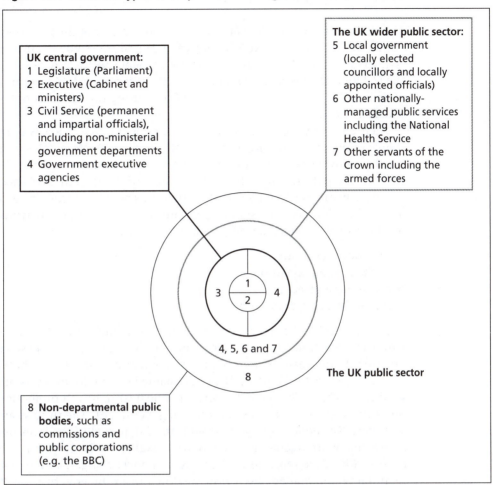

UK central government:
1 Legislature (Parliament)
2 Executive (Cabinet and ministers)
3 Civil Service (permanent and impartial officials), including non-ministerial government departments
4 Government executive agencies

The UK wider public sector:
5 Local government (locally elected councillors and locally appointed officials)
6 Other nationally-managed public services including the National Health Service
7 Other servants of the Crown including the armed forces

8 Non-departmental public bodies, such as commissions and public corporations (e.g. the BBC)

4, 5, 6 and 7

8

The UK public sector

In health, the NHS Purchasing and Supply Agency was established in April 2000 to be the NHS' centre of excellence on matters of purchasing and supply and to modernise and improve purchasing and supply for the NHS. Whilst operating for, and on behalf of, a complex network of organisations which forms the NHS, the Agency is in fact part of central government (the Department of Health). In this capacity the Agency is directly accountable to government ministers and is called on to contribute to the development of government policy and to advise and support ministers on issues associated with supply and the interface between health and the commercial sector.

However, prior to 2000 the situation was different. There was no single organisation with this remit, or this close to central government. There was an NHS body a 'special health authority', called the NHS Supplies Authority – that attempted to pull together fragmented spending in the NHS from 1991 to 2000. This case study tells the story of the development of NHS Supplies and its impact on NHS spending. The next section describes the NHS situation in 1991, when this story starts.

# The NHS in 1991

The National Health Service was formed in 1948 as part of the great post-war creation of the Welfare State. The NHS is not part of central government, and is not staffed by civil servants; the NHS is part of the wider UK public sector and, as such, a member of the Cabinet (the Secretary of State for Health) is accountable to Parliament for its overall performance and delivery, and for securing the funds from the Treasury to enable it to operate.

There are many characteristics which describe the NHS (such as a public service, a source of funds, a gathering of processes, a bank of assets, a collection of organisations, a knowledge pool, and many more), but in legal terms the NHS is defined through legislation, through successive Acts of Parliament, and their subsequent Statutory Instruments, Orders and Directions. There is no 'corporate' mission statement, as the NHS is not a single corporate body; however, many within the service would recognise a general description that the NHS:

- provides health care
- to the whole population
- according to need and
- free at the point of delivery.

In organisational terms, when the NHS was created, separate administrative systems were established for the three main strands of health care and service provision. The first strand was primary care, including family doctors, who became independent contractors to the new NHS, but remained organised, much as before, through local committees. The second strand – public health, health promotion and disease prevention – was retained as part of local government. The third strand – hospitals and specialist services – was removed from the myriad of predecessor funding and management arrangements (such as local taxation, voluntary contributions, insurance, charities and religious institutions, and direct charges) and 'nationalised', with its funding and management flowing down from the government, 'through' the minister, and then through a geographical hierarchy of public bodies.

For the first time ever, health services were funded largely from general taxation and for the first time ever the entire population had access to the most advanced services available to medicine. Today, the NHS has an annual budget for 2000/01 of more than £50bn. Approximately one million people are employed in the NHS. In any single day it is estimated that one million people visit their family doctor, 33 000 have an outpatient appointment with a specialist, and more than 25 000 operations are performed. Over one year, nearly five and a half million people are admitted into hospital for some form of diagnosis, treatment or monitoring.

However, from its earliest days, there have been funding pressures on the NHS, which have contributed to the emergence of waiting lists for treatment and to continuing differential service levels across the country. As a result, not only does the funding method come under periodic scrutiny by successive governments, but ways of improving performance are constantly being sought in an effort to make the money go further.

In 1974, huge structural change took place in an effort to integrate the three service areas more closely, in particular, bringing hospitals and community services closer together. A three-tier organisational structure was introduced with (i) 14 regional, and

(ii) 90 area health authorities and (iii) sub-sets of areas known as 'districts'. A major feature of the time was the introduction of 'consensus management'– a management partnership of clinical and managerial professionals – heading up each newly constituted health organisation at each of these levels. ('Areas' were abolished in 1982, so that districts became statutory health authorities in their own right.) At this time, most general hospital and community health care was planned, managed and delivered by these district health authorities, including the running of the large acute hospitals, and consensus management was replaced by general management during 1984.

Since alternative funding methods for the NHS (such as insurance) continued to be rejected, governments continued to be concerned with finding other ways of reducing the constant pressure on resources – performance management, output measures and targets, resource management, compulsory competitive tendering, performance pay, and the rise of public accountability through increasing numbers of audit bodies, which all became features of the NHS environment of the 1980s. But perhaps the most profound change to the NHS since its inception came about in the early 1990s with the creation of an 'internal market' for NHS health care provision; central to this was the split between the roles of 'purchaser' (or 'commissioner') of health care and 'provider' of health care. The internal market was intended to improve efficiency and effectiveness, and respond to consumer preferences through the introduction of competition, this competition remaining 'internal' to the NHS. The internal market was 'structured' through the placing of contracts for health care by the planning and funding organisations (health authorities) with provider units (hospitals and groups of clinics) which were potentially 'in competition' with each other. These provider units became NHS trusts (about 450 were created), independent of the NHS management hierarchy, and given a range of freedoms previously unknown, including pay levels and the ability to earn income. They moved nearer to commercial management, with the requirement to make a return on investment each year, and to pay the equivalent of interest on the capital tied up in their facilities. Innovation, competition (for patients/contracts) and efficiency measures were bywords of the culture.

Meanwhile, within central government, an executive board for the whole NHS had been established within the Department of Health, with general management principles also being introduced, but with a clear internal separation between the executive functions of leading and managing the NHS at the top, and the central government civil service functions of working with ministers in the development and implementation of 'policy'.

It was into this environment of devolved and 'hands-off' management (frequently viewed as a time of fragmentation of the NHS) that NHS Supplies was born – providing another phase in a long history of different arrangements for supply in the NHS which had fluctuated between centralisation and devolution since 1948.

## The formation of NHS Supplies

In 1991 there was a mixed pattern of arrangements for purchasing and supply throughout the NHS, determined, in the main, by the 'policies' of the 14 different regional health authorities (some of whom had highly integrated and centralised state-of-the-art purchasing and logistics organisations, and others who had the opposite, see Figure 40.2).

**Figure 40.2 Purchasing and supply in the NHS pre-1991**

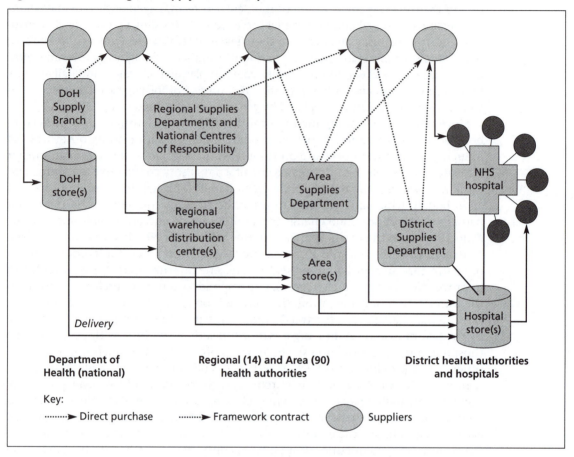

There was a significant amount of criticism of procurement in the NHS at this time. A National Audit Office report in 1991 was highly critical of the variety of buying processes for the same products. At that time there were estimated to be over 127 000 order points in trusts, health authorities and directly managed units, all placing orders with the upstream supply market. Whilst no one knew precisely how many suppliers the NHS as a whole was dealing with, it was estimated from various data files, purchase ledgers and reports to the Department of Health that there were over 50 000 suppliers contracting with the NHS.

In some trust hospitals, an item may have been ordered by a nurse using a hand-written order, in others the same item may have been ordered by staff in a supplies department. In some hospitals there was reasonable budgetary control, in others budgets were devolved and used inconsistently. Supplies managers frequently complained that clinicians placed orders by telephone, had goods delivered directly to them, then sent the invoice to accounts for payment, having authorised the purchase from their budget. There were over 30 different information systems across the NHS being used for purchasing. Whilst a 'national' coding system for products was in existence, its uptake and interpretation varied significantly across regions and there was no common coding of services and suppliers. Purchasing practice varied enormously across the entire portfolio of spend. For some parts of the portfolio, such as pharmaceuticals, pharmacists were relatively autonomous in their ordering, storing and distribution of drugs, and guarded their role from supplies staff. There were some regional consortia for purchasing in some parts of the country and not in others. Some specialist centres across the country, such as heart transplant units, coordinated their spending; others acted separately and independently, and did not actively share information with other similar organisations with similar patterns of spending. Furthermore, it was clear that there was variable capability and competence across NHS sites to ensure that purchasing activities were compliant with EU regulations on public procurement.

As a result of the criticism by the National Audit Office, and of top NHS management in the subsequent Parliamentary Accounts Committee hearing based on this report, new organisational arrangements for supply in the NHS were considered, and the decision was taken to create a single, national body within the NHS to remedy the problems of inconsistency and variable standards and facilities. NHS Supplies was formed as a Special Health Authority in 1991.

Established by Statutory Instrument, and authorised by Regulations and Directions, NHS Supplies was given the responsibility for the majority of staff and assets associated with purchasing and supply throughout the English NHS; this included:

- transferred employment of more than 5000 staff from more than 70 different district and regional health authorities throughout England and from the Department of Health, and based in more than 200 locations
- transferred ownership and management of more than £34m of fixed assets, including 70 stores and distribution centres, and £42m of stockholding
- absorption of more than 39 different computer and information systems
- transactions amounting to more than £500m in value per annum
- systems, procedures and relationships extending from manufacturers right into the heart of NHS hospitals.

Within six months of its establishment date, it had completed these transfers and had a baseline for a consolidated business, which included a complete balance sheet and a working P&L. A corporate headquarters was fully operational and a clear corporate identity well established, and a sense of purpose enshrined in its new mission statement:

'NHS Supplies works within the National Health Service to provide a reliable, responsive and forward-looking service that guarantees its customers the best value for money on the goods and services they need to deliver health care.'

## NHS Supplies – the early years

Despite the scale of this organisational upheaval and operational change, NHS Supplies delivered on its mission without any operational failure to the NHS – a notable achievement welcomed by both ministers and departmental officials. However, from this point a major task for NHS Supplies was not simply to 'do' purchasing and supply for and on behalf of the NHS, but to ensure that standards, values and ethics were in line with good purchasing and supply practice, and were consistent throughout the NHS.

In order to gain some control, one of the first main decisions taken in NHS Supplies was to form six regional (geographical) operating divisions. Each division managed relations with, and delivered the full range of services to, the hospitals and clinics within its boundaries. The management structures of these divisions were very similar, each with a top management team responsible for the following key functions:

- purchasing (product range, contracting with suppliers)
- logistics (storage and distribution) – including the operations of the warehouses and distribution centres
- customer services – including the management of some 1500 staff based in hospitals carrying out local transactions
- finance and information (financial planning, management and performance reporting; income collection; information and operating IT systems)
- human resources (each division employed more than 1000 staff)
- communications and business management.

Each division was led by a chief executive, who was accountable to the National Director (chief executive) of the authority.

At national (corporate) level the National Director was supported by a team of four directors (for purchasing and contracting, finance and IT, communications, and human resources), whose responsibilities crossed all divisions, who provided professional leadership to divisional functional directors, and who, together with a non-executive chairman and five non-executive directors, formed the *authority*. The National Director of Purchasing also created a new central purchasing unit, which incorporated some Department of Health staff and was able to serve common divisional requirements and manage relationships with key national suppliers, thereby gaining national economies of scale and also the ability to specialise in key markets. The National Director of the authority, the four national functional directors and the six divisional chief executives formed a strategic management group known as 'G11'.

Whilst the divisions had a considerable degree of operational autonomy, other issues of 'control' were also addressed during this early stage, including centrally designed and controlled sets of standards, values and ethics. Rigorous internal procedures were established – not only operational procedures for purchasing, warehousing and customer services, but also financial and performance management, business planning and communications. NHS Supplies had to ensure that employees were trained and acted in a consistent, professional manner, abiding by the appropriate regulations for public sector procurement. One of the ways it did this was by recruiting professional purchasing staff qualified with the Diploma of the then Institute of Purchasing and Supply (now the Chartered Institute of Purchasing and Supply) and by encouraging supplies staff in hospitals to pursue qualification.

There were some very early successes; for example, in the first six months, £27m of audited savings were made for the NHS from purchasing (nationally and locally), and a reduction of warehouse floor space of nearly 10 per cent was achieved. Plans were also put in place which were to lead to further warehouse rationalisation, increased stock-turn, reduced stockholding, improved service levels, and major inroads into the inconsistencies and variations in product range, product prices and customer charging mechanisms which existed not only across the six divisions but also within them. In the first two years of its existence, NHS Supplies invested about £8m in replacing outdated IT systems in order to rationalise and reduce the number of systems, initially to six as a first stage towards complete national standardisation. Similar plans were put in place relating to data management, product and supplier coding, and catalogues.

## Calming customers and suppliers

Prior to NHS Supplies being formed, hospitals in many parts of the NHS, particularly where there had previously been poorly developed supply organisations at regional health authority level, were acting relatively independently as business units; they therefore had their own responsibility for purchasing the goods and services they needed. Clinically trained staff, such as nurses and doctors, as well as administrative supplies staff, were involved in ordering items that they required from suppliers. This took up time and there was concern that this detracted from their core roles as clinical service providers. Individual purchasers were not able to manage the supply market in any way. For example, each ambulance trust in the country was buying ambulances to their own specification and making individual contracts with suppliers of ambulances. Every trust had a slightly different specification. The private sector chassis manufacturers and ambulance body builders typically received orders from the trusts at the start of the financial year when capital budgets became available, or at the very end of the financial year when budgets were being cleared out, therefore these companies saw most of their demand in about two months of the year. Despite taking on extra workers during the demand peak, they were unable to adjust capacity to meet demand peaks and troughs. This lack of coordination caused problems for the hospitals, which were frequently unable to receive goods and services when they were required, but it also caused significant problems for suppliers. All hospitals were forming contracts with similar sets of suppliers and using different methods of ordering, different codes for items, and were negotiating different contracts with different prices. For both customers and suppliers the transaction costs of these many, separate and different exchanges were higher than if there had been some coordinating hub acting as an intermediary. As a way of getting control over the external relationships between hospitals and suppliers, and with a view to adding value in both these areas, new initiatives were required. On the supply side, NHS Supplies' supply portfolio was divided in the product/service groupings shown in Table 40.1. A Purchasing Executive was appointed to manage each supply group. The relative spend importance of each of these areas is shown in the pie chart in Figure 40.3.

Each purchasing executive was tasked with forming plans to ensure:

- purchasing would be conducted on a once-only principle, acknowledging that project purchasing would require a local presence
- divisional boundaries and current locations for purchasing activity could be disregarded; purchasing should be conducted on a reduced number of sites
- purchasing tasks currently being undertaken by other functions should be examined to ascertain whether they should be performed by purchasing.

### Table 40.1 Supply portfolio groups

| Supply group | Product/service categories |
|---|---|
| Hotel | • Office equipment/furniture<br>• Office consumables<br>• Furnishings<br>• Clothing/bedding/linen<br>• Cleaning/laundry |
| Facilities | • IT<br>• Telecoms<br>• SET<br>• Capital equipping |
| Food | • Canned<br>• Frozen<br>• Chilled<br>• Ambient<br>• Catering equipment |
| Estates | • Transport<br>• Energy/utilities<br>• Building<br>• Engineering |
| Pharmacy | • Pharmaceuticals<br>• Vaccines/gases<br>• Dressings |
| Medical and Surgical | • Cardiology<br>• Orthopaedic implants<br>• Specialised IV devices<br>• Theatres<br>• Anaesthesia/obstetrics and gynaecology |
| Diagnostic Medical Equipment | • X-ray/pathology<br>• Diagnostic laboratory |
| Patient Appliances | • Orthotics/prosthetics<br>• Patients' aids<br>• Urology/ostomy |

Each portfolio of spend was examined and key product/service areas that appeared to provide opportunity for a national approach were identified. Also, key suppliers for whom key supplier management would be appropriate were highlighted. For example, it was calculated that £30m was being spent on X-ray film across the NHS, £30m on contract hire of cars, £15m on chilled food, £30m on vending services, £10m on disposable examination gloves, £44m on incontinence products, £50m on vaccines, and so on. The total spend on goods and services was about £8bn per year at that time. Major lines of spend were ripe for national contracting or some coordination of the supply market.

NHS Supplies systematically set about *influencing* NHS spend to ensure that the £8bn spent was providing best value for money. Some of this spend – about £0.5bn – was on common items that were suitable for national storage and distribution.

**Figure 40.3 Spend in the NHS**

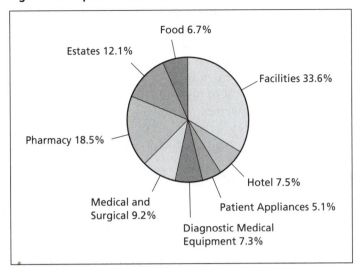

Items such as sutures, tinned food, surgical wipes, etc. that were in common use by most NHS sites were not only contracted for by NHS Supplies, but physically received, owned as stock, stored, sold and distributed through its centrally controlled logistics operation. A further £1.3bn was influenced through NHS Supplies placing framework agreements or 'contracts' with suppliers to ensure one price for the NHS. Individual trust hospitals then purchased those items direct from the supplier using that national 'contract'.

As logistics rationalisation was maximised within the six operating divisions, opportunities for cross-divisional services and economies of scale were sought, with a national logistics strategy being developed under the leadership of a newly created National Director for Logistics, making a twelfth member of the top management team.

On the customer side, NHS Supplies sought to increase efficiency through: the introduction of account management; the design, implementation and servicing of automated stock control and top-up systems within hospital wards and departments (called 'materials management'); and the development of a larger, nationally available product range available from all its stores, and accessible through new streamlined, standardised catalogues, using standard consistent product codes.

At this time, many of the plans put in place by NHS Supplies in its first year of operations came to fruition and in these ways NHS Supplies was able to improve efficiency of the contracting and physical distribution activities across the NHS and start to improve on the dissatisfaction of the NHS and suppliers with the previous, uncoordinated arrangements.

## Strategies to improve customer service

NHS Supplies took two main strategic initiatives, both supported by collaboration with leading academic groups. First, it embraced marketing strategy and, through collaborating with the marketing group of Cranfield School of Management, underwent education and the development of a strategic approach to marketing. Second, it sought to be more strategic at the supply side of the organisation and collaborated with the Centre for Research in Strategic Purchasing and Supply (CRiSPS) in the School of Management at the University of Bath.

In between these two initatives, major internal restructuring took place. First, the purchasing function – like logistics, and for similar reasons – was brought into a single national management structure. Second, the six geographical operating divisions – which without control of logistics and purchasing were no longer viable units – were replaced by three new nationwide and nationally managed 'business streams' covering the separate activities of purchasing (contracting for the NHS); wholesaling (bulk buying, storage and distribution); and customer services (on-site operational supplies staff in NHS trusts).

Marketing planning was introduced in the organisation based on a completely new application of 'customer segmentation'. Previously, each NHS organisation (for example, each NHS trust) in its corporate form had been assumed to be a 'customer', making corporate judgements and representing aggregated demand. Now, individual budget and department managers in different hospital specialities *within* these organisations were recognised as individual 'customers'. Also, in order to achieve sensible segmentation for planning purposes, NHS Supplies categorised these individual customers *across* organisational boundaries and *according to the similarities of their daily activities* and the demands they would make on the supply systems which serviced them and their operations. So, for example, rather than focusing on 'acute trusts', 'community trusts', etc. departments and functions such as 'operating theatres', and 'diagnostic services', were regarded as identifiable customer segments for planning and development purposes. This approach allowed the new organisation to be more critical of its existing service, more investigative and supportive of customer requirements, and more responsive in the 'offers' (of 'products' and of service packages) it developed and delivered to the NHS.

During this time, and as part of this approach, the organisation also introduced customer account management principles and dedicated product managers. Matrix management was introduced to provide a framework for business planning, drawing together those involved in the demand side with those involved in the supply side, and supported by regular and extensive customer research and by standardised approaches to business planning and product development prompted by customised planning workbooks, all with a view to systematising service planning and significantly improving customer responsiveness.

To bring the customer and supply side of the business together strategically, the organisation embraced the newly emerging concept of 'supply strategy'. Supply strategy is an integrative concept of the strategic management of operations in inter-organisational settings which draws on existing bodies of knowledge from a variety of fields, particularly operations management and purchasing and supply management, but also logistics, industrial and relationship marketing, and service management. It focuses on the existing and future requirements of end customers and how supply networks can collaborate to provide these.

A structured, planned approach to supply strategy formulation was taken at this time, building on the experiences already gained through marketing planning. A workbook was created to take users through a staged approach to supply strategy formulation; each stage contained a methodology, tools and techniques to help form strategies appropriate to their supply and customer market contexts. Senior staff of the Purchasing Division attended presentations given, and workshops led, by CR*i*SPS. The workshops focused on briefing managers on the use of the *Supply Strategy Workbook*.

Below is an extract from a communication from the Purchasing Director to launch the project.

*'The recent removal of divisions requires a new approach to the formulation of strategy to supply customers that integrates purchasing, logistics, marketing and customer service. A project is underway to formulate an overarching supply strategy and a portfolio of differentiated supply strategies for different product/service commodity groups...'*

A working group comprising senior purchasing and marketing personnel from NHS Supplies and CR*i*SPS was formed to design and manage the project of formulating a supply strategy that was appropriate to customers and the new NHS Supplies organisation. This group comprised:

NHS Supplies:    National Director, Purchasing
                 National Director, Communications
                 National Director of Finance and IT
                 Heads of Purchasing (two, reporting to the National Director of Purchasing)

CR*i*SPS:        Senior Research Fellow
                 Research Associate (also Chairman of the IFPMM*)

The supply strategies aimed ultimately to serve end customers – the last individual or buyer group in a supply chain to take a product/service differentiation decision – to ensure they get best value for money from the supply network that serves them and that they will continue to wish to be served by that network. For example, end customers for cardiovascular products were identified as including cardiologists, perfusionists, radiologists, theatre managers, business managers, technicians and any other budget holders.

Supply strategies were underpinned by a framework, shown in Table 40.2, containing:

● clear identification and understanding of end customer segments and their requirements, through integration of purchasing with marketing and customer service
● development of a service concept to serve end customer segments
● development of a service package to support the concept, including the design of the service and its delivery, through integration of purchasing with marketing, customer service and logistics

Portfolio teams selected high priority product/service families within their portfolios to target supply strategies. For example, in pharmaceuticals, 82 per cent of the total pharmaceutical spend of £761m was on the following product families:

● Pharmaceuticals, generic
● Pharmaceuticals, proprietary
● IV fluids
● Medical gases
● Enteral feeds

---

* IFPMM – the International Federation of Purchasing and Materials Management

**Table 40.2 The supply strategy framework**

| End customer segment requirements | Service concept | Service package | Supply strategy | |
|---|---|---|---|---|
| | | | Supply structure | Supply infrastructure |
| • Price (cost)<br>• Delivery speed<br>• Flexibility<br>• Product/service quality<br>• Innovation<br>• Range<br>• Reliability<br>• Competence<br>• Access<br>• Courtesy<br>• Communication<br>• Credibility<br>• Security<br>• Understanding the customer | • Aim of the service | • Service design<br>• Service delivery | • Capacity – size, volume and timing<br>• Supply network players configuration<br>• Supply network facilities configuration e.g. fleet, buildings, materials handling systems<br>• Do-or-buy | • Supply network human resource policies<br>• Supply network quality systems<br>• Supply network operations planning and control<br>• New offer development<br>• Supply network organisation<br>• Performance measurement, reward and incentivisation |

- Procedure packs
- Wound management products
- Absorbents.

In each portfolio, therefore, strategies were formed that were focused on end customer requirements and how the supply network could support the delivery and satisfaction of those requirements.

## Providing leading edge thinking and innovation from the supply network

Between 1995 and 2000, experience from the implementation of the supply strategy approach led to important changes in views of what NHS Supplies could and should contribute to the NHS. Corporate goals changed, as did the expectations of members of the NHS and the Department of Health. Instead of focusing on dyadic relations with NHS trust budget holders and private sector suppliers, directors and purchasing personnel widened their perspective to consider supply networks and the impact of network performance on the end customer.

However, the potential for a strategic role was greater than formulating and implementing strategies to improve performance to support the satisfaction of end customers. Potentially, NHS Supplies could take a sector-level perspective, considering the interests of the National Health Service as a whole, rather than only the needs of individual hospital trusts.

NHS Supplies increasingly viewed its future role as more strategic, becoming not just a centre of excellence for all matters relating to supply for and on behalf of the NHS, but taking a policy lead on supply issues on behalf of the NHS. Its role included taking decisions on the appropriate type and level of intervention in any supply context. In this way it became more proactive and innovative for the NHS, leading rather than supporting. It was able to provide economies of scope for the NHS through providing specialist services not justifiable in any one individual NHS organisation. For example, in addition to negotiating framework agreements for energy, the estates team gained expertise in energy management and was able to advise hospitals on how to become more energy efficient. Each trust hospital could not justify having its own specialists in the Private Finance Initiative or in strategic outsourcing, so NHS Supplies could offer an additional service by developing its expertise in these areas.

The role of NHS Supplies was formally changed in April 2000 when the strategy and purchasing functions of the organisation were formed into the NHS Purchasing and Supply Agency and taken into 'head office' – the Department of Health. The wholesaling and logistics functions of the organisation remained in the special health authority (with a reporting role to the new agency) and was renamed the NHS Logistics Authority. Figure 40.4 shows the revised arrangements for purchasing and logistics in the NHS.

**Figure 40.4  Revised arrangements for purchasing and logistics in the NHS**

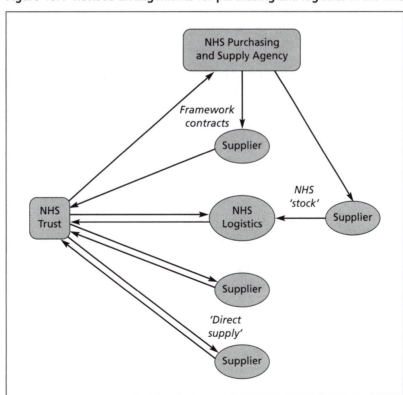

*Source*: NHS Purchasing and Supply Agency – 2001

## Questions

1 *Map the supply network for the NHS in 1991.*

2 *Do a SWOT analysis for NHS Supplies in 1991 – what were the main strategic alternatives for dealing with supply for the NHS at that time?*

3 *NHS Supplies went through distinct stages of development. At each stage, what enabled NHS Supplies to move to the next stage and what blocked it?*

4 *Assess the relative merits of privatisation of all or part of NHS Supplies.*

5 *What are the main contextual differences for a chief executive of a public sector organisation operating at the level of the sector, such as NHS Supplies, as opposed to one operating as an individual private sector firm?*

# PART 6

# Quality planning and control

# Introduction to Part 6

We are undergoing a 'quality revolution', and there is a growing realisation that high-quality goods and services give an organisation a considerable competitive edge. Good quality reduces the cost of rework, scrap and returns and, most importantly, generates satisfied customers. Some operations managers believe that, in the long run, quality is the single most important factor affecting an operation's performance relative to the competition.

Figure P6.1 illustrates the various ways in which quality improvements can affect other aspects of operations performance.

**Figure P6.1 Higher quality has a beneficial effect on both revenues and cost**

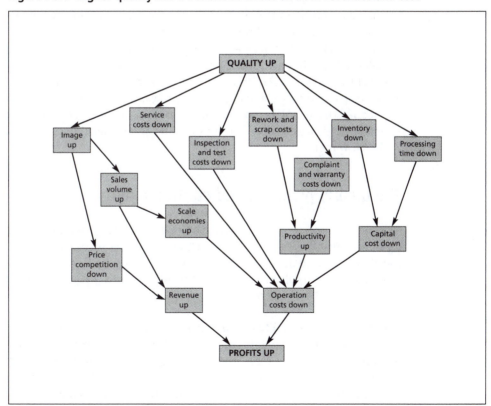

*Source*: Based on Gummesson, E. (1993)

Quality is often defined as 'consistent conformance to customers' expectations'. This definition does not take account of the fact that the quality of a product or service may be perceived differently by different customers. A definition that integrates the operation's view of quality, concerned with trying to meet customers' expectations, and the customer's perceived view of quality: 'quality is the degree of fit between customers' expectations and their perception of the product or service'. If the product or service experience was better than expected, then the customer is satisfied and quality is perceived to be high. If the product or service was less than his or her expectations, then quality is perceived to be low and the customer may be dissatisfied. If the product or service matches expectations, then the perceived quality of the product or service is acceptable. (See Executive Holloware for a good discussion of the importance of quality.)

## Diagnosing quality problems

The gap between expectations and perceptions may be caused by four related gaps, as illustrated in Figure P6.2.

1 *The customer specification – operations specification gap* Perceived quality could be poor because there may be a mismatch between the organisation's own internal quality specification and the specification that is expected by the customer.
2 *The concept – specification gap* Perceived quality could be poor because there is a mismatch between the product or service concept and the way the organisation has internally specified the quality of the product or service.
3 *The quality specification – actual quality gap* Perceived quality could be poor because there is a mismatch between the actual quality of the service or product provided by the operation and its internal quality specification.
4 *The actual quality – communicated image gap* Perceived quality could also be poor because there is a gap between the organisation's external communications or market image and the actual quality of the service or product delivered to the customer.

## The quality planning and control activity

Of the four gaps described above, the one for which operations managers bear the most responsibility is to ensure that the product or service conforms to its required specification (Gap 3). Quality planning and control tries to ensure that Gap 3 does not exist. This involves six sequential steps (the first four are dealt with here and the remaining two in Part 7):

### Step 1 – Define the quality characteristics of the product or service
The detailed design specification of the product or service should provide operations managers with a clear understanding of the characteristics of that product or service and how it is expected to perform – see Smithy's Brewery (Case 41). The characteristics will include functionality, appearance, reliability, durability, recovery (ease of repair) and contact (the nature of person-to-person contact involved in the delivery of the product or service).

**Figure P6.2  A gap between customers' expectations and their perception of a product or service could be explained by one or more gaps elsewhere in the model**

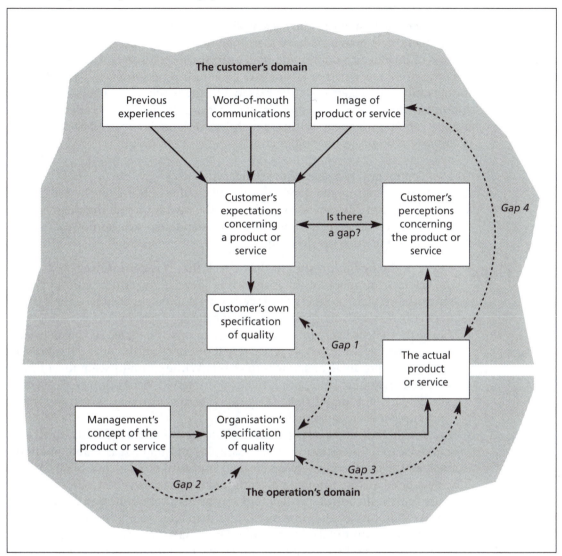

### Step 2 – Decide how to measure each quality characteristic

For every product or service these characteristics must be defined in such a way that they can be measured and then controlled. This involves taking a very general quality characteristic, such as functionality or appearance, and breaking it down into its constituent elements. Measures for each element need then to be established, either objectively in the case of size or shape for example, or subjectively in the case of customer perceptions of courtesy or empathy.

The measures used by operations to describe quality characteristics are of two types – variables and attributes. Variable measures are those that can be measured on a continuously variable scale, for example length, diameter, weight or time. Attributes are those which are assessed by judgement and are dichotomous (that is, have two states), for example right or wrong, works or does not work, looks OK or not OK.

### Step 3 – Set quality standards for each quality characteristic

When operations managers have identified how any quality characteristic can be measured, they need a quality standard against which it can be checked, otherwise they will not know whether it indicates good or bad performance. The critical task for operations managers is setting reasonable and achievable targets which will be appropriate to the level of customers' expectations. In the case of variables these are usually called 'tolerances' within which the variable is required to conform (for example plus or minus one millimetre).

### Step 4 – Control quality against those standards

After setting up appropriate standards that are capable of being met by the operation and that will meet customers' expectations, the operation will then need to check that the products or services conform to those standards – see Fastflowers.com (Case 45). This involves three key decisions:

- Where in the operation should they check that it is conforming to standards? The key task for operations managers is to identify the critical control points at which the service, products or processes need to be checked to ensure that the product or services will conform to specification.
- Should they check every product or service or take a sample? Having decided the points at which the goods or services will be checked, the next decision is how many of the products or services to check. While it might seem ideal to check every single product being produced or every service being delivered, operations usually work on samples since 100 per cent inspection may be too costly, time-consuming or even dangerous.
- How should the checks be performed? There are two main methods which can be employed to help operations check samples and make reasonable predictions about all the products or services created. Statistical process control (SPC) aims to achieve good quality through prevention rather than detection. Once a process is under statistical control, predications can be made about how it should behave. Regular sampling of the process enables managers to make rational decisions about what action to take, if any, in order to maintain control. Acceptance sampling is concerned with whether to regard a complete incoming or outgoing batch of materials or customers as acceptable or not, on the basis of inspection of a representative sample.

Valley District Council Cleansing Services (Case 43) illustrates the application of SPC in a service setting. The case also brings up the issue of the 'total quality' nature of the business environment in which SPC is used. Sun Products (Case 44) provides an exercise in control charting and data is supplied to enable the calculation of process capability indices and to compile run charts.

### Step 5 – Find and correct causes of poor quality and Step 6 – Continue to make improvements are dealt with in Part 7 of this book.

## Recommended reading

Bergman, B. and Klefsjö, B. (1994), *Quality – from Customer Needs to Customer Satisfaction*, McGraw-Hill.

Slack, N., Chambers, S., Johnston, R. (2001), *Operations Management*, (3rd edn), Financial Times/Prentice Hall, Harlow, Chapter 17.

## References

Gummesson, E. (1993), Service productivity, service quality and profitability, *Proceedings of the 8th International Conference of the Operations Management Association*, University of Warwick, UK.

# Smithy's Brewery

Case date
2001

Robert Johnston

Smithy's Brewery is a small independent brewery in the UK supplying real ale to its 200 pubs in the south-west of England. It brews a range of quality beers, the most popular of which is Anvil Ale, a traditional, light tawny-coloured beer with a slightly fruity taste and malty finish with an original gravity (OG) of 1038, alcohol by volume (ABV) 3.8%. Its stronger beer is Old Smithy, a dark-brown, well-rounded old ale, OG 1045, ABV 4.6%. In the summer a lighter addition to the range is Thirstquencher with a dry hopped aroma and clean bitter taste, OG 1035, ABV 3.4%. All of the brewery's pubs trade under the Anvil name, for example the Anvil and Hammer and the Anvil Arms, and are located within about 100 miles of Weston-Super-Mare. Many of the pubs are featured in *The Good Beer Guide* published by CAMRA (Campaign for Real Ale). (For more information visit *www.camra.org.uk*, *www.real-ale-guide.co.uk*, and *www.greatbritishbeers.co.uk*.)

Dick Nowak is the owner and General Manager and he inherited the brewery from his father 10 years ago, since which time he has doubled the output of the brewery to its present size. He explained the problems that he is facing:

'Everything seems stacked against us at the moment. Beer drinking is really on the decline and has been for the last 10 years. Not only are people spending less and less in pubs but the younger market is shifting away from traditional real beers to keg beers and the nitro-kegs (smoothflow beers). They also go in for novelty cocktails and non-alcoholic health drinks. The older market also seems to be drinking less beer and more wine.'

There is some evidence to support his views. Between 1990 and 2000, British beer consumption fell by 13 per cent to around two billion pints per year and during the same period wine consumption doubled (Brewers and Licensed Retailers Association, 2001). Whilst this movement is the result of changing consumer tastes, it has also been exacerbated by the strengthening grip on the market by the big breweries.

In the early 1990s the British Government, following a review of the beer industry by the Monopolies and Mergers Commission, tried to force the six big breweries to relax their 'complex monopoly' on the industry. At that time these breweries accounted for 75 per cent of beer production. The legislation required the breweries to open up some of their pubs to non-tied beers, that is allow their tenants to buy one draught beer not produced by the brewery that owned the pub. Rather than free their pubs of some of the tie to the brewery, the major breweries embarked on a number of different strategies, including selling thousands of their pubs to new pub-owning companies, often set up with money from the big breweries. These pub companies were outside the remit of the legislation.

Many smaller brewery owners, such as Dick Nowak, felt that the legislation had been totally ineffective, indeed the evidence was that it had made the situation worse. By 1999 there were just four major national breweries now controlling 85 per cent of the county's beer production and the new pub companies (pubcos) had emerged as a major retailing force in the industry, with about four companies controlling over 10 000 pubs between them. These new, powerful pubcos could now not only demand heavily discounted beer but also require a product that does not need too much looking after. Handling cask beer (real ales), unlike keg beer, involves a great deal of care. It requires an ability to monitor the development of each living cask until it has reached maturity with the correct level of natural condition before it can be served. It also demands routine stock rotation to ensure each cask is used within three days, before oxidation sets in, and that a replacement cask is ready, in prime condition, to replace it.

Dick bemoaned the demise of the traditional manager with the skills of tending real beer:

'Traditional pub managers selling traditional beers have been ethnically cleansed by the country's big brewers. The old managers have been replaced by salaried managers paid by vast pub-owning chains, trained to maximise profits and even to call their customers "traffic" as though they were running petrol stations not pubs. They don't want a living organism in their cellars. They haven't got the time. They just want ease of use and no worries. These management types have been responsible for the demise of the traditional pub, ripping out good fixtures and fittings and creating themed pubs which all look the same: characterless, compulsory music, mediocre food, and "have a nice day" service.'

## Smithy's solution

Retail General Manager, Karen Lees, is responsible for overseeing Smithy's 200 pubs through a network of seven district managers, each responsible for about 30 pubs. She explained how the brewery should face up to the decline in sales and in particular the decline in beer sales.

'There is a need for any brewery that is to survive in the beer, wine and spirit retail trade to be able to differentiate itself from the competition. This is not an easy task as all our competitors have similar locations, with similar products at similar prices. Even when a competitor brings out a new product, it is relatively easy for us or anyone else to either reproduce it at similar prices or buy it in from the competitor. The problem is that Anvil does not have a unique selling point (USP). There is nothing that differentiates us from the competition.

'We need to position ourselves as a traditional brand with good honest values of good beer, good food and homely service provided by people who care. By all means we should provide a full range of drinks including alcopops (blends of alcohol and juices) but we also need to focus on how we relate to our customers. As a USP I think this will help us achieve real market growth and be difficult, if not impossible, for the major players to follow. It will, however, need changes, not only in the pubs themselves but to overall company culture and central control systems. This I believe could be difficult for a less forward-looking and flexible company to follow.'

There was some evidence to substantiate Karen's views. A recent survey commissioned by the brewery had found that good service was important to customers. The survey of 40 Anvil pubs reported that customers felt that staff attitudes were crucial in creating the right atmosphere and that customers expected them to be friendly, happy, smiling, polite and efficient. Every single person in the survey agreed that pubs should provide a friendly, warm and happy atmosphere. Furthermore, customers believed that the high turnover of staff was an indication of poor management.

Karen continued:

'We already have good traditional beers and many excellent pubs where the character has been maintained and cherished. What we need to complete our vision is a high standard, of service. If we can do this, I believe our turnover and profits will increase. In all fairness, many people believe that we are not doing badly at the moment. The company only receives about 10 written complaints a month. This, you must realise, is out of thousands of sales every single day. However, this really says that we are not giving "bad" service but it does not say that we are giving "good" service. I believe that if we could make an improvement in this area, and move from providing not bad service to providing good or even outstanding service, we will be far ahead of the competition. One problem is that we are not sure what constitutes "good" service as each and every customer's idea of what is good service might be different. Another problem is that our service has been getting worse in some pubs where they are experiencing declining sales. The first thing the managers do is cut back on staff and it seems that some customers are just walking out because they are not getting served fast enough. Then they find they are not able to sell the contents of a barrel within three days and are left with stale beer which we then have to buy back as ullage. Some bar staff have told me that they feel pressurised to serve customers as quickly as possible and are often stressed from having to deal with impatient and irritable customers who have had to wait.'

The brewery has segmented its pubs into four pub types based broadly upon the clientele that they each tend to attract, which usually depends upon the location of the pub:

- The local – small town or city pubs, usually on the outskirts, with a regular clientele, with darts and dominoes and a snack menu
- The traditional town pub (young people) – town centre drinking pubs with music, serving snacks at lunch time and early evening, transient clientele with large numbers of customers at weekends
- The traditional town pub (older people) – town centre quiet pubs with bar meals, real fires and quiet background music
- The traditional country pub – destination pubs requiring car journeys from nearby towns, with family-friendly facilities, wide range of meals available all day, piped music and beer gardens.

Karen added:

'However, realistically, we have 200 different pub types as each and every one of our pubs is different and attracts different people. You see, we are not branded, and I don't think we want to be. Our customers don't have a McDonald's expectation of what they are going to get.'

## The staffing problem

Karen explained the problem:

'The main problem is that our pub managers rely predominantly on part-time staff, and part time can be anything from one evening a week to every lunchtime and evening. The typical bar person is a married housewife who is trying either to supplement the family income or save up for a particular need, like a holiday. Most of our pub managers experience difficulty in recruiting good staff. They require someone who is neat, numerate, reliable and honest but who will work for quite low pay.

'The crux of the problem is that our staff change more often than our customers. Our staff turnover is not unusual for the industry. We have about 2000 staff in our pubs and we employ about 3000 new people each year and they stay with us an average of six months. This is not quite as bad as it seems for we have a core of good people, about 38 per cent of the total workforce, who have been with us for some time. There is only a small turnover in this core.

'You will realise that training staff is a bit of a headache! My small central training staff cannot deal with that many new staff each year and, quite rightly, we leave it to managers to train their own staff. However, we give them a lot of help and support in this area. We provide videos and written guidelines and we also provide a training programme for the pub manager. This involves one-to-one instruction and also training the managers on how to train their staff. This is a relatively new idea in the business. Already 100 pub managers and their partners have been through this programme. We are hoping to have had all of them through it by the end of this year.'

## Central control

There is strict control of the performance of each pub and pub manager. Each pub manager reports directly to a District Manager (DM). Each year the District Manager negotiates with the Licensed House Manager (LHM) and discusses the budget for the future year and the possible promotional campaigns. The pub's budget is based on the previous year's contribution plus a bit more to account for proposed changes in prices, volumes, costs and promotional efforts. The LHM receives bonuses on a sliding scale depending on their performance over the agreed target. There is careful and frequent monitoring of their performance in terms of turnover, profits, stocks, food sales, staff turnover, general effectiveness and competence by the District Manager, who is seen to be there to help and advise and, if necessary, remove.

Dick outlined a problem with control systems:

'The problem is that we employed a guy with a management degree a few years ago as our financial controller. We thought if he shaped up we might offer him a place on the board in due course. However, he implemented many control systems that were more appropriate to a large chain, not a family-owned business like ours. I think they have changed the culture of our business and we now need to get back to our traditional values. Thankfully he left to work for one of the major breweries last year.'

Karen added:

'He also developed a customer service report that he used to check out one or two pubs each month (see Appendix 41.1). When a pub scored less than three overall, which happened quite often, he would inform the pub's District Manager of the unsatisfactory performance. We now use the form as an auditing tool and we use all of our senior brewery staff, visiting pubs incognito, who send the audit sheet to the DM as additional feedback on his or her public houses. We are concentrating on three areas at the moment. First, the "welcome" – we believe that every customer wants a good welcome which includes acknowledging their presence when they arrive at the bar. Second, good facilities – everyone wants to see a clean and tidy pub. Third, we are trying to get the staff to always provide a "good-bye".'

## Improving the service

Karen again:

'Not only do we need to start understanding what the regular customers see as good service, but we must also try to understand what attracts passing trade, because today's passing trade could be tomorrow's regular.'

A second survey of 100 pubs found that 84 per cent of the customers described the pub as their 'local' – the pub that they usually frequented and that passing trade only accounted for 16 per cent of the business. The most common reason for visiting the pub, according to the survey, was that of convenience. Friends, friendly staff, good service and food were secondary. The type of beer also appears to have little significance on pub selection. Forty per cent of those surveyed came into the pub unaccompanied, suggesting that the pub is a place for social gathering and companionship for the lonely.

Karen readily admitted that it is not easy trying to improve customer service.

'The problem is that our performance measurement of the LHM is very much financially orientated. 'A lot of LHMs even have their own laptops and spend hours analysing, their own profit and loss accounts. While this shows real financial keenness and control, it significantly reduces the time that they spend with their staff and customers.'

Dick added:

'The company is, understandably, financially orientated and our control systems mirror this. It would be a bit of an overstatement to say that all DMs assume that all LHMs are thieves, but in reality the control systems that have been developed seem to imply it. Just as it would be a bit of an overstatement to say that all LHMs assume that their staff are incompetent but, again, some of their house rules imply it. For instance, managers were not allowed to permit their staff to accept a cheque for over £10 without the manager checking it first, despite the fact that most bar staff have bank accounts and handle the family budget. They are just as able and competent as the manager to make sure the cheque is in order. This has now changed and the limit is £50, which is much more sensible. We also need to change the delivery system, which "our friend" developed, which results in deliveries to one of our busiest country pubs on a Saturday lunchtime, one of its busiest times of the week! There are a lot of other crazy things that have been set up and we need to stop them.'

Karen continued:

'The biggest difficulty is the bar staff. How do I interest an eight-hour-a-week part timer, who is only with us for six months to get some spending money for the summer holiday, in providing good service? Most staff don't even see it as a "real" job and they feel that it has low status not only because of its low pay but also because they think that anyone can do it. Despite the fact that in a recent survey all staff said that coping with the customer is the most difficult aspect of the job, none of them had received guidelines on it and even felt that the only formal training they did require was on how to use the electronic cashtill. My worry is that if we try a "put people first" type campaign they may either feel that they know it already or they will see it as a "two day wonder" package.'

## The way forward

Karen outlined what needs to be done:

'Somehow we need a training or communications exercise to increase people's awareness of the problem. I don't believe we can change our level of customer service, especially people's attitudes to the customer, just by saying that it is a problem. Somehow we need to create awareness and appreciation. We need an output called "customer service". But it is almost against current culture, not only at HQ level but also in the pub, where unless you are in the right circle of locals you may not get good friendly service. Somehow we have to be able to define good customer service and we have to measure it and somehow reward it. We have to change the bar staff from being beer pushers and money takers to being good traditional service providers.'

The signs are hopeful that the company can achieve this. Recently one DM organised a staff training session in an evening. Attendance was entirely voluntary but there was a buffet at the end of the evening. The DM's colleagues said that no one would turn up as he was not going to pay people to attend. The DM hoped that about 20 people would attend. On the day, 50 people turned up and it was a great occasion. At the end of the evening the DM concluded that not only were staff desperate to learn more, they were also desperate to contribute more.

Karen concluded:

'Most of our bar staff are housewives and mothers with families; we need to understand what makes them give only adequate service at work when they give good service to their families at home. Also, we need to get managers to demonstrate good service and to set high physical and interpersonal standards. Somehow he or she has to become a coach, not a cop.'

### Questions

1 *Why was Smithy's Brewery considering improving its customer service?*

2 *How good or bad was its service?*

3 *What do you think are the barriers to improvement?*

4 *Evaluate the customer service report form as a means of measuring service quality.*

5 *Apply the 'gap model' to the case, describing each gap and explaining why you think it exists.*

6 *How would you suggest the company goes about improving its service?*

## Appendix 4.1

## Customer service report

PUB _____  DATE _____
DM _____  TIME _____

| | 1 | 2 | 3 | 4 | 5 | NOTES |
|---|---|---|---|---|---|---|
| **WELCOME** | | | | | | |
| Acknowledgement | | | | | | |
| The greeting | | | | | | |
| Invitation to purchase | | | | | | |
| **DRINK** | | | | | | |
| Correct drink | | | | | | |
| Passing off if appropriate[a] | | | | | | |
| Correct glass | | | | | | |
| Ice | | | | | | |
| Fruit | | | | | | |
| Cleanliness of glass | | | | | | |
| Selling up[b] | | | | | | |
| Correct price and change | | | | | | |
| **FACILITIES** | | | | | | |
| Clean toilets | | | | | | |
| Clean and clear tables | | | | | | |
| Clean ashtrays | | | | | | |
| **FOOD** | | | | | | |
| Menu | | | | | | |
| Availability | | | | | | |
| Selling up[b] | | | | | | |
| Clean plates | | | | | | |
| **STAFF** | | | | | | |
| Appearance | | | | | | |
| Speed of service | | | | | | |
| **GOODBYE** | | | | | | |
| Goodbye and thank you | | | | | | |
| **OVERALL SCORE** | | | | | | |

*Notes*:
[a] Passing off is the offering of an alternative product to the one that is requested because it is not stocked.
[b] Selling up is the offering of a more expensive alternative to the one that is requested.

# Executive Holloware

Case date
2002

Kevan Scholes*

'We must get to the bottom of this quality problem,' said Hugh Preston, Managing Director of Executive Holloware Ltd, at one of his regular monthly meetings with senior managers in June 2002.

'I've just seen some figures from Jean Lipson's accountants and it appears that it may be costing us more than £12 000 each month – and that's only reworking costs and customer returns, heaven only knows what the total cost might be. I've asked Paul Stone from Quality Assurance to look at this problem and report back to me by the end of July. I hope you'll all give him every assistance in sorting this one out'.

Quality had always been of importance at Executive since many of its products were aimed at the top end of the market and commanded high prices. Its most important product line was its hand made, silver-plated Georgian tea sets retailing at anything from £400 upwards. Other products included hand made, silver-plated candelabra, small items of giftware (silver-plated) and tea sets made from pewter and stainless steel.

Executive had been founded in 1948 in Birmingham and began by manufacturing a wide range of cutlery and tableware items. The company had gradually narrowed its range and by 2002 had become one of the leading UK suppliers of top-quality holloware as well as continuing to produce items for the less expensive end of the holloware market. Turnover in 2001 exceeded £18 millions, although pre-tax profits of only £160 000 had been very disappointing compared with the company's profit performance over the previous 10 years. The Chairman's report for the year had sought to explain this poor profit situation:

'The results are, of course, a disappointment but are largely a result of production inefficiencies during this period of transferring our traditional craft methods to a batch production, light engineering type system. We are confident that the new methods will give us the necessary competitive edge and help us return to, and exceed, our previous levels of profitability.'

Paul Stone, the Quality Assurance Manager, decided to approach his brief in two ways. Firstly, his department would undertake a quality survey on a sampling basis to assess the scale of the problem and, secondly, he would talk to people in the company who were either directly or indirectly concerned with quality. He decided to concentrate his efforts, in the first instance, on silver-plated teapots since they were by far the most important item made at Executive.

---

* This case is based on a real organisation and was written by Kevan Scholes and adapted by Robert Johnston. The author gratefully acknowledges the financial assistance of the Nuffield Foundation who supported the writing of this case study. All rights reserved to the author. Copyright © H.K.Scholes 2002

**Figure 42.1 Production route and responsibilities**

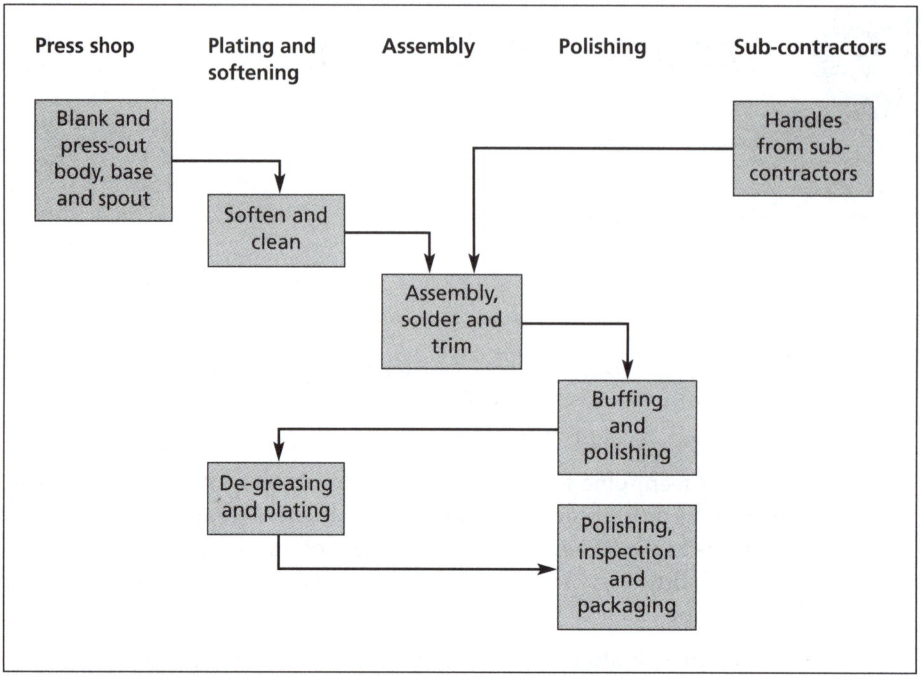

## Quality control at Executive

The Quality Assurance Department's task was to ensure that goods leaving the factory were of the required quality. In addition, the department dealt with customer complaints. Internal quality assurance was performed on a batch sampling basis (10 per cent for most items) of goods leaving the final polishing process (see Figure 42.1). In the case of teapots, they were inspected for both dimensional accuracy and surface finish (scratches and bruises). Batches rejected on a sampling basis were subjected to 100 per cent inspection and rejects either renovated or scrapped (depending on the nature of the defect). Certain items, for example candelabra and top-quality tea sets, were subjected to 100 per cent inspection as a matter of course.

The Quality Assurance Department was, from time to time, involved in investigating quality problems arising during production or with bought-in components, teapot handles for example. The majority of these investigations arose as a result of complaints from the Buffing and Polishing Department about the number of scratched or bruised items they were having to deal with.

## Paul Stone's quality survey

Paul first checked through sales records for the last 12 months and found that out of every 100 teapots sold, around five were returned by the retailers with complaints about bruising, scratching or slightly misshapen pots. Paul then checked through the final inspection records for the last 100 teapots which showed that five had been rejected at that stage. All five had scratches and one also had a bruise

**Table 42.1 Quality survey – silver-plated teapots**

| Stage of production process | Percentage sub-standard[a] | | | |
|---|---|---|---|---|
| | Dimensional accuracy | Scratches | Bruises | Total[b] |
| Leaving press shop (bodies only) | 2 | 24 | 6 | 28 |
| Prior to assembly (all items) | 2 | 32 | 6 | 32 |
| Leaving assembly | 0 | 30 | 8 | 32 |
| Leaving buffing and polishing | 0 | 20 | 1 | 20 |

*Notes*:
[a] Sample size 100
[b] Some teapots were rejected on more than one count.

above the spout. Paul decided to take a random sample of 100 teapots at various stages in the production system and assess their 'quality' in terms of dimensional accuracy and surface condition. The results of his survey are shown in Table 42.1.

Having completed the survey, Paul decided to discuss his findings with Andrew Keegan, the new Production Director at Executive. Andrew Keegan's reaction to the figures was as follows:

'Well, Paul, on the face of it, it looks as though I should have asked you to do a survey like this when I first arrived – there certainly does seem to be a serious problem, particularly on scratching. I know that nickel silver's not the easiest material to deal with but I'm surprised at the scale of the problem. What I find difficult to swallow is the fact that most of these scratches and bruises are being removed by reworking so why did they get through the system in the first place? I think we'd both better have a word with Jim Dyer, the Senior Shop Foreman.'

Knowing Jim's reluctance to speak too frankly when Andrew Keegan was around, Paul decided that he had better have a chat with Jim by himself if he was going to get any useful information on the quality angle. He met Jim later that day in his office. Paul explained the results of his survey and asked for Jim's opinion. Jim said:

'I don't doubt that your people have done a good job Paul, but you know the problems as well as I do. First of all, how do you decide what is a scratch and what is not a scratch? Even after 20 years I'm not sure how consistent I am on that one. Then of course there's Keegan breathing down my neck all the time about output – I mean he can't have it both ways, can he? What's more, the workers in the shop can't spend all day worrying about every little scratch – what would their pay packets look like at the end of the week if they did? I think it'd be quite a good idea if you had a chat with Alan Jones in the Buffing Shop. He had a go at me only last week about this one!'

Paul decided to take up Jim Dyer's suggestion and managed to speak to Alan Jones a couple of days later. He told Alan he was particularly interested in his views on the scratching and bruising problems. Alan was only too willing to tell him!

'You probably know that I had a bit of a barny with Jim Dyer over this last week. It was about one batch of teapots we got from assembly which were in a dreadful state. Apart from some deep scratches, half of them were bruised and should never have been let out of the shop. Jim seemed to feel I was being too fussy but, quite honestly, if we've got to sort out rubbish like that, we'll never earn a living wage – I don't think the

Assembly workers care any more. When I worked up there we used to do our own buffing and polishing and problems like this never arose, but with the new set-up, the sooner they get them out and on the worksheet the better seems to be the attitude. They don't seem to care if we send half of them back – it gives them more work to do.'

Paul decided that before he could put his report together he needed to see John Wells, the Sales Director, and Jean Lipson in Finance. He managed to see John Wells the following week and asked him about the customer complaints situation. John told him:

'Frankly, you probably know as much about this as I do since it's your people who investigate the complaints. As you know, most complaints come from the shops – very few from the public, although this may not be a fair picture as the shops may not be passing on customer complaints. In the case of Georgian tea sets, I'm sure that we're very often accepting responsibility for scratching that isn't our fault – but it's difficult to prove that of course. The trouble is that the tea sets usually need to go back to Buffing and then Replating, which must cost a great deal. One thing I find funny is that we've had very few complaints about the new range – probably because they're fighting each other to get hold of them as they're selling like hot cakes, apparently. The thing that worries me most at the moment is that the backlog of work in the factory is lengthening my delivery times.'

Paul met with Jean Lipson, the Finance Director, that afternoon and asked for her opinion on the whole quality problem. Jean told him:

'I raised this with the MD because it's something that worried me for a long time. The trouble, as I see it, is that we really don't know what's going on. For example, it's almost impossible to sort out reworking from normal work and even if you manage to do that, it's only guesswork as to the costs of reworking. I know that Andrew Keegan seems to think that a lot of the overtime in the Buffing Shop must be due to reworking and he'd like to cut it down.'

Following this chat, Paul decided it was about time he sat down and started work on his report if he was to meet the MD's deadline. The situation certainly didn't seem so straightforward as he had assumed it might be!

## Questions

1  *Why is quality important to Executive Holloware?*

2  *What do you understand by the term 'quality'?*

3  *How would you specify 'quality' for Executive Holloware?*

4  *What are the underlying causes of the problems at Executive Holloware?*

5  *How should Executive Holloware measure quality at each stage of the process?*

6  *What steps would you advise Paul Stone to take to improve quality?*

CASE
43

# Valley District Council Cleansing Services

Case date
March 1996

John Bicheno and Alan Harrison

## Introduction

The party was in full swing. Everyone who was anyone connected with the Cleansing Service at Valley District Council was there. Dustmen, street sweepers and civic amenity site workers rubbed shoulders with the mayor, councillors and chief officers. Why? To celebrate the success of Valley Council's 'Cleaner Environment' campaign.

It all began some 10 years ago when Teresa New, the chairperson of the Environment Committee, visited the United States on holiday. She had used the opportunity to call in on the 'Keep America Beautiful' organisation, and had been impressed by their systems approach to reducing the sources and causes of litter. Each source should be specifically targeted and improved through a combination of awareness, education, enforcement and facilities such as litter bins. Rapid response to litter accumulation was also part of the organisation's approach, since it had been shown that a cleaner environment tended to remain clean, while litter promoted yet more littering. One particular point that stuck in Teresa's mind was 'if you don't measure the incidence of littering, you will never know if you are wasting your ratepayer's money, and you won't know how to focus your campaign'. As a hard-nosed accountant, this had particular appeal to Teresa.

On returning home, Teresa made a beeline for the Tidy Britain Group (TBG). This is an independent charity, part-funded by the Department for the Environment, Food and Rural Affairs with a specific brief as the national litter abatement agency. TBG works through six initiatives:

- *Awards* – recognising excellence through campaigns such as *Britain in Bloom*
- *Consultancy* – through the group's Environmental Research and Consultancy Unit
- *Research* – such as developing standard ways to measure litter
- *People and Places* – working at community level
- *Campaigning* – to raise awareness and the need for action
- *Education* – targeting schools in particular.

TBG offered invaluable assistance, and recommended use of the international 'Tidyman' symbol shown in Figure 43.1.

Several years and seemingly innumerable meetings later, Valley Council had adopted a complete package of measures proposed by the Environment Committee. Today's party was being held to celebrate the achievements these measures had

**Figure 43.1 International 'Tidyman' symbol**

made, that is a 40 per cent reduction in the litter count from an average 27 pieces to the current 16.

Valley District Council is one of three local authorities in a county in South Wales. The Council's area includes one town of moderate size, four smaller towns and over 40 villages. The population and most of the industry is concentrated in the south. The Council undertakes the normal range of services required of a non-metropolitan district council. Services include recreation and tourism, environmental health, housing, planning and economic development, and cleansing services.

The Cleansing Service basically undertakes refuse collection and disposal and street cleansing. It runs civic amenity sites where garden waste and bulky objects can be left, and container services comprising both compacted waste from office buildings and other waste removed in open skips. The Cleansing Service has been subjected to compulsory competitive tendering and the compactor vehicles used for refuse collection are now run by contractors, with crews supplied by the District Council. For operating purposes, the Cleansing Service is divided into three depot areas, known simply as North, Mid and South, each controlled by a superintendent.

Street sweepers at Valley have a routine which requires them to cover all high street areas on their 'beat' once per day. Other areas are covered in a specified frequency which ranges from twice per week to once per month. Actual sweeping may not be needed, so the sweepers spend much of their time picking up litter with a scoop which looks like a domestic dustpan with a long handle. Their other equipment comprises a trolley with bins and brushes. A proportion of each day is left to the sweepers' own initiative. During these periods, sweepers can clean whatever area they think has highest priority. Since all of the sweepers live close to or on their beat, this has proved quite successful.

Apart from competitive tendering, several innovations have been undertaken in the last few years. These include new crew sizes, different plastic bags, trials with wheeled containers for business uses, mechanised sweeping in the Mid region, more litter bins of various types, and most recently 'doggy' bins. The doggy bin scheme had enjoyed priority since a private member's bill had gone through Parliament. A dog owner who did not clear up after their pet could now be fined up to £1000. Councillors and officers were now considering how the law could now be enforced, and in the light of the success with the litter campaign, how it might be measured.

Over the last two years, Valley had embarked on a Total Quality programme. Senior and middle-ranking officers had attended courses and were encouraged to adopt a 'TQ' philosophy by becoming more 'customer focused'. Several of the courses, however, made use of manufacturing examples and it was not always clear how the tools and techniques discussed in the courses could be adopted for use within the District Council.

## Measuring performance

The principal performance measures used at Valley are based on quality and productivity. Productivity is measured by sacks per man per year, and by cost per sack and per tonne removed. Where possible, these figures are compared with corresponding national data, but there is always controversy over such comparisons. Areas with relatively poor performance go to considerable lengths to explain why they are 'different'. 'Quality' of the Cleansing Service has traditionally been measured by complaints received. A recent analysis is shown in Table 43.1 for the Mid depot area.

**Table 43.1 Analysis of complaints received during 20 days last month**

| Complaint | Number received | Maximum in 1 day |
|-----------|-----------------|------------------|
| Late collection | 158 | 31 |
| Missed collection | 29 | 4 |
| Spillage | 89 | 16 |
| Broken bags | 22 | 3 |
| Bags not delivered | 67 | 6 |
| Litter | 10 | 4 |
| Dog fouling | 14 | 2 |
| Dangerous driving | 5 | 2 |
| All other | 18 | 2 |

Since her visit to the United States, Teresa had been convinced that measurement was fundamental to the success of the litter campaign, and insisted that additional measures to these must be devised. Eventually, the Cleansing Service decided on a modified version of methods recommended by TBG and 'Keep America Beautiful'. This required that 12 sites should be selected, each comprising 200 metres of typical high street pavement. Each day, four of the sites would be selected at random, and all pieces of litter would be counted, whatever their size, between the building line and the roadside edge of the gutter. Thus sweetpapers, cigarette ends, matches, soft drink cans and newspaper pages each count as one item. The sites themselves were kept secret, known only to four people within the Cleansing Service. Even the method used was kept confidential to a selection of council officers and councillors on the Environment Committee. In particular, neither the method nor the sites were disclosed to street sweepers or to shopowners adjoining the sites. Table 43.2 gives a sample of recent measures.

## At the party

During the party the Chairman of Valley District Council, Kevin Anderson, was introduced to staff by the Chief Cleansing Officer, Stan Verrier. In talking to one of the street sweepers, A. J. Williams, Councillor Anderson asked A. J. what he thought about the state of the streets. A. J. replied that he thought that while some areas had improved, 'there are still some very bad streets where people just don't seem to care. No matter how many times I clean them, they're always a mess the next day.'

**Table 43.2 Items of litter by sample area**

| | | Area | Items | Area | Items | Area | Items | Area | Items |
|---|---|---|---|---|---|---|---|---|---|
| Week 1 | Mon | S | 111 | N | 10 | M | 109 | S | 90 |
| | Tue | M | 3 | N | 12 | N | 8 | N | 16 |
| | Wed | S | 29 | M | 15 | N | 20 | M | 14 |
| | Thurs | N | 11 | S | 36 | M | 69 | N | 13 |
| | Fri | S | 27 | N | 6 | S | 3 | N | 5 |
| Week 2 | Mon | M | 90 | N | 13 | N | 14 | N | 15 |
| | Tue | S | 24 | M | 24 | M | 14 | S | 18 |
| | Wed | N | 19 | N | 11 | S | 27 | N | 11 |
| | Thurs | S | 11 | S | 22 | S | 12 | N | 6 |
| | Fri | M | 4 | S | 15 | N | 1 | S | 28 |
| Week 3 | Mon | N | 15 | M | 144 | S | 44 | N | 8 |
| | Tue | M | 15 | N | 13 | M | 10 | S | 28 |
| | Wed | M | 14 | S | 25 | M | 5 | S | 34 |
| | Thurs | M | 16 | M | 18 | N | 19 | S | 31 |
| | Fri | N | 21 | S | 37 | N | 10 | M | 12 |
| Week 4 | Mon | S | 49 | M | 88 | S | 83 | M | 120 |
| | Tue | M | 9 | M | 16 | N | 15 | M | 17 |
| | Wed | S | 22 | N | 9 | S | 35 | N | 17 |
| | Thurs | M | 15 | N | 13 | S | 24 | M | 6 |
| | Fri | M | 19 | M | 5 | N | 4 | M | 18 |
| Week 5 | Mon | S | 73 | S | 44 | M | 60 | M | 127 |
| | Tue | N | 3 | M | 17 | M | 18 | N | 10 |
| | Wed | M | 54 | N | 9 | S | 25 | M | 38 |
| | Thurs | S | 15 | S | 20 | N | 10 | N | 19 |
| | Fri | S | 27 | S | 29 | S | 34 | M | 7 |

Councillor Anderson took Stan to one side, and said 'People like A. J. are just trying to protect their jobs. We have to translate the success of our litter campaign into cost reductions that we can pass on to the ratepayers.'

In another part of the room, Councillor Teresa New was speaking to two of the street sweepers. 'But how do you know that there has been a 40 per cent reduction in litter?' asked Dai Jones. This put Teresa on the spot. 'We have a measurement system', she said, 'but you'll have to ask Mr Verrier how it works.' This rather spoiled the evening for the two sweepers. Were they being spied on, they wondered?

Later at the party, Stan Verrier was speaking to Councillor Gareth Edwards, a management consultant and member of the Environment Committee. Gareth suggested to Stan that the litter data could be plotted on an SPC chart. Stan said that he had heard about SPC at the Total Quality courses, but was reluctant to try SPC because 'no one in Cleansing Services is a statistician'. Gareth then said to Stan that SPC really stands for making a process 'Stable, Predictable and in Control'. 'I had never thought of it that way', said Stan.

1 *Should the measurement system for the litter campaign be more widely understood?*

2 *What do you think about Councillor Anderson's remarks about 'protecting jobs'?*

3 *How could SPC be used at Valley to analyse the number of litter items by sample area? (Clue: use a Number of Defects (c) control chart, and analyse the data by depot area ignoring Mondays.)*

$$\bar{c} = \Sigma c/n, \text{ and UCL} = \bar{c} + 3\sqrt{\bar{c}}, \text{ LCL} = \bar{c} - 3\sqrt{\bar{c}}$$

*What do the control charts suggest about the litter process at Valley?*

4 *Which of the other '7 Tools of SPC' could be used to analyse the litter problems at Valley, and how?*

CASE
44

# Sun Products Company: An exercise in variables control charting

Case date
March 1996

Alan Harrison

## Sun Products Company

Sun Products Company (SPC) makes a range of components for various customers in the automotive industry at home and abroad. One of these customers made an approach a year or so ago with a quality concern about the sunroof which was supplied by SPC. The customer delegation told the Sun QA Manager, Fred Jarvis:

'This is on our top 40 list of quality concerns at present. The height of the glass on the roof is often noticeably uneven, or sits too proud of the car body. We'd like to take a look around your processes to see if there are any immediate improvements we can make.'

After looking round the sunroof line at SPC, the customer delegation suggested to Fred that some improvements should be made to materials handling within the Sun works, and in the way that parts were transported from Sun suppliers. A detailed inspection of the production process with Fred and his colleagues had been made, and a process flow chart drawn up. But attention had eventually focused on the profile setting operation where the glass was fitted into the sunroof mechanism. A sketch of this is shown in Figure 44.1. A 100 per cent inspection of the profile was made by probes at the end of the production process. The probes measured the height of the glass at four points on the sunroof near to the corners, represented by P1, P2, P3 and P4.

The customer specification called for a profile measure with a tolerance of ±1.00mm for each point P1 to P4. If the probes detected a condition which was out of specification for one of these points, the inspector called for the profile setting to be altered.

A month later, the customer delegation returned to Fred, and told him that they had made further investigations of their own assembly process.

'We have made a number of immediate improvements on our assembly line, such as giving the operator a step block to make the fitting process more exact and less visual. Now we want you to introduce variable control charts on your profile setting operation. You are generating a lot of data at the inspection stage, but you're not doing enough with it! Further, you're reacting to events rather than controlling them.'

These comments had come as rather a shock to Fred, who thought that Sun had installed the best kit, and that it was virtually impossible (given 100 per cent inspection of the profile) for defective products to be shipped. Nevertheless, Fred got to

**Figure 44.1 The sunroof at Sun Products Company**

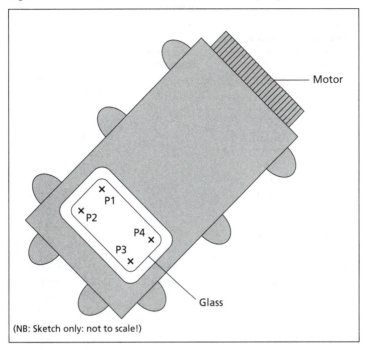

(NB: Sketch only: not to scale!)

work, first tackling a process capability study. This came as an even greater shock! The process was clearly out of control. It seemed very difficult to maintain specification on all four points at the same time. Thus $C_{pk}$ values of less than 1 were initially quite common. Fred concentrated first on getting rid of special causes of variability. For example, he found that when the glass supplier changed batches, the curvature of the glass could change significantly and cause problems at Sun. But once these problems had been recognised and dealt with, Fred was satisfied that control charting could start.

Although the inspection process would be left at 100 per cent for the time being, Fred decided on taking two samples each hour and recording the difference to specification for all four points P1 to P4. Samples would be taken for the two readings made closest to the hour. Tables 44.1 and 44.2 show the data which were used for calculating the grand average, and the upper and lower control limits for the averages chart (X Bar Chart) for point P3. They also provide the data used to calculate the upper control limit for the range chart (R Chart) for P3.

## Table 44.1 P3 data used to calculate the process capability indices

| | | Reading 1 | Reading 2 |
|---|---|---|---|
| Saturday 2/12 | 06.00hrs | +0.6mm | +0.2mm |
| | 07.00 | +0.3 | +0.2 |
| | 08.00 | +0.4 | +0.1 |
| | 09.00 | +0.1 | −0.3 |
| | 10.00 | −0.2 | +0.0 |
| | 11.00 | +0.0 | +0.0 |
| Monday 4/12 | 06.00 | +0.2 | +0.2 |
| | 07.00 | −0.3 | +0.1 |
| | 08.00 | −0.3 | +0.0 |
| | 09.00 | +0.1 | +0.3 |
| | 10.00 | +0.6 | +0.4 |
| | 11.00 | +0.0 | −0.2 |
| | 12.00 | +0.5 | +0.0 |
| | 13.00 | +0.1 | +0.2 |
| | 14.00 | +0.1 | +0.0 |
| | 15.00 | +0.2 | +0.3 |
| | 16.00 | +0.4 | +0.3 |
| | 17.00 | +0.1 | −0.1 |
| Tuesday 5/12 | 06.00 | +0.0 | +0.6 |
| | 07.00 | +0.2 | +0.0 |
| | 08.00 | −0.3 | −0.1 |
| | 09.00 | +0.0 | −0.2 |
| | 10.00 | +0.5 | +0.2 |
| | 11.00 | +0.1 | −0.2 |
| | 12.00 | −0.2 | −0.1 |
| | 13.00 | +0.0 | +0.1 |
| | 14.00 | +0.1 | +0.1 |
| | 15.00 | +0.0 | +0.4 |
| | 16.00 | −0.3 | −0.1 |

## Table 44.2 P3 data from a subsequent day's production

| | | Reading 1 | Reading 2 |
|---|---|---|---|
| Thursday 18/1 | 06.00 | −0.3 | −0.1 |
| | 07.00 | −0.4 | −0.1 |
| | 08.00 | −0.2 | −0.3 |
| | 09.00 | −0.2 | −0.2 |
| | 10.00 | −0.5 | −0.2 |
| | 11.00 | −0.4 | −0.8 |
| | 12.00 | −0.7 | −0.3 |
| | 13.00 | +0.1 | −0.1 |
| | 14.00 | −0.1 | −0.3 |
| | 15.00 | −0.3 | −0.1 |
| | 16.00 | +0.1 | +0.2 |
| | 17.00 | +0.1 | −0.1 |
| | 18.00 | −0.2 | −0.1 |
| | 19.00 | −0.1 | +0.2 |
| Friday 19/1 | 06.00 | −0.6 | −0.4 |
| | 07.00 | +0.0 | −0.4 |
| | 08.00 | −0.3 | −0.8 |
| | 09.00 | −0.5 | −0.2 |
| | 10.00 | −0.5 | −0.2 |
| | 11.00 | −0.5 | −0.2 |
| | 12.00 | +0.0 | +0.0 |
| | 13.00 | +0.1 | −0.2 |
| | 14.00 | +0.2 | −0.1 |
| | 15.00 | +0.0 | +0.6 |
| | 16.00 | +0.2 | −0.1 |
| | 17.00 | +0.2 | −0.1 |
| | 18.00 | +0.0 | +0.0 |

## Questions

1 Why was Sun's process before SPC implementation prone to giving problems to its customer in spite of 100 per cent inspection?

2 From Table 44.1, calculate the grand average and the upper and lower control limits for the P3 profile height setting process at Sun. Use the formulae and constants given on the control chart. Plot the hourly data on the chart. Given that action on special causes is called for if there is any point outside the control limits, or if there is a run of seven points all above or all below the central line, is the process under statistical control? Does this mean that Sun no longer ships defective product?

**3** Given the ±1.00mm engineering tolerance for all four profile points, calculate the $C_p$ and the $C_{pk}$ of the process.

For a sample size of 2, assume that $6\sigma = 5.319\,\bar{R}$.

$[C_p =$ tolerance $÷6\sigma$ of the process,

$C_{pk} =$ the smaller of (the upper specification limit – the grand average) $÷3\sigma$
and (the grand average – the lower specification limit) $÷3\sigma]$

**4** Table 44.2 shows data for P3 that was collected on a subsequent day. Again, plot the data on the $\bar{X}$ and R chart. Comment on the degree of process control this indicates.

**5** The customer is now pressing for the engineering tolerances to be reduced to ±0.5mm. What effect would this have on process capability at Sun?

**6** Comment on the sequence of events leading up to the introduction of control charting for the sunroof at Sun Products.

Jane Babson set up FastFlowers.com three years ago to provide a small range of cut flowers to customers over the Internet. The site shows a range of wreaths, bouquets, buttonholes and table displays suitable for 'all occasions'. Unlike her competitors who promise delivery sometime during the day, she offers delivery within one hour either side of an agreed delivery time, any time between 8.00 a.m. and 6.00 p.m. Despite initial scepticism from friends and colleagues in the trade, she had successfully managed to negotiate with flower delivery companies, including some national and international chains, to meet her delivery targets. Indeed a survey of delivery times undertaken by a student friend last year showed that the average delivery time was 29.5 minutes after the agreed time with a standard deviation of 13.3 minutes.

In the first year the business managed a turnover of £30 000 which has grown to £150 000. Jane now employs one person to help her deal with the orders which arrive by Internet, e-mail or phone. This involves sending e-mail acknowledgement of the order, and arranging delivery with a national flower delivery chain. If she is unable to find a company that is able or willing to fulfil the order on time, she arranges for her local florist to make up the order which she then sends by courier.

With a margin of less than 10 per cent Jane was unwilling to employ extra staff as yet, but she was finding much of her time was taken up with dealing with what seemed to be a rapidly increasing number of complaints about the late, and in a few cases, the early, delivery of flowers. When analysing the complaints she noticed over half of them would have been delivered by just three of the seven national chains that she uses, Interflower, Fleuro and BloomsUSA. She was reluctant to complain to the companies as good relations were essential because she had to negotiate prices and delivery times on every occasion. Furthermore, she did about 60 per cent of her business with these three. The alternative, sending flowers by courier, was much more expensive.

Jane needed to understand what was happening so she selected one customer who should have received flowers from each of the suspect organisations on each day for the last two weeks (excluding Sundays). The results, in terms of minutes late/early as reported by the customers, are shown in Table 45.1.

**Table 45.1 Results of delivery survey late/early**

|  | Mon | Tue | Wed | Thu | Fri | Sat | Mon | Tue | Wed | Thu | Fri | Sat |
|---|---|---|---|---|---|---|---|---|---|---|---|---|
| Interflower | 60 | 45 | 40 | 70 | 60 | 50 | 60 | 65 | 40 | 20 | 40 | 70 |
| Fleuro | −15 | 45 | 70 | 80 | 0 | −20 | 50 | 50 | 0 | −20 | 40 | 70 |
| BloomsUSA | 20 | 30 | 15 | 20 | 30 | 25 | 30 | 15 | 80 | 40 | 20 | 40 |

*Note*: A minus signifies an early delivery.

## Questions

1 *Evaluate the performance of FastFlowers' suppliers.*

2 *What do you think Jane should say to each of them?*

# PART 7

## Improvement

# Introduction to Part 7

Even when an operation is designed and its activities planned and controlled, the operations manager's task is not finished. All operations, no matter how well managed, are capable of improvement. In recent years the emphasis has shifted markedly towards making improvement one of the main responsibilities of operations managers. This section deals with four main areas:

1 *Performance measurement* If organisations are concerned to improve what they are doing, they need to know how good or bad they are at the moment and also know by how much they are improving. Performance measurement is therefore a prerequisite and essential tool for improvement.
2 *Types of improvement* There are two different and, to some extent, opposing philosophies on improvement: breakthrough and continuous improvement.
3 *Improvement techniques* There are many techniques that can help improve an organisation's operational performance.
4 *Total quality management (TQM)* This is probably the best known philosophy of improvement.

## Performance measurement

Performance measurement is the quantification of the performance of an operation. This may be carried out at a broad level in terms of the operation's performance objectives, quality, speed, dependability, flexibility and cost, although this does not help operations managers make decisions about exactly what to change. These performance objectives will usually be measured using a variety of more detailed second order measures, some of which may impact on one or more performance objectives. Some examples of performance measures are:

- *Quality* – number of defects, scrap level, customer complaints, or a customer satisfaction rating
- *Speed* – order lead-times, customer processing times, frequency of delivery
- *Dependability* – percentage of late orders, adherence to schedule, availability of products or services
- *Flexibility* – time to market of new products or services, range of products and services, ability to make changes to schedules (volume and timing)
- *Cost* – variance against budget, utilisation of resources, added value.

Measuring performance in itself is often sufficient to bring about improvement in an organisation as it shows that management is concerned about the activity being measured. However, by adding performance targets, managers can provide a better means to display the amount of change required and check progress against it. Several types of targets can be used:

- *Historical standards* Historical standards allow organisations to assess improvement against previous performance as historical standards are based on what has been achieved in the past.
- *Competitor performance standards* Competitor performance standards compare the achieved performance of the operation with that which is being achieved by one or more of the organisation's competitors.
- *Benchmarking* This is used to compare an organisation's performance with other organisations, often using organisations from quite different environments. The purpose is to help the organisation search out new ideas which might be copied or adapted. Deciding which organisations to benchmark against is not an easy decision and is explored in the Bristol & West Building Society case study (Case 48).
- *Absolute performance standards* An absolute performance standard is where perfection is required. Although this might be very difficult, if not impossible or extremely expensive for organisations to achieve, some organisations have to work hard to try to achieve it, such as safety levels at nuclear waste processing plants or railways.

The problem of setting appropriate performance standards is addressed in the case of Newtown Customer Service Centre (Case 46).

## Types of improvement

### Breakthrough improvement

Breakthrough improvement, or step-change improvement, looks for dramatic changes to the operation. This might involve the creation of a new factory, the total redesign of a computer-based reservation system or a total redesign in the methods of working. Such changes are usually costly and do not necessarily realise the required improvements quickly. Business process re-engineering (BPR) is one such approach. Underlying the BPR approach is the belief that operations should be organised around the total process which adds value for customers, rather than around the functions or activities which perform the various stages of the value-adding activity. BPR is about undertaking a radical rethink and redesign of all business processes, not just operations processes.

### Continuous improvement

Continuous improvement involves a more incremental approach to improvement, concentrating on encouraging many small step improvements. Continuous improvement is also known by the Japanese word *kaizen*. Continuous improvement is less concerned with the size of the steps taken but more with the nature of ongoing improvement activities. The repeated and cyclical nature of continuous improvement is best summarised by what is called the PDCA (Plan, Do, Check, Act) cycle:

- *Plan* – the examination of the current method or the problem area being studied and the formulation of a plan of action
- *Do* – the implementation of the plan
- *Check* – the evaluation of the plan against expected performance improvement
- *Act* – the consolidation or standardisation of successful change and the re-planning, doing, checking, acting of unsuccessful change.

## Improvement techniques

There are many techniques that can be used by organisations to help gain improvements in performance:

- *Flow charts*. Flow charts provide a detailed picture of the flows of materials, information or customers. This technique can quickly show poorly organised flows, highlight areas where procedures do not exist, identify non-value-adding delays and movements, and allow managers to assess where control and measurement should take place. The Executive Holloware case (Case 42) uses a simple flow chart to understand the points where quality problems might occur.
- *Scatter diagrams*. Scatter diagrams are a quick and simple method of identifying whether there seems to be a connection between two sets of data. It will highlight the strength of their relationship though is not necessarily evidence of a cause–effect relationship.
- *Cause-effect diagrams*. Cause-effect diagrams are used to search for the root causes of problems. This is done by asking what, when, where, how and why questions. Cause–effect diagrams (which are also known as 'fish bone' or *Ishikawa* diagrams) have become extensively used in improvement programmes.
- *Pareto diagrams*. Pareto analysis attempts to identify what is most important and what is less so. It is a relatively straightforward technique which involves arranging information on the types of problem or causes of problem into their order of importance and/or frequency. This can then be used to highlight areas where further analysis will be useful.
- *Why – why analysis*. This technique starts by stating the problem and asking *why* that problem has occurred. Once the major reasons for the problem occurring have been identified, each of the major reasons is taken in turn and again the question is asked *why* those reasons have occurred, and so on.
- *Failure detection*. There are several ways of trying to detect whether a failure has occurred so that not only can it be put right but also the organisation can learn from the mistake and improve its operation, such as by process control (statistical process control – see Part 6), diagnostics checks by machines, customer interviews or phone surveys and complaint cards.

## Total quality management

Total quality management (TQM) is arguably the most significant of the new ideas which have swept across the operations management scene over the last few years. TQM is concerned with the improvement of *all* aspects of operations performance, not just quality.

TQM is a philosophy, a way of thinking and working, that is concerned with meeting the needs and expectations of customers. It attempts to move the focus of quality away from being a purely operations activity into a major concern for the whole ('total') organisation. Through TQM, quality becomes the responsibility of all levels, departments and sections in the organisation. TQM also embodies the process of continuous improvement.

Specifically, TQM can be seen as being concerned with the following:

### Meeting the needs and expectations of customers

The TQM approach is about more than just meeting the expectations of customers; it is about seeing things from a customer's point of view. This involves the whole organisation in understanding the central importance of customers to its success and even to its survival. It requires that the implications for the customer are considered at all stages in corporate decision making and that decisions are made and systems created that will not detract from the customer's experience. Prye, Byll and Runne (Case 47) and London Zoo (Case 49) are examples of the processes involved in gaining understanding of customer expectations and/or perceptions.

### Covering all parts of the organisation

One of the most powerful aspects to emerge from TQM is the concept of the 'internal', customer and supplier. This is a recognition that everyone is a customer within the organisation and consumes goods or services provided by other internal suppliers (or micro-operations), and too is an internal supplier of goods and services for other internal customers (or micro-operations). The implication of this is that errors in the service provided within an organisation will eventually pass through the internal supply chain and affect the product or service which reaches the external customer.

### Including every person in the organisation

TQM is sometimes referred to as 'quality at source'. This notion stresses the impact that each individual staff member has on quality as well as the idea that it is each person's own responsibility to get quality right. Everyone in an organisation, not just those with direct contact with customers, has the potential to impair seriously the quality of the products or services received by customers. They also, therefore, have the ability to improve quality. The Eurocamp Travel (Case 52) is an illustration of how one organisation involved all its workforce.

### Examining all costs which are related to quality

TQM is concerned with examining all the costs associated with quality. These costs of quality are usually categorised as prevention costs, appraisal costs, internal failure costs and external failure costs. In traditional quality management it was assumed that there was a trade-off between improved quality and increased costs, and hence reduced profits. Furthermore it was assumed that there is an optimum amount of quality effort to be applied in any situation which minimises the total costs of quality. TQM rejects the 'optimum' quality level concept and strives to reduce all known and unknown failure costs by preventing errors and failures taking place.

### Getting things right first time

The emphasis on TQM, as indicated by its approach to quality costs, is on prevention. TQM therefore tries to shift the emphasis from reactive (waiting for something to happen) to proactive (doing something before anything happens). This change in the view of quality costs has come about with a movement from an inspect-in (appraisal driven) approach to a design-in ('getting it right first time') approach to quality. 'Design', of course, involves the original design of the product or service and of the macro and micro-processes.

### Developing the systems and procedures which support quality and improvement

Improving quality is not something that happens simply by getting everyone in an organisation to 'think quality'. Very often people are prevented from making improvements by the organisation's systems and procedures. Indeed there is a belief that direct operators can only correct a small percentage of quality problems, the majority are management's responsibility because they are due to 'the system', or the lack of one.

### Developing a continuous process of improvement

TQM is not a one-off activity but an ongoing process of development and improvement. As such it is a mistake to consider it as an 'initiative' or 'programme'. TQM is a way of thinking, and, simply put, just good management practice.

Many of these elements of TQM are not easy to mobilise in an organisation that has become accustomed to managing quality only in traditional ways described in Part 6 as 'quality control'. Changes in management style and culture are required, as well as the use of new quality tools and techniques. These difficulties are illustrated in Executive Holloware (Case 42) and E-Cab (Case 53).

## Implementing TQM

Many organisations have launched a TQM initiative with high expectations as to the likelihood of fast pay-offs. This is contrary to the nature of TQM as described above and not surprisingly has resulted in many failures. A number of factors appear to influence the eventual success of performance improvement programmes such as TQM:

- *A quality strategy*. This means having clearly thought-out, long-term goals for TQM, including setting out the role and responsibilities of various parts of an organisation in its implementation and planning the resources to pursue it.
- *Top management support*. The full understanding, support and leadership of an organisation's top management emerges as a crucial factor in almost all the studies of TQM implementation.
- *A steering group*. Successful implementation requires a steering group to plan the implementation of the improvement programme.
- *Group-based improvement*. TQM programmes are usually implemented by teams as improvement usually involves people from several departments in an organisation, each of whom will have direct experience and understanding of the processes involved.

- *Success is recognised.* Formally recognising success stresses the importance of the quality improvement process as well as rewarding effort and initiative. Celebration of individual, team or organisational success may be crucial.
- *Training is the heart of quality improvement.* Improvement techniques should be provided to help people work towards the basic objective – the elimination of errors.

The evolution of TQM implementation is illustrated in the Eurocamp Travel case.

## Summary

The task of improving operational and organisational performance is emerging as a key task of operations managers. It involves measuring performance in order to help managers make decisions about what to change and understand the impact of their decisions, not just on quality but the other operations performance objectives, speed, dependability, flexibility and cost. There are many techniques that can be used to help gain improvements in performance, including flow charts, scatter diagrams, cause–effect diagrams and Pareto diagrams.

Total quality management (TQM) is one of the best known improvement philosophies and involves:

- meeting the needs and expectations of customers
- covering all parts of the organisation
- including every person in the organisation
- examining all costs which are related to quality
- getting things 'right first time' – designing-in quality rather than inspecting it in
- developing the systems and procedures which support quality and improvement
- developing a continuous process of improvement.

### Key points

- Performance measurement and appropriate choice of targets underpins performance improvement.
- Improvement activities are usually either breakthrough activities or continuous improvement programmes.
- There are many techniques which can be used to help organisations improve their performance, such as Pareto analysis and cause–effect analysis.
- TQM is a philosophy which applies to all parts of the organisation. If everybody in the organisation can detract from the organisation's effectiveness, then everyone also has the potential to make a positive contribution. A central concept of TQM is its use of internal customers/suppliers to enable each part of the organisation to identify its contribution to overall quality.
- TQM puts customers at the forefront of quality decision making and places considerable emphasis on the role and responsibilities of every member of staff within an organisation to influence quality.

## Recommended reading

Feigenbaum, A. V. (1986), *Total Quality Control*, McGraw-Hill, New York.

Fitzgerald, L., Johnston, R., Brignall, S., Silvestro, R. and Voss, C. (1991), *Performance Measurement in Service Businesses*, The Chartered Institute of Management Accountants.

Heskett, J. L., Sasser, W. E. and Hart, C. W. L. (1990), *Service Breakthroughs: changing the rules of the game*, Free Press, New York.

Imai, M. (1986), *Kaizen*, McGraw-Hill, New York.

Ishikawa, K. (1985), *What is Total Quality Control? – The Japanese Way*, Prentice Hall, New Jersey.

Slack, N., Chambers, S. and Johnston, R. (2001), *Operations Management*, (3rd edn), Financial Times/Prentice Hall, Harlow, Chapters 18, 19 and 20.

Taguchi, G. and Clausing, D. (1990), 'Robust Quality', *Harvard Business Review*, Jan–Feb, 65–75.

# CASE 46

# Newtown Customer Service Centre

Case date
2002

Carole Driver

The customer service call centre at Newtown is a high-volume operation answering approximately 25 000 customer queries per week. 'To provide customer service that delights' is its key strategic objective. To reflect this priority, customer satisfaction is a key performance indicator and the Operations Manager's bonus depends on the achievement of service level targets. Of these, the speed of response target has the highest weighting and is set at 85 per cent of calls being answered within 20 seconds.

As at other call centres, 20 seconds is believed to be the threshold beyond which customers become dissatisfied with the speed of response. Some research sponsored by the Operations Manager has confirmed this belief. It was found that 98 per cent of customers who were answered within what they thought to be 20 seconds were happy with the speed of answering. The percentage dropped dramatically to 69 per cent when the perceived speed of answering was greater than 20 seconds. Interestingly, although 82 per cent overall said they were happy with the speed of answering, the call centre statistics from the time of the survey indicated that only 42 per cent were actually answered within 20 seconds. These statistics are produced automatically by the phone system and displayed continuously on the manager's PC.

The speed of response target is not used to assess the performance of the employees because the manager believes that setting such targets would cause them to rush calls, which results in errors and rework as well as customer complaints. Although the number of customer complaints is also used as an indicator of customer satisfaction, the only complaints counted are those addressed to the Managing Director (MD). These are sorted by the MD's office and relevant ones sent to the call centre for immediate action. The office also provides monthly statistics on the nature of the complaints.

Complaints statistics highlight areas for improvement and the quarterly customer satisfaction survey provides feedback on that improvement in the form of a satisfaction index. A sample of customers are asked by a firm of market researchers to rate their satisfaction with various aspects of the call centre's service and the responses are multiplied by importance weightings for each aspect to arrive at an overall index. Provided the index is no worse than in the previous survey no further action is taken. Periodically the weightings, which are calculated by regression analysis, are checked. If they are found to have changed substantially, the new weightings are used, but this can result in an unwelcome decrease in the index which the manager believes is probably caused by the method of calculation.

## Questions

1 *Critique each of the measures used at the Newtown Customer Service Centre. How useful are they as measures of customer satisfaction?*

2 *Suggest alternatives and explain in which ways they might or might not be better than the measures currently being used.*

# Prye, Byll and Runne, Chartered Accountants

Case date
2002

Robert Johnston

Prye, Byll and Runne (PBR), founded in 1880, is one of the large UK-based accountancy firms. It has offices in 20 towns and cities and a staff of about 3000. The company's largest office, which includes the national office, is in London and has over 60 partners and 1000 staff. In common with all the other large accountancy firms, PBR offers a range of specialised services including accounting and auditing, taxation advice, management consultancy, business investigations, insolvency, trust administration and technical training.

PBR recognises that in many ways it is no different from all other large accountancy firms. It provides the same sort of services, in the same locations, with similar fee structures, and pays about the same wages to staff as all other companies. However, PBR does pride itself on its efficient, personal and friendly service. Every enquiry is directed through a partner who becomes the account holder. The partner then always deals personally with that client. This approach also rubs off on the firm's recruitment of staff. One recently appointed junior member of staff explained it attracted her into the firm

'There was really little to choose between the top companies, however PBR really stood out. There was a better atmosphere, the people were informal and friendly and very helpful and there were no great divisions between partners, managers and staff. It is a good place to work.'

PBR partners believe that this approach is the reason for the success and growth of the company. Indeed the firm has opened up two new offices in the last three months and aims to open at least three more within the next 12 months. Spencer Dobson, a senior partner, explained the increases:

'Most of our "new" offices are not new but are small independent firms which we buy out. We then take over the existing client base, together with the partners, with the intention of attracting new clients by using our name and reputation.'

## Attracting new business

Most of PBR's business is performing audits for companies. Once a company uses PBR they would tend to use them each year and as a result there is a relatively stable client base. Spencer added:

'We have never lost any clients by avoidable causes but sometimes we feel we have little control over the size of the business as changes often happen in the market – mergers and takeovers for example. If one of our clients is taken over by the client of another company, we would tend to lose the business to our competitors because it makes more sense for all the subsidiaries in a group to use the same firm. Clearly, you win some and you lose some.'

Spencer went on to explain how they attract business.

'Organisations out looking for accountants are not too common. If they are, it is usually because they are fed up with their current accountants or have grown out of the services that their accountants are able to provide. Some firms may not be able to provide the degree of specialism that the organisation may now require.

'We are allowed to carry out advertising campaigns, but not only is this expensive, it also does not seem to be necessary. You see, most of our new clients come from recommendation from our other clients, bank managers or solicitors. Some new work is on the basis of competitive tendering. This has been a fairly recent development. Sometimes we might be asked for a competitive proposal for a whole group of companies. This could be a very big job. Our success rate has been reasonably good in this area.'

Spencer explained some of the problems associated with tendering for work:

'We may occasionally put out a low price if we want to get a foot in the door or think we can get ancillary work, but it is rare. Otherwise, putting in a low price on a tender can work against you. Firstly, because our prices are relatively fixed, we know how long the job will take and how many and what sort of staff it will require. Secondly, because we tend to know what other firms will charge, and usually we all charge roughly the same rate. After all, it is the same job, requiring the same resources and time, and we all pay roughly the same rates. Also, the price of an audit is not a big cost to the client. An organisation with a turnover of £20 millions may pay £10 000 for its auditing. It scarcely matters whether it is £9000 or £11 000. For some organisations, however, the price is important, in particular government services.

'What I think does matter in attracting work is how the clients feel they will get on with the auditors, who they have to work with for some time. It's like choosing a doctor: the auditors will be inside your organisation and can mess things up for you. Decisions are usually made on whether they feel good about you or not.

'The main thing that makes our firm different from all the others is that we try to sell our staff rather than our skills. I reckon the thing that clinches a deal is the individual that the clients meet at this end. The clients can't easily assess skills at the first meeting but they can assess if they like what they see. They like to see someone who gives the appearance of being bright, cheerful, competent and willing. Usually the first point of contact is a partner. It is important then that we know how to sell ourselves. We have training for senior staff on client management which includes how to make formal presentations, how to address people and write to people. Client relationships are very important to us. Besides working hard getting clients, we work hard on keeping them. I believe it's the best way to keep a thriving practice. We have a programme of visiting all our major clients so we keep in close touch with many organisations. Sometimes our contacts within the organisations come and go, so we try to deal with several people. If one of us deals with the old guard, we will bring someone in who can deal with the new guard as well. We need to be alert to management changes.

'An important part of managing our relationship with the clients is making sure our staff in the field do a good job, so we spend a lot of time on student recruitment in order to try to get hold of the best people possible. We don't necessarily pay more than other firms, indeed pay scales are comparable, but we do try to get better people by selecting better.'

As a senior partner, Spencer is keen to make sure that client relationships are managed well. Though there is no systematic method of monitoring client relationships, Spencer keeps his ear to the ground.

## Audits

An audit is the act of checking the client's records to make sure that they are accurate and fairly represent the situation. It involves examination of an organisation's financial statements and the performance of detailed tests and procedures on the accounting and other records to form the basis of a professional opinion (audit report) on the fairness of the financial statements. The audit report provides the statements with credibility and enables third parties, such as banks and other creditors, to rely on the statements with confidence. Auditing has become increasingly sophisticated with the development of many techniques, including flow charting, statistical sampling and analytical review techniques. Although many techniques have become standardised, there is still a major need for professional judgement, which is required because clients operate in many different industries, each with characteristics that create special audit issues and problems. In addition, clients use a wide variety of accounting systems and vary significantly in the competence of their accounting staffs.

Professional judgement is also required because audits must frequently be carried out under considerable pressure. Deadlines for completion are imposed by regulation or client reporting requirements. Audit staff are, therefore, commonly required to make trade-offs between completing audits within the required time and ensuring that the procedures performed are appropriate, sufficient and properly executed. Spencer added:

'We are quite hard pressed at times, but we don't turn work away. Also, clients sometimes change their plans but we always do our best to accommodate them. We have never yet failed to staff a job. If it comes to it we can always borrow staff from London or other offices or use overtime if the work builds up. Sometimes we can delay part of the work – there is always a bit of slack.'

The pressure is further increased by the seasonality of the workload. Audits are performed at a client's year-end. Many of PBR's clients have a 31st December year-end which means that January, February and March are very busy months. Most of the other clients have a March year-end so the heavy workload is actually spread over about six months. One junior commented,

'We are quite frantic at times but we always meet our deadlines'.

The length of time needed to complete an audit varies and depends largely upon the size (turnover) and complexity of the organisation. The audit for an organisation with a turnover of around £2000 may only take one person one day. A large job for an organisation with a turnover of £200 million may take 3000 hours.

A central London-based Professional Standards Committee is responsible for controlling the professional performance of the individual offices. The Committee sends out inspection teams to each office on a regular basis, every couple of years, to monitor their performance on a selection of their audits. The team report on any shortcomings or difficulties encountered. The Committee then advises the office as to how it should deal with them. The teams are made up of partners from other branches. They select a number of audit files at random and review them for compliance with the firm's accounting procedures.

## Audit teams

Each PBR office creates an internal audit team for each audit assignment. Typically a client will see an Audit Senior and two or three assistants, usually 'students', working in the field. The students are graduates who are doing their three years training, during which time they take their professional exams. There is an Audit Manager to whom the Senior reports. The Audit Manager would normally be permanently assigned to a set of clients. It is his or her job to arrange the audit assignment, assign staff, visit and review the audit team and keep in contact with the client throughout the audit. A partner oversees the operation, keeps in regular touch with the client and reviews the work of the Audit Manager.

Audit Managers plan the staffing of the team in conjunction with the Administrator who runs the Planning Board. This is a large chart showing all the staff below manager level, with the dates of known jobs and all the staff allocated to them. When an Audit Manager is planning an audit, they will go to the Administrator to book the number and grades of staff that they require for the weeks they will be required. There is usually never quite enough slack in the system for the Audit Managers to have exactly what they want when they need it. This is resolved in cooperation with the other managers and by minor adjustment to the job schedule.

## Staff assessment

One student explained:

'We are formally assessed twice a year by one of the partners. The basis for this is the performance report sheet [Appendix 47.1]. It is really quite useful and it is very fair. We have to fill in our comments as well and we then discuss all the points. It's a very good learning document. It gives you feedback on how you are improving and in what areas you need to improve. All the managers are assessed in the same way.'

Spencer added.

'We also keep our ears to the ground and listen to the gossip; we are a small community, so we know what is going on.'

Each branch of PBR has a considerable degree of autonomy. All performance targets are set by the local partner in discussion with Head Office. Spencer Dobson explained:

'I don't have any specific targets set by Head Office. Any targets that are set, I set, and I will be measured against them. Most branches are well established and if they want to expand they have to look for new clients and new markets – they have to achieve something new from a current base. The bright people in the business will work out how to do it and then do it. They see it as a challenge for themselves and they will be acknowledged as bright people.'

In general, performance criteria are set at local level. They are, however, examined by Head Office and discussions may follow, but as Spencer said,

'If they don't know where we can get any more business then there is no point in demanding that we increase it.'

There are five main performance criteria: manpower utilisation, collections, variance, profit and pricing.

## Manpower utilisation

Everyone (including partners) in the organisation, with the exception of the administrative staff, fills in time sheets. These documents show how many hours each person has spent on which job and how many hours have been spent on things that cannot be charged to any job. Spencer added:

'These sheets are not used as a stick to beat people with but so that we know what we have to charge each client for. We do check them to make sure that any non-chargeable time on the sheet is our fault and not the auditors' fault. If a junior only fills in three days work, there may be nothing wrong with this if we were only able to provide him/her with three days work that week. Utilisation is a management problem, not a problem for the individual.'

## Collections

Spencer explained,

'In the office we check our rates of billing and collections. If we have done the work then we hope to collect money for it. Like all organisations, we have to monitor our cash flow.'

## Variance

Spencer explained:

'Variance is the difference between the actual cost of a job and what we charge the client for it. This checks that our original estimate of time, number and grade of staff required is accurately reflected in the cost of the job. It also ensures that we don't stoke time on to a job. For example, if you agree a fee of £5000 with a client you could allocate time on the job to say £15 000 and still only charge £5000. The variance would be £10 000 and would obviously not be a good thing. These figures are checked locally by the partners and then centrally.'

## Profit

Profit is influenced by several factors including the combined variances of all the jobs. It is important to monitor profit as all the partners share in the profits of the firm, so a partner's share is expected to be covered by the profits from his/her office. Also, if any office wants another partner, it has to demonstrate that there is enough potential profit to cover another share.

## Pricing

Spencer explained how the firm sets charging rates:

'Pricing and budgeting are basically the same proces. We work out how many people we are going to have and how much we are going to charge for them on an hourly basis. This is based on the hours we expect them to work, the expected utilisation of each, last year's charges and this year's pay increases. We have a computer program in London that provides us with a new set of charging rates based on all of these. When they appear, we check them against what we think is possible in our local market and, if necessary, amend them and rerun it. Head Office may come back and say that the proposed rates are not high enough. Then we will debate them as Head Office will not necessarily know about any new competition in our area or if a big job has recently been lost.'

Generally PBR quote for the job based on the hours and grades of staff required, but it is equally possible to quote per hour. The budgeting process starts each April with ideas about salary increases due in July. The process has to be complete by July when the rates have to be entered into the central computer.

### Questions

1 *How is PBR's operational performance monitored and controlled?*

2 *What seem to be the weaknesses in PBR's systems?*

3 *Identify the improvement priorities for PBR using the importance–performance matrix.*

4 *What steps would you recommend PBR to take?*

## Periodic performance report

NAME _____ OFFICE _____ DEPT/GROUP _____

GRADE _____ PERIOD COVERED _____

CLIENTS

OTHER WORK

This report is for completion and discussion by the person in charge of the work who completes sections A1, B1 and C, and by the person whose work is reported on who completes sections A2, B2 and D. The person in charge of the work should then forward the report to the staff or group partner for completion of section E.

A        NATURE OF WORK UNDERTAKEN

A1        Describe the nature of work undertaken during the period and comment on the degree of difficulty of the results required in relation to the individual's grade.

A2        Comment on how demanding you have found the work over the period and identify areas that were new to you.

B        LEVEL OF ACHIEVEMENT

In section B level of achievement should be summarised on a scale of 1 to 7 where the following definitions apply: 1 very low, 2 low, 3 less than satisfactory, 4 satisfactory, 5 more than satisfactory, 6 high, 7 very high.

B1        Identify aspects of performance which exceeded or fell short of the level of achievement required. Summarise achievements under each heading using the scale 1 to 7 defined above.

         Technical

         Planning and organisation

         Staff relations

         Client relations

         Personal and professional

B2     Identify under each heading areas in which you experienced difficulty and areas which were helpful to your development.

C     EFFECTIVENESS OF CONTRIBUTION

Comment on the progress made during the period and identify the particular respects in which clients and/or the firm have benefited from the individual's work and business understanding.

What specific recommendations would you make to assist this individual's development in the next few months?

Signed _____ Grade _____ Date _____

D     COMMENTS

I discussed this report on _____ and my comments are:

Signed _____ Date _____

E     ACTION

Describe the action taken as a result of this report.

Signed _____ Date _____

# Bristol & West Building Society

Case date
2002

Robert Johnston

'We are doing well but we cannot afford to be complacent,' said Peter Woodrow, the Information Management Manager with Bristol & West Building Society.

'To keep us on our toes and help us keep improving what we do, I think we need to benchmark ourselves against other organisations. Though the problems are which measures do we use and which organisations should we benchmark ourselves against?'

With a head office in Bristol and 132 branches mostly focused in the south and south-west of England, Bristol & West is one of the top 10 building societies in the UK. Bristol & West has assets in excess of £13 billion and employs around 3000 staff. The Society specialises in mortgages, savings and investments and manages over 200 000 mortgage accounts and over one million savings and investment accounts. It does not offer services and accounts outside of these categories. By specialising in these financial products the Society believes it can be more responsive to customers' needs. It also offers its customers convenience and provides specialist sales and service teams who ensure that the highest levels of customer service are provided by phone, post, Internet and in person.

Peter explained how the Society has been trying to develop its performance measurement systems.

'We are currently using the EFQM Business Excellence framework to help us develop our measures and improvement activities and we have found, maybe not surprisingly, that we have quite a few measures of "the results" but that we are less good at measuring "the enablers".

'We obviously have a lot of information in terms of volumes about all of our products, mortgages, savings and investments, and details of all money flows on a daily basis – all the "day-to-day measures" needed for running such a business. We use these performance measures to compare the activities of our various branches. We also have lots of measures of "competitiveness" and we send monthly returns to the Building Society Association (BSA) and Building Society Commission (BSC). The material they produce allows us to compare ourselves with the rest of the building society sector, though not on a one-to-one basis. We do measure customer satisfaction and employee satisfaction but maybe not in a particularly sophisticated way, though we are working on this at the moment.

'We want to do some benchmarking to see how we can improve what we are doing and also to try to ensure that what we do is adding value to our customers and other stakeholders. Should we look, for example, at the Cheltenham & Gloucester Building

Society, it is very focused in terms of its products and services, or should we look at the Halifax because it is the biggest, or Midshires because it has a good reputation for customer service ... or British Airways? I don't want us to waste our time creating measures for the sake of measuring things. I want us to chose things that will help us improve and know how far in front or behind we are.'

## Questions

1 *What is the purpose of benchmarking?*

2 *What advice would you give to Peter Woodrow?*

# London Zoo

Adrian Watt and Stuart Chambers

## Introduction

Dr Jo Gipps, the Director of London Zoo, turned away from his window:

'I have quite a good view of Regents Park and the zoo from here. I can also see the visitors arriving and walking to the main entrance from the car park or the tube station on the other side of the park. You get quite a good feel for the attendance numbers just from watching the stream of people walking along the pavement. By late morning on really busy days we have quite a queue building up at the ticket kiosks. Of course, that doesn't happen as often as it did some years ago, but we would like to see if we could bring the crowds back. We have a huge fluctuation in daily numbers. Our busiest times are obviously weekends and the summer holidays when we regularly get attendance levels of between 4000 and 6000. On the Easter and August Bank Holidays we can easily reach 10 000. The busiest day we have had in the last few years was on a special "Save Our Zoo" day when visitor numbers topped 18 000; the zoo was packed, you could hardly move, the whole operation was bursting at the seams, there were queues everywhere, we were running out of food, it was chaos! Yet our lowest budgeted attendance figure is for Christmas Eve with just 48 people. The place is like a ghost town, it lacks any atmosphere and there are hardly any staff around as they are all getting on with their work behind the scenes.

'We certainly need to increase our visitor numbers, but it is vital that we still provide a high quality of service; and there lies our problem. We have had all the usual market research done for us: we know the age range, group size, average length of visit, where the visitors come from, and even which newspapers they read. We also know which animals they like best: the monkeys, big cats, elephants and penguins are always popular, but we do not really know what the public thinks of the quality of the service we provide throughout their visit. Apart from providing the animals, what are we doing right and when? If we do not know that, how can we improve and build on our successes? Marketing is all very well at getting people here, but once they are here we have to keep them and organise our operations to give them a good day out.

'The second problem is largely concerned with society's attitude to animals, and this is really one of the reasons for the zoo being in the difficulty it is today. The public's views have changed a great deal over the past few years: they have become far more aware of issues such as animal rights and welfare, and conservation, they are far more sceptical of the need to keep animals in captivity, and they are questioning the role of zoos in today's society. London Zoo (and the Zoological Society as a whole including the

Institute of Zoology) has long been primarily dedicated to animal welfare and conservation, but in the past there has been no real need to emphasise this because people did not really seem to care. All they wanted to do was to come to the zoo to see some exotic large animals and did not think about the welfare of the animals in the zoo or the wild. Now things have changed completely! Many people now still want to see the animals, but are worried about their happiness, their well-being and their conservation in their natural habitats. Some people think that zoos are one of the problems rather than part of the solution.

'I suppose this encapsulates our problem; having got the visitors to come, are we treating them well by giving them a good quality service, and indeed are we giving them what they want?'

## Background information on London Zoo

Ever since it opened in 1828, London Zoo has played a major part in the country's interest in natural history both as a scientific and recreational activity, and has frequently been in the news headlines. London Zoo is the UK's premier zoological collection and has one of the most prestigious animal collections in the world. It was designed to house and display the 'grand collection of live animals', for the Zoological Society of London. Although initially only occupying a small corner of Regents Park, it expanded rapidly to reach its present size of 36 acres. From the start the zoo had a wide range of exotic species including Indian elephants, llamas, leopards, kangaroos, bears and numerous birds. The collection grew rapidly with the addition of an orangutan, an Indian rhinoceros, giraffes, and chimpanzees all arriving over the next 10 years. The first of a series of gorillas arrived in 1887.

As the collection expanded so building work continued, with major periods of construction and refurbishment occurring in the 1830s, 1850s, 1880s and 1920/30s. For the first 65 years all the animals were permanently housed inside in the mistaken belief that they would not survive the cold outside. The world's first aquarium was built in 1853. The original lion house was replaced in 1876, and the first reptile house which opened in 1849 was replaced in 1883. The existing aquarium was built in 1924, the present reptile house in 1927, the penguin pool in 1934, and the Cotton and Mappin Terraces were also built during the 1930s. The latter are closed awaiting refurbishment, and have been for a number of years. These, and many of the other buildings, are listed and cannot simply be demolished, but must be renovated within strict guidelines.

There was a severe lack of capital investment in the zoo's infrastructure in the 1960s and 1970s. However a spate of building did occur in the 1970s with the Sobell ape and monkey pavilions opening in 1972, followed by the big cat enclosures, and the Snowdon Aviary. In the late 1980s and 1990s there was the redevelopment of the Clore Small Mammal House into the Moonlight Centre and the rebuilding of the Children's and Petting Zoo (which has been present in some form since 1924), the construction of the Lifewatch Centre, Macaw Aviary, and Barclay Court and the fountain area. Recently the zoo has been awarded £2 million from the National Lottery Heritage Millennium Fund to go towards building an education centre.

Visitor attendance levels have always fluctuated as fashion and public interest have increased and waned with the introduction of new exhibits and developments, or as investment declined. In the 1830s annual attendance levels exceeded 250 000, but fluctuated considerably during the latter half of the century. The zoo's popularity increased after the turn of the century with a sustained period of expansion, attendance figures reaching 2 million per annum before the Second World War. After the war, attendance figures leapt to 3 million due to the desire for post-austerity recreation, but by the mid-1950s the visitor numbers had settled back down towards their pre-war 2 million level and remained stable for some time. In the late 1960s and early 1970s a new decline began and by 1975 attendance levels started to fall rapidly. By the early 1980s visitor levels were just over 1 million, and the budgeted 1995/96 attendance level was just 900 000.

This decline in attendance levels was due to a number of socio-economic changes including changing social habits, growth in car ownership, leisure preferences and inflation. In the 1950s there was very little competition from other animal or general leisure attractions. Coupled with this there was a general lack of transport, usually only public transport being available and there being very little private means of transport with only a few cars. This restricted the ability of people who lived in and around London to travel widely beyond the city, or for other people to go anywhere far except to the capital. With the expansion of the road network and increased car ownership, as well as the growth of foreign travel, people found it easier and were more willing to go further for their leisure activities. Competition also grew rapidly with respect to animal based organisations; there were nine zoos in Great Britain in the 1950s but there are now over 250 attractions which include animals. The fastest growing visitor segments were leisure, amusement and country parks. Historical buildings, and the museums and galleries sector remained constant, and wildlife attractions showed the lowest consistent absolute growth, and as a consequence a fall in percentage terms. Thus London Zoo was in a market sector which had a rapidly increasing number of new entrants and competitors, but at the same time its segment was showing a relatively decreasing market size while other visitor attractions expanded rapidly.

The proportional decrease in the attendance of animal attractions was coupled with the change in the public's perception of the rights of animals, the care of animals in captivity and the effect of caging animals on their health, behaviour, and psychology. The morality, function and need of zoos was also questioned with an emphasis being placed on the requirement for conservation to occur in the wild.

Over the last 25 years there has been a general lack of investment in the zoo's infrastructure, new attractions, facilities, educational and conservation development or its image. This occurred just at the time when alternative leisure attractions, both animal based and otherwise, were starting to present substantial competition. The performance of the zoo in the early 1960s to mid-1970s had generated considerable profit which could have been used for the reinvestment in the zoo's infrastructure, but the Zoological Society decided to use the money to support and expand its scientific work at the Institute. In the mid-1970s attendance levels fell sharply and the zoo went into a major financial deficit. At the same time many private donations dried up, and the government was no longer willing to provide money for capital development. A severe money shortage resulted at the very time when capital investment was desperately needed. The zoo reached a desperate position by 1981/82. It was realised that it was imperative to increase gate revenues by developing new exhibits and improving the facilities and the service offered to the public. Between 1985 and 1988 government grants totalled £7.5m, without which the operating deficit would have been £6.5m. In 1988 the zoo applied for £13m for immediate work and £40m for long-term development. The government gave a one-off £10m grant, and informed the zoo that it had to be self-supporting.

Following a number of strategy reports in 1990 the society announced its plans for major changes in the collection. There was a large reduction in the number of species kept, and many animals were moved to its sister collection at Whipsnade in order to reduce costs. Throughout 1991 the zoo produced 80 per cent of its revenue from gate receipts but remained open due to private donations received. Further development plans and fundraising activities took place throughout 1991 and 1992. The incumbent Director of the zoo resigned and was replaced by Dr Jo Gipps, the present Director. Following disappointing attendance levels to early summer 1992, it was announced that the zoo would close by Christmas. However at a special council meeting this decision was reversed by the Fellows, and this was confirmed at the Annual General Meeting in September 1992. A new Council was elected by April 1993.

## The 1992 development plan

With the support of the zoo's staff, Dr Gipps' development plan was published and adopted in June 1992. This would cost an estimated £21m over 10 years. The plan focused on the conservation of animals with breeding programmes for endangered species including Asiatic lions, Sumatran tigers, and Lowland gorillas. The aim was summarised in the statement that 'there will be less emphasis on the zoo as a good day out. We are going to appeal to people's intelligence. Zoos have no right to exist in the late 20th century unless they can show they are good for animals.' The plan also detailed the proposed infrastructural changes and reorganisation required as well as the finance required, and the consequences of the changes. Developments were to include a children's zoo, an education centre, the long-term restoration of the dilapidated Mappin Terraces and the reintroduction of the bears. The reorganisation and rationalisation involved the shedding of 90 staff and a reduction in the size of the animal collection, although the remaining animals had enlarged enclosures. An emphasis was placed on cost-cutting and the evaluation of the species in the collection, with particular consideration to those for which the captive breeding programmes were an integral part of their conservation, and in line with the zoo's mission statement.

The 1993/94 period was largely one of financial structural and organisational consolidation after years of upheaval so stabilising and equating income and expenditure and thereby ensuring a secure future that did not exceed income. A new charter and mission statement was ratified in 1994/95. The Zoological Society's mission statement is summarised in Appendix 49.1. There was an organisational restructuring into a series of departments with defined roles and responsibilities. These included the departments for animal management, education, marketing, events, projects, visitor operations, general services and the retail departments, with outside franchises awarded for catering and peripheral visitor activities e.g. face painting. Attendance figures still continued to fall.

## Conservation in action

In 1993, in association with the launch of its marketing campaign, summarised by its slogan 'Conservation in Action', London Zoo commissioned its first ever market research poll to establish a visitor profile and to measure the public's awareness of its advertising campaign. This indicated the family and children orientated nature of the visitor profile, that 41 per cent came from London and 14 per cent from overseas. Overall views were positive, with 76 per cent saying that they were likely to return within two years. The decision to visit was largely at the request of the children, was only made a few days prior to the visit, and was strongly influenced by the weather on the day. There was also a high awareness of the zoo and its advertising campaign.

Throughout 1994/95 a small rise was seen in visitor numbers although there was an underlying deficit in revenue of £600 000, offset by a £900 000 private donation. Further market research revealed that the average visit was of four hours, and that the apes and monkeys, big cats, elephants and penguins were the most popular exhibits.

## The management of London Zoo

London Zoo consists of eight departments, the heads of which report to Dr Jo Gipps, the Director of London Zoo. The departments consist of the animal management division, marketing, development, general services, projects, retail and visitor operations. In total the zoo directly employs 161 staff. In addition there are catering and other franchise staff employed by outside contractors. The permanent staff are supplemented by temporary staff employed during peak periods such as school and bank holidays. These are largely used at the catering and retail facilities.

## The service quality research project

In June 1995, Jo Gipps was addressing a meeting of the monthly management committee:

'For us to manage the budget and to break even we must maintain an attendance level of at least one million visitors a year ... but even then there will be very little money available to carry out the much needed modification of the infrastructure, and the addition of new exhibits. A secure financial future would enable us to carry out our development and expansion plans, and to adapt further as views and perceptions of the public and of society as a whole change. It is therefore essential that we accurately define our target market segments, identify what our customers expect when they come to the zoo, and then provide them with their needs and requirements at a consistently high quality of service. Of course, we must target and attract these customers using accurate and effective marketing, promotions and PR, but to build and maintain a reputation we must be able to deliver what the customers want, or they will not come back. If we fail to do that, the customer will be disgruntled and dissatisfied, and when they return home they will spread their dissatisfaction or disappointment by 'word-of-mouth'. The consequence will be that visitors will not return, and new visitors will not be attracted. If, however, the service is as wanted and expected, or even exceeds expectations, the visitors will leave satisfied and delighted. They will spread the zoo's positive reputation, returning themselves and helping to increase the level of new visitors.

'In order to ensure that we achieve our aim of providing the visitors with an excellent day out and so attract them back again in even greater numbers, it is essential that we find out how they rate their visit. This involves two basic issues: the first is to discover how the zoo performs with respect to the service it provides, and the second is to ensure that it is delivering the services that the customers want. It is only after we have some measure of these things that we can hope to fine tune our operating procedures, and develop a plan of action to tackle problem areas in some order of priority. I have decided to seize an opportunity to use an MBA student, Adrian Watt, to undertake a major customer research programme over this summer, so I hope you will all find the time to assist him when necessary. His work should give us a much better understanding of what we must do, but first it is important to ensure that an accurately defined segment of visitors is targeted. We have three general categories of visitors: school and education groups; large parties and coach trips; and individuals, couples or family groups. Each category requires different services from the zoo during their visit. The latter group represents our largest category of visitors, particularly during the summer months, so Adrian should only target these this year. Overseas visitors can be included as long as they are fluent in English, because they account for about 15 per cent of the total visitors, and could provide us with a valuable means of international competitive benchmarking. Perhaps Adrian could explain to you all how he intends to go about his project?'

## Designing a questionnaire

Adrian explained that he would first need their help in designing the questionnaire:

'What I would like to do is to use a list of the "18 determinants of service quality" [see Appendix 49.2] as a guideline for the design of the questionnaire. I would like you all to help me translate these into a comprehensive list of appropriate questions that we could ask about the zoo and the visitors' day here. We should word them so that people can make a judgement of their perceptions of the quality of the service they have experienced, on a 1 to 5 scale, where 1 is very bad and 5 is very good, and hence 3 is average. The scores will then be analysed using statistical software.

'It is essential that our questions also reflect the areas that are relevant and of importance to the zoo, and that are within the control of the zoo, so that you can act to alter or influence the provision of the quality of those aspects of the service. It is equally important that the questions are not ambiguous, too complex, or leading. Consequently the wording must be kept simple and the phraseology might use terms such as "how did you rate" to avoid leading statements such as "how good" or "how bad", which may influence the respondents' rating score.

'Having ascertained how the visitors perceive the quality of the service the zoo provides, the second part of the questionnaire will be designed to discover what customers expected from the zoo during their visit. This can be achieved by providing a list of short statements derived from each of the questions asked in the first section of the questionnaire. Each statement will be a non-committal sentence which does not indicate that this is the standard actually provided by London Zoo, but rather it is a desired standard that should be provided. The respondent will be asked to consider their expectations of the zoo, and to select and rank the top ten statements. This would enable us to obtain an indication of exactly what visitors wanted from their visit to the zoo.'

After several attempts at designing the questionnaire, including a reduction in the number of questions to manageable levels, a final version was agreed (see Appendix 49.3). It was necessary for visitors to have experienced a large proportion of the zoo's facilities and service process, as a result all respondents had to have been at the zoo for at least two hours prior to the interview (half the average visit duration) in order to be allowed to complete a questionnaire, assisted by Adrian. As a result, interviewing only started after 12.30 p.m. on any given day so that visitors could have been at the zoo for the requisite time, and interviewing continued until 5.30 p.m. when the zoo closed. Because each interview took approximately 15 minutes, it was considered necessary to approach potential interviewees who were already resting, as would often be the case for visitors who had already been at the zoo for two hours.

As a result the areas used to select potential respondents were predominately those in which people were likely to be resting and eating, namely seating areas and near to the restaurant and cafe facilities.

The interviews were conducted on a group basis with all members of the group taking part. It was stressed that the questions should be answered with respect to the group as a whole. For example, the visibility of the animals would include a child's ability to see as well as an adult. Access would include the ability to gain access for those with pushchairs and small children or elderly people as well as adults. Other questions involving perceptions were usually answered following a discussion which gave rise to a consensus; if a strong divergence of views occurred, which was rare within a group, either those with the strongest (not necessarily the most extreme views) or a majority vote usually prevailed. A consensus group view was also obtained for the second part of the questionnaire to obtain a top ten priority ranking of those aspects of the visit that they felt the zoo should provide.

The expected subjective variability of the responses that would be obtained, required a large sample size over a broad range of attendance levels. The survey was carried out over the summer months of July, August and September 1995. This included the school summer holidays, a bank holiday and a pre and post-holiday period. This would sample a wide range of attendances, which were predicted to be between 1000 and 9500 visitors per day. The sample days selected reflected this range. The size of the overall sample was therefore determined by the fact that each individual day had to have a potentially statistical credible size group, the size only being limited by the number of people that could be questioned on any given day. The target number of completed questionnaires per day was 20.

Having agreed the design of the questionnaire, and selected the appropriate segment of visitors for interviewees, the range of sample days, the sample times and other criteria, Dr Gipps concluded:

'All our previous market research has been on a very different track. We know a great deal about our visitors' demographics, where they come from, and the newspapers they read. However, I can now appreciate that we didn't find out anything about what they thought about their visit, or how we performed in giving them a good day out, nor what they actually wanted or expected from us or their visit in the first place. The one commonality with Adrian's work is that we also carried out the survey on a wide range of days from the slowest to almost the busiest, so that when we averaged the results we got a really representative view of the average visitor on an average day. The only days we didn't survey were the really busy ones, because we felt that it might only add to any problems. If people were tired due to queues and the general bustle, the last thing they would want to do was answer a list of questions!'

## Results

Over the three-month period of the survey (July, August and September 1995), a total of 755 questionnaires were completed on 38 separate days. The first was carried out on 20 July before the school summer holidays had begun, and the last on 18 September after the schools had gone back. The attendance levels varied between 1046 on 18 September and 9554 on the August Bank Holiday Monday. The total number of people to visit the zoo on these days was 183 395, with an average daily attendance level of 4826 visitors. The mean group size was 3.6 with a modal group size of 4. This represented mainly family parties, and of these a mean of 1.9 or 43 per cent of all visitors were children under 16. Most people arrived between 11.00 a.m. and 12.29 p.m., and the mean visit time was four hours 50 minutes. The weather was consistently excellent during the entire research period, as the UK experienced one of its hottest and driest summers on record.

The results for the performance and priority sections of the survey were digitised and fed into a spreadsheet in order to analyse the huge quantity of data, using a combination of standard and specially written software. The results were analysed and the scores scaled onto a 1 to 5 scale, with 1 representing the poorest performance or of very low priority, and 5 representing an excellent performance or the highest priority to be provided by the zoo. This scaling was simple for the performance ratings as the visitor had already awarded a score of 1 to 5, and so the final rating was simply an average of the scores achieved for each day or appropriate attendance band. The scaling of the priorities assigned to each aspect of a visit was more complex. The priorities were given as rankings and were therefore relative. Each priority ranking was assigned a score with the highest priority (1) receiving the highest score, the lowest priority (10) receiving the lowest score, and all those not included in the top ten list were given a score of zero. All the scores assigned to any given aspect were added together for any given day or attendance band, and these were then ranked in order of scores, with the highest overall score representing the highest overall priority. To scale these scores onto a 1 and 5 scale, the highest score achieved by any aspect in any attendance band was awarded a score of 5, and then all the other scores were scaled by the same factor to achieve a score between 0 and 5. As only the highest score achieved in any set of attendance bands was awarded a 5 it enabled a true comparison to be made between attendance bands, to see how priorities changed under different conditions.

The results were collected and presented in four categories:

1  The overall results averaged for all the data sets obtained
2  The data divided into three groups of daily visitor attendance levels:
   - 0 to 2999 visitors per day;
   - 3000 to 5999 visitors per day;
   - over 6000 visitors per day.

The performance and priority results are tabulated in Appendix 49.4 and 49.5 respectively.

At first sight the data appeared to show that the zoo was performing well overall, although there was significant variation between different attributes of quality. Also, as could be expected, there was a wide variation in the priority rankings with some factors scoring almost a maximum score of 5, and others only a quarter of that.

Adrian's task was the interpretation and use of the data to help the zoo's management derive some idea of how it was performing in providing visitors with a good day out and where it was failing to provide a reasonable quality of service, and under what conditions this occurred. He would have to summarise the visitors' rankings of the zoo's performance and of what they expected from the zoo. And finally he would have to help the zoo determine a prioritised plan of action to improve its service delivery system.

## Questions

1 (a) *Using the 18 determinants of service quality, devise your own questionnaire for the zoo. Compare your questionnaire to the one actually used.*

(b) *Which determinants of service quality are investigated by which question?*

2 *What do the various sets of figures tell you about the zoo's performance from the visitors' perspective? In which are the zoo performing best of all, and where are the areas of poor performance? Which areas and type of the operational processes do they reflect? How and why do they vary?*

3 *Do the visitors' priorities vary in a similar manner and why?*

4 *Derive a plan of action and priority list which will help the zoo decide which aspects of its service provision to tackle first. What factors may need to be taken into account while formulating this order of action?*

5 *Evaluate the strengths and weaknesses of the questionnaire in its objective of providing a priority agenda for improvement to operations.*

## The mission statement of the Zoological Society of London

To promote the worldwide conservation of animals and their habitats by presenting outstanding living collections, breeding threatened species, increasing public awareness through information and education, conducting relevant research, and undertaking action in the field.

The Society pursues this mission by:

1 keeping and presenting animals in accordance with best practice;

2 giving priority to species that are threatened in the wild;

3 increasing public understanding of animals and their welfare and of the issues involved in their conservation;

4 maintaining an outstanding education and information programme, particularly for school children and families;

5 undertaking field conservation programmes, both in the UK and abroad;

6 developing its role as a leading centre for research on conservation biology and animal welfare;

7 fulfilling its role as a learned society and force for zoology and animal conservation through publications, scientific meetings, lectures, the award of prizes for outstanding achievement and the promotion of conservation policy.

*Source: The Annual Report 1994–95 of The Zoological Society of London.*

# Definitions of the 18 determinants of service quality

| Determinant | Definition |
|---|---|
| Access | The physical approachability of service location, including the ease of finding one's way around the service environment and clarity of route. |
| Aesthetics | Extent to which the components of the service package are agreeable or pleasing to the customer, including both the appearance and the ambience of the service environment, the appearance and presentation of service facilities, goods and staff. |
| Attentiveness and helpfulness | The extent to which the service, particularly contact staff, either provide help to the customer or give the impression of being interested in the customer and show a willingness to serve. |
| Availability | The availability of service facilities, staff and goods to the customer. In the case of contact staff this means both the staff/customer ratio and the amount of time each staff member has available to spend with each customer. In the case of service goods availability, includes both the quantity and range of products made available to the customer. |
| Care | The concern, consideration, sympathy and patience shown to the customer. This includes the extent to which the customer is put at ease by the service and made to feel emotionally (rather than physically) comfortable. |
| Cleanliness and tidiness | The cleanliness, neat and tidy appearance of the tangible components of the service package, including the service environment, facilities, goods and contact staff. |
| Comfort | The physical comfort of the service environment and facilities. |
| Commitment | Staff's apparent commitment to their work, including the pride and satisfaction they apparently take in their job, their diligence and thoroughness. |
| Communication | Ability of the service to communicate in an understandable way with the customer. The clarity, completeness and accuracy of both verbal and written information, and the ability to listen to and understand the customer. |
| Competence | The skill, expertise and professionalism with which the service is executed. This includes the carrying out of correct procedures, correct execution of customer instructions, degree of product or service knowledge exhibited by contact staff, the rendering of good advice, and the general ability to do a good job. |
| Courtesy | The politeness, respect and propriety shown by the service, usually contact staff, in dealing with the customer and his or her property. This includes the ability of staff to be unobtrusive and uninterfering when appropriate. |
| Flexibility | A willingness and ability on the part of the service worker to amend or alter the nature of the service or product to meet the needs of the customer. |

| Determinant | Definition |
| --- | --- |
| **Friendliness** | The warmth and personal approachability (rather than physical approachability) of the service, particularly of contact staff, including cheerful attitude, the ability to make the customer feel welcome. |
| **Functionality** | The serviceability and fitness for purpose or 'product quality' of service facilities and goods. |
| **Integrity** | The honesty, justice, fairness and trustworthiness with which customers are treated by the service organisation. |
| **Reliability** | The reliability and consistency of performance of service facilities, goods and staff. This includes punctual service delivery and ability to keep to agreements made with the customer. |
| **Responsiveness** | Speed and timeliness of service delivery. This includes the speed of throughput and the ability of the service to respond promptly to customer service requests, with minimal waiting and queuing time. |
| **Security** | Personal safety of the customer and his or her possessions while participating in or benefiting from the service process. This includes the maintenance of confidentiality. |

*Source*: Johnston, R. (1995), 'The determinants of service quality, satisfiers and dissatisfiers', *International Journal of Service Industry Management*, Vol 6, No 5, 53–71.

## Appendix 49.3

## London Zoo customer questionnaire

---

**The first page of the questionnaire recorded details of the respondents' group size, ages, times of arrival and of anticipated departure, the time and date of the interview, and the weather conditions.**

These questions are intended to be answered relatively quickly to reflect your general perceptions of your visit. If you are completing the questionnaire as part of a group, please feel free to discuss your answers briefly within your group.

Questions 1–29 are scored on a 1–5 scale, where 1 reflects the lowest degree of satisfaction and 5 the highest, or you can leave it blank (*a separate card as below was provided for reference*).

---

1 = **Very bad / very disappointing / unacceptably poor / never or rarely.**
2 = **Bad / disappointing / poor / not frequently enough.**
3 = **Average /usually / could be improved.**
4 = **Good / above average / most of the time.**
5 = **Very good indeed / very satisfactory / delighted / always.**

    **Or leave blank**

---

Please answer questions 1–28 on the separate answer sheet (*not included in this case*) by ringing the appropriate number (1 ... 2 ... 3 ... 4 ... 5)

  1 How do you rate the parking facilities (being able to find a parking space)?

  2 How do you rate being able to find your way around the zoo?

  3 How do you rate the access and being able to move freely around the zoo?

  4 How do you rate the visibility of the animals?

  5 How do you rate the happiness of the animals with their environment?

  6 How do you rate your overall impression of the appearance of the zoo?

  7 How do you rate the attentiveness and helpfulness of:
    (a) The staff?
    (b) The volunteers (Information *etc.*)?

  8 How did you rate the level and usefulness of the contact with staff?

  9 For your needs:
    (a) How do you rate the number of animals available to see?
    (b) How do you rate the number of events and presentations?

10 How would you rate how London Zoo looks after its animals?

11 How do you rate London Zoo as a conservation organisation?

12  How would you rate how London Zoo looks after you, its visitors?

13  How would you rate your visit to London Zoo as an educational experience?

14  How do you rate the cleanliness and tidiness of London Zoo?

15  How do you rate the smartness and tidiness of the staff at London Zoo?

16  How do you rate the comfort of the animals at London Zoo?

17  How do you rate the quality and provision of toilet facilities throughout the zoo?

18  How do you rate the quality and provision of catering facilities throughout the zoo?

19  How do you rate the commitment of London Zoo to:
    (a) The animals?
    (b) You, its visitors?
    (c) Conservation and Education?

20  How do you rate the degree to which the information available around the zoo answered any questions or interests you had?

21  How do you rate the professionalism of London Zoo at:
    (a) Caring for their animals?
    (b) Customer care?

22  How do you rate London Zoo as a friendly place to be?

23  Overall how do you rate your day out at London Zoo?

24  Having been to London Zoo, how do you rate the honesty of London Zoo in its aim of *Conservation in Action*?

25  How do you rate the quality of the events and presentations?

26  How do you rate the time you spent queuing at London Zoo?

27  How do you rate your safety and that of your group during your day at London Zoo?

28  How do you rate London Zoo for value for money?

29  When thinking about today's visit to London Zoo, **which 10 of the factors** listed below would you consider that a zoo should provide generally or during your visit when you are deciding whether to come again and/or recommending London Zoo to friends or family? **Please number these in order of priority (1 = highest priority).**

    **For example**; If you think being able to see the animals is the factor of highest priority when you consider visiting London Zoo again, or recommending it to friends and family, put a '1' in the priority box in row 4. Then put a '2' in the priority box of the next most important factor, and so on until '10'.

| No. | Factor | Priority |
|-----|--------|----------|
| 1 | It is easy to find a parking space. | |
| 2 | It is easy to find your way around the zoo. | |
| 3 | There is good access and it is easy to move freely around the zoo. | |
| 4 | It is easy to see the animals. | |
| 5 | The animals are happy with their environment. | |
| 6 | The zoo is in a good condition. | |
| 7a | The staff are attentive and helpful. | |
| 7b | The volunteers are attentive and helpful. | |
| 8 | There is plentiful contact with the staff. | |
| 9a | There are enough animals to see. | |
| 9b | There are enough events and presentations to see. | |
| 10 | The animals are looked after well. | |
| 11 | The zoo is an important conservation organisation. | |
| 12 | The visitors are looked after well. | |
| 13 | A visit to the zoo is a good educational experience. | |
| 14 | The zoo is clean and tidy. | |
| 15 | The staff are clean and tidy. | |
| 16 | The animals are comfortable. | |
| 17 | There are enough high quality toilet facilities. | |
| 18 | There are enough high quality catering facilities. | |
| 19a | The zoo is committed to its animals. | |
| 19b | The zoo is committed to its visitors. | |
| 19c | The zoo is committed to conservation and education. | |
| 20 | There is sufficient information available to answer your questions and interests. | |
| 21a | The zoo is a professional organisation with respect to the care of its animals. | |
| 21b | The zoo is a professional organisation with respect to the care of its visitors. | |
| 22 | It is a friendly place to be. | |
| 23 | Overall a visit to the zoo is an enjoyable day out. | |
| 24 | The zoo is honest in its aim of Conservation in Action. | |
| 25 | The events and presentations are of high quality. | |
| 26 | There is minimal queuing. | |
| 27 | It is a safe place to spend the day. | |
| 28 | It is good value for money. | |

**Any other comments:**

## Performance scores

This table shows the mean performance scores achieved by each attribute investigated. The mean scores are calculated overall, and for three bands of attendance levels.

| Question number | Aspect of visit | Adjusted mean performance score (1–5 scale) | | | |
|---|---|---|---|---|---|
| | | Overall | 0–2999 visitors | 3000–6000 visitors | over 6000 visitors |
| 1 | Parking | 3.36 | 4.31 | 3.53 | 1.82 |
| 2 | Find way around zoo | 2.41 | 2.38 | 2.66 | 1.99 |
| 3 | Access, free movement | 3.49 | 4.46 | 3.57 | 2.45 |
| 4 | Visibility of animals | 2.08 | 2.18 | 2.17 | 1.96 |
| 5 | Happiness of animals | 1.96 | 2.23 | 2.13 | 1.78 |
| 6 | Appearance of zoo | 2.08 | 2.28 | 2.65 | 1.32 |
| 7(a) | Attentiveness & helpfulness: staff | 2.45 | 2.70 | 3.03 | 1.76 |
| 7(b) | Attentiveness & helpfulness: volunteers | 3.69 | 3.58 | 4.27 | 3.80 |
| 8 | Contact with staff | 1.10 | 0.60 | 1.62 | 1.07 |
| 9(a) | Number of animals to see | 2.88 | 2.79 | 3.08 | 2.64 |
| 9(b) | Number of events and presentations | 2.01 | 1.77 | 2.53 | 2.19 |
| 10 | Care of animals | 3.77 | 4.07 | 3.88 | 3.46 |
| 11 | Conservation organisation | 4.01 | 4.90 | 3.91 | 3.44 |
| 12 | Care of visitors | 2.31 | 2.08 | 2.69 | 1.86 |
| 13 | Educational experience | 3.58 | 4.12 | 3.57 | 3.01 |
| 14 | Cleanliness and tidiness | 2.76 | 4.46 | 2.99 | 1.73 |
| 15 | Smartness and tidiness of staff | 2.54 | 3.13 | 2.79 | 2.03 |
| 16 | Comfort of animals | 1.73 | 2.43 | 1.87 | 1.51 |
| 17 | Quality and provision of toilets | 2.46 | 2.79 | 2.56 | 1.49 |
| 18 | Quality and provision of catering | 1.72 | 1.67 | 2.29 | 1.18 |
| 19(a) | Commitment to animals | 4.37 | 4.47 | 4.47 | 3.99 |
| 19(b) | Commitment to visitors | 2.86 | 2.11 | 3.24 | 1.97 |
| 19(c) | Commitment to conservation/educn. | 3.37 | 3.93 | 3.56 | 3.13 |
| 20 | Availability of information | 2.66 | 2.38 | 2.89 | 2.31 |
| 21(a) | Professionalism: care for animals | 4.37 | 3.77 | 4.58 | 4.01 |
| 21(b) | Professionalism: customer care | 2.29 | 1.87 | 2.64 | 1.72 |
| 22 | Friendliness | 3.36 | 2.29 | 4.02 | 2.33 |
| 23 | Overall as day out | 4.39 | 3.10 | 4.35 | 3.32 |
| 24 | Honesty of aims of London Zoo | 3.09 | 3.34 | 3.22 | 2.66 |
| 25 | Quality of events and presentations | 3.42 | 3.02 | 3.99 | 2.67 |
| 26 | Time queueing | 3.22 | 4.36 | 3.46 | 2.64 |
| 27 | Safety of you/group | 3.40 | 3.33 | 3.43 | 3.43 |
| 28 | Value for money | 2.68 | 2.27 | 2.99 | 2.45 |

## Appendix 49.5

### Priority scores

This table shows the mean priority scores achieved by each attribute investigated. The mean scores are calculated overall, and for three bands of attendance levels.

| Question number | Aspect of visit | Adjusted mean performance score (1–5 scale) | | | |
| --- | --- | --- | --- | --- | --- |
| | | Overall | 0–2999 visitors | 3000–6000 visitors | over 6000 visitors |
| 1 | Parking | 2.48 | 1.29 | 2.66 | 3.28 |
| 2 | Find way around zoo | 3.29 | 3.17 | 3.39 | 3.47 |
| 3 | Access, free movement | 3.27 | 3.21 | 3.05 | 3.40 |
| 4 | Visibility of animals | 4.78 | 4.72 | 4.94 | 4.69 |
| 5 | Happiness of animals | 4.79 | 4.89 | 4.52 | 5.00 |
| 6 | Appearance of zoo | 2.60 | 2.86 | 3.04 | 2.03 |
| 7(a) | Attentiveness & helpfulness: staff | 3.01 | 2.63 | 2.89 | 3.46 |
| 7(b) | Attentiveness & helpfulness: volunteers | 2.83 | 1.92 | 2.86 | 3.50 |
| 8 | Contact with staff | 3.07 | 2.88 | 3.09 | 3.36 |
| 9(a) | Number of animals to see | 3.78 | 3.57 | 3.83 | 4.01 |
| 9(b) | Number of events and presentations | 3.30 | 3.08 | 3.17 | 3.74 |
| 10 | Care of animals | 4.65 | 4.78 | 4.31 | 4.76 |
| 11 | Conservation organisation | 3.07 | 3.30 | 3.22 | 2.88 |
| 12 | Care of visitors | 2.38 | 2.37 | 2.12 | 2.87 |
| 13 | Educational experience | 3.67 | 3.51 | 3.29 | 3.75 |
| 14 | Cleanliness and tidiness | 3.54 | 3.44 | 3.19 | 3.79 |
| 15 | Smartness and tidiness of staff | 2.19 | 1.88 | 2.43 | 2.05 |
| 16 | Comfort of animals | 3.53 | 3.47 | 3.70 | 3.44 |
| 17 | Quality and provision of toilets | 2.73 | 2.87 | 2.60 | 2.73 |
| 18 | Quality and provision of catering | 2.37 | 2.52 | 2.14 | 2.54 |
| 19(a) | Commitment to animals | 3.82 | 3.84 | 3.58 | 3.87 |
| 19(b) | Commitment to visitors | 3.39 | 3.52 | 3.22 | 3.77 |
| 19(c) | Commitment to conservation/educn. | 3.51 | 3.62 | 3.41 | 3.48 |
| 20 | Availability of information | 2.99 | 2.99 | 2.68 | 3.27 |
| 21(a) | Professionalism: care for animals | 3.08 | 3.52 | 2.86 | 2.87 |
| 21(b) | Professionalism: customer care | 2.68 | 2.54 | 2.32 | 3.08 |
| 22 | Friendliness | 3.00 | 2.73 | 2.92 | 3.10 |
| 23 | Overall, as day out | 4.10 | 3.96 | 4.16 | 4.42 |
| 24 | Honesty of aims of London Zoo | 2.89 | 2.85 | 2.51 | 3.17 |
| 25 | Quality of events and presentations | 2.31 | 2.88 | 1.87 | 2.73 |
| 26 | Time queuing | 3.23 | 3.17 | 2.88 | 3.06 |
| 27 | Safety of you/group | 2.81 | 3.08 | 2.33 | 3.16 |
| 28 | Value for money | 3.18 | 3.26 | 2.66 | 3.66 |

# Bulmers Cider

Case date
2001

Stuart Chambers

## ● Background

Bulmers is the world's largest producer of cider (an alcoholic beverage made from apple juice), with an output of approximately 350 million litres per year. Its main factory is located at Hereford, near the England/Wales border, where some 85 000 tonnes of apples were processed in the 2001 harvest. A visitor's first impression of this site might be that they had entered an enormous speciality chemicals factory, with banks of towering stainless steel silos, kilometres of stainless steel pipe, and a generally very tidy and well laid-out plant. In stark contrast, however, they might notice a procession of farm tractors delivering trailer loads of freshly picked apples to the collection hoppers, or the large numbers of articulated lorries departing with their valuable cargo, their huge curtained sides emblazoned with the 'Strongbow' cider logo.

The production of cider involves a relatively straightforward set of tasks within a very large and complex macro-operation. Most stages of production are modern and highly automated, not only to reach high levels of productivity, but also to ensure the consistency and quality of the final products. The fresh apples are first washed and cleaned, and are then conveyed to a machine that chops them into smaller pieces. This material is continuously pressed to release the juice, which is then evaporated to form a light syrup which can be stored safely, without fermentation, for future use. At a later stage the concentrated juice is re-diluted and fed into a large fermentation vessel along with a specialist preparation of the appropriate yeasts. After no more than 10 days, the juice will have fully fermented; the majority of the fruit sugars will have been converted into alcohol, at about a 10 per cent strength, which is a much higher level than required for finished cider. After separating the yeasts, the liquid is diluted and blended with other ingredients, ready to be packaged. The majority of the cider that is to be sold in 50 litre stainless steel barrels (kegs) or plastic bottles is first pasteurised. There is a large automated production line for filling kegs, and another line which blows (prepares) plastic bottles, fills and labels them. The remaining cider is automatically filled into glass bottles and cans, which are then pasteurised. These products are outer-wrapped in point-of-sale packaging such as cardboard multipacks. Finally, the packed materials are palletised and warehoused, ready for despatch.

# Evolution of manufacturing in the 1990s

Each stage of this operation presents its own set of technical difficulties, complexities, and quality challenges. There are several reasons for this. One is that the natural raw materials (apples and yeasts) have a high level of variability. This results in the need constantly to monitor and adjust the downstream production processes. A bigger impact on the operation comes from the market. Consumers and retailers require ongoing innovation in both product and packaging, which has to be accommodated within each stage of production. Demand varies seasonally, cyclically and randomly and the operation needs to respond to this to avoid storing large quantities of inventory.

Additionally, there are numerous human resource issues that add to the complexities faced by the operations managers. The past decade has been a period of intense change since almost every technology has been replaced, with higher levels of automation displacing much of the manual labour tasks. In consequence, skills and working practices have had to change, while at the same time the company's volume growth has required new shift patterns. Reorganisation and retraining have been undertaken at an unprecedented scale. Chris Jones, the Training Manager, described some of the achievements and problems of the last few years:

'Increasingly, during the first half of the 1990s, the management team became aware that the levels of productivity and quality achieved in operations were not matching the pace of investment in new technology. For example, downtime was increasing as a result of inadequate maintenance and long changeover times. We knew that some fairly radical change would be required, but we were also aware that help would be needed because of the scale and scope of the tasks ahead. We investigated several change consultancy companies that specialised in manufacturing operations, and eventually chose a local company, MPI, to help us. They were particularly attractive to us in that they had the skills and personalities to work well with shop floor personnel. They introduced us to what they called "total productive manufacturing" or TPM. This has many of the elements of "total productive maintenance", but really goes much further. Let me explain...

'The main thrust of the consultants' early work involved improvements to routine maintenance and working practices. They worked with selected individual production teams, identifying all the areas of machines that had to be lubricated, cleaned, adjusted, or otherwise regularly maintained. These areas were all labelled so that they could be clearly identified by everyone. Then each team prepared comprehensive work instructions that clearly set out the responsibilities, routines and procedures required to maximise the overall productivity of the processes, using the previously referenced areas of the machines. Not only did this release the plant technicians to undertake other more complex work, but it also ensured that the day-to-day condition of the plant was greatly improved. With hindsight, we now realise that the technicians had never had sufficient capacity (or time) to complete all the routine maintenance required in the increasingly large, complex and automated plant. Ownership by the operations team of these routine tasks increased their own interest and commitment, and several of the teams have achieved dramatic improvements in productivity and quality. Overall equipment effectiveness (OEE) was measured and generally improved as a result of the TPM activities. In addition to this work, the consultants began training each team in problem solving and resolution techniques. Whilst these were often not immediately applied, most teams did at least manage to maintain the improvements they had achieved. But the consultants knew this was only the first step in TPM, and that the real gains would only come from subsequent steps in the TPM methodology.

'These activities take time, and this was recognised from the outset. Hours were set aside for TPM work, and no production was scheduled for these periods of up to four hours per week. Some team leaders, supervisors and managers were unhappy with this because they were simultaneously under pressure for output. In some ways, I think this limited our progress to the later steps of TPM. It was never intended that the team activities should be confined to routine maintenance and cleanliness. What we really wanted was ongoing continuous improvement, for example process improvements and changeover time reduction. But there was often little support from the supervisors and team leaders for continuing along this route, so only a few teams have really gone on to this type of activity. One of the few examples of ongoing success is the "Keg Team", which has dramatically improved performance in its area.

'In my view, the problem lay both with our existing organisation structure and with the capabilities, personalities and motivation of some of the supervisory and management staff. We had a complex organisation structure in manufacturing, with six levels between the Operations Director and the shop floor. For a company with less than 500 employees in manufacturing, this was clearly excessive! [The existing manufacturing organisation structure is shown in Appendix 50.1(A)]. We had large numbers of shift-based supervisors, some of whom also had "relief supervisors", or assistants, and many of these had only been given supervisory responsibility as a consequence of experience and long service in their area. Many were of the "old school" of manufacturing supervision ... good at following routines such as record keeping, and focused on the immediate output of their shift, which is often referred to as "getting pallets out of the door". Indeed, our performance measurement system encouraged this culture, and this was recognised at an early stage by the consultants. They even recommended that the supervisors should be excluded from involvement with the TPM teams so that the teams could concentrate on improvement, isolated from the immediate pressure for output. Earlier, in a few areas of the factory, supervisors had been superseded by team leaders (who were from an engineering or technical background). These proved to be more amenable to the TPM processes, but even then, progress towards the improvement stages of TPM was often slow. More significantly, I believe that the potential benefits of employing these more capable team leaders were not always fully appreciated by our manufacturing managers, so the role was underdeveloped for a while.

'With the benefit of hindsight, the exclusion of supervisors from the teams was a mistake because we never achieved buy-in from them. During TPM activities, they often went to their offices to catch up with paperwork or other tasks, and were not seen to support their teams at all. Their involvement, if any, was clearly reluctant, and this did little to motivate their teams to migrate to further steps in the TPM process. The practical consequence of this was that when the pressure for output increased, the time for TPM meetings was locally withdrawn on an ad-hoc basis, sending strong messages to the workers that improvement activities were no longer important. The enthusiasm of the teams was undermined, and this was a management problem – it was our fault! We were sending out mixed messages.'

## A manufacturing reorganisation

At the beginning of January 1999, a significant reorganisation of manufacturing was implemented. The supervisor roles were removed and replaced by 22 team leaders, all now qualified at NVQ (National Vocational Qualification) Level Four, which is a respected management qualification. These team leaders were to be front-line managers in every area and on every shift. Existing supervisors, shift managers and team leaders were invited to re-apply for these new jobs, but during the rigorous assessment process, few met the capability requirements of the new role. Several accepted redundancy, and one shift manager returned to a shop floor role. The revised organisation structure is shown in Appendix 50.1(B). The team leader's role now unambiguously encompasses many aspects of human resource management, including training, motivation, facilitation, employee development, team support, and obtaining the necessary resources to support improvement activities. In addition, of course, they continue to be responsible for planning capacity, achieving output targets and maintaining quality in their areas of responsibility. Chris Jones observed:

'Despite these radical changes, the TPM programme did not progress as much as we expected under this new arrangement. In some areas, significant improvements were made by TPM teams, but this was not widespread and universal. In mid-1999, attempts were made to relaunch and revitalise TPM, highlighting set-up reduction and eliminating bottlenecks as important target areas for team activities. Further training (in problem finding and solving, and in the use of simple tools and techniques of analysis) was made available to the teams. I think that we failed to encourage team leaders and engineers to get involved, and without their support little new would happen. Some or all of the time allocated to TPM meetings continued to be taken for production as the whole system was under intense pressure of growth. Team leaders often felt that TPM was the domain of teams and not of themselves! TPM was never included as a core objective of their role, and some would not even be able to explain clearly what TPM was all about. Despite this, some teams did very well, but others made little progress in the move towards continuous improvement.

'As far as the shop floor was concerned, people got involved to a very varied extent. Within a team, some didn't want to be included in improvement activities at all; others enjoyed being involved with TPM meetings, but maybe in order to avoid the intensive cleaning activities that took place concurrently! Some actually valued the training, as well as the thinking activities and discussions that took place in special meeting rooms. Critical mass is an issue. One forceful character in a team can exert a big influence on it, either positive or negative. Some teams have worked extremely well because they passed the critical mass and gained support from the influencers; others have achieved much less because they have insufficient enthusiasts and; too many obstructive influencers.'

## How successful is TPM?

A good example of TPM teamwork bringing results was described by Simon Cornock, a former team leader on the keg-filling line, who has gone on to facilitate further TPM activities following its 1999 relaunch:

'The TPM meetings in the keg-filling line involved all three shifts' team leaders working together. This meant the night shift team leader coming in early to participate in part of the 12-hour (10 a.m. to 10 p.m.) weekly activities. The keg-filling line involves heavy physical work, and hence there is a wide range of abilities including a significant proportion of highly manual labour. We designed a training programme that involved nearly everybody, starting with clear work instructions, developing our own spreadsheets for planning and controlling all cleaning and lubrication tasks. Much of the routine maintenance that had previously been carried out by technicians could then be transferred to production personnel. The overall equipment effectiveness (OEE) of the keg line had been running at around 68 per cent, and we needed extra output to cope with high demand. Analysis conducted by the TPM team indicated that a large number of short duration stoppages had been occurring which eroded our efficiencies. The team used a "measles chart" to record areas of the machinery where these problems had arisen, and this allowed us to home in on root causes which required enhanced levels of maintenance or further process improvements. We also kept improved records of problems arising throughout the plant, keeping a detailed log of where they were occurring and how they had been rectified. As a result of this type of activity, the OEE is now consistently higher than 85 per cent. More importantly, we have developed a real sense of team ownership, which has made work more satisfying for everyone.

'I have subsequently worked with other teams, continuing to train them in TPM activities and methods. Part of this involved using the keg line experience as a demonstration of best TPM practice. Where this has been successful, it is good to see the change from a "command and control", blame-orientated culture, to an open, ideas-based one. It's been very interesting and exciting work!'

Dave Turner, the newly appointed Manufacturing Improvement Manager (MIM), commented on the TPM work carried out within the cider production team, where he previously headed the quality support team:

'We held weekly meetings involving personnel from each of the three shifts. This group worked extremely well and achieved some impressive improvements in productivity. One area we tackled was the blender, where there were repetitive small stoppages throughout the day, triggered by automated alarms. Applying logical root-cause analysis, using a combination of the more experienced operatives and good technicians, we reduced the number of alarms from 200 to less than 10 per shift! We invested a lot of time in people development, which enabled us to solve many problems at a very low engineering cost.

'I would like to think that in my new role I will be invited to help teams as an internal consultant. I will be able to facilitate, resource, and advise on improvement projects, but inevitably I will be a gatekeeper for scarce technical resources, rationing them to the best value-added projects. I have already been asked by the team running the glass-filling line to help them reduce cleaning times from the current six hours to a target of two hours. They know that the remaining four hour period is spent following procedures that include many time-consuming steps such as removing safety guards. We hope that this project will demonstrate the approach to, and value of, set-up reduction. There are at least 50 other improvement projects in progress now which may require my involvement.'

Alan Stokes, one of the three Manufacturing Managers, was formerly a team leader on the keg line, and is now responsible for people development. He had clear views as to why this area was relatively successful in implementing TPM:

'Firstly, we allowed sufficient time for these activities: the full 12-hour period every Wednesday. There were at least a dozen people involved, and their ideas were backed up with sufficient money and resources to allow implementation. Above all, the team leaders took responsibility for the TPM process, while avoiding excessive interference in details. We didn't use the consultants much, except for seeking their advice on specific techniques or on the process to be followed. Our team was of mixed capabilities: some were content to do cleaning of the equipment, drains, and pits while others got involved in analysing processes and coming up with improvements. We had our own dedicated engineering resource, which allowed us to undertake some minor modifications relatively quickly. The team owned and measured their own performance on a PC, and displayed the figures on white boards in the rest area. We even had exchange visits to other companies that were pursuing continuous improvement to learn from them.

'We achieved some impressive results. For example, the changeover time on a line was reduced from fifteen minutes to seven. We removed many non-value-added tasks. We clarified all work instructions and ensured that everything was clearly labelled and stored in the correct place – every tool, every consumable. We reviewed the need for taking microbiological samples, and created a new sampling regime.

'I think that we have learnt the crucial importance of team behaviour. Every team member now has an annual appraisal, and there is an increasing emphasis on social skills development. Of course, team leaders must have some basic training to give them technical knowledge of their processes, but they are now also trained in coaching, mentoring and avoiding confrontational behaviour. Their responsibility is to develop the people within their team, so "sales skills" are needed to persuade team members to cooperate. Team leaders now have annual "360 degree" appraisals, where their performance is discussed with their boss, their peer group and also their team members!'

Martin Keene, one of the other two Manufacturing Managers, responsible for the packaging lines, explained how the process of improvement was becoming somewhat more structured:

'We did the TPM training, and expected the teams to go away and get on with it! The actual level of uptake was quite variable, as my colleagues have already explained. We have certainly achieved a base level of TPM, but the progress towards continuous improvement has been patchy. We have found it best to target specific lines and activities, for example the glass-packing line set-up reduction project. This can then be used as an example for others to follow. At the moment we can only handle these isolated pockets of continuous improvement, therefore we need plans from each area that commit every team to relevant future improvement activities.

'We have decided to base these plans directly on the structure of the company's strategy statements. Each team's plans for improvement projects are entered into a master spreadsheet, which is categorised into the eight elements of our strategy. These are time-phased over the next two to three years so that we can clearly see the resource requirements across the company. Some teams, such as the keg line, have very few entries for the next 12 months because they are already well ahead with their TPM activities, and are already achieving good plant performance and output. Some projects need capital, others are just methods changes. Some measure cost reduction, and others evaluate the benefits in terms of OEE. We have no single vision of what constitutes a good project, but each must now be justified by its alignment to strategic intent. Every one of the manufacturing management team is convinced that we now have the organisation structures and processes in place to allow us to forge ahead with continuous improvement. Our futures depend on it! '

## Questions

1 *To what extent has the consultant's TPM (total productive manufacturing) approach at Bulmers incorporated the five goals of total productive maintenance, or surpassed these goals? These are outlined in the companion book,* Operations Management *by Slack, N. et al., Chapter 19.*

2 *What were the advantages of the early focus on 'basics', such as cleanliness, maintenance and working procedures, in advance of the wider scope offered by continuous (process) improvement activities?*

3 *In what ways did the organisation change in 1999 influence successful TPM implementation?*

4 *How has the role of team leader developed to support the improvement activities?*

5 *Using Bessant and Caffyn's six generic organisational abilities, described in the companion book, identify those behaviours within Bulmers' manufacturing system which reinforce the commitment to continuous improvement. What additional behaviours should be encouraged and/or developed to accelerate and sustain the pace of such activities?*

## Appendix 50.1

## Organisation structures in manufacturing

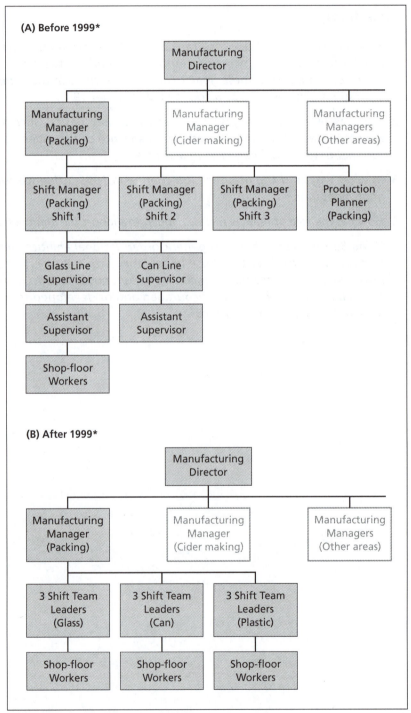

**(A) Before 1999***

**(B) After 1999***

* Note that only part of the organisation structure is shown.

# TPM at Filmco UK

Case date
1996 Alan Harrison

The Newbury factory of Filmco produces polypropylene film for food and packaging markets. The process of film making, described in Appendix 51.1, is basically very simple. Polypropylene granules are melted, extruded and then stretched first lengthways (machine direction) and then horizontally (transverse direction). After making, the film is *wound* onto a mandrel, and left in a *lag store* to relax for a minimum eight-hour period. It can then be *slit* to customer-specified widths and lengths, after which it is *packed* in various ways depending on the size and weight of the reel. Filmco's customers are the converters who print the film for packaging products like Mars chocolate bars and Weetabix breakfast cereal.

Film making is a 24-hour, 360 days/per year, continuous process carried out on capital-intensive lines. As the market in polypropylene film boomed in the 1980s, more and more capacity was added to cope with demand, and three new lines were added to the Newbury plant to take the total number to four. As new investment went in, the opportunity was taken to increase the widths and running speeds of the making lines. While the old Line 4 produced film in 5m widths and ran at 90m/minute, the last line to be added was Line 7, which produced film in 8m widths and which ran at a theoretical speed of 300m/minute. Table 51.1 compares Lines 4 and 7.

However, competitors had also been attracted to the booming market, and overcapacity in the industry was a feature of the early 1990s. Filmco found itself struggling with uncompetitive costs and delivery performance. Factory practice was holding up staff promotion progress. Packing was the job for new starters and from there a man progressed to slitting, then winding, and finally reached the top job of control panel operation. Maintenance and quality were jobs for non-production specialists.

## Operation restructure

A clear objective was set to address these issues: increase production by 30 per cent with 20 per cent fewer employees. A new production structure was implemented as follows:

- A new grade of *process technician* would replace the numerous former grades, such as winder, packer and panel operator. The new grade would attract additional payments for developing skills such as quality control, mechanical and electrical maintenance and forklift truck operation.
- The number of shifts would be increased from five to six but overall manning would be reduced. The purpose of the sixth shift would be to allow a week on days every sixth week so that the extensive training programme could be undertaken.

**Table 51.1 Physical differences between Lines 4 and 7**

| Aspect | Line 4 | Line 7 |
|---|---|---|
| *Products* | Mostly 35μ, 40μ pearlised films<br>Four different product formulations | Clear 'B' films + metallised<br>One product formulation |
| *Lead times* | More even, average | Short (10 days) on 'B' film<br>Long (4 weeks) on 'M' films |
| *Width* | Narrow: 5m line, mill roll average 1.4 tonnes<br>Reels max 640mm outer diameter | Wide: 8m line, mill roll average 6.3tonnes<br>Reels max 2m wide, 770mm outer diameter |
| *Campaign size* | Average 40 tonnes (20 mill rolls) | Average 100 tonnes (30 mill rolls) |
| *Markets* | Confectionery and biscuits, specialist applications | High-volume snack business, commodity products |
| *Standard conditions* | Set and documented<br>Most established, least variable | Fewer standard conditions, less to set up, simpler product range |
| *Charting* | More difficult: more offcuts which cannot be sold<br>Edge trim a problem (yield ↓) | Easier: 'width is good in this business'<br>Edge trim much less of a problem |
| *Slitting* | Manual set-up, 67 mins average<br>All mechanical drive system | Automated set-up, average 34 mins<br>Computerised drive system controls |
| *Age* | Commissioned Mar. 1978 | Commissioned Sep. 1989 |

- Each shift would be developed as a team, with a *team leader* in charge of a group of process technicians covering each line. The team leaders reported to a *shift manager* who had overall responsibility for that shift. The six shift managers reported to a *production manager*, who was on days.
- Technical support was organised by line, thus there were four *unit managers*, each with a unit technologist, working on days.
- Maintenance on days was retained as a central group under the *engineering manager*. The shift maintenance team (led by a *craft team leader*) reported to the shift manager.

In a subsequent round of changes, the factory was divided into two business units: Lines 4 and 5 comprised *North Factory*, Lines 6 and 7 *South Factory*. The shift team for each factory was headed up by a *business team leader* (BTL) with 10 other people in each team covering the two lines: two panel operators, two winders, four on slitting and two on packing.

## Performance of Lines 4 and 7 compared

The main performance measure used by Filmco was overall equipment effectiveness (OEE). This had three components, which were calculated as follows:

**Figure 51.1 Trend of demonstrated capacities expressed as six-month moving averages, Lines 4 and 7, trend of demonstrated capacities, Jan 1995 to Aug 1996 as six-month moving averages (tonnes/day)**

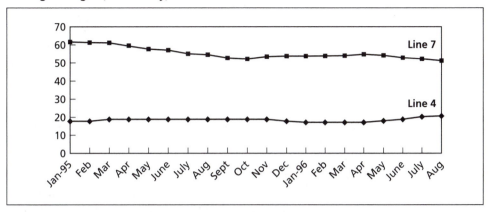

- *uptime*: the running time as a percentage of the total time for the month
- *linespeed*: the average line running rate for the month compared with target
- *quality*: Grade 1 slit film output compared with resin input.

Appendix 51.2 shows the history of OEE for the two lines over a 20-month period. The target for 'world-class' performance had been identified as 80 per cent. While the performance of Line 4 had been steadily improving, especially over the last few months, that of Line 7 had deteriorated considerably. This was also evident in the trend of demonstrated capacities of the two lines, which measures the output tonnage (see Figure 51.1).

What was driving Line 4's comparative success? Line 4 management had addressed the improvement challenge by a major programme of engineering improvements on the line, combined with simplification and standardisation of methods (standard conditions), and by reducing the number of products made on the line. In terms of standardisation, only four process variables had been left from some 200 possibilities. The rest had been fixed completely, for example by removing the wheels from the stenter chain profile adjusters, or by fixing the variables for a given type of film. Quality performance had apparently reduced, although this was attributable to the shrinking batch sizes on Line 4 (76 per cent lower in 1996), combined with greater product complexity. Linespeed had not been specifically pursued, although it had been raised from 90 to 130 metres per minute over the previous three years. One member of the unit team argued:

'Chasing speed is the wrong philosophy. It is essential to get the fundamentals right, like the correct film profile, maintaining pressure in the die, and a stable extrusion rate.'

Another member stated that Line 4's linespeed had been:

'...nudged up 5m/min every six months: when I feel everyone's got their confidence in it [increasing the linespeed] and they go straight into it without even questioning it. Obviously the higher you go, the longer it takes – the more things can go wrong.'

**Table 51.2 Targets for Line 7 linespeed for 1996 (m/min)**

| Film type | Jan | Feb | Mar | Apr | May | Jun | Jul | Aug | Sep | Oct | Nov | Dec |
|-----------|-----|-----|-----|-----|-----|-----|-----|-----|-----|-----|-----|-----|
| B25 | 209 | 213 | 217 | 221 | 225 | 229 | 233 | 237 | 241 | 245 | 249 | 253 |
| B30/B20 | 200 | 205 | 210 | 214 | 219 | 224 | 229 | 234 | 238 | 243 | 248 | 253 |
| B35 | 194 | 197 | 200 | 202 | 205 | 208 | 211 | 214 | 217 | 220 | 223 | 225 |
| B40 | 176 | 178 | 180 | 182 | 184 | 186 | 186 | 190 | 192 | 194 | 196 | 198 |

The Line 7 unit team, on the other hand, had specifically pursued linespeed as the primary goal for productivity improvement. Specific minimum linespeeds (in metres per minute) from the first of each month had been issued on plastic cards (see Table 51.2).

Indeed, it was claimed in August that 'we've had Line 7 running at 253m/min for B30, which is December's target. This trial highlighted some issues at that speed.' The string of major breakdowns on the line in 1996 was described as special causes which would not recur. However, Line 7's linespeed policies provoked intense disagreement elsewhere in the plant. One process technician commented:

'Can you imagine anything going at 250m/min, 24 hours a day, 50-odd weeks a year? It doesn't ring true to me that they can do it. It isn't going to last very long. Something's got to wear out. And that's exactly what's happened to Line 7. Things have started to go on it now because they've been pushing the shit out of it.'

Two fundamentally different improvement strategies were creating very different results in terms of line performance. Also, the improvement in Line 4 film making was impacting on the downstream activities of slitting and packing. The members of the slitting and packing team were under continuous pressure because of the improving performance of the line:

'We're always cutting corners, we don't weigh every reel. If we did it all properly, that [the making line] would shut down.'

Slitting and packing on Line 4 were of necessity closely integrated with the making line. Geographically, the operation was relatively compact, too, with these end-of-process activities taking place close to making in the open shop. However, there was evidence that slitting and packing activities on Line 7 were operating at much lower performance levels than the equivalent Line 4 activities. Lack of pressure from making, the relatively severe discontinuity between making and slitting (the lag store had 40 spaces) and extension of effort can all be regarded as contributory factors, but there also appeared to be a resistance to improvement that was absent from other areas. In spite of TPM projects, the changeover time on the Line 7 slitter remained stubbornly at 34 minutes when the unit team considered that it should be just 17 minutes. Packing took place behind the brick firewall that obscured the process technicians from other parts of the factory; it was 'newspaper hourly in there', cups of tea brought in from the refreshment room, and a standard of housekeeping that was 'a God-awful mess'. Yet a member of the Line 7 slitting and packing team said:

'Now they've reduced it and reduced it ... but nothing's changed out there. All it's done is make it harder for the people that are out there, and people get down – despondent about it because they're getting under pressure from the job because it's not easy.'

## Questions

1 *Explain the differences in approach between the management of Line 4 and of Line 7.*

2 *Which line had the better strategy? Why?*

# The process of film making at FILMCO, Newbury

As has been indicated, the process is basically very simple: melt, extrude and stretch. Most films produced at Newbury have three layers: a central core ('homopolymer') between 18μ and 38μ thick, sandwiched between two outer layers of 1μ each. The outer layers are made from various mixes ('co-polymers') which create additional special properties for the film, such as non-stick coatings, ease of printing and heat sealing. Polypropylene granules are fed from bulk storage silos into a main extruder where they are melted and *extruded* to form the homopolymer, while the co-polymers are fed via two satellite extruders (for a layout diagram, see Figure 51.2). Immediately after extrusion, the resulting 'sandwich' is *chilled* by passing it over a water-cooled roller, which has the effect of 'setting' the plastic in a manner analogous to curing rubber. It is the speed of the chill roller that governs the speed of the whole line. This critical process also determines the crystalline structure of the film and hence its gloss and surface properties: faster chilling creates a smaller crystalline structure. The extrudate is next fed into the first of two stretching processes that greatly increase the mechanical strength of the film by orientating the polymer molecules. This first stretch is in the machine direction (along the length of the film), and the process is called a *machine direction orientation (MDO)*. It is executed by a series of rollers that successively heat, stretch and relax the film; output speed is 4–5 times faster than input speed. Once out of the MDO, the film is input to the stenter oven, where the edges of the film are clamped in chains on either side and stretched widthways, called a *transverse direction orientation (TDO)*. Output width is 10 times the input width. The thick edges of the film, where it has been gripped by the stenter chain, are then removed (edge trim removal) and recirculated to feed the extruders via a *reclaim* section which converts the trim back into granules. One or both surfaces may then be treated by *corona discharge* to etch them for future printing at the next stage in the supply chain. The film is then *wound* onto a mandrel to become a *mill roll*, and placed in a *lag store* to relax for a minimum eight-hour period. The film is then *slit* to customer-specified width and length on the line slitter (*primary slitting*). *Charting* the reels involves planning which of the mill rolls will be slit to customer specification, and in what sequence (see Figure 51.3).

The quality of the roll is usually known at the mill-roll stage, and the areas that may be suspect can be selected for downgrading to *Grade 3* status, which means that they are sold off to a third-party processor at material cost. Finally, the slit reels are *packed* in various ways depending on the size and weight of the reel. If they cannot be slit to size on primary slitting because they are too narrow or too short, part-finished reels are transferred to *secondary slitting* for completion.

**Figure 51.2  Film making at Filmco, Newbury**

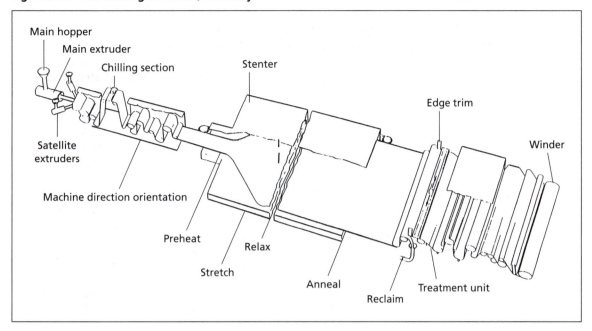

**Figure 51.3  Possible chart for 6m reel**

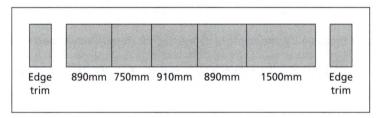

| Edge trim | 890mm | 750mm | 910mm | 890mm | 1500mm | Edge trim |

## Appendix 51.2

# Data for overall equipment effectiveness (OEE)
OEE calculations and demonstrated capacities (tonnes/day) for Line 4

| Month/Year | Uptime % | Linespeed % | Quality % | OEE % | Demonstrated capacity |
|---|---|---|---|---|---|
| 1/95 | 79.0 | 82.5 | 78.9 | 51.4 | 17.9 |
| 2/95 | 88.1 | 86.0 | 79.9 | 60.6 | 19.4 |
| 3/95 | 92.8 | 86.2 | 86.2 | 68.9 | 20.3 |
| 4/95 | 86.6 | 88.2 | 83.7 | 64.0 | 19.3 |
| 5/95 | 85.0 | 85.7 | 83.4 | 60.7 | 18.8 |
| 6/95 | 83.1 | 87.2 | 82.1 | 59.5 | 17.8 |
| 7/95 | 7.0 | 88.1 | 79.7 | 55.5 | 17.4 |
| 8/95 | 78.2 | 87.8 | 71.5 | 49.2 | 16.7 |
| 9/95 | 87.0 | 93.0 | 82.0 | 67.0 | 20.8 |
| 10/95 | 75.0 | 85.0 | 81.0 | 53.0 | 20.2 |
| 11/95 | 76.6 | 87.4 | 74.8 | 50.0 | 16.8 |
| 12/95 | N/A | N/A | N/A | N/A | N/A |
| 1/96 | 59.0 | 81.4 | 50.0 | 29.7 | 14.1 |
| 2/96 | 78.7 | 79.1 | 75.6 | 47.9 | 16.2 |
| 3/96 | 93.8 | 84.2 | 88.2 | 69.6 | 20.6 |
| 4/96 | 92.4 | 86.1 | 84.4 | 67.4 | 21.1 |
| 5/96 | 87.8 | 86.0 | 73.6 | 55.6 | 19.7 |
| 6/96 | 82.2 | 88.6 | 78.2 | 57.5 | 18.1 |
| 7/96 | 92.4 | 88.8 | 79.0 | 65.0 | 21.2 |
| 8/96 | 91.8 | 92.2 | 76.2 | 64.6 | 20.7 |

OEE calculations and demonstrated capacities for (tonnes/day) Line 7

| Month/Year | Uptime % | Linespeed % | Quality % | OEE % | Demonstrated capacity |
|---|---|---|---|---|---|
| 1/95 | 83.4 | 84.2 | 85.6 | 60.1 | 64.0 |
| 2/95 | 80.4 | 78.5 | 8.7 | 52.2 | 54.3 |
| 3/95 | 87.3 | 83.4 | 86.4 | 62.9 | 59.9 |
| 4/95 | 78.3 | 81.7 | 88.4 | 56.5 | 56.6 |
| 5/95 | 79.5 | 77.2 | 88.1 | 54.0 | 51.7 |
| 6/95 | 87.4 | 72.7 | 81.8 | 52.0 | 53.7 |
| 7/95 | 78.9 | 75.5 | 75.8 | 45.1 | 50.8 |
| 8/95 | 85.7 | 75.9 | 78.8 | 51.2 | 53.2 |
| 9/95 | 77.3 | 76.0 | 82.4 | 48.4 | 49.1 |
| 10/95 | 75.2 | 72.9 | 85.8 | 47.0 | 52.3 |
| 11/95 | 79.3 | 77.6 | 81.8 | 50.3 | 57.6 |
| 12/95 | 54.1 | 71.9 | 76.9 | 30.0 | 55.0 |
| 1/96 | 75.0 | 73.3 | 80.5 | 44.3 | 53.1 |
| 2/96 | 86.3 | 75.7 | 85.1 | 55.6 | 53.5 |
| 3/96 | 77.3 | 76.6 | 84.9 | 50.3 | 47.1 |
| 4/96 | 88.0 | 78.7 | 85.6 | 59.3 | 58.7 |
| 5/96 | 83.6 | 79.2 | 77.5 | 51.3 | 53.2 |
| 6/96 | 73.7 | 74.1 | 83.2 | 45.4 | 44.9 |
| 7/96 | 75.4 | 76.3 | 70.1 | 40.3 | 50.8 |
| 8/96 | 74.9 | 78.0 | 78.7 | 46 | 48.6 |

# Eurocamp Travel

Stuart Chambers and Jim Crew

## Background

Eurocamp Travel was founded in 1974, specialising in the provision of family camping holidays in France, based on car travel. The service package initially comprised ferry crossings from the UK, fully-equipped tent or mobile home accommodation on high specification campsites, the services of on-site couriers, and insurance. The company soon gained a reputation for the high quality of its equipment and services, and became market leader in this rapidly-growing sector, with high levels of repurchase and recommendations. Growth averaged around 15 per cent per year in the period 1985–90, and at the same time, the business became much more complex: sales offices were opened in The Netherlands and Germany, and the geographic coverage was extended to include sites throughout Europe, totalling 160 by 1990. The service package also offered more choice, including en-route hotels, short stays on sites, and a range of company-provided site services including sports equipment, children's entertainments, baby-packs, etc. As the business became larger and more complex, the demands placed on the office systems also became greater, reinforcing the need for functional specialisation of staff, yet requiring more interdepartmental understanding and cooperation. At this time, batches of customers' files were moved physically between departments for each stage of processing, and this resulted in delays and excess costs when amendments or corrections were requested by customers. Feedback from customers has always been valued, primarily through analysis of questionnaires issued to every customer. Levels of satisfaction with many aspects of the services, including the initial reservation, were closely monitored throughout each season and from year to year.

## The quality challenge

By 1990 it was clear that almost every element of Eurocamp's service package could be, or was being, copied by competitors eager to attract away some of the premium customers. The best defence would be to reinforce quality at every stage in the process, since this was believed to be the main criterion that already differentiated Eurocamp, and this was also potentially the most difficult for lower priced competitors to follow. Under a UK Government Department of Trade and Industry (DTI) initiative, a consultant was brought in to initiate and facilitate a major quality improvement programme. This was conceived as a 'top-down' approach, whereby important projects would be identified and tackled by trained teams. It was intended that the entire workforce would eventually be affected and involved by this 'cascade learning' approach, but it soon became apparent that these early projects were not achieving the anticipated sustainable improvements. It became clear that the failure of the early work was largely the result of only involving senior managers, who couldn't devote the time required to projects, and did not fully understand the processes concerned. Conversely, those employees who did have a very detailed understanding of the processes and the problems had been excluded from the problem definition, evaluation of potential solutions, and implementation of changes (although few projects actually reached the implementation stage). It was decided to learn from these failures, and to continue in the quest for sustainable, tangible improvements in quality. A complete rethink of the company's approach would be required.

## Introduction of Total Quality Management

Now free from the constraints of the prescriptive approach of the consultant, the quality manager reviewed the latest thinking on TQM, and found inspiration in the clear approaches described in the book *Total Quality Management* by Oakland (1989) which then became compulsory reading for the members of the board of directors. In 1991, the company launched the Quality Management System (QMS) initiative, but also decided *not* to pursue ISO 9000 registration. A clearly structured organisation for quality was set up, headed by the directors, Quality Council. Each department established a Quality Steering Committee which comprised at least one director, a trained facilitator, and volunteers from every grade of employee. The emphasis at this stage was on the identification and improvement of internal processes, with emphasis on satisfying the internal customer. Each departmental committee initially chose three such processes to analyse and improve, not necessarily including the biggest known problems. Early successes demonstrated the validity of this approach, and generated a high level of enthusiasm throughout the company.

One example of a project involved analysis of the process of entering telephone bookings data onto the computer system. The objective was to reduce the number of key strokes, so that the length of telephone calls could be minimised without affecting the quality of the customer–staff interaction. Unnecessary steps were identified and improvements were made to the booking screens. The number of key strokes was reduced from 123 to 85, a saving of 32 per cent.

In 1992, a new approach was developed to tackle specific problems concerning processes that affected operations in several departments. These problems were initially identified and selected by individual departmental managers, but their selection was then controlled more rigorously with structured feasibility studies, before release to the ad hoc 'Improvement Teams' of around five to seven people. These were established and given substantial training, both in the tools and techniques of quality improvement, and more significantly in a compulsory 'seven-stage project methodology', which is outlined in Figure 52.1. In the early projects the team leaders were usually junior managers, but now almost any grade of employee, including part-timers, may act as leader. An example of a successful project of this

**Figure 52.1 Eurocamp's Seven-stage Methodology for improvement projects**

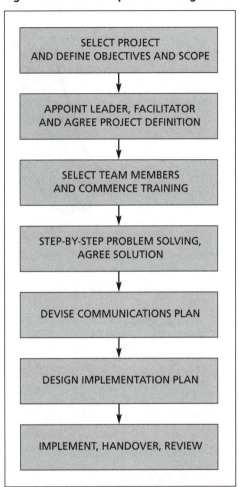

type was the redesign of the brochure requests system, which brought together formally disparate parts into a single operations centre, which included the brochure requests telephone lines, label printing facility, assembly and enveloping operations and despatch.

Although many of these projects were unquestionably successful, and had brought great credibility to the programme, it was increasingly apparent that further stimulation of the process would be required if results were to be sustained. It was decided to introduce occasional elements of fun or humour, and 'Dragon Days' were conceived and implemented. Briefly, this involved the search for hidden green dragon eggs (dyed hard-boiled hens' eggs) throughout the offices, prizes were awarded for their discovery, and a mechanism was introduced for employees to report problems called 'hatched dragons' which still had to be identified and slayed! Employees were issued with a number of blank 'Dragon Cards', on which they could detail any problems, however minor, that were affecting them or their work, (an example is shown in Figure 52.2), for example:

**Figure 52.2 Example of typical 'Dragon Card' completed by an employee in Reservations**

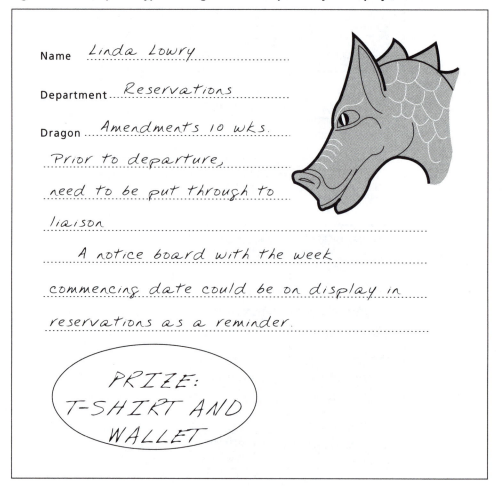

Name  *Linda Lowry*

Department  *Reservations*

Dragon  *Amendments 10 wks.*
*Prior to departure,*
*need to be put through to*
*liaison*
*A notice board with the week*
*commencing date could be on display in*
*reservations as a reminder.*

*PRIZE: T-SHIRT AND WALLET*

- a process that they did not fully understand
- a slow process
- a process that they found difficult to do
- discomfort, such as distracting noises, poor seating position, draughts, etc.

Usually these cards were then passed to the person that owned the process, for action or further analysis as appropriate. Some of this 'slaying of dragons', or problem resolution, could be done individually, with a reward of appropriate T-shirts, but more complex problems were handled by improvement teams. Prizes were also awarded for the best dragon problems, as judged by the Quality Steering Committees and Quality Council. Some examples of prize-winners were:

1 suggested changes to the late-amendments system, including a new form of reminder to reservations staff;
2 amendments to brochure information concerning opening and closing dates in Scandinavian sites in relation to complex ferry schedules, to reduce customer confusion.

No attempt was made to quantify the number of problems identified, or solved. The success of the system relied simply on the interest and enthusiasm of the staff, and on the culture of continuous improvement, rather than on numerical targets or quality cost reductions.

Having concentrated efforts on satisfying the internal customers and improving the processes that linked them, it was then decided to refocus the programme on satisfying the end-customers: the paying holidaymakers. In 1994 the company launched a Customer Focus Programme, beginning with two half-day consultant-facilitated workshops in a local theatre, for all employees. This programme emphasised the value of a customer, both in terms of retaining existing and gaining new ones. One outcome of this programme was a recognition of the need to re-examine the handling of complaints, which led to a more generous, professional, and respectful, service recovery policy. This considerably enhanced the empowerment of all contact staff to resolve customer complaints or disappointments without having to get permission from managers. Sometimes this involved issuing free days, discounts, or upgrading, but often was simply a more personal way of responding quickly, sensitively and constructively to genuine problems as they arose. The customer-orientation approach of the organisation is reflected in recent independent customer research, which reported one of the highest scores was for Eurocamp's telesales which came near the high scores of Hewlett-Packard. For the 1995 season, the telesales and booking administration departments received an average score of 9.3 out of 10, with 57 per cent of respondents giving a rating of 10 out of 10! This excellent performance was also recorded by Eurocamp's own highly developed market research; nearly 50 per cent of customers go to the trouble of completing and returning a post-holiday questionnaire, which gives feedback on a wide range of quality attributes. An annual bonus based on a customer satisfaction score is paid equally to all employees. Managers feel that the early resolution of customers' problems through greater staff empowerment has saved the time and costs involved in handling ongoing disputes, and has therefore had a significant role in improving the productivity of the overall system.

The latest initiative to create an even greater customer orientation is the 'Listen and Learn' programme. As with most large organisations, there is considerable specialisation of work, whereby individuals develop knowledge and skills in their own role, but lack experience in, and understanding of others. The company devised an initial menu of ten 'modules' in which employees could experience other customer-oriented jobs within the company, either actively or passively, as observers. These experiences focused on getting people into customer contact roles, either directly or alongside customer-facing staff. Participation in the programme was voluntary, and each module of experience was clearly defined in a booklet and advertised internally. Table 52.1 lists the available modules and points awarded for each experience, and Appendix 52.1 describes a typical module. As can be seen, each completed module earned a number of points which an employee could record and collect towards an award on the scale: Green Standard (250 points), Red Standard (500 points), and Gold Standard (750 points). The directors showed their commitment by each promising to achieve Green Standard by a certain target date, and they were soon seen taking telesales bookings, analysing customer feedback questionnaires, and working in the Customer Services Department. A 'Heros and Heroines' awards ceremony is now held annually, when attractive rewards are presented. All award

**Table 52.1 'Listen and Learn' programme contact modules and points earned**

| Contact module | | Points | | Maximum points | |
| --- | --- | --- | --- | --- | --- |
| No. | Description | Number | Per | Number | Equivalent |
| 1 | Reservations / Reception | 25 | 2 hour session | 125 | 5 sessions |
| 2 | Reservations / Liaison: Listen-in facility | 15 | 2 hour session | 75 | 5 sessions |
| 3 | Customer call-back: Post travel-pack, pre-hol | 2 | call | 80 | 40 calls |
| 4 | Customer call-back: Post-holiday | 3 | call | 150 | 50 calls |
| 5 5 | Adopt-a-customer calls per customer | 10 | customer | 100 | 10 customers |
| 6 | Site visits | 5 | customer | 250 | 50 contacts |
| 7 | Work as a courier | 250 | 5 days | 250 | 1 visit only |
| 8 | Work as a cleaner | 85 | 3 days | 85 | 1 visit only |
| 9 | Read questionnaire comments | 6 | Batch of 50 | 60 | 500 questionnaires |
| 10 | Questionnaire call-back | 2 | call | 100 | 50 calls |

winners receive a customer focus memento such as an inscribed mug and passport holder, plus gift vouchers for purchases in a popular store. It had been hoped that this scheme would be of interest to backroom staff, such as the accountants and IT people, but to date their involvement has been considerably below average, as indicated in Table 52.2.

**Table 52.2 Analysis of 'Listen and Learn' programme involvement**

| Category | Number (Percentage) of category achieving | | |
| --- | --- | --- | --- |
| | Green Standard 250 points (%) | Red Standard 500 points (%) | Gold Standard 750 points (%) |
| Directors | 3 (75) | | |
| Senior managers | 2 (33) | | |
| Supervisors | 4 (40) | 1 (10) | |
| Customer sales/support | 20 (25) | 7 (9) | 2 (2) |
| On-site service | 5 (14) | | |
| Accounts | 2 (33) | | |
| Computer department | 2 (16) | 2 (16) | 1 (8) |

While the programme is considered to have been a success, the directors now feel that there is a need for it to be revised and updated to maintain interest, and to bring in those whose participation has not yet been significant. The menu of contact options certainly needs regular review and updating, and the points allocation will have to be adjusted. Currently, the programme encourages the 'easier' passive activities, such as observing and reading, so greater rewards will be needed for more proactive tasks involving direct customer contact. New objectives for 'Look and Learn' might include greater staff flexibility, continuous improvement, and personal development.

## Towards the paperless system

Since the early beginnings of the company, an envelope-style file had been used for every booking, to hold all the associated information and correspondence including copies of invoices, acknowledgements, letters, amendments, and handwritten 'Contact Sheets' which recorded details of every telephone conversation with the customer. The file was also used as a trigger for each specialised stage of the processes involved in completing the associated administrative requirements of the order.

The file, in a colour representing the start-of-holiday month, was prepared in 'Bookings Reception', and this triggered an acknowledgement of order being sent to the customer. This department then passed on the file to the required next stage in the process, such as the 'Travel Department' which booked ferries and/or Motorail if required by the customer. It would then be passed to 'Hotel Reservations' if appropriate, or to the Sales Ledger Department for invoicing, and then to the Records Department to await receipt of deposits, and so on.

At each stage of this essentially 'batch' process, staff used computers and had access to the basic details of each order, but the file remained the core of the system. No work could be done by any department without the file. Where amendments were required, either at the request of the customer, or as a result of problems in providing exactly what the customer wanted, this was dealt with by specialists in the 'Liaison Department', who also needed the file to be fully informed about all previous discussions and negotiations with the customer. Under these circumstances the file had to be found from within the normal system, and temporarily diverted to Liaison until the problem was resolved. When not in immediate use and when completed, the file would be returned to 'Filing'. In 1994, a total of 50 large filing cabinets were in use, holding 40 000 files, and occupying a large area of office space. At the end of the season, all this paperwork was carefully sorted, and archived in a warehouse for five years.

This file-based system had been the stable core of the bookings administrative system, and had been constantly improved and adapted while the departments developed and used more computer systems and electronic links to the suppliers and external operations. Most ferry bookings, for example, are now made online with direct links into the operators' systems, and communications with hotels and campsites are usually by fax. The use of conventional files was, by contrast, slow and labour-intensive. Sometimes it was also far from ideal in terms of flexibility, for example when amendments were required, and a few files could be mislaid, affecting dependability.

The biggest problem was when files entered the Liaison Department, since they would have to be held there until the amendment was confirmed by the supplier, such as a ferry company, French Motorail, or a hotel. This could delay the file by many weeks, delaying later critical stages such as invoicing.

The difficulties of locating files resulted in delays in responding to customer queries, often leading to anxiety and a general impression of substandard service. Equally serious was the cost of unproductive searching for files by liaison staff, the most skilled and highest paid administrative grade, and the time and cost of extra telephone calls back to customers. Customer files had to be found quickly in the event of cancellations, and everyone involved with that booking alerted, so that associated external reservations could be reversed. All of this took large amounts of staff time and effort, which could have been used more productively and proactively in direct contact with customers.

In 1994 it was decided to change the system, with the objective of 'reducing or eliminating the dependency on customer files, such that costs are reduced and service is improved'. A six-person improvement team including members of each department involved in the process and a computer systems expert, was established. It carried out its work in accordance with Eurocamp's well-tried 'Seven-stage Methodology' (Figure 52.1) described earlier. The objective was to develop new systems and procedures that would reduce the need for customer files, and that these would be working before July 1994, the start of the 1995 booking season. Targets were set for the proportion of customer files still in use: 50 per cent for 1995, and 20 per cent for 1996. There was significant resistance to this project, since physical files had been a normal part of everyone's job, and there were implicit threats to employment levels.

The improvement team brainstormed the issue with all the departmental managers, and collected data on all the existing uses of files. Many further meetings refined the specification of the proposed system changes. Involvement with users in this way helped to reduce resistance to change, and facilitated the later implemented work. The recommendations were that the new system should be installed in three phases. Phase one transferred all existing routine correspondence including acknowledgements and invoicing onto an internal paperless system, the customer receiving the only hard copies. Phase two involved 'electronic contact sheets' to replace the handwritten ones. All discussions with customers were now keyed directly into the system, which recorded the date and time and member of staff involved. This record could not be amended, and also provided immediate communication of required actions to other departments for action, along with a 'to do' list for every user. Phase three, not yet implemented, will involve scanning all incoming correspondence, which is the only remaining reason to open a conventional customer file.

The targets set for the project have been exceeded, with only 9.5 per cent of conventional files in 1995, and only 1 per cent in 1996. The system has clearly worked extremely well, and has had significant effects on productivity. Table 52.3 indicates the changes in permanent staff levels and bookings made over the last three years. It is believed that most of the improvement in productivity has been as a result of the new system. The reduction in staffing during this period has been through natural wastage and voluntary redundancy.

**Table 52.3  Productivity of bookings system 1993 to 1995**

| Year | Number of permanent staff (excludes seasonal staff) | | | | Bookings processed | | Productivity Bookings / Staff | |
|---|---|---|---|---|---|---|---|---|
| | Administration | Liaison | Reservation | Total | Gross | Net[*] | Gross | Net[*] |
| 1993 | 62[‡] | | 30 | 92 | 34937 | 31231 | 380 | 339 |
| 1994 | 48.6[‡] | | 24 | 72.6 | 39880 | 36091 | 549 | 497 |
| 1995 | 25.6 | 14 | 19 | 58.6 | 41525 | 37997 | 709 | 648 |
| Productivity improvement 1993 to 1995 | | | | | | | 87% | 91% |

[*]Net refers to the final number of bookings after deduction of cancellations.
[‡]Refers to combined number of staff for Administration and Liaison before they were separated organisationally (no separated figures available).

## The future

Jim Crew, Eurocamp's Managing Director, believed that the past five years demonstrated the value of TQM for the business:

'One of the most striking effects has been our ability to analyse and improve our processes. This has resulted both in improved quality as experienced by the external customers, and in increasing productivity. With the current adverse economic conditions for our market in Europe, our growth has slowed somewhat, so the savings that we have achieved have been essential for the ongoing development of the business. Now is certainly not a time for complacency. We will need to consider how we can continue to motivate everyone to continue to look for the thousands of little improvements which are so essential in sustaining the vitality of the business. We have to ensure that the individual initiatives, such as the "Listen and Learn" programme, are developed or replaced. We must also give more thought to quality improvements in the back office. How important is it for our computer experts and accounts staff to learn to interface with our external customers? And what about our campsite couriers? Every year we take on over one thousand employees, mostly students, to look after our customers on sites spread all over Europe. They are all very well trained and supervised, but perhaps there is much more we could do to get them involved in improvement, in addition to their basic "maintenance" tasks of cleaning equipment and being helpful to customers.'

### Questions

1 Why has Eurocamp's 'Seven-stage Methodology' been so important in managing the company's quality improvement projects? How does this compare with 'best practices' for project management in general?

2 What are the main features of Eurocamp's approaches to quality improvement, and why have these been so successful? How has the company avoided 'Quality Droop'?

**3** *Should the 'Listen and Learn' programme be reviewed or scrapped now that the level of participation is declining? Could it be modified to encourage more proactive participation and to identify more opportunities for process improvement?*

**4** *Why was there a lower than average participation in the 'Listen and Learn' programme by back-room staff? How could this resistance be overcome, and what benefits, if any, would acrue from their involvement?*

**5** *Would it be possible to get the active involvement of temporary staff, and particularly of the couriers, in continuous improvement activities?*

**6** *Now that many of the larger process improvements have been achieved and customer satisfaction ratings are so high, further changes will inevitably be less spectacular. How can the momentum of improvement be maintained? Should improvements be recorded and counted? Should Eurocamp undertake self-assessment under the European Foundation for Quality Management (EFQM) Quality Award model?*

### Reference

Oakland, J. S. (1989), *Total Quality Management*, Butterworth-Heinemann.

## Appendix 52.1

## Example of 'Listen and Learn' module

---

6 Site Visits

Manager: Ruth Stubbs

WHAT'S INVOLVED: meeting and talking to customers on the campsite. This would include:

- Making an initial contact.
- Asking a short series of questions and recording the responses.
- Asking a specific series of questions if required for any special market research.
- Following these up with general discussion as appropriate.
- Feed-back of information including record of additional anecdotal information.
- Post-holiday response to customer if appropriate.

TRAINING AND PREPARATION: staff wishing to undertake this module will be provided with a pack including a preparation sheet for their guidance and a set of question sheets for completion. Further support will be available from Ruth Stubbs, Marketing. Points will be accrued for each set of responses returned.

TIMING: for many employees, site visits will have to be carried out during holidays, staff educationals etc. However, staff taking up module 8 (Cleaner) would finish work at 3.00 p.m. and would have the opportunity to use 'time off' to speak to customers.

---

**CASE 53**

# E-Cab

Case date
1995

Stuart Chambers

## Introduction

'I was brought in to sort out manufacturing, and that is what I'm going to do – and fast! Honestly, I was shocked by what I saw in my first week here, but I am sure that you will both want to help get to the bottom of the problems, and sort them out. Materials management must be our top priority if we are to get back on course and bring manufacturing here at least up to the high service standards shown by other departments, such as Design and Sales. At the moment all I can see is scrapped materials, shortages, wasted effort, and a large overhead which seems to be there only to make absolutely sure that good products reach our customers. We've certainly got a big task ahead, but I need your input. First, however, I am bringing in an experienced materials manager to take overall responsibility for planning, materials handling, inventory management and performance measurement within manufacturing. I would like you both to work directly with me and the new manager, over the next year, to develop our improvement strategies and to get them into action.'

Pierre Dumas, the new VP of Operations at E-Cab's Lille factory, in northern France, was talking at his first meeting with Sara Montenay and Jean Brasfort, two young graduate production engineers who had joined the company about nine months earlier as trainees in the operations department. The previous VP of Operations had recognised the importance of giving them an important, but not high-risk project based on their recent training in the latest thinking in manufacturing. He had decided to ask them to prepare outline plans for introducing 'best practice' manufacturing to the company, with a particular emphasis on halving the 10-week lead-time needed to produce the products. They had then drawn up an outline project plan which involved them in a series of activities such as capacity planning, 'de-bottlenecking', the introduction of *kanban* control, inventory planning and facilities layout. They would also work on improvements to the basic MRP system that had been allowed to fall into disuse because of outdated data, failed working practices and inaccurate data entry.

E-Cab is one of the leading European manufacturers of customised metal cabinets (known in the business as 'cabs'), of various sizes and designs. These are sold to a wide range of high-technology industries to contain, support and securely protect electrical and electronic control systems from dirt ingress, the weather and accidental or deliberate interference or damage. They often included built-in air conditioning systems to maintain uniform temperatures in the electrical circuitry. The main applications include cabinets for cellular telephone transmitter base stations (these are often seen at the side of autoroutes and on the roofs of large commercial buildings), large traffic signalling systems, industrial controls and cable television equipment. E-Cab had experienced rapid growth in sales and profits (see Appendix 53.1) during the last four years, for three main reasons.

Firstly, the market in general had grown rapidly during this period, with substantial new opportunities in the development of cellular communications networks, the rebuilding of Eastern Europe's infrastructures, modernisation of railway signalling in several European countries, and huge growth in cable/satellite television systems. Similar growth was starting in South America and SE Asia. Suppliers who could cope with rapid increases in volume were highly valued by the electronic system manufacturers. This was because they often wanted to concentrate on their core competencies of electronic design and system development, outsourcing their more traditional manufacturing requirements.

Secondly, E-Cab provided excellent technical support, designing increasingly sophisticated products which exactly met the customers' technical and aesthetic requirements. This was supported by E-Cab's ability to make prototype cabinets very quickly, sometimes in less than a month, if required.

Finally, E-Cab had been particularly willing and eager to do more of the value-added work on these products, initially fitting and testing many of the electrical and electronic systems, and more recently, purchasing these components directly from vendors. The company was also accredited to quality systems standard ISO 9002 and had passed all external quality audits with rarely more than trivial errors found in records, and high levels of adherence to documented procedures. However, the management team had always recognised that there must come a time when these factors would no longer play such a big part in E-Cab's growth. Maturing markets might not require constant technical revisions, and there was even an increasing risk that customers might take back the value-added assembly work and do it in-house.

CEO, Philippe Legrand, spoke at the last board meeting about his concerns:

'At the very least, we should expect the market prices to become tighter over time, and customers will start to pay more detailed attention to schedule adherence and the quality of what they are getting, so there will be no room for complacency. We must start raising productivity throughout the business if we are to survive and prosper.'

Most of Sara and Jean's time had been spent acting as the improvement team for the 'Nokia Cell' which had been established just before they joined the company to assemble cabinets for one of the largest customers, accounting for over 4000 cabinets per year. In line with their work plan, they had spent the last two months beginning to look at quality issues in this area. They had decided to share the analysis by dividing it into two categories. Jean would concentrate on the physical aspects of the processes, looking at work specifications, at the causes of damage in material handling and at assembly faults. Sara would look at the human side of quality, starting with an attitude survey to determine employees' views on quality in the company and in this cell. She would also recruit and train 'Improvement Teams' on the cell to demonstrate the benefits of *kaizen* principles in gradually eliminating the causes of faults on the cabinets. This approach would then be extended to the whole factory with teams for each area.

## Jean's experience

'Some of the most critical components used in these particular products are the corner posts and cross members, since if they have been processed incorrectly, the cab built can be completely disrupted. These components are made from long lengths of bought-out, purpose-made aluminium extrusions which are first cut to length and then fixing holes are made using dedicated punching and drilling jigs. They are then sent out to subcontractors who provide a special chemical EMC finish (Alocrom), and they are finally returned to the company for painting, if required, and then to mechanical assembly to be built into cabinets: [Appendix 53.2 gives an indication of the process route involved].

'When I started looking for quality problems, I didn't have to look far! A brief inspection of the scrap bins revealed hundred of posts and cross members in amongst the normal offcuts and scraps of metal associated with the cutting and drilling processes. Many of these had obviously been through most of the operations. I decided to start by evaluating the cost of the scrapped posts and cross members, and then tried to identify the causes of the scrap. Some of these components were obviously bent or scratched, but what or who had caused this was not at all obvious. I then collected samples of all types of defect that had been found, and showed them to the supervisors of the component supply areas concerned. I have written down some of their comments to highlight the nature of the problems we face [see Appendix 53.3]. Lack of product standards was seen to be a big problem: people seemed to have little understanding of what level of quality was actually required or acceptable – for example, the position, depth, length of any scratches. Surprisingly, many of the technical drawings issued to the shop floor included dimensions without clear tolerances, or with ambiguous ones. Most people in the assembly areas admitted that they had absolutely no idea of what they were looking for in terms of the visual appearance of the components, and when in doubt, they tended to use rather than reject them, to save money and to keep to the build schedule.

'The first shock to both of us had been the enormous variety and cost of all this scrap. A typical finished post costs around FFr200 (French francs) and a typical cross member FFr80! I prepared a Quality Standards Board for the Mechanical Assembly area, which used physical components and photographs to show the assemblers (for the first time) what were the acceptable standards of finish. Posts and cross members below this standard were to be put aside for reasons to be identified and recorded. Data for two months was analysed, and the true cost of scrap was highlighted. [This is summarised in Appendix 53.4] Unfortunately, this only emphasised that scratching was the biggest problem, but did not tell us precisely where it was coming from.

'To highlight where we should focus our efforts, I then looked at cross members in more detail. I introduced random sampling at the four check points [see Appendix 53.5]. A sample of four components was taken at each point every hour, and was thoroughly inspected against the standards. The percentage failure due to scratching was recorded in this way for a period of five weeks, and the results were recorded [see Appendix 53.6]. This exercise focused our initial improvement efforts on the saw and pierce activities, where the scratching problem was greatest. Analysis of these processes highlighted three areas where scratching occurred: on the saw table; at the pierce operation where the cut length of aluminium is pushed into the punching jigs; and in transit between the saw, deburring and piercing operations.

'Jigs were designed to prevent the extrusion coming into contact with the metal table of the saw. Swarf (sharp metal cuttings) from the saw and punching operations was removed by the addition of a constant controlled supply of compressed air, preventing build-up of swarf that could cause scratching. Special tubular plastic carriers, similar to large crates for beverage bottles, were designed to protect the components between operations. Further monitoring at the check points [see Appendix 53.7] indicated that our efforts were paying off, with noticeable improvements downstream. Unfortunately, at this point in the project I was asked by M. Dumas to work with Jules Lecabec, the new Materials Manager, on the scheduling system for the press shop, so I was no longer able to pursue this work.'

## Sara's experience

'My first task was to determine the attitudes of the workforce to quality in general, in order to discover whether the quality problems we had seen around the factory were due to carelessness or inability of the people to do their jobs well – perhaps due to problems with the design of products or processes, lack of training, inadequate tools and equipment, and so on. I started by talking informally to the Nokia Cell management and supervisors, and finally to a small cross-section of the shop-floor employees. Extracts from some of their replies is included in my report. [see Appendix 53.8]

'Clearly, while the managers and supervisors were emphasising the importance of good quality, their generally held view was that the shop-floor workers didn't care about quality, and were the source of most of the mistakes and damage. I therefore decided to find out the views of those on the shop floor, so conducted a more structured employee survey, initially in the Electrical Assembly section. Most of the questions required the employee to rate their opinions on a 1–6 scale, but the last few questions were more open, asking for descriptions of good and bad quality practice. [A copy of the main findings of the questionnaire is included as Appendix 53.9] What I want to do next is to repeat this in other parts of the Cell, and then to present the results of these surveys to the managers and supervisors for comment. The results might also be a valuable introduction to the second Improvement Team, which I hope to get under way in the next few weeks – but I don't know if it's a good idea to start with that or not. I know that Pierre is very keen to get teams established in every area within the next few months.

'I believed that membership of improvement teams should be voluntary, and so arranged for Pierre to authorise overtime to allow meetings be conducted after work to avoid conflict with production output requirements. In practice, however, Anne preferred to nominate some brighter and more company-minded people in her section, and to conduct the meeting in working time. On balance, I felt it was best to agree to this because if I were to go against this I might lose her cooperation and interest. Unfortunately, in practice, two of the team members are not as keen as the others, but even so, have started to make a useful contribution to the work. Another problem I had to face is how a team should be run. I had assumed that we should allow them to identify problems and solve them, supported by my training sessions in "tools and techniques". Anne and Pierre, however, both felt that we must direct the agenda – setting a limited number of important problems to be solved. I don't know how we will get their full support and enthusiasm that way, but only time will tell!

'I devised and ran a training programme with the team to teach the basic ideas of quality and some problem-solving techniques such as brainstorming, cause-and-effect analysis, SPC charting and preparation of simple graphs. The team now meets on an ad hoc basis, often with only two members involved, to solve problems which have shown up recently on the inspection of finished cabs. I am now aiming to have the team meeting held twice a week to work on problems, and once every two weeks to review progress and for further training. They are already producing some good solutions, and are establishing the root causes of some of the more obscure problems. However, they are still very dependent on me. Over the next three months, I would like gradually to hand over more responsibility, until they are telling me about their meetings and the problems they have solved. One obstacle that I have encountered is the way in which the company is geared up to productivity. Everyone is working flat out to meet production targets, so I am finding it almost impossible to pull people off production to solve quality problems – so I tend to resort to doing the implementation work myself! That is not what I had intended, but at the moment, if I don't do it, nobody else will!'

## Questions

1 *How important is quality to the company, given its current growth situation?*

2 *What are the underlying causes of the quality problems in this company?*

3 *What action is being taken by management to overcome these problems, and is this sufficient to create lasting improvements?*

4 *Should more inspectors be recruited and/or trained to cope with the growth in output?*

5 *What other actions could be taken to improve quality in the company?*

## E-Cab – financial performance 1992–1995

| | Year ended 31 March (FFr million) | | | |
| --- | --- | --- | --- | --- |
| | 1992 | 1993 | 1994 | 1995 |
| **Turnover** (continuing activities) | 115 | 252 | 310 | 750 |
| Cost of sales | (72) | (167) | (215) | (575) |
| Gross profit | 43 | 85 | 95 | 175 |
| Other operating income and charges | 29 | 67 | 70 | 104 |
| **Operating profit** (continuing activities) | 14 | 18 | 25 | 71 |
| Retained profit | 2 | 2 | 11 | 41 |
| Fully diluted earnings per share | 31 | 32 | 47 | 124 |

## Appendix 53.2

### Process routes for main components of Nokia cabinets (white areas are used for other products)

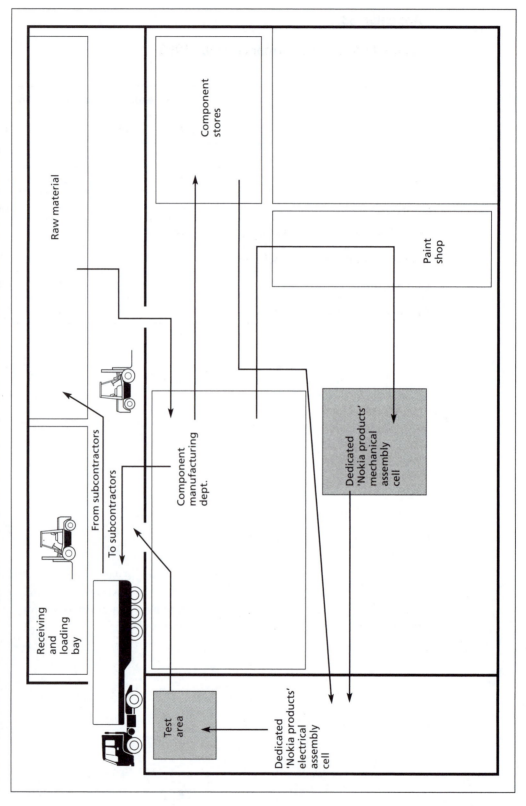

## Extracts from Jean Brasfort's notes

**Some of the causes of non-conformance on Nokia cabinet posts and cross members, as reported by supervisors**

### Charlotte Lorcy, Final Inspection

'We have to reject a completed cab if we find any visual defects on the posts, either inside or on the outside. If there are obvious dents or bent edges, this needs assemblers to remove the electrical parts (about three person-hours' work), change the offending posts, and rebuild the cab. Scratches and damaged paint are more of a problem because they show up a lot in our section's strong lighting, but are not always so obvious in the factory. I have to admit, however, that we've had very few returned because of this type of fault, but it certainly doesn't convey a good impression of the company if these are seen by the customer's engineers. M. Cahor, the Quality Manager, has often told us that we (in the Quality Department) are here just to make absolutely sure that only good cabs get to the customers, so we are usually quite careful in our final checks, and record every blemish we can find. It's then up to management to decide what to do.'

### Anne Cardignac, Electrical Assembly

'Being in the same area of the factory, we work closely with Charlotte, so we try to pick up any faults for her before we start our work, but that's not always easy because we aren't qualified to say whether a small scratch or dent *is* acceptable or not. Very often we find holes missing which we need for fixing parts to. This is really frustrating, particularly if we have already done most of the assembly and have to take everything out again. I have to admit that sometimes we do a little damage getting some of the larger and heavier electrical assemblies into position in the cabs; they are a tight fit at the best of times, but sometimes they have to be pushed in hard. A small variation in the size of the inside of the cabinet creates an interference fit which I don't think is what the designers intended, and this can cause paint damage.

'I must say that most of the problems seem to be caused by Mechanical Assembly. I've seen them walking over posts and cross members rather than picking them up! There's a lot of bad work like that – lack of care, poor discipline. What really annoys me is that they manage to assemble the cabs wrongly – all the posts and cross members upside down and back-to-front, not once, but over and over again! However, for many of the cabs there aren't any clear Build Instructions to show the new employees in Mechanical Assembly, so it's really no surprise that mistakes are made. Taking cabs apart again not only takes time, but also almost always causes some damage. We used to run out of cabs when this happened, so now I keep a reserve of cabs to work on, in case there are any problems in Mechanical. They are a bit in the way, in the corridor near the office, but it's nice to have the back-up stock. As you know, at the end of every week all the managers are accountable for their output achieved. It's really the only performance measurement taken seriously here, so it tends to make me angry when these problems make me miss my target.'

### Quentin Latour, Mechanical Assembly

'Many of the people on my section are temporary staff and they're new to the job, so that's a problem for a start. Trying to achieve high targets for efficiency is bad enough without having to train temporary contract people to do it. Management thinks that our job is as straightforward as assembling Lego, but our components are not always that consistent, and we have to constantly watch out for missing holes and damaged components, while suffering from constant shortages from our suppliers. We often get batches of components which are well outside the tolerances (when there are any!), which I am told is because of a backlog of repairs on worn tooling or machines. If we were to do our job properly, we would stop production every time we see a problem, but, of course, we wouldn't be allowed to do that! I think the manager should stop criticising us and look at where the posts and cross members are coming from before they get to us. We get bad quality from the Alocrom subcontractors for a start – bits of the post are sometimes untreated so the paint falls off, and I know for certain that they damage good posts. The Sawing and Piercing Section is very bad as well. There's a complete lack of care in there. We sometimes get cross members which are sawn off a few millimetres too long or short, or with holes punched out of place – we only find this out when we can't get the cab doors to fit properly! The manager of the Components Department has been complaining that the dimensional tolerances on new designs of cab are often tighter than he can achieve with the existing machines and tooling, but since we don't use any SPC, he'll have a job convincing management that this is the cause of all of his problems! The first thing they taught me on my quality course at the local technical college was how to use SPC, and it amazes me that we haven't got that going here! How they expect us to do a good job with all this rubbish I don't really know. One thing's certain: it's always us that gets the blame if a bad one gets out, and they don't want to listen to our explanations.'

### Hubert Montielle, Components Manufacturing Dept.

'I know that everyone feels it is always our fault when bad components are found, but I really don't agree. You specifically highlighted posts and cross members, but these are only a few of the thousands of different things we make. Because these components are large and are easily seen on the final cabs, we take every precaution to protect them in our department. We have made containers with tubular plastic inserts which we drop the posts into for protection when they are ready to go to the Alocrom subcontractors, so they certainly aren't getting damaged by us. I admit that there have been problems with the occasional missing holes or wrong lengths, but now that the employees are more experienced at making these parts, these mistakes don't happen any more. We all get better at a product the longer we have been doing it! We try to get well ahead with production of the posts so that if any get damaged or incorrectly Alocromed, it doesn't stop Mechanical Assembly.

'I'm not always happy with the long lengths of aluminium extrusions which come from our suppliers. Because they are banded in bundles with a cardboard outer protection, the outside ones are sometimes crushed by the banding, or have obviously been damaged by other things on the truck. We only find this when we come to open up the bundle, and we take care to avoid using the damaged pieces. This is the price we pay for going to the cheapest supplier of extrusions! I think that our buyers should stop being proud of the savings they screw out of the suppliers, and spend a little time down here looking at the problems we have to cope with. For example, I'm not really happy with the attitude of the Alocrom subcontractors. We try to keep the posts and cross rails clean, but it's inevitable in our environment that some oil and grease gets on the parts, which we wipe off as best we can. When they get a bad batch of Alocrom finish, their excuse is that our material is contaminating their liquids, but they are supposed to degrease everything first anyway. It seems like a feeble excuse for their bad work, if you ask me! Our buyer should look for a better supplier – and quickly too, before they damage our reputation for quality cabinets.'

### Gaston Cahor, Quality Manager

'This site has expanded very quickly over the past two years with all the new business. What this has meant is that the products have been introduced very quickly so that we can fulfil our orders. Often, there have been a lot of design and assembly problems which had not been foreseen, and it usually takes some time to iron them out. I know that the Design Office has a huge backlog of changes to do, largely because most of their time is taken on new products. Quality isn't really considered enough – a problem will be solved but not at its root cause, so it'll show up again and again.

'We need to build quality into the design and the process before manufacturing starts but this isn't easy – our design and prototyping facility is on the other site 200km away, so generally communication is poor. We can go back and try to improve everything on a piecemeal basis, but inherently it's our way of doing things as a company which should be addressed by senior management. To be honest, I just haven't got the resources or authority to do that! All I can do is to solve problems as they're found now, and allow the general build standard to improve that way.

'It's very difficult to get people involved in quality when they're so preoccupied with output. Also, and let's be honest here, most of them think that quality should be the responsibility of somebody else, usually me! I can't really accept their excuse that they haven't got time for quality. They've got time to rebuild it, that is to build it twice, but they haven't got time to build it once, properly!'

## Identification of scrap causes on mechanical assembly

**Two-month period: 23/03/95 to 23/05/95**

| Part no. | Description | Scratches | Operation omissions |
|----------|-------------|-----------|---------------------|
| SP-1361501 | X Member | 40 | 0 |
| SP-1361502 | X Member | 91 | 10 |
| SP-1361701 | X Member | 60 | 0 |
| SP-1361702 | X Member | 172 | 0 |
| SP-1361800 | Rear Post | 100 | 23 |
| SP-1361900 | Hinge Post | 44 | 0 |
| SP-1361902 | Lock Post | 43 | 20 |
| SP-1404200 | X Member | 27 | 0 |
| SP-1404300 | X Member | 122 | 15 |
| SP-1405000 | X Member | 99 | 0 |
| SP-1643301 | R/Post | 20 | 6 |
| SP-1643302 | R/Post | 15 | 10 |
| SP-1643401 | Hinge Post | 10 | 0 |
| SP-1643501 | X Member | 15 | 30 |
| SP-1643502 | X Member | 10 | 10 |
| SP-2103801 | X Member | 51 | 0 |
| SP-2103802 | X Member | 110 | 50 |
| SP-2116101 | X Member | 79 | 30 |
| SP-2116501 | Hinge Post | 40 | 21 |
| SP-2116502 | Lock Post | 150 | 15 |

*Costing*
Average cost for posts          FFr200
Average cost for X Members      FFr80

*Cost of scrap over the two-month period*
Posts                           FFr103 400
X Members                       FFr81 680

## Appendix 53.5

### The detailed process route for posts and cross members

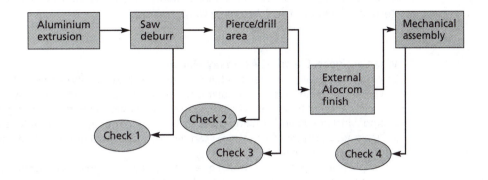

## Appendix 53.6

### Initial analysis of cross member faults

Four components selected at each check point every hour. Inspected against 'scratch standard' on Quality Board

| Check point | | | | Weekly failure rate % | | | |
|---|---|---|---|---|---|---|---|
| Number | Description | week 1 | week 2 | week 3 | week 4 | week 5 | Average |
| 1 | Saw | 45 | 37 | 50 | 43 | 38 | 43 |
| 2 | Pierce | 31 | 28 | 36 | 30 | 31 | 31 |
| 3 | Drill | 22 | 28 | 19 | 25 | 21 | 23 |
| 4 | Mech. Assy. | 24 | 19 | 20 | 28 | 16 | 21 |

## Appendix 53.7

### Continued analysis of cross member faults

Four components selected at each check point every hour. Inspected against 'scratch standard' on Quality Board

| Check point | | | | Weekly failure rate % | | | |
|---|---|---|---|---|---|---|---|
| Number | Description | week 1 | week 2 | week 3 | week 4 | week 5 | Average |
| 1 | Saw | 35 | 32 | 28 | 26 | 25 | 29 |
| 2 | Pierce | 21 | 21 | 19 | 23 | 20 | 21 |
| 3 | Drill | 18 | 19 | 19 | 20 | 17 | 19 |
| 4 | Mech. Assy. | 13 | 14 | 13 | 14 | 13 | 13 |

## Sara Mountenay's interviews

Some representative extracts from Sara Mountenay's interviews with employees in the Mechanical and Electrical Assembly Departments

### Anne Cardignac, Electrical Assembly Manager

'I have a lot of quality problems in here – I don't really know where to start!

'One of the main causes of problems is just lack of care. Nobody accepts responsibility for their work around here! For example, in one cabinet we found this morning, there are holes missing which we need for fixing parts to. Now we're going to have to take everything out and start again. It's very frustrating, I can tell you – and we'll probably find a few more like it before the end of the day!

'Suppliers are a problem as well. For example, with one type of connection cable we had to go over to just one supplier to get the lowest price, but they're often causing a problem – they're not made properly and we have to adjust them when fitting them. Their delivery is also bad. I've complained but it takes ages to get anything put right here and when it is, we don't hear about it until weeks afterwards.

'I do think that improvements are beginning to happen, though. We'll be moving to our new layout soon and that should tidy things up – all the stock at one end, and lines for assembly. They're also going to start using the MRP system properly which means that my shortages should be a thing of the past!'

### Fabrice Tripont (Electrical Assembly Team Leader: 5 years' service)

'I agree that in theory we need better quality, but it's not so easy in practice. We've just been told that we have to produce *25* per cent more cabinets each week. To meet that target, we're just going to have to use everything in sight or we'll end up with shortages!

'The problem with the Improvement Team is that we just haven't got the time to do it. If I lose people from the line it'll affect productivity, and I can't afford to do that! Anyway, why should we do it? We're here to build cabs, and it's management's responsibility to sort out the quality of the suppliers and the Components Department! I think that we really need more quality engineers to solve all the problems we get. The Quality Department is too small here – it definitely needs to be bigger and more effective. It has never kept up with the expansion that we have been through!'

### Sophie Lambert (Assembly: 3 years' service)

'The problems we face are really unnecessary. We get cabs from Mechanical Assembly that look okay, but right at the end of our work we find something wrong. Last week it was a few which had no hole for the earth strap. We had to strip about ten cabs right down so that the faulty post could be removed and replaced. All this wasted time could have been avoided if they employed inspectors in the Mechanical Assembly to make sure everything's right before we get it. We haven't got time to do all this extra work – Pierre Dumas keeps telling us that we have to make more cabinets every week or we'll let the customer down badly, and the company will lose money too.'

### Bernard Dupond (agency worker in Assembly: 2 months' service)

'I fit doors to the finished cabs, which is the same for every type of cab, and so was quite an easy job to pick up. I reckon that I do it just as well as the old-timers now! Training? Well, somebody showed me what to do and that was it, but I wouldn't really say that was training, would you?

'My basic wage is fairly low, but we end up with a good bonus if we reach the output targets, which we do almost every week unless there have been problems with cabinets coming late from Mechanical Assembly. Some of the tools here are a bit worn but we have to make do with what we've got. I had trouble with the torque wrench slipping, but if you set it a little on the high side, it seems to do the job okay. I had to ask Quentin to get me a new one, but he told me that the manager had said that the old one could be repaired, but it never was. Management here seem to pass all the problems back to the shop floor … that's what they called "empowerment" at my last factory, but it really didn't seem to work! I mean, I think that at the end of the day, nothing really improves unless management get down onto the shop floor and start putting a few basic things right. The only time we see them here is when there's a problem to sort out!'

### Amandine Fouquet (Union Representative in Electrical Assembly: 2 years' service)
'We're under far too much pressure here – it's getting ridiculous! I know that Anne has been threatened with the sack if we don't get out the scheduled cabs, which is hardly the way to get morale up in the Cell. Because she's the supervisor, she isn't in our union, but she does seem to take it out on us. There is a very aggressive style of management right from the top, and all this pressure ends up on our shoulders. Of course, we'd have no trouble meeting the targets if supplies were good and came in on time, but there are problems with shortages both from here and outside.

'I don't think that the management respects or appreciates the workforce at all. We pull out all the stops for them, time and time again, to meet deadlines and we don't get anything back at all. It's hardly surprising that nobody cares around here.'

### Emile Verpeau (Electrical Tests Inspector: 5 years' service)
'Having worked here so long, I know from experience what the customers will accept and what they won't. Although our main job is to check out the circuits with the computerised testing equipment, we also look for visual and mechanical faults: parts missing, scratches, poor paint finish, and so on. This is the last chance before the cabs are packaged up and sent to the customer. If we find one of these faults, it is usually on several cabs which quickly build up on our section and get in our way. What we need is quick decisions from management, but because of meetings, it may be hours before they get down here to sort things out. And nine times out of ten, they decide to let cabs go out of the door that shouldn't go – then a week later they shout at us for having missed a quality problem, and inevitably the cabinets come back!

'Sometimes we find damage caused by lack of clearance between the components, for example, doors that won't shut tightly because of a build-up of tolerances on the hinges and posts. I think these could be sorted out by the designers, but we get the same problems over and over again. They don't solve these problems at the design stage and leave us to sort it out the best way we can, even if someone has to use a hammer!'

### Charlotte Lorcy (Final Inspection: 5 years' service)
'Scratched and damaged components shouldn't be there, they should be rectified or replaced, but we have regularly been completely overruled by the Cell Manager or even by M. Dumas, and these cabs are immediately sent out to the customer.

'As the number of cabs has gone up, we're having to take short cuts with inspection and we're sure to miss faults occasionally because of the rush to get products out of the gate. We could really do with at least two more inspectors to add to our current four, to ensure that everything is checked, and so that we don't hold up dispatch. My biggest fear now is that we will find a batch of bad cabs and the customer won't get the scheduled delivery.'

**Francoise Alon (Electrical sub-assemblies: 2 years' service)**

'I've been doing assembly work of this type for 15 years now, so I've worked in quite a few places, but I've never come across anywhere as chaotic as this! I mean, there doesn't seem to be any proper understanding of what needs to be done and how! Some of the girls don't even know which spanners and screwdrivers to use!

'We're under a lot of pressure here. If management wants better quality, they should give us the right tools and training and take the pressure off output! But I really think that the main problem is with Inspection. There just aren't enough qualified inspectors.'

## Appendix 53.9

# Extracts from the results of the Employee Survey

### Section 1: The respondents and their jobs

*Question 1.1: What is the length of your employment with the company?*
41% of the respondents had worked for E-Cab less than three years.

*Question 1.2: What was the extent and quality of your training to do your current job?*
82% of respondents said that they had been trained, although opinions varied about the extent of that training. 73% rated their training as below average or poor. In many cases they commented that the quality of their training could not really be rated because it had simply been a demonstration of the specific task to be done, given by a more experienced worker.

*Question 1.3: What information are you regularly given to do your job correctly, and what is the standard of that information?*
The most widely available information provided within the departments were Build Instructions and Check Sheets, used by 41% and 82% of respondents respectively. Most of this information was rated as incomprehensible and/or incomplete.

*Question 1.4: What is the quality and condition of any equipment that you use in your job?*
70% of respondents expressed dissatisfaction with the quality and/or condition of the equipment that they used.

*Question 1.5: Do you carry out regular checks on the quality of your own work?*

Unsurprisingly, 100% replied that they did!

### Section 2: Quality and the company

*Question 2.1: What importance do you think the company places on quality?*
41% felt that the company placed below average importance on quality, and only 27% felt that priority was given to quality.

*Question 2.2: What importance should be placed on quality in the company?*
In contrast to the responses to Question 2.1, 86% considered that quality should be given priority. There is a large credibility gap here.

*Question 2.3: Who do you think is responsible for quality in the company?*
Although 59% said that every individual had a responsibility for quality, 32% considered the Quality Department to be primarily accountable.

*Question 2.4: Who do you think should be responsible for quality?*
65% recognised that the individual should be responsible, but 18% still felt that quality should be the responsibility of the Quality Department.

*Question 2.5: List two things that E-Cab does badly regarding quality:*
A wide range of problems were identified here, with 'Inspection' and 'Attitudes of the Management' cited as the top two, each representing 18% of the total list of problems.

*Question 2.6: List two things that E-Cab does well regarding quality:*
The most popular answer was 'Can't think of any', with 41% of respondents only providing that answer! The second highest response, surprisingly, was 'Company attitude to quality'. Unstructured questioning of respondents revealed that most were referring to the sophisticated *design* (quality specification) of the new products, and not to conformance quality.

*Question 2.7: What do you think are the two main causes of quality problems in your part of the company?*
'Tooling' and 'Attitude' were the top answers at 18% each, followed by 'Training', 'Pressure of work' and 'Quality of parts', all at 10%.

*Question 2.8: What is your opinion on the following statements?*
This series of statements was adapted from the company Quality Systems Manual (shown in Appendix 53.10).

| Statement | % Disagree strongly | % Disagree | % Slightly disagree | % Slightly agree | % Agree | % Agree strongly | % Don't know |
|---|---|---|---|---|---|---|---|
| I am fully aware of the standards the customers expect from our products | 0 | 5 | 0 | 5 | 55 | 35 | 0 |
| It is necessary for everyone to check their own work | 0 | 0 | 9 | 18 | 55 | 18 | 0 |
| In this company, we are striving for products with no defects | 0 | 13 | 5 | 14 | 50 | 18 | 0 |
| This company is geared towards action and improvement | 0 | 9 | 5 | 23 | 50 | 13 | 0 |
| There is an emphasis on teamwork in this company | 18 | 18 | 14 | 27 | 18 | 5 | 0 |
| People here are recognised for their achievements | 41 | 27 | 18 | 9 | 5 | 0 | 0 |

## Extracts from the E-Cab Quality Systems Manual
Dated Nov 1994, and signed by Philippe Legrand

---

**Mission Statement**
To completely satisfy our customers' needs by...

**How Will We Achieve This?**
Delivery of a quality product, on time, every time.

We will undertake to monitor and improve our processes on a continuous basis. Our aim is constantly to improve in all areas of our operation to:

1  reduce the manufacturing cycle time;

2  bring product to the market quicker;

3  reduce costs;

4  strive for zero defects;

5  keep to our promises and plans.

**Our People**
To achieve the goals we have set, we must aim to develop an environment with:

1  a bias for action and improvement;

2  emphasis on teamwork;

3  integrity and respect for others;

4  training and development of our people;

5  recognition for achievement.

---

# Index